D1453275

THROUGH FAITH & FIRE

St. Joseph's Abbey, Spencer, Massachusetts. Aerial view from the southwest.

YORKVILLE PRESS

NEW YORK, NEW YORK

Library of Congress Cataloging-in-Publication Data

Bertoniere, Gabriel.
Through faith & fire: the monks of Spencer,
1825-1958 / Gabriel Bertoniere.
  p. cm.
Includes bibliographical references (p. 562) and index.
ISBN 0-9729427-9-3
1. Trappists—Massachusetts—Spencer—History.
2. Spencer (Mass.)—Church history.
I. Title. II. Title: Through faith and fire.
BX4110.S64B47 2005
271'.12507443—dc22

    2005008414

Photo credits appear on p. 597
Text credits and permissions appear on p. 597

Edited by Robert Somerville
Design by Tina Taylor

Printed in the USA by Quebecor World
JMS 10 9 8 7 6 5 4 3 2 1

THROUGH FAITH & FIRE
The Monks of Spencer 1825-1958

GABRIEL BERTONIERE

In memory of Frank A. Bartimo and Katherine Toomey Bartimo,
dear friends and benefactors of Saint Joseph's Abbey,
whose kindness made possible the publication of this history.

Contents

List of Illustrations

Figures

Acknowledgments

FIVE YEARS OF RESEARCH have put me in debt to many who offered their kind assistance with this book. I have haunted many archives, since twice in its history the community's records were destroyed by fire. The assistance offered by other monasteries and dioceses as well as several public archives has been crucial. I am deeply grateful to their archivists for generous permission to consult and make use of materials in their collections.

Thanks are due, first of all, to Dom Bernardo Olivera, General of the Cistercian Order of the Strict Observance, for his permission to consult the archives of the Generalate of the Order in Rome, and to Father François de Place, who was serving as its archivist in 2003 during my visit there.

Also to the monasteries of Bellefontaine (Spencer's motherhouse), la Trappe, Westmalle, Melleray, Sint-Sixtus, Mount Melleray, Timadeuc, Gethsemani, Oka and to Spencer's first daughterhouse, Guadalupe, for offering Spencer a complete copy of the diary of Father Maurice Malloy, without which the account of the Valley days from 1930 to 1949 would lose much of its detail and color.

Special thanks to Spencer's own archivist and senior monk, Father Laurence Bourget, who after the fire at Our Lady of the Valley in 1950 recovered many of the monastery's early historical records and now ably continues to manage its archives. Not only has he submitted to frequent and lengthy interviews about his monastic past, which reaches back as far as 1933, but he has also kindly read my manuscript both in its early phases and in its final form, offering crucial corrections and suggestions.

I am also indebted to the directors of the archives of the following institutions: the Archdiocese of Quebec, the Archdiocese of Baltimore and the United States Province of the Society of St. Sulpice (both of which now form part of the Associated Archives at St. Mary's Seminary and University), the Rhode Island Historical Society in Providence, Rhode Island, the Archdiocese of Halifax, and the University of St. Francis Xavier in Antigonish, N. S., which at the time of my research housed a portion of the archives of the Diocese of Antigonish including the important papers of the Reverend A. A. Johnston, eminent historian of the Church in Eastern Nova Scotia.

The Augustinian community of St. Augustine's monastery in Tracadie, which in 1938 took over the buildings of Petit Clairvaux, warmly welcomed Brother Bernard Mathews and me on two separate occasions, and when their monastery was forced to close due to declining numbers, they generously donated to Spencer numerous documents and other items that they had inherited from the last Trappist monks who lived there.

Among the many monastic archivists, special thanks to Father Alfons Vanden Brouke of Sint-Sixtus, who for over forty years not only patiently gathered materials pertinent to our history from his monastery's archives but also wrote detailed reports on his findings for three successive researchers into Spencer's history; Brother Philippe Roussier of Bellefontaine, who provided an unending stream of copies of crucial documents; Dom Emmanuel Coutant, Bellefontaine's former abbot, who shared with me a substantial portion of his private archives concerning his period of service as our Father Immediate during the last years covered in this book; Father Bruno, archivist of Oka, who patiently answered many e-mailed questions with great promptitude and kindly read sections of the book that pertain to the relations between our two abbeys; and Father Félix Héno, archivist of Timadeuc, who gathered important materials for me at lightning speed in the course of my single-day visit to the abbey.

I also wish to thank others who contributed in a significant way to my work, among whom are: Bill Degenhard, who over a long period of time has dedicated himself to obtaining photocopies of material pertinent to my research not only in archives located in Baltimore but in libraries and other collections elsewhere in Maryland and even further afield; Kathy M. MacKenzie, archivist of the University of St. Francis Xavier in Antigonish, friend and guardian spirit during our visits to the university; Kathy White of the Archdiocese of Halifax; the Reverend Robert Hayman, historian of the Diocese of Providence, for his generous permission to consult and make extensive copies of materials in his personal archive; the Reverend J. Appelman, MHM, assistant archivist of the Diocese of Kingston, Ontario, for coming to my assistance at the eleventh hour with photocopies of letters written by a hitherto elusive figure in the monastery's history, a certain Father Dominic of Petit Clairvaux; and Alan Hudon for the important information he shared with me in the course of several long interviews concerning his days as builder and later as treasurer of the abbey. A debt of special gratitude to Father Chrysogonus Waddell and Terryl Kinder for their help in the special areas of their high competency.

Father John Barry, pastor of St. Peter's church in Tracadie, offered us kind hospitality during our visits to Nova Scotia and has been a faithful friend over the years. Mr. Lloyd Boucher of the same parish supplied firsthand information concerning the Tracadie area and served as our guide to Arichat and l'Ardoise.

Thanks to Paul Sagendorph for photos, plans, and other memorabilia of the Sagendorph family, and to Ms. Jessie Brown and her brothers, James and David, for their reminiscences of early days on Spencer's Alta Crest Farms.

In addition to those already mentioned, thanks in a particular way to all those who patiently read the text—in some cases many times over: Brother Bernard, Sister Grace Forster of Wrentham, Brother Anthony Maggiore, and Mr. Jonathan Montaldo, as well as to those who read sections of the book dealing with individual foundations of Spencer: Dom Robert Barnes, abbot of Berryville; Dom Joseph Boyle, abbot of Snowmass; Father Ceferino Leardi of Azul; and Father Martinus Crawley of Guadalupe. The same is true of the many brothers of Spencer whom I interviewed and who recounted for me tales of the early days. Among these Brother Leo Gregory, Spencer's senior laybrother, holds a special place, due to the important role he played in the monastery's growth. Brother Anthony has been a faithful companion along the way, sharing in concerns over the layout of the book as well as its text and illustrations. Brother Daniel Charpentier offered professional assistance in the preparation of the maps that appear in the book. Brother Bernard not only provided the inspiration for this work but has been a constant source of encouragement and information both here at Spencer and along the roads of Nova Scotia, where we explored Petit Clairvaux and other sites pertinent to our history. Several important photos of Spencer were taken by Brother Emmanuel Morinelli.

My thanks go out in a special way to Kate Hartson of Yorkville Press, who graciously agreed to oversee this publication and coordinate the efforts of the exceptional team of Tina Taylor, gentlest and most capable of designers, Judy Lyon Davis, who created a splendid index for the book, and Bob Somerville, my editor, who immersing himself fully in the monastic world of this book not only ferreted out many errors and inconsistencies but helped me keep in focus the needs of the broader non-monastic readership.

Finally, a word of gratitude to my abbot, Dom Damian Carr, and to my community for their support and patience with me over these years of writing. At this point gratitude for help on the book blends almost imperceptibly in my mind with gratitude to Spencer itself, our town, our monastery and all its brethren past, present, and future.

—GABRIEL BERTONIERE

Introduction

O N A RIDGE BETWEEN two valleys north of the town of Spencer, Massachusetts, surrounded by fields and woods, lie the stonework buildings of St. Joseph's Abbey. This Roman Catholic monastery of contemplative monks belongs to the Cistercian Order of the Strict Observance—known familiarly as Trappists. Its origins date back to 1811, when a group of French monks fleeing from persecution set out for Baltimore, Maryland. It wasn't until 1825, however, that a small community finally took shape—not in the United States but in the village of Tracadie, Nova Scotia. After seventy-five years of monastic life in Canada, two disastrous fires occasioned still another move—to Cumberland, Rhode Island, where in 1900 Our Lady of the Valley came into existence. After years of patient toil and rebuilding, fire struck again in 1950, and the community moved yet again, this time to the hills and farmlands of central Massachusetts. All these experiences schooled the community in the twin values of perseverance and adaptation, which would remain important components of its heritage.

But Spencer's origins stretch even further back in time. Its fountainhead was the monastic movement of the late third and fourth centuries, when certain Christians began to respond to the call of a life dedicated to prayer and contemplation, far away from cities—either in solitude or in small groups. History favored those who shared a common life, and this form of monasticism, in which the Gospel reality of mutual love and support found powerful expression, became more typical in the West. Gradually, various "Rules" of life embodying the ideals of these communities appeared. By the end of the eighth century the Rule of St. Benedict of Nursia (died c. 547 A.D.) had become predominant in the West, where it would hold sway throughout subsequent history.

Because of its emphasis on moderation, the Rule of Benedict provided a livable framework for a well-balanced—if nonetheless challenging—life of prayer and work. The Rule concentrated largely on the life of individual monastic communities, however, and in the course of time experience showed that, just as individual monks needed the support of their brothers, so too monasteries themselves needed the support of other monasteries in order to remain faithful to their shared ideals. This became crucial when a voice of authority from outside a community proved necessary to address problems not easily resolved from within. The bonding of monasteries came about almost naturally when a fervent monastery gave birth to other monasteries that wished to preserve the charisma of the founding house. It was in this context that the Cistercian Order came into being.

Early in 1098, Abbot Robert set out with a group of twenty-one monks from the monastery of Molesme in Burgundy for a property that had been given to them in an uncleared forest area about twelve miles south of Dijon. Here they hoped to live more faithfully according to the Rule of Benedict, paring away the complexities of life they had known at Molesme. At first, their monastery was known simply as the "new monastery." But it eventually adopted the name of the property, Cistercium or Cîteaux, which, in turn, gave rise to the name of the Cistercian Order itself.[1] The work of clearing the land and erecting the first buildings amid inhospitable surroundings took its toll on the new community, and in little more than a year they were faced with a new crisis. Through the intervention of the bishop of Langres, the monks of Molesme were able to bring about the return of Dom Robert to Molesme, and a considerable number of those who had come with him to Cîteaux now returned. It is possible that only eight monks remained at Cîteaux.

After Robert's departure Cîteaux's subordinate superior, Alberic, who had been an important figure in the founding group, was elected its second abbot in 1099. Under the new leadership, the monks made a firm commitment to the work they had taken on. During this period of consolidation, Alberic sent two monks to Rome, where they won the approval of Pope Paschal II. After Alberic's death in 1108 Stephen was chosen as abbot. The new abbot, who had himself been a prominent member of the founding group, would prove an even more dynamic leader, as he faced the unexpected developments of Cîteaux's subsequent history.

In 1113 the monastery's personnel was dramatically increased by the arrival of a group of young Burgundian noblemen under the leadership of Bernard of Fontaine-lès-Dijon, who was destined to become the Order's most famous son. Within the year this led to the creation of a new monastery, Cîteaux's first daughterhouse, la Ferté. Others would follow. By 1119 there were nine, and it became imperative to define just what the ongoing relationship of these "foundations" would be to the motherhouse. The basic outline of a working solution had already begun to take shape in a document called the Charter of Charity, which was now submitted, with a request for renewed support, to the newly elected pope, Callixtus II. Confirmation came on December 23, 1119, in the form of a papal bull, *Ad hoc in apostolicae*.[2]

This document outlined a form of organization in which the monasteries, while maintaining their essential independence, were bound together by the common values expressed in their manner of life, and by the mutual control exercised by a "General Chapter." This yearly meeting at Cîteaux brought together the abbots of all the monasteries. While in its early phase the role of the abbot of Cîteaux was predominant, eventually each of the abbots came to have a voice in its deliberations. Its governing powers increased over time, and it became more and more the determinative authority in the Order. As Cîteaux's foundations grew in terms of personnel and of experience, they in turn began to make foundations of their own, resulting in an increasingly complex network.

The arrival of Bernard and his companions initiated a period of spiritual flowering for the new Order. In 1115, not long after his novitiate Bernard himself was chosen as the superior of Clairvaux, one of Cîteaux's new foundations, situated about seventy-five miles north of the motherhouse. Over the years his prestige continued to grow, and he was called upon to undertake activities outside the monastery and indeed outside France itself. Thanks to the spiritual vision communicated by his preaching as well as by his writings, candidates for the Cistercian life continued to multiply, and new foundations spread over a wide area that included most of Europe, and beyond. The monastic culture of this new international generation of monks was passed on to future generations by a host of writers, including among others William of Saint-Thierry, Guerric of Igny, Isaac of Stella, Aelred of Rievaulx, and Baldwin of Forde.

For all their fidelity to the Rule of St. Benedict, the founders of Cîteaux realized that, in order to remain faithful to its insistence on self-support, they must adapt to new economic conditions prevalent five hundred years after the death of Benedict. For example, it was difficult for the monks to dedicate themselves completely to the prescriptions of the Rule and still effectively manage the operations of agriculture and animal husbandry by which they provided for their own needs of food and clothing. The lands necessary for such a program normally consisted of a variety of holdings known as granges that were not usually contiguous to one another or to the main property of the abbey itself. These needed to be staffed on a regular basis, but this was impossible for the monks themselves since it would involve living outside the enclosure of the main monastic property. The solution was the establishment of a corps of laymen who, though they shared in the spiritual life of the monastery, were not required to participate in the full round of liturgical services of the monks or even to remain within the enclosure of the monastery. Thus these "laybrothers," could not only dedicate themselves to staffing the various granges essential to the abbey's economy, but also be available for types of labor that required more intensive supervision than the monks themselves could provide.

Future development was closely linked to the evolving shape of European civilization. In one way or another, monasteries managed to respond to challenging new situations as they presented themselves. The rise of the mendicant Orders in the thirteenth century presented one such challenge, offering powerful competition for prospective candidates to Cistercian monasteries. Later on, the Hundred Years' War of the fourteenth and fifteenth centuries, the Wars of Religion in France during the second half of the sixteenth, and the Thirty Years' War of the first half of the seventeenth all wreaked havoc on the Cistercian monasteries of Europe, and those of France in particular. In addition to these physical and spiritual challenges, the gradual fragmentation of Europe into nationalistic states frequently at war with one another made communications difficult, and sometimes large numbers of abbots were not able to attend the General Chapter. For the same reason it became difficult for abbots to visit their daughterhouses in other countries. This led to a scheme of administrative "provinces" conceived along national lines. These remained within the larger organizational structure of the entire

Order. Similar concerns motivated the creation of "congregations," which continued to live according to Cistercian traditions but separated themselves from the effective jurisdictional control of the Order.

The most serious threat to monastic life, however, was the institution of commendatory abbots. The practice originated as a means of assigning the care of a diocese or a monastery to an individual on a temporary basis during a period when there was no incumbent in the office of bishop or abbot. Such an appointee need not even be a cleric. Eventually one receiving such a benefice was also given the right to enjoy the revenues attached to it. The practice first threatened the Order in the second half of the thirteenth century but became a particularly acute problem in France when the French monarchs themselves began assigning abbeys to commendatory abbots of their own choosing. To make matters worse, in 1516 Pope Leo X sanctioned this practice. Monasteries were more and more turned into mere sources of revenue for non-resident "abbots" who cared little for monastic life and who effectively controlled any efforts at raising the spiritual tone of the monasteries over which they ruled. In such circumstances there was little hope of community fervor and still less hope of attracting serious candidates. Indeed, the number of monks in each monastery was limited to a number determined by the commendatory abbot with a view to reducing the amount of money needed to support the monks.

Between the devastation of war and the evils of the system of commendatory abbots, monastic life in the Order had fallen to an all-time low. Fidelity to the celebration of the Liturgy and the fundamental values of separation from the world, silence, and sacred reading were seriously compromised. Reduced to extreme financial deprivation due to the demands of commendatory abbots, many monks were forced to seek funds from relatives and to manage their own personal affairs. These were the abuses that reformers would eventually address.

Nonetheless, efforts at renewal were not wanting. The reform of the monastery of Feuillans near Toulouse deserves special mention. In addition to the fact that it survived until the time of the French Revolution, it illustrates what would be an important factor in dealing with the debilitating problem of commendatory abbots, namely, the conversion of such abbots to true monastic life and the subsequent regularization of their status into that of "regular" abbots. Their new status then gave them a free hand in carrying out reforms in their monasteries. In 1577 the "converted" commendatory abbot of Feuillans, Jean de la Barrière, set in motion such a reform. His efforts were successful, and he was able to make a number of daughterhouses. This in turn led to an interesting new development: the gradual creation of an independent congregation focused on reform, whose juridical links with the Order in the course of time became more and more tenuous.

Of even greater importance was the more widespread "Strict Observance" reform movement, which operated within the Order itself. Seen by some as springing from the efforts at reform promoted by the Council of Trent, this movement had modest beginnings in the early years of the seventeenth century. As in the case of Feuillans, it was a converted commendatory abbot who led his monastery into reform. Octave Arnolfini, commendatory abbot of la Charmoye, made his profession in 1603, became regular abbot, then undertook the reform of his abbey. Under the aegis of Denis Largentier, abbot of Clairvaux, the reform movement spread to Clairvaux itself and eventually to other monasteries it had founded. Their program was expressed by a declaration signed in 1622 by a considerable number of abbots. This called for

> ...integral observance of the Holy Rule, namely perpetual abstinence from flesh meat and from the use of linen garments, fidelity in the established laws of fasting and silence and all other [regulations] which had been followed most faithfully from ancient times by our predecessors.[3]

Though "strict" or integral observance of the precepts of St. Benedict's Rule was stressed, abstinence from meat became a hallmark of the movement, and the reformers became known as "abstinents," while other members of the Order were referred to as the "ancients."

The history of the efforts to contain the movement within the structure of the Cistercian Order and to regulate its relationship with monasteries that did not embrace the reform was a stormy one, in which the players were not only the authorities of the Order and individual monasteries and abbots, but also various other figures of church and state. Though monasteries that adhered to the movement lingered on until the French Revolution, the torch of effective reform passed to the monastery of la Trappe, which after a period in which it espoused the ideals of the Strict Observance, finally distanced itself from it. And here the story proper begins.

✑ Dramatis Personae

Despite the vicissitudes of history, the basic structure of the Order remained amazingly stable throughout the centuries and in its essential lines is still in place today. Thus, before venturing into the venerable cloisters of the monasteries from which Spencer drew its own life, it will be well to have a look at the cast of characters that the reader will encounter in these pages and to see what daily life was like in a Cistercian monastery.[4] Many changes have taken place in the Order's thousand-year history, but the present description covers in a broad way the Cistercian lifestyle during the period covered in this book.

Until the time of the French Revolution, the *abbot of Cîteaux* continued to exercise an important role, presiding each year at the General Chapter and, when it was not in session, managing the Order's business—within prescribed limits. Nonetheless, the Order's "genealogical" structure based on the lines of paternity remained a central feature. A key figure in this organization was the *Father Immediate,* the abbot of a monastery's founding house. He formed a crucial link between the General Chapter and each of the monasteries that he or his predecessors had founded. These taken as a whole were referred to as the filiation of his monastery. By his vigilance he fostered a spirit of fidelity to the vision that inspired the foundation of Cîteaux itself. His own role was a delicate one, since he had to respect the authority of the local abbot as well as the independence of the monastery.

The most important exercise of the Father Immediate's authority took place in the course of an annual *visitation* of the daughterhouses, carried out either by himself or by another abbot whom he delegated. During the visitation the monks had free access to the *visitor* in order to express their judgment on the state of the monastery. It was eventually prescribed that at the end of his visit, the visitor should draw up a *visitation card* that outlined for the community the results of his findings, stressing points that deserved special attention. During the interim between visitations, the local abbot was expected to keep in mind the points the visitor had made. It was even read in public on several occasions during the year. Outside of the time of visitation, the amount of ongoing contact between the Father Immediate and the local superior and community varied according to need.

In terms of life in the individual monasteries, a new monastery that had passed successfully through its early stages of growth and achieved financial independence was normally granted independence from the motherhouse and could proceed to the election of its own superior. If it fulfilled certain conditions it would become an *abbey*, and its members would proceed to the election of their own *abbot*. Monasteries with more reduced numbers or limited means might be given the status of *priory*. Here the elected superior would hold the title of *prior*.

Whatever his title, a superior in office was referred to by the honorific title "*Dom*," in line with St. Benedict's prescription that he be called *Dominus* (Lord), since he was believed to hold the place of Christ in the monastery.[5] Within the restrictions inherent in the setup of the Order and in accordance with canon law, his authority in the monastery was absolute. In some monasteries where his quarters consisted of a suite of rooms or even a separate building, this might be called the *abbatiale*.

According to the prescriptions of the Rule, he would choose one of the monks as *prior* to assist him in his functions and to substitute for him when he himself was away or, for some other reason, unavailable.[6] Further assistance was offered to the abbot in his administration in the form of a *private council* composed of a small number of monks.[7]

Another important figure, likewise appointed by the abbot, was the *cellarer*, who was largely responsible for the materialities of the monastery. His exact functions differed from period to period and from monastery to monastery. He might be assigned a *subcellarer* to help him in specific areas.

The life of the community was centered around the daily celebration of the Eucharist and of the *Divine Office*, which St. Benedict called the "work of God." (This is sometimes referred to simply as *the Office*, or in the case of single liturgical celebrations, an *Office*.) Since Vatican II, this has been called *the Liturgy of the Hours*. As the name suggests, it consisted of a series of liturgical gatherings for prayer at various hours during the day and night: *Vigils* at night; *Lauds* in the early morning; *Prime, Tierce, Sext,* and *None* marking the first, third, sixth, and ninth hours of the day according to Roman reckoning; *Vespers* in the early evening; and finally *Compline* before retiring.

Of a more personal character, the second important element in the day of the monk was *lectio divina*, or meditative reading of Sacred Scripture and other religious writings. The third element consisted of *manual labor*, which enabled the monastery to provide for its own needs instead of relying on others for its support. At the same time it offered a healthy counterbalance to the more spiritual and intellectual activities of the day. In actual fact, due to a wide variety of needs, the "labor" often turned out to be other than "manual."

New candidates were placed in the *novitiate* as *postulants*. Here they received training in the monastic life under the direction of the *novice master*, who not only was responsible for introducing them to the externals of their new way of life but also assisted them in their spiritual development. The candidate was often given a new name on this occasion. After a period of a month (six months for laybrothers) the postulant became a *novice*, receiving a habit consisting of white robe, scapular, and cincture. Outside of times of work, a full white cloak was worn over this habit. The novice followed the life of the community according to the category to which he belonged. In the case of the *choir novices*, priestly studies were frequently begun sometime during this period, often after only one year of the novitiate. The choir novices were called *Frater* (Latin for "brother") to distinguish them from the *lay novices*, who were called simply *Brother*.

Originally, after a period of two years as a novice, the person was eligible to make a permanent commitment to the monastery in the form of *profession*, in which he promised fidelity to three vows specified in the Rule of St. Benedict: stability, obedience, and *conversatio morum¸* which signified an overall fidelity to the monastic way of life. In 1868, however, Rome insisted that this permanent commitment be preceded by *temporary profession*, which bound the monk for a period of three years. This has been in force since then. The novice's admission to this new status depended on the deliberative vote of the *conventual chapter*, which was made up of all the solemnly professed choir monks.

The place where the conventual chapter met was called the *chapter room* or *chapter house* in cases where, as was traditional, it consisted of a separate building normally perpendicular to the eastern range of the cloister. Such a meeting took place each day and might itself be referred to as a "chapter." For the acceptance of a novice for temporary profession, an absolute majority of votes of the chapter was necessary. Upon making his profession, the new member exchanged his white scapular for a black one, and his cincture for a leather belt. In place of his white cloak, he received the cowl, an ample over-garment with hood attached. Finally, he received the monastic tonsure, his head being shaved, save for a band of hair in the form of a "crown," symbolizing the saying, "To serve God is to reign."[8] As a professed monk, limited responsibilities might be given to him in the line of work, and priestly studies would be continued. Until his ordination as a priest, he would continue to be called *Frater*.

At the end of his period as a temporarily professed monk, the monk or brother was eligible for *solemn profession*, whereby he made a definitive commitment to monastic life in the monastery that he had joined. In this case also the conventual chapter was called upon to vote, but their vote was only consultative, and the final decision remained with the abbot.[9]

The monk or brother was now an integral part of the monastic community, although only the monks became members of the conventual chapter with voting rights. After an additional year or two of studies, the monk was normally ordained a priest, at which time he exchanged the name *Frater* for that of *Father*.

One of the most important functions of the conventual chapter was to elect a new abbot when the ruling abbot or prior died or resigned. In such cases the Father Immediate once again appeared on the scene and presided over the election. If, in his judgment, circumstances dictated that for the time being it was not prudent to hold an election, he appointed a provisional superior called a *superior ad nutum*.

The life that tentatively took root in the third and fourth centuries, and was taken up in monasteries that followed the Rule of Benedict, then renewed and tailored by Cîteaux to conditions of twelfth century society—that same life further adapted to the difficult conditions of later history still inspires the generation of monks who now live in the stonework buildings of St. Joseph's Abbey in Spencer. This book is the story of how they got there.

FIGURE 1. *Dom Augustin de Lestrange.*

Chapter One

The World of
Dom Augustin de Lestrange

T HE ABBEY OF la Trappe lies in the Perche region of France, some eighty miles west of Paris. Founded in 1140 as a Benedictine monastery, this venerable abbey was incorporated into the Cistercian Order in 1147. In 1638 its commendatory abbot was a twelve-year-old boy named Armand Jean le Bouthillier de Rancé. He began his ecclesiastical career in 1635 and within three years had come into possession of a windfall of ecclesiastical benefices that included, in addition to la Trappe, four other religious establishments, two of them abbeys and two priories belonging to other Orders.[1] He was ordained a priest in 1651 but continued to live the worldly life of a courtly cleric. By 1657, however, he began to show signs of a conversion, eventually resolving to embrace the monastic life and become the regular abbot of one of his abbeys. After obtaining the king's permission to change his status from commendatory abbot to that of regular abbot he went to the monastery of Perseigne for an official novitiate. On June 19, 1664, Rome gave its approval, and on June 26 he made his profession as a monk. Three weeks later he received the abbatial blessing from Patrick Plunket, the Irish bishop of Ardagh in exile, and the next day took over his new office as regular abbot of la Trappe.[2]

The movement of the Strict Observance had been in existence for a long period by the time of de Rancé's conversion and provided an ideal juridical setting for the newly reformed monastery of la Trappe. Indeed, de Rancé became a leading force in the movement through the power of his personality and teaching. In the same year that he became a monk and regular abbot, he was chosen as one of two delegates sent to Rome to defend the Strict Observance in one of the unending conflicts between the "abstinents" (as the reformers were called) and the "ancients." Rome's reaction to these discussions came only on April 19, 1666, when the constitution *In suprema* was issued. It dictated concrete norms for the functioning of the two observances that remained in effect up to the time of the French Revolution. Most importantly, *In suprema* designated the Strict Observance as a distinct legal entity within the structure of the Order.

However, when the constitution was promulgated at the General Chapter of 1667 (the first and only one de Rancé ever attended), he challenged the accuracy of the official account of what had transpired at Rome and objected strenuously to the provisions made for the Strict Observance in the papal document. For a number of years he continued to be a rallying point for the adherents of the Strict Observance in their attempts to reverse the decision of the Order to accept the papal brief. In 1675 he attended a meeting of the Strict Observance abbots in Paris and in the same year composed a letter to Louis XIV asking for the king's support in this endeavor. But the king's council pronounced in favor of the "ancients."

From this time on, de Rancé distanced himself more and more from the movement, as well as from the Order as a whole. He remained almost uninterruptedly at la Trappe until his death in 1700. Although he maintained an attitude of respect for the authority of the Order, he himself resolved to determine the concrete observances of his own monastery, a move that was tacitly accepted by the Order. He did continue to offer support to certain other monasteries of the Strict Observance, such as Sept-Fons, Tamié, and Orval. During the eighteenth century, despite the criticism of religious life by the Enlightenment, the monasteries of la Trappe and Sept-Fons continued to win new vocations and at the time of the Revolution they could boast of being the two houses of the Order in France with the largest number of monks.[3] La Trappe's ongoing strength was no doubt linked to the fact that all of de Rancé's nine successors up to the time of the Revolution were appointed by the king as regular—not commendatory—abbots.[4]

⌘ La Trappe and the French Revolution

Like all religious institutions in France, the monastery of la Trappe had grounds for fear when it learned of the expropriation of ecclesiastical properties decided upon in 1789. On February 13, 1790, the blow fell closer to home when the Constituent Assembly voted to no longer recognize religious vows. Nevertheless, many at la Trappe still hoped that their monastery would prove the exception to the rule and be permitted to continue in existence. But one man, who would play a major role in la Trappe's subsequent history and indeed set the stage for its move into the New World, was more farseeing than his fellows. Augustin de Lestrange, la Trappe's novice master, believed that the time had come for la Trappe to make provisions for what promised to be a grim period in the Order's history. After considerable efforts he discovered that the abandoned Carthusian monastery of la Valsainte in Switzerland might be available as a refuge for the monks.

La Trappe's prior (the monastery was without an abbot at the time) and others who hoped for better times opposed Lestrange's efforts, but then, in November 1790, a new decree specifically included la Trappe in the general decree of suppression, and all hope vanished. Augustin was finally granted permission to go to la Valsainte to see what could be done. His mission was successful, and an agreement was reached with the Senate of Fribourg, the most important stipulation of which was that the number of monks would be limited to twenty-four.

⌘ La Valsainte

On April 26, 1791, Lestrange and the chosen group set out in covered wagons, trying to live the monastic life as best they could along the way. Though they suffered from some taunts as they passed through Paris, the authorities did not hinder them from proceeding—emigration was outlawed only on August 6 of that year.[5] They eventually crossed the Swiss border and arrived safely at la Valsainte on June 1, 1791.[6]

The years spent in their new location constituted an important, formative period for the little community, even though they would remain there for less than seven years. Removed from the stress of the turbulent Revolutionary times in France, they were able to settle down once again to monastic living. It was a time for getting used to new surroundings and to living, at least at first, in smaller numbers. The expense of having to repair and refurnish a monastery that had been in large measure abandoned for ten years reduced their financial resources to such an extent that they were forced to live a life of extreme hardship.

The mystique of the new la Trappe slowly evolved during the years at la Valsainte. Soon after arriving there, the monks began to study the Rule under Lestrange's direction with a view to drawing up their own detailed "code" of behavior, designed to supplement the prescriptions of the Rule. In 1794 these usages appeared in print with the title, "Regulations of the House of God of Our Lady of la Trappe, by the Abbé de Rancé, its worthy reformer, newly arranged and augmented by the particular usages of the House of God of la Valsainte of Our Lady of la Trappe in the canton of Fribourg in Switzerland. . . ."[7] The key word here is "augmented." La Valsainte not only preserved the special austerities of la Trappe but also added to them. No doubt the Spartan demands of everyday life at la Valsainte played a role in the formulation of these new observances.

December 8, 1794, proved to be an important date in the history of the community, with far-reaching implications. Through the good services of the papal nuncio in Switzerland, the monastery was elevated to the status of abbey. At the request of Lestrange himself the nuncio even went beyond the terms of the Roman decree, granting the new abbot wide-ranging authority not only over the monastery itself but over any foundations it might make:

> We wish not only that the abbey of la Valsainte be subject to the authority of the new abbot, but also whatever colony sent out from the said monastery and established in whatever part of the universe; in such wise that the abbot of la Valsainte should be regarded as the Father Immediate of these colonies or of these religious, and that he should have all the powers necessary to govern them in a holy manner, as well as all such powers as the Constitutions of the Order of Cîteaux grant to Father Immediates.[8]

Lestrange's image of himself as a kind of Superior General of a "Congregation" no doubt traces its origin back to this decree and would characterize his activities throughout his life.[9]

Over the next years there were other important developments. In 1796 a group of women religious from various Orders began to gather together to live the Trappist life under Augustin's direction in the village of Sembrancher, which lay about forty miles south of la Valsainte. To this was added a new institution that Lestrange called his "Third Order":

groups of men and women formed into communities whose purpose was the education of young people. Novitiate training for the men took place at la Valsainte itself, and at Sembrancher for the women. The rule they followed was far less severe than that followed in what Lestrange began to refer to as the "Great Order," represented by the full monastic life as led at la Valsainte.

✑ EXPANSION

The community of la Valsainte prospered so well that from early on Lestrange had to consider establishing other monasteries to accommodate the growing numbers that threatened to violate the government's limitation of la Valsainte's membership to twenty-four. The New World of America appealed to him, removed as it was from the turmoil in Europe. Lestrange had a connection in America; Father François Nagot, who had been his mentor when he was a seminarian at St. Sulpice, in Paris, was now in charge of a Sulpician seminary in Baltimore.[10] The support of such a person would be invaluable. Accordingly, in June 1792 Lestrange wrote to Nagot to bring him up to date on developments at la Valsainte and to broach the possibility of a foundation somewhere in Maryland.[11] In 1793, however, Father Jacques-André Emery, the Superior General of the Sulpicians, suggested to Lestrange that it would be better to aim for a foundation in Canada. Although it was ruled by Britain, Lower Canada (now the province of Quebec) was steeped in French culture, which had been established there long before the period of British rule. Lestrange took Emery's advice and dispatched a group of monks with England as their destination, the idea being that they could apply there for permission to go to Canada to establish a monastery.[12] It was, in at least one sense, an impetuous move, since Lestrange failed to make any contact with Bishop Hubert of Quebec explaining his intentions.

As the little band made their way toward the English Channel, they found that, due to the unsettled conditions in the region, it was difficult to find a ship to carry them across the Channel. Taking advantage of this situation, the bishop of Antwerp sent word to Lestrange, asking if a foundation could be made in his diocese. Lestrange agreed, and the monastery of Westmalle came into being. Eventually, though, Lestrange ordered some of the monks to continue on to England, again with Canada as their ultimate goal. This group set off under the leadership of Father Jean-Baptiste Desnoyers, their numbers strengthened by additional men sent to join them in the venture.

They were well received in London, where they found a friend in Jean-François de La Marche, the French bishop of Saint-Pol-de-Léon in Brittany, then living in exile in England. He was an important figure in the ecclesiastical life of London, having been chosen by the Vicar Apostolic of the Southern District (to which London belonged) as Vicar General of the diocese, with jurisdiction over all French exiles—both ecclesiastical and lay—living there.[13] De la Marche was able to find passage for the monks on a ship headed for Canada, but whether due to carelessness or willful intention, they were not on the boat when it left. Instead, they accepted an offer from Sir Thomas Weld to establish a monastery on his property at Lulworth, in Dorsetshire. In October 1794 they moved into temporary quarters on the estate while a proper monastery was being built for them.

Lestrange now, belatedly, communicated with the Diocese of Quebec. His letter of March 24, 1795, to Bishop Hubert was somewhat apologetic in tone because of his earlier silence. He described to the bishop his interest in making a foundation in Canada, tracing it to the suggestion made by Father Emery.[14] He explained that the first expedition sent out in 1793 had failed, but that this had resulted in the foundation of Lulworth. He also sent a brief description of the life of his monks, asking the bishop's opinion as to whether or not vocations might be found in Canada.[15]

Bishop Hubert's response was welcoming, but it also sounded a note of warning. The rigors of the climate would make their already austere life difficult in Canada, and it would be hard to find novices willing to embrace it. For this reason, when coming to Canada, it would be best to temper the austerities of la Valsainte during the winter months. Secondly, it would be imperative to have full permission from the British Government for such a venture.[16]

✂ THE ODYSSEY

Nothing immediate resulted from the communication with Bishop Hubert, but the question of a new location soon became urgent. In February of 1798, French forces invaded Switzerland, and la Valsainte's very existence was threatened. Once again it became necessary to look for a refuge—not, as before, to house the overflow from la Valsainte, but

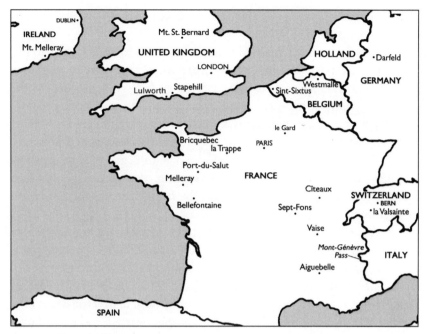

FIGURE 2. *European Trappist monasteries of particular interest to this study.*

rather to find sufficient place for all of Lestrange's followers.

Help came from an unexpected quarter. Six months earlier the Princess Louise-Adelaïde de Condé-Bourbon, cousin of Louis XVI, had become a novice at the monastery of La Sainte Volonté de Dieu, founded by Lestrange in the Bas-Valais region of Switzerland. As a young woman she met Czar Paul I of Russia, who spent some time at her family's chateau at Chantilly when he was still czarevitch. This fact inspired Lestrange with the bold idea of asking for a refuge in Russian lands. The princess, now Sister Marie-Joseph, sent the request, and before an answer came back, the whole band of the Lestrange establishment—monks, nuns, and Third Order members, along with many of their pupils—set out eastward in separate groups. The czar's reply finally reached Lestrange in Bavaria: He was willing to provide havens for them but set a limit of fifteen monks and fifteen nuns.

Disappointing as this was, Lestrange decided to accept the offer but first brought the entire contingent to Vienna, in the hope of finding a place of refuge for those who would not be going to Russia. He then continued on for Russia in July 1798 with the two bands destined for the monasteries there. The others were temporarily left behind in Austria and Bohemia.

When the travelers reached Russia, they were taken to Orsha, to the east of Minsk in present-day Belarus, where the two monasteries promised to them were located.[17] Lestrange himself proceeded to St. Petersburg and was received at the royal court. The czar made an additional offer of certain monasteries in the traditionally Catholic area of his realm—what are now the eastern portions of Belarus and Ukraine. Word was sent to those who had remained behind, and they began their journey just before winter set in. By spring, the various groups had assembled in the town of Terespol, on the Bug River, which at the time constituted Austria's border with Russia.

After crossing over to Brest Litovsk, the monks were organized into six monasteries in the immediate territory, and the nuns were given a convent near one of the monasteries. Two other communities were set up farther south in Volhynia and Podolia. After more than a year of uncertainty, it seemed that they would finally be able to settle down into a regular monastic life. But less than another year later, they all faced another uprooting. After a defeat at the hands of the French, the czar decided to abandon his alliance with England and to go over to the side of Bonaparte. Consequently, in March of 1800 all of Lestrange's monks and nuns were ordered to leave their newly found homes. The various groups made their way down the Bug River towards Danzig in Prussian territory. They eventually sailed to Lübeck and by summer had made their way to Hamburg. They spent the next winter there in houses that Lestrange had managed to rent for them.

This long and trying experience of more than two years "on the road" tested the mettle of Lestrange's troops. Not only had the Russian winter proved to be extremely taxing, but all along the way there they had done their heroic best to maintain their observances. A considerable number lost their lives due to the extreme cold. But it all served as an additional binding force for the group and showed Lestrange just how ready his followers were to accept situations of extreme hardship. More importantly, it forced him to resort to an innate gift of improvisation that would characterize his efforts to find refuge for his religious over the coming years.

◈ Resettling in Western Europe

With the need for a permanent home once more confronting Lestrange, Canada again entered the picture. The year before he and his followers had been forced out of Russia, a French priest of noble extraction living in England, Jacques-Ladislas de Calonne, had traveled with a group of priests to settle on Prince Edward Island, then known as St. John's Island, where they shared a common life and worked as missionaries. Soon after arriving, or perhaps even before they left England, de Calonne considered inviting Lestrange to come to the island to make a foundation. When he heard of this, Bishop Denaut, who had succeeded Hubert as the bishop of Quebec, wrote on July 7, 1800, expressing openness to the idea but wondering if St. John's Island would be the right place for a novitiate.[18] De Calonne respectfully acknowledged the bishop's concern but gently continued to insist.[19] He received a some- what emphatic answer from the bishop's coadjutor[20] at the time, Joseph-Octave Plessis:

> Let us settle this matter of your religious of la Trappe. I personally continue to desire to have them come to this diocese. Just what do you have in mind for them? What other advantages are you offering them? I need this information in order to be able to tell you if they would be better off here rather than there.[21]

Then, on August 3, Lestrange wrote to Bishop Denaut himself. He explained the new predicament in which he found himself after the fail- ure of the Russian expedition and made an even bolder request than he had in 1795 to Bishop Hubert. He proposed coming to Canada not only to found a monastery of monks but also a convent of nuns and an estab- lishment of his Third Order for the purpose of educating children. He even went so far as to suggest that he would establish his own head- quarters in Canada.[22] He never received an answer. Plessis, writing to de Calonne more than ten months later, explained the reason for this silence and offered the possibility of an alternative:

> The abbot of la Trappe lost several of his religious in Russia; they were unable to adapt to the climate of that empire. He wrote to the bishop of Quebec expressing a desire to set up two establishments in this dio- cese, one for women, another for men. . . . For one thing, one should not even dream of introducing new women religious into Canada. Secondly, the climate of the country argues against establishing even one for men; they would succumb as they did in Russia. I have

nonetheless written to the seminary of Montreal to learn if that institution would be disposed to offer land in case the abbot should persist in his project. The superior of the seminary showed that he was well disposed to this. But he believes that the abbot has changed his plans and wishes to settle in England.[23]

Indeed, early in 1801, Lestrange had gone to England to see for himself what could be done to obtain permission from the British government for such a venture in Canada. He had the devoted backing of Bishop de la Marche, but the government was not favorable to the idea. It did, however, offer some generous monetary support for each member of his Order, even those residing outside the British Empire.[24]

During this trip Lestrange also took the first steps towards the creation of a foundation of nuns there, with a view to resettling some of his nuns still living near Hamburg. By the middle of March things were in sufficient readiness for a group of nuns to set sail for England on this new venture. Upon arrival they were settled in temporary quarters, until on October 21, 1802, they moved into Stapehill, a property of the Arundell family adapted for them near the monastery of monks at Lulworth, who would provide for their pastoral care.

After settling matters Lestrange returned to the Continent to take up once again the task of finding a place for the other veterans of the Russian expedition. By that time, there was only one remaining monastery in Europe that could boast of relative peace and prosperity, and Lestrange turned his attention to it in attempting to find room for the wanderers.

∽ DARFELD AND BEYOND

Only a month after its foundation in 1794, the monastery of Westmalle, Lestrange's first foundation, had been threatened by advancing Revolutionary forces, and its monks were forced to flee to Westphalia. Received at first by the Capuchins in the city of Münster, then in the Cistercian Abbey of Marienfeld, they were eventually offered a property at Darfeld by Baron Droste zu Vischering, where they took up monastic life in October of 1795 with Father Eugene de Laprade as their superior. (Fig. 2) Over the intervening years the monastery had grown and prospered. By 1800 it had 126 members. Consequently, Darfeld served as base of operations for resettling large numbers of Lestrange's monks and nuns. Some of the original buildings at Darfeld were adapted for use by the nuns. As the nuns' community continued to grow, these arrangements proved insufficient, and the monks were transferred to Klein Burlo, an abandoned Cistercian priory situated nearby, leaving the original Darfeld property to the nuns.

Other monasteries also participated in the process of repatriation. Lulworth took some of the refugees, and the monastery of Westmalle, which had been closed in the wake of the Revolution, was now re-opened. In addition, the Swiss government gave permission for the re-opening of la Valsainte in 1802, providing yet another haven.[25]

More ambitiously—and more significantly for the Order's future—Lestrange's original plan of attempting to establish a foundation in the United States came back to life. The Sulpician General, Father Emery, who had originally suggested a Canadian home for Lestrange's émigrés, made a generous financial commitment to the American project of the Order. As things turned out, the group of Trappists would be able to count not only on the moral support of the Baltimore Sulpicians, but also on Sulpician funds that would be advanced to them on credit as needed.[26]

In March of 1803, Lestrange sent a letter to Bishop John Carroll of Baltimore, informing him of his plans and asking the bishop to take the group under his protection, gently reminding him, however, that their pastoral ministry to the Church at large would be limited:

> Although they are not called by their vocation to preach, they will not for that reason be useless to our holy religion, as long as they remain faithful to the accomplishment of the duties of their state, because in this way they will preach by their example, a form of preaching that is often more efficacious than the other.
>
> Besides, according to the Rule they must apply themselves to educating children in piety and innocence without neglecting learning. In this way they will be able to prepare for you worthy ministers of the altar.[27]

This amazing statement, which rules out preaching but stresses the education of children, fails to distinguish between the two branches of Lestrange's movement: the strictly monastic one and the "Third Order," with its role of education. Perhaps this misleading statement betrays the fact that Lestrange himself was looking for a formula to describe what would be his American "mission." Dom Augustin's biographer, Laffay, goes so far as to suggest: "Dom Augustin was not simply looking for a new place of refuge in the United States but above all for a field of apostolic activity. In missionary territory, this action was to consist in the education of local youth."[28]

✑ FATHER URBAIN GUILLET

Lestrange lost no time in putting his American plan into action. On May 29, 1803, just two months after writing to Bishop Carroll, Lestrange dispatched the first of two groups, thirty-two monks under the leadership of Father Urbain Guillet, a veteran of Lestrange's wanderings across Europe. Urbain had entered la Trappe in 1786 and was the last of the novices to make profession there before the move to la Valsainte. After his ordination in 1794 he was given various responsibilities, the first of which was an abortive attempt to found a community in Hungary. Then in 1796 he was sent to set up a monastery in Sembrancher. Father Urbain's group set sail from Amsterdam and arrived in Baltimore on September 25. The Sulpicians in Baltimore had apparently already decided to set the monks up on a property that was in the personal care of Father Nagot, Lestrange's former mentor.[29] This thirty-nine acre tract in Pennsylvania, known as Pigeon Hill, seemed an ideal place for the Trappists. The community lived there for almost two years, but on June 10, 1805, they set out for the West on an ill-fated adventure that was to last ten years. One by one the places they chose— in Pennsylvania, Kentucky, Missouri, and Illinois—proved unsuitable.

Urbain was not without support, from both sides of the Atlantic. Early in 1806, la Valsainte sent assistance in the form of Father Marie-Joseph Dunand, who with two companions sailed for Baltimore, arriving there in August. Urbain met him there, and two weeks later Dunand headed to Kentucky to join Urbain's monks. Meanwhile, the former coadjutor of the bishop of Quebec, Joseph-Octave Plessis, who had become bishop himself in January of 1806, had established a connection with the Trappists. Sometime in 1806, one of Plessis's priests went to join Father Urbain, and a correspondence between Urbain and Plessis began that served to sustain the bishop's interest in the Order.[30] As the years go by, one senses Plessis's growing sympathy for the monks. He provided financial assistance for Father Urbain in the form of Mass stipends. He even expressed his desire to be associated spiritually with the monks and adopted the practice of offering Mass once a month for Urbain's group. He also made an attractive offer of land for a possible foundation in Canada, which Urbain failed to accept.

The image of Father Urbain Guillet that comes through in these letters is one of a man harried by the constant battle for sheer survival in impossible circumstances. Nevertheless, it is also clear that some of his problems arose from his own indiscretion, a fact that was not lost on Plessis. In one notable example, Plessis had to discourage Urbain from overreaching his means by going to the Senate in Washington to consolidate his claim to property at Cahokia, in present-day Illinois, site of one of the largest centers of Native American life in North America. Plessis suggested that Urbain be content with the 400 acres he had, and not try to obtain a concession of 4,000 more! Plessis proved to be right: The entire Cahokia establishment failed, like so much else undertaken by Father Urbain.

✐ FATHER VINCENT DE PAUL MERLE

FIGURE 3. *Father Vincent de Paul Merle.*

Some years later another group would be sent to the New World under the leadership of Father Vincent de Paul Merle. Jacques Merle was born on October 29, 1768, in the town of Chalamont, about fifty miles from Lyons.[31] His father was a physician and surgeon in the town, and both he and his brother received an education from the Jesuits at Lyons. In the course of time Jacques was attracted by what he learned of the monastic life at la Valsainte and entered the monastery in its early years.[32] He spent six months in the novitiate, but his health was poor, so he decided to return to France.

On his way to the French border, Jacques met up with one of his friends who was headed south to Saint-Maurice in the Valais region of Switzerland, where he was to be ordained to the priesthood. Jacques decided to accompany him, and he remained there for several months. In this setting he made new contacts, and it is even possible that he received one or other of the Sacred Orders there. He returned to France sometime in the summer of 1794, where he dedicated himself to eccle-siastical ministry during a period of five difficult years.[33] At first he functioned as catechist and teacher but was eventually ordained priest on April 7, 1798, (Holy Saturday) by Bishop Charles-François d'Aviau du Bois de Sanzay, archbishop of Vienne, an ancient town on the Rhône River fifteen miles south of Lyons.[34] The ordination took place secretly in Lyons, in a home near the Rhône.[35]

After his ordination Jacques was attached to a mission in the town of Bourg-en-Bresse and the surrounding area, where he administered the sacraments clandestinely. But he soon was found out and after a trial condemned to deportation. He somehow managed to escape, and in 1799 was functioning as professor at Franclieu, then in 1802 as professor of rhetoric at the seminary in the town of Marboz. The same year, how-ever, when the seminary was transferred from Marboz to Meximieux, Vincent set out once again for la Valsainte, determined to give the monastic life another try.[36]

Much had happened since Jacques's first stay there—most notably the abandonment of the monastery and the subsequent exodus to Russia. But by May of 1803, la Valsainte was formally reestablished, and during or shortly after the month of January 1804, Jacques Merle received the habit and was given the name Vincent de Paul. On October 13, 1805, he made his profession.

✑ BONAPARTE AND LESTRANGE

With the turn of the new century the Church in France faced a new political situation, brought about by the appearance of Napoleon Bonaparte. Because of the military importance of the mountain passes near France's southern borders, in 1801 Napoleon's administration com-missioned the former abbot of the Cistercian monastery of Tamié, Dom Gabet, to organize and open a monastery in the pass of Mont-Cénis. He was authorized to assemble a community and even to assume the title of abbot. The monks were to staff a hospice for soldiers traveling through the pass.

Then, in 1805, on the occasion of Bonaparte's visit to Genoa on his way to France after his coronation in Milan, the superior of Lestrange's nearby foundation of la Cervara sent a message to Napoleon asking his protection for the monastery. Since the idea of using monks to staff the hospice at the mountain pass of Mont-Cénis had worked so well, it was decided these monks should also create a hospice, this time at the mountain pass of Mont-Génèvre. (Fig. 2) Lestrange got wind of the offer and proceeded to take over the project himself.

The new monastery was placed under the care of Father Vincent de Paul as prior. On August 21, 1806, three monks were appointed to direct and oversee the construction of the hospice. Elaborate architectural plans were drawn up for the new monastery, but these were destined to remain on paper, since it was eventually decided to transfer the main hospice to the Sestrières Pass. The Mont-Génèvre establishment became a simple halting place for soldiers. Accordingly, its buildings finally took shape along more modest lines.[37]

In any case, Lestrange made the most of this newly acquired imperial favor, and thanks to the cooperation of Napoleon's Minister of Worship, Portalis, he was able to assure the existence of la Valsainte, Cervara, and Westmalle, and even make several small monastic establishments near Paris.

∾ DARFELD THREATENED

During this period of relative peace a serious problem arose at Darfeld, in Westphalia, that was destined to have important repercussions on the future of Lestrange's entire operation. The drain on the community caused by Lestrange's modifications of the monastery to receive more religious was becoming a source of discontent. Furthermore, Darfeld's superior, Father Eugene de Laprade, felt that his monastery was being neglected in the management of the funds that Britain was making available to Lestrange's monasteries. Without asking permission, de Laprade went off to England to try to remedy the situation. When Lestrange arrived at Darfeld for an official visitation, he was amazed to find that its superior was absent without his permission. Upon returning to la Valsainte he deposed de Laprade and appointed Father Amand Lévêque to replace him.

When the new superior arrived at Darfeld, its subprior, Father Germain Gillon, who was in command during de Laprade's absence, refused to accept him, and after consultation with the local bishop, boldly proceeded to organize an abbatial election on June 6, 1806. The outcome was that de Laprade was elected abbot in absentia. The matter was referred to Rome, and despite Lestrange's own appeal the monastery was provisionally removed from Lestrange's jurisdiction, though he was invited to come to Rome to discuss the matter. He demurred, however, and on June 21, 1808, Darfeld was constituted an abbey of the Order of Cîteaux, (which continued to exist outside France and areas under its control), and Eugene de Laprade's election was officially confirmed by Rome.

It is not clear to what extent the lifestyle at Darfeld began to change in the wake of its independence. It seems that as late as 1814 the monastery was still following the regulations of la Valsainte. Eventually, however, they distanced themselves more and more from the exaggerated austerities that characterized that tradition.

We know little of the stages of this development, but the point of view eventually adopted by Darfeld was that of a return to the way of life as led at la Trappe during the time of de Rancé himself. Consequently their "regulations" came to be known as the "usages" of de Rancé as opposed to those of la Valsainte published in 1794.

It is well beyond the purpose of the present work to enter into the differences between the regulations of la Valsainte and those of de Rancé. By far the most significant "additions" made by la Valsainte had to do with a reduction in the amount of food and of sleep permitted to the monks. The importance of the opposition between the two observances was eventually accentuated, as the foundations of both Lestrange and Darfeld began to multiply after the restoration of the French monarchy in 1814.

∞ Worsening of Relations with Bonaparte

As time passed, Napoleon's relations with the Church worsened, and his friendly feelings toward the Trappists began to erode as well. When he annexed the Papal States to the Empire, Pope Pius VII retaliated on June 10, 1809, by excommunicating "all robbers of Peter's patrimony" (without specifically mentioning Napoleon himself). On July 6 the Pope was taken prisoner and led away to exile in Savona in Piedmont. Lestrange was able to visit him there, a fact that was noted by Napoleon's administration.

More trouble was brewing. The monks of la Cervara, who had taken the oath of fidelity to the regime that had been demanded of them in 1810, were now ordered by Lestrange to make a public retraction. What better indication than this that Lestrange was burning his bridges? The retraction took place on May 4, 1811, and on Lestrange's orders was made public from the pulpit of the monastery church on July 16.

In light of this Lestrange began laying plans once again for the transfer of his monks and nuns to America. The first inkling we get of this comes in March of 1811, when the pupils living at Mont-Génèvre were sent home and Father Vincent, who was chosen to lead the group to America, successfully obtained permission from the government to go to Baltimore.[38] Then in April Lestrange himself applied for a passport to the little seaside town of La-Teste-de-Buch near Bordeaux, where he planned to organize the whole operation. He actually received the passport, but this aroused the curiosity of a town officer of La-Teste-de-Buch who, suspicious of Lestrange's high-class manners, initiated an inquiry, and Lestrange was placed under temporary house arrest in his hotel room. The matter was pursued at central headquarters in Bordeaux, and, in the meantime, Lestrange was permitted to reside at the seminary of Bordeaux.[39]

It became imperative to expedite the sending off of the ones chosen to go to America. In addition to Vincent, two other monks had been singled out for the project, along with a group of five nuns. While the monks were cleared for departure by the authorities, the nuns encountered difficulties and delays. As things turned out, only one of them was able to depart. We learn from Vincent's *Mémoire* that this sister "was also going in order to begin a community and . . . for that reason wished to go before the others; but afterwards she found herself alone because the authorities did not wish to grant passports to her Sisters."[40]

In haste, on June 15, Lestrange penned a letter to Bishop Carroll of Baltimore, informing him of his project and asking for his support, noting: "Although . . . our monasteries are subject directly to the Holy See, we are always full of regard for the bishops who welcome our establishments in their dioceses."[41] It was probably on the same occasion that he sent Father Nagot a letter to the same purpose, hinting in this case that funds would be needed for their operation.[42] In both letters Lestrange requested the bishop to help Vincent de Paul find a suitable location somewhere either in Philadelphia or New York.

∽ A New Contingent Leaves for America

On June 15, 1811, the little band sailed from Bordeaux, arriving in Boston on August 6.[43] Father Matignon, who was working in Boston under Bishop Cheverus, welcomed them warmly and even proposed that they settle there. They decided, however, to keep to their original orders, and Vincent headed on to Baltimore to meet with Bishop Carroll and Father Nagot. The others were to remain in Boston until he called for them. Another version of this story throws a little more light on the possible reason for this decision:

> A group of Trappists exiled from their country by the Revolution, having learned of his high reputation [the reference is to the Bishop Cheverus of Boston], came to him to try to re-establish in his diocese their scattered community. He welcomed them with his usual kindness, offering them generous and loving hospitality for as long as they wished, as well as his help and protection in successfully establishing themselves in the place; but he placed as condition that they mitigate their Rules, several points of which, according to him, were incompatible with the extreme rigor of the climate. He felt that the night Office above all could not take place in a land where the cold was so extreme. These good religious wanted in no way to consent to this and so went on to another place.[44]

The nun that had accompanied Vincent on his journey made a good impression on Cheverus, as he related to Carroll two months later:

> The Sister is a very sensible woman and would, I think, make an excellent instructress of youth. Should her expected companions not arrive, I think she would be a valuable acquisition to the Sisterhood at Emmetsburg.[45]

When Vincent arrived in Baltimore, the bishop, after some difficulties in finding a place for them, finally found a farm belonging to the Jesuits. In the meantime those left behind in Boston were growing anxious after six weeks without any news.[46] Finally, after two months had passed, Vincent sent for them. By the time they arrived and settled down into their new temporary quarters at the farm, it must have been well into the fall.[47] The sister was placed in a separate house.

It is not clear just when Vincent was offered a tract of land near the town of Milford, Pennsylvania, on the Delaware River at Pennsylvania's eastern border, about a hundred miles from Philadelphia. (Fig. 4) It is conceivable that before the winter set in he was able to make a brief, preliminary visit to the site, but given the severity of the winter in this mountainous territory, it could not have been until the following summer that he made a more detailed exploration of the property. This he did in the company of two young men who had expressed interest in

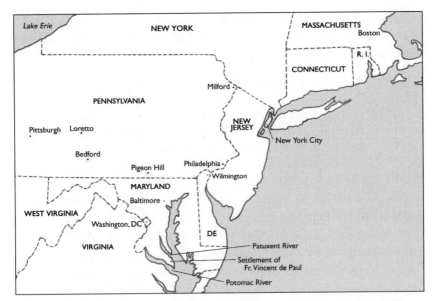

FIGURE 4. *Sites in the eastern United States related to the work of Fathers Urbain Guillet and Vincent de Paul Merle.*

embracing his way of life, and whom he describes as "novices."[48] Their way was through a dense forest, where they did their best to avoid an encounter with the local bears and managed to keep alive by munching on blueberries and whatever else could be found in the way of food. The adventure proved to Vincent that the property offered to him did not suit his needs.

∽ SETTLEMENT IN MARYLAND

After a year spent in the United States, Vincent turned his attention to an area in Maryland that was recommended to him by both Bishop Carroll and the Sulpicians. Late in 1812 or during the early months of 1813 Vincent moved his group to the new location. By this time they were joined by three others whom Lestrange had sent to America: Father Francis Xavier Kaiser, who was to play an important role in the future of Vincent's later foundation in Nova Scotia, Brother Claude, and Brother François de Paule.[49] Vincent's account does not identify the exact spot where they settled; he describes it as being "near the Patuxent [which he calls Potoxen] and not far from the Potomac" and "near the sea."[50] Local tradition, however, situates their property more precisely in the southern part of St. Mary's County, Maryland, which saw the beginnings of settlement in the state in 1634 by a group of English colonists.

> At the beginning of winter, 1813, they arrived in St. Mary's county, bought land near St. Nicholas', built a log-house, cleared an acre and a half, and, helped by negroes, began to cultivate. . . . The only memorial of their brief sojourn near St. Nicholas' is the name Trappe, and the graveyard where some of them were buried.[51]

St. Nicholas was then a small church served by the Jesuits from the nearby Church of St. Ignatius, some ten miles to the south. This account, which depends in part on Vincent's own account of his stay there, suggests that the Trappist settlement was near this church. There happen to be two streets bearing the name Trapp (Trapp Road and Trapp Way) in existence today only a half mile from the Church of St. Ignatius itself, which might indicate that Vincent's group was closer to St. Ignatius, but street names alone hardly constitute strong evidence.

In the course of the winter they set up log cabins and began to clear land. In the spring they planted a garden—things seemed promising. With the onset of summer, however, they learned what it meant to wage war on mosquitoes and ticks, and eventually all of the monks came down with fever.

The aftermath of this experiment seems to have been a move back to Baltimore, where the community was welcomed by one who proved to be a faithful friend during the rest of their stay in the United States: Father Jean-François Moranvillé. Born in Cagny near Amiens, Moranvillé had joined the Holy Spirit Fathers and was ordained in 1784. After a number of years spent ministering in the French colony at Cayenne, French Guiana, he came to Baltimore in 1794 or 1795, and in 1804 became pastor of the Church of St. Patrick at Fells Point.

> To the Trappists, coming to Baltimore after an unsuccessful attempt to establish their Congregation in Southern Maryland, Moranvillé offered first the hospitality of his house, with additional accommodations in a rented building adjoining the church property; and later, he set them up in "Whitehall," a large property opposite the church on Market Street, which he rented for that purpose. One of their members had died on the trip to Baltimore, and Father Moranvillé, as an added mark of courtesy, had the body interred at the foot of his Calvary. The following is a transcript from the burial records:

FIGURE 5. *Jean-François Moranvillé.*

2d 8ber [October 2], 1813, was buried the Reverend Father Franciscus Xaverius of the Order of the Trappists, deceased last night, in the Chesapeake Bay, brought sick from St. Mary's County, in the 37th year of his age. [Signed] Moranvillé.[52]

Father Moranvillé also offered his hospitality to Father Urbain Guillet, who from the rectory of St. Patrick's wrote a letter to his brother in France recounting the latest news of the Trappists in America. There had been much illness and death among his own men, and as a result he had decided to leave the Midwest and come east with the survivors. After settling them in "a small hut, big enough to house two cows, on an island near Pittsburgh in Pennsylvania," he proceeded to Maryland to assist Vincent's group. He had hoped to bring them back to Pittsburgh, but finding them unable to undertake the arduous journey of more than 200 miles, he had decided instead to lead them "to a place between Baltimore and Philadelphia."[53] One supposes that, when he himself arrived in Baltimore, he found Vincent and his group in their temporary home near St. Patrick's, and that by the time the letter was written he had already transferred them to the spot "between Baltimore and Philadelphia."

Whatever its precise location, the new site of Vincent's community must have been reasonably close to Philadelphia, since Vincent was able to administer the sacrament of Baptism in St. Joseph's Church there on August 22, 29, and 30, October 22, 29, and 30, 1813, and then again on January 18 and 23, 1814.[54] Vincent's concern for the needs of parish ministry would characterize his entire life in North America. For his part, in typical never-say-die fashion, Father Urbain still had plans afoot to find a suitable site for a foundation, as he tells his brother in the same letter quoted above:

> I am hoping to leave next Tuesday to visit those in Pittsburgh, after which I will go to visit two parcels of land eighty miles from Pittsburgh, which I want to buy. If this location suits me and I can come to some agreement with the owner, I will immediately bring there those who are on the island; otherwise I will try inasmuch as my means permit, to bring them together with the others. Then I will go to see a site in Virginia, only 100 miles from there. It is said to be promising for us.[55]

By the fall of 1813, the stage was finally set for the appearance of the person who would determine what the next move would be: Dom Augustin de Lestrange.

Chapter Two

Adventures in Martinique and the United States

∞ LESTRANGE IN FLIGHT

WHILE LESTRANGE'S MONKS in America were struggling with their own situation, Dom Augustin was facing his own challenges back in Europe. About a month after Vincent and his group left France in June of 1811, Lestrange managed to get permission to leave the seminary in Bordeaux and return to la Valsainte on what he described as urgent business. He traveled as a hunted man: The monks of la Cervara had announced the retraction of their oath of loyalty to Napoleon's regime on July 16, and the news had spread quickly. The blow to Lestrange's monasteries came swiftly. On July 28 all Trappist monasteries in lands controlled by Napoleon were closed. In many cases the monks continued to live in small clandestine groups awaiting better times. The community of la Cervara suffered most of all, and its monks were exiled to Corsica.[1] Darfeld, which had successfully weathered the Revolutionary storm of the late 1700s, was now also forced to close its doors. Lestrange himself, who had arrived in la Valsainte by August 1, was forced to flee yet again, "disappearing" for almost a year along the various roads of Europe.

During this period, the rumor spread that he had been captured and executed. This news led to the celebration of Requiem Masses for him at Lulworth and Stapehill in England. Lestrange himself put the rumors

25

FIGURE 6. *Bishop Edmund Burke, Vicar Apostolic of Halifax.*

to rest by resurfacing in England towards the end of 1812. Once again he approached government officials for permission to go to Canada.

✎ FATHER EDMUND BURKE

Having failed at least twice before to make arrangements for settling in Canada, Lestrange this time changed his tactics. He had heard of a Father Edmund Burke in Halifax, Nova Scotia, a dynamic figure, originally from Ireland, who would play a highly significant role in the future of Father Vincent's community. Quebec's Bishop Plessis, who had been long acquainted with Lestrange's movement and who still maintained a guarded interest in it, named Burke Vicar General for this distant colony, entrusting to him the organization of the local Church there. Sometime in January of 1813 Lestrange decided to write to Burke. The letter has not survived, but Burke apparently forwarded it to Bishop Plessis, expressing his own enthusiasm for the possibility of "a good establishment of these good Fathers in Upper Canada and even in Lower Canada."[2] He promised to offer them lands for cultivation as well as some financial help. From the tone of his letter, it seems that Burke saw the Trappists as something of a missionary force, particularly in Upper Canada, where a community would be more effective than scattered missionaries.[3] Plessis's reply shows that he was still open to the idea of their coming but insisted once more on the need for getting British government approval for the project. He promised to take the matter up with the authorities.[4]

By the time Burke answered the bishop's letter in July of 1813 his interest had shifted from Upper and Lower Canada to Nova Scotia itself. He had taken the initiative to speak with Sir John Sherbrooke, lieutenant-general of Nova Scotia (1811-1816):

> While speaking to our Governor the other day I took the opportunity to speak to him of Father Augustin of la Trappe, saying that he would be of great help to me with the Indians. This good man [the governor], who sympathizes with my fate of being all alone, answered me that I must send for him [Augustin] immediately to help me here until I find some others. "And after that," said he, "we shall see." This was all I was asking for, for as soon as I can build a house for him on a property which I have just acquired at Antigonish, no one can hinder my doing what I want in this matter. Furthermore, this community will be more useful in this province than in the Canadas. Besides, an establishment here will be a step toward [setting them up in] the other colonies. There are several Irishmen in the community in England [Lulworth], whom I can subsequently bring to Upper-Canada without [obtaining] the consent of anyone else. We Irish are not in the habit of asking permissions to enjoy privileges which the laws themselves give us. . . .
>
> I have written to the good Father [Lestrange] and will send the letter on a boat leaving today. I have also written to a merchant who is a friend of mine asking him to pay the expenses of his voyage.[5]

This is vintage Burke. Impatient with red tape, he goes straight to the governor and, playing on his concern for the ever acute problem of British relations with the Indians, he gets a verbal go-ahead to bring in the community "for now." Nor does he lose time in making arrangements to bring Lestrange over immediately. His penchant for the grandiose also comes through in his plan to bring some of his fellow countrymen from the Lulworth community to Upper Canada, which had been the first field of his missionary activities.

Plessis's cautionary reply is no less characteristic, and would continue to be a mark of their respective dealings with Vincent throughout the coming years. He reminds Burke of just how much pastoral help he could expect from the Trappists:

> I admire your views concerning this good Father. Is it probable that, if he comes to America, it would be to work in the ministry? Do you think that the religious who would come with him or after him would put aside the exercise of contemplation or manual labor to give themselves to instructing the savages? Are you so little familiar with their vigils, their fasting, their flight from the world to [word illegible] that they could adapt themselves to so severe a climate as Antigonish or any other place in Nova Scotia or Lower Canada? I am counting a great deal on the secular clergy which you will get from Kilkenny.... But as far as the Trappists go, don't expect anything else from them except fervent prayers and the clearing of a little land, and that in some other climate than ours.[6]

As he mentioned in his own letter, Burke made contact with a merchant in Liverpool and had him purchase a ticket for Lestrange to come to Nova Scotia. Unfortunately, by the time Burke's letter of invitation reached England, Lestrange had already embarked on a new adventure in his ongoing saga. Despite his best efforts, he had been unsuccessful in getting the British government to allow him to go to Canada, but he had been able to procure permission to go to the British colony of Martinique, in the Caribbean. He set sail on April 25, 1813.

✑ MARTINIQUE AND THE UNITED STATES

Lestrange's choice of traveling companions was as ill-fated as the timing of his departure. Among those he selected were three young monks of Lulworth: Two of these, Francis Flynn and the Canadian Martin Chéneguy, were ordained to the priesthood for this new venture, while the third, Thomas Power, because of his young age, received only the subdiaconate. Trouble was not long in arising. First of all, according to reports, Power became the captain's drinking companion. Then Martin Chéneguy turned against Lestrange and denounced him to the captain. History has not preserved what reasons Chéneguy gave, but when they arrived at Martinique he repeated his accusations to the governor, and Lestrange was imprisoned. Chéneguy subsequently fell desperately ill and in a dramatic scene of repentance retracted his accusations. Lestrange regained his freedom, but in the meantime had lost his two other companions; both Power and Flynn moved to the island of Ste. Croix to undertake an apostolate of their own.[7] Flynn eventually ended up in Pennsylvania, where he died in 1831, and Power returned to England.[8]

Lestrange's own position remained precarious, because it seems that he had only been granted permission to fill "a vacant parochial post in the colony . . . as a simple priest."[9] Despite this proviso, he insisted that he had come to Martinique to found a monastery. To make matters even worse, he did not hesitate to appear in public wearing pontifical insignia.

Conditions were obviously far from ideal in Martinique, and Lestrange soon took steps to move on. By December 7, 1813, Dom Antoine Saulnier de Beauregard, superior at Lulworth, had received news that Dom Augustin was planning to go with his remaining religious "to Baltimore or to the banks of the Missipipy"[10] undoubtedly with a view to joining his two lieutenants who were already there: Fathers Urbain Guillet and Vincent de Paul Merle.[11]

The Martinique episode represented something of a turning point in Lestrange's reputation as a leader. His lack of judgment in the choice of his three traveling companions was not lost on Bishop Plessis of Quebec, who also noted that Lestrange had hastily arranged for Chéneguy's ordination to the priesthood in 1814, while he was still a novice. Plessis wrote to his Vicar General in London, whom Lestrange had talked into granting the promotion: "This worthy abbot must have had little judgment in order to be duped by this rascal and to show such confidence as to present for Sacred Orders a man who does not know three words of theology, philosophy or rhetoric. . . . This whole enterprise was poorly planned."[12] This latter judgment would have been heartily underwritten by Dom Antoine de Beauregard, the superior of Lulworth, who had seen his own community tapped for personnel for Lestrange's venture. Years later, reporting to the Roman Congregation of Propaganda, Dom Antoine described this adventure as:

a voyage so poorly organized and which had such regrettable consequences and was painful in more ways than one for our little
monastery in England, to which Dom Augustin came to take, arbitrarily and without discretion, subjects who were doing well, who were
useful to me [and yet] for whom this unfortunate journey was a disastrous reef.[13]

The process of division within Lestrange's movement, which began
with the independence granted to Darfeld in 1808, would gain strength
from now on.

The first stage of Lestrange's journey to the United States was from
Martinique to the Island of St. Bartholomew, for which he received a
passport on November 20, 1813. Sometime after this date, he seems to
have gone to Baltimore to meet Bishop Carroll and no doubt got in
touch with Urbain and Vincent, but little else is known about how he
spent the first months of 1814 in the United States.[14] As for the other
Trappists, we left Vincent and his group at some location between
Philadelphia and Baltimore after their stay with Moranvillé in
Baltimore. Father Vincent's pastoral activities in Philadelphia, which
continued at least until January 23, 1814, suggest that the group was still
in their same location at that time.

A less reliable document in the form of a series of historical notes in
the archives of the abbey of Bellefontaine suggests that Urbain's group,
after leaving the island near Pittsburgh, eventually made their way to
Bedford, Pennsylvania, on the old military road leading west from
Philadelphia. From here they made one last abortive attempt at a foundation in a wilderness area near Loretto.[15]

✑ The Trappists in Manhattan

Whatever Lestrange's activities might have been during the first
months of his stay in the United States, a new idea had certainly begun
to take shape at least by the spring of 1814, if not earlier: to transfer all
of his religious to New York City. The Trappists would enter the city at
a difficult moment in its history. Even before the outbreak of war with
Britain in 1812, the economic situation had begun to deteriorate due to
President Jefferson's 1807-1809 embargo prohibiting international
trade either out of or into American ports. Furthermore, from the end
of 1813 until the end of the war in February 1815, the port itself was
closed because of an extensive British blockade of the northeast coast,

including the entrance to Long Island Sound. Unemployment was rampant, particularly in activities linked to the shipping industry.[16]

Despite this lengthy period of uncertainty, the city had already begun to expand beyond the settled areas at the southern extremity of the island. The first plans for a grid of regular streets appeared in 1811, and by the time of Lestrange's arrival, some buildings already existed in the area to the north. Among these was the New York Literary Institution, a Jesuit school situated on what would one day be Fifth Avenue between Fiftieth and Fifty-first Streets. In 1813 the Jesuits decided to close the establishment, and the property was offered to Lestrange as a gathering place for his followers.

A letter that Lestrange later wrote to Baltimore's Bishop Carroll gives some idea of how the project was to be financed:

> I thank Your Excellency for the fears which you expressed concerning my acquisition of the college of New York, for this is a proof of your sincere concern for me; but I must put Your Excellency at ease by saying that I did not contract any obligation. With these gentlemen we had only agreed that I would give them $2,000 [gourdes] and that the other $10,000 would be covered by a mortgage on the property.[17] I had only consented to that because a business man promised me these $2,000, which I did not have.[18]

Lestrange's plans were for a diversified use of the property. First, he called together and combined into a single community under his personal direction the three groups of monks: those of Urbain, those of Vincent, and finally those who had come with him from Martinique.[19] Then, near the newly acquired property he set up a small convent for nuns. One of Vincent's occupations during his sojourn in New York was to serve as confessor to the convent of Trappistines, as well as to the nearby convent of the Ursulines. On Sundays he went to celebrate Mass in each of these convents. Finally, a school was set up for thirty-three poor children, almost all of them orphans.

We learn more about this school from a document Lestrange had printed in English on June 1: "A Prospectus Shewing the advantages of the Houses of Education under the direction of the Order of LA TRAPPE, and particularly in behalf of Orphan Children."[20] This sets forth Lestrange's ideas on the sort of education that would be offered in the prospective school, along with more practical details concerning the admission of students. Thus the original scholastic orientation of the property would in some measure continue, albeit in the Lestrangian mode, alongside the two monasteries.

Things were already in place by the feast of Corpus Christi on June 10, 1814, for Vincent describes a public procession of the Blessed Sacrament with stations set up in the field adjacent to their house.[21]

✑ THE RETURN TO FRANCE

Despite these seemingly promising beginnings, the New York establishment was to be short-lived. Before two months had elapsed, Lestrange decided to return to France with his entire company, as he makes clear in a letter of July 25 to Bishop Carroll. There seems to have been a shortage of funds and possibly some opposition to what he was trying to do in New York.[22] More importantly, the restoration of the monarchy in France opened the door to the exciting possibility of making foundations in France itself. Accordingly, Augustin and his troop of monks and nuns set sail in the autumn of the same year, arriving at Le Havre on November 22, 1814.[23]

Vincent was left behind with six brothers to close down the operation in New York. By the spring of 1815, they too were ready to undertake the voyage home to France. The sisters of the little Ursuline convent nearby were returning to Cork, Ireland, and they invited Vincent to travel with them (at their expense) and serve as their priest during the crossing. So the whole group finally set out on April 27, 1815, on the *Mars*, which was heading for England.[24]

The ship, a British transport vessel, was due to make a stop at Halifax, then continue on to England. But when it arrived in Halifax on May 10, it was ordered to proceed to Quebec, and the passengers were put off at Halifax. The little troop was warmly received by Father Burke, who had earlier solicited so diligently for the establishment of a Trappist community in Nova Scotia. He was able to obtain free passage for them on the *Ceylon*, another British transport heading for Plymouth, their only expense being the provisions needed for the crossing. The boat was scheduled to leave in two weeks' time, and when the day arrived, they boarded the ship. Vincent's account of what followed is worth citing in its entirety:

> The vessel was headed straight for Plymouth, a port not far from Lulworth, where our monastery is situated. I had already been on board with my brothers for two days, when at the suggestion of these

brothers as well as of several officers on board, I went to get provisions. At the time the wind was altogether contrary, and I noticed that several fellow passengers were going to Halifax. There seemed to be no question of the boat leaving right away. Hardly had I reached Msgr. Burke's house when all of a sudden the wind changed and became favorable. As soon as I became aware of this, I ran to join my brothers, but it was too late, the vessel was already far off.

Although it pained me to be separated from my brothers, my conscience did not reproach me for having wanted this to happen. Before leaving the ship I had suggested to Br. Francis Xavier that he go to Halifax for these provisions. It was only after he said that he would not be able to get certain things we wanted, that I decided to go myself, not, however, without some anxiety. Yet, I was so convinced that I would return—and that very soon—that I did not even bring a Breviary with me. I left just as I was, in an old habit. Fortunately, I had a guinea with me which served to obtain some necessary things. So I can assure you that at the time I had no plan of remaining in America, having decided to join my brothers in England. I might be at fault, (and I certainly am) for having desired some time before that such a thing happen; however, I would not have wanted this to come about from my own doing, but from God. I had several times told my brothers how sorry I was to leave America without having accomplished anything there, and that I had an attraction to remain there at least for a while longer. What I wanted God did not want; it was only when I had renounced my own will, that he willed or permitted this event to happen.

To get back to my brothers—they left without me on the ship *Ceylon* on May 26, 1815. There were six of them: Brothers Francis Xavier, Ignatius, Eutymius, Dominic, as well as two children who had been with us in the house.[25]

Ordered into a harsh, difficult world, Vincent had been subjected to all sorts of hardships, and now found himself abandoned, literally on the dock. He took on his duty willingly, of course. And yet, the whole experience had clearly become something more. His sense of mission went far beyond a mere sense of duty. He had taken this new land into his heart. Henceforth, he would be facing an entirely new chapter in his life. For the moment, he had little choice but to return to Father Burke, who had shown such great kindness to the little group during their brief stay in Halifax.

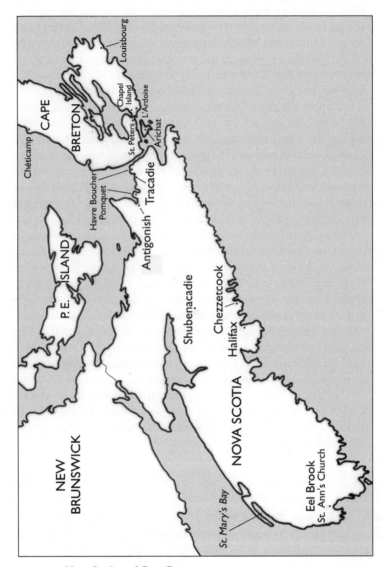

FIGURE 7. *Nova Scotia and Cape Breton.*

Chapter Three

The New World of Nova Scotia

V INCENT ARRIVED AT a crucial moment in the development of the Church in Nova Scotia. Bishop Plessis of Quebec, in whose vast diocese it was situated, was at that very time on his third pastoral tour of these outlying areas and would be arriving in Halifax just six weeks after Vincent. Furthermore, in two years' time Father Burke, who had welcomed Vincent in Halifax, would be ordained bishop and put in charge of the Church in Nova Scotia with the title of Vicar Apostolic. Thus, very shortly after his arrival Vincent would meet the two most important ecclesiastics responsible for the Church in this area. Both of them knew of the Trappists, and Burke had for some time been trying to get them to come to America. So for the future bishop what seemed at first a chance meeting with one of Lestrange's monks turned out in God's providence to be the beginning of a lasting relationship with Father Vincent. The first Lestrange monastery in the New World would eventually be set up in the territory of his new Vicariate Apostolic.

But all that still lay in the future. As for now, Burke willingly took Vincent under his wing. From Burke's own perspective, the timing could not have been better. Burke himself was soon to be heading home to Ireland to undergo surgery on his knee, and given the scarcity of priests, Vincent's presence would be a great boon to the only other priest in the city of Halifax, Father Mignault. Meanwhile, as they all waited for the bishop's imminent arrival, Vincent undoubtedly spent some of his time making his first acquaintance with the day-to-day realities of city life in Halifax.

✍ THE BISHOP'S PASTORAL VISITATION

On May 31, 1815, Bishop Plessis—accompanied by an entourage of three priests and a servant—set out by boat for his official canonical visitation of part of the lands at the easternmost extremity of his large diocese. During the course of this arduous four-month trip, the bishop visited the local clergy, conferred the sacrament of confirmation, and inspected places of worship. Beginning at Arichat on Cape Breton, the visitors worked their way around the southeastern portion of the island, finally arriving at Halifax on July 14. The bishop kept a careful journal of his experiences and impressions along the way, as he had done on his first two pastoral visits, in 1811 and 1812. Written in the third person, these accounts are of unusual interest not only for the information they provide, but also for their lively style and attention to many details of human interest.[1]

The impression that Father Vincent de Paul Merle made on Plessis is evident from the space given both to the story of Vincent's mishap of "missing the boat" and to a lengthy description of Lestrange's work from the time of the occupation of la Valsainte up until his return to France from America in 1814. There is even an account of the unpleasant experience of Martinique, with this wry comment concerning Chéneguy: "Dom Augustin expiated by this unexpected persecution his imprudence in promoting an unworthy person to Orders."[2]

Plessis's meeting with Vincent was his first face-to-face contact with these Trappists of whom he had heard so much. The bad impression made upon the bishop by Lestrange's lack of judgment in the Chéneguy affair now gave way to fascination with an idea that had surfaced in a July 6, 1813, letter he had received from Burke.[3] A community could have greater pastoral efficacy than a number of individual missionaries in caring for the needs of the local population. This would be especially effective, felt Burke, were a Trappist community established near a settlement of the local Native American people, the Mi'kmaqs. At the time, Plessis was not convinced, but now he was able to discuss these ideas more fully with Burke, who by this time had certainly done some further thinking on his own concerning the rich possibilities offered by the presence of a real Trappist.

FIGURE 8. *Archbishop Joseph-Octave Plessis of Quebec.*

In any case, a plan slowly took shape for a foundation of Trappists who would lead their secluded life but would do so near a settlement of Indians for whose spiritual needs they could care. Such an arrangement would undoubtedly appeal to the British government. Since their earliest contacts with the Mi'kmaqs, the British had had great difficulty dealing with the native peoples. The French, on the other hand, had from the times of their earliest settlements developed a kind of symbiosis with them, often sharing in their lifestyle to some extent and frequently intermarrying with them. The early French missionaries had made a particularly strong impression on the Mi'kmaqs. One of these, Father Maillard, who had arrived in Nova Scotia in 1735, was able to consolidate the efforts of those who had come before him and he was single-handedly responsible for the conversion of the whole tribe to Catholicism. So close was this bond between Mi'kmaqs and the Catholic Church that after the British takeover in 1760 Maillard was appointed official missionary to the Indians and Acadians of Nova Scotia, with a base in Halifax itself.[4] This, the British felt, was the only effective way of keeping some control over them. After Maillard's death in 1762, the Indians continued to ask for a Catholic missionary, and though appointments were made, there never seemed to be enough priests to satisfy their demands. Thus it was an ongoing problem.

High on the list of government plans regarding the Mi'kmaqs was the task of bringing them in line with the British work ethic. As the British saw it, this meant above all getting them to settle down to farming. For this reason one would imagine that Plessis's idea of a Trappist foundation would be appealing. Farming had always been an important part of Trappist life, and if such a community were founded to care for the spiritual needs of the tribe, it could also educate them in farming and itself provide a strong visible image of how the government was trying to get *them* to live.

Soon after his arrival in Halifax in 1815, Plessis paid an initial visit to the Lieutenant Governor, Sir John Sherbrooke. The subject of the Mi'kmaqs and their need for spiritual and material assistance came up. Plessis must have outlined his plan for the Trappists, which seems to have been well received by the Lieutenant Governor.[5] Plessis lost no time in setting down his ideas in a letter to Sherbrooke written on the last day of his stay in Halifax. In this he outlined Burke's old idea that a stable community was the best way to provide for the needs of the Indians. He then went on to present the Trappists as the ideal group to manage such an establishment:

> In all the world there is perhaps no community more apt to accomplish these different ends than the religious of la Trappe. High on the list of duties of these highly respected men is that of instructing the ignorant. They are also well versed in different kinds of work, above all the cultivation of grains and vegetables. They are accustomed to living on little, and far from being a burden to the countries where they settle, they bring to such places their own hard work and are ready to offer their hospitality to others.
>
> They [the Mi'kmaqs] are children who must be taught how to work. If one succeeds in doing this, all else will be easy. . . . [When they become] attached to their fields, they will find in them a source of their clothing, their nourishment and will no longer have a pretext for wandering here and there throughout the city, begging and dragging through the streets in a state of drunkenness. But who is to inspire them with a love for work, which is a value so foreign to them and for which they have so little aptitude? Your Excellency was kind enough to permit me to express my ideas to you on this matter. It will be an honor for me to submit them to you freely.
>
> These Mi'kmaqs were brought up in the Catholic religion and although deprived of missionaries for about fifty years now, they

nonetheless hold fast to its principles, to such a degree that there is not even one among them who has yet abandoned this religion. They feel the need for a missionary to reestablish themselves in their former religious ways; they insistently ask for one, and experience has shown that missionaries will always have more influence on the Catholic savages, than do any civil or military officers that one might place in charge of them. Nonetheless in the state of apathy and degradation into which the Mi'kmaqs of this province have fallen, an isolated missionary would not be sufficient, as is the case with other tribes of the British Provinces of this continent. They need the assistance of a vigilant and industrious community.[6]

It is clear from the letter that Plessis was seeking not only Sherbrooke's personal approval but also official confirmation from the British government. He explicitly asks the governor to communicate the request to "His Majesty's ministers." His thinking in this matter was that if the establishment were set on a firm footing from the British side, it would be able to survive a change of governor, which might bring in someone unfavorable to the Church.[7]

Vincent took part with Fathers Burke and Mignault in the events of the bishop's visitation at Halifax and was even invited to accompany the bishop on his visit to the village of Chezzetcook, eighteen miles up the coast from Halifax. They were taken there on a vessel supplied by Admiral Griffiths. As they attempted to land, the ship's launch was almost overturned by a huge wave that thoroughly doused them all. Fortunately, no one was harmed, but Plessis notes with his characteristic attention to detail that Vincent lost his hat.[8]

Vincent was forced to stay home on the day of the bishop's day trip to the village of Prospect, some miles south of Halifax on the coast, in order to care for Father Mignault, who was ill. Vincent assisted in making the final preparations for the Confirmations that took place on the last day of the bishop's stay in Halifax.

By the time he left Halifax, Plessis had already taken a first step in implementing his plan for the Trappist venture: He had written to Sherbrooke. He would still need to interest Lestrange in the project. The importance the bishop attached to this new plan is shown from the fact that he penned a letter to Lestrange while still on his way through Nova Scotia, as he continued his pastoral visitation. In this letter he outlines the plan, attempting to show that it would not disturb monastic observance, pointing out that it would be:

a means to exercise your brothers in the active life, in works of charity and of ecclesiastical ministry, without prejudice to monastic observances, because applying themselves to the formation of the savages near the monastery, they would be able to take turns in giving themselves to this activity and still be able to return to solitude from time to time so as to be renewed and sustained in the spirit of their way of life.[9]

This might seem a venturesome way to present matters to Lestrange, considering the exclusively contemplative bent of the monks in his monasteries. Yet there was earlier evidence that in Lestrange's thinking his monasteries in the New World had a definite, if limited, missionary thrust: His letter to Bishop Carroll in 1803 proposing just such a role indicated as much. Furthermore, given the existence of his Third Order, room might be found also for this new plan. Pushing matters a bit, Plessis adds in the same letter:

> As for novices, you will easily find them in whatever spot you should choose in Nova Scotia, which abounds in Catholics of all nationalities, as well as [in] the neighboring islands and in Canada which is not very distant.

There is, perhaps, no clearer indication of the degree to which Plessis's thinking had changed since the days when he offered Burke little hope that the Trappists would be able to find vocations in Nova Scotia.

On August 6 Plessis sent to Vincent the letter he had written to Lestrange (which Vincent was to forward to France) along with a copy of his letter to Lieutenant-Governor Sherbrooke.[10] Even before Vincent had a chance to send them off, however, he himself had received a letter written by Lestrange on July 7, giving him permission to remain in Nova Scotia "and to begin to establish a monastery there."[11] On August 29 Vincent finally forwarded Plessis's packet of letters to Lestrange at Lulworth in care of its abbot, Dom Antoine. There is no indication that Lestrange ever answered the bishop's letter. So it seems to have been on the strength of the permission given in Lestrange's July 7 letter that Vincent pursued his work in Nova Scotia over the coming years.

∽ Vincent's Early Days in Halifax and Vicinity

In his covering letter sent with the documents to be forwarded to Lestrange, Plessis informed Vincent that his first assignment would be to spend the coming winter with Father Jean Mandé Sigogne, in St.

Mary's Bay on the old Acadian coast. Coming from England in 1799 where he had taken refuge from persecution in France, this dedicated priest had settled in the Eel Brook area near the southwestern tip of Nova Scotia, where he established the parish of St. Ann. (Fig. 7)

"For the winter you will have a warm church, a warm room for yourself, and much tranquillity and freedom to give yourself to your exercises."[12] The bishop's main intent was to give Vincent a more suitable atmosphere than could be found in Halifax. But with Sigogne he would also be able to begin studying the Mi'kmaq language, which would stand him in good stead in his work with this native people, if Lestrange were to approve of their plans.

As it turned out, the plan to spend the winter with Sigogne proved unfeasible, for in Halifax Father Mignault's increasingly poor health made it imperative that someone remain there not only to care for him, but also to serve the needs of the Church, since Burke had by this time left for Ireland to care for his own health. When Plessis learned of Mignault's plight he permitted Vincent to remain in Halifax. He suggested, however, that Vincent make several excursions to places where the Mi'kmaqs gathered in order to get a feel for their way of life—warning him, however, that he should not give the impression that he was starting an establishment before permission came through. But Vincent was nonetheless authorized to minister to them spiritually. In response to the bishop's suggestion, Vincent visited the two places nearest Halifax where the Indians gathered: Shubenacadie and Chezzetcook. (Fig. 7) Furthermore, while Plessis waited for an answer to his letter to Lestrange (at the time of writing this letter he was still waiting), he and Vincent agreed that Vincent would remain in Nova Scotia "without taking into consideration any orders he might receive from his abbot, unless the abbot should send these orders to him after having received my own letters."[13] In other words, Plessis wanted Vincent to remain in Nova Scotia until Lestrange had answered the bishop's letter.

So Vincent was based in Halifax for the time being. The town in which he now found himself had always been one in which the tone was set by the military. This was particularly true during the years immediately preceding his arrival. Britain's war with France had only come to an end in the spring of 1814 with the fall of Napoleon, and the conflict with the United States on Christmas Eve. In addition to the splendor of the Great Parade, when the king's troops daily mounted guard in their colorful uniforms, there was also the seedier side of military life represented by the brothels on Barrack Street and the drinking establishments on Water Street. Add to this the constant roving of drunken military men and of the navy's press gangs out to forcibly recruit civilians, and you have the picture of a town that was, for Vincent, a decided change from Maryland's mosquitoes.[14]

As fall set in, Vincent found himself alone for a whole month ministering to the Catholics of Halifax, for Mignault had gone to Arichat for a rest sometime around the middle of September. One of the greatest challenges for Vincent was dealing with a congregation that consisted principally of English-speaking Irish who had settled in Nova Scotia. He occasionally ventured to preach in English, as he was to recount some years later:

> [During the month Mignault was away] I had to baptize, hear confessions, marry, visit the sick in the city and in the countryside, be available day and night, sing the Mass on all Sundays and feasts. Although I did not know much English, I twice preached in that language in the Catholic church of the city, and at that time there were more than two thousand Catholics in the city, most of them Irish.[15]

During this early period, he seems to have found time to help out at least occasionally in the Eel Brook area of the missionary territory of Father Sigogne.[16]

Mignault, on his return to Halifax, wrote Plessis an apologetic letter excusing himself for not having asked permission for the trip to Arichat. The matter was urgent, however, and, as he put it, having consulted "God and Father Vincent," he had set off.[17] His frequent and chatty letters to the bishop almost always make mention of how Father Vincent was faring.

One important decision they made was to find a location that would provide solitude for Vincent but would be not far from Halifax in case Mignault needed him. Mignault had at first considered having him spend the winter at an important Mi'kmaq site, Shubenacadie, which was about forty miles from Halifax.[18] In fact Vincent visited it briefly at the beginning of the winter season and once again during it, but he found that in their pattern of shifting settlements few of the natives had returned there, as had been expected. Eventually Vincent set his sights on another option: the village of Chezzetcook.

Chapter Four

Chezzetcook and Beyond

∽ CHEZZETCOOK

CHEZZETCOOK WAS NOT new to Vincent. He had visited there with Plessis during the summer months of 1815 on the occasion of the bishop's pastoral visit. Although only eighteen miles east of Halifax, the settlement was isolated from the traffic of the big city because access was principally by sea. (Fig. 7) The heart of the area is a deep, ten-kilometer inlet, and the complex pattern of water flow created by the tides inspired the Indian name, which refers to water flowing in several channels. The area was a favorite summer haunt of the Mi'kmaqs even before it was settled by the Acadians. Of the five small villages that today cluster around the inlet, West Chezzetcook seems to have been the first one settled in any systematic way. This process began in earnest when, around the end of the 1760s, certain Acadians who had been held prisoner in Halifax during and after the deportation were released and permitted to settle here. They were joined by others who had been released from Cape Breton.

A missionary by the name of Father Bailly had touched down there in 1768 to minister to both Indians and Acadians. Others had paid brief visits, but there had never been a resident priest.[1] When Bishop Denaut made his pastoral visit in 1803 he found things in a state of dilapidation and ordered that a new church be built. Since then, a priest had come once a year to spend some time with the people, but he had become old and infirm and had to discontinue his visits after 1810. Apart from a brief visit from Father Mignault in 1814, the people had been without spiritual assistance. When Plessis arrived on July 18, 1815, the new church was almost completed, and Mass was offered there on three occasions in the course of his two-day visit. Confessions were heard, twenty-nine people were confirmed, and the little church was dedicated in honor of St. Anselm.

After settling down in Halifax Vincent himself began to visit Chezzetcook in the course of his ministry and was so taken by it that twice in January of 1816 Mignault wrote to Plessis complaining that he was finding it difficult to get Vincent back to Halifax: "The Father [Vincent] is still at Chezzetcook. I wrote him several times asking him to return, but he always finds some excuse."[2] Then two weeks later: "I can't get Father Vincent back from Chezzetcook. He left here for one week, and now he's been absent for two months."[3] It must have seemed like paradise to Vincent after the noise and military bustle of Halifax. Bishop Plessis understood this, and at the end of January approved the plan for making Chezzetcook the center of Vincent's activities.[4] While enjoying the solitude of the village Vincent would be close enough to Halifax when Mignault needed his help. Mignault's appreciation for his helper is apparent from a letter he wrote to Plessis on another occasion: "Father Vincent is very well; I thank the Almighty that he was graciously pleased to send me so pious a man."[5]

By April 26, 1816, Vincent could report to Plessis that he had made an extended stay of two months at Chezzetcook and another of two weeks, in addition to his visits to Shubenacadie during the winter.[6] This shows that while Chezzetcook remained his home base, Vincent continued to range over a wider area.

The plan for a Trappist foundation near the Mi'kmaqs encountered a setback when Nova Scotia's lieutenant-governor, Sir John Sherbrooke, suffered a stroke that led to his resignation on June 27, 1816. Without his support there was little hope of success for the project. He was succeeded by George Stracey Smyth, whose tenure was limited to a period of several months. On October 24 George Ramsey, Ninth Earl of Dalhousie, assumed the office. Already in August, Sherbrooke had warned Bishop Plessis that the prospect of the proposed Trappist foundation was not good.[7] Nonetheless, Plessis pressed on, and in March 1817 he would write to Mignault asking him to approach the new lieutenant-governor for his support. Nothing concrete came of this.

In September of 1816 Vincent considered once again going up to St. Mary's Bay to spend some time learning the Mi'kmaq language, but the trip never materialized.[8] On September 11 Lestrange wrote urging Vincent to dedicate himself for the moment to pastoral work. Vincent answered him on October 9 with a description of Chezzetcook and his work there. He added:

> As soon as I received your letter dated September 11, 1816, from Lulworth, in which you condemn my ideas of solitude considering them to be a temptation, they disappeared. I gave them up immediately, persuaded that it was God who spoke to me through your mouth. I thought that it would be more in conformity with your intention that I give myself to the work of the missions and particularly the salvation of the savages.[9]

✎ A New Problem

During the winter of 1816-1817, Plessis and the priests working for him in Nova Scotia were appalled by what they considered an intrusion into their spiritual territory. An Englishman named Walter Bromley had come to Nova Scotia in 1813 under the auspices of the British and Foreign School Society. In Halifax he founded the Royal Acadian School, which offered nonsectarian education to the local population. He was also interested in bettering the condition of the Mi'kmaqs. According to Mignault, during the winter in question he received 800 pounds sterling for distribution among the Indians. (The money seems to have come from a Protestant missionary society.) As the Catholic missionaries saw it, this was a deliberate attempt to woo the Indians away from Catholicism towards Methodism. It is more probable that Bromley's aims were principally humanitarian. He was unable to obtain the financial support he needed from the government, however, and the project was discontinued. Nonetheless, Plessis considered what seemed a Methodist threat to the Catholicism of the Indians as one more reason for continuing to pursue the plan of committing the Mi'kmaqs to the care of the Trappists, in spite of the government's seeming loss of interest.[10]

✎ Halifax Becomes a Vicariate Apostolic

Both Bishop Plessis and his Vicar General, Father Burke, realized that the unwieldy size of the Quebec diocese called for some type of subdivision in order to provide more effective spiritual care for the population. The bishop's hope was for the ordination of a number of assistant bishops who would be given the care of specific areas in the diocese but would remain subject to the bishop of Quebec. Burke, for his part, was in favor of the creation of new ecclesiastical territories, each with its own local bishop, immediately subject to Rome and therefore not under the jurisdiction of Quebec. Burke set to work to bring this about for Nova Scotia. As we have seen, with the permission of Plessis he had set out for Ireland in July 1815 in order to seek medical treatment. After spending two and a half weeks there, however, he headed for Rome in early August. There he spent five months promoting his ideas at the Congregation of Propaganda, which was responsible for the Church in areas where there was no Catholic hierarchy in place. As a result of these negotiations Rome agreed to set up in Nova Scotia a Vicariate Apostolic directly under the jurisdiction of this congregation, to be administered by a bishop holding the title of Vicar Apostolic. The boundaries of the new vicariate were limited to Nova Scotia itself, to the exclusion of Cape Breton, which would remain under Plessis's jurisdiction. Bishop Plessis was, of course, consulted, and on October 15, 1816, he gave his approval. Finally, on July 26, 1817, Burke himself was officially appointed head of the new vicariate.

The new situation left Father Vincent somewhat caught in the middle. His attachment to Bishop Plessis would incline him to favor the idea of a foundation in Cape Breton, which Mignault urged upon him.[11] Apparently, this idea also had the backing of Laurence Kavanagh Jr., a prominent Catholic of the town of St. Peter's on Cape Breton. On the other hand, Burke was offering Vincent lands at Antigonish and had promised him other assistance. Mignault wrote to Plessis of Vincent's dilemma:

> Father Vincent is wavering; Cape Breton is to his liking. Mr. Kavanagh has strongly encouraged him in this direction. The Mi'kmaqs will give him as much land as he would desire. Mr. Burke, no doubt, will do all that he can to keep him.[12]

To complicate matters, Vincent had received a letter from Lestrange putting pressure on him to return if he were not able to get something started. Furthermore, the news that the ancient monastery of la Trappe was once again functioning left Vincent torn between his inclination to join his brethren there and his desire to see a foundation of the Order established in America. Plessis wrote to console him, expressing some partiality for the Cape Breton plan, but also advising him to keep his options open for the Antigonish offer.[13] On the very same day, the bishop wrote to Burke, urging him to do all he could for Vincent and, curiously enough, saying that he had counseled Vincent to opt for Nova Scotia instead of Cape Breton![14]

Perhaps what finally swayed Plessis in this direction was the likelihood that Burke would be better able to deal with the delicate subject of the permission of the British government, which Plessis felt was needed for the foundation. He confided to Mignault: "I recently wrote to Dr. Burke asking him to try to keep for himself at least the Trappists, since he has the boldness (which I do not) to intend establishing them without the permission of the Government."[15] It was, however, not an easy decision. Even a year later the bishop wrote to Father Lejamtel, who was caring for the church at Arichat:

> Father Vincent is wavering and he cannot make a decision. The bishop of Sion [Bishop Burke] would like him to make his establishment in Nova Scotia. If the Indians of the province could profit from this, I too would be in favor, since they have been so terribly neglected. On the other hand, an establishment on Cape Breton, which is part of my diocese, is something too precious for me not to desire.[16]

By May of 1817 Vincent had received another letter from Lestrange, who this time made it clear that he wanted Vincent to remain in Nova Scotia at least a little longer.[17] Although he was happy to comply, Vincent's own convictions about the suitability of Nova Scotia for a foundation were beginning to waver, and the nostalgia for his brethren was growing. "I am beginning to be a little tired of America. For I see that there is little good our Order can do here, and I personally feel the need of being with my brothers."[18] In any case, Vincent seems to have taken Lestrange's letter as a go-ahead for starting what was in effect a monastic experiment at Chezzetcook. When Mignault heard of Lestrange's letter to Vincent he wrote to Plessis concerning Chezzetcook: "Father Vincent is overjoyed at the permission which his superior is giving him. We are going to begin, without making a stir; Chezzetcook will become the headquarters, unless Your Grandeur should order otherwise."[19]

Vincent's own reply to Lestrange fills in some of the details. He not only speaks of having "a brother with me, although he is only half so, since he is not able to fully follow the Rule," but also mentions that he was providing nourishment for four people.[20] Fifty acres of land had been purchased and a large garden planted. Moreover, he felt that several of the young people in the village had religious vocations. There was even some hope that their friend from the days in Baltimore, Father Moranvillé, might send them some vocations and even come to join them himself.

Despite all the excitement about the possible foundation, the Mi'kmaqs were not neglected. In the spring of 1817 Vincent accompanied them to a nearby island, where he taught them to plant potatoes and turnips. On July 26 two hundred Mi'kmaqs gathered on the feast of St. Ann for a lively celebration, in which they themselves provided the music for the Mass and the closing *Te Deum*. Thus, even though the project of the Indian "foundation" had begun to founder after the disappearance of Sherbrooke as lieutenant-governor, Vincent continued his pastoral work among the Mi'kmaqs and was even taking a hand in their agricultural education. He also continued to help out in Halifax, where in August of 1817 we find him busy answering correspondence that had been sent to the rectory there.[21]

✎ VINCENT MOVES TO TRACADIE

For all its idyllic qualities, the Chezzetcook experiment was doomed to a brief existence. Vincent, writing to Dom Urbain in France to ask for seeds for his garden, was more and more skeptical about success. This attitude was shared by Dom Urbain, as well as Father Moranvillé. Burke, for his part, was continuing to press for an establishment in Antigonish. Not only did he have land for Vincent there, but he was no doubt also concerned for the pastoral needs of the area to the east of the city. The priest that Plessis had hitherto provided to care for these places would no longer be available, since after the creation of the new Vicariate Apostolic, most of the Quebec clergy opted to remain part of their diocese of origin. If Vincent were to accept the idea of an establishment in the Antigonish area, he would be able to care for three small missions, for the moment at least.

Burke had hoped that Vincent would be able to leave for this new assignment at the beginning of the winter of 1818, but instead Vincent waited out the bad weather. By March 29, 1818, however, he was in Halifax waiting for the boat that would take him to Tracadie. He would

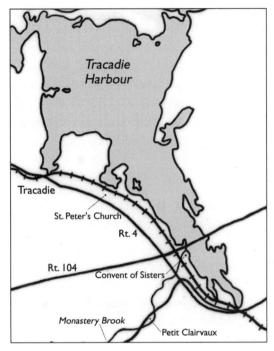

FIGURE 9. *Tracadie area, Nova Scotia.*

be in time to permit the faithful there to fulfill their Easter duties.[22]

The exact date of Vincent's departure from Halifax has not been recorded, but he arrived at his destination by April 30, the date on which his signature first appears in Tracadie's parish records.

This new setting would take some getting used to. For all its rusticity, Chezzetcook was within fairly easy reach of Halifax, where the new bishop would reside. In the vast area at the northeast extremity of Nova Scotia in which Vincent now found himself, each of the few priests available was assigned to a district, in which he moved from place to place to serve the needs of the people. The district that would be served by Vincent consisted of a series of three villages along the coast, the principal one being Tracadie, flanked on the west by Pomquet at a distance of twelve miles and on the east by Havre Boucher at a distance of eight miles. All three were close to the narrow Strait of Canso, which separates Nova Scotia from Cape Breton. (Fig. 7)

Like all priests who worked in Nova Scotia and Cape Breton, Vincent occasionally had to substitute for other priests who were ill, overworked or otherwise hindered from ministering to their flocks.

Apart from the work in his own district, his help was needed most frequently in Cape Breton with its Acadian parishes and Mi'kmaq missions. His *Memoir* recounts some of the trips he made to minister to the Mi'kmaqs at the Bras d'Or Lakes in Cape Breton.[23]

The situation was further complicated by the fact that the faithful these priests ministered to were of two different ethnic backgrounds: French-speaking Acadians and English-speaking Irish. Later on the influx of Catholic Scots would add Scots Gaelic to the list of languages a priest needed.

✂ THE ATTRACTIONS OF CAPE BRETON

Although situated close to the mainland, Cape Breton constituted an entirely separate British colony with its own administration. Though this division was soon to come to an end in 1820 with its annexation to the colony of Nova Scotia, the particular flavor of life on the Cape would perdure, even into modern times. Vincent himself would be increasingly attracted by what he saw. In early May of 1818, soon after arriving in Tracadie, he went to Arichat to visit the venerable Father Lejamtel, who had spent many years serving the needs of the Church on Cape Breton. Lejamtel offered him encouragement and proposed taking him to inspect the area of the Bras d'Or lakes for a possible site of a permanent foundation. With this in view, Vincent returned to Arichat again sometime in the summer. (Fig. 7) A specific property became available in the fall, and he returned once again in early November to inspect it, although nothing came of the visit.[24] The winter months brought on attacks of rheumatism.[25]

Ever mindful of the financial needs of a new establishment Vincent for some time had been planning a visit to Quebec to seek funds and to confer with the bishop on the question of a choice of site. Burke convinced him, however, that the time was not ripe for seeking alms in Quebec, and the trip was delayed for several years. Writing to Plessis to explain his failure to appear as planned, Vincent shared with him his continuing dilemma in choosing between the needs of the new vicariate and the good prospects offered for a community on Cape Breton.[26] He finally came up with a classical Lestrangian proposal: opening *two* houses, one in Nova Scotia and another on Cape Breton, each to be connected to an Indian settlement—all of this with still only himself available as personnel for the venture.

From these first activities in Tracadie and Cape Breton, it is clear that Vincent's objectives still lacked focus. On the one hand, there was the drive to found a monastery in Nova Scotia—or Cape Breton—either in proximity to the Mi'kmaqs (which seemed increasingly unlikely) or as an independent establishment. On the other hand, he was, for the moment, much involved in pastoral work among the Acadians as well as among the Mi'kmaqs. Soon, however, he would be taking a first step in the direction of founding a monastery.

✌ Vincent Purchases the Property Destined to Become Petit Clairvaux

Despite his interest in Cape Breton, Vincent was by no means neglecting Tracadie. Soon after his arrival in the spring of 1818 he made a trial planting of three bushels of wheat on a piece of land fairly close to the center of the village. The results were promising, and soon thereafter he purchased 253 acres of land in the vicinity of the patch where he had carried out his experiment. By June, seventy-six acres of this land had already been cleared, and he lost no time in planting once again.[27] Furthermore, he already had his eye on a nearby piece of property for an Indian settlement. He even sent a memorandum to Bishop Burke with his ideas on how such an establishment for the Mi'kmaqs might be organized.[28]

In addition to ministering in the three villages and among the Mi'kmaqs, Vincent had concerns about the black people of Tracadie. While caring for their spiritual needs, he also worked towards providing a school for them.[29] He even found time to help train one of Burke's seminarians in theology.[30] Besides all of this pastoral activity, he was also carrying out renovations on the church buildings of Tracadie. He wrote to Lestrange on May 27, 1819:

> I have . . . to build a small monastery this year, [and] remodel the former chapel of Tracadie in order to turn part of it into a church for the religious of the Order, and the other part into a sacristy for the new church of the Tracadie parish.[31]

A year later he could report that the project was nearing completion:

> The house which will serve as monastery and which is rather well suited for religious will be completed next month. It can easily accommodate twelve to sixteen persons. It is joined to another small house

which is attached to the church, all in a straight line. This consists of a series of three separate buildings.[32]

The renovations at the parish church of Tracadie were carried out partially with a view to providing temporary quarters for his prospective community until he could complete the buildings on the land he had purchased for the permanent monastery. His expenses were covered in part by the little money he received from his parishioners. It is not clear to what extent Burke was able to help out, but the scanty funds that Plessis was able to send him over the next years were also of great help. The money due for the purchase of land in Tracadie was paid only gradually.[33] In a letter to Lestrange on June 1, 1819, he could report that of the two young men who were helping him, one showed some interest in joining.[34] There were other prospective vocations waiting in Halifax, and it was his hope to call them to Tracadie once the renovations were complete. (He was also still holding on to the idea of two foundations.)

After a year at Tracadie, Vincent began to feel the need of a lengthy retreat. Accordingly, he proposed to Lestrange a trip to France in order to experience monastic life once again in its fullness. This would also be a chance for him to discuss with his superior his experiences in Nova Scotia and make plans for the future. Most important of all, he hoped that Lestrange would be able to send back with him several men to help out in the new foundation. But his letter of November 17, 1819, never reached Lestrange, and he had to repeat his request in two more letters written over the next year.[35]

Lestrange, as it turned out, was by no means indifferent to Vincent's project, but these were busy years for him, in which he was coming to grips with the problem of how to settle the relationship of his own monasteries in France to the authorities in Rome. In any case, in an appeal to Rome in 1820 Lestrange makes indirect mention of Vincent's house, thus showing his interest in it.[36] His interest had perhaps been kept alive as a result of two visits he received from Bishop Plessis himself, who had been traveling in Europe in 1819-1820 on his way to Rome for his official *ad limina* visit.[37]

‰ THE DEATH OF BISHOP BURKE

In the course of 1820 Bishop Burke himself visited Vincent's establishment and expressed his approval of the property that had been acquired.

It would be his last visit, for on November 29 of the same year he died, and thus Vincent lost his old friend and protector. The years ahead were not easy ones for the new vicariate. Affairs of the diocese were looked after by the bishop's nephew, Father John Carroll, and it was only in 1827 that Msgr. Fraser, Burke's successor, was finally consecrated. Without a bishop at its head the vicariate had undergone a period of instability.

By the summer of 1821, Vincent had begun a small school. That summer he finally made the much deferred trip to Quebec to look for financial help, but the bishop felt that the time for such a collection was not opportune. Vincent had hoped also to find vocations in Quebec, but, though two young people expressed some interest, they did not return with him to Tracadie.[38]

Around this time another prospective postulant came to Vincent, a young man named William Edge. This may have been the person Vincent described in a letter to Lestrange in 1821:

> Providence sent my way a young Irishman, twenty-six years old, who has done well at his studies and who knows theology rather well. He wants to become a religious. I took him with me to Quebec to have him receive Orders.[39]

Later we learn that Edge was a cleric and perhaps had received one or other of the Minor Orders. By the next summer, Vincent had to report to Plessis that Edge's vocation had been in crisis but was now once again firm. He was finding the penances of the full Trappist life too exacting, and Vincent thought that he would do better as a member of the Third Order.[40]

While Vincent was in Quebec, Father Roux, the superior of the seminary of Montreal where Vincent spent some time while in Lower Canada, generously helped him lay plans for a group of sisters who would work as teachers at Tracadie. The Sisters of Notre Dame at Montreal invited Vincent to send three girls from Nova Scotia for training in their novitiate.

Vincent returned to Tracadie at the end of July, and made plans to set aside for these sisters part of the buildings he had renovated. It should be noted that in various letters of this period Vincent gives the impression that the project was a foundation of the Congregation of the Sisters of Notre Dame of Montreal in Nova Scotia, rather than a convent of the Lestrange Third Order, still less of Trappistines. He lost no time in choosing the girls to be sent: Anne Coté (24), Marie Landry

(18), and Marie Olive Doiron (25), and by June they were on their way. Apparently, the agreement reached with the sisters was that they would, without remuneration, undertake the training of the girls but would not themselves sponsor the foundation. No doubt this eventually led Vincent to consider them as part of the Third Order.

Still desperately waiting for permission from Lestrange to visit France, Vincent wrote yet another letter to him on August 4, which was to be delivered by hand thanks to the good services of Father Rice, a local priest who was traveling to France in order to recuperate from an illness. Unfortunately the poor man died in Paris that winter and nothing further is known of the fate of the letter.

Illness struck Vincent again sometime during the following September in the form of an epileptic attack, the second that he had suffered in Nova Scotia.[41] He also had a scare during the fall, from an unannounced visit to his property by an English colonel. Though the man was impressed by what he saw and made no show of having been sent in an official capacity, a local priest suggested to Vincent that he might indeed have been sent by the government. Then there were the payments on the land he had purchased—he still owed half of the sum he had agreed on. All of this was added in Vincent's mind to the increasingly pessimistic views expressed by Father Roux, superior of the seminary of Montreal, and the other Sulpicians stationed at the seminary, as well as by his friend, Father Moranvillé, concerning the very feasibility of a Trappist foundation.

✑ Vincent Decides to Visit France

Weighed down with all this, Vincent wrote a pathetic letter to Plessis seeking counsel, more specifically asking whether it would be prudent, in the light of Lestrange's failure to answer his letters, for him to return to France to speak to Lestrange face to face. On the occasion of this letter, Vincent also took the opportunity to gently chide the bishop for his rather cool reception during Vincent's visit to Quebec.[42] Plessis did not respond immediately.

William Edge agreed to accompany Vincent on this proposed trip to France, although he had been reticent at first. Vincent eventually decided not to take the chance of bringing him along, since he had finally come to appreciate the young man's inconstancy. Instead he urged Edge to return to Canada to report to his religious superior (presumably the bishop), but Edge decided to spend the winter in Tracadie, living, as Vincent put it, "as a simple cleric and pretty much on his own."[43] A year later Vincent could report that Edge had spent his time during that winter teaching school and giving catechism lessons to the children of the parish. There seemed to be some improvement, and he was talking again of going to Europe to become a religious.[44]

Finally, sometime during the winter of 1822-1823 a letter from Lestrange arrived. Far from bringing the good news that Vincent might indeed return to France for a rest and for discussions with Lestrange, the letter indicated that he was to close down the operation in Nova Scotia and proceed to Kentucky to see if something could be done in the diocese of Bardstown, whose bishop, Benedict Joseph Flaget, was friendly to the Trappists. Faced now with an explicit command from Lestrange, Vincent wrote once again to Plessis on April 8 to ask: "Do you think that I would sin against obedience if I were to go to France beforehand so that there I might be renewed once again in the spirit of my way of life? . . . I need to make a good retreat in one of our houses. I need to speak to my superior concerning many points. . . ."[45]

Plessis answered on May 20. No doubt smarting from Vincent's remark about his coolness towards him, he reminded Vincent of all that he had done for him over the years and pointed out that, when Vincent had arrived in Quebec, he was still worn out from his European voyage. On the other hand, as to Vincent's current plan to return to France, he reassured him:

> I do not hesitate to take upon myself to convince you to return to France instead of going to Kentucky. You deserve a rest. Furthermore, when Father Abbot takes into consideration that you are fifty-five years old and when you inform him of your weakened health (above all of the threat of epilepsy) I am convinced that he will not insist on the trip to Kentucky.[46]

Vincent made his decision, then wrote to the Sisters at Montreal to inform them of his impending departure, enclosing a letter to the three young girls. He urged them to make plans to return immediately to Tracadie so that there would be time before he left to discuss the future with them. By June arrangements had been made for their passage by ship from Quebec. William Edge had generously written to his aunt in Montreal to pay for the expense of the return journey.[47] Unfortunately we know little of what their life was like upon their return. At first they set up house in the parish of Pomquet, where they arrived by August 6, 1823.[48] Anne Coté was appointed superior.

The ever-changing Edge had decided once again *not* to accompany Vincent on his journey and sometime in the summer headed for Arichat, where he was to spend the winter of 1823-24 teaching school and assisting the pastor, Father Hudon, with catechism instruction.[49] Hudon was annoyed when he discovered that, during Edge's visit to Arichat in September, he had without informing Hudon sought ordination from Bishop MacEachern, Plessis's Vicar General for Cape Breton.[50] Hudon wrote Plessis in March of 1824 expressing his doubts about Edge's suitability for receiving Orders, noting that his behavior during the winter had left much to be desired.[51] He had to admit that Edge's behavior during Lent had shown some improvement, but the situation deteriorated once again, to such an extent that Hudon had asked him to leave.[52] Edge decided to go to Tracadie with the intention of teaching school there.

A ray of light during this difficult period was the support of two ecclesiastics who were involved in the care of Catholics in Cape Breton. Bishop MacEachern, who by this time had been appointed Plessis's Vicar General for Cape Breton, sent Vincent a letter spelling out the many reasons he felt that the enterprise that had been begun should not be abandoned.[53] Two years later when Vincent returned, the bishop had his eye on a property on the Cape which he planned to offer to him for a foundation.[54]

Another source of friendly support was Father Henry McKeagney. This young priest had been sent by Plessis to Arichat as assistant in November of 1822, then to l'Ardoise as its first resident priest on January 8, 1823. Vincent went to spend some time with him at his new quarters during part of July and August of that year, and they worked together for a while at the Indian mission of Chapel Island.[55] During their conversations McKeagney stressed how important it was not to abandon the work that had been begun and urged Vincent to communicate to Lestrange how strongly he felt about this.[56] Like Bishop MacEachern he also was hoping that a foundation could be started in Cape Breton itself.[57] Thus when Vincent set sail for Europe in October he did so with some hope in his heart. ✠

Chapter Five

Laying the Foundations for Petit Clairvaux

⁘ DEVELOPMENTS IN FRANCE 1815-1823

VINCENT LEFT NOVA SCOTIA sometime in October of 1823. As the ship made its way across a particularly stormy Atlantic, he may well have wondered what he would find in his homeland after an absence of twelve years. It had been nine years since he bade farewell to Lestrange in New York, and though news filtered through to him about all that Lestrange had accomplished in France, he must have been eager to see the results for himself.

Lestrange's departure from New York had been prompted by the return of the Bourbon monarchy in May of 1814, which offered hope of a thoroughgoing restoration of Cistercian life in the country of its birth.[1] Lestrange had indeed been busy in France since his return, and by the time Vincent arrived, several important monasteries had been founded or restored under his allegiance—most important of all, la Trappe itself. Dom Eugene de Laprade, the abbot of Darfeld—the Westphalian monastery that had achieved independence from Lestrange in 1808 and had adopted the usages of de Rancé as opposed to those of la Valsainte—had already begun negotiations for the reacquisition of the property of la Trappe, but he generously offered to turn the project over to Lestrange and even offered him the funds already collected for this purpose. Lestrange was not one to pass up such an opportunity, and he accepted in February of 1815. By December monastic life was able to begin there again in earnest.

Various other properties were also acquired (some of them former monastic establishments), and new foundations begun under Lestrange's auspices. (Fig. 2) The year 1816 saw the foundation of Bellefontaine, which was the crowning effort of Lestrange's faithful old lieutenant, Urban Guillet, who died in 1817 less than a month after the finalization of the purchase of the property. Also in 1816 Lestrange refounded the ancient Cistercian monastery of Aiguebelle in the south of France. During the same year, the community of Lulworth came upon hard times. The British authorities decided that ". . . the Abbot and the Religious had gone beyond the intentions of the Government which was only to offer a refuge to French émigré religious and not to perpetuate their presence."[2] As a result Lulworth's superior, Dom Saulnier, took advantage of the new winds blowing in France to acquire the Cistercian monastery of Melleray in Brittany, which had been confiscated during the time of the Revolution. Royal favor was not wanting; the community was gloriously transported to its new home in a frigate of the French navy, sent by command of King Louis XVIII himself. With its sixty or so monks, the new Melleray was now the largest Cistercian monastery in France.[3]

This period also included the restoration of monastic life for Lestrange's nuns. The convent of Michael the Archangel was set up in May of 1816 at Forges, a site near la Trappe, and already in 1817 the new community of nuns was in a position to found a monastery near Bellefontaine.[4] On May 18, 1820, they began still another foundation at Vaise, near Lyons.

Despite his chivalrous gesture of ceding la Trappe to Lestrange, Abbot de Laprade of Darfeld had the honor of establishing what would be the first Trappist monastery in France after the Revolution. The Napoleonic ban on Trappist monasteries had affected the monks of Darfeld as it had so many others, and the community had been broken up into small groups. Most of these were situated in various German towns, and at the chateau of Borsut in the town of Verlaine in Belgium, where Dom de Laprade himself took up residence. With the fall of Napoleon Darfeld was once again opened, and many of de Laprade's exiles began to flow back towards France. The monastery of Port-du-Salut was established for them in February of 1815, the same month when Lestrange accepted de Laprade's offer of la Trappe. Father Bernard de Girmont, a monk of Darfeld who had been instrumental in this first move back to France, was named superior.[5] Dom de Laprade died on June 16, 1816, but the return of the exiles to France continued. Soon thereafter, under the new superior, Dom Germain Gillon, the remainder of the original community of Darfeld was transferred with all its rights and privileges to le Gard, near Amiens, and the nuns attached to Darfeld transferred to the monastery of Laval.[6]

Also in 1816 Dom Bernard de Girmont was elected abbot of Port-du-Salut, and with the help of Monsignor Rafaele Mazio in Rome, he cleverly obtained not only the erection of the monastery as an abbey but also the confirmation of his own election as its abbot. Most important of all, the monastery was placed directly under the jurisdiction of a new figure in the Order. Towards the end of 1816 the Vatican conferred upon Dom Raimondo Giovannini, the abbot of San Bernardo alle Terme in Rome, the rights and privileges of Abbot General of the Cistercians, giving him the title of President General (*Praeses Generalis*).[7] This move would set the new monastery and eventually all the monasteries of the Darfeld Observance on a secure footing vis-à-vis the Church, freeing them definitively from the threat of Lestrange's control. It would also set Lestrange scurrying to establish his own relationship to the new figure in Rome.

Thus with the establishment of Port-du-Salut, another "line" of Trappist monasteries was planted in France, a line that would continue in the foundation of other monasteries. Westmalle, the Belgian monastery from which Darfeld itself had originated, was also detached from the jurisdiction of Lestrange and placed under that of the bishop of Malines. It would eventually form the nucleus of a still third grouping of monasteries constituting a Belgian Congregation. Though it was to adopt the Observances of de Rancé it remained separate from the Port-du-Salut group.

Both of these "Observances," of de Rancé and of la Valsainte, had to face the problem of adapting to the new political scene in France brought about by the restoration of the Bourbon monarchy. As time went on, it became increasingly clear that the new monarchy was not a restoration pure and simple of the ancient order of things. Two major problems faced the Trappists of both camps. First of all, there was the delicate question of financing the construction or restoration of monastic buildings and indeed of all the materialities that go to make up a monastery. While some public funds were forthcoming, they were extremely limited. Second, there was the question of the monasteries' legal status.

Monasteries had been legislated out of existence in the early years of the French Revolution. Relations between France and the Church had been regularized by the Concordat of 1801 concluded between Pius VII and Napoleon; the state was given certain powers of policing religious affairs, but the legitimacy of the Church was recognized and public worship officially restored. No stipulations were made, however, regarding religious Orders that before the Revolution were subject directly to Rome and were largely exempt from control by local bishops. This meant that henceforth *all* ecclesiastics in the country were subject to the jurisdiction of the bishops. Thus, while monasteries began to reappear during the Napoleonic period, there was no firm legal basis to rectify the situation brought about by the Revolution. It was hoped that the restoration of the monarchy in 1815 would address this problem, but all the efforts of both Lestrange and Dom de Girmont of Port-du-Salut to bring about a change were in vain. (The bishops themselves were none too ready to lose their newly acquired control over blossoming monastic communities.) Some years later, after the little Nova Scotian monastery had come into existence, an echo of this problem would be sounded by Lestrange in the closing words of an appeal he made to the Archbishop of Paris:

> We were recognized as religious of la Trappe even in the savage wilds of America amidst tigers and bears who in the midst of the forest came to warm themselves peaceably at the same fires as ourselves; would it only fail to be recognized in our country, in a reborn France, in a France where religion and legitimacy have returned once again?[8]

In addition to these problems common to both Observances, special difficulties lay ahead for Lestrange. Monsignor Alexis Saussol, the bishop of Séez, in whose diocese la Trappe was located, began to raise objections to the situation at the newly restored abbey. On May 30, 1821, he gave Lestrange a list of nine complaints, most of which centered around what he considered to be his rights to jurisdictional and economic control in the affairs of the monastery. In addition, the bishop pointed out that Lestrange held the abbatial title to the monastery of la Valsainte, *not* to the newly acquired property of la Trappe. The bishop also inveighed against the practice of medicine carried on in the monastery by a former doctor who had become a monk. He further objected to the practice of exits from the enclosure for purposes of fundraising. Lestrange in turn countered with a document that responded to the points raised by the bishop. Eventually both parties appealed to the Papal Nuncio in Paris, who in turn consulted the Holy See.

Before Rome's answer arrived, however, a new confrontation led the bishop to place the monastery under interdict. Lestrange responded by ordering the monastery to be evacuated. Leaving only two or three priests with a small group of laybrothers, the main body of monks was sent to join the monks of Bellefontaine in June 1822. The nuns of Forges had already transferred to les Gardes by October 1821.

✂ LESTRANGE APPROVES OF VINCENT'S WORK

This, then, was the state of affairs that Vincent found upon his return to France in December 1823.[9] It was to be a relatively short but fruitful visit, and Vincent would be back on his way to Nova Scotia a year and a half later, on May 10, 1825.

Lestrange was obviously impressed with Vincent's work, including his missionary efforts among the Mi'kmaqs, and he decided to spread the news among various ecclesiastical circles in France. He had Father Vincent and Father Marie-Joseph Dunand draw up separate accounts of their experiences.[10] They were then published in 1824 under the title, *Account of what happened to two religious of la Trappe, during their sojourn with the savages.* Vincent's account, which appears first, bears the title: "Memoir concerning what happened to Father Vincent de Paul, religious of la Trappe, and his observations when he was in America where he spent about ten years with the approval of his superior."[11] Lestrange prepared several circulars on the subject and even had Vincent draw up another brief report on his work with the Indians for the *Annals of the Propagation of the Faith.*[12] During the difficult times that lay ahead, Lestrange would proudly refer to this American connection by including in a list he later drew up of his foundations: "Monastery of St. Ann in Eastern America, in Nova Scotia, near the barbarian people called Micmacks."[13]

Apparently Lestrange at one point had second thoughts about all this, as we learn from a letter which Dom Saulnier of Melleray wrote to the superior of Stapehill, Madame de Chabannes:

> Reverend Father Augustin came to see us three or four months ago with two religious who had come from America, Father Vincent and Father Marie-Joseph. The Father Prior [of Melleray] said [to Dom Augustin]: "Father Vincent speaks English rather well, he is pious, gentle and serene; his health is not good, and he is getting old; you

should . . . send him to our sisters at Stapehill." "Oh, my friend, how little charity you have! And what will become of these poor savages?" . . . What was my surprise then when several days ago I received a letter from Father Vincent dated from Rennes in which he asked my advice and my prayers, because he was being sent by the Reverend Father Abbot to make a foundation in the Diocese of Coutances and to be its superior. . . .

I answered Father Vincent that since he asked my advice I felt obliged in conscience to give it to him, and that he could blame me and say that he acted upon my advice; but that in conscience, without the authorization of Rome neither he nor his brothers should undertake such a commission. . . . But Father Vincent has been named superior. For that matter, he is a weak person, and I can hardly believe he has the strength to follow my advice. . . .[14]

✆ VINCENT'S CHIEF COMPANION: FATHER FRANCIS XAVIER KAISER

Nonetheless, by the spring of 1825 Vincent was free to return to America. Lestrange appointed a group of four religious to accompany him to Nova Scotia in order to set the prospective foundation on a more secure basis. Chief among these was a monk who had been a companion on his earlier venture in the United States. Johannes Baptist Kaiser, who was to become Father Francis Xavier, was born in Freiburg, Germany on May 13, 1785. He was the son of Franziscus Kaiser and Emerentine Ketterer.[15] After working as a schoolmaster for some years, he entered the community of Burlo in 1807, a monastery that had been founded as part of the expanded facilities near Darfeld created to accommodate the monks and nuns returning from Lestrange's Russian adventure. Kaiser remained here as a novice for eight months but left when the monastery changed from the Observances of la Valsainte to those of de Rancé.[16] He then headed for la Valsainte itself, where he entered on January 1, 1808 as Brother Francis Xavier.

In 1812 he was chosen along with Brothers Claude and François de Paul to join Vincent in America. Francis Xavier was permitted to make his profession on January 2, 1813. There is no record of when he was ordained priest. He went to New York along with Lestrange's other religious and later on, when it was decided to abandon the project, Francis Xavier was among those chosen to remain behind under Vincent's direction to settle the community's affairs. Together they traveled to Halifax and were separated only when Vincent was left behind in Nova Scotia.

Upon returning to France, Francis Xavier was sent to Bellefontaine, arriving on June 5, 1816. He apparently served as the monastery's first cellarer. In a letter to Lestrange filled with much self-accusation, he expressed his great distaste for the assignment:[17]

> I ought to think only of working, praying, doing penance, not getting mixed up in anything, of weeping over my sins which are almost numberless, and yet I have not yet shed one tear. I am greedy, immodest, disobedient, I swear, I am a liar, a chatterbox, slanderous, proud, negligent, lazy, curious. . . . . You can judge from all this whether or not I am a good cellarer. I have all the vices that are opposite to the virtues St. Benedict calls for. I beg and entreat you, Reverend Father Abbot, help me, poor and unworthy child that I am, by your holy prayers. I would like to be tranquil and not mixed up with all sorts of people, with people of both sexes, in the midst of so much trouble. I throw myself at your feet and beg you to give me your holy blessing.

FIGURE 10. *Father Francis Xavier Kaiser.*

Perhaps as a result of this request Francis Xavier was relieved of the job, and was henceforth occupied with the monastery's building programs.[18] A year later, however, he wrote once again to Lestrange asking for still more seclusion. After an introduction filled with the same kind of self-accusation, he wrote:

> If you have some house that is more solitary, I would be ready to go there, if you should so wish. I fear distancing myself from the holy will of God by asking you to go here or there, but fully convinced of your prudence I would be happy to reveal my weaknesses and miseries to you, then letting the good God declare his will through your mouth, I will place all my confidence in his graces. . . . Nonetheless, I would like to go to another house, if you should so wish, for I fear the jobs that will be coming up this summer. . . .[19]

The other members of the group sent to Nova Scotia with Vincent were Brother Benoît Nozet of Aiguebelle, by trade a farmer; Brother Étienne Normand of Bellefontaine, a native of Cognac, by trade a stonemason (his baptismal name was Joseph); and Brother Bruno, a farmer, who had made profession at la Trappe on Oct 1, 1821.[20] Of these Brother Étienne would remain at Petit Clairvaux until 1845, when after twenty years of service he returned to Bellefontaine. Brother Benoît got involved in practicing medicine outside the monastery and was reprimanded; he decided to return to France, leaving on December 24, 1826. Brother Bruno left religious life completely sometime after 1837. He eventually married and settled on Cape Breton.[21]

The founders belonged to various monasteries: Vincent and Francis Xavier had been monks of la Valsainte; Benoît a brother of Aiguebelle, and Bruno a brother of la Trappe itself. Only Brother Etienne belonged to Bellefontaine. Yet because the founding party had set out from Bellefontaine, and indeed Lestrange himself had taken up residence there, the connections to this monastery were strong, and would remain so throughout the organizational struggles that would in the future plague the community. In fact, although Petit Clairvaux was not strictly speaking a Bellefontaine foundation, its founders consistently aspired to be united to it as a "filiation."

✑ DEPARTURE OF THE FOUNDERS

The little band set out from Bellefontaine on March 19, 1825, but set sail from Rochefort only on May 10.[22] The "missionary" slant of their future activities appears once again in the letter of obedience that Lestrange made out for one of the members of the group:

> Inasmuch as the Lord has inspired in you a very great desire to con-
> tribute, at least as much as you can, to bring the knowledge of God
> and of the true religion to the most barbarous pagans and savages . . .
> we expressly enjoin upon you to go to America . . . with Reverend
> Father Dom Vincent de Paul, superior of the monastery which we
> have founded in this area. . . .[23]

Somehow they managed to get passage on a ship of the French navy heading across the Atlantic, although further details are wanting.

∾ LESTRANGE'S LAST YEARS: 1825-1827

Only three days before they left, Lestrange received a hand-delivered letter summoning him to Rome. It was the beginning of the last chapter of his life. He arrived there by the end of July 1825 and would remain for almost two years.

Several issues were at stake. First of all, of course, there were Lestrange's own difficulties with Bishop Saussol, in whose diocese la Trappe was situated. This was symptomatic of the more general question of the relationship of formerly exempt monasteries to local bishops—a delicate issue for Rome in its dealings with the French political authorities, as well as with the French bishops themselves.

There were also the complaints received by the Holy See concerning Lestrange's administration in general. As the inquiry proceeded, it was decided that the matter would be treated by a small group of four cardinals of the Congregation of Bishops and Regulars. Participating as consultants in the inquiry were the members of the Italian Congregation of St. Bernard, the President General at their head. On March 11, 1826, it was decided that the French bishops themselves should be officially consulted in the matter, and that, while waiting for their responses, Lestrange should remain in Rome.

After the reports of the bishops came in, Cardinal Pedicini presented to his colleagues a summary of their remarks. These centered around Lestrange's abuse of his authority by failing to consult local bishops before opening monasteries in their dioceses, as well as the manner in which he dealt arbitrarily with the monasteries themselves, failing to observe any procedure in naming superiors, in transferring them without reasonable cause, and in disposing of monastic property as he saw fit. Notwithstanding these objections, the bishops' responses were almost unanimous in praising the monasteries themselves.

The result of all these deliberations was to propose that Lestrange resign his position and that "a new Abbot General" be elected.[24] On July 4, 1827, Pope Leo XII gave his approval, and letters were sent to the nuncio in Paris to outline the plan and to ask what sort of reaction could be expected in France. At the same time it was decided that Lestrange would now be free to leave Rome. It is not clear just how much of all of this information filtered down to Lestrange himself, since, once the reports from the bishops came in, Lestrange was left in the dark concerning the proceedings. In any case, he took it upon himself to leave Rome even earlier than this date, and by June 15 he was already back in France, heading for Bellefontaine. He was convinced that, even though the pope had not yet made a final decision, he, Dom Augustin Lestrange, was still in power.

But the old man's days were numbered. On the way to Bellefontaine, he visited the little monastery of la Sainte Baume in southern France, where he had a bad fall. Nonetheless, he pushed on to Aiguebelle and from there to the nuns' convent at Vaise. By then his health had run out, and on July 16, 1827, he died at the age of eighty-one.

Despite the many inconsistencies of a long career, Lestrange had been largely responsible for assuring the Order's survival over the difficult years of the Revolutionary and Napoleonic periods. Not only had he brought the little "remnant" from la Trappe to la Valsainte, but in the course of time he had seen to the establishment of a significant number of new foundations. Among all these, Petit Clairvaux could boast of having been the last—his "Benjamin."

✥ The Founders Land on Cape Breton

All of this happened a little over two years after Vincent and his group sailed for Nova Scotia. They landed on June 10, 1825, at St. Pierre de Miquelon, an island possession of France near the south coast of Newfoundland. Vincent wrote to Bishop Plessis on June 30 to announce his arrival with four new Trappists and his intention of heading for Tracadie. He also mentioned an accident that had occurred on their first landfall:

On June 10 we entered the port of Saint-Pierre de Miquelon. As we arrived there, two men fell into the sea. Only one was saved; the other lost his life.[25]

This simple statement has given rise to the idea that the two who fell overboard were monks. But nothing in the letter or in other early sources suggests that this was the case.[26]

From there, thanks to the good offices of the French Minister of the Navy, the captain of their boat was ordered to transport the monks to Louisbourg, on Cape Breton. Though the war with France had ended in 1814 with the fall of Napoleon, the arrival of five monks on a French naval vessel caused some consternation to the British authorities:

> The Lieutenant Governor made many objections to that Gentleman [Vincent] on account of [his] being from old France and coming out in a French frigate. He also said he was afraid he was a spy sent out to tamper with the Indians. . . .[27]

Fortunately, nothing came of this.

By the time Vincent wrote to Plessis, he seemed already in touch with the situation at Tracadie. Conditions in the Nova Scotia Church were far from settled. Bishop Burke, before he died in 1820, had committed the affairs of the vicariate to his twenty-two-year-old nephew, Father John Carroll. Bishop Burke no doubt thought that this situation would not last long, but as things turned out, his successor would take over the vicariate only in 1827. This long period of interregnum had its effect on the level of clergy discipline.[28] Anxious for the monks to be free from pastoral concerns, Vincent appealed to Plessis in this letter to send someone to serve the Tracadie parish, even though the village was now outside the bishop's jurisdiction:

> Since we do not wish to take over the parish, desiring to follow our Rule and preserve our solitude, and since M. Carroll has no priest to assign there, as I have learned, you would do us a great favor by helping us in this matter.[29]

They managed to find passage to Arichat only two days after the letter was written, and there they were received by Vincent's old friend, Father Hudon. A new idea had surfaced: By way of experiment, they proposed going to l'Ardoise and living in the rectory there, which was under Father Hudon's care. (Fig. 7) The community might be able to succeed better there than at Tracadie. It seemed to offer a better means of livelihood, and their work with the Mi'kmaqs might be easier, since the Cape Breton Mi'kmaqs were more disciplined than those of Nova Scotia. In another letter he wrote to Plessis, to ask the bishop's advice concerning this, Vincent also hinted at the disorder reigning in the Vicariate of Nova Scotia.[30] Vincent's old love of the Cape was obviously coming back into play. Judging from the parish records of l'Ardoise, they were already there by July 17, when Vincent's first entry in the book appears. Bishop MacEachern, who was responsible for Cape Breton as Vicar Apostolic of Quebec, got wind of their arrival and hoped that they would stay. He even had a property in mind for them on the Cape.[31]

✑ FATHER VINCENT DE PAUL IN L'ARDOISE

Vincent remained at l'Ardoise for a considerable time, perhaps until November of 1826, as the parish's record book suggests.[32] It is less clear when plans for the community itself changed, but it was eventually decided that the others should go to Tracadie to take up residence there. They certainly left before Vincent did. Father Francis Xavier seems to have been in Tracadie by the second half of July 1825, and it is probable that the others went with him.[33] Vincent must have at least accompanied them to Tracadie to introduce them to the situation there before returning to Cape Breton.

While at l'Ardoise Vincent received an answer from Plessis. The bishop welcomed him back and was open to the possibility of his settling on Cape Breton. As so many times in the past, however, he warned him that he must seek permission of the government and recommended that he enlist the aid of Laurence Kavanagh Jr., who by now had become a member of the legislature.[34] Whether or not Vincent contacted Kavanagh is unknown. In November, however, he sent an appeal directly to Sir James Kempt, lieutenant governor of Nova Scotia, requesting to set up a foundation along the lines worked out with Plessis many years before: permission to exist as a community with primary emphasis on the mission to the Indians.[35] There is no record of an answer to his petition. Despite the concern expressed by the lieutenant governor over the manner of Vincent's arrival in a French frigate, there seems to have been at least no positive rejection of the petition, since the community *de facto* began and continued its existence unchallenged.[36]

During his stay at l'Ardoise, Vincent received a first postulant. He recorded the event in an official tone that contrasts with the fact that it was scribbled on the back of his rough copy of the letter to Kempt: [37]

> Brother John, called in the world John Donn [sic], born in the county of Northumberland of James Dunn and of Marie Souane, aged 28 years, a Protestant converted in 1812 at Batiscan, Diocese of Quebec, arrived at l'Ardoise where he began to follow the rule of la Trappe on August 12, 1825. (A good, pious boy). Drawn up at l'Ardoise, August 15, 1825.
> He left the house on the twenty-fifth of the month in the morning.

Local tradition at l'Ardoise points to a spring alongside a country road as being linked to the memory of Father Vincent. It is said that as Vincent passed along a new road that was still under construction, the workmen he met complained that there was no water for them to drink. He pointed out a spot where they would be able to find water. Accordingly they began to dig, and soon a fine spring began to flow.[38]

∽ FATHER FRANCIS XAVIER IN TRACADIE

During Vincent's stay in l'Ardoise, Francis Xavier back in Tracadie also found himself sharing in some of the pastoral work in the area. Even though the records at Tracadie have been lost for this period, we know that he baptized Father Hubert Girroir sometime in July of 1825. Also his name appears for the first time in the Pomquet church records on September 18 of the same year.

On December 19, 1824, Father Doucet, pastor of Tracadie, died suddenly after a brief tenure of only six months. Since no one else was available, Father Francis Xavier accepted his responsibilities and had to assume full care for the parish and its dependencies until the return of Father Vincent in the summer of 1826. Vincent's appeal to Bishop Plessis for help had been in vain.

Nothing is known of what the life of the community was like without Vincent during that first year in Tracadie. There are no surviving documents that speak of an official opening of the Nova Scotia monastery. The closest thing we have is the letter of obedience that Lestrange gave to Brother Étienne Normand. This refers to "Reverend Father Dom Vincent de Paul, superior of the monastery that we have founded in this area . . ." Nonetheless, September 1, 1825, has been considered the date of the official opening of Petit Clairvaux, even though

FIGURE 11. *Tracadie, Nova Scotia. Convent of Our Lady of Seven Sorrows.*

Father Vincent had not yet returned from l'Ardoise.[39] At this early point, however, there is still no clear indication of what the monastery would be called. Only much later does the name "Petit Clairvaux" begin to appear in documents.[40]

Francis Xavier also cared for the Sisters of the Third Order in Vincent's absence. After their arrival in 1823 they moved from their original location in the parish of Pomquet into the small house Vincent had built near the parish church of Tracadie to function as a rectory. The author of the *Anonymous Life* adds some details that are difficult to situate chronologically:

> They also founded a school at St. Patrick, a small Irish village two miles from Tracadie. This school was at that time cared for by several companions who had joined them. The house at Tracadie, transformed into a school, was not large enough to serve also as a convent. While waiting for their present monastery to be built (and this was only begun at this time), Father Vincent had a temporary convent built on the hill opposite the monastery of the monks, on the other side of the river. The poverty of this first monastery can be gathered from the fact that it as well as the chapel were built in the space of nine days. This was the place where the three first religious pronounced

their vows in the hands of Father Vincent; after this they could receive novices.[41]

A new convent was later built on the shore of the Bay of Tracadie not far from the point where the access road to the monastery of the monks meets the present-day Route 4. (Fig. 9) It is not known exactly when this construction began, but by 1838 its central building was a "two-storied structure about fifty feet long and thirty wide containing a small chapel which can hold thirty persons."[42] An undated photograph of this later convent (much retouched) shows a considerable complex of small buildings. (Fig. 11)

Vincent was still at l'Ardoise when he received the news that Bishop Plessis had died, on December 4, 1825. Without the support and counsel of this old friend, who was ultimately responsible for the Church on Cape Breton, the idea of remaining on the island must have seemed less attractive. This no doubt was at least one factor in Vincent's decision to return to Tracadie. Indeed, on June 3, 1826, the pastoral care of l'Ardoise reverted to Father Hudon, and Vincent was free to join the others at Tracadie. In any case he was certainly there by July 22, 1826, when his name first appears in the records book of the parish of St. Peter's in Tracadie. The monastic experiment at l'Ardoise had come to an end.

When Vincent returned to Tracadie it was not a return to the full monastic life. Judging from the records book, he took over as pastor of St. Peter's and remained such until he was finally replaced in 1836 by John Quinan.[43] Furthermore, there are many indications that Vincent continued to travel—at least casually—to other areas of Nova Scotia. In 1827 we find him in Halifax and even farther afield, in Eel Brook near Tusket on the opposite end of the island.[44] Later, in the fall of 1834, he is reported as having made several more trips to Halifax to care for the population during the terrible cholera epidemic that had broken out there.[45] Closer to home there are records of visits to l'Ardoise and Arichat.[46] Despite all this he retained the title of prior and continued to take an active role in caring for the monastery's needs.

FIGURE 12. *William Fraser, second Bishop of Halifax, later first Bishop of Arichat.*

Chapter Six

A Dearth of Vocations

∾ BISHOP WILLIAM FRASER, SECOND VICAR APOSTOLIC OF HALIFAX

I N 1827, THE LONG YEARS of waiting for a new bishop to replace Burke came to an end when Father William Fraser was consecrated second Vicar Apostolic of Halifax. Part of the reason for the delay had been the problem of finding a suitable candidate to care for the growing number of Irish and Scots Catholics in the vicariate. After serving for eighteen years in his native Scotland as a missionary in the Highlands and eventually becoming rector of the seminary on the island of Lismore, near Oban, Fraser had come to Canada in 1822 to work with the Scots who had immigrated to Cape Breton.

The first Catholic Scots had come to Prince Edward Island in 1772. Other groups arrived in 1791, some settling in Nova Scotia itself. More Scots settlements emerged after the turn of the century in response to growing immigration from Scotland, a trend that continued for the next half century.

Fraser's arrival in Cape Breton created something of a sensation. Many heard the Word of God in their native Scots Gaelic for the first time in many years. In 1824 he took over the parish of Antigonish, a stronghold of Scots culture—both Catholic and Protestant—that was to remain dear to Fraser throughout his entire life. A description found in a letter of Joseph Howe catches something of the spirit of the place:

At the hospitable board of R. N. Henry, Esq., the then Postmaster of Antigonish, I met four men, each differing in training, profession and character, but each in his own time sufficiently remarkable to make his society very attractive. These were Dr. Fraser, who became Catholic bishop of the diocese, Dr. McDonald, then in the full enjoyment of a large county practice, the Rev. Thomas Trotter, Presbyterian pastor of the village congregation, and our old friend Sandy MacDougall. They were all Scotchmen or of Scotch descent, were fast friends and cronies. Each would stand up for his own Church or his own snuff box, but they would all stand up for old Scotland, and fight to prove a thistle more fragrant than a rose. I would have given a trifle to have seen and heard our four old friends once more chaffing each other in Latin, English, Greek and Gaelic. With these four men I remained on terms of intimacy and friendship while they lived. Nothing impressed me so much as to hear questions of philosophy, of practical or abstract science, or of European politics, discussed in the county of Sydney with the keenest of logic and fullness of information scarcely met with in the capital.[1]

Fraser's appointment to the See of Halifax could have meant his leaving behind the mission field, in which he had worked so successfully, to take up residence in a city where the Catholic population was chiefly Irish. Instead, a compromise solution was reached: Fraser would administer the diocese from his beloved Antigonish, without abandoning his missionary work; in Halifax two Irish priests, appointed by Fraser, would care for the city's Catholics. Father James Grant became his Vicar General and Father John Loughnan rector of the cathedral parish. Fraser's consecration took place at Antigonish on July 7, 1827, and was performed by his friend and fellow Scot, Bishop Angus Bernard MacEachern, who himself had become bishop of Charlottetown, Prince Edward Island. Fathers Vincent de Paul and Francis Xavier were present and assisted him in the ceremony.[2]

On the occasion of Fraser's appointment, Rome decided that Cape Breton would henceforth be attached to this vicariate rather than to Quebec. And with the creation of the new, independent Diocese of Charlottetown, Quebec's authority over Prince Edward Island had also come to an end.

∾ LIFE IN THE MONASTERY

Little is known of the life of the monastery during these early years. Its archives were lost in the fire that destroyed its buildings in 1892, and only scanty information filters through from various other sources.

In 1828 Vincent addressed a problem that concerned both the monks and the neighboring farmers in the Tracadie–Havre Boucher area: There was no grist mill nearby, and the local inhabitants had to have their grain milled at some distance. On March 17 Vincent sent a petition to the Secretary of the Council of Nova Scotia, Sir Rupert D. George, asking him to seek financial assistance from the governor for the construction of such a mill in Tracadie. Nothing came of the request, but by February of 1830 Vincent had mustered enough funds to build a mill for the monastery and made it available to the local population. He was able to fit it out to mill wheat, but it could not handle barley or oats. Accordingly, he sent a new petition, this time to the General Assembly of Nova Scotia at Halifax, asking for financial assistance to improve the machinery. This time the petition was signed not only by Vincent and Francis Xavier but by twenty-nine local people. Once again no help was forthcoming. He repeated his request on January 25, 1832, but still received no funds. Finally in a later petition (unfortunately undated) he reported having brought the mill up to standards for milling various types of grain, and once again asked financial help for expenses incurred. Yet again he received no assistance.[3]

Only in the 1830s do we learn of the first brothers entering the monastery: Brother Charles (Charles Broussard) of nearby Pomquet, and two Irishmen, Brother Bernard (James Kilmartin) of County Limerick and Brother James Mary (James Hynes) of County Kilkenney.[4] All three persevered and made profession together, as lay-brothers, on December 12, 1841. Their memory lingered on in the community for many years, and Father Ambroise of Bellefontaine, writing decades later in 1881, spoke of "all three, disciples of Father Vincent and much esteemed for their virtue, above all Brother James who had the reputation of being a saint."[5]

∽ The Aftermath of Lestrange's Death

After Lestrange's death in 1827 there was talk of convening a General Chapter and electing a successor to Lestrange. But by September the suggestion of Cardinal Lambruschini, the Papal Nuncio in Paris, had won the day, and Dom Saulnier of Melleray was appointed as provisory superior and Visitor General. His outstanding record as superior of

Lulworth and then of Melleray, as well as his notable skill in diplomacy, made him an obvious choice. Upon appointment, he was ordered to carry out a visitation of all the houses of both Observances in France. He set about this without more ado and in less than a year had visited eighteen houses of monks and nuns. Apparently during this time Vincent wrote to Saulnier asking for directives concerning Petit Clairvaux. Dom Saulnier wrote back on several occasions saying that they should remain where they were.[6]

A detailed report of the visitations was sent to Rome on September 1, 1828. The main points the report touched on were: 1) the need to suppress houses that were too small and poorly run, 2) abandonment of the Third Order concept, and 3) mitigation of austerities in the houses of nuns, where needed. In the course of these visits Dom Saulnier showed himself to be respectful of the Houses of the "other" Observance, namely that of de Rancé. His proposal for the future was the adoption of the same monastic lifestyle for all the houses of both Observances. This presumably would mean some give and take on both sides.

In the near term, little was done about the report. The rapid succession of popes after the death of Leo XII, as well as the repercussions of the 1830 Revolution in France, meant that the question of these monasteries was placed on the back burner.

Meanwhile Dom Saulnier had come upon hard times. The new government established by the 1830 Revolution had taken great exception to certain political connections he had made. The community of Melleray became the object of reprisals, and the abbot lost much of his prestige. In light of these difficulties Dom Antoine decided to send out a group of the Irish and English monks in his community to found a monastery in Ireland under the leadership of his prior, Father Vincent Ryan. The monastery of Mount Melleray was officially opened in 1832. Three years later a small group of Irish and English monks were sent to establish the monastery of Mount St. Bernard in England, which Vincent would visit two years later.[7]

By the time it became clear that Rome was getting ready to take up once again the question of the "Trappist" monasteries, Dom Saulnier's influence in the matter had waned, due to the loss of face occasioned by his conflict with the French government. Two new figures now came to the fore. Dom Fulgence Guillaume, abbot of Bellefontaine since 1830, and his friend, Dom Joseph-Marie Hercelin, the newly elected abbot of la Trappe, came to Rome in the spring of 1834 in order to further the cause of the Lestrange foundations with the four cardinals who had been chosen to study the matter. While there, Hercelin received the abbatial blessing at the hand of one of them, Cardinal Weld, son of the founder of Lulworth. Hercelin also brought with him a document signed by all the monks of la Trappe in which they listed certain points of Lestrange's Observance on which they were willing to compromise, in order that some elements of their lifestyle, at least, might be saved.

Rome finally took up the matter again, and on October 3, 1834, issued a decree of unification of the two Observances.[8] It stipulated that henceforth there would be only one entity, to be known as the Congregation of the Cistercian Monks of Blessed Mary of la Trappe. As regards lifestyle, "The whole Congregation will observe the Rule of St. Benedict and the Constitutions of Abbot de Rancé." Exception was made, however, in the matter of fasting, where communities were left with the option of following either the Rule of St. Benedict *or* the Constitutions of de Rancé, "according to the established custom of each monastery." Though the ruling clearly alluded to two Observances, there was no mention of either Lestrange or la Valsainte. The Observance of monasteries founded by him now appeared in the guise of "the Rule of St. Benedict."

Of great importance was the decision to entrust the new Congregation to the jurisdiction of the President General of the Italian Congregation of St. Bernard, which was considered by Rome as replacing in some measure the functions of the abbot of Cîteaux. This policy had already been implemented in the case of certain de Rancé houses, which had earlier appealed to Rome for clarification of their status. It would henceforth be his right to confirm the elections of individual abbots. In France itself there would be a Vicar General to administer the Congregation, and this office would belong by right to the abbot of la Trappe.

Also of importance was Rome's decision to temporize on the thorny question of episcopal jurisdiction over the monasteries: "Even though the monasteries of Trappists are exempt from episcopal jurisdiction, they are nonetheless, because of particular reasons (and this until it is otherwise established), subject to the jurisdiction of the bishops, who will act as delegates of the Apostolic See."

When the decree was promulgated, Hercelin—by virtue of his role as abbot of la Trappe—became Vicar General for the Congregation in France. Henceforth it would be his office to preside over the yearly

General Chapters, and he would have the right to make visitations at all the houses of the congregation, either personally or through someone he delegated. These extensive powers would make him a key figure in the Congregation during the coming years.

℘ VINCENT LEAVES AGAIN FOR EUROPE

When the news of the reunion of the Observances in 1834 reached Petit Clairvaux, it became obvious that something had to be done about their own situation. For one thing, the decree from Rome showed that the

FIGURE 13. *Dom Joseph Hercelin, abbot of la Trappe.*

Observances of Lestrange would no longer be integrally observed by any of the houses. The letter that Hercelin had brought to Rome from la Trappe made this clear. Father Francis Xavier reacted strongly to this, and throughout his life he would chide those who had tampered with the "Reform."

To complicate matters, the major concern that gave rise to the promulgation of the decree was the situation of the Trappists in France. There were problems enough there without dealing with such a tiny foundation as the house in America. This attitude would continue to plague Petit Clairvaux throughout the coming years, as they attempted to link themselves to some house of the Order in France and to find monks to help in Nova Scotia. It was to Bellefontaine's abbot, Dom Fulgence Guillaume, that Francis Xavier appealed for help, since it was from Bellefontaine that the little band of founders had set out. Francis's dedication to Lestrange's Observances, which he refers to as the "Reform," appears clearly in this letter of November 9, 1835:

> I charge you before God. It was from Bellefontaine that I began this establishment with great difficulty. All those you have, stem from the Reform. I believe that we are legitimate sons of the Order and it seems to me that, without going against justice, you should help us. This was certainly the intention of Rev. Father Augustin. And if you are not able to come and join us, send us several brothers who are solidly attached to the Reform. . . . The more we are abandoned by men, so much more does our trust in God increase.[9]

This same letter noted that the Nova Scotia community consisted of two priests and five laybrothers.[10] Comparing these figures with the names of monks found in the *Petit Clairvaux Records Book* provides the first ascertainable community list of the monastery:

- Father Vincent de Paul
- Father Francis Xavier
- Brother Étienne
(one of the founders)
- Brother Bruno
(another one of the founders, who would leave after 1837)
- Brother Charles
- Brother James
- Brother Bernard

As was the case with earlier appeals for help addressed to Bellefontaine, there was no reply. Vincent then turned to another plan: to attempt to transfer his foundation to Quebec. Years before, Vincent had received an offer to settle at a site described simply as St. Joachim.[11] He wrote to Bishop Turgeon, coadjutor of Quebec, to see if this would still be possible. He was under the impression that not only land but also certain buildings would be available. The bishop's answer indicated that at most a portion of uncleared land might be available. He recommended that they remain in Nova Scotia.[12]

When all else failed, Vincent decided around the middle of 1836 to go to Europe himself to see what could be done.[13] His first known stop was at la Trappe, where he must have arrived sometime in the fall of the year.[14] During his stay, Hercelin criticized him for the time he spent working in the missions and made it clear that he felt Vincent should remain at la Trappe "to work towards perfection and the salvation of my soul." Vincent considered the idea for a while, but felt called to return to America when the question of their relation to the new Congregation would be finally settled.

From la Trappe he set off for Paris, where he saw the Papal Nuncio, who counseled him to go to Rome to discuss the matter. For the time being, in December Vincent simply sent a letter to the Prefect of the Congregation of the Propaganda Fide in Rome, describing the monastery for men and the one for women and showing how important they were to the Church in Nova Scotia.[15] In this he specifically requested: "If the Reverend Father General of the Order of Cîteaux, to whom we beg Your Eminence to communicate the present letter, decides that we may continue in America the establishment which we have begun, I beg him to obtain the approbation of the Holy See for the Great and Third Order of la Trappe."[16]

While in Paris Vincent also sought advice from Father Dubois of the Seminary of the Foreign Missions. During his stay in the capital he received a letter from Hercelin apparently once again urging him to return to la Trappe. Vincent shared this with Dubois, affirming that he was ready to return to la Trappe if this priest felt it was God's will. But Dubois suggested instead that he go to the Abbey of le Gard for a period of two weeks, which he did. That Vincent should fail to follow Hercelin's advice to return to la Trappe and then go instead to le Gard, a stronghold of the de Rancé Observance, to seek counsel surely did not sit well with the Vicar General.

Vincent remained at le Gard for two weeks. The abbot of the monastery approved of his desire to continue Petit Clairvaux as well as his plan to visit the newly founded monastery of Mount St. Bernard in England to join his "brothers who were forced to leave Melleray of Nantes and come to their own country to establish a monastery there."[17] Vincent went to Mount St. Bernard probably around the middle of February 1837, and after he had been there for two months, he wrote to Hercelin to keep him abreast of his movements since leaving la Trappe. He once again turned down Hercelin's invitation to come back to la Trappe and expressed his inclination to return to America, although he agreed not to carry out any further missionary activity.

A new idea had surfaced, however. In the event that it became impossible to continue Petit Clairvaux, he now began to consider bringing its monks to join forces with those of Mount St. Bernard. The prior of the new monastery, Dom Odilo Woolfrey, was enthusiastic and assured Vincent that they would be welcome. Furthermore, the benefactor of the monastery had promised help in starting a monastery nearby for the Sisters of Tracadie.

The time spent at Mount St. Bernard was also a time of waiting for answers. First and foremost, the decision of the Congregation of Propaganda Fide had not yet arrived by April.[18] He was also waiting for word from Bishop Fraser, to whom he had written, passing on the favorable impressions he received from European abbots and other French clergy concerning the Nova Scotia foundations. The choice of whether to try to remain in Nova Scotia or come to Mount St. Bernard, regardless of what the Propaganda Fide might rule, would rest with the bishop and with Father Francis Xavier, both of whom were more in touch with the situation at the monasteries themselves.

Writing to Francis Xavier would be a delicate matter. He was an ardent devotee of the Lestrange regulations and even took exception to the current Observance of la Trappe itself. As Vincent wrote in his letter to Hercelin:

> I fear that Father Francis Xavier will cause you some trouble because of his views or claims concerning the rule as observed at la Grande-Trappe, which is not altogether in conformity with that of the Reform of the deceased Dom Augustin de Lestrange, to which he clings as to a rock.[19]

While Mount St. Bernard's Observance was in many ways close to the Rule of St. Benedict, it too did not follow the Lestrange Observance in all matters. Vincent wrote at least twice to Francis Xavier while he was in England. The first letter has not survived, but it must have broached the question of a possible transfer of the community to England. The second one, written on March 14, 1837, contained a checklist of things that had to be attended to in the event that the transfer should actually take place. Vincent included the promising news that Dom Vincent of Mount Melleray (who was responsible for the foundation in England) had written saying that he was doing all in his power to assure that the Rule of St. Benedict would be followed. Dom Odilo included a letter of his own, welcoming Francis Xavier and urging him to make the move, since Vincent's efforts at finding subjects in France for Petit Clairvaux had failed.[20]

∾ VINCENT APPEALS TO ROME

By October of 1837 Vincent was at the Convent of Vaise near Lyons.[21] Since his written petition to the Congregation of Propaganda had received no answer, by January 1838 he decided to go to Rome to present his case in person, as had been originally suggested by the Papal Nuncio early in 1836.[22] The moment seemed opportune. A year earlier Rome had received favorable news of the two monasteries in a report sent to the same Congregation by a promising young priest named Colin MacKinnon, who had just returned to Nova Scotia after studies in Rome and was destined one day to succeed Fraser.[23]

While in Rome Vincent pressed his case. First of all, since the Third Order had been, practically speaking, suppressed in France, it was important for him to make some provision for the Sisters of Tracadie. Accordingly, he made a request for the approbation of the rule of the Third Order for the New World.[24]

Then, on March 24, 1838, he drew up a document for the President General of the Cistercians and submitted it to the Congregation of Propaganda Fide.[25] It contained a brief description of the two monasteries, their personnel and their buildings, with a request that the General take their case in hand. The description of their Observance did not sit well with the General. The letter was sent back to the Congregation with the suggestion that they adopt the Observance of de Rancé and that they be placed under the authority of the Papal Nuncio to Canada.

Rome settled the matter on April 30, 1838, without entering into the question of Observance by simply placing the two Tracadie communities under the authority of Bishop Fraser.[26] This obviated the necessity of making pronouncements on the questions of Observance or officially approving the rule of the Third Order, which had, after all, disappeared in Europe. The local bishop could deal with such things.

Thus, alongside the various Congregations of the Order now subject to the limited jurisdiction of the President General in Rome, this decree made provision for still another way of incarnating the old Cistercian charisma: submission of the two tiny Nova Scotia monasteries to the jurisdiction of the local bishop—a canonical solution, to be sure, but one which did not dissolve their link with the Cistercian heritage. Rome had still not found a final solution for restoring to the Order the unity it lost as a result of the French Revolution and its aftermath.

Vincent sent a copy of the decree to Bishop Fraser, and by August received a reply in which the bishop expressed his conviction that Vincent's presence was necessary for the well being of the two houses in Nova Scotia.[27] He also requested Vincent to recommend the needs of his diocese to the board of the French Society of the Propagation of the Faith in Lyons. So Vincent headed back to France and by July was in Lyons.[28] He remained at the nearby convent of Vaise serving as their chaplain at least until May of the following year (1839),[29] during which time he drew up the lengthy document Fraser had suggested.[30] He also managed to visit his birthplace, Chalamont, about twenty miles from Lyons.[31] Sometime in 1839 Hercelin carried out the regular visitation at Vaise. One wonders if Vincent was present at the time. In any case, nothing is mentioned concerning him in Hercelin's report of the visit.[32]

By July Vincent was at Le Havre finally making preparations for his return home. He was still there in August but we lose track of him after August 27.[33] He next appears the following year (March 13, 1840) in Cottin de Vire, a little town in Normandy, from where he wrote Hercelin for the last time, asking for his blessing before setting out. There is no record of an answer.[34]

Chapter Seven

Father Francis Xavier,
Acting Superior

∞ Vincent Returns

V INCENT FINALLY SET SAIL for Nova Scotia sometime in the spring of 1840, landing on May 6 after an absence of almost four years. Upon arrival he discovered that while he was still in France Hercelin had written an inflammatory letter to the young pastor of the church of Arichat denouncing Vincent in no uncertain terms. The priest in question was Father Jean-Baptiste Maranda of Quebec.[1]

In 1835 Maranda had been sent from Quebec by Bishop Signay to become pastor of the Arichat parish. Over the years he kept up a correspondence with his friend Father Charles-Félix Cazeau of Quebec, a prominent young cleric who was the secretary of the diocese and chief spokesman for the bishops with the government. When Maranda set out from Quebec, Cazeau had asked him to keep him abreast of the religious scene in Arichat and environs.[2] The tone of Maranda's letters is familiar, such as one would use in writing to a close friend, and often filled with gossip. He does not hesitate to express his own likes and dislikes in vivid terms. For this reason these letters provide an important firsthand account—albeit a strongly biased one—concerning life in the area during the fifteen-year period between 1835 and 1850, when an aging though still active Vincent was winding down from a long career of leadership.

Already in May 1836 we find Maranda piqued with Vincent for

having gone to a Protestant merchant to obtain Mass wine instead of coming to Maranda himself.[3] A month later he writes: "If you see Mr. Edge, get him to tell you all he knows about la Trappe and the Trappists. The honor of the bishops (who, I am told, want to have this scum in Canada) demands it."[4] Later that year he reported that "Father Vincent now seventy years old has gone to Boston or Philadelphia trying to promote an establishment there. He is, I believe, somewhat demented. . . ."[5] Later on, having picked up a rumor of Vincent's imminent return from Europe, he wrote:

> We expect Father Vincent during the spring along with a French priest. The Father is in a kind of second childhood, if he has not always been. Father Francis Xavier is still furiously irritated with me and the Canadian *magnums*. I don't flatter him. Mr. Edge would say that on several occasions he deserved to be hanged."[6]

All of these negative comments about Vincent, Francis Xavier, and their establishment lead one to wonder if Hercelin's letter to Maranda might not have been an answer to a letter that Maranda himself sent to Hercelin on the subject of Petit Clairvaux. There is no positive evidence for this, but it is difficult to imagine what other occasion there might have been for a letter from such a lofty personage to the pastor of a relatively small town on Cape Breton.

Hercelin's letter itself, which was written on February 1, 1840, has not survived, but we get some idea of its content from a letter of complaint that Father Francis Xavier sent to Hercelin in September. As a witness to Francis Xavier's devotion to Vincent as well as his impatience with the improprieties of Hercelin's letter to Maranda, it is worth citing in its entirety:

Tracadie, September 1840

My Very Reverend Father,

Your letter of February 1, 1840, to the pastor of Arichat arrived and was read and passed around, causing a considerable stir. Many persons (not to say all) were scandalized. Judge for yourself, my Very Reverend Father, what the consequences of this will be. Msgr. Fraser our bishop, first superior of our monastery, showed it to me himself and said that one could see by the expressions used in the letter, that it betrayed passion and jealousy. But here is the meaning of the word vagabond, which you used of Father Vincent: "He is a person given to all sorts of abomination and the foulest of crimes against morals." Judge what impression this made in our land. My Very Reverend Father Abbot, what a letter written by the hand that probably touched the Body of Jesus Christ who himself *is* charity, and on the same day at that, alas! Your own heart will tell you that which I do not wish to write here. Catholics and Protestants all have great respect for Father Vincent. Upon his return he was received with as much honor as would be shown a bishop in Europe, with great rejoicing, church bells ringing and rifles firing away.

If it was out of zeal that you wrote, permit me to tell you, my Very Reverend Father, that this zeal was not good zeal, nor was it prudent, because it was not of the kind that St. Benedict teaches us. What is the cause for such a letter? Do you have some charge based on the Rule of St. Benedict, on the Gospel, which should be the only support that a superior should follow, since a superior has no other authority save through Jesus Christ, which should make him act in his name. My Very Reverend Father, I do not believe that you would have wanted to write such a letter at that time when I had the honor of speaking with you at N.-D. des Gardes, alas! God has not changed. So, after having followed the orders of the abbot whose commands are to be preferred over those of any other person (Rule of St. Benedict, Chapter 71) [sentence unfinished] Then, Reverend Father Dom Augustin of happy memory, our legitimate superior, sent us to America. Rev. Father Antoine having been consulted concerning what we should do answered: "Let them remain! Let them remain!"

In 1838 God by his representative, his Vicar, made himself clear in our regard. *Sanctitas sua benigne in omnibus probavit et confirmavit.* [His Holiness has graciously considered and confirmed all matters— a reference to Rome's decree of April 9, 1838, entrusting Petit Clairvaux to the care of Bishop Fraser.] It seems to me that my stubbornness is neither against the Rule or against the Gospel, nor against charity. Our conduct will have doubtlessly occasioned your great displeasure, to see that we expose ourselves to many miseries so as to hold on to the Reform. It must have caused you much pain, that you should pursue Father Vincent de Paul, pursuing him indeed even as far as America itself. Since God by His Church approves our undertaking we would hope that you would love us and do all you could to promote that others should do what you cannot do yourself. You can believe that I have a great desire to be in a house where regularity is observed. The only reason that keeps me from going to France to one of the houses to follow the Rule there is the mitigation that has been set up in all of our monasteries and that causes me displeasure. The Holy See had its own reasons to bring this about, and I respect its authority. But since it does not order us to embrace this, I am delighted and even obliged to fulfill the promises that I made to God. . . . You are a man and I am also, you are a Christian and I also, you are a religious and I also at least in name; you are a priest and I also, even though unworthy; you are a superior and an abbot, and I thank God that he gave me neither the talent nor the responsibility [for this] that I consider as fearsome before God, and I believe that all superiors are worthy of compassion because of the terrible account to be rendered, according to the word of St. Benedict. Let us look to what we should be and we will see in what we may rejoice, and in what be sad. *Ut sint unum sicut et nos unum sumus Ego in eis et tu in me ut sint consum[m]ati in unum.* [That they may be one, as we are one, I in them and you in me, so that they might be made perfect in unity. John 17:23] Does he who said these words tell you that your letter is in conformity with his will? I hope so, but the contrary seems to me to be true. You were misinformed when you were told, Reverend Father, that I was going to the missions. Far from it!

1) This is not my state. 2) As you yourself said, I am not capable of it, and even if I were, I see too much danger in it and have too much repugnance to undertake it. If you doubt this, Father Vincent and the bishop could bear witness that I am speaking the truth. If, Reverend Father, you have some complaint to bring against Father Vincent and myself, you should speak to the bishop, I think, and not to a young priest such as the pastor of Arichat, about whose maturity and whose prudence you know nothing, and it seems to me that in so doing you are acting in an offensive way towards the bishop.

I recommend myself to your prayers and have the honor of being, my Very Reverend Father, your very humble and obedient servant.

f. f. Xavier[7]

The Vicar General was probably not used to receiving such strongly worded missives from lesser mortals. This, added to the fact of Francis Xavier's poor command of French grammar and spelling, must have made the reading of this letter an indelible experience for Hercelin.

Despite all the furor caused by Hercelin's letter, Vincent's return was the occasion of renewed hope for the little community. The three laybrother candidates, Charles, Bernard, and James, after a long wait were finally permitted to take the novice's habit on November 13, 1840, and made their profession the following year on December 12. Even more ambitiously, the community sent to Rome the following petition, which apparently received no answer:

The monks of the monastery of Our Lady of Loretto in the Diocese of Halifax in Nova Scotia, living according the Constitutions of la Valsainte, bowed down at the feet of Your Holiness humbly pray that you may deign to raise the said monastery to the status of abbey and to confirm the election of Reverend Father Vincent de Paul Merle, whom the entire congregation with unanimous accord has elected as abbot and to bestow on him the use of Pontificals. . . .

[Signed] F. F. Xaverius, priest, subprior, Father Martinus priest, Brothers Cyprianus, Barnabas, Lucianus, Stephanus, Bernardus, Carolus, Jacobus, Emmanuel, Paulus, Franciscus.[8]

ᴄ⁄ᴼ Vincent Retires to the Convent

According to the *History of Petit Clairvaux*, shortly after returning from Europe, Vincent went to live at the sisters' convent, leaving the daily affairs of the monastery to Francis Xavier.[9] It is clear, however, that during the coming years he continued to act as superior, particularly in the important matter of making provisions for the continued existence of the monastery. From this time on he curtailed his pastoral ministry in the parish, perhaps as a result of Hercelin's criticism of his earlier missionary activities. Necessity was to intervene, however, when at the tragic death of Tracadie's pastor, Father Anssart, on February 12, 1844, Vincent was forced once again to take over as pastor until May 21, 1845.[10]

We get an idea of life in the monastery at this time, as well as a picture of what the monastery itself was like, in two letters written by Father Vincent:

The monastery of the religious consists of a house of about thirty feet square which serves as guesthouse, cellar and kitchen. Another building forty feet long and twenty feet wide that is two-storied contains the dormitory, workspace, and refectory. There is a large building for the cattle and for their fodder, also two mills, a forge, etc. The chapel that is linked to the monastery is small yet sufficient to hold 36 persons.

The house of the Sisters is a two-storied structure about 50 feet long and 30 wide containing a small chapel that can hold 30 persons. There is a balcony in the chapel from which the young girls who are pupils there assist at Mass.[11]

. . . We are seven (not counting several others who will join us), three choir religious, and four laybrothers. Among the latter, there is a gardener, a shoemaker, a cook and another who is capable of heavy work. Although we are only a few choir religious, we sing the Canonical Office, save for Matins which is sung *recto tono*. Several other brothers sometimes help us chant. We observe the Rule of St. Benedict as best as we can, above all the fundamental points such as Vigils, fasting, work, silence, the penances of the Order, etc.[12]

The little community continued to receive a few aspirants. Shortly after returning in 1840 Vincent established a "Living Rosary" group and appointed the members of the community as participants, adding to the list enough friends of the monastery to make up the fifteen necessary people.[13] Here we find the same names as in the 1836 list, with the exception of Brother Bruno, who had returned to France. There are in addition several new ones: Brother Francis, Brother Jean Baratt, and Brother Michel Noël, a Mi'kmaq.[14]

Most of those who entered received the status of "familiar" or "donate brother." These men shared the daily life of the monastery in varying degrees but never took monastic vows.[15] In any case very few of those who appear in Vincent's record book over the next years persevered. Thus the question of recruitment remained an urgent one.[16]

There were practically no aspirants to the choir, and even among the laybrothers, none of those who entered persevered to profession, with the notable exception of the faithful three. It is understandable that it was difficult to find vocations for the choir in this part of the world, where knowledge of the Latin language, so important for this type of life, was in short supply. Throughout the coming years the preponderance of laybrothers over choir monks would remain a characteristic of Petit Clairvaux.

In an effort to keep afloat during these years Vincent and Francis Xavier tried to obtain personnel from other monasteries and even considered transferring the monastery to another location where there was better hope of finding candidates. To prepare for such a move Vincent apparently asked Bishop Fraser for a letter of introduction. The document that Fraser created serves to show how reluctant he would be to see them go:

> The bearer, Reverend Vincent de Paul, is superior of the monastery of the Order of la Trappe established in this Vicariate Apostolic; he lived in my immediate neighborhood for a number of years, and during that period, his conduct, as well as that of those under his spiritual direction, has been most edifying and exemplary. Should more flattering prospects induce him to leave this Diocese, and remove his present Establishment to a more favourable situation, I would view such a

change as a loss to myself individually and to those under my spiritual jurisdiction in general.[17]

The option of relocating the monastery had already been proposed earlier on, when Vincent considered transferring Petit Clairvaux to Mount St. Bernard. Indeed, if we are to believe Maranda, even before leaving for Europe he had traveled to the United States, looking for a place there.[18] In 1844 he would write again to Bishop Turgeon trying to revive a former project of a transfer to some spot near Quebec, informing the bishop that they now had the explicit sanction of the Holy See for their monastery.[19] Nothing would come of this either.

A glance at Vincent's record book and other documents of this early period shows a predominance of Irish among those who came to the monastery seeking entrance. While there are seventeen Irish, there are surprisingly only two Acadians, one French Canadian, and one, or possibly two, Scots. Of the others, one is Mi'kmaq, one Black, one Flemish, one Dutch and four of uncertain origin.

This stands in striking contrast to the ethnic composition of the convent of sisters, where up to 1850 we find seven Acadian names, two Scottish, and one English. In subsequent years we find nine Acadian names and four Scottish ones.[20]

Maranda looked on all these goings and comings with a jaundiced eye, although for once he showed some esteem for Vincent in this remark to Cazeau in 1842:

> Great troubles at la Trappe! Truly, I would like to see the venerable Father Vincent with you, and see the rest committed to fire, along with anything that might serve to remind us of it.[21]

Even though the continuing influx of prospective postulants led to few permanent vocations, it was sufficient to provide the upkeep and even further development of the physical plant of the monastery, which continued to grow. By 1843 work had begun on a new chapel, although the lack of funds was slowing things down.[22] The situation of the farm was also a source of encouragement. Thanks to Vincent the monastery could boast of a fine mill to support its own needs as well as those of the surrounding villages. Throughout the coming years the three professed laybrothers working with the familiars and donates would continue to provide personnel to staff the farm.

Years later when Francis Xavier wrote to the abbot of Westmalle offering to turn over the monastery to his care, he would be able to boast:

> We have no debts. The monastery, whose church is, for these parts, a beautiful one, is situated in a charming, solitary spot far from all the noise of the world. . . . [It] possesses 400 arpents [about 338 acres] of land, a great part of which is arable, the rest consisting of woods, pastures, and grasslands. . . . There is a barn with stables, eighteen cows, three pair of oxen, two horses, and a small flock of sheep, pigs, and heifers. Two mills are attached [to the barn], one of them for wheat (which can handle 50 to 60 bushels per day), and we are not able to mill all that the neighbors bring us. This mill is able to support a large community.[23]

Nonetheless, despite the joy that Vincent's return from Europe brought to the community, the situation of Petit Clairvaux remained precarious. As Vincent related to Bishop Walsh of Halifax, a fire broke out during the night of February 19-20, 1843, in the older building containing guesthouse, cellar, and kitchen. After vain attempts to control the blaze,

> Brother Stephen made a sign to me and to the others to go back to bed since there were still two hours before the beginning of Vigils, which were due to begin at 2:00 AM that day. We followed his advice. When the time came for us to rise, we went to the chapel and recited the Office, while the fire was still burning.[24]

Unimpeded by any further efforts of the brothers, the fire completely destroyed the building. Thus, in the middle of winter, they found themselves without provisions.[25]

✒ Developments in the Vicariate of Halifax

All of these ups and downs of the little monastery were played out against the larger background of important developments that were taking place in the Vicariate of Nova Scotia from 1840 to 1850. Throughout this period Fraser continued to live in Antigonish even though he held the office of bishop of Halifax. The precarious situation of a bishop residing far from the region's major city was proving unfeasible. In Halifax conflicts arose between Fraser's Vicar General, the Irish Father Loughnan, and two priests who had come from Ireland to work in the city. Letters of complaint began to arrive in Rome around 1840.

In a lengthy document drawn up in 1844 Monsignor (later Cardinal) de Luca summarized the history of the problem for the cardinals of the Congregation, laying special emphasis on the differences between the Irish in Halifax and the Scots in Eastern Nova Scotia.

The idea of appointing a coadjutor as a solution to the problem was first proposed by Vincent himself in a letter to the prefect of Propaganda, Cardinal Fransoni, who had befriended him in Rome and who had been responsible for getting the decree of 1838 that placed Tracadie under Fraser's authority approved:

> After 20 years of silence, and seeing no change for the better in the Vicariate Apostolic of Nova Scotia, in which I have been living since 1815, I feel obliged, for the good of religion, to let the Sacred Congregation know the deplorable state in which it is. From the time when this province was separated from the Diocese of Quebec ... the lower clergy has given, and is still giving, nothing but scandal. . . . Ecclesiastical discipline here has no force. Necessity has compelled the employment of young priests for the missions, priests who have no experience or even learning, since they had only half of a course of theology. . . .
>
> Msgr. Fraser is really doing everything he can for the benefit of the flock under his charge. He is an excellent priest and a holy bishop. But the gift of administration to govern well a vicariate as difficult as is that of Nova Scotia is not given to every bishop. As long as there are no statutes, or discipline among the clergy, or retreats from time to time, etc., things will never go well, and I firmly believe that there is need of a coadjutor with the qualities of a good administrator. Msgr. Fraser is good and has good intentions. His coadjutor would be happy with him and would carry out his functions happily.[26]

Rome moved into action on January 9, 1842, appointing as coadjutor William Walsh, a priest of the Diocese of Dublin, and at the same time raising the vicariate to the status of diocese. Amazingly enough, all of this took place without Fraser being consulted or even informed—he learned of the decision from the public press and from a letter written to him by Walsh *after* he had already been consecrated! The backwash from this tactless move delayed matters somewhat, but Walsh finally arrived in Halifax in October 1842, and during a meeting of the two men in Antigonish it was decided that Walsh would care for the needs of Halifax. However, due largely to the continuing presence of Father Loughnan, who remained Vicar General, problems continued to emerge,

FIGURE 14. *Archbishop William Walsh of Halifax.*

to such an extent that Walsh stormed off to Rome in March 1844.

The final solution to the problem turned out to be a suggestion Fraser himself had made in May 1842, even before he learned of Walsh's appointment—namely, to divide the single diocese into two. Walsh opposed the idea when Rome first proposed it, but it eventually won the day, and on July 20, 1845, Walsh formally took over the Diocese of Halifax, while Fraser became the bishop of the new diocese of Arichat, which would encompass Cape Breton and Western Nova Scotia. Fraser continued, however, to reside in Antigonish.[27] Petit Clairvaux would thus remain under Fraser's care.

A new figure who began to emerge during this long struggle was Father Colin MacKinnon, recently returned to Nova Scotia from his studies in Rome. In the course of the deliberations as to what should be done to remedy the situation of the Church in Nova Scotia, he was consulted by the Holy See, and after the final decision was reached, he served as an important link between the two dioceses, since he was on friendly terms with Walsh as well as with his own bishop, Fraser.

Both Bishop Walsh and Father MacKinnon (who was to succeed Fraser as bishop of Antigonish) represented a new look for the Church in Nova Scotia. The days of the two great missionary bishops, Burke and Fraser, were passing away. These pioneers gave their best efforts to serve the immediate spiritual and material needs of their fellow countrymen, Burke in the urban context of Halifax and Fraser on Cape Breton and later in Antigonish. The new men were above all capable administrators, able to deal with the delicate problems of personnel, and concentrated on coordinating the efforts of others. This is not to say that they neglected the more immediate spiritual needs of the faithful. MacKinnon, in particular, represented the class of Roman-trained clerics who would take over the leadership of the diocese after Fraser's death. This change of style in the local episcopate would not be without meaning for Petit Clairvaux.

The Trappists of Petit Clairvaux had been able to count on the esteem and benevolence of Bishop Fraser. He had graciously accepted the jurisdiction over them that Rome assigned to him and was happy to underwrite their request for unification with the Order when that seemed the best thing to do. He was even willing (albeit with regret) to accept Vincent's proposal to transfer the community elsewhere. Nonetheless, it is clear that he took little initiative to find a solution for Petit Clairvaux's problems, an attitude that is understandable given the many problems of a higher level he had to deal with during these years. This would change with the accession of Bishop MacKinnon, who took very concrete steps to improve conditions at Petit Clairvaux, not only in terms of its spiritual tone, but also with regard to its canonical situation.

✑ Relations with Bishop Walsh

The "new look" was not unwelcome to Vincent. He was never comfortable with the spiritual atmosphere of the vicariate either during the years of interregnum between Burke's death and Fraser's accession, or during the reign of Fraser himself. It was do doubt for this reason that over the coming years he would frequently turn to Walsh for advice. Indeed, even as early as February 16, 1843, he wrote to the newly arrived Walsh asking if he might take up a collection in Halifax to help complete the new chapel. Only three nights later a disastrous fire destroyed the monastery's older building, and Vincent was writing to Walsh again on March 6 to ask once more for help. On May 4 he wrote yet again, this time in a mood of despondency, taking stock of Petit Clairvaux's situation:

> A church and a monastery to complete, and no means to do so. Debts to pay, no hope of receiving candidates, the priests being against us. Father Francis Xavier and your servant will soon be incapable of fighting because of age and infirmities. . . .
>
> I told His Grandeur that I believed it would be appropriate and more advantageous for us to go and finish our days in the midst of our brothers in France who want us to come, rather than vegetating here without being able to do any good. It has been over twenty years that I have been in Nova Scotia in order to make a foundation of our Order, and I have not been able to succeed. The small number of candidates who would have come to become religious have mostly been turned away by neighboring priests.[28]

He asked Walsh's advice in the matter and even asked him to try to come to visit in the spring to see the conditions there for himself.[29] Apparently things had come to such a pass that the monastery was actually put up for sale in the newspapers, as we learn from the ever-vigilant Maranda:

> After gadding about the world for twelve months, Father Martin has re-entered the Trappists. The monastery has been advertised in the papers for sale. Three brothers arrived from France to help Father Vincent take up a collection to support the riffraff and help to fill the house. They have [received] their faculties.[30]

The person alluded to was Martinus Hermsen. Of Dutch origin, he was a monk of Bricquebec in France who had been brought to Halifax by Bishop Walsh in 1842, presumably to engage in ministry. He turned out, however, to be a source of unending problems.[31] Such a person was hardly a welcome addition to the monastery, which is described in a document Walsh received from Rome sometime after April 25, 1844:

There is a small monastery of Trappists, and another of women who make their vows annually, and this in Tracadie. In the monastery there are two priests, both very old, and one of them, the prior, a man of saintly and edifying life, is held in high esteem throughout the Province. This institution is rapidly going downhill into decadence; the sale of the monastery and of a large tract of surrounding land was announced. The good old prior cannot maintain the necessary discipline because there is really no one to back him up. He says that the Sacred Congregation, some years back, placed the monastery under the jurisdiction of Msgr. Fraser "until other provision is made." But every time that he goes to the bishop, he always refuses to get mixed up in any of their affairs.[32]

The overall situation, along with Vincent's mood of despondency, eventually led Walsh to oppose the continuance of the monastery. Johnston summarizes a document that Walsh wrote to Rome around this time:

Walsh opposes the continuance of the Trappists at Tracadie. They have only 2 priests besides Father Vincent. Father Martin, a Dutchman, is no good. He came from Europe to Halifax in 1842. Irregularities there. Then to Tracadie, where he quarreled. Got faculties from Fraser. Left and went to Halifax; more trouble. To Canada, to Cape Breton, to Newfoundland, to Halifax, to Boston.[33]

In 1845, shortly after Walsh became bishop of Halifax, Vincent wrote asking his advice concerning an offer of land to settle in that part of Nova Scotia.[34] He seems to have received a positive response from Walsh, and in October sent him a letter to be forwarded to Hercelin:

In line with the wish of our brothers and the desire of Msgr. Walsh . . . to have us in his diocese I have decided to send Father Francis Xavier to Europe to try once again to obtain several good choir religious from our houses of Europe. I hope, Reverend Father, that you will not oppose this move.[35]

Nothing would come of this project, but Walsh continued to show his respect for the monastery. Years later, writing to Cardinal Fransoni in 1850 to urge that MacKinnon be made coadjutor to Fraser, he said: "His [MacKinnon's] church, vestry, presbytery and Parish are models, and with the exception of the little Trappist Convent at Tracadie, the only green spot in the whole diocese."[36]

✒ FATHER FRANCIS XAVIER LEAVES FOR EUROPE

Faced with the increasingly acute problem of recruitment, Francis Xavier set out for Europe in early November 1845 in the hope of seeking help and possibly winning the approval of Hercelin for incorporating Petit Clairvaux into the Congregation. On his way there, he stopped in Halifax, where he celebrated High Mass at the cathedral, the Halifax *Register* calling attention to the importance of his mission abroad.[37]

Francis Xavier's plan was to visit Ireland and England as well as France, although it is not known if he did so. In France he arrived at Bellefontaine on November 26, 1845, bringing with him Brother Étienne. Vincent wrote to Hercelin: "I sent back the laybrother, Brother Étienne, to Bellefontaine. He merited to end his days in a house that is more regular than ours. He was a good brother while with us. But he will become better with you."[38]

More importantly, Francis Xavier paid a visit to the Papal Nuncio in Paris, as well as to the bishop of Séez to enlist their help. As a result of this the bishop (in whose diocese la Trappe was situated) wrote to Hercelin urging him to accede to the request of the American monks for affiliation, pointing out, however, (as had the Nuncio) that Rome's approval would be needed due to the fact that Petit Clairvaux was under the jurisdiction of the local bishop.

There is no direct record of his encounter with Hercelin, but from the letter that Francis Xavier wrote to him before returning to America it is clear that they actually met:

> I undertook this trip from America to France out of obedience, and this is certainly trying at my age, but it was for the good of the Order of which I am a member, and to which I must dedicate myself until my death. The purpose of my trip was 1) to affiliate ourselves with the Cistercians, 2) to learn about the organization of the Order, both the Rancé party as well as the Cistercians, in case of the need to save our Order, 3) in order to find members to sustain our establishment in America, and 4) in order to have help for my return trip.
>
> God be blessed! God has his own ideas, and I adore them, for they are always just and holy. But I do not despair of seeing our Order established in America. The more opposition there is, the more hope will I have; because the works of God are always thwarted in this way.
>
> As regards myself my life does not amount to much; I will return with tranquillity to the side of Father Vincent, so old and worn out as he is, and I will *not* abandon him in his old age. He is no

longer able to cross the sea. For the rest, the abbots indeed *did* tell me to remain, but I told them of my situation and asked whether if they were in my place they would remain. Not one of them said yes, all said no; they [too] would return. Thus God wants me to return and wait to see the arrival of brothers who are solid and are able to spread our Order in all America.[39]

It seems clear that Hercelin must have asked Francis Xavier to remain at la Trappe as he had done in the case of Vincent, an invitation that Francis Xavier could not accept.

∽ FURTHER EFFORTS TO DEAL WITH HERCELIN

Notwithstanding the continuing negative attitude taken by Hercelin concerning Petit Clairvaux, when Francis Xavier returned to Nova Scotia, Vincent decided to proceed with the suggestion of the Nuncio and the bishop of Séez, and he drew up a request to Rome for affiliation "with some house of the Order." It was signed by the entire community:

> Father Vincent de Paul, superior of a colony of Cistercian or Trappist religious, in Nova Scotia, forming two separate communities, one of men, of the Strict Observance of the Reform of la Valsainte, in Switzerland, founded by Dom Augustin de Lestrange, and the other, of women, following the Rule of the Third Order of la Trappe, established by the same reformer, which rule has been praised, and encouraged by the Sovereign Pontiffs, as can be seen at the end of the book of the Rule of St. Benedict written in French.
>
> The aforementioned Father Vincent de Paul having obtained a decree of the Holy See on April 9, 1838 which, until further order, placed these two communities under the dependency and jurisdiction of Msgr. Fraser, formerly Vicar Apostolic of Nova Scotia, and now bishop of Arichat.
>
> But seeing with sadness that this establishment of religious will necessarily fail because of the lack of subjects to maintain it, his brothers as well as himself, cast down at the feet of His Holiness, humbly beg him to grant them another decree to affiliate them to some house of the Order among those that are most regular and austere, such as that of Melleray in France.[40]

This text is followed immediately by the endorsement of Bishop Fraser himself, written in his own hand: "I recommend and strongly approve this request." The signatures of the community follow. The decree, however, was not sent to Rome but rather to Hercelin for him to present to the Holy See. There could hardly be any hope of success without his *placet*. No answer was forthcoming, and the request was repeated, the petition being sent to Dom Fulgence of Bellefontaine, who now resided in Rome as Procurator General. Finally in 1848 Vincent wrote once more to Hercelin in pathetic tones:

> Your Reverence has waged war against us up until the present. You persecuted and treated me harshly, but not as much as I merit. Now I hope that peace will be between us and that you will finally have pity on us who are your brothers, or rather your abandoned children, forsaken as we are, and exiled from the flock. . . . It is in your power to grant us the affiliation in question. For we sincerely desire to be associated with our Cistercian brothers. If you establish a house of this Order in Canada, or elsewhere in America we are disposed to go there and to follow the rule.[41]

∽ The Division of the Congregation of Our Lady of la Trappe

It is likely that Francis Xavier's trip to Europe in 1845 and Vincent's petition to Rome in 1846 were inspired to some extent at least by developments taking place in Europe itself. The years since the decree unifying the two Observances in 1834 had not been easy ones for the new Congregation. Little by little the union had come apart at the seams. The year 1843 saw the last General Chapter, and the notion of a redivision of the two Observances was in the air. This finally took place on February 5, 1847, when Pope Gregory XVI approved a plan to create two separate Congregations: the Old Reform of Our Lady of la Trappe (followers of the de Rancé observances) and the New Reform of Our Lady of la Trappe (the Lestrange group who were now to be known as followers of "the Rule of St. Benedict and of the primitive constitutions of Cîteaux:").[42] Each Congregation would have its own Vicar General under the jurisdiction of the President General in Rome, and each would hold its own General Chapter.

A striking feature of the new Congregation of the New Reform was its willingness to admit into its ranks monasteries outside France. Already in 1832 Melleray had founded Mount Melleray in Ireland, and in 1835 a group of monks from both these monasteries had founded

Mount St. Bernard in England. Then on October 26, 1848, just a year after the creation of the new Congregation, the Abbey of Melleray in France sent out a band of forty-four of its monks to make what would be the first successful Trappist foundation in the United States.

A New Monastery in the United States

The site chosen for the new foundation was in the diocese of Bishop Flaget in Louisville, Kentucky. After a long journey over sea and land the monks arrived there on December 21, 1848, and in an amazingly short time, took up monastic life in earnest. By 1849 they had torn down their original huts and set up more substantial, albeit temporary, living quarters. They were already thinking of erecting permanent buildings.[43]

The monastery's superior, Dom Eutropius Proust, went to Europe in September 1849, where for the first time he and the superiors of the other non-French houses, Dom Bruno Fitzpatrick of Mount Melleray and Dom Bernard Palmer of Mount St. Bernard, attended the General Chapter of the Congregation.[44] Dom Bruno announced his own project of a new foundation in Dubuque, Iowa, to be known as New Melleray. Dom Eutropius profited from his trip to Europe by engaging in a fundraising tour, which he planned to continue in America upon his return home.

FIGURE 15. *Bishop Colin MacKinnon.*

Chapter Eight

Bishop MacKinnon and Petit Clairvaux

THE ACCESSION OF Bishop MacKinnon brought new hope for Petit Clairvaux. An official document from Rome confirmed his jurisdiction over the monastery, renewing the arrangement that had been made at the time of Bishop Fraser.[1] His esteem for the community would show itself over the coming years in a number of ways.

Little more than a year after Mackinnon's appointment, Father Vincent passed away quietly on January 1, 1853, at the age of 84. Seeing his end approaching, he had asked the bishop to come to the monastery to discuss the question of the ownership of the monastery's properties. As Ambroise relates:

> He had the bishop of Arichat come, and he placed in his hands all his goods, declaring that he was giving 200 arpents [about 169 acres] of the land to the monks and the other hundred to the sisters. The two communities were to share the remaining goods in equal measures and to peacefully enjoy these as long as the communities should continue to exist, but, if they should disappear, all of these goods would come to the bishop who would dispose of them as he saw fit, in pious works.[2]

Vincent's death left the community only one priest to serve both houses, Father Francis Xavier. Six months later MacKinnon sent a report to Rome on the situation in the two monasteries, showing that he had already set to work to help the community find personnel:

I have already written to several houses of this Order requesting that they send several religious who are priests to come to our aid. They all refused to do so. The common opinion is that the severe discipline of the Order is not suited to this region, especially because of the rigors of our winters. However, when I consider how useful these monasteries can be, as well as the love which our people have for them, and what great good such institutions can produce if well administered, I truly prefer to change somewhat the laws and rules of the Order rather than see these houses be abandoned. If therefore there were two religious priests who were [available] for us, and who would adopt some mitigation of the laws and constitutions, I believe that great good would truly come of it.[3]

This document brings out several points: the bishop's esteem for the monasteries, his awareness of the need for additional priests, and the perceived need for tempering the rigors of the Rule to make it more livable in the severe climate of Nova Scotia. This last point had been one stressed by Plessis at the time of his first contacts with Lestrange. Francis Xavier (whom we might well expect to be "not amused" with the last proposition) apparently learned of this, and writing to the Procurator General he noted in passing that Switzerland was every bit as cold as Nova Scotia.[4]

Little seems to have come from MacKinnon's appeal to Rome, and he turned to the Congregation's Vicar General in the hope of obtaining the personnel he needed. Indeed he wrote to Hercelin on three different occasions without receiving an answer. In 1854 he made still one more attempt. One of MacKinnon's priests, Father John Cameron, was returning home after studies in Rome and MacKinnon asked him to pass through Paris and contact Hercelin. Cameron dutifully obeyed and passed on MacKinnon's request for priests, adding also a request for five nuns.

The letter arrived while Hercelin was away on visitations, but his secretary answered, explaining that Vincent and Francis Xavier had separated themselves from the Congregation and that the General Chapter had laid down that neither monks nor nuns were to be sent to Tracadie.[5]

Apart from pressing the matter of their need for personnel, the bishop helped to involve the monastery more closely in the life of the diocese by establishing an annual retreat there for his clergy. The first of these took place in September of 1854 under the personal leadership of the bishop. It was also the occasion of a diocesan synod.[6] The bishop also established the practice of sending priests to spend time there for disciplinary purposes.[7]

✺ Gethsemani's American Fundraising Tour

On June 19, the Feast of Corpus Christi, just a month after his election as abbot, Dom Eutropius launched his American fundraising campaign before a large crowd gathered outside the gates of Gethsemani. The preacher for the occasion was a certain Father Dominic, about whom we know little. He was not a monk of Gethsemani, and his name does not appear in the monastery's register.[8] He had made the rounds of several monasteries before coming to Gethsemani, where he apparently intended to settle down. Eutropius was glad to make use of his skill as a preacher, especially since English was his native tongue. His first appearance in Gethsemani's story is precisely this sermon that he preached on Corpus Christi.

The campaign thus launched was to be extended far afield, and in July of 1852 Eutropius and Dominic set off to raise funds in Upper and Lower Canada. Their trip was interrupted by a letter from the Congregation's Vicar General, which Eutropius received in Montreal. The fundraising tour did not find favor with the General Chapter, since this practice had been forbidden by the Holy See. The letter also brought the disturbing news that Dominic's monastic past was not all it should have been.

When he learned of the Order's displeasure at his fundraising, Eutropius headed home via Cincinnati. As luck would have it, the Apostolic Delegate was also in Cincinnati at the time, and Eutropius was introduced to him. Upon hearing of Eutropius's plight he assured him that in the circumstances it was acceptable, even necessary, to engage in fundraising! Eutropius reported this to the Vicar General, adding an apologetic postscript concerning Dominic:

> As for the reproach made against me for taking Father Dominic with me given the fact of his past history, I knew nothing and still know absolutely nothing as to what this might have been. Knowing only that he had changed monasteries several times, I thought that he must be inconstant, but I am ignorant of the scandals he was involved in anywhere, (if indeed there had even been any such). Besides, I had no one else who spoke English. Whatever might have been his past, I can assure you that in our travels, his conduct was edifying and that he did much good by his preaching and made a good impression everywhere.[9]

Encouraged by the Apostolic Delegate, Eutropius eventually returned north with Dominic, visiting the Dioceses of Halifax, Arichat, St. John, and New Brunswick.

So it was that around the middle of August 1854, the two Trappists arrived at Antigonish, where they preached on two Sundays, Eutropius at Mass and Dominic at Vespers. The list of contributors still preserved at Gethsemani is headed by Bishop MacKinnon himself, followed by Father Girroir (who bettered the bishop's offering by five dollars).[10] Bishop MacKinnon was obviously impressed with Father Dominic. He received a number of letters from him, replying on April 10, 1855, with the details of a plan that would involve Dominic in a thoroughgoing modification of Petit Clairvaux's setup:

> In reply to all the letters I have received from you since I had the plea-sure of seeing you last, I beg to state and inform you that I have made up my mind at last to tell you *to come.* I assure you that it has cost me a good deal of mental pain to arrive at this conclusion. You will natu-rally ask why? If we both live to see one another I will tell you. I will tell you this much now: a countryman of your own, and one in high station has cautioned me, etc., etc.
>
> The good Père François has written for you. You will therefore come in the name of God, and with the consent and blessing of the Father Abbot, you will take as many as you can of the good brothers with you. A Belgian Father has just arrived at the Monastery at Tracadie and has been received. We expect soon a German Priest from the States. He will soon be in Tracadie.
>
> The good Père François is unwell just now. After your arrival we shall hold a general meeting or Chapter, and try to bring about an organization which shall be in harmony with the place, circumstances and persons. We shall appoint a Superior, and aided by the grace of God we shall do our best to put the place upon a good footing.
>
> I do not wish to do anything clandestinely. You will hand the accompanying letter to the Most Reverend Father Abbot. In this let-ter I request his Paternity to allow you and as many as wish to follow you, to come to the house in Tracadie. It is merely a request. I hope he will not be displeased with me.[11]

Dom Hercelin of la Trappe must have somehow gotten wind of these plans, for already on April 4 he had written to Francis Xavier to warn him about Dominic, as he had already done when we wrote to Dom Eutropius in 1853:

> A certain monk named Dominic who seems to be at Gethsemani has probably offered you his services to help sustain your faltering house, but I must tell you that he is a bad sort, a very dangerous man, and that you must refuse him strenuously.[12]

It seems unlikely that Francis Xavier would not have communicated this information to Bishop MacKinnon. Perhaps Hercelin's letter was received only after the bishop had issued the formal invitation.

✑ The Arrival of Father Dominic

By 1855 the community at Petit Clairvaux seems to have been reduced to Father Francis Xavier and four laybrothers, one of whom was only a novice. For this reason, whatever his take on Hercelin's letter, the bishop must have been happy to witness the arrival of Dominic and three choir monks from Gethsemani on June 15, 1855.[13] The monks were Brothers Gregory, Malachy, and a third whose name is not certain. This brought the number of the community up to nine.

It is likely that the bishop intended to eventually make Dominic superior, a move that cannot have been congenial to Francis Xavier, who was already smarting from the bishop's desire to introduce mitigations into the life of the community. Notwithstanding all this, Francis Xavier "officially" joined the bishop in inviting Dominic, no doubt with some prompting from MacKinnon.

The bishop apparently had little time to devote to the monastery during the first eight months of 1855, as he was much taken up with various educational projects for the diocese. Though there is no indication that he actually appointed Dominic superior, it seems clear that he expected him to take initiative in improving conditions in the house. The bishop would not be around to monitor how things were going, however, since he would be leaving for Europe at the beginning of September for what would be a ten-month absence.[14] In any case, Francis himself was not long in confronting Dominic with Hercelin's letter.

Alarmed by the description of himself as "a very dangerous man," Dominic began writing to four different bishops in the hope of interesting one of them in the possibility of a Cistercian foundation to be led by himself. It would be necessary, of course, to have proof of good standing if such a venture was to succeed. Accordingly, Dominic approached MacKinnon (probably before the bishop left for his *ad limina* trip to Rome) and asked for "a letter of leave to go home, in which His

Lordship testifies that I am under no ecclesiastical censure."[15] He requested a similar letter of Father Francis Xavier, saying that he was undecided as to whether to return to Gethsemani or to Melleray. Both the bishop and Father Francis Xavier provided the letters requested, little suspecting what was really afoot.

One of the four letters of appeal Dominic sent out has survived in the papers of Bishop Patrick Phelan, who was functioning as Apostolic Administrator of the Diocese of Kingston, Ontario. He had met Dominic in the course of the fundraising tour of Dom Eutropius in 1853. In his letter of appeal, written on September 14, Dominic outlined the situation at Petit Clairvaux and offered to bring a group of the (according to him) disgruntled monks of Petit Clairvaux to Kingston, provided a suitable agricultural property could be found for them. Dominic proposed opening a school of boys and even suggested that "one of the Priests of the Community would attend to the Missionary duties, so far as requisite in the vicinity of the Monastery."[16] He requested that the bishop send his response in care of Father James Duffy, pastor in nearby Guysborough, a priest of Irish origin like himself, who was also interested in the new foundation. (Duffy had actually entered Petit Clairvaux in 1850 but stayed for only a brief while.)[17]

By November 3 he had received a favorable reply from Bishop Phelan, who also proposed a house and property near a church, which could eventually be served by the monks. Sometime after this Dominic set out for Salem, Massachusetts, with Brother Malachy, one of the choir religious who had come with him from Gethsemani. While there, on November 13 he received a letter from the bishop inviting him to come to Kingston with his followers. Dominic answered Bishop Phelan the same day thanking him for the invitation and informing him that he would be setting out with Brother Malachy around November 19 or 20. On the same day he wrote another letter announcing the good news to Father Christian Kauder, another diocesan priest, who was a lodger at Petit Clairvaux and who also hoped to follow Dominic in this venture. This young priest, a native of the Grand Duchy of Luxembourg, had come to America in 1844, where he joined the Redemptorists and made profession in 1845. He eventually left the Order due to poor health and came to Nova Scotia, where he resided as a guest at Petit Clairvaux. Kauder was crucial to Dominic's plan, since he could serve as liaison with those still at Petit Clairvaux who hoped to join Dominic.

These ambitious plans, however, came to naught. The letter to

Kauder was somehow intercepted and fell into the hands of Francis Xavier and, needless to say, was never delivered to Father Kauder. Infuriated with what had happened, Father Francis Xavier wrote Bishop Phelan on November 28, including a copy of Dominic's letter and citing the words he had received from Dom Hercelin concerning Dominic.[18]

In the meantime, having arrived in Ontario Dominic and Malachy were sent by Bishop Phelan to Wellington on the bay of the same name in Lake Ontario, where Dominic was named pastor of the church of St. Frances of Rome. Not having received an answer from Kauder, Dominic wrote again on December 5 to reiterate the messaage that all was ready and that Kauder was to take a group of others and set out as soon as they could. This group was to comprise four brothers— Gregory, Anthony, Patrick and Bernard—and three laymen. Father Duffy was to follow in the spring.

On December 11, however, Dominic received a letter from Bishop Phelan asking for an explanation for the letter he had received from Father Francis Xavier, a copy of which he included in his own letter. Dominic wrote back on December 13:

> The letter from Tracadie was from the old Father Prior, and it is any-thing but agreeable, for it is full of crossness and scolding. In it he accuses me of causing trouble in the little community.
>
> As Your Lordship is now my spiritual father and Superior in Christ, I can have nothing to conceal from Your Lordship, and there-fore I unbosom myself to you.
>
> In the little community of Tracadie there are but six members. Two of these followed me from Gethsemani, and made no vows what-ever to the Prior of Tracadie. One of the four laybrothers is but a novice, and altho' he is three years there, he would not, on any account, make his vows in Religion to the Prior, hoping, at all times, to leave, as he has a right to do, for some other well-regulated monastery of our holy Order.
>
> The other three Lay-Brothers never made any vows to the Present Prior, so that, according to our holy Rule and Constitutions; as also according to the Canons of the Church and Decrees of Sovereign Pontiffs, they are at liberty either to make their vow of stability to the present Prior; or to leave for another house of the Order, where Discipline is observed, which, unhappily, has never been observed in Tracadie, now thirty years in existence.
>
> The good young priest, Rev. Mr. Kouder [sic], belongs, by no means, to our Order. He followed me to Tracadie, to board and lodge

there, so long as I would remain there. One of the three professed Lay-Brothers wished to leave and follow me, with the prime intention of observing our holy Rule, according to the Primitive Observance.

Four out of the six in community, before I left, promised to follow me. They most earnestly begged and supplicated me, for the love and honor of God; for the sake of their salvation, to make out a place, somewhere or another and send for them as soon as practicable. Some of them even declared that, if necessary, as Brother Malachy can testify, they would beg their way in order to come to me.

After I had the honor and happiness to receive your Lordship's kind invitation, I wrote to the Brethren, thro' Rev. Father Kouder, and invited them to come to Kingston. They, I presume, told the Prior their intention to leave; and this is what the Prior calls a cabal and disturbing the community.

Three out of the six made no vows whatever in Tracadie; and the other three made their vows to Father Vincent, who died nearly three years ago, but never renewed the vow of stability to the present Prior, so that, if they wish, they have the *right* to leave for any other monastery of the Order that would be willing to receive them. This, my dear and beloved Lord, is, I might say, an every day practice in the Order, where the vow of stability has not been made. Such is my own case, with regard to Gethsemani, as your Lordship had seen by the Abbot's letter, as also by the letter of the Prior of Tracadie.[19]

Dominic wrote again the very next day with a few remarks about Father Duffy (explaining that he was a diocesan priest also interested in joining the group) and adding significantly, in case the bishop might have some idea of establishing contact with the Order in Europe:

Under existing circumstances and for several grave reasons, which I shall at a future day communicate, I think it would be better and more desirable that the Cistercian Monastery should be, in all things, subject to Your Lordship's jurisdiction, at least for a time, on trial.[20]

By January 1, 1856, Francis Xavier had intercepted a second letter from Dominic and had sent copies of both letters to MacKinnon, who was still in Rome. He also sent a second warning to Bishop Phelan to be on his guard with Dominic.[21]

What with the confiscation of Dominic's letters to Kauder, the little troop of hoped-for members had still not been informed of the new foundation, but in a letter of February 27, 1856, to Bishop Phelan, Dominic indicated that Father Duffy had promised to visit Petit Clairvaux and break the good news to them so that they could be ready for departure in the spring. Duffy also reported (in Dominic's words):

> He says that the old Russo-German General, Father Frank of the
> Tracadie-Sebastopol [Father Francis Xavier], is furious as he greatly
> fears that not so much as even one sentinel will remain to guard the
> shattered remains of that old and nearly abandoned fortress.[22]

Judging from the last letter in this dossier, written on March 10,
1856, it is clear that although Dominic was still hoping for men from
Petit Clairvaux and environs, the old fortress was still standing and
guarded by the same small platoon. Dominic himself was becoming
increasingly absorbed in his work in the parish. He remained there until
his death on Palm Sunday April 7, 1857, and was buried next to the little church he had served during the last years of his life. Brother
Malachy eventually returned to Petit Clairvaux and changed over to the
laybrothers, although the date of his return is not certain.[23]

Another account of the events just described has come down to us
from the pen of Father Ambroise Baugé of Bellefontaine, who wrote in
1885-86 during his sojourn at Petit Clairvaux. His version is based on
conversations with old Amable Coté, the brother of Mother Anne:

> A certain Father Dominic arrived on June 15, 1855, . . . an Irishman,
> choir religious, priest and professed of Gethsemani, who remained at
> Petit Clairvaux only two years. This religious had been chosen by the
> bishop of Arichat to replace Father Francis as superior, at the instiga-
> tion of several who could not always get along with this latter. The
> bishop himself was very much in favor of this change, for he could not
> always manage to tame the Germanic tenacity of Father Francis and
> make him obey as exactly as he would have liked.
>
> A day was chosen for this new installation that the bishop was to
> carry out in person, but at the moment when he called to the chapter
> the one newly chosen, he learned that suddenly he had just left the
> monastery in order to go to found a new house in the Diocese of
> London in Canada. I was not able to discover why Father Dominic
> behaved in this manner. (The reason given to me was that, since
> Father Francis had to remain in the monastery, Father Dominic feared
> some sort of rivalry.)[24]

Based as it is on the recollections of a layman concerning events that
transpired thirty years earlier, there are several inaccuracies. First of all,
Dominic's time at Petit Clairvaux did not last two years, but only for a
period of six months during 1855. Secondly, the diocese to which

Dominic went was not London, Ontario, but rather Kingston. Finally, the operatic dénouement of the bishop calling a chapter to appoint Dominic superior only to find that he had taken off is pure fiction, since Dominic did not leave Petit Clairvaux until after Bishop MacKinnon had left for Europe.

Brother Gregory, who had accompanied Dominic when he came to Petit Clairvaux from Gethsemani, remained after Dominic's departure. A Fleming by origin, he was originally a choir monk of le Gard. He had been sent away from his monastery and had come to America. He eventually became Petit Clairvaux's secretary, an office he was still holding in 1862.[25] Over the coming years he was to be a controversial figure in the monastery.

Not long after writing to Francis Xavier to inform him of Dominic's past, Dom Joseph Hercelin died on July 13, 1855. Francis Xavier decided to take advantage of the change of Vicar General and to send to the General Chapter that would be meeting in September yet another request for integration into the Order.[26] He also sent a letter to Dom Fulgence of Bellefontaine presenting his case and indirectly asking for his support.[27] The chapter opened on September 12 under the presidency of the newly elected abbot of la Trappe and Vicar General, Dom Timothy Gruyer. Francis Xavier's letter was read at the chapter's second session that afternoon, but little came of it during the course of the meeting.

In 1856, however, Bishop MacKinnon arrived in Rome for his first *ad limina* visit. While there he visited the Procurator General of the Congregation of the New Reform of la Trappe, Dom Francis Regis de Martrin Donos. Stressing the great potential of the monastery despite the lack of sufficient personnel, he once again made a plea for two priests and possibly another religious. The Procurator wrote to the new Vicar General submitting the bishop's request and suggesting that, since Dom Eutropius had already been to the Antigonish area to raise funds, he might be the one to help out. He gave the letter to Bishop MacKinnon to present to Dom Timothy.

The bishop's original intention had perhaps been to visit la Trappe, but as things turned out, he simply wrote to Gruyer on his way through Paris, enclosing the Procurator General's letter. In this he expressed his readiness to see the monastery pass from his own jurisdiction to that of the Congregation of the New Reform of la Trappe, stressing the need of speedy action to put the affairs of the little monastery in order.[28]

By way of answer Dom Gruyer promised that the matter would be taken up by the next General Chapter. In the meantime they were urged to see what Gethsemani could do to help. A barb, however, was attached:

> Already several times the case of the monastery of Tracadie (concerning which Your Reverence wrote to us) was taken up, and the opinion of the Reverend Capitular Fathers was not favorable, because from the beginning Fathers Vincent de Paul and Xavier separated themselves from our Congregation. If now, however, led by necessity and as well as by the grace of God, the monks of Tracadie show themselves less alien to regular observance, for this disposition (on their part) we render thanks to God. However, considering the renewal and formation of this monastery in a distant land to be an extremely difficult and arduous undertaking, we do not wish to make a private decision in this matter, but in the next session of the General Chapter, we will propose it and consider with the Lord's help what is to be done.[29]

∽ HOPE FROM WESTMALLE

After the debacle with Dominic, the suggestion of applying to Gethsemani for help must not have been very appealing to the bishop. A new suggestion was made by Brother Gregory, who was acquainted with Dom Martinus of Westmalle. Why not appeal to this abbot for help? The bishop liked the idea, and he urged Francis Xavier to follow the advice of Brother Gregory and write to Dom Martinus to offer Petit Clairvaux to him, which Father Francis Xavier did in these terms:

> I beg you in the name of our glorious Father, St. Benedict, to send here a colony of your dear children, along with a prior to govern this house. As for myself, I will abandon all to the one whom you wish to send, and I will retire to prepare myself for death during the few days which still remain for me to live. This house would be a filiation of your abbey and you would have full authority over it. [This is followed by a vivid description of the property and its many assets.][30]

To make the decision easier for Dom Martinus, Francis Xavier offered to pay the travel expenses of the little colony he hoped the abbot would send. More immediately, he proposed that Dom Martinus send one of his own trusted religious to inspect the property for himself. Francis Xavier explained that they were under the jurisdiction of the bishop, but that the bishop was not only willing to cede the monastery to Dom Martin, but was of the opinion that this was the best course to follow. The poignancy of this decision for Francis Xavier was all the greater given that the monastery to which he was offering Petit Clairvaux was one that followed the usages of de Rancé.

The monastery of Westmalle was, almost by accident, among the very first of Lestrange's foundations. Like la Valsainte itself, it had to live through the difficult times of the Revolutionary and Napoleonic periods. Like Darfeld, it became legally separate from Lestrange's jurisdiction and was eventually placed under the local bishop. But unlike Darfeld, Westmalle remained faithful to the regulations of la Valsainte. In 1835 Westmalle sent two of its monks to Rome to seek approbation for its usages. Instead they were told to adopt the usages of de Rancé. On the same occasion Rome decided to set up a Belgian Congregation of the Order under the jurisdiction of the President General of the Italian Congregation of St. Bernard. Westmalle now became an abbey, and its abbot henceforth served as Vicar General of the new Congregation.

There was only one other monastery in Belgium at the time, the little priory of Sint Sixtus that had been founded not by Westmalle, but by the French monastery of le Gard.[31] It would henceforth be part of the Belgian Congregation and was raised to the status of independent priory. It would still need help from Westmalle.

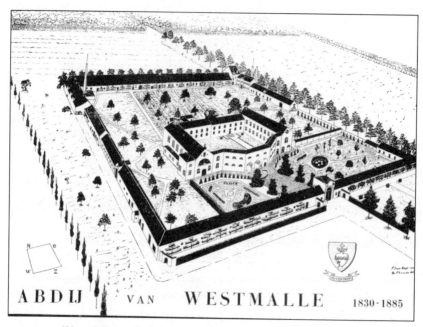

FIGURE 16. *Abbey of Westmalle, Belgium during the period 1830–1885.*

FIGURE 17. *Dom Martinus Dom, abbot of Westmalle.*

Father James Deportemont had entered Westmalle in 1831 as a diocesan priest, shortly after Belgium achieved statehood. His priestly experience and his own personal qualities were to win for him a series of important offices in the course of his monastic career. In 1836, when Sint Sixtus became a member of the Belgian Congregation, Dom Martin sent Fathers James and Dositheus there to help staff the little monastery. Along with the other members of the monastery, they made stability in the monastery of Sint Sixtus on November 12 of the same year.[32]

Dositheus became Sint Sixtus's superior, and James was appointed its novice master and also served as secretary to Dositheus. In addition to these offices, James seems to have been singled out to draw up the new usages of the Congregation, which were based on those of de Rancé. Things went peacefully for eleven years, then in 1847 Dositheus resigned, and Father Francis Decroix was elected prior. James was named subprior. Not long after this, problems arose when Francis got involved in a scandal, and James apparently urged Abbot Martinus to make a visitation of Sint Sixtus in 1850. In July, shortly after this visitation, Francis created the foundation of Chimay in order to take refuge there from judicial pursuit, and James took over the role of interim prior (probably in virtue of his role as subprior). Some voices were raised in criticism of James's regime, although it is not clear how valid this criticism really was.[33] Finally in 1856 Dom Martinus declared the office of prior at Sint Sixtus vacant and organized an election, at which Dom Dositheus was reelected.

When Father Francis Xavier's request to Dom Martinus arrived, the abbot decided that Father James would be the man for this new project. While there is no evidence to prove this, it seems likely that James was chosen as the leader of the group going to Tracadie precisely to remove him from Sint Sixtus.[34]

∞ RETROSPECT

The retirement of Father Francis Xavier brings to an end the first phase in the history of Petit Clairvaux. Father Vincent had dedicated himself to the establishment of Petit Clairvaux and throughout his life had its best interests at heart. But most of his time was spent ministering to the needs of the local population. His dedication to the Christians of Nova Scotia and Cape Breton from 1815 to his death in 1853 inspired a corresponding esteem among the Mi'kmaq, Acadian, Scottish, and Irish populations. Even after his death the memory of his devotion to the Church in those lands lingered on and eventually led to a petition for his beatification in 1905, a petition largely inspired by the local population.

Despite the community's sorrow at the loss of their beloved founder, little actually changed at Petit Clairvaux after Vincent's death, since all along it had been Francis Xavier who provided continuity in the life of the community. Looking at the one surviving photograph of Father Francis Xavier, it is hard to believe that this smiling old man was the world's last literal follower of Lestrange's observances. As a novice at Darfeld's foundation of Burlo, his decision to leave the monastery and to transfer to la Valsainte had been motivated by his devotion to the observances of la Valsainte, and throughout his entire career these observances were the inspiring light in his life. During his years at Petit Clairvaux he continued to insist that the community remain faithful to them, long after they had been considerably modified by Lestrange's followers in France itself.

FIGURE 18. *Abbey of Sint Sixtus, Belgium.*

Nonetheless, for all his dedication to this ideal at Petit Clairvaux, the reality was otherwise. Limited as they were to a group of six or seven members (only two or three of whom were choir monks), the community could not come near to carrying out the Lestrangian observances in their entirety. What was important, however, was that they did what they could to live a monastic life and to keep it alive in that remote corner of Nova Scotia. Others would now take over.

Beyond all matters of observance, however, what was perhaps the most engaging quality of Francis Xavier was his devotion to Vincent. It would have been all too easy for him, with his high ideals, to look askance at Vincent's pastoral activities. But his reaction was just the opposite; we have seen with what vehemence he struck out in defense of Vincent in response to Hercelin's imprudent letter to Maranda. Then there was his unsinkable trust in God in the face of opposition and seeming failure, so well expressed in his last letter to Dom Hercelin:

> God has his own ideas, and I adore them, for they are always just and holy. But I do not despair of seeing our Order established in America. The more opposition there is, the more hope will I have; because the works of God are always thwarted in this way. . .[35]

FIGURE 19. *Dom James Deportement.*

Chapter Nine

A New Beginning

✍ FATHER JAMES SETS SAIL FOR NOVA SCOTIA

WHEN JAMES SET OUT for Nova Scotia on December 25, 1857, he had considerable experience behind him. He had lived under both the Lestrange and the de Rancé usages. He had experienced monastic life in the older, well-established atmosphere of Westmalle as well as in the small priory of Sint Sixtus.[1] He had held the offices of novice master, subprior, and even superior, and was thus well acquainted with what it meant to deal with monks and their problems.

Abbot Martinus provided James with a document stating that he was sending him to Nova Scotia to govern the monastery and that he was to have all the rights attached to such a role. In addition, Martinus renounced all rights of jurisdiction over the monastery, leaving James free to seek affiliation with some other monastery. This last proviso, while it assured James liberty in the matter, also assured that Martinus himself would not be forced eventually to assume jurisdictional responsibility for Petit Clairvaux.

James's very first letter to his prior, Dositheus, was penned shortly after he got to Tracadie.[2] After narrating his experiences crossing the Atlantic, he described his arrival at Halifax on the cold morning of January 16, 1858. James's long trip to Tracadie through Nova Scotia's fir forests took eighty hours. He was first received at the sisters' convent, where he met the famous Amable Coté, brother of the mother superior and overseer of the domestics who lived at the convent. By then what was left of the school was run by "a little old man" and was relegated to a small house; the sisters no longer participated in teaching but were still providing for the monks' needs, making some of their clothes and doing their washing.

James's first impressions of Petit Clairvaux seemed to belie the enthusiastic description that Francis Xavier had sent to Abbot Martinus. He wrote to Dositheus:

> Here we find great poverty right in the midst of great abundance. There are many buildings, but they are not very usable because of the builders' lack of skill. There are two places that serve as the church, one for summer, and the other for winter, but everything is very poor. Nothing is visible but bare boards, sometimes with a bit of plastering here and there. The tabernacle is a small chest, just high enough to accommodate a modest chalice. There is no porter's lodge, or guest-house or infirmary. Yet it would be possible to provide for these things; if we had your Thomas, it would be possible to arrange things much better. That is why I hope you will do us this favor, and also that you will send Father Robert and several other brothers whom I list, but I will write once more before Easter or before May to give you more details about how they should travel, and to give you fuller assurance that all will go well with their interior life and with regular discipline. For I fear rather strongly that there will be difficulties arising from the change that must necessarily take place. Up until now we have had only words and promises, and we have not yet spoken with His Excellency; I hope, however, that all will go well. For this intention I ask you to unite your prayers to our own prayers that the Lord might grant us all the graces necessary to bring the work that has been begun here to a good end. Hoping for this, I remain . . .[3]

The tone of his closing words shows that, despite his fear concerning what effect the changes he must make would have upon the community and the prospect of all the work that lay ahead, he was enthusiastic about his new assignment and had in mind a list of those he wanted as helpers in the new venture.

By February 24, 1858, he could report to Dositheus that the meeting with the bishop turned out to be a productive one. Francis Xavier was happy to step down, and the bishop gave James authority over both monasteries with full powers to introduce the Constitutions of de Rancé. James enthusiastically added seven names to the list of brethren he had already requested of Dositheus. There was also urgent need of various practical things in this remote corner of eastern Canada. "Here we are, as it were, outside the world; we must travel twenty-three miles to find a doctor; the parish priests sometimes have to serve five parishes, and the bishop himself has but one chaplain."[4]

Francis Xavier eventually retired to the convent of sisters and spent his last days with the Lestrange flag held high:

> He desired to be left in peace to follow the Rule that he swore to observe. Not being able to obtain what he desired, he applied to the bishop and obtained permission to retire to the convent of the Sisters, as Father Vincent had done, there to follow the Rule of la Grande Trappe. He brought along Brother Charles for his consolation.[5]

In March James decided to send someone to Belgium to offer assistance to the new contingent that Dositheus would be sending to Nova Scotia, and the man chosen was the ubiquitous Brother Cyprian, who, since 1845, had actively devoted himself to the promotion of Petit Clairvaux's survival.[6] His knowledge of both French and English would be of great use, as would his acquaintance with the procedures involved in traveling across the Atlantic.[7]

∽ NEW ARRIVALS

In addition to five of the men James had requested, Dom Martinus sent two more. In all, there were two choir monks, Fathers Paul Meulemeester and Arsenius Ruyssers, and five laybrothers, Brothers Bernard Van Nieuwenhuise, Innocentius Van Seynhaeve, Bartholomeus De Bonte, Marcus Lacayese, and Clemens Van Bellegem. They arrived on October 20, 1858. This group would prove faithful over the years; all save one would persevere at Petit Clairvaux until death.[8] The two choir monks were ordained shortly after arriving. One of them, Father Paul, would play a crucial role in the development of the monastery.[9] He was appointed to the important office of cellarer, and in subsequent years he would make several trips to Europe to look for prospective vocations. In a less apparent way, Father Arsenius would also become a pillar of the community, serving as a popular confessor to monks and guests alike.[10] He was subprior from 1871 until the time of his death in 1892.[11]

Four more Europeans arrived in the spring of 1859. Once again Sint Sixtus sent two choir religious—one of them a priest, Father Andrew—

along with a laybrother postulant. A laybrother from Westmalle came with them.[12] Unlike the first group none of these men would remain at Petit Clairvaux. By January 12, 1860, Bishop MacKinnon had ordained Paul and Arsenius, and in his diocesan report of that year he could boast of a community of three priests and thirteen brothers.

This great influx of Belgians into the monastery shifted its ethnic composition. Writing to Rome shortly after their arrival, Bishop MacKinnon reported that before the newcomers arrived there had been in the community one priest and six professed brothers,[13] three identifiable as Irish, one German, one Acadian, and one Belgian. Now a strong majority would be Belgian. Furthermore, there seems to have been little local recruitment once the Belgians took over. This meant there would never be a solid base of membership from Nova Scotia itself, and the monastery's survival would depend in large measure on continued influx of personnel from Europe.

After his ordination, Father Paul made his first journey to Belgium to find new candidates. He began the return trip on April 16, 1861, with nine new members. All of them were from Sint Sixtus, most being novices or postulants, but included in the group was one simply professed choir monk and three solemnly professed laybrothers.[14] These last three proved to be the most stable members of this group, further contributing to the preponderance of laybrother vocations that was characteristic of the monastery throughout much of its history. They remained in the monastery until their death.[15] Also included in these nine was the colorful Brother Placid Gubbels, who eventually left the monastery at the time of its transfer to Rhode Island and became a diocesan priest of Antigonish.

✍ A Bold Move: Attempts to Make a Foundation

Of those who had arrived in the spring of 1859, Father Andrew was soon to find life hard under Father James, and he began asking him for permission to go to Lower Canada to see if a community might be started there.[16] James refused, and eventually Andrew appealed to the bishop. The Bishop agreed and Andrew went to Montreal to see what opportunities he might find there. But nothing materialized, and after six months he returned to Petit Clairvaux, where he was received back, albeit with some coldness. After a year he convinced James to consult the community on the question of a foundation, and the result was positive.

Accordingly on January 16, 1862, James wrote this time to the auxiliary bishop of Quebec, Msgr. Baillargeon, and received a favorable and even enthusiastic reply. James himself had come to see the value of having a foundation in Quebec, as he reported to Dositheus:

> I told him [Father Andrew] to go to Lower Canada with a view to starting a new house; the Archbishop of Quebec promised us his support. On the 21st of this month Father Andrew is going to prepare a place and to see if it might be possible to establish our holy Order in these very cold lands. We hope to get more results there than we have in Nova Scotia.[17]

Andrew set out as planned, stopping first at Montreal where the Sulpicians offered him property (it would one day become the Abbey of Notre-Dame du Lac at Oka). He declined their offer and instead continued on to Quebec to consult with the bishop. While there he met Father Louis-Théodore Bernard, pastor of the church in Sainte-Claire, a small town some thirty miles southeast of Quebec City. This priest invited him to found the monastery in his area and even came up with three benefactors who were willing to purchase the land necessary. The lots were situated in an undeveloped forest less than twelve miles from the present United States border of Maine, not far from the center of the present town of Sainte-Justine. Andrew accepted the offer, and the land was officially donated to the Archdiocese of Quebec (the deeds never passed into the hands of the monks). These lands were totally uncleared, and much work lay ahead for the new community.

James sent a small group of his monks as founders to join Father Andrew: Father Placid, and Brothers Edmund and Clement. They left on Pentecost Monday, 1862. On their way they passed through Quebec and were received by the bishop. They then went on to Sainte-Claire, where Father Andrew was waiting for them, and spent several days as guests of Father Bernard at his rectory. Then on June 24, 1862, Father Placid, Brother Edmund and Brother Clement set out from the church of Sainte-Claire accompanied by laymen who served as guides and helpers. Local people provided wagons for their trip to the forest, but for the last twelve miles they had to carry all their provisions on their backs, since it was impossible to get through with the wagons.[18]

Over the coming months, it became evident that Father Andrew's ascetic demands on the little group went beyond what was reasonable in the severe climate of Quebec. News filtered back to James, and he decided to visit the little foundation. He arrived there on August 14, bringing with him Brother Francis Xavier de Brie and Brother Maur. Assessing the situation, James decided to send Andrew to Europe under the pretext of gathering postulants for the foundation. After Andrew left, James appointed Brother Francis Xavier de Brie temporary superior, even though he was not yet a priest.

While in Europe Andrew managed to find four men willing to come to Quebec. Two were professed priests (one from la Trappe itself and one from Achel in Holland), one was a novice and the fourth was a postulant of Sint Sixtus. These he brought to Mount St. Bernard in England to await departure for Canada.[19] When Andrew learned of Brother Francis Xavier's appointment after his departure, he sent the men on to Quebec and resolved to remain at Mount St. Bernard. He died there on February 20, 1867.

✑ Official Opening of the Monastery of St.-Esprit at Sainte-Justine

The new candidates Andrew had gathered arrived in Quebec on June 12, 1863. They were welcomed into the Bishop Baillargeon's residence where they rested for a few days. On June 14, the bishop canonically established the monastery, which took the name of St.-Esprit in honor of the Holy Spirit. It was to be under the jurisdiction of the Archdiocese of Quebec "without depending on any other house, until such time as circumstances permit its affiliation to or union with a community already established either in Europe or America."[20] The new brothers arrived at Sainte-Justine on June 18, and on June 20 an election was held. The young Brother Francis Xavier de Brie was elected, even though he was not a priest and had not even made his solemn profession. To remedy this situation he made his profession on the same day as the election, and on September 27 he was ordained priest in Quebec.

Almost immediately he began the construction of a large monastery, its plan measuring 120 feet square, designed to meet the needs of eighty monks. The farm was developed, a mill was built, and the monks seem to have been the first ones in the area to collect sap from the maples for making syrup.

Despite the material progress made by the community of St.-Esprit over the first years of its existence, recruitment proved to be a problem. As in the case of Petit Clairvaux, the community had to depend on vocations from Belgium. Canadian vocations were not wanting, but few of them remained.

Immediately after the election at St.-Esprit, James returned to Nova Scotia with one less responsibility resting on his shoulders now that the bishop had assumed complete control of the new foundation. He was back in time to serve as archdeacon to Bishop MacKinnon at Brother John Baptist's ordination to the subdiaconate on November 1, 1862.[21]

✏ FURTHER EFFORTS TO OBTAIN PERSONNEL FOR BOTH MONASTERIES

With five of his monks at St.-Esprit and Father Andrew off in England, James was beginning to feel the need of more personnel. There remained only seven professed in the choir and eleven in the laybrothers. Local vocations were not forthcoming. There had been a windfall in 1862 when a professed priest and two postulants from Belgium volunteered to come, but only one of these (Brother Romuald) was to persevere. On August 19, 1863, James appealed to Dositheus once more for help.[22] In 1864 Father Paul made his second recruiting trip to Belgium, but once again the results were meager, and of the four men he brought back to Nova Scotia, only one laybrother would still be there in 1894.[23]

The year 1865 saw the monks busy with building plans. Father Paul, the cellarer, reported to Dom Dositheus that a quarry of fine stone was opened, and there were some attempts (albeit unsuccessful) at brick making.[24] Though he had hoped to begin work on a new church, the barn and stables were in such bad condition that it became imperative to replace them with an entirely new facility (measuring eighty-four by thirty feet), which included space for a barn, as well as stables and storage areas for food. (Fig. 22 shows the probable position of this building, which was destroyed by fire in 1896 and rebuilt afterward.)

Back at St.-Esprit it was decided in 1865 that Father Placid should go to Europe to look for prospective postulants. He returned with only two but had managed to interest seven others who would eventually make their way to Canada in 1870. Thus Petit Clairvaux itself would no longer be burdened with providing further candidates.

One exception was Brother Bernard Van Nieuwenhuise, who was a member of the first group to come to Petit Clairvaux from Sint Sixtus. He was sent by James to St.-Esprit, an assignment that was not without its sacrifices.[25] This brother wrote home to his former superior, Dom

Dositheus, on January 23, 1866. His letter, which goes far beyond the realm of monastic officialdom and its busy-ness, serves as a witness to the sap of real monastic life that flowed in the veins of the little community:

> I, Brother Bernard, take the occasion to let you know how things are going. God be praised, I am in very good health, and I hope with God's grace to be able to stay in our new monastery until my death. Here in the winter it is very cold, but it seems to me that it is very good for one's health, because in our monastery there are in general few that are sick. In the summer the fathers as well as the brothers have to work very hard, because the summer is very short, but, God be praised, our superior realizes that we must perform our spiritual exercises and readings on time and hear Mass every day. And we also may attend conferences throughout the year. And in contrast to the past we are allowed to say 10 Our Fathers and 10 Hail Marys instead of Vespers, and also the same for Matins and for Lauds. And when it is a Holy Day for the Fathers it is also such for us. All this is agreeable to me. Honored Father, I ask you and all the others to pardon the scandal that we have given especially in the garden by talking too much, much more than was necessary, also in other places. . . . I shall never be able to thank God and you enough for having received me into the Order and shown great care for me, as well as for the teaching that you gave me. I beseech you especially that all of you would pray for me, and I shall pray for you, because I see here, Honored Father, that we in all places and at all times need very badly the help of God, so that we all together might come to the great monastery of paradise for all eternity. But in order to come there we will have to persist in doing good until our death. So I am and remain son and servant, Brother Bernard.[26]

After the eventual closing of St.-Esprit, Brother Bernard would return to Petit Clairvaux, where he ended his days in fidelity to his profession.

In October of 1865 Father Paul set out on his third recruiting trip to Belgium to find candidates for Petit Clairvaux. This time he brought back six secular postulants, three of whom would persevere. Foremost was Dominic Schietecatte, who would one day become the monastery's first abbot.[27] For one last time the indefatigable Father Paul set out for Belgium in 1869 to look for candidates. He came back on May 10, 1870, with four secular postulants, two for the choir and two laybrothers. The only one to persevere, however, was his own blood brother, who as laybrother took the name of Francis.

Around this time we learn of a spirit of discontent at Petit Clairvaux concerning the drain on the monastery's energies caused by the creation of St.-Esprit. On June 16, 1866, Father John Baptist Doughe wrote to Dositheus:

> First of all, concerning Father Andrew who has since completely ruined our monastery by persuading our Reverend Father to make a foundation in Canada. . . . We were then in a good position to form a beautiful monastery and a fine choir, but since then all is lost. Expensive trips were undertaken, that turned out to be of little use, for when the Fathers and the postulants arrived and saw the situation here, most of them lost courage and went away from here to Quebec and elsewhere, and they are currently wandering around. Others such as Gerard and Felix have left everything in the lurch and can now be considered I know not what! When Father Paul arrived here we were altogether seven in choir. . . . You yourself and Reverend Father no longer dare to encourage people to come here; we have no means of receiving postulants because of these migrations of the tribes, and thus we must struggle along in a house which is separated from all [others], not knowing to whom we should have recourse in our every need.[28]

The author of this letter was himself a controversial figure in the monastery and eventually returned to Sint Sixtus in 1872. Yet the tone of his criticism in this matter seems to ring true. The Belgian resources had been spread too thin, and local vocations were not forthcoming. Nonetheless, in March of 1868 James could affirm that there were twenty-four religious at Petit Clairvaux.[29]

∾ Toward Incorporating Petit Clairvaux into the Congregation of the New Observance of la Trappe

Throughout this period the question of the incorporation of Petit Clairvaux into the French Congregation of the New Observance of la Trappe remained a high priority for both bishop and community. Ever since his meeting with Dom Eutropius and Father Dominic during their fundraising tour from Gethsemani, the bishop himself had looked to Gethsemani for help in this matter. Even though the project of "importing" Father Dominic as potential superior proved to be a failure, Gethsemani still remained in the forefront. The bishop's contacts with the Congregation's new Vicar General also suggested appealing to Gethsemani directly, as a possible source of help. In the meantime, the arrival of the Belgian monks seemed to offer stability to the situation. It

FIGURE 20. *Dom Benedict Berger, second abbot of Gethsemani, first Father Immediate of Petit Clairvaux.*

might have been hoped that the monastery would eventually be invited to join the Belgian Congregation, but Petit Clairvaux's continued demands for personnel from Belgium must have made the abbot of Westmalle wary of taking full responsibility for the community.

Nonetheless, by 1862 the many appeals made over the years by the bishop as well as by Petit Clairvaux itself finally had their effect. The matter of Petit Clairvaux's incorporation into the Congregation was put on the agenda of the General Chapter of the Congregation of the New Reform of la Trappe of that year. The chapter was also willing to consider a similar request for incorporation made by the newly established Canadian monastery of St.-Esprit.

The official Acts of the General Chapter of 1862 simply report that Dom Benedict of Gethsemani was given the charge of visiting both of these monasteries to study the feasibility of their incorporation into the Congregation. A letter of instructions written to Benedict by the Vicar General, Dom Timothy Gruyer, in the name of the chapter provides more details:

> The General Chapter does not wish to permit the erection of a province in America, this being contrary to the Constitutions of the Order, nor, consequently, an annual meeting of the four superiors in a Provincial Chapter.
> To remain in the limits of the Charter of Charity, these monasteries will constitute the filiation of America [la filiation d'Amérique], united to the Congregation by Melleray as Father Immediate for Gethsemani, and Mount Melleray for New Melleray.[30]

With the prospect of incorporating two new monasteries in America, the General Chapter had to face the challenge of having *four* monasteries in a country outside of France. The situation in Ireland and England, with one monastery in each, was less challenging.[31] In the minds of the Fathers, the thought of having four monasteries in America raised the specter of an independent "American Congregation," with its own provincial chapters. This was ruled out, however, and in its place they proposed that these monasteries would be juridically linked to the Order by the normal means of the traditional institution of Father Immediates. The curious term "the filiation of America" seems to have been coined to describe the prospective new situation.

On the practical side, the difficulties connected with multiple Atlantic crossings were handled thus:

> The filiation of America having been thus constituted, one of the four superiors must come to the General Chapter every year, and visitations will take place among these houses according to the powers granted by their respective Father Immediates, if these Father Immediates are not there themselves present. . . . Every nine years, an abbot from Europe will visit each of the monasteries of the filiation of America as delegate of the General Chapter.[32]

On September 3, just nine days before the chapter met, Petit Clairvaux's beloved co-founder, Father Francis Xavier Kaiser, died. His agony lasted two days, and, as Sister Géneviève was later to write, during that time he walked about hither and yon without speaking.[33] We may believe that his own prayers from heaven helped to bring about

Petit Clairvaux's reunion with the Order, a union that he had so long worked for on earth.

✍ Dom Benedict Berger's First Visit to Petit Clairvaux

One would imagine that Dom Benedict of Gethsemani would have visited Petit Clairvaux sometime shortly after this chapter, yet it seems from one of his later letters to the Vicar General that his first visit took place only in 1865, if his memory was indeed accurate.[34] From this and other letters to the Vicar General it is clear that he was impressed with the monastery. He proposed union with the Congregation of the New Observance of la Trappe, with Gethsemani serving as motherhouse.[35] Dom James wrote to Cardinal Barnabó of the Congregation of Propaganda, describing the reaction of the community:

> On the occasion of this visit all seven of the professed choir Fathers at first expressed their desire to unite with the house of Gethsemani adopting their constitutions, but after having had a closer look at the differences there were between the Constitutions of Rev. Father de Rancé and those practiced at Gethsemani, the greater number no longer opted for reunion, save on the condition that they would be able to retain the Constitutions of de Rancé.
>
> If the union could take place in this manner, all of the Fathers would be happy, and the house of la Trappe that is in Canada and that is an affiliate of our own would also like to unite.
>
> By order of the same visitor, Rev. Father Abbot Benedict, I went to visit this house in Lower Canada, since I was the one to send there the first Fathers and Brothers as founders, but the bishop tells me that I have no right to visit this monastery and that it was entirely under his direction; the abbot of Gethsemani maintains the contrary opinion. If Your Eminence might deign to counsel me in this matter I would be most obliged.[36]

The matter of James's proposed visitation to St.-Esprit caused a stir not so much with the bishop as with St.-Esprit's superior, Father Francis Xavier de Brie. James's letter to Rome was taken up by the Congregation, and, according to ordinary procedure, those involved were consulted. The results of this inquiry were sent to James by the Congregation: "We respond to the Father Prior of the monastery of Our Lady of la Trappe [Petit Clairvaux] that the impediment in opposition to the visit of the house of his Congregation in Lower Canada does not come from the part of the bishop but from that of the prior of that house who is striving with all his might to free himself from such a visitation."[37]

In 1868 James tried another strategy to achieve incorporation. He wrote to Dom Martin of Westmalle begging that Petit Clairvaux be admitted into the Belgian Congregation, which by now numbered four houses.[38] This was a logical choice, not only because of the many members of the community who had come from Belgium, but also because the Constitutions of de Rancé were in force in Belgium.[39] Nothing came of this, however, and later that year James reported to Dositheus that the community was now waiting to be united with Gethsemani.[40] As a matter of fact Ambroise's version of the story seems to suggest that some pressure was put on the community by the bishop:

> Having learned of the dispositions of a certain number of religious who were favorable to the union, he [the bishop] felt that he need not take into account the contrary opinion of Father James and of a large segment of the community which had accepted this alliance almost unwillingly, and he resolved to profit from the occasion to recommend the matter to Dom Regis, then procurator of la Grande Trappe in Rome. This latter, having consulted the Congregation, joined with the bishop of Arichat in having the alliance confirmed by the Pope, and the abbot of Gethsemani named visitor of the monastery.[41]

The response of the Holy See came in the form of a decree issued on March 21, 1869, officially uniting Petit Clairvaux to the Congregation of the New Observance of la Trappe with Gethsemani as its motherhouse. The following July 23, the decree was read at the General Chapter held that year. It should be noted that this Roman decree specified Gethsemani as the motherhouse, a point that would come up later when the General Chapter transferred this right to Bellefontaine.

The little monastery of St.-Esprit in Lower Canada did not follow suit in seeking incorporation into the Congregation. Instead, its superior went to France in October of 1869 to pursue the possibility of incorporating into either the Belgian Congregation or that of the de Rancé Observance in France.[42] Not only was this objective not achieved, but the days of the monastery itself were numbered.

The year 1869 also marked the passing of one of the laborers of the first hour. The venerable Brother Charles Broussard, who had retired to the convent with Father Francis Xavier, fell from a hay wagon and was killed, leaving behind Brother James Hines as the last of the three who had made profession at Father Vincent's hands in 1841. (Brother Bernard Kilmartin had died in 1859.) Brother James would follow in 1872, thus bringing to an end the first generation of Petit Clairvaux.

It did not take Father James long to appreciate the security that incorporation into the Congregation brought to Petit Clairvaux, as he wrote to Dositheus on August 8, 1870:

> I would like you to know that we are all still in good health and very happy under the direction of the French Congregation that follows the primitive Constitutions of Cîteaux. It seems that our Father Immediate, the abbot of Gethsemani, is a man very experienced in everything that concerns the monastic discipline of our holy Order, so that nothing is left for us but to remain for better or for worse in humble submission. This puts me at ease so that in any case of doubt I may say: "We shall lay it before the Reverend Father Abbot or the Procurator General of the Cistercians or the General Chapter, and we shall say with one of the holy fathers: *"Roma locuta est. Causa finita est."* That is a great consolation for a superior.[43]

Chapter Ten

Petit Clairvaux, an Abbey

✎ LIFE AT PETIT CLAIRVAUX IN 1871-1872

OM BENEDICT BERGER began his first official visitation of Petit Clairvaux on July 2, 1871. Little is known of what transpired, save that one of the important matters taken up was the question of the sisters and their dependence on the service of the monks. He decided that if the bishop were not able to give the sisters a chaplain of their own, one of the priest monks might celebrate Mass for them and give Benediction on Sundays and Feasts. A monk would also be available for confessions every two weeks.[1]

In September of 1871 Dom James attended the General Chapter for the first time. It took place, as usual, at la Trappe. Dom Benedict of Gethsemani praised the community of Petit Clairvaux for its spirit of charity, but pointed out several irregularities, which James publicly promised to address.

James came to the chapter that year with a set of plans for a new main building for the monastery. They were approved with the proviso that he proceed carefully and not go beyond his financial means in carrying out the project. No doubt work began rather soon after his return, for by 1873 the graves of the monks buried before that year were transferred to a new cemetery laid out near the spot where the new chapter house would be. It is conceivable that the older cemetery occupied part of the site chosen for the new complex. It is not known when this new building was completed, or where exactly it was located in relation to the present buildings, since it was later destroyed in the fire of 1896. A rather complete description of its layout has survived, however, in the *History of Petit Clairvaux*.[2] Schrepfer was able to interview Charles Brean, a villager who had seen it before its destruction, and on the basis of his findings he made a reconstruction sketch.[3] It might well have been located in the area between the agricultural buildings and the later monastery constructed after the 1896 fire.[4] A map of the monastery made after 1903 shows the approximate position of the old main building as well as other buildings destroyed by the 1896 fire. (Fig. 22)

The 1871 census of Nova Scotia shows that there were twenty-seven people in the monastery, of whom ten were choir monks and sixteen laybrothers.[5] Only four priests are identified as such, but other records indicate that by the end of that year there were seven.[6] One of these, Father Stephen, was Bishop MacKinnon's nephew.

A letter of Dom Benedict of Gethsemani to the Congregation of Propaganda dated December 12, 1872, complains that the bishop was trying to force Petit Clairvaux, against its wishes, to accept a Father Gregory into the community. From the description it is clear that this is the same Gregory who had come to Petit Clairvaux in 1855 from Gethsemani with Dominic. He was still there in August of 1862 and was serving as secretary to James.[7] Apparently at some point he had left the monastery (or perhaps had been *asked* to leave) and went to live at the convent. The bishop's favorable attitude towards Gregory was no doubt based on his own estimation of Gregory's character, but there is also the fact that it was Gregory who had urged Father Francis Xavier Kaiser to write to Westmalle for assistance, an act that proved to be the turning point in the history of Petit Clairvaux.

The affair dragged on into 1873, the bishop writing to the Congregation insisting on Gregory's worthiness, and the General Chapter of that year supporting the view of Dom Benedict and James concerning some apparent misconduct of his.[8] The bishop returned to the attack in December with a letter to the prefect of the Congregation once again appealing in favor of Gregory, who, he said, was old and living in great misery.[9] Gregory himself wrote to the same prefect in December begging re-admittance to the monastery. He included a covering letter from the bishop. No further documentation concerning this is found in official sources, but Gregory's name does appear in the 1881 census, so presumably his wish was granted.

FIGURE 21. *Petit Clairvaux before the fire of 1896. Reconstruction drawing by the Rev. Luke Schrepfer, O.S.A., on the basis of a description of the building by Charles Brean, who had seen it before the fire.*

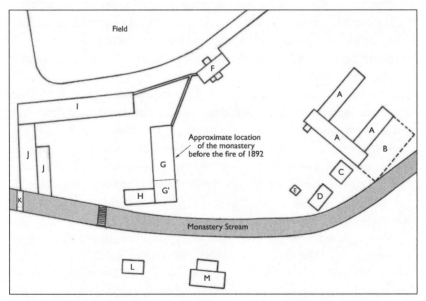

FIGURE 22. *Petit Clairvaux after 1903. A. Central monastery buildings. B. Cemetery. C. Extension of main buildings. D. Woodshed. E. Tool shed. F. Porter's lodge. G. Shed for agricultural equipment. G'. Carpenter's shop. H. Forge. I. Haybarn and stable. J. Mill buildings. K. Dam. L. Bakery. M. Laundry.*

Apart from this, life in the monastery seemed to continue peacefully, judging from the absence of specific information in the sources. The monastery was legally incorporated in Nova Scotia by an act of the legislature on April 18, 1872.[10] Father Paul made his last trip to Europe to find vocations in the autumn of 1872, returning with four candidates in the spring of 1873. The only one to persevere, the laybrother Aloysius Van Enschot, would be the only one of the Belgian monks to take part in the transfer of the monastery to Our Lady of the Valley in Rhode Island in 1900.

∽ Last Days of St.-Esprit

The year 1872 marked the tragic end of the community of St.-Esprit in Lower Canada. After having reached a high point in 1870 with forty members, decline set in, and by 1872 there were only about twenty left. One of the basic problems in the community was the unwillingness of its superior, Father Francis Xavier de Brie, to adapt the life of the monks to the severe climate in which they lived. As a result, several of the Canadian vocations died relatively soon after entering.

Furthermore, on more than one occasion the superior lamented that, though vocations were not lacking, the quality of the candidates often left much to be desired. This situation was certainly not improved by the departure of three professed monks, who had set out to start a foundation in Missouri.[11]

Also serious was the lack of contact with any other monastery that could offer support for the community's monastic needs. Such a role was normally played by the founding house, but in this case Archbishop Elzéar-Alexandre Taschereau of Quebec, who had succeeded Baillargeon, was adamant in asserting his own authority over the community and insisting that no other monastery would have claims over it, until such time as a stable house would be found to which it could be attached and thereby become part of the Congregation of la Trappe.

What proved to be the final blow was a conflict with the bishop over the ownership of the land on which the monastery was built. The original deeds were made out in the name of the bishop. The bishop's intention was to hand these over to the monastery, but only when it had entered into union with a well-established monastery that could assume responsibility for its spiritual well-being, with the further condition that the Rule be adapted to the rigors of the Canadian climate.[12] The General

Chapter of 1872 was to consider the matter, but by May of that year the situation in the monastery had deteriorated to such an extent that Father Francis Xavier de Brie drew up for the bishop an estimate of the value of the monastery's goods and began to make preparations for the dispersal of the brethren. They were all gone by the beginning of June, save for Father Francis Xavier de Brie himself, who decided to remain as parish priest of the little parish and caretaker of the monastery's property.

Some of the monks returned to Europe; others remained in Canada. Nine of them appeared on James's doorstep at Petit Clairvaux on June 4 with nothing but their religious habits.[13] Though James complained to Bishop MacKinnon of this suddenly imposed burden of feeding nine more mouths, he must have realized that these additional members would give greater stability to his community.

Many of the dispersed monks were still trying to sort out their ecclesiastical status early in 1873, and on January 10 the Trappist Procurator General wrote to the Congregation of Propaganda concerning a brother who had written to Rome:

> The dispersal of this community has been truly sorrowful, and we have not yet heard the last word. There are a number of religious who left their cloister; it seems that the few who went to the monastery of Tracadie in Nova Scotia did well. But a certain number of others are wandering about hither and yon, and the better ones are having recourse to the Holy See to regularize their status. I believe this is the fifth request that we received from Propaganda.[14]

Taking his cue from this particular problem, the procurator went on to gently suggest to Propaganda that in cases such as this the Trappists would be better off if they had a General of their own instead of being under the authority of the President General of the Cistercians in Rome. This idea would gain popularity among the Trappists over the coming years, and though it would have to surmount serious objections raised against it in 1879, it would eventually win the day when the various congregations of Trappists were united under a General of their own in 1892.

✑ PETIT CLAIRVAUX AN ABBEY

With the arrival of the nine men from St.-Esprit, Petit Clairvaux seemed to enter a period of prosperity. The construction of the new monastery was probably far along at this time, if not complete. In 1875 Father Paul as cellarer negotiated the purchase of seventy-five additional acres of land, bringing the total holdings to 275 acres.[15]

This happy state of affairs was reported to the General Chapter that year by Dom Benedict of Gethsemani, requesting that the monastery be raised to the dignity of abbey. The chapter was favorable, and steps were taken to contact the Holy See. The decision was not long in coming. On May 3, 1876, the election for the new abbot took place. Bishop MacKinnon was delegated by the Holy See to preside over it, but due to illness, he delegated his coadjutor, Bishop Cameron.[16]

We last heard of Father Cameron in 1854 when, as a young priest returning from his Roman studies, he had intervened with Dom Hercelin (at MacKinnon's request) asking for the admittance of Petit Clairvaux to the Congregation of la Trappe. In 1870 he was ordained bishop in Rome and appointed coadjutor to MacKinnon. A Scotsman like MacKinnon, he was of much the same mold. Trained in the ways of Roman curial practice, he kept his sights focused on the higher administrative tasks that were to fall to him, first as coadjutor and then as successor to MacKinnon. The election he had been chosen to oversee turned out to be something of a challenge, and his handling of it shows his ability to deal with the unforeseen. The best account of what happened that day is Cameron's own:

> When the time came to count the votes, suddenly I could not help noticing with amazement the conduct of the youngest of the scrutators, who had just received Sacred Orders at my hands a few days before. Now he would sneer and show clear signs of intense pleasure, then his face would cloud over and he would grind his teeth together and with fiery eyes seemed to threaten woe to such a one as had dared to cast the vote which he was now reading, almost trembling with anger and torment. This alternating spectacle lasted until the end of the scrutiny, when he gave me to understand that one of the votes had been written without the required precision, and that if it were not counted it would be necessary to begin the scrutiny again. What he objected to was that Father Dominic [Schietecatte] was called prior instead of subprior, which he really was. No one doubted that the subprior was indeed the man intended in this vote, because his name and surname were clearly written on it, and no one else could have been intended but himself. Besides, it was a known fact that not all the electors were experts in the language of Latium [Latin] and that in writing their votes they gave ample proof of this fact. Thus one vote in favor of Father James, called him "Jacobum prior," but no one thought

the voter was thinking of arrogating to himself the dignity of prior instead of attributing it to the true prior.[17] Finally, calling *prior* the one who substitutes for the prior did not seem to me sufficient in these circumstances to justify rejecting the vote in question, and thus I declared that without a doubt the vote was to be counted. But before doing so, holding up the Ritual I asked the Father Prior if this book had some rule to follow in order to determine when a vote was not to be counted. He answered that he did not know of any. In the meanwhile the young scrutator mumbled out loud in a language I could not understand, but the few English words that were mixed in left me no doubt that he was resolved to fight the vote in question until the end. When he first heard my decision declaring that the vote was to be counted, he rose from his chair, hurried away from the table of scrutators and went to a corner of the chapter room where he sat down on a bench. When it came his turn to sign his name to the act, he scornfully refused, and his confreres seemed distressed and scandalized, but he did not want to bend to their insistent entreaties. Several times I looked over to the Father Prior and observed that he took no steps at all to use his authority to put an end to this sad scene. In the end I judged it my duty to say a few words to him by way of disapproval of his inflexibility. Then without listening to all that I had to say, turned his back on me and signed the act. After this all sang the Te Deum and a short time after the young scrutator went around the rooms asking pardon for his most strange conduct. The Father Prior shows himself to be very satisfied with the election of Father Dominic, but observed that Bishop MacKinnon would be very unhappy with it because His Excellency hoped that the Father Prior would be elected. As for myself, I must say that my sympathy was all in favor of the election of the venerable prior whom I had known and loved for not less than twenty years, while Father Dominic was a stranger to me. I thank the Lord with all my heart, because I cannot believe that any motive of partiality might have been able to incline my judgment concerning the decision I gave in favor of the validity of the vote mentioned above. As soon as the documents to be sent to Rome were completed and placed in the hands of the prior, I left to go home the same day.[18]

The episode did not end there, however. Ten days after returning home Cameron received a letter from MacKinnon complaining about what had happened during the election. Judging from what he says, it is clear that he had misinterpreted the facts. A letter from James to Cameron cleared up the matter, and at the prudent suggestion of Dom Benedict the bishop's letter announcing the election was sent to Rome with a postscript briefly describing the unusual events connected with it.

Thus Dom Dominic Schietecatte was finally able to settle down as the monastery's new superior.[19] The affair was definitively put to rest when, at the General Chapter of 1877, Dom Benedict reported: "The irregular circumstances of this election are the result of a misunderstanding."[20]

Things seemed to calm down quickly after the election, and there is little to relate concerning the life of the monastery during the ensuing years. After the election, the venerable Father James served as prior of the monastery until his death in 1883. Bishop MacKinnon held him in great esteem and asked him to direct one of the yearly retreats for his priests. Father Ambroise went so far as to say that even after the election, Father James "in some sense continued to govern the community on the spiritual level."[21]

The General Chapter of 1876 assigned Petit Clairvaux's rank among the Order's other houses on the basis of the date of Rome's decree uniting it to the Congregation. After the chapter Dom Benedict went to Petit Clairvaux to install Dom Dominic on October 25, 1876, and on November 1 the new abbot received the blessing from Bishop Cameron in the abbey church. Dom Benedict took the opportunity to carry out the regular visitation of the monastery. He was able, with the

FIGURE 23. *Community of Petit Clairvaux during the abbacy of Dom Dominic Schietecatte (undated).*

help of Mother Anne Coté, to study some of the early documents dating from the time of the foundation. He urged her to send to Dom Jean-Marie Chouteau, abbot of Bellefontaine, some further information along the same lines. In a letter to the Vicar General of the Congregation he provided what is perhaps the finest tribute to Father Vincent de Paul that has come down to us:

> Good Father Vincent was a man of rare courage and profound humility. From what remains of his works it is evident that he was a man with a heart and a man of sacrifice. At the present time few would be willing to undertake in our Order what he dared to do. When I contemplate this first monastery built with simple planks in the midst of the forest with the bears that roamed through them at that time, I ask myself how they were able to live. This spirit of sacrifice has not been appreciated. Isn't the finger of God there, when we see that despite all of this and despite more than one superior, Petit Clairvaux is today an abbey.[22]

In 1878 Dom Dominic attended his first General Chapter on September 12–16 and continued to assist at these meetings at intervals of four years (1878, 1882, 1886, 1890, 1892).

∽ THE CONVENT OF THE SISTERS 1869–1916

After the union of Petit Clairvaux with the Congregation of la Trappe it soon became evident that something would have to be worked out with regard to the sisters. They themselves had no doubt been considering various options, and by April 13, 1869, the bishop was aware of the situation. In a report sent to the Vatican he explained the difficulties:

> Now, with regard to the Sisters' Monastery, which is established on the same Tracady [sic] property, and about which Your Eminence desired more accurate information, I reply: Father James, prior of the Monastery of Trappist Monks, has stated—and the Sisters themselves are of the same mind—that the Sisters belong to the Cistercian Third Order of St. Benedict. Theirs grew up at the same time as that of the Trappists; it was founded about forty years ago,—namely at the time when the two holy priests, Fathers Vincent and Francis, both of Trappist Order, one a Frenchman and the other a Swiss, founded the Trappist monastery in the district of Tracadie.
> These two Monasteries possess a common fund of great value, a

third of which belongs to the Sisters. By the will of the prior, Father Francis, this fund was left to the local Ordinary for the use of the two Monasteries. Now, in order that the desired union of the Trappist Monastery with the Mother House may be affected, the Fathers of the Order lay down an indispensable condition, namely, that the fund and everything belonging to the religious be transferred to the Trappist Order or the Mother House by a legal document drawn up by the Ordinary, all of which I am prepared to put into execution. However, the Sisters are unwilling to transfer their share of the common fund to the Trappist Order or the Mother House, fearing that, with the loss of their land, they may be reduced to extreme penury. For this reason they prefer to have their lands remain under the care and good faith of the Ordinary, as they were left by Father Francis, the former prior.

Meanwhile, with these lands of the Sisters remaining *in statu quo,* I should greatly like to have this Monastery of Sisters subjected in discipline and spiritual matters to the Religious Priests of the Monastery of Monks; otherwise they will be left without law, without discipline, and without progress in religion or true piety. The Sisters live by manual labor, for they actually till the soil.

At present the Father Prior of the Monastery of men and most of the monks are Belgians, but all of the Sisters are natives of this district. Hence a certain diffidence has arisen among the Sisters towards the Belgians. However, since under the new regime there is a possibility that the new prior may come from France—if he is a pious, learned and prudent man, especially since the Mother Superior and most of the Sisters are of French descent, there is no doubt, but that all things in both Monasteries will daily tend to the ever greater increase of religion and piety.[23]

Thus the bishop's solution was to leave things in the status quo regarding the temporalities of the convent, but to transfer the spiritual responsibility for them to Petit Clairvaux, presumably without effecting a union with the Trappist Congregation. Dom Benedict took an interest in the convent and its problem. At the time of his first visitation of Petit Clairvaux in 1871, his own point of view was that they would be best off if they were to become full members of the Congregation, and in order to facilitate this he proposed that several nuns be sent from France to help the process along.

The bishop was once again won over by the idea and personally appealed to the General Chapter to receive the nuns into the Congregation. In the meantime, however, Amable Coté, Mother Anne's brother, was demanding compensation for property he had given the monastery at an earlier period, and Dom Benedict was deterred from pursuing the project of uniting the sisters to the Congregation. After his report the chapter of 1871 gave its decision: "In the light of the unfavorable report given to us concerning the temporalities of this house, the state of mind of its members, and the difficulties of carrying out a reform there, it is decided that it will not be possible to accede to the request of the venerable prelate." It was no doubt in light of this decision that the bishop had forbidden the sisters to receive any more novices.[24]

Around the time that Petit Clairvaux was preparing for its elevation to the status of abbey, Mother Anne, undaunted by the bishop's move, exchanged several letters with Dom Chouteau of Bellefontaine, sending him "relics" of Father Vincent and Father Francis Xavier as well as materials concerning the life of Father Vincent. She promised the sisters' prayers for Bellefontaine "from which they [Vincent and Francis] came forth, and which is esteemed as the most holy monastery there is among the Trappists of France, hoping one day to be united to the said monastery of Bellefontaine and not to any others, in accordance with what our poor old Fathers told us."[25] She was clearly leading up to asking the support of Bellefontaine in their increasingly difficult position. She wrote again two months later:

> Our good Fathers Vincent and Francis at the time of their death, expressly ordered us to unite ourselves to the Abbey of Bellefontaine, in order to be sure of preserving our Holy Order here after our own death, since we have all become extremely old and are on the point of appearing before God who will call us soon. There are now only five of us from the time of Father Vincent and Father Francis; there are ten in all. Formerly we were as many as twenty. . . . It seems that the Third Order would be the one best adapted for America considering the good that it could accomplish. . . .[26]

Clearly they were still hoping to save the idea of a Third Order establishment. After all, that was the way they had lived from the beginning. Dom Chouteau became interested in helping the sisters, although it is unlikely that he supported the Third Order idea. Mother Anne's correspondence with Chouteau continued and on March 17, 1877, in her last letter to him we learn that the abbot had suggested that help be sent from the monastery of Gardes, which was near Bellefontaine. She had obviously won a convert to the cause of her little monastery. On August

30, 1877, however, she passed away, leaving Sister Mary as superior.

Another important event in the life of the Church in Nova Scotia occurred about the same time. In July 1877, at Rome's insistence, Bishop MacKinnon resigned his office and Cameron took over as bishop of Arichat. The new bishop immediately turned his attention to the convent and sent Father Girroir, who was pastor of nearby Havre Boucher, to insist that the sisters sign a document promising to relinquish their exclusive rights to their current properties to such nuns as would be sent with the approval of the bishop to assist them, and to recognize as superior whichever of these nuns might be sent to fill that office. Girroir was in fact able to obtain such a document from Mother Mary Landry and the other sisters. He also obtained a document signed by Amable Coté, Mother Anne's brother, and by his niece renouncing rights to all their properties in exchange for complete care for the rest of their lives.[27] Father Girroir sent these on to the bishop along with a list of the sisters and their ages.

In the meantime Dom Chouteau was won over to the idea of the sisters' entering the Congregation of la Trappe and had apparently brought it up at the General Chapter of 1878, as indicated by its Acts:

> The religious called "Trappistines of the Third Order" of Tracadie in Nova Scotia have approached the General Chapter, asking for the constitutions of our Sisters and desiring to become true religious of our Order. The Reverend Father Abbot of Bellefontaine is asked to communicate to them that we gladly agree to consider their request. The Reverend Father Abbot of Petit Clairvaux in collaboration with the Reverend Father Abbot of Gethsemani is asked to undertake a study of this question; the latter would become their superior if this union should take place.[28]

Once again, nothing came of all this, and Bishop Cameron decided upon another tactic: to attempt to interest the sisters of some other Order to send a contingent to Tracadie to take over the convent. Accordingly, early in 1879 he approached the Montreal Sisters of Charity of Providence asking if they would incorporate the Trappistines into their institute. This too, however, was doomed to failure.[29] Mother Mary Landry, the superior, died sometime before February 9, 1881.

The Trappists themselves, however, had not completely abandoned the idea of a union. The Vicar General of the Congregation of la Trappe seems to have been wavering in his attitude concerning the sisters. In

1882, Benedict had chided him for this: "If I understand your letter, and if I understood you last year, a great change has taken place. Last year you seemed to me not only opposed to a community of Trappistines in America, but you were arguing in favor of relieving the Congregation of all nuns. Times change and so do men."[30] The implication is that the Vicar General had once again taken up the cause. Chouteau himself in the *Ordo Notes* of 1882, musing over the advantages of assuming the paternity of Petit Clairvaux, listed as one of these, "The prospect that I would perhaps be able to reform the tertiaries of Tracadie, who live near the monastery, a reform ardently desired by the Sisters and one that would permit them to do much good in a country where the poor French Acadians have been sorely neglected."[31] During his first visitation of Petit Clairvaux he paid a visit to the sisters and was struck by conditions there: "My impression is one of sadness. It seems to me that I would be assuming a great responsibility to send [to them] Sisters from France. I place this affair in the hands of God."[32]

As a matter of fact, at the chapter of that year in July, Chouteau presented the request of the sisters, but the decision was not favorable: "The General Chapter after hearing the arguments of Dom Jean-Marie does not feel able for the moment to undertake this project, which is all the more interesting in that it is recommended by the bishop of Arichat."[33] This seemed to put the project definitively to rest. The sisters were aging rapidly. Finally on November 20, 1885, those remaining in the convent petitioned the bishop to turn over all their properties to Petit Clairvaux in exchange for what was needful for their support.[34] They had never been a numerous community. Father Ambroise, who left Petit Clairvaux on May 31, 1887, reported that there were only six graves of sisters in the cemetery. These added to the nine who were still living made a total of fifteen.

The last sad chapter in the history of these heroic sisters was the transfer of the last four survivors to the Convent of the Sisters of Filles de Jesus at Arichat in 1903. The last of them, Sister Marie, died on December 31, 1917. The buildings of the convent disappeared one by one. Schrepfer writing in 1947 noted that there was still one small structure in existence. Since then it was moved, and today it still stands near the old railway station of the town of Monastery, Nova Scotia—a final vestige of the sisters' presence in Tracadie.

FIGURE 24. *Dom Jean–Marie Chouteau, abbot of Bellefontaine and second Father Immediate of Petit Clairvaux.*

Chapter Eleven

Bellefontaine, Motherhouse of Petit Clairvaux

∾ TROUBLES AT BELLEFONTAINE AND A NEW FOUNDATION IN THE UNITED STATES

THE YEAR 1880 brought new religious persecution to France, and on November 8 Dom Jean-Marie Chouteau and the monks of Bellefontaine were expelled from their monastery. Most took refuge in the neighboring villages. Though their exile lasted only five weeks, Dom Chouteau realized that provision must be made for the future possibility of expulsion from France itself.

Less than four months after the monks returned to Bellefontaine from their brief exile, Dom Chouteau and Father Jean-Baptiste set out for Canada by boat, arriving at Montreal on April 11. They had come to inspect the lands that were being offered to them by the Sulpicians for a foundation near Montreal. The property in question was in an idyllic spot near the Lake of Two Mountains. Though Montreal was only a short distance away, the site was cut off from the metropolis by the lake, thus offering an ideal setting for monastic life.[1] After visiting the site and discussing the matter with the Sulpicians, Chouteau accepted the proposal and the next months were spent finalizing the transfer of the property and adapting a small existing building as the future home of the founders.

✍ Dom Chouteau Pursues His Interest in Petit Clairvaux

In the course of his stay in Montreal and Oka, Dom Chouteau decided to pay a visit to Petit Clairvaux from May 6 to May 10. He had been interested in the little monastery for a number of years, and as early as 1876 showed signs of a desire to assume the paternity of Petit Clairvaux. The idea of a change of paternity had actually been proposed to the General Chapter of 1876, and Dom Benedict of Gethsemani even went so far as to offer his resignation as Father Immediate. The offer was rejected, however, and the proposed change went no further, for the moment.[2]

After his brief visit to Petit Clairvaux Chouteau returned to Montreal and Oka and on May 26, 1881, he left Father Jean-Baptiste in charge of the preparations at Oka and went to Gethsemani for a visit, no doubt to pursue once again the question of a change of paternity for Petit Clairvaux. From there he headed back to France. By August 12 all was in readiness for the departure of the founders of Oka, and on that day two priests and two brothers left for Canada. After a brief stay with the Sulpicians in Montreal they arrived at the Oka property on September 1, which is still reckoned as the official date of the foundation. Lestrange's dream of a foundation in Lower Canada had finally become a reality. The new monastery took its name from the lake near which it was situated, Notre-Dame du Lac at Oka.[3] Late in 1881 it received its first Canadian postulant.

On April 26, 1882, musing once again over the question of the possible change in Petit Clairvaux's paternity, Chouteau drew up a list of reasons why this move was appropriate. His own community was still devoted to the memory of the monks of Bellefontaine who had been sent to Tracadie as founders. Then there was the possibility that he could help the sisters of Tracadie solve their problems. And now that Oka had been founded he would have to make the trip to America in any case for purposes of visitation; Petit Clairvaux could easily be included in his rounds.[4]

Perhaps due to Dom Chouteau's insistence, the subject was once again put on the agenda of the chapter of 1882, which took place in June. Dom Benedict wrote to the new Vicar General, Dom Étienne Salasc, before the chapter to make it clear that he had no objection to the move:

In 1876 when I saw that the Reverend Father Abbot of Bellefontaine wanted to re-assume his former rights, I requested the chapter to declare him Father Immediate and clearly offered my resignation. The capitulants did not wish to accept it, but I have not changed. Consequently I declare that I no longer regard myself as Father Immediate of Petit Clairvaux. . . . So, the matter is settled and the Reverend Father of Bellefontaine can take peaceful possession. Amen![5]

Despite the strong affirmative tone of the letter, a note of pique is definitely sounded. Dom Benedict did not attend the chapter that year but eventually learned that it had chided him for failing to send in his visitation report of Petit Clairvaux, adding significantly:

The visit of Petit Clairvaux was carried out by the Reverend Father Abbot of Gethsemani, who failed to send us his report. Since this monastery was founded by the religious of Bellefontaine, and since the foundation of Our Lady of the Lake [Oka] makes it possible to visit it in a more regular fashion, the General Chapter has decided that it will henceforth be one of the daughterhouses of Bellefontaine.[6]

The fact that these two provisions come one directly after the other probably owes more to the synoptic nature of these Acts than to anything else. But Dom Benedict may very well have been offended by the possible implication that the changeover had something to do with the caliber of his administration. In any case, after having expressed his agreement with the change of paternity in an earlier letter, he now wrote again to the Vicar General vehemently objecting to it:

In 1869 the General Chapter announced to all the houses that Petit Clairvaux had been united to our Congregation by the authority of the Apostolic See, under the filiation of Gethsemani. Since at that time Rome's intervention was judged necessary, we cannot undo what Rome did without submitting to it the reasons for the change and asking for its ratification. My resignation not having been accepted in a legal way, I remain in Rome's eyes Father Immediate until such time as Rome accepts my resignation.[7]

There is no record as to how this matter was settled, with or without consulting Rome, but things eventually calmed down, and Dom Chouteau took over his new charge.

Looking back over the years of Dom Benedict's administration, one becomes aware of his deep appreciation of Petit Clairvaux's origins.

He wrote to Dom Étienne Salasc, Vicar General of the Order on May 30, 1882:

> Since 1849 this house has been held in much scorn and considered as a lost cause. When I was called there the first time, 17 years ago, I became convinced that many of the scorners would not have had the courage to carry out what was being practiced there.[8]

Dom Dominic of Petit Clairvaux began corresponding with Oka's superior, Father Guillaume Lehaye, that same year. The relative nearness of the Tracadie foundation, as well as its French origins, made it an ideal source of moral support for the new community during the hard times of its early days in Canada. Father Guillaume confided his difficulties to Dominic. In one of his replies, on August 31, 1882, Dominic evoked as an example to be imitated the heroic times of Petit Clairvaux's own beginnings:

> Don't be discouraged by the difficulties you might encounter. Think of our forebears, Father Vincent de Paul and Father Francis of blessed memory. Imagine how long they lived here, abandoned, so to speak, by everyone. I think that they never had as many vocations as you already have, yet these heroes of courage always bore up under their difficulties, their privations and their sufferings. They persevered until the end, and the good God finally blessed their works, and they now are receiving their reward.[9]

The letter is also interesting for the details it gives of life at Petit Clairvaux in 1882:

> As for the summer schedule, we have the High Mass after chapter, when there is work on the hay; after Mass we work for three hours and say Tierce and Sext at 10:55. Otherwise we follow the Regulations. We rarely prolong the work periods here, but it is up to the superior of each house to judge of local circumstances, and in need, he can, according to the rule, require extraordinary work.
>
> Our diet, it seems to me, is the same as everywhere else: milk, potatoes, rice, cheese (which we make ourselves), vegetables, such as cabbage, carrots, [illegible word], beans and peas. Vegetables are not as abundant in these lands as they are in Europe.
>
> Our drink is beer that we make ourselves; we serve it only at dinner and supper; in the morning we have milk or chicory with milk. For dessert we have apples, rhubarb and cheese. We have no other fruits.

We have very few contacts with women; we never hire them, not even to wash the altar linens. We do it all ourselves. We have no chapel where they can assist at Mass. We have no exterior ministry, save that we celebrate Mass on Sundays and feastdays at the Sisters' convent, which was founded by Father Vincent and which is ten minutes from our monastery.

The novices are never hebdomadaries for Mass. We have the lay-brothers serve at High Mass and during processions; this year's General Chapter decided that they may wear the surplice but not the alb.

We have two brothers in charge of our mill. . . . Each brother has his turn to work in such a way that they do not lose any of their interval time; they have time to do their reading, etc.

The first canonical visit of Oka was carried out in 1882 by Dom Eugene Vachette, abbot of Melleray, with the collaboration of Dom Benedict Berger, who at the time was still Petit Clairvaux's Father Immediate. The report he made to the chapter that year shows that their impressions were positive. On January 8, 1883, Oka received its second Canadian postulant, Richard Murphy, who would eventually become Petit Clairvaux's superior. And on March 24, Dom Chouteau, who had continued to send men to staff the foundation, arrived with a choir novice of Bellefontaine, Brother Ambroise Baugé, whose historical sketch of Petit Clairvaux has already been noted for its valuable information.

✑ Chouteau's First Visitation of Petit Clairvaux

After spending several weeks at Oka, Chouteau traveled on to Petit Clairvaux, where he made his first visitation as its new Father Immediate. He arrived on April 28 and remained there until May 8. In his *Ordo Notes* of 1883, he provides a good description of the monastery as it was at that time:

> The monastery is complete; three wings are in brick and are well constructed. The fourth, also in good condition, is built of wood. [Description of the wings:] 1. Church and guesthouse, 2. Infirmary and various rooms, 3. Kitchen, work space, refectory, dormitory, 4. Sacristy, chapter and dormitories. The stables are built of stone, with a wooden barn of excellent construction above them. There is a cellar and area for storage of manure; fifty horned animals.[10]

A detailed description of the property follows. By now the holdings amounted to 450 arpents (about 380 acres). The health of the community seemed excellent. The only one in the infirmary was Father James, and none of the monks required a special diet.

He found little to criticize in terms of observance, although he noted that there was not a sufficient appreciation of Holy Orders and of the Eucharist, due to the lack of instruction and to the practice of ordaining the monks without sufficient preparation. Yet he affirmed that there were several holy and excellent priests, citing as an example the Father Master (whom he does not name). Recreation took place for an hour and a half after dinner and for an hour after supper, much of this time taken up playing dominoes!

Dom Chouteau also paid a visit to the sisters and took stock of the situation by way of preparation, no doubt, for his presentation of their request for unification at the coming chapter the same year. As will be recalled, however, this request was turned down.

Little more than a week after Dom Chouteau left Petit Clairvaux Father James died on May 14, 1883. He had been the leader of the Belgian monks that came to give new life to the monastery, and even after the election of Dom Dominic, he remained its spiritual mainstay. The old guard was gradually disappearing. Two years earlier James's faithful companion and cellarer, Father Paul, had died, on July 6, 1881. Father Paul's activities as cellarer and his many efforts to find new candidates for the monastery must have been sorely missed. These two deaths left their mark on the community.[11]

Our chief source for the history of the next few years is the series of letters Dom Dominic exchanged with the superiors of Oka. Much of this correspondence involved a lively discussion of the agricultural activities of both monasteries. Dom Dominic's emphasis on this aspect of the community's life tallies well with what we learn some years later from Dom Chouteau's reflections on Dominic's character. Another fact that stands out clearly in these letters is the fragility of Dom Dominic's health. Despite constant promises to come to Oka for a visit, he always excuses himself, blaming his poor health. This was also true when Chouteau asked him to carry out the 1885 visitation at Oka in his stead.[12]

∽ Father Ambroise Baugé

During the summer of 1885 Dominic received a letter from Guillaume requesting him to receive a monk who was undergoing difficulties at Oka. On July 23, 1885, Dominic wrote back saying that he was willing to receive him. There seems to be little doubt that the monk in question was Father Ambroise Baugé, who had already made his temporary profession at Oka on June 24, 1883.[13] Ambroise arrived at Petit Clairvaux sometime that summer or in the early fall of 1885, and on October 17 Dominic wrote to Father Guillaume to report on his progress. It is an important letter, demonstrating that, on occasion at least, Dominic could be an understanding father:

> Concerning your recent request for information about how Brother Ambroise is doing, I can tell you that he is rather well. The letter that he wrote you and that you will receive at the same time as mine will help you to understand very well his present dispositions, and I believe that he has made a strong resolution to put them into practice. He suffers from headaches from time to time, but as he says, not as much as at Notre-Dame du Lac. I have not dared to permit him to follow the exercises of the community, because he came here to rest from fatigue. I feared that since he is not strong and above all with these headaches, that this change would tire him out even more. It is impossible for him to remain here, because he does not at all want to make a change of monastery, and I believe that it would be good to call him back as soon as possible.
>
> Since you knew that he had been suffering from headaches for a long time both at Bellefontaine as well as at Notre-Dame du Lac, and since the community admitted him to simple vows, he is consequently now a religious, and I think the time of "testing" him in any serious way has come to an end, but rather that the time has come to treat him gently, inasmuch as the rules permit this, if you want to keep him in the monastery. For if you force him or put him too much to the test, he is in danger of losing his vocation or of losing his head. On the contrary, if you treat him gently he can still be useful to you, for he has several good qualities. He is well educated, etc., and perhaps with a little kindness and patience this will all pass away after a while, and he will be still able to become a good religious, as indeed I hope. Let us pray to God for him.[14]

It seems certain that Dominic's concern was felt by Ambroise himself, and that it had an effect on his healing. It may even be that Ambroise's efforts to record the history of the little monastery that had welcomed him was, partially at least, a gesture of gratitude. Though he admits that he depended heavily on the testimony of old Amable Coté for earlier periods in the history of the monastery, his description of life at Petit Clairvaux as he himself experienced it is an eyewitness account of great importance.[15]

✍ AMBROISE'S ACCOUNT OF PETIT CLAIRVAUX

Ambroise offers a description of the physical landscape of the monastery as well as of the monastic buildings as they were before the fire of 1892. Constructed of brick and stone, the monastery was a two-storied edifice laid out on a quadrangular plan in the space between the river and the road that gave access to the property.

Curiously enough, the main entrance was in the west wing, which faced towards the farm buildings. It contained the infirmary, the abbot's quarters, the kitchen and refectory for guests, as well as some rooms for guests. The north wing, facing the main road, contained the guesthouse and the church. The south wing, on the side facing the river, housed the monks' refectory, the kitchen, dormitory, and a work area. The east wing was a crowded one; it contained the sacristy, the calefactory, the chapter house, classrooms, library, rooms for the Father Masters, wardrobe, and bookbinding workplace.[16] The cemetery was on this eastern side outside the quadrangle and near the chapter house. In describing the cemetery, Ambroise listed all those buried there in the order of their date of burial.

Ambroise then proceeds to describe the farm buildings, which he qualifies as magnificent. These dated from the time of Dom Dominic and were built under the direction of Brother Benedict. Facing the principal façade of the monastery and parallel to it lay the wing with the flour mill. It occupied the three stories above the ground floor; the shingle mill was on the ground floor, which also served to store some of the farm equipment. (Fig. 22: J) Perpendicular to this great building and running parallel to the road was a barn for the animals and for storing fodder. (Fig. 22: I) There were plans for still another wing to house various workshops. This was to be laid out along the river and would have tied in the mill with the monastery buildings. However, it was never built.

Ambroise also gives a brief description of a small stone quarry and lime pit behind the mill, followed by words of high praise for the farm produce that the monks were able to coax out of the poor soil.

He then describes the nuns' convent, which he calls "Notre-Dame de Grâces." In another document written in his hand, however, he refers to it as "Notre-Dame des Sept Douleurs" (Our Lady of Seven Sorrows).[17] (Fig.11)

Finally, he gives the current statistics of the community, with a complete list of persons including the date of their entry into the monastery and an indication of their ethnic origin. In the choir there were eleven professed religious, four novices and one oblate; among the laybrothers there were twenty professed and one oblate—a total of thirty-seven.

During these years of material prosperity, important to the running of the monastery's departments were various secular workmen:

> The monks and lay brothers were helped in the running of the farm by about twenty men in summer and a smaller number in winter; labor was cheap in those days. Eight or ten men stayed at Tracadie all the year round to help run the flour mill, the shingle mill, and a carding mill for preparing wool for the manufacturer; they were also there to attend to the raising of horses, to be sold later on.[18]

During the summer of 1885 Oka received another young man who was destined to play a crucial role in the community's later history. John O'Connor was born in Ventry, Ireland, on February 11, 1864. After receiving his primary education there, he emigrated to Nova Scotia with his family; they settled in Halifax. After finishing his secondary education he decided to enter religious life at Oka at the age of 20 on June 20, 1885. Why he chose to go to this distant monastery instead of joining Petit Clairvaux is a mystery. He did not receive the habit at Oka, however, and by December he had moved to Petit Clairvaux, where on December 20 he received the choir novice's habit. He kept a rather low profile during his early years there, difficult times that no doubt made a lasting impression.

◢ DOM ANTOINE OGER BECOMES SUPERIOR OF OKA

A new development in the life of the monastery of Oka was the appointment of Father Antoine Oger as its superior. He arrived to take over on September 2, 1886, and less than a year later the monastery was raised to the status of priory. An election was held on May 10, 1887, and Father Antoine was elected titular prior.

During the General Chapter of 1886 (which was attended by Dom Dominic), Dom Eugene reported his findings concerning his visitation at Petit Clairvaux:

At Petit Clairvaux, there is prosperity in the area of temporalities, but there are several religious animated by a bad spirit that makes for opposition to the Father Abbot. In his visit the Reverendissime tried to set things aright. Father Ambroise, a professed of Notre-Dame du Lac has been at Petit Clairvaux for several months. The General Chapter decides that he will return to Notre-Dame du Lac.[19]

Given the context of this report, Father Ambroise was apparently one of those "animated by a bad spirit." Judging from Chouteau's correspondence with Oka's new superior, Dom Antoine Oger seemed opposed

FIGURE 25. *Dom Antoine Oger, Superior and later abbot of Oka, third Father Immediate of Petit Clairvaux and Our Lady of the Valley.*

to receiving Ambroise back despite Chouteau's insistence that he obey the decision of the chapter. Chouteau himself was very supportive of Ambroise, and shortly after the General Chapter decided to solve the problem by accepting Ambroise back into the community of Bellefontaine. Accordingly he delegated Dom Dominic of Petit Clairvaux to receive Ambroise's solemn profession as one of Chouteau's own monks of Bellefontaine. This took place on October 22, 1886.

In 1886 for the first time in history we get an accounting of the monastery's personnel in the official report submitted to the Congregation's headquarters at la Trappe. Out of a total of forty-five members, there were twenty-one professed laybrothers and twenty-four choir religious—of whom nineteen were professed, four novices and one an oblate or postulant. The number of priests is not indicated. This is the highest figure recorded in the whole history of Petit Clairvaux. (In 1860 there had been only four priests and nineteen other religious.) It was a high-water mark. In 1898, for example, there were eight choir religious and twenty laybrothers at the beginning of the year, and only twelve men remaining (their status unreported) by year's end.

✑ Dom Chouteau's Visitation of 1887

In February of 1887 Dom Chouteau wrote to Bishop Cameron to make preparations for Ambroise's ordination to the priesthood during the coming visitation of Petit Clairvaux in May. Although he had hoped that Ambroise's ordination to the diaconate would take place before Easter, it was apparently deferred until May. Shortly after his arrival in the area Chouteau was invited to supper with the bishop on May 14 and on the following morning Ambroise and Placid (who had become prior) were both ordained to the diaconate.

On May 24 the visitation opened, and to judge from the official report it must have been a rather quiet one, the points covered in it being such as would become staple standbys for visitation cards throughout all ages, such as exhortations to silence, promptitude in arriving at the Offices, and a reminder that the brethren should salute one another with a bow when meeting in the cloister. Apparently the use of snuff was getting out of hand, and the visitor had to remind the brethren that its use was *only* permitted to seasoned addicts and was not available to new users! Chouteau reported that among the choir religious there were now ten professed, four novices and one oblate. The professed laybrothers numbered twenty,[20] for a total of thirty-five.

After the visitation was over, Father Ambroise's ordination to the priesthood took place on May 29, and on May 31 Chouteau left Petit Clairvaux, taking Father Ambroise with him for the return trip to Bellefontaine. In gratitude for what Petit Clairvaux had done for Father Ambroise, Chouteau left a contribution of 150 francs.[21]

In August Dominic wrote for the first time to Oka's new superior, Dom Antoine Oger. True to style, he once again declined an invitation to come to Oka, excusing himself on the basis of poor health. In the coming months, the two superiors played the game of swapping prospective candidates and other personnel. Oger had sent an Irishman to Petit Clairvaux and was himself toying with the idea of receiving one of Dominic's disgruntled monks, Brother Alphonse Laliberté, who was displeased at not having been admitted to the priesthood. Oger eventually accepted him despite Dominic's warnings. (Things went from bad to worse and eventually Oger sent him to Bellefontaine, where he appeared unannounced in October 1890, much to Chouteau's surprise. Chouteau was unwilling to receive him into the community, however, and Alphonse eventually sought laicization.[22]) By early January of 1890 Dominic had had enough of such transfers and said he would never support them in the future.[23] The two superiors continued to compare notes on agricultural and other subjects, and Dominic came to Oka's help by sending three chasubles for the community, promising to obtain others when he next visited Belgium.

These cordial relations between Petit Clairvaux and her new sister-house at Oka are confirmed in the correspondence between Dom Oger and Dom Chouteau, their common Father Immediate.[24] This link between his two daughterhouses must have seemed promising to Chouteau, who was beginning to realize that it was difficult to offer ongoing help to Petit Clairvaux due to the distance between France and Nova Scotia. Indeed, this may have been when he first toyed with the idea of turning over the paternity of Petit Clairvaux to Oka, a move that was to finally take place at the General Chapter of 1898.

In the winter of 1887-88 typhoid fever broke out at Petit Clairvaux. Fortunately, of all those stricken, only Brother Pacôme Leloup died, on March 3, 1888. Nevertheless, the outbreak served as an excuse when Dominic turned down another invitation from Oger to come for a visit to Oka.[25] In the fall of 1888, however, Oger himself paid what seems to have been an informal visit to Petit Clairvaux.[26]

The report of the 1887 visitation of Petit Clairvaux made at the General Chapter of that year struck a note that did not appear in Chouteau's own *Ordo Notes*: "At Petit Clairvaux, the Father Abbot is a good administrator of the temporalities of the community, but he does not concern himself enough with the spiritual direction of his religious."[27] The report lingers a bit on the first point, noting the monastery's freedom from debt and its increasing prosperity.

∽ Dom Chouteau's 1889 Visitation

Chouteau made his third visitation to Petit Clairvaux in 1889, arriving on September 20 and leaving on October 2. The community had diminished slightly; there were now thirty-one, four fewer than in 1887. The census of 1891 would show a total of thirty, with twelve in choir and eighteen among the laybrothers. Chouteau's notes to himself continue to stress the two points singled out in the previous General Chapter, namely, material prosperity on the one hand but an increasing awareness of the abbot's limitations from a spiritual point of view on the other:

> The community is prospering on the material level. The property consists of about 350 hectares [about 865 acres; this figure includes land received from of the sisters.]. . . . While I was here, they purchased a dozen hectares [about 30 acres] and another since then; this gives the community a self-contained block of holdings.[28] The Reverend Father continues to reclaim fields by means of drainage, a procedure that is very difficult but that makes the soil very fertile.
>
> The mill is a great resource. People come from very far, and the railway is used to make shipments.
>
> The personnel leaves much to be desired both as regards numbers and quality. For without slighting anyone, the Reverend Father has no religious on whom he can depend, either for temporalities or for spiritual matters. This latter point is more grave, since the Reverend Father feels no aptitude for this and does not have the necessary health. He is not able to speak in public, and not even very much in private without suffering great fatigue. The community is suffering from these conditions, since there is no one to care for their interior lives. And it happens that, if the Reverend Father gives a certain latitude in some matter, the religious do not know how to make use of it with moderation; if he acts with severity, people suffer, sometimes more than they should have to, because the Reverend Father does not always realize people's needs.

My job as visitor is very awkward, because I am dealing with a sickness, the remedy for which I know but cannot obtain. There is need of a true spiritual director on whom the Reverend Father could lay the burden of the care of his religious.

The formation of novices is impossible. The religious who is most capable cannot be counted upon; he is pastor of a parish several miles from the monastery. The area has such a great need of priests.[29]

Chouteau adds a series of observations about agricultural detail that show him to be every bit as interested as Dominic and Antoine in the daily ins and outs of farming. In a letter to Oger he confides: "Reverend Father Dominic is today a bit tired. His community is really suffering and he sees it. He would like to retire, but in favor of whom and for what reason. The status quo is still the best option."[30] On a more optimistic note he adds: "Brother John [O'Connor], the former Brother Macaire, who was brought here from Oka, seems to me at this time to be the hope of the house."[31]

The early months of 1892 brought with them an epidemic of the grippe that took the lives of two of the monks: old Brother Malachy, the senior of the community, veteran from the days of Father Francis Xavier; and Brother Edmund, one of the brothers who had come from Belgium. They both died on March 12, 1892. Only five days later, the beloved Father Arsenius, prior of the monastery for many years, passed away.[32] These events were harbingers of the more disastrous event that would take place later in the year.

Chapter Twelve

Crisis

✍ FIRE!

ON MARCH 28, 1892, Chouteau came to Oka to preside over the abbatial election that was to result in Dom Antoine Oger becoming the monastery's first abbot. He was installed on June 6 and received the abbatial blessing on June 29 at the church of Notre Dame in Montreal. Dom Dominic, though a reluctant traveler, was on hand for the occasion.

Chouteau then traveled to Petit Clairvaux for the 1892 visitation, which opened on June 15. It must have been a fairly quiet one, since the notes in his Ordo are few, mostly dealing with problems concerning two individual monks.

The General Chapter of 1892 turned out to be of great importance in the history of the Trappist Congregations. It met in Rome from October 1 to October 17, and as a result of its deliberations the Congregations of la Trappe, Sept-Fons and the Belgian Congregation were united to form a single entity, the Order of Reformed Cistercians of Our Lady of la Trappe. The Italian Congregation of Casamari chose not to join. Chief among the administrative changes was that the figure of Vicar General, which had been of crucial importance in the past, now disappeared, since the Order now had its own Abbot General. The General would henceforth have a council made up of five *definitors* chosen from various language groups in the Order. Elected by the

General Chapter for a period of five years, the definitors would "assist the Abbot-General in his administration." Together they were known as the *definitory*.[1]

While the chapter was in progress in Rome, during the early hours of October 4 a fire broke out at Tracadie in a wooden building next to the new monastery and soon spread to the main building. By morning, nothing was left but the bare walls. Father John O'Connor was an eyewitness and many years later recorded the following account:

> A disastrous fire consumed the greater part of the principal buildings, including the pretty little church, a quantity of Sacred Vessels and Vestments, the valuable library, in fact all the furniture. This fire must have started about one o'clock in the morning, because when the religious rose at two o'clock, as usual for the Divine Office, they found an old wooden building adjoining the monastery, all in flames. This wooden building which was the first monastery, constructed by Father Vincent himself, was at this time used as a dormitory for the workmen, a bake shop, a laundry, etc., and contained great quantities of wood and coal. The flames consequently spread very rapidly and soon caught onto the main buildings. As we had no means of fighting the flames, except the little water we carried in buckets from the brook which flowed close by, the fire soon got beyond control, and the poor religious, exhausted by their futile efforts could do no more than fold their arms and stand by, watching their beloved retreat reduced to ashes by the demon fire. In fact, some of the religious were so exhausted by their efforts to save some, at least, of the books, furniture, etc., that they fell ill, and never afterward recovered their health. Everything was a complete loss as there was no insurance. The poor abbot was greatly to be pitied, as he stood there disconsolate, looking at the labors of the past twenty-five years of his life, reduced to cinders in a few hours.[2]

To make matters worse, Dom Dominic (despite Dom John's affirmation) was away at the General Chapter in Rome on the night of the fire. Word reached him the next day, and he set out immediately for Nova Scotia. A collection was taken up among the other abbots, and Dominic was able to return with a donation of about 500 French francs.[3]

The immediate aftermath of the fire was trying in the extreme for the community, and the primitive conditions in which they were forced to live continued for several years. Once again Father John tells the story:

For about one month after this disaster we could observe no rule, we did not say the Divine Office in Choir, we slept in a loft over the grist mill, and took our meals in a tent in one of the fields. The people of the surrounding country were extremely kind to us and supplied us with everything necessary for food, clothing and bedding. It was now the month of October, and as Winter was approaching, we made haste to provide a temporary dwelling for ourselves where we could pass the Winter; so we fitted up as best we could an old dwelling which had been used as a carriage shed and a place for stowing away old lumber. Here we partitioned off all the regular places, and immediately began to observe our rule and perform all our religious duties with all possible fidelity. We passed five years in this poor abode, and as there was no plaster on the walls of this shed—for it was nothing more—we were buffered severely from the cold in the winter. It was so cold that the bread would sometimes freeze on the table in the refectory, and the water would be frozen in the pitchers, the ink even, would freeze on the pen of the religious who might be writing. . . . Shortly after entering the new building, four of the brothers died in quick succession, their death was no doubt hastened by the cold and other hardships endured.

Father Columban Conaghan was sent out on a fundraising tour. In the spring of 1893 Dom Edouard Chaix-Bourbon of Gethsemani wrote to Oger of Columban's visit:

I recently had a visit from Father Columba [sic] of Tracadie; our pupils arranged a little party in his honor, which produced $25 to $50. He obtained permission from the bishop of Louisville to raise funds in his diocese sometime around July, but I strongly doubt that he will be well received by the priests. . . . I do not think that our poor Father will have any luck, despite his talents as a fundraiser. He wrote to me several days ago from Chicago: 'I am heartily sick of the whole . . . [The bottom margin of the page is worn away.][4]

After the fire letters also went back and forth between Dominic and Dom Antoine of Oka. Chouteau even urged Antoine to go to Petit Clairvaux to see the state of things. Dominic himself invited Antoine, urging him to "come and see the ruins of your sister as well as to have a look at the beautiful chateau we are living in."[5] He said that they were finally getting a little peace now that the place had burned down. "Things are very quiet now; no one comes here since the fire. Deo Gratias!" They were bravely trying to follow (with slight modifications) the grueling Lenten schedule.[6]

✑ THE IMPORTANT 1894 VISITATION

On January 18, 1894, Chouteau wrote to the General of the Order, Dom Sebastian Wyart, to discuss his plans for the visitation of Petit Clairvaux that year, broaching the subject of Dominic's possible retirement; Chouteau had been thinking of Columban as a provisional superior. He wisely proposed that Bishop Cameron be brought in as part of an ad hoc council to study the question of the monastery's continued existence. At the end of the month Wyart approved the visitation, and Chouteau made immediate plans for departure. He set sail for Halifax in the company of Father Ambroise as secretary, arriving at Arichat on March 18.[7]

Coming so early in the year, the visitors were treated to a full spate of Nova Scotian snow during their stay, as Chouteau noted in his *Ordo Notes*. At a meeting of the abbot's private council held on April 1, before the visitation officially began, the importance of getting a building program under way was discussed. Some guidelines were set down. The current year would be spent gathering building materials for a new construction, of similar design to the one destroyed in the fire. Bricks from the destroyed building were to be saved for reuse and a sufficient supply of new ones obtained to make up what was needed. Construction would begin only in the following year, and that in stages. In order to provide more manpower for the building operation, work on clearing land would then be discontinued.

Chouteau's lengthy notes on this important council meeting and his own personal reflections on the situation at Petit Clairvaux fill four pages in his Ordo. They center largely on matters of finance, the need to cut back drastically on the farm program, and the deficiencies of the monastery's bookkeeping. Musing to himself in his notes, the visitor continued to reflect on the deficiencies of Dominic as abbot:

> The Reverend Father has lost courage. He has no hope for the future of the monastery; everyone thinks that *he* is the obstacle (save perhaps Brother Hilarion, the subcellarer). He is totally taken up with matters of the farm, particularly the horses. [A list of examples of poor management follows.] For the future of the community, the Reverend Father seems repulsed at the idea of receiving novices; he thinks that it is impossible in America. As a matter of fact, the Reverend Father is harsh in his way of acting. He gives no encouragement; and does nothing to satisfy the spiritual needs of his religious, either in the matter of piety, or that of regularity, or that of instruction. *Blind obedience, work,* and *penance.*[8]

At the same time, Father Columban, the prior, whom Chouteau had considered as possible superior, had his limitations:

> Father Columban, with his many good qualities is too [unintelligible word or phrase, perhaps: *sans gêne*, inconsiderate], and is not sufficiently a "man of the Rule." He would perhaps take too much initiative; not all would accept him. We must wait and pray.[9]

Chouteau also records a lively exchange between abbot and prior on April 7:

> The Father Prior wanted to play the role of the one in charge and give orders to the abbot. [Columban said,] "People are afraid that you will do nothing after I leave. [He was planning to continue his fundraising shortly after the visitation was over.] Why don't you give the religious what is due to them when there is no reason not to?"[10]

Yet Dominic was unwilling to take the initiative to resign. Chouteau concluded that the moment was not yet ripe to talk of appointing another superior. Accordingly in his interview with Dominic before the beginning of the visitation Chouteau urged: "Insure the monastery's farm buildings without delay. Do not lose courage and, above all, do not show discouragement. Don't talk of resigning. Explain the situation to the General Chapter. . . . Sell the horses. . . . "[11]

The official visitation finally opened on April 14, and since so much preparation had been devoted to the situation beforehand, it lasted only four or five days. Chouteau's notes list a series of impressions: a general mood of anxiety and discouragement in the community, the abbot too taken up with materialities, a sense of a house without a superior. "Reverend Father with his desire to see each one obey, puts up with irregularities and hopes to prevent them by refusing as much as possible; or at least, not taking into account real needs, he refuses what should be given and thereby contributes to the malaise felt by all."[12] He notes that the subalternate superiors must use their authority under the abbot to be vigilant that the Rule be observed.

Chouteau urged Columban to be more submissive to his abbot, and to moderate his zeal for exterior ministry. Nonetheless, it is clear that Chouteau appreciated his gifts. Indeed, Columban accompanied Chouteau on a visit to Bishop Cameron on April 16. It may be somewhat surprising to discover at this point that the prior was only temporarily professed; he made his solemn profession, along with Brothers

Benedict and John, on April 19.[13] The following day Columban was sent out on a fundraising tour, but not without a warning from Chouteau to behave like a monk. Shortly afterwards, on April 22, Brothers Benedict and John received Minor Orders. (Columban had entered as a priest.) This is of some significance in that Chouteau had written to Bishop Cameron on April 7:

> The Father Abbot has been thinking for several years of having his youngest religious, Father John (29 years of age) ordained, and I proposed that I confer on him the four Minor Orders before my departure; however, he fears that he will encounter some difficulty in this regard with Father Benedict who, despite the amputation of two joints of the index finger of his right hand, persists in asking to be ordained to the priesthood, to this extent, that he makes it a condition for his making solemn profession. To put an end to these entreaties, the Father Abbot wishes to refer this religious to you, leaving you to judge in this case of irregularity. . . . He will be satisfied to rely fully on your judgment and your decision.[14]

Since the ordinations to Minor Orders took place, we can only assume that the bishop's reply was positive. On the same day a lay-brother novice, Brother Vincent, made his first profession. After these happy events, Dom Chouteau left the monastery for Montreal on April 23, arriving at Oka on April 26 for what would be a brief informal visit.

✌ AFTERMATH

Despite the resolution taken during preliminary meetings before the visitation to postpone rebuilding for a year, it must have begun soon after the visitation, for in December Dominic was writing to Oger that three wings of the new building were almost complete. At the architect's suggestion it was decided that the new building would be a "case brick building," namely a building of wood with brick facing. Once again Father John O'Connor takes up the story:

> Plans were drawn up by Mr. O'Donahue, an architect of Antigonish; these provided for three wings of a large monastery, 350 feet of building in all. We utilized as much as we could of the brick and stone of the burnt buildings, and made the remainder of the brick necessary to complete the building, on the premises. These buildings, however, proved very unsatisfactory; they appeared very nice on paper, but

when finished looked like a big mill or factory of some kind. In 1894 the exterior of the three wings was completed, but that is as far as we went; we never finished the interior. Our intention, of course, was to complete it, but another disaster befell us which upset all our plans.[15]

In 1895 a series of letters were exchanged between Oka and Petit Clairvaux concerning Columban. It is not at all clear what had happened, but by June 20 he had returned to Petit Clairvaux, and it became obvious that fundraising would no longer be possible.[16] Whatever was involved here, the General Chapter on September 12 officially forbade Columban to engage in any more fundraising.[17] This was a severe setback for the monastery in its need for funds to complete the new building. A lottery was organized in December to help the cause along.

ᴥ Still Another Fire

In May 1895 Chouteau delegated Oger to make the regular visitation of Petit Clairvaux, but it does not seem to have taken place.[18] At Petit Clairvaux Columban continued to function as prior, an office that he was still holding in 1896 according to the *Catholic Directory* of that year. By September Chouteau noted that the new building was still not ready for use. On July 13, 1896, an indult was granted to the monastery permitting it to engage once again in its fundraising operation, but on October 2 disaster struck again.[19] According to Father John's account:

> In 1897 [sic] the remaining buildings of the monastery were destroyed by another terrible conflagration, even more disastrous than the former. . . . It was the beginning of the month of October 1897 [sic], one evening as we were making an examination of conscience, just before retiring, we heard the cry of Fire! and coming out, we found the flames already penetrating through the roof of the barn. This barn was at least 200 ft. in length and was just at this moment filled with all the crops of the season, it contained consequently large quantities of hay and grain. The cellars too, were filled with turnips and mangles for the cattle. All the cows were saved; two beautiful horses perished in the flames, the rest, ten in all, were rescued, but not without difficulty. The hen houses which were attached to the barn were also consumed, and at least two hundred hens perished. Under the barn was kept a number of swine. These managed some way to get out of their dens, and roaming about fell over the bridge into the dam and got drowned, the following day we found them scattered along the banks of the stream

that flows by the monastery. The horses for several weeks roamed at perfect liberty through the fields and woods, the cows too, without any protection from the inclement weather. They were herded together in a small enclosure where they were fed and milked, under the most trying circumstances for the poor Brothers, who were often drenched with rain while waiting on the cattle.

Attached to the barn was a large building which contained a cording mill, a grist mill, and a shingle mill, these were all destroyed with every part of their machinery. There was also a kiln for drying grain, and a general storehouse, all consumed. Unfortunately these buildings were all joined together, so that there was no possibility of saving them.

Once more the good people of the surrounding country gave us many instances of their kindness and charity, giving us clothes, provisions, and their labor gratis. By their aid, we, in a few weeks, re-constructed the barn, and were thus enabled to shelter the cattle before the severe weather set in.

Immediately after this conflagration we entered the newly unfurnished monastery, and suffered great hardships during the severe winter which followed.[20]

After the news of the fire reached him, Chouteau wrote to Bishop Cameron, the General, Dom Sebastian Wyart, and Dominic himself, though none of this correspondence has survived.[21] In a letter to Oger he suggested that there may have been foul play at work in this second fire: "What is most surprising is the fact that this fire took place on the same date as the first one. Can this one be due to some kind of malicious intent? or is it pure chance?"[22] He later wrote that some of the monks of Petit Clairvaux believed (without certainty) that the fire had been started by a novice who had left a few days before.[23]

∽ A Special Visitation

By November 19, 1896, it was decided that the visitation of Petit Clairvaux and other North American monasteries would be carried out by a person of some importance in the Order, Dom Eugene Vachette, abbot of Melleray.[24] Dom Eugene had headed the old Congregation of la Trappe as its Vicar General until the reunion of the Trappist Congregations into the Order of Reformed Cistercians in 1892. Subsequently, in 1894 he was chosen as vicar of the new General, Dom Sebastian Wyart. Dom Eugene was no stranger to Canada. He had come in 1882 to carry out Oka's first regular visitation. Now, delegated by the Abbot General, he would carry out the visitations of all the North American houses together with Dom Carthage Delaney of Mount Melleray in Ireland. It is not known exactly when the visitors arrived at Petit Clairvaux, but it was most likely in April 1897, before the two abbots arrived at Oka to begin the visitation there.[25] Dom Chouteau had some correspondence with Dom Eugene before they left for the visitations and advised him not to hesitate to send away three of the religious of Petit Clairvaux who were causing trouble. Upon his return to France, Dom Eugene paid a visit to Chouteau on July 22 to report on the visitation.[26]

FIGURE 26. *Dom Dominic Schietecatte, first abbot of Petit Clairvaux, in his later years.*

The results of this visitation were no doubt communicated to the Abbot General, Dom Sebastian Wyart, who in turn wrote to Bishop Cameron on September 23 asking his advice about the future of the monastery and requesting that the bishop himself carry out a careful visitation of the monastery. He provided a list of concerns, most of which centered on the current state of the monastery's materialities and the small number and the quality of the personnel still remaining, although there are some remarks about the abbot that betray the voice of Chouteau: "Is the present abbot the man needed to re-establish this house from a material as well as a spiritual point of view? Is it not to be feared that the abbot lets himself get too absorbed in temporal concerns to the detriment of spiritual ones?"[27] Unfortunately, Cameron's answer (if there ever was one) has not been preserved, nor is it known whether he actually carried out a formal visitation.

Sometime late in 1897 Oger had given Dominic some glimmer of hope, writing to say that he might be able to send a little colony to help Petit Clairvaux. Dominic's reply was:

On receiving your last letter I had decided to come see you with respect to what you say of being able to send us a colony, if you have someone to place at its head, but I believe that I must give up the idea since I don't have a penny to spend for this trip. Consequently, I must resign myself to remaining here. I have not yet spoken to the community concerning what you wrote in your last letter, but if you intend to do something I will speak to them of it, and, if things can be worked out, it will be easier for you at the time of the General Chapter. It goes without saying that nothing can happen before this time, nor without the consent of the superiors. Let me know what you think.[28]

Dom Dominic's letters to Dom Oger during this period reflect his despondency over the increasingly hopeless situation. The death of Father Stephen on October 26, added to four others during the preceding twelve months, further depleted their forces. Moreover, a number of brothers had left the monastery, either returning to the world or going to other houses of the Order. Basically, he was awaiting word from Bellefontaine or from Rome as to whether he should even assist at the forthcoming chapter that was to take place in April of the following year. There was little else to do but wait and hope. Dom Eugene apparently felt that it would not be necessary to have another visitation before the chapter. Dominic personally could see no need to assist at the chapter:

In any case, I don't see the need of going, for the abbot of Bellefontaine having given an order to our Father Prior to send a complete report to the Sacred Congregation concerning our monastery, of our situation, of all that is going on there and of all that is happening, etc., etc.; consequently, I think that everything will be worked out by the Sacred Congregation before the chapter in such wise that the chapter will have nothing to do but to pronounce the decision of the Holy See. I have no idea what he has written. All was arranged by the abbot of Bellefontaine between prior and company (the superior having been excluded). All the better for me; there is nothing I have to do, nor have I any responsibility.[29]

Whatever information was submitted by Prior Columban has not survived, but a letter sent by Brother John O'Connor to the Abbot General on January 13, 1898, outlines a point of view that perhaps reflected the "and company" of Dominic's phrase "prior and company":

It is certain, that under the present system of government—under the present superior, no order or regularity shall ever exist in the community. It never did exist to any great extent, for Father Dominic our present abbot is incapable of maintaining it, nor did he ever exert himself much to that effect. He never took sufficient interest in the duties and obligations imposed upon him by his office, and he has frequently declared both publicly and privately that he could heartily wish to be relieved of his burden.

If he had applied himself from the beginning of his reign as much to the maintenance of order and regularity, and the spiritual welfare of his community, as he did to the management of temporal and external affairs, without doubt we would not be in the apparently hopeless condition to which we find ourselves reduced at the present day.

We feel convinced, however, that order and regularity can be established, in the present community, and the monastery rendered prosperous, by adopting the proper means—by sending us an efficient and wise superior.

What you are to do, then, is simply to depose Father Dominic, and place here another superior sending with him a few religious who are capable of discharging some of the more important offices in the community. . . .

But, if you do not approve of the idea of sending a colony hither immediately on account of the unfinished condition of the buildings, etc. we would suggest that after you have relieved Father Dominic of the burden of the Abbacy, you would appoint one, or two, if you order [illegible word] good [f]inanciers, men capable of transacting business, and give them charge of the affairs of the monastery until such time as the buildings are completed, the present debt paid off and the place put in a proper condition to receive a new colony.

We would recommend Father Columban our present prior as one whom we feel confident could conduct the affairs of the monastery in a satisfactory manner. Father Columban was a parish priest for a number of years before he entered the monastery, and ever since he became a religious, has been extensively employed in missionary labors so that he has considerable experience in worldly affairs and besides a good business education, we know that he would certainly do his utmost to keep the house in existence if the affair were placed in his hands. . . .[30]

∽ THE GENERAL CHAPTER OF 1898

All of this gives us some idea of what was brewing at Bellefontaine and in Rome. The fruits of this planning became apparent at the General Chapter on April 21-26, 1898, which was held at the monastery of

Tre Fontane in Rome on the occasion of the eighth centenary of the Cistercian Order. It would also be the occasion of an important change at Petit Clairvaux.

Despite his great reluctance to go, Dominic was asked to be present at the chapter. He went to meet Oger at Oka, arriving on March 22 in Montreal, and together they traveled to Europe. When they reached Italy, they visited Subiaco.[31] The chapter that year took place on April 21–26. The Commission delegated to treat the question of Petit Clairvaux met on April 23. After some deliberation, Dominic's resignation for reasons of health was accepted. No doubt by this time he was all too happy to offer it. With the approval of Chouteau the filiation of Petit Clairvaux was turned over to Oka, and Chouteau himself could gracefully retire from the scene. (Oger later confessed feeling that during this chapter Chouteau had pressured him into accepting the office.)[32]

Looking back over Chouteau's term as Father Immediate of Petit Clairvaux, one cannot help but wonder how the monastery would have fared had it remained under the tutelage of Gethsemani. Dom Benedict Berger's esteem of the monastery and his willingness to help might have inspired an influx of personnel from Gethsemani itself. In any case, Petit Clairvaux would now have as its Father Immediate the man who was to do more for it than all of its previous Father Immediates, Dom Antoine Oger.

The most important aspect of this decision was, of course, the chapter's act of faith in Petit Clairvaux itself. But much would depend on Dom Oger. Fortunately, he had been in close and genial contact with Dominic over the years and faced the challenge square on. First of all, he addressed the question of just where Dom Dominic would henceforth reside. Before returning to Canada, he visited Dominic in Belgium, where he had gone to spend some time in his birthplace, S. Blasius-Boekel in East Flanders. Oger invited him to come to Oka; he also consulted the abbot of Westmalle to find out if he would accept Dominic, if he should so wish. Dominic eventually chose to retire to Sint Sixtus, which was in his native land and which, after all, had such close ties to Petit Clairvaux.[33] Before doing so, however, he returned to Nova Scotia to accompany Oger to Petit Clairvaux.

Chapter Thirteen

Enter Father John Mary Murphy

∞ DOM OGER VISITS HIS NEW DAUGHTERHOUSE

O N JUNE 27, 1898, Oka's prior, Father John Mary Murphy, met Dom Oger and Dom Dominic at the Quebec railway station, and together they set out for Petit Clairvaux, arriving there two days later. The very next day, Oger and John Mary paid a visit to Bishop Cameron to learn what they could about the situation of the community. On July 1 Oger sent his first impressions of the situation to the General:

> The brothers are for the most part old and infirm. Out of eleven (ten professed and one novice who has been here three or four years), one is blind and out of his mind, one paralyzed, one with a broken leg. [These] are asking to go elsewhere. Another, Brother Stanislaus, is asking for a dispensation. That leaves four, of whom one is very good. Out of four [choir] religious, there is one who is very good, and for the rest I wouldn't be willing to pay much! I could send several religious if I had a good superior; otherwise it would be better to close the place as soon as possible. There *are* two postulants here, but who knows what they are like, alas!
>
> I have provisionally named as superior my Father Jean-Marie Murphy, my good and dear prior, and things are going well, but this is clearly only a temporary arrangement. Also I would be very grateful to you if you would send me a good superior for this house or give me instructions as to what I should do.

It is a beautiful and vast property, although too isolated; fine har-
vest, good animals, etc. but along with all that there are debts for 2,000
and some hundreds of dollars. In addition there are seven old nuns
(seventy-six to ninety-five years old) and an old familiar, who must be
cared for, and a chaplain. Perhaps we could leave several religious
while waiting for these old people to die and then look for a good
chance to sell.[1]

Oger proceeded to interview the entire community and came to
realize that, indeed, personnel was the major problem. Considerable
numbers were opting to leave the monastery, either to go to some other
house or to return to the world. Brothers Matthias, Anthony, and
Joseph were asking to return to Belgium with Dom Dominic, who had
been told by Oger that his continuing presence at Petit Clairvaux would
make anything like reformation impossible.[2] Oger wrote to ask the
abbot of Westmalle if he would receive them.[3] (He also made so bold as
to ask the abbot if he could send some other men to help out at Petit
Clairvaux.) In the long run, only Brother Joseph returned to Westmalle;
the other three went to Sint Sixtus.[4] Father Columban and Brother
Stanislaus had made requests for dispensation from their vows, and
Oger sent these along to the General with his letter of July 1, urging
that indults be granted.[5]

Columban himself wrote to the General a few days later to explain
his situation and to formally request the indult:

> I had been Prior since 1892 and was installed [sic] in this position
> while in Simple Vows. After the first fire, I undertook extensive
> fundraising to obtain resources to build a new house. In the midst of my
> work, our Father Immediate of Bellefontaine came to our monastery.
>
> There were two other choir members with Simple Vows. Rev.
> Father Jean-Marie (Chouteau) ordered me to prepare the two others
> for the ceremonies of Solemn Profession, without saying one word as
> to whether or not I myself was prepared to take this important step.
> The morning of the third day, he came to our room and commanded
> me not to celebrate Mass, since it is necessary to wait for the High
> Mass so as to receive Holy Communion from his hands.
>
> "But, Reverend Father," I said, "you did not say a single word con-
> cerning this serious matter; you simply told me to prepare the other
> two. I need time to reflect. After the fundraising is over, I will have
> enough time to reflect. "No," he answered, " it is contrary to our rules
> to have a father in Simple Vows acting as prior. You must make your
> Solemn Vows today or another will take your place." Then pride and

FIGURE 27. *Father Columban (later Joseph) Conaghan.*

shame at being deposed had such an effect on my heart that I said, "Well, all right, I will make my vows."[6]

Columban added that after an almost nonexistent novitiate he spent much of his monastic life engaged in parish activities. He also admitted that when at home he was extremely negligent of monastic observances. There is no record that the indult of secularization was ever given to him, or, if it were, that he accepted it.

Father Columban left on July 8 to go to Lincoln, Nebraska, where he had been accepted by its bishop for work in his diocese. Apparently, this did not succeed, for by July 20 he was back at Petit Clairvaux.[7] He continued to send out inquiries. By July 29 he had received a negative reply from the bishop of Portland.[8]

In the case of Brother Stanislaus, however, Rome refused to grant an indult and made instead the following curious recommendation:

> In order to remove the scandal which he is giving to the community as well as to ease his conscience you are authorized to keep this poor Brother as a familiar. Thus he will be able to maintain the substance of his vows, while using whatever permissions you may give him to eat, drink, smoke, etc. . . .[9]

On August 1, Dom Oger brought him to Oka and placed him in the infirmary, which seemed to satisfy all parties. He may later have returned to Petit Clairvaux. In an undated letter Father John Mary wrote to Father Pacôme: "Bro. Stanislaus is a first class sleeper and he does many other things in good style also."[10]

By July 5 Oger was ready to make a fuller report to the General. His account of his initial visit to the bishop is of special interest in that it summarizes Cameron's own opinion about the situation:

> I found that His Excellency was most anxious to keep the Trappists, who are the only religious established in his fine diocese, the most Catholic one of all Nova Scotia. Here are the remarks he made to me: 1. There are many priestly and religious vocations here. If there are no vocations for la Trappe, it is first of all because there is nothing that attracts people to Petit Clairvaux, no cleanliness, no order, no sung Offices, no charity, for a long time an impossible regime, a foreign tongue, etc. If the house were decent and put in order and the personnel weeded out, with a new superior whose native tongue was English, there would be a chance for vocations. 2. Why is the community not in a better condition? The founder, Father Vincent de Paul, the bishop told me, was a saint but was without education; he remained a missionary rather than a superior. His successor, Father James, was also a holy man, but was so good-natured that everyone did what they wanted. In theory the rule was excessively severe, but in practice no one followed it. Father Dominic, continued the bishop, was always a good religious but with little education. He came to power in these conditions with religious who were lax and whom he found very disagreeable. Discouraging, is it not?[11]

Oger continues, offering some insight into Chouteau's administration as Father Immediate:

I add what the bishop himself noticed, namely that the visitors only encouraged the poor spirit by criticizing the superior with the religious and the religious with the superior. The Very Rev. Father Immediate ordered the extraordinary Visitors to send away the prior and subprior (which these visitors preferred not to do), and then several months after, he himself ordered these [same officers] to write to the Sacred Congregation of Bishops and Regulars against their superior. The secondary actors in this sad comedy told me so themselves, and I was able to see fully authentic written proof of this.

∽ FATHER JOHN MARY MURPHY APPOINTED SUPERIOR OF PETIT CLAIRVAUX

Oger dealt with the other members of the community with a strong hand, insisting that those who wished to remain would be expected to follow the Rule. He named Father John Mary superior and removed all of the former office holders. The remaining ten professed (three choir and seven laybrothers) and a promising laybrother novice, Brother Anthony Chisholm, showed every sign of good will and were disposed to embrace a reform.[12] Bishop Cameron registered his satisfaction with the situation.[13] Still more men were needed, however. While promising to send some from Oka, Oger realized that the few he could spare would not be enough. Accordingly, he asked the General for help.

With winter coming on, it was urgent to continue work on the main building, which had never been completed. John Mary requested permission from Oger to borrow money. In a letter to the General, Oger raised for the first time the question of compensation that he felt was due to Oka for the resources it would be supplying to Petit Clairvaux. It was a theme that would continue to surface in his relations with the little community both before and after its transfer to Rhode Island.

Dom Dominic and the three laybrothers set sail from Quebec for Belgium on or shortly after July 9 and Dom Oger returned home to Oka on July 13.[14] Faithful to his promise, Oger sent the first contingent of brothers to Petit Clairvaux, three men who were of Irish extraction. On July 11, Brother Bonaventure Walsh left Oka, followed on July 25 by Brother Thomas Boothly, a choir religious, and Brother Zephirin, a laybrother. The choice of a superior and three brothers whose native tongue was English made it clear that Oger had decidedly opted for an English-speaking community.

In a personal note Murphy confessed to his friend and fellow reli-

FIGURE 28. *Dom John Mary Murphy, Superior and later prior of Our Lady of the Valley.*

gious at Oka, Father Pacôme Gaboury: "Alas, I am doomed to remain here for some time longer, how long I do not know, but I hope it will not be long."[15] (It is well to remember that not only was John Mary's presence at Petit Clairvaux seen as a temporary measure, but that he officially continued to hold the office of prior at Oka.) The two friends would continue to correspond over the coming two years. Pacôme occasionally sent Murphy a bit of snuff to cheer him up and provided him with cedar powder to fight off the fleas, which were proving to be one of Petit Clairvaux's greatest annoyances.

Meanwhile Brother John O'Connor, who had come to Petit Clairvaux from Oka as a postulant in 1885, was preparing to return there—temporarily—for his theological studies. He would take with him old Brother Hilarion, who was going to Montreal for an operation. There were unending delays, however, since Brother John had to train Brother Thomas to take over his assignment as guestmaster. Brother Bonaventure had taken over the infirmary and was doing a good job at it.[16]

Father John Mary seemed pleased on the whole with the seculars who lived and worked in the monastery, particularly the "big Scotsman," a reference, no doubt, to Angus MacRyan.[17] More important was his satisfaction with the newly reconstituted community. On July 20 he wrote to Oger: "Everyone puts lots of good will into all I ask of them, and I have no complaints about anyone."[18] He was clearly warming to the challenge of his new assignment. Pacôme's packages of snuff continued to arrive to help matters along.[19] On August 2 two promising laybrother candidates received the habit, Brother Anthony Chisholm as a novice, and Brother Paul Charlier as an oblate. Both were destined to persevere and would end their days at Our Lady of the Valley. And on August 8 Brother John finally set out for Montreal where he left Brother Hilarion for treatment, then continued on to Oka. After his treatment, Hilarion also returned to Oka, where he died on November 29, 1900.

The farm operations continued through August. The purchase of a sheaf binder for the grain is an indication that the little group was still optimistic about Petit Clairvaux's future.[20] On September 4 Brother Thomas returned to Oka and was replaced by Brother John Baptist Daigneault on September 12.[21] By mid-September Father Columban had found work as a priest somewhere in the United States.[22] By December, however, he had left his position and was asking Father John Mary to return to Petit Clairvaux.[23] There were plans to rebuild the mill sometime during the coming spring, a project of which Oger seemed to approve, although the General urged that Oger should move slowly and keep an eye on his budget.[24]

Early in the fall, new problems were brewing for Oka itself. In 1892 it had begun its first foundation, Our Lady of Mistassini, in the far north of the Province of Quebec. Now the situation in the new monastery seemed to call for immediate help. A new superior was needed, and Chouteau felt that, despite John Mary's love for Petit Clairvaux, he should be sent as superior of Mistassini and that Petit Clairvaux be reduced to the status of a simple grange with Father Jean-Baptiste Daignault as its "director."[25]

But Oger put his faith in the future of Petit Clairvaux and decided that John Mary would remain there, a move that after all pleased Chouteau, whose own affection for the little monastery apparently remained strong.[26] He was happy to learn that John Mary was going to Oka for a visit, and that he would be able to see him during his own upcoming visit there.

✒ FATHER JOHN MARY'S INTERLUDE AT OKA, MISTASSINI, AND KINGSTON IN LOWER CANADA

On September 3 Oger set out for a visit to Mistassini, after which he proceeded to Petit Clairvaux; he was planning, as Oka's chronicle puts it, "to reform, if possible, this monastery."[27] After his visit he left Petit Clairvaux towards the end of September, taking Father John Mary with him to Mistassini. John Mary remained there for two days but then took up once again his activities as Oka's prior. He left for Kingston on October 14 to represent Oger at the consecration of Bishop Gauthier, then returned to Oka on October 22 in order to update the abbot by letter on conditions there. The letter shows that while at Oka he was still keeping an eye on things at Petit Clairvaux:

> I received about 17,000 dollars on the monastery, barn, and stock of Tracadie. Mr. Laurin was more than happy, and we can pay him by small payments. I also got 1000 dollars on the buildings of the sisters.[28]

This remark, which seems to refer to a mortgage taken out on some of the monastic property at Tracadie, witnesses to John Mary's continuing resolution to save Petit Clairvaux. He received additional support when on October 26 Father Remi Baron left for Petit Clairvaux with the official title of subprior. In September, Chouteau had already recommended a change for Remi since he was not happy under Oger's regime.[29] He would eventually go with the community to Valley Falls, where he served the monastery for many years until his death on March 17, 1934.

John Mary's travels continued. He was in Montreal on October 29 in order to meet Dom Chouteau, who was arriving from the monastery of Prairies, and to accompany him to Oka.[30] The very next day, after a brief talk in chapter, John Mary brought him back to Montreal, no doubt to catch the train to Mistassini.

Chouteau arrived at Mistassini on November 5 for what would be a brief friendly visit. Nonetheless, he must have discussed the situation at Mistassini with Oger, and it was probably as a result of their deliberations that on November 8 the superior, Dom Jean de Dieu Grolleau, tendered his resignation, invoking his poor health. (On December 2 Oger would decide to take over as superior himself, a role that he continued to fill until March 15, 1899, when he named as superior Dom Cléophas Roy, who was also called Desjardins.) Finally, Chouteau and Oger set off once again for Oka on November 10, arriving there on the 12th.[31]

The next day Chouteau officially opened Oka's own visitation. At the morning chapter, John Mary was officially named prior of Petit Clairvaux. Father Marie Beauregard was named prior of Oka in his place, and the young Father Pacôme Gaboury became subprior. The new prior's role took on added importance in light of the fact that Dom Oger would now be filling two roles: that of abbot of Oka as well as temporary superior of Mistassini. The very next day, November 14, John Mary left to return to Petit Clairvaux.

One wonders what provisions had been made for Petit Clairvaux during John Mary's absence. Perhaps he left Father Placid in command as priest with Brother Richard in charge of materialities, as he would do the following year when he went to the General Chapter.

With Father John Mary back at Petit Clairvaux, on December 1 Brother John Baptist, after much vacillation throughout the year, finally left to return to Belgium, where he was received at Sint Sixtus. Brother Thomas also continued to threaten returning to Oka, which he finally did on January 23, 1899.[32] Writing to Pacôme on December 4, John Mary gave him the latest version of the community list: twelve members, of whom six were choir monks and six laybrothers.[33] Only the priests are mentioned by name: John Mary Murphy (prior), Bonaventure Walsh (who now is shown as subprior), Placid Gubbels, and Remi Baron.

With the cold growing more intense, John Mary asked that a plasterer be sent to finish off the interior walls of the monastery to protect against drafts. The ram that had been long promised by Oka finally arrived on December 24 as a kind of Christmas present, and before the end of January they would be receiving from Oka a fine Berkshire hog, whose singing John Mary praised in a letter written to Pacôme on January 30.[34] January also brought with it the community's usual bout with the grippe.

◈ First Ideas of a Transfer of Petit Clairvaux

On January 9, 1899, John Mary's correspondence with Oger makes its first mention of the possibility of transferring Petit Clairvaux to another location. He had received a letter from a certain Father Tetreau of New York inviting him to make a foundation there. There was even some money available from a prospective benefactor:

> I received a card from Father Tetreau of New York, inviting me to make a foundation in New York. I find this very tempting, and I see in this the salvation of Oka and Mistassini because we could give you without difficulty at least $3000 a year for ten years. The Father Abbot of Bellefontaine tells me that he would be happy to see a house of our Order in New York, and that is why Dom Edmund [Obrecht] is going to do all he can to make a foundation, if we do not found one before him. Here we could still manage to keep going, but I think it would be very difficult to say that we will make progress. If you permit me to write to the Father General and explain the situation to him, I will first go to see the farm which the Father is speaking about, and if it is suitable I will get in touch with the General. I think, Rev. Father, that it is worth the trouble. For the present, we will place the whole affair in the hands of good St. Joseph and the Holy Virgin.[35]

Already in 1895, in the course of his fundraising tours as prior of Oka, Father John Mary had come to realize that a location in the vicinity of New York or Boston would be of great advantage.[36] Now that a concrete proposal had been made he was all the more enthusiastic. This insight concerning the importance of such a foundation was not lost on Father Edmund Obrecht (then a simple priest), who in 1895 was living in New York, where he had his base of operations for a fundraising campaign on behalf of the Order itself. According to Murphy, Obrecht at that time had plans for a foundation in the Diocese of Brooklyn.[37] Though this did not materialize, in March of 1898 Obrecht was made superior of Gethsemani, and less than a year after his appointment, he was already considering the possibility of reviving this plan for an east coast foundation. On the basis of Murphy's correspondence alone it is not possible to know just how Oger felt about Murphy's proposal, but one presumes that it met with his approval, since Murphy continued to consider it a feasible option.

Probably about the same time, Father John Mary received word from Oger that by a decision of Oka's council he would be expected to pay Oka $350 a year. While the purpose of these payments was not stated, it probably relates to a subject that Oger broached with the Abbot General during the preceding summer: "Notwithstanding the spirit of abnegation that a good religious should have, would I be permitted to sacrifice my best religious without any kind of compensation?"[38] On this occasion Oger had nothing concrete to propose, but it seems likely that the present arrangement of a yearly payment to the motherhouse was an attempt to set things straight. Murphy expressed his willingness to make the payment, but over the years Oger would continue to press his point, and Murphy would eventually appeal to the Abbot General to complain of the situation.

Another monetary concern that continually surfaces in Murphy's correspondence is the question of money that Father Dominic owed to Petit Clairvaux. Dominic's nephew in Belgium was somehow involved in this debt, but it is not clear what the nature of the debt was or how much money was involved.[39]

∽ CHANGES IN PERSONNEL

The personnel situation continued to evolve. By the end of January 1899 both Brother Thomas and Brother John Baptist Jochem were gone. Thomas returned to Oka, while John Baptist went home to Belgium, but two new men had arrived the month before: Father Caillault and "Jacob." Father Caillault was a French priest who, having come to Canada because of some irregularity in his situation in France, had been living at Oka for some time. John Mary assigned him to replace Brother John Baptist in the garden.[40] He served in that capacity for a number of years, both in Nova Scotia and after the move to Rhode Island. Nothing more is said of Jacob.

The following summer brought several more changes. Father Remi was made master of the laybrothers. Brother Bonaventure applied for a dispensation from his vows and somewhat impatiently went to wait for an answer from Rome at the rectory of a priest in St. Brigitte near Montreal.[41] The ever-changing Thomas returned to Petit Clairvaux from Oka in June. He was to remain there until September 9, 1900, when he left definitively to return to Oka.[42] Brother Macaire arrived from Oka and would soon prove to be a source of trouble. Brother Francis, a promising young laybrother novice, entered in the course of the summer.[43] Brother Benedict, who had become a sub-deacon by this time, was "still dreaming of the priesthood; he says that he will not die before becoming a priest."[44] His request for dispensation from the three years of studies required before ordination had been turned down by Rome on January 20, 1899, and presumably there was no opportunity to begin these studies in the unsettled conditions at Petit Clairvaux.[45]

∾ THE GENERAL CHAPTER OF 1899

During the summer Father John Mary continued to reflect on the question of a possible New York foundation. He even went so far as to share his thoughts with Dom Obrecht of Gethsemani, a move that he later regretted.[46] The General Chapter was not far off, and although Oger would not be attending the meeting this year, Dom Chouteau had suggested to John Mary that he himself come.[47] John Mary decided to follow his advice, trusting that Father Placid and Brother Richard could together keep things in order at Petit Clairvaux while he was gone.[48] He was attracted by the idea of setting before the Abbot General his plan for transferring Petit Clairvaux. He set sail on August 29 from New York, but not before paying a visit to the bishops of New York and Trenton.

John Mary had the special pleasure of assisting at a chapter that was held for the first time at the historic monastery of Cîteaux, which had been purchased by the Order the previous year. During it he broached the subject of the proposed foundation to the Abbot General, and the matter was duly taken up by the assembly in its sixth session on September 15. The results of the discussion appear in the chapter's minutes: "The monastery of Petit Clairvaux being no longer able to survive in its present location, it has been proposed to transfer it to several possible locations in which offers have been made to the community. Another possibility is its incorporation into N. D. du Lac." Further discussion in the seventh session led to the resolution: "It is decided that the monastery of Petit Clairvaux will be transferred to a property offered to this community near Boston."[49]

Another decision of the Order in response to an invitation by Rome itself was the change of the Order's official name to the "Order of

Reformed Cistercians," without the addition of the phrase "of Our Lady of La Trappe."[50]

Explaining how all this had come to pass, Murphy wrote to Oger from Mount Melleray, where he had gone for a visit after the chapter at the invitation of its abbot:

> Now I will tell you of several things of which I have not spoken of before, fearing that perhaps Father Tetreau would learn of it. Several days after your departure from Tracadie I received a letter from a friend in Boston offering me 1000 arpents of land, situated 24 miles from the city with many advantages and on very easy terms. Then without saying anything to anyone I went to visit this farm which I found to be quite beautiful. In brief, having arrived at Cîteaux I explained this matter to the General and to the commission; they rejected the offer of Tetreau. Then I asked for a transfer of [Petit] Clairvaux to the Diocese of Boston, and although Rev. Father Edmund [of Gethsemani] strongly opposed it, the permission was granted to me. I have not seen the bishop of Boston, but the owner of the farm has undertaken to obtain the Archbishop's permission in due course. Reverend Father, I ask you to please keep this for yourself for fear that the rumor be spread abroad and that the bishop will come to know that we are trying to come to his diocese. This gentlemen has undertaken to bring the matter to completion if we leave it up to him.[51]

It is clear that Murphy was aware of all this before he set sail, and that his visits to the bishops of New York and Trenton before leaving for Europe were intended to keep these options open in case the offer from Boston should not materialize. Indeed, at the chapter he began by proposing the New York offer. He was obviously ready to take a considerable amount of initiative, not to say responsibility for orchestrating the entire scenario, all without the knowledge of Oger. Furthermore, he showed himself able to deal with the Abbot General, as well as the formidable and extremely well-connected Obrecht, and to come away with what he wanted. No mean showing for his first appearance at a General Chapter. Nonetheless, the chapter's decision to specify a concrete location for the transfer was based on Murphy's exaggerated trust in the ability of his contact in Boston to convince Archbishop Williams to accept the venture.[52] As we shall see, he would be disappointed.

From Chouteau's pen we get an independent view of Murphy's showing at the chapter:

You will have heard that this question was asked: "Should Petit Clairvaux be suppressed?" And an affirmative answer was being upheld and would probably have won the day, had it not been for the good impression made by Rev. Father John Mary Murphy on all the members of the chapter and for the confidence that he was able to inspire. They were ready to grant all that he was asking, and he won his case despite the opposition that Rev. Father Edmund of Gethsemani made to the transfer.[53]

Murphy's experience at the chapter was clouded by bad news from home that Brother Macaire had been causing difficulties in the community. Father John Mary took the occasion to gently upbraid Oger for sending problematic monks to Petit Clairvaux:

I am amazed at the news which you give me of Petit Clairvaux. My opinion would be to send Father Macaire away immediately. . . . Before his arrival everyone was happy. I think that this is the first time there has been a letter of complaint written to you from our house and I hope that this will be the last time. How can you hope that people who do not give satisfaction elsewhere would be able to do so with us at Tracadie? So I beg you, Reverend Father, take back Father Macaire, please; he will be better off at Oka than anywhere else.[54]

Apparently this failed to make an impression on Oger, for once again in December Oger was proposing to send another monk whom John Mary did not want, as we learn from Murphy's letter to Oger: "Concerning this good brother of whom you speak, I do not know what to say; he has some very wild ideas, and here we are so few that people notice everything that happens."[55] Chouteau himself would later complain to the General concerning Oger's tendency to do this.[56]

On his way home Murphy visited several monasteries and even went for a brief visit to Sint Sixtus in order to see Dom Dominic. Dominic, who related the event, stressed the fact that it was very brief—several hours long. It seems likely that they discussed unsettled financial matters. John Mary also stopped off in New York before returning to Petit Clairvaux. He had some explaining to do to Father Tetreau and to the bishop. He may also have visited Oka to discuss matters with Oger before returning to Petit Clairvaux.[57] In any case, he did not return until sometime after October 28.[58]

∞ Not Boston, but Providence

One wonders how closely Murphy was able to monitor the progress of negotiations in Boston. There was still no news by November 27 when he wrote to Oger, asking to be informed as soon as the archbishop contacted Oger. An undated letter to Oger written from New York after this date, however, reports that Murphy had received word from Boston that he was to go to see the archbishop. Whatever the outcome of this visit, Murphy was still waiting for news on December 4, when he received a letter from Oger saying that, though a letter had not been received from Boston, it seemed that the bishop's response was negative.[59] Obviously disappointed but far from giving up, Murphy wrote Oger saying that he would go to Boston himself to see what could be done:

> Since the Abbot General and the chapter grants us [permission for] the transfer, don't you think that it is worth the trouble to do all we can? I accept with resignation the refusal of Bishop Williams, but I am going to try one last time.
>
> Since Dom Edmond is so tenacious in his idea to found a house in the East of the United States, that shows us that the project is worth the effort. Well, Reverend Father, I will do all I can to have a foundation before he does, because once he has the permission to come to the East it will be very difficult for us to act.[60]

Murphy would indeed have his foundation in the East but not in the place he was thinking of. Writing to Oger from Boston on December 21 he could announce:

> I have good news to give you. Bishop Harkins of Providence is very favorable to us and is offering me a farm of more than 300 arpents [about 253 acres], and he gives me to believe that it will all be a gift.
>
> I like this place much better than the farm near Boston; it is 7 miles from the city and in perfect solitude.
>
> The bishop tells me to make the request in regular fashion. He will be having a meeting of his consultors towards the first of the year, and afterwards he will give his answer. But I have met several of the more distinguished pastors, and they are truly desirous of having us. I am leaving for Tracadie immediately, and I will be there on Saturday.[61]

During his fundraising for Oka, Father John Mary had passed through Providence in the spring of 1893 even though the policy of the diocese was not to permit religious to seek funds there. On that occasion, he had noted that the bishop held the Trappists in high esteem.[62] Around the same time, John Mary's sister Sarah, Sister Aldegonde, a sister of the Congregation of Notre Dame in Montreal, was superior of their convent in Providence, and it is possible that the bishop had come to learn of the Oka Trappists through her.[63] There was, of course, no question of a foundation at that time. Now, some years later, when he found himself faced with the failure of the Boston project, perhaps Murphy's thoughts turned to his former meeting with Bishop Harkins and he decided to contact him.[64]

Murphy wrote immediately to Dom Sebastian, the General, to bring him up to date on recent developments; he was hoping for an answer around January 10, 1900.[65] Unfortunately, we have no details concerning Oger's exact reaction to the news save that by December 27 Murphy had received a disturbing, accusatory letter from him:

> I have just received your letter of the twenty-second. I tell you humbly that it caused me much pain. All that I did to come to this day was for the good of our three houses; now to see that I caused you suffering and you have almost abandoned me, I feel my courage ebbing away.[66]

Whatever the reasons for this, the storm blew over. Nonetheless, Oger was pondering the possibility of merging the community of Petit Clairvaux with that of Oka. John Mary made it clear to him, however, that the community was opposed to this. "If I told you that no one here would like to go to Oka, it is not that they do not respect your authority, but only that they prefer to live in an English[-speaking] community."[67]

Amazingly enough, only two days after Murphy saw Bishop Harkins, the Providence Diocesan newspaper, the *Providence Visitor,* published the story of Murphy's plan for a foundation in Boston, apparently not aware that this entire project had failed and that a foundation near Providence itself was already in the making. The account is important, however, in that it gives us details about the Boston venture, which appear nowhere else:

> The Rev. Father Murphy, the head of the Order of Trappist Monks in the United States and Canada, has returned from Rome after a seven weeks' visit, with permission from the general of the Order for the building of a monastery in Medway, Mass. The only thing remaining to be done before the deal can be consummated, is to have it ratified by Archbishop Williams, and his sanction has been asked by the authorities at Rome.

The tract of land to be used embraces nearly 700 acres.

It is understood that the building will begin early in the spring and that the monastery will accommodate about 50 monks.

There is but one monastery of this order now in the US, near Louisville, Ky. . . .

The Order of Trappist Monks is one of the most austere in existence. The "brothers" till the soil.

The tract purchased at Medway is about three-fifths woodland and is one and one quarter miles long, extending from the Medway town line on Village street, to the N. Y., N. H. & H. railroad tracks.[68]

∽ BISHOP HARKINS OF PROVIDENCE APPROVES THE FOUNDATION

In early January the good news of the bishop's definitive approval of the foundation finally arrived from Providence. Bishop Harkins had discussed the matter with his Board of Consultors on January 8, 1900, and their response was favorable, on condition that "no general collection be taken and no appeal be made having the purpose of general collection, unless with the consent of the bishop expressed in writing."[69] Murphy sent word on to Oger and went to visit Bishop Cameron the next day.[70]

> He answered me, saying that this would be painful to him and that he would prefer to see us remain in his diocese. I asked him if in case of our departure, he would take care of the sisters. On this question he answered that he would not be able to, that Dom Dominique placed the sisters under the protection of the monastery for ever, accepting their goods in exchange for care [to be provided] for them as well as food.

This meant that Murphy would have to find some way of providing care for the sisters himself. He promised Oger that he would refrain from going to see Bishop Harkins until he had heard from Rome and had come to Oka to receive orders from Oger. While there is no indication about an answer from Rome, Murphy met with Oger on January 24-26 and returned to Petit Clairvaux on January 27.[71]

Murphy made a brief trip to New York, where he received a gift of $200 for the new monastery along with promises of more money. He left for Providence on February 20 in order to make arrangements for the act of incorporation and to try to obtain free transport and exemption from duty for the farm animals he planned to send to Rhode Island. By the 28th he had to report that getting this free was proving to be out of the question but that he was still hoping for a reduction.[72] During his stay in the city (at St. Mary's rectory) the *Providence Visitor* got wind of the news and on February 24 it published a brief story about the proposed foundation.[73] The news was soon taken up by the *Providence Journal* in its Sunday issue on March 4. The article affords some information about the origin of the property:

> Some years ago this property comprising over 300 acres, within a mile and a half of the village of Lonsdale, was purchased by the Rev. Father Kane, then pastor of St. Patrick's Church in Cumberland, the intention being to establish a theological seminary on the place. The project was, however, abandoned, and the property was placed in the hands of Bishop Harkins.[74]

Back in Petit Clairvaux, Father Murphy made the final preparations for the move. It was decided to ship the horses and the majority of the cows to Providence, but the sheep, pigs, and several of the older cows, along with what remained of their farm gear, would be sold at auction. The 1,000-pound ox was a problem. Murphy hoped to sell it in Halifax at a good price. There is no record of the auction or of what finally happened to the ox.[75] More delicate was the question of the "familiars" who had lived in the monastery and worked there. Some of them were claiming compensation, which Murphy seemed willing to meet—within reason.[76] Some of the local population were also asking for the money that they had contributed to the monastery.

Far more important was the question of providing care for the sisters. Murphy finally decided to hire a Mr. Somers, the monastery's chief supplier in Antigonish, to provide them with all their material necessities. Ben Petitpas, who was to be left in charge of the farm and the monastery buildings, would also look out for them.[77] Finally, a certain Father Noel offered his services to them as priest in exchange for room and board. This met with the bishop's approval.

Finally, John Mary was able to leave on March 26. The original plan was to take three or four men with him to get things started. Spring plowing would be the first order of business: Nothing superseded the importance of planting vegetables that would keep them going that first year.[78]

Chapter Fourteen

Our Lady of the Valley

℘ CUMBERLAND

R HODE ISLAND, new home to the community of Petit Clairvaux, was the most industrialized State in the Union, thanks to the textile mills along the Blackstone River and several lesser watercourses nearby. The demand for cheap labor to man these mills gave rise to an intense wave of immigration. The Irish were the first to come, around 1820, followed by the French Canadians between 1860 and 1870, and the Italians after 1890. These three remained the principal immigrant groups, but there were also smaller ones such as the Portuguese and Capeverdians.

The fact that these immigrants were predominantly Catholic meant that by 1905 Catholicism had become the religion of the majority of the state's population. Yet relations between these various immigrant groups were tense, even in the religious sphere. These tensions gave rise to a typical feature of Catholicism in Rhode Island: the creation of parishes based on ethnic groups, rather than on strict geographical limits.

In response to the needs of individual immigrant groups, priests—both religious and diocesan—came from the old countries to minister to them. Each group was thus able to receive instruction and celebrate certain parts of the liturgy in its own language. These parishes also tended to promote the survival of the secular cultural traditions of each ethnic community.

The intense concentration of Catholics in the state made it an ideal seedbed of vocations for the new monastery. In its turn, the monastery offered the state its first experience of contemplative religious life for men. Alongside the dedicated religious of other Orders who ministered to the needs of Catholics in parishes, schools and other institutions, the monastery would eventually become a fixed beacon of church life to which the faithful could come to share in its liturgy and to spend quiet time in retreat.

The monastery also offered a new kind of outreach to the local population. Unlike other groups, it was not ethnically oriented. Though the founders included a significant number of monks of Irish extraction (four), there were also two monks from France, one French Canadian, a Flemish Belgian, and a Nova Scotian Scotsman. Father Remi Baron, who had been curate of the famous Cathedral of Rheims in France, had joined Bellefontaine and been sent to the foundation of Oka in Canada; at the new site in Rhode Island he would become a beloved spiritual guide to the people of the area, English-speaking as well as French. Furthermore, Fathers John Mary, John O'Connor, and Alberic, though of Irish extraction, were all fluent in French. Thus, while the community decided to use English in its daily routines, all of the other ethnic groups of the area would find a welcome, particularly the French Canadian immigrants who clustered in the nearby towns of Woonsocket, Central Falls and Pawtucket.

Bishop Harkins's property was situated in the town of Cumberland. Nestling snugly in the extreme northeast corner of the state, Cumberland had been carved out of territory that originally belonged to Massachusetts. The great Blackstone River, at the town's western edge, had long brought prosperity to the area—to such an extent that the little village of Woonsocket Falls at Cumberland's northwest corner had by 1867 become the independent town of Woonsocket.

The property offered to the monks was on the southern portion of Diamond Hill Road, which at this spot runs along a ridge between the Blackstone River on the west and the much smaller stream known as Abbott Run on the east. The original holding of 227.5 acres was limited to the area adjacent to Diamond Hill Road and extending as far as a bog fed by a small stream flowing in a north-south direction through the area. In 1909 a further purchase of 106 acres would extend the monastery's holdings beyond the line of the stream.[1]

Unlike Woonsocket Falls, the other villages within Cumberland's

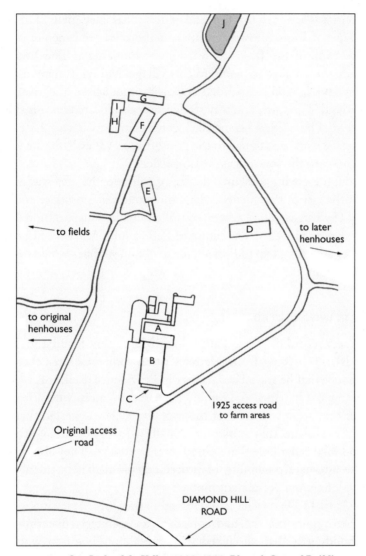

FIGURE 29. *Our Lady of the Valley, 1900-1938. Plan. A. Central Buildings (see Fig.32 for detail), B. Courtyard of guesthouse, C. Porter's lodge, D. Garage and later barn, E. Original 1900 monastery, F. Old cow barn, G. Ice house, milk processing area, and various utility areas, H. Hay barn, I. Horse barn, J. Pond.*

limits never achieved independence. Nonetheless they held on to their individuality in one way or another, not least by retaining their original place names. Lonsdale, the Cumberland village to which the new

monastery was assigned for its postal address, was itself "new." The original village of Lonsdale was situated in the town of Lincoln, on the
opposite bank of the Blackstone from the monastery.[2] The Lonsdale
Company, which gave its name to this village, had built many mills in
the area and in 1860 expanded its operations across the river into
Cumberland. The town's railway station was also located on this side of
the river.[3] Thus "New Lonsdale" came into existence. Later the
monastery would be assigned to the post office at Valley Falls, the village
immediately to the south of New Lonsdale.[4]

Though enjoying a relative degree of solitude, the area was in easy
reach of the city of Providence, where the monastery's produce could be
sold. By 1895 an extensive system of trolleys made transportation to and
around the big city easy. The figure of Father John Mary on his way to
the trolley stop for a trip to Providence to obtain supplies would become
a familiar sight.[5]

✎ Getting Started

There is no record of where Father John Mary spent his first nights in
Rhode Island. Judging from a letter written sometime later, there is a
good chance that he stayed at a rectory in Providence itself, at least some
of the time.[6] On April 5 Dom Oger came to meet with him, and
together they went to look over the property. Oger suggested that, as a
temporary measure, they construct a small two-story building on top of
an abandoned cellar hole that existed on the property. They also considered the alternate possibility of proceeding immediately to the construction of a more permanent monastery.

By April 11 Dom Oger had left, and Father John Mary was already
writing to report that he had consulted an architect concerning the
larger building he had discussed with the abbot. The cost would be
$12,000, a figure that was prohibitive for the time being. Father John
Mary then decided to go ahead with the plan of constructing a temporary monastery over the existing cellar hole.[7] A cabin to house the workmen had already been built. The faithful Angus arrived from Nova
Scotia the next day and, as Murphy put it, "took up residence in his
chateau." Additional accommodations were provided in a house rented
from Elisha Waterman on the other side of Diamond Hill Road just
opposite the monastery property.[8]

The architect Father John Mary had consulted was the Worcester-born Ambrose Murphy. Upon completing his studies he had entered the service of his uncle, James Murphy, who specialized in ecclesiastical architecture. After his uncle's death he joined the firm of Martin and Hall. He would eventually start his own office in partnership with Franklin R. Hindle and himself become a popular ecclesiastical architect, with many Catholic churches to his credit, along with schools and other buildings in Rhode Island and Massachusetts—seven of them churches in the city of Providence. But in April of 1900 when Father John Mary met him, Ambrose Murphy was still at the outset of his career. It was the beginning of a long friendship and collaboration with the Cumberland monastery.

Things were moving fast by April 14. Preparations had been made for plowing and planting a small vegetable garden. A horse had been purchased along with some agricultural tools. More importantly, the temporary two-story monastery, measuring twenty-eight by fifty feet, would soon be going up. The ground floor was to contain the chapel, chapter room, and refectory; the upper floor would serve as dormitory. It is not clear whether this whole plan was ever carried out, but Brother Vincent Madden, who entered the community on August 17, 1905, affirmed that the door of the building gave access to a reception hall that was flanked on the left by the chapel.[9] The cellar, over which the structure had been built, remained accessible by stairs.

FIGURE 30. *Our Lady of the Valley. First monastery, 1900.*

By April 26, with work well under way, Father John Mary was able to make a brief trip to Tracadie to take care of business there. He brought Father Remi back with him as a helper.[10] On May 28 he could report that the temporary monastery was going up and would be finished in three weeks. By this time, work had begun on a barn,[11] and the vegetable garden was growing apace—tended by Fathers Caillault and Flesselle, two of the diocesan priests from Petit Clairvaux who by now had also arrived at Lonsdale.[12]

Early in July Father John Mary returned to Tracadie to make ready for the transfer of the livestock. With all he had to do at Lonsdale, he was beginning to feel the pressure and asked Oger to send Father Alberic Crotty for a period of six months to help him with the accounts. This request was frequently repeated over the coming year before it was finally granted.[13]

On July 16 three railway cars left Tracadie with the livestock aboard. Although Father John Mary was expecting them to arrive around the 20th, the trip took eight days, the faithful Brother Richard traveling with the animals in their freight car.[14] By then a small stable for the horses had been built, and the barn, although still under construction, was sufficiently ready to receive the cows. In light of all this activity John Mary begged Oger to put off plans for a regular visitation, since in all the chaos of the move there was nothing regular there to visit! To add to the hustle and bustle, Fathers John Mary and Remi went out to do parish work on Sundays.

A letter of Murphy to Oger written on July 18 gives us the first known address of the new monastery: "Abbey of Petit Clairvaux, Lonsdale, R. I., P. O. Box 11." It is worthy of note that the monastery was still considered an abbey, and was still called Petit Clairvaux. All of this was consistent with the fact that the move from Tracadie was a transfer and not the foundation of a new monastery. The same title was used in the monastery's report drawn up later in August, probably for presentation to the General Chapter.

For all its hard work and confusion, July brought some exceptionally good news. A Canadian widow, angered at the way her son was treating her, resolved that he should not receive anything by way of inheritance. Instead she made over $15,000 in bonds to the monastery. By this a foundation of Masses was set up, according to which Masses were to be offered for as long as the monastery continued to exist. Murphy cashed in one of the $5,000 bonds to pay for the new buildings he had constructed: the temporary monastery, the barn, and the small horse stable.[15] The other $10,000 was carefully stored away as a nest egg for the future, and the interest was applied to paying off a standing debt from the days at Petit Clairvaux.[16]

⁘ MONASTIC LIFE UNDER WAY

On August 1 five of the laybrothers arrived.[17] Father Placid and Brother Benedict were still in Tracadie. Brother Richard had apparently returned to Tracadie after accompanying the animals to Lonsdale and was staying on a while longer, no doubt to oversee the final arrangements there. The household goods were shipped out only on August 13.[18] Conspicuously absent was Father John O'Connor, who was still at Oka. Despite Oger's offer to send John to Lonsdale after his ordination to the priesthood on July 6, Murphy preferred for John to remain at Oka for a while longer and to have Alberic sent to Lonsdale instead.[19] On August 16, John Mary noted that there still were not enough choir monks present to perform the Divine Office in choir. The full monastic life had not yet begun.

Although it was out of the question for John Mary to go to the General Chapter of 1900, a document drawn up in his hand was undoubtedly intended for presentation at the chapter:

Report of the Abbey of Petit Clairvaux Aug 29, 1900

We purchased 230 acres of land from Right Rev. Bishop Harkins of Providence RI for $3,000 payable in 15 years without interest.

We built a house 50' x 30'; a cow stable of the same size, and a small building close by cost us $3,700 which is all paid. The barn when completed will cost $890, and we have the money on hand to pay for it. We have no debt but the old debt contracted at Tracadie of $4,000 on which we are pay[ing] an interest of 4%. To settle this debt we have $10,000, ten thousand dollars in bonds drawing 4½%, so that we have a surplus of $6,000 in the bank and a property worth $12,000; we have 2 acres of land under cultivation at present and next year we expect to have close onto 100 acres under cultivation.[20]

Murphy went to New York to meet Oger, probably on his return trip from the chapter, and it is possible that Oger came to the new monastery for a visit. Father John O'Connor finally left Oka for Lonsdale on January 30, 1901. Due to a mix-up in communications, no one was at the Boston Station to meet him, and in alarm he went to St. James parish, where the pastor sent him on to Providence, providing him with the money he needed for the fare.[21]

Oger had told Father John Mary to appoint O'Connor subprior. John Mary also wanted to make him novice master, but Remi strongly objected to the young man's assuming both of these important roles. Consequently, John Mary appointed him only novice master but gave him permission to speak to others during his own absences from the monastery, thus giving him a measure of authority over the community. O'Connor settled down to life at his new home and found it quite to his liking, as he wrote to Father Bernard of Oka: "I am quite delighted with this place. I do not know how it is, but I was never so happy and contented at Oka. I feel very confident that this shall be a great and flourishing monastery in the near future."[22] In the same letter O'Connor reported that there were fifteen in the community—six choir religious, and nine laybrothers. The farm counted thirty cows, six horses, some pigs and chickens. With the arrival of Father John, the core of the community had finally come together.[23] Only one key figure was still missing, Father Alberic, and he would not be arriving until the summer.

Father John Mary managed to find the time for a visit to Tracadie and discovered that both Fathers Benedict and Placid, whom he had been counting on to come to Lonsdale, were instead asking for dispensation from their vows. By early March Father Placid was accepted by Bishop Cameron for the Diocese of Antigonish, and on June 4 he was granted definitive secularization.[24] Brother Benedict, however, threatened to ask for a dispensation from his vows, but finally agreed to go to Oka, at least temporarily.[25] This move was perhaps inspired by a suggestion of Dom Dominic, who from his new home at Sint Sixtus continued to show concern for the old brother. He wrote to Dom Oger:

> I wrote to Father Benedict this week, and I strongly urged him to join the community, or if he does not want to go with Father Jean-Marie to write to you, that you were his Father Immediate and perhaps you would receive him or help him to go to another monastery, either to Tilburg or somewhere else. If he writes to you, I beg you, Very Reverend Father, to help him and to do for him all that is in your power. Perhaps you will win him over and save his soul.[26]

The fate of the Petit Clairvaux property was still uncertain. There was talk of the government purchasing it to use as a hospital. But in late

December the community of Timadeuc in France showed interest in the property as a possible refuge in case the community should have to leave France due to political pressures. By March 3, 1901, they had purchased it for $10,000, agreeing to a down payment of $5,000 and an additional $5,000 in a year.[27]

In early spring the monastery received a brief friendly visit from Dom Chouteau. Father John Mary went to New York to meet his boat and brought him to Lonsdale.

Chouteau may have been motivated by concern for the future of Bellefontaine, itself still threatened by renewed government opposition to religious communities. If the community were forced to leave, at least some of its monks might find a home at the Lonsdale monastery. Two years later he would write to Murphy asking if he were willing to receive several monks and brothers of Bellefontaine.[28] Murphy was delighted at the prospect, but nothing came of it.[29] Chouteau's remarks in his Ordo concerning this visit were positive.[30]

✐ CANONICAL ISSUES

Sometime that spring Dom Oger began to show concern for the canonical status of the Lonsdale monastery, a concern that may have been prompted by the affairs of Oka's foundation at Mistassini, near Lake St.-Jean in northern Quebec. Mistassini had been founded in 1892, and after many difficult years finally began to prosper under the direction of Murphy's old friend, Dom Pacôme Gaboury, who was named superior in 1901. In an undated rough draft of a letter to Dom Augustine Marre, the Abbot General, Oger asked for clarification concerning "the relations that should exist between a foundation that had not yet been canonically erected (Our Lady of Mistassini, for instance) and the motherhouse, Our Lady of the Lake." [31] The questions dealt with practical matters: Who was to vote on candidates for profession, the motherhouse or the filiation? Which place was to be mentioned in the document of profession? When did a person belong definitively to a foundation and no longer to the motherhouse? Although his chief focus was Mistassini, which still had not been canonically erected, he felt that clarification was also needed concerning Lonsdale:

> What are the relations between Our Lady of the Lake and the new
> monastery that is being established in the Diocese of Providence in
> the United States, where only three of the religious came from

Tracadie? Should this monastery be considered as the former monastery of Our Lady of Petit Clairvaux or as a new foundation analogous to that of Our Lady of Mistassini?

The fact of the matter was, of course, that the General Chapter of 1899 had decreed a transfer of Petit Clairvaux to a new location; it was not to be a new foundation. Indeed, this would be repeated at the chapter of 1901. Behind Oger's question, however, lay a more practical consideration, which surfaces in his last paragraph:

> Our Lady of the Lake is heavily in debt but is well-provided with vocations, while the house at Lonsdale (Providence) is without vocations but is assured of financial resources. Can Our Lady of the Lake, or rather should it, demand compensation since it provides personnel, which have to be replaced by hired workers [at home]. The Reverend Father Immediate had counseled me to ask for Mass stipends. Last year we asked for $100 per priest, namely approximately 1/3 of the stipends of Masses and $50 from the non-priest choirmonks and laybrothers.

Oger's motives were obviously not without some degree of self-interest. Judging from Murphy's letters to Oger, the latter seems to have been pressing for funds to such an extent that Murphy wrote to Rome to complain of the matter. Dom Louis Carew, the definitor for the English language, laid the matter before the Abbot General and his council. A decision was made in Murphy's favor. Murphy then wrote to Oger, quoting the letter he had received from the definitory:

> Yesterday I received yours of 5 Oct. and this morning brought the question between yourself and Abbot Anthony [Oger] before the General and the other definitors. It is scarcely an exaggeration to say that all here were scandalized with his mode of acting, for it is an attempt to introduce into the Order a mercenary spirit instead of the hospitality for which it had ever been famous, not merely towards its members, but even to strangers.
>   The General will not permit such a thing and has directed me to tell you not to attempt paying for anyone whom you have received from Oka nor for any whom Oka has received from you.
>   If heretofore the custom of paying has existed in Oka and Petit Clairvaux, the sooner it is at an end, the better. It may be that Dom Antoine might be referring to the custom that exists for the superiors

to pay when at the General Chapter. There is no parity, as anyone can see that a struggling community like Cîteaux could not be at the expense of entertaining the members of the General Chapter.

On becoming Father Immediate Dom Antoine has adopted the role of a stepmother. I am sorry you did not mention this matter before now.

Brother Louis [Dom] O. C. R[32]

Notwithstanding all of this, the question of Petit Clairvaux's canonical erection as an abbey had to be settled. The first step taken in this direction was to propose that the Oka monks change their stability to the new monastery.[33]

Accordingly Dom Oger came to Lonsdale on May 17 for this purpose. Father Remi and Brothers Theophane and Zephyrin wanted more time to reflect on the matter, however. So on Friday, May 18, it was Father John Mary alone who changed his stability, as he reported to Father Pacôme.[34] In his letter he also chided his friend:

Do not address us as Trappists any more. We are no longer Trappists, but Cistercians. This is the Abbey of Little Clairvaux, not the Trappist Monastery; we are doing all we can to get this into the minds of the people here.

This seemingly strong statement does not refer to a change of affiliation but rather to the growing conviction that the Order's true ideal was twelfth century Cîteaux and not the seventeenth century reform of la Trappe.

The next important step was to ask Bishop Harkins to write a letter requesting the canonical erection of the monastery in his diocese. The bishop was all too happy to oblige, and a letter was sent to Oger for presentation to the General. Oger in turn forwarded it to Rome with his own covering letter to the General.[35] The matter was duly taken up at the General Chapter of 1901, which met in September, and the following decision was given:

The community of the former Abbey of Petit Clairvaux, legitimately transferred to the town of Cumberland, should enjoy its former privileges, and in particular the right to receive novices. It is composed of seventeen persons, of whom five are priests able to confess.

Nonetheless, it is certain that, in order to have an election of the superior, the place needs to be canonically erected, which would confer on it a title; but in order to request the canonical erection of the new monastery, it [the chapter] feels it is fitting to wait until there is a suitable building and a more numerous community.[36]

This important decision confirmed the fact that Petit Clairvaux was, indeed, truly transferred to Lonsdale and that it was not a new foundation. Taken literally, the text suggests that the canonical erection was above all needed in order that the election of a superior could take place; Father John Mary was still no more than an interim superior appointed by Oger. But the further implication is that the capitulants wanted—by means of holding out on the canonical erection—to postpone for the moment the affirmation of the abbey's rightful privileges. The deliberations that led to this decision were described in a letter that Chouteau sent to Murphy the day before the decision was made:

Letter to Rev. Father Murphy. Petit-Clairvaux approved as an autonomous community with novitiate. The plans for construction have been approved. When the community will be more numerous and the buildings completed, we will ask for the erection as an abbey. Next year, if things are ready. (The name might be changed.)[37]

The delay was seen, by Chouteau at least, as being relatively brief, but this was not how things were to turn out. Moreover, the chapter's approval for the creation of a novitiate was to give rise to further problems, since the admission of novices and the professions that took place at Lonsdale subsequent to this chapter were eventually looked on as being out of order.

In the context of pre-1917 canonical legislation (which was anything but clear), it is understandable that this case must have caught the chapter somewhat by surprise, since the question of transferals of monasteries was not one commonly encountered at these meetings. In any case, the burden of indicating the precise course of action for the Lonsdale monastery would rest upon the Order's curia in Rome, or at least on Dom Oger, who was the Father Immediate of the new monastery. Murphy, for his part, remained in close contact with Oger concerning admissions to the novitiate as well as the professions he received.[38]

The bishop was duly informed of the chapter's decision. A further measure adopted at the chapter, even though this does not appear in the

Acts, was that Petit Clairvaux had to cede its name to the new community that would be sent by Timadeuc to take up the monastic life once again at the venerable old site in Nova Scotia.

In light of this development, Murphy approached Bishop Harkins, as he explained in a letter to Dom Oger:

> I proposed to His Excellency the names which you suggested to me for our monastery. He did not like "New Clairvaux," nor did he react very much to the name, "Our Lady of Providence." But he said that, as we were in the Blackstone Valley, "Our Lady of the Valley" would be more fitting. So I told him that since this came from him, I thought that you would have no objection. What do you think?[39]

Oger did not answer for some time, but eventually agreed that henceforth the Lonsdale monastery would be known as Our Lady of the Valley.

FIGURE 31. *Our Lady of the Valley. Second monastery, 1902. Facade.*

Chapter Fifteen

Early Years

✍ Early Growth and Plans for a Permanent Building

ACED WITH THE CHALLENGE of erecting a more permanent building, Father John Mary must have rejoiced when the long-awaited
Father Alberic arrived in July 1901.[1] The monastery's finances
were in good condition, thanks to the money remaining from the foundation of Masses set up by their Canadian benefactress, as well as the
first installment of money received from the sale of Petit Clairvaux. As
a former businessman Father Alberic had acquired an expertise in financial matters that would be crucial to the management of these and other
funds necessary to get work started on a permanent monastery. Indeed,
his good judgment in other matters would be a key asset in the development of the monastery over the years.

As early as March 1901 Dom Chouteau had noted that the monks
were planning to set aside the money to be received from the sale of
Petit Clairvaux for the building of a permanent monastery 100' x 30' in
size.[2] In the fall, Father John Mary spoke of these plans to the bishop,
who was pleased at the prospect. The bishop had suggested taking out a
loan for the estimated $15,000 that would be needed to complete the
buildings. However, the standing debt remaining from the monastery's
days at Tracadie made Father John Mary leery about such a move, at
least for the present.[3] In any case, it would not be until March of the following year that the new building would begin to rise.

Meanwhile, everyday life at the monastery went on. During the winter Father Remi had got to work pruning one of the apple orchards, and considerable work had been done to clear the swampland. By spring farm activities had begun in earnest.[4] Brother Aloysius planted vegetables on four of the acres that had been cleared the preceding fall.

With the arrival of Alberic the core of the community was in place: Fathers John Mary Murphy, John O'Connor, Remi, Alberic; Brothers Aloysius, Richard, Anthony, along with Brother Paul, who was still a novice.[5]

Novices and oblates came and went. June 14 saw the profession of Brother Francis MacKinnon, who had entered as a novice at Petit Clairvaux and came with the community to Lonsdale. By 1905, however, his name had disappeared from the roster. On September 23, 1901, a familiar face showed up at the door: the former Father Columban Conaghan of Petit Clairvaux. He had with him a letter from an official at the Order's curia at Rome affirming that the Abbot General was not opposed to his entrance into the Order. John Mary in some panic wrote to Oger to ask advice about what he should do. He was not happy about receiving Columban at the Valley.[6] In a letter to Oger written the very next day on various subjects he added: "If I am forced to receive Father Columban, I intend to give him the oblate's habit for a year."[7] As a matter of fact, Father Columban *was* admitted as an oblate on October 17. His new monastic name was Father Joseph.[8] A community list of 1921 notes that on October 26, 1920, "he received [the] cowl." It is not clear whether this indicates a change in status from oblate to professed monk, or simply a concession permitting him to wear the garb of a professed monk, while still remaining an oblate.[9]

On October 20, 1901, the monastery appeared for what seems to be the first time in the pages of Providence's principal newspaper, the *Providence Journal*.[10] Throughout its history, the Valley would be a favorite subject for the *Journal*. This first article provides sympathetic coverage of what the new monastery seemed like to secular eyes, stressing the neatness and order of the establishment in its country setting. It provides an interesting detail not known from other sources: Cheese was being produced for sale.

Late in the year a decision was made to rent a property adjacent to the monastery known as the Jason Sprague farm. A letter of Murphy to Oger shows that he was even thinking of purchasing the property, for which the owner was asking $1,900.[11] The reason for Murphy's concern was that the right of way this farm could claim through or near the monastery grounds could be a serious threat for the future of the community. For the moment problems were averted by renting the property, but eventually the monastery purchased it in 1909. From Murphy's letter we learn that the Sprague farm had a house in good condition as well as a barn in less good condition. Its fields would be used as pasturage for the cows.

A decision was finally made to proceed with construction. Father John Mary once again approached Ambrose Murphy, who by this time was in partnership with Hindle, and a contract was signed. The new building would be rectangular in plan, parallel to the public road and at a relatively short distance from it. Though much of the building's structure was to be of wood, the main façade would have revetment in fieldstone.[12]

The figure decided upon in the contract was $16,729—exclusive of plumbing and heating. Work did not begin until March or April 1902.[13] But by April 21 Murphy could already announce that the building was going up quickly and that they hoped to be in it around November 1.[14] This date receded more and more as the work progressed. Murphy received periodic bills that had to be met, and he took up with Oger the necessity of borrowing money. The bishop was willing to help with one of the mortgages.[15] Later on, Oger himself decided to lend them $10,000 at four percent interest.[16]

Despite the confusion that must have been associated with this large building project, the monastery continued to expand its operations in different directions, as we learn from Malloy's *Annals*:

> Our dairy promises to be our most successful industry. A team of horses, driven by our family brother, began this year delivering all the milk we produced to restaurants and convents in Pawtucket and Central Falls. Two or three times, in order to keep these customers, we bought milk from a neighboring farmer. That happened when three of our cows were drowned or suffocated in the bog and in the canals that drain it. . . .
>
> In the course of the year 1902 we sunk an artesian well near the northern end of the new monastery, to a depth of 530 feet. The engineers told us they had to drill 300 feet through solid rock. The well yields twelve gallons of excellent water a minute. We began selling this water to hotels and institutions in Providence and its suburbs, and continued to do so for almost ten years.
>
> A dwelling house on the hilltop near the south-eastern extremity of the property was this year fitted out as a ladies' guesthouse, in

charge of Father Superior's sister. It is a source of some income to us.

We have 8 horses, 40 cows, an indefinite number of pigs and chickens, and are trying to raise Belgian hares. In the latter experiment we did not succeed according to our expectations. This year we planted 100 apple trees, just south of the new building, mostly late maturing fruit.[17]

A letter of August 6, 1902, from John Mary to Oger informs us that old Brother Benedict was living at the Valley. In the spring of 1901 he had agreed to go to Oka instead of seeking a dispensation from his vows. Sometime in the spring of 1903, John Mary must have seen his way to obtaining permission to ordain him, for he proposed this to Brother Benedict. Amazingly enough, after all those years of pleading for ordination, Benedict turned down the invitation and once again began to ask for secularization:

> Brother Benedict has refused to be ordained priest for the monastery, so I sent his response to the General; he is asking for secularization. He is asking me to let him leave; I told him that he would be obliged to wait for the answer of Rome—poor old Father, it is a pity he is so foolish.[18]

Once again in December 1903 he had changed his mind: "Now he is at it again, and if what he desires is not granted to him it is possible that he will leave the community."[19] When Benedict learned of the reopening of Petit Clairvaux, he asked to go there and was given permission to do so. He left during the summer and arrived there on August 5, 1904. Father Guénolé of the "new" Petit Clairvaux noted:

> August 5, 1904. Father Benedict Angement arrived from the Valley, USA with all due authorization. He was a native of Gennep, Limburg, Holland. He had strongly missed Petit Clairvaux. Upon learning that there was once again a community there, he asked and obtained permission to come to us. He worked especially at the mill. He died June 12, 1905.[20]

The monastery sustained another, more significant loss on November 5, 1902, when Brother Aloysius Van Enschot died. He was the only Belgian member of Petit Clairvaux who had come to the Valley as one of its founders and was the first of them to die. His expertise on the farm would be sorely missed, and Father John Murphy wrote to Dom Oger asking if it were possible to send someone to replace him.[21]

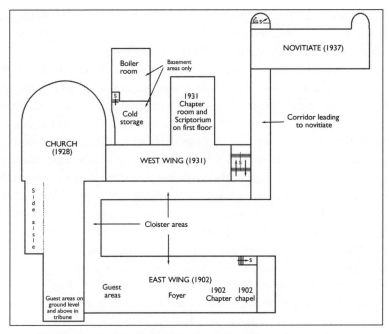

FIGURE 32. *Our Lady of the Valley. Plan of central buildings, 1902–1937.*

This must have been a hectic time for John Mary, especially with the approaching move into the new monastery.

∾ THE COMMUNITY MOVES INTO THE NEW BUILDING

Things were in a sufficient state of readiness for the monks to begin transferring the furniture to the new building on December 29, although they themselves moved in only on January 1, 1903. The occasion was apparently somewhat subdued. The bishop had offered to say the first Mass, and Father John Mary wanted things in perfect shape before inviting him to come. His plan was to have a low Mass for the occasion.[22] However, there is no indication that the bishop actually came. The blessing of the new building was deferred until March 21, 1903, when a Solemn Pontifical Mass was celebrated in the new chapel.[23]

While the layout of the building provided an enormous amount of space compared to the small house in which they had been living for over a year, it was a far cry from the traditional plan of the monastic quadrangle, which separated the various areas of monastic activity into distinct spaces. In the new building everything had to be fitted into this one wing. The community would have to wait more than twenty-five years for a further enlargement of their living facilities.

The overall layout of the new building left no doubt about the intentions of the monks to welcome visitors. Broad steps led up to a large outdoor porch from which guests entered the foyer, where they were greeted by the porter or the guestmaster. Furthermore, a considerable portion of the entire building was devoted to the reception of transient guests and of retreatants who came to spend some days with the monks. The area to the left of the foyer contained parlors, a room for the guestmaster, and a refectory reserved for the guests. At the back of the foyer a flight of stairs, very much in evidence, led to the second floor, the entire south side of which contained rooms for guests and retreatants. From the foyer itself guests and retreatants could assist at the services in the chapel, albeit somewhat awkwardly, by means of windows that were opened into the chapter room and beyond that into the chapel.

All of this made for a considerable amount of hustle and bustle in close proximity to the chapel, and Father John O'Connor noted that, due to the thinness of the wall separating chapel from reception area, this proved to be a disturbance for the monks during their services: "Worldly conversations are easily heard through the light partition, both during the Office and the time of meditation."[24] The porch also turned out to be a popular spot for conversations of visitors, a matter that would eventually come to the attention of the General Chapter. A further point of contact between the monastery and its environs was the guesthouse for ladies opened in 1902.[25]

The areas in the building for the use of the monks themselves were concentrated on its north end. On the main floor the foyer area was flanked on the right by the chapter room and beyond that the chapel. A long corridor about nine feet wide ran along the back side of the building and served as the "cloister" where the monks could read and pray. (The Stations of the Cross were situated here.) At the southern end of this corridor was a room for the superior.

The second floor's north end housed the novitiate, the library, and the wardrobe area, where the monks' habits were sewn and mended. The third floor was reserved entirely for the monks. On the north side was the dormitory, which along with its lavatory took up most of the space on this floor. The remaining area to the south was occupied by a small infirmary.

At its southern end the basement of the building housed the

kitchen, scullery, and monks' refectory. A dumbwaiter sent food up to the guests' refectory on the first floor and to the monastic infirmary on the top floor. The rest of the basement was used for storage and also housed the heating equipment for the building.

For its day the building offered a number of amenities. In addition to central heating, there were two fireplaces on the first floor and two others on the second floor along the path of the same chimneys. The one in the foyer was double-sided, offering heat to both the foyer and the parlor behind it. Each floor had a lavatory in the guest area; the one on the top floor included a bathtub.[26]

In the spring of 1903 some landscaping was carried out around the building, and a wide new access road leading from Diamond Hill Road to the new building was put in, accentuating still further that visitors were welcome. Though the choir monks as well as the brothers worked on this project, ten laymen were hired to hurry the work along.[27]

∽ Growing Pains

The regular visitation of 1903 was carried out during the early summer. At Oka itself this was a busy year. Plans were being discussed for the building of a new monastery to replace the one that had been destroyed by fire in the summer of 1902, and developments at the monastery's agricultural school were taking up the attention of Dom Oger. This is probably why Dom Obrecht of Gethsemani was asked to conduct that year's visitation at the Valley. This would be a taste of things to come, as he was destined to take over as Father Immediate of the Valley in 1914. Amazingly enough, Malloy's *Annals* do not even comment on this unusual event, and the only mention of it that has survived is Obrecht's signature in the account books of the monastery, and Father John Mary's remark in a letter to Oger that the visitor seemed pleased.[28]

On April 29, Brother Paul le Chartier, who had been an oblate at Petit Clairvaux for many years, finally made his simple profession. For its part, Oka continued to send men to help. Father Edward Villeneuve left for Lonsdale on August 4, 1903. Two others came in 1904, but none of these remained permanently at the Valley.[29]

On December 23 Father John Mary sent an eight-page letter to Oger on various matters. One of these is of some importance. It is clear from Murphy's words that Oger had requested that both English and French be used at the Valley, apparently in some kind of official way.

Murphy's response (written, as usual, in French!) was a strong affirmation of his policy of maintaining English as the official language of the monastery without outlawing the use of French in his private interviews with those for whom French was their native tongue:

> Reverend Father, I believe that there will be difficulties in having two languages in the house; here we live in the midst of a population which speaks the English language, and we are forced to speak this language. For myself, I much love the French language, and never do I oblige those who speak it to speak English. We have here two Canadian lay-brothers, who know English very well. Nonetheless in my room I always speak to them in French. Likewise with Father Remi, Father Edward and Brother Paul. I never oblige them to speak English.
>
> You tell me that you are expecting a Canadian postulant from Fall River [Massachusetts]. Well, during the summer *we* have received two from Montreal for the simple reason that we speak English here, and I am expecting another from Manitoba, not far from Our Lady of the Prairies, for the same reason. The same is true of still another who should be entering tomorrow and who is coming from Nova Scotia for the same reason. It is natural, Reverend Father, for a postulant to seek a house where his own language is spoken. There are only four houses to the east of Chicago and isn't it right that, of these four, at least one of these houses be reserved for the English language?[30]

Oger's request should be seen in the context of the situation of the Church at large in the Diocese of Providence, where tensions tended to surface between the various ethnic groups that were concentrated in individual parishes. Oger would have been well aware of this situation, and there is even reason to believe that he solicited funds for Oka among parishes of French-speaking Canadian immigrants in the area around Cumberland. There is a record of at least one visit he paid to nearby Fall River in Massachusetts, on the occasion of one of his trips to the Valley.[31] Thus it is possible that in his letter to Murphy, Oger was taking the part of the French-speaking parishes of the region when he asked him to consider making French one of the official languages of the monastery. In Chouteau's notes on his 1904 visit to the Valley there are echoes of the displeasure caused by Murphy's decision to insist on the use of English as the monastery's official language: "The Canadians near the monastery and the parish priests do not want this monastery, because everything there is English. The parish priests refuse to send their subjects there because of this."[32] Much later on, we still find what might be a lingering trace of this opposition in Oger's report to the General on his 1907 visitation.[33]

Things were looking grim during January of the new year of 1904. Extensive strikes at the mills in the neighborhood were causing havoc to the economy of the area. Milk sales in the monastery were down, and offerings for Masses were nonexistent.[34] In May Oka reinforced the ranks of the Valley by sending Father Francis of Assisi Quézel. He definitively changed his stability on July 14, 1905.[35]

Perhaps the biggest event of the year was another brief visit by Chouteau around May 21. The personal notes in his *Ordo* of 1904 provide an outsider's view of things:

> They follow the former customs of Tracadie along with others which Dom Jean-Marie Murphy would like to introduce in conformity with the regulations. They have the new books, but Father Joseph, the oblate, the former Father Columban, wants to direct [things] in his own way. Father Murphy is often absent. Father Remi has no influence. Father Joseph, Father Benedict and Father John of the former Tracadie [monastery] are on top. The fact that the priests go out to parishes is certainly lamentable. Sometimes there is only one priest left. There is no common work, or hardly anyone of the personnel of the monastery goes to it. If there is a novice, they simply send him to some job or other. There are eighteen lady guests, and there are conversations on the porch.[36] On Sundays there is a procession of visitors of both sexes from 1:00 to 7:00 in the afternoon.

True to form, Father Joseph (the former Father Columban) is once again trying to run things. Chouteau's remarks reveal three problematic situations: the practice of the priests' going out to help in parishes on Sundays (which they had been doing since they arrived in Rhode Island); the disturbance caused by visitors, particularly acute since it mostly took place near the chapel; and finally the ladies' guesthouse. At the end of his *Ordo Notes* Chouteau's remarks about the new building are more favorable (although his figures are inaccurate):

> Great cleanliness and well-ordered appointments. Toilets, lavabos, without any bad odors. Everywhere toilets and bathtubs. The plumbing (including toilets) and the installation of the silo together cost $2100. $450 spent on lighting. Placing of [illegible word] $5. Purchase of a farm that is supposed to be 105 arpents for $2000. The whole property consists of approximately 500 arpents.[37]

Dom Oger made the regular visitation of 1904 at the beginning of June. One of the questions that must have surfaced was the increasing difficulty of securing their livelihood exclusively from farming the rocky soil of their property. It is true that the very rockiness of that soil had opened the way to a small new industry. The contractor Denis Shea, who had used stones from the property in building the new monastery, offered to buy more for use in his construction work. Thus later in 1905 we have a record of four buildings in which monastery stone was used.[38] Nonetheless, prospects for making a livelihood out of the land seemed bleak, as Malloy reported in his *Annals*:

> This farm, a stony waste, does not pay. We must buy food to eke out that which we grow. The sale of stones "harvested" from our fields, and of "mineral water" from our artesian well, along with an occasional money gift, barely help us to keep ourselves going. But God will provide! We live for Him alone.[39]

Ever resourceful, on June 12 Father John Mary sought to address the problem, writing to the Abbot General in Rome to discuss the possibility of an industrial venture of manufacturing malt, the equipment and expertise to be furnished by a layman.[40] But the project went no further.

Notwithstanding the economic pinch, on September 28, 1904, Murphy was able to send Oger payment for the balance of the loan of $10,000.[41] By the time the General Chapter opened in October, all had been settled.

Malloy's *Annals* relate that by June 1905 one hundred fruit trees had been planted in the new orchard. In August Father Guillaume Guillaume of Oka came to the Valley for three months to give chant lessons to the community. A native of Nancy in France, he had entered Oka as a priest in 1897. During the summer of 1904 he had studied chant in England at Appuldurcombe House on the Isle of Wight, where the community of Solesmes had taken refuge after their expulsion from Solesmes in 1901.[42] He was, as a result, personally acquainted with Dom Mocquereau and Dom Desrocquettes. Both of these prominent figures in the restoration of Gregorian chant at Solesmes later paid a visit to Oka.

During Dom Oger's 1905 visitation in August he brought up several points that would surface once again at the forthcoming General Chapter in France, to which Oger must have traveled directly from the Valley. The General Chapter had some stern remarks about the community:

Several serious abuses have been pointed out in the monastery of Our Lady of the Valley. The General Chapter imposes on the Father Prior the following orders: 1. To suppress the regular exits of priests on Sundays and feastdays; 2. To do away with the communication that exists between the rooms of the guests and the regular places; 3. To close the guesthouse in which women guests are received. Besides this, the prior is asked to come to the General Chapter of 1906 to render an account of the manner in which he will have carried out these prescriptions.[43]

Dom Oger had called the community's attention to the first and third points during his visitation in August.[44] Indeed, all three had been noticed by Chouteau during his brief visit in May 1904, and his observations had probably played an important role in the chapter's decision. Foregoing the income brought in by the parish work would be a great sacrifice for the community in its still fragile economic situation, and it is not clear how faithful Dom John Mary was in implementing the General Chapter's injunctions. In any case, as late as the mid-1920s Fathers Remi and Alberic were still active on Sundays in the parish of Notre-Dame-du-Sacré-Cœur in Central Falls.

∽ Petit Clairvaux Reopened; Movement to Beatify Father Vincent de Paul

During these years of early growth at Our Lady of the Valley, Petit Clairvaux itself once more came back to life. As conditions for the Trappists in France had worsened in 1903 with an anticlerical government in power, Timadeuc had finally sent a colony of monks to begin life at Petit Clairvaux. Not long after arriving, on August 30 the monks transferred the remains of Father Vincent from the convent of the sisters to the cemetery of Petit Clairvaux itself. The remains of Father Francis Xavier and of Brother Charles were likewise transferred on September 11. The superior, Dom Eugene Villeneuve, also paid a visit to the four surviving sisters from the convent, who had taken up residence with the sisters known as the *Filles de Jésus* at Arichat. He reported that they were doing well.[45]

The General Chapter of 1904 had discussed a project for the beatification of Father Vincent de Paul Merle and appointed the abbot of Timadeuc to work along with Bishop Cameron in the diocesan process of investigation. It also requested that a life of Father Vincent be prepared and printed for the monasteries of the Order;[46] Father Etienne Ozenne of Timadeuc was assigned the task of composing this biography.[47]

When the chapter met again in 1905, a commission composed of several abbots (among them the abbot of Timadeuc) was set up to examine the completed biography. And it was noted with pleasure and gratitude that Bishop Cameron had officially introduced the cause of Father Vincent.[48]

Petit Clairvaux's superior, Father Eugene Villeneuve, had already prepared a circular letter that was sent to the priests of the diocese relating the facts of Father Vincent's life and supposed miracles and asking that each ascertain from the parishioners any other favors that might have been obtained through the intercession of Father Vincent. The letter was also printed in the local Catholic newspaper, *The Casket*:

> Not long after my arrival in this country, I sent to the Chapter General of the Order of Cîteaux, to which Father Vincent belonged, and to which we also the Religious of Petit Clairvaux have the honor to belong, a relation of his alleged miracles and extraordinary virtues, all gathered from well authenticated sources. This relation having been carefully considered it was unanimously decided to request the Rt. Rev. John Cameron, Bishop of Antigonish, to appoint a Canonical Commission for the purpose of examining into the nature of these reputed miracles or preternatural favors, as well as into the heroic character of his virtues.
>
> Father Vincent of Paul was the founder and first superior of the Monastery of Little Clairvaux. He died in the odor of sanctity in the Little Convent, better known as the Convent of the Sisters of La Trappe, on January 1, 1853, and his mortal remains were laid in the cemetery adjoining. There they lay until August 28, 1903, which day the Rev. Michael Laffin, delegated by His Lordship, Bishop Cameron, translated them to the Monastery of Little Clairvaux. The solemn ceremony took place in the presence of a large concourse of the faithful of Tracadie and surrounding parishes, who were glad to pay a tribute of veneration to the memory of Father Vincent. His venerated remains now repose in a vault at the foot of the Cross in our cemetery. The vault is covered with a marble slab, the gift of pious citizens of Halifax and upon it are inscribed the principal events of his life.
>
> The exhumation was made by myself assisted by Fathers Abraham and Corentin of our Order. In the grave we found but his bones, his monastical [sic] cincture, 48 grains of his beads, a copper cross and fragments of the monastic habit in which he was buried according to the custom of our Order.[49]

Chapter Sixteen

The Valley 1905–1910

∽ SETTLING CANONICAL ISSUES

E VEN THOUGH NOTHING appeared in the Acts, better things for the Valley were in the making at the General Chapter of 1905. Soon after its completion John Mary sent to the General (at his own request) a brief report on the monastery, outlining the main steps in the transfer from Nova Scotia. This included a community list as of August 1905, as well as a list of all juridical acts performed at the Valley since 1900: receptions of the habit, simple and solemn professions, changes of stability.[1] The procurator presented this to the Congregation of the Propaganda Fide, and on February 24, 1906, the Congregation sent to the General an act of sanation[2] of the irregularities supposedly incurred by the community in connection with its transfer:

> Augustine Marre [Abbot General] . . . most humbly sets forth what follows. The Monastery of Petit Clairvaux . . . since it found it difficult to support itself because of various difficulties, and especially since there seemed to be no promise of vocations to our form of monastic life in that region, the General Chapter of 1899 decided that a more fitting location be sought for that small community, care being taken to follow all that is laid down concerning the transfer and the erection of monasteries. Thus the superior of the said community having carried out a search with great care, found a site apt for founding a Cistercian monastery near Lonsdale in the Diocese of Providence in

the United States. At the end of February 1900, he himself went there
to prepare a property and a building destined for the future community; and this was done with the approval of the Ordinary of the
Diocese of Providence.

Gradually the other six members of the community of Petit
Clairvaux, of whom three were still novices, following the superior
moved to the new dwelling place, to which the name of Our Lady of
the Valley . . . was given; so that at the end of the month of July 1900
the entire community of Petit Clairvaux was gathered together there.
Several days later, on August 2, the regular exercises were begun and
monastic life was established with exactitude according to the rule and
the usages of the Order, and indeed that little community (clearly in
all good faith, but for which it is now sorry) comported itself as if the
new dwelling had already been canonically erected, for seven young
men were one by one admitted to the reception of the habit—two to
the choir novitiate, and five to the laybrothers' novitiate, and three
novices made simple vows, one of whom after three years made
solemn vows. This suppliant, therefore, having obtained the consent
of the Ordinary for the canonical erection of the house of Our Lady
of the Valley (hereto attached) eagerly asks Your Holiness

1. to deign to ratify the transfer of the monastery of Petit Clairvaux to
the aforesaid place,

2. to deign to erect the house of Our Lady of the Valley as a priory of
the Order of Reformed Cistercians and to declare it erected,

3. to deign to ratify both the new stability of the monks who were
already professed and came from Petit Clairvaux to that place, as well
as the time of novitiate spent at the house of Our Lady of the Valley,

4. to deign to validate and rectify [*convalidare et sanare*] the profession
of both simple as well as solemn vows made in this house too quickly
and incorrectly [*praepropere et perperam*],

And God.[3]

From an audience with His Holiness which took place on
February 24, 1906.[4]

On April 21 the Procurator General informed Murphy by letter of
the favorable decision of Rome.

Whatever the ins and outs of the complicated story, this canonical
fluttering of feathers seems to have brought satisfaction to all concerned, save on one point. If the monastery had been "legitimately
transferred" with all its "former privileges," how was it that the Valley
now found itself no longer an abbey but rather a simple priory? Surely

this was a point that constituted the most important of its "former privileges." As Chouteau's commentary on the 1901 decision indicated, the restoration of the monastery's right to abbey status was clearly intended back then. What had happened in the meantime to change this policy? It is hard to believe that if the word "abbey" had been substituted for "priory" in the request to Rome, it would not have been accepted. Indeed, such a procedure would have been more in accord with Canon Law, since abbatial status is not lost by transfer or even by diminution in the number of an abbey's members. Perhaps someone on the level of the Order had decided that the Valley would have to wait. Given his opposition to the transfer of Petit Clairvaux to New England, not to mention his disappointment earlier on at not having been able himself to make a foundation in the eastern United States, one wonders if this might have been Obrecht. In any case, there is nothing found in the decisions of the General Chapter to suggest that this deliberation was the result of a vote of the assembly as a whole.[5]

The documents that John Mary drew up after the chapter of 1905 show that from 1900 to August 1905 a total of twenty-seven novices had been received, eleven for the choir and sixteen for the laybrothers. Only one of these (Brother Robert Morin) was to make his simple profession. Three other laybrother novices made simple profession, but they had come as novices from Petit Clairvaux.

Despite these disappointing figures, the local population was showing a noticeable interest in possible vocations at the Valley. During the first year alone, there were three novices for the choir and three more for the brothers.

In 1906 the monks of the Valley created a pond by damming the stream that ran through the northern portion of the property and fed the bog. In winter this would provide ice to refrigerate the milk produced by the monastery's dairy. The ice was removed in blocks and placed in two storage buildings, the walls of which were insulated with sawdust.[6]

At the General Chapter, which took place in September, a general principle was enunciated concerning procedure in opening new monasteries. The chapter seemed intent on profiting from the lesson of the preceding year:

> For the canonical erection of a monastery, the Reverend Father Capitulants declare that one must, first of all, ask the chapter's permission to make a foundation. Then recourse is had to the Holy See,

which, if the opinion of the local bishop is in favor, then authorizes the establishment of the house, *positis ponendis*, namely, on condition that the regular places be ready, that revenues or means of support be assured, and that there be sufficient personnel.[7]

✑ The Cause of Father Vincent de Paul Merle

Among its other acts, the chapter appointed Dom Vital Lehodey, abbot of Bricquebec, to examine the biography of Father Vincent de Paul Merle, which was finally ready for publication. Dom Vital, one of the great lights of the Order in the first decades of the twentieth century, was largely responsible for the shift of emphasis away from the Trappist ideal towards a return to authentic Cistercian sources. In 1910 the General Chapter entrusted to him the redaction of a new *Spiritual Directory*, designed to translate this ideal into concrete practical advice for the monks and nuns of the Order.

Dom Vital set to work examining the manuscript. By October 20 he had already had it read publicly in his community. On November 5 he sent his impressions to Dom Bernard at Timadeuc in a lengthy letter. His remarks touch not only on the biography itself, but also on the figure of Father Vincent as it emerges from Father Étienne's pages:

> As regards the substance of the work. Father Vincent must have been a holy man, since many extraordinary events took place during his life and after his death and since he left behind in the area a widespread and lasting reputation for holiness. But it must be admitted that in reading the work right down to its last chapters, this comes as a true surprise—something not expected. One sees an excellent religious, of whom there are so many, but heroic virtues are not in evidence. This is not the fault of the narrator; he simply did not have documents at his disposal.
>
> Thus the chapter on the Revolution is very interesting, but little is said of our hero. The facts presented give us an idea of what his activity must have been like, but personal documents are lacking. Nothing positive is known of his novitiate, nor of his work at Mont Génèvre; nor of his first days in America, save several trips and isolated facts.
>
> Understandably one could easily excuse the fact that the first part of his life is enveloped in darkness. But there is still more obscurity concerning the second half. There is no evidence that he did much to found his monastery (and yet that was his principal duty). He seems rather to have become absorbed in his missions. And even there, one

does not sufficiently see whether his zeal was heroic. We know the places where he exercised his ministry; we also know his method [of work]; we see his love for souls, but we look in vain for those little details that would show uncommon zeal.

As for his religious life, first of all, we know of it only by the letter in which he expresses his regret for not following the Rule; he admits that he eats meat and that he eats three times a day. Was this because he was not able to do better? It is said later on, that even during his travels he followed the Rule, but this is merely mentioned in passing. In all of this second part of the *Life* we do not sufficiently see the Christian, the religious in his interior life. Thus we have to guess at his virtues rather than see them. . . . And when he brings religious back to Tracadie on two occasions he seems to neglect them too much in favor of his mission or even in order to live tranquilly with the Sisters. Is it really the trait of a founder to appear in his Community only once a week, or at least only rather seldom?

I submit all of these observations to you because others will make them, and you will have to answer them. I do not doubt the sanctity of this person, because of his miracles and the renown of his great virtues. I believe that in order to begin the canonical process there is everything that is needed, and it would be good to act soon while a good number of witnesses who knew Father Vincent are still to be found, the bishop himself among them. If they can be found and made to speak, you will discover a multitude of small facts that will make it possible to draw up a definitive and interesting history, because it will be documented. . . . In the present state of things, it would have been better to create a brochure; for a book, there are not enough facts. . . .

I do not believe that Father Vincent could be accused of disobedience. His conduct is in each case understandable; however, it does need to be explained. Likewise, I believe that Dom Joseph-Marie [Hercelin] was acting fully in accordance with his office, given the decision of the chapter and the very correct judgment made not to authorize missions.[8] But the good intentions and ideas of the superior need to be brought out more, (and this would not have been difficult) as well as the well-founded conviction of Father Vincent that his duty kept him in America. This violent situation is not imputable to the superior; this was the great suffering of Father Vincent in the second half [of the book]. I think that this could be better brought into light.

Father Francis of Assisi [he means Francis Xavier] who so well assisted Father Vincent is truly sympathetic; he even seems to be more the founder than Father Vincent. He is the one who lived with the community and sustained it by his courage. But his first letter is scandalous. He speak of his faults (and he has all of them) as if they were intentional; subsequent history would indeed show that he fought against them and that he was also speaking only out of humility; but the first impression one gets is unfortunate. The letter to Dom Joseph-Marie is somewhat violent; it shows more love for the old rules than obedience towards present superiors.[9]

He then goes on to criticize certain aspects of the biography from the point of view of style and presentation, taking exception, for instance, to the frequent lengthy citations:

> Summing up, I am not opposed to the publication of the work. I admit however that I was disappointed; I am persuaded that there would be much to be gained for the public by waiting until after the diocesan process in order to use the remarks of the witnesses.
>
> In any case, if you decide to publish that work now with the authorization of the General it would be good to make the several corrections that I pointed out; this would not call for much work.

As things turned out, the biography was never published. Nonetheless, the next year's chapter (1907) decided to introduce the cause at Rome. A Vatican official eventually responded, noting that the cause could probably be sustained with success, but that "the procedure would be long and difficult because of the scarcity of sufficient documentation of a precise nature." When this letter was read at the chapter of 1909, it was decided by secret ballot to suspend the cause "for the moment."[10] The propitious moment was never to come again. No doubt Dom Vital's own reaction had its own role to play in the chapter's final deliberation on this theme.

✎ THE ELECTION OF A PRIOR

With the matter of the sanation behind them, the monks of the Valley were able to prepare for the election of their prior. Dom Oger arrived at the Valley for a regular visitation, which opened on the morning of May 2, 1907, and closed the next day with the reading of the visitation card to the community assembled in the chapter room.[11] According to a time-honored formula, the report listed the numbers of current personnel (a total of twenty), affirmed that the visitor interviewed all the choir monks "and a few of the laybrothers," and carried out the prescribed inspections of the various parts of the monastery and of its financial accounts. In his general remarks Dom Oger praised the "noticeable improvement in the number and the quality of the members" and noted on the basis of his interviews that "all of them [the brethren] were satisfied with the noticeable improvement in the condition of the community." Among the things pointed out for further improvement was the poor condition of the building where the workmen lived. He also showed some concern for the modest increase in the debt.

Dom Oger next paid a visit to Bishop Harkins to announce the plans for the election, and without further ado, it took place on May 4, 1907.[12] In accordance with law, two witnesses from outside the monastery were called in.[13] At that period in the Order's history only the priest-monks were eligible to vote. Thus the electors were only five: John Mary, Alberic, Remi, Francis, and John. Father John Mary was unanimously elected prior save for one vote (presumably his own).[14] The good news was taken up by the *Providence Sunday Journal* on May 7, which did not fail to note the more picturesque elements of the ceremony:

> One of the features of the ceremony was the "announcement to the four winds" of the name of the elected candidate. . . . During the election all the doors and windows were securely fastened and the keys were deposited in the centre of the chapter room.

The process was not over, however. The election required confirmation by the Abbot General. The following day Oger wrote to the General to announce the results and to ask for his confirmation of Dom John Mary as prior. He also gave his own comments on the regular visitation. His remarks are all the more important in that we have few documents from his hand that reflect his thought about conditions at the Valley throughout these years. The positive tone of the letter shows that his encouraging remarks to the community in the visitation card were sincere:

> Spirit. In general, very good. There is a very noticeable improvement. All of the choir and lay novices whom I saw privately after the visitation were edified concerning what they saw, save for the too frequent visits of women. The same remark was made to me by His Excellency. However, there is a noticeable improvement and, practically speaking, it would be very difficult to do better. . . .
>
> The guesthouse is better screened off, but there are always numerous visits that are sometimes rather bothersome . . . .

Temporal Affairs. The situation is rather stable. There is an augmentation of debts compensated for by urgent improvements: enlargement of barns, ice house, land clearing and above all weeding. Given the natural poverty of the soil, I am rather of the opinion along with His Excellency and the neighboring parish priests that some small industry would be very useful, not to say necessary to secure the community's future well-being on a material level. The soil which is very rocky and porous requires much fertilizer and this is expensive.

The Reverend Father is esteemed, indeed much esteemed by His Excellency, the clergy and his community. The clergy (with the exception of several individuals) and the public in general have great esteem for the community which made a very good impression also on myself.[15]

The General's confirmation eventually arrived, and the installation of the new prior took place on the Feast of St. Bernard, August 20, 1907. A sung Mass was celebrated by Father Francis, at which a number of notable guests assisted, including Monsignor Doran, the Vicar General of the diocese. The Office of Sext was sung, and the monks gathered in the chapter room, where the Abbot General's letter of confirmation was read. The prior was then installed and the monks made their promise of obedience to him. The visiting clergy were served a luncheon after the ceremony.[16] Dom John Mary would get a chance to relax after all the bustle of these events, when in January 1908 he went for a visit to Oka to celebrate the twenty-fifth anniversary of his entrance into monastic life.

✌ 1908–1910

Life seemed to continue peacefully over the coming months of 1908. There is little to report, since the volume of Murphy's correspondence with Oka was beginning to diminish around this time. We are largely dependent on the remarks of Malloy in his version of the monastery's *Annals*. Oger went to the Valley for the regular visitation in late June, but there is no record of what transpired during it.[17] In the fall Murphy attended the General Chapter at Cîteaux. The year also saw two simple professions, that of Brother Augustine Herran on August 15 (the first profession of a choir monk in the new monastery), and that of Brother Vincent Madden on August 23 as a laybrother. Brother Brendan Kelly's profession on December 24 of the following year was the second profession to the choir.

For 1909 Malloy relates in his *Annals*: "Seven of our cows were condemned by the state veterinarian. Potato bugs wrought havoc whilst we fought weeds and insects in other parts of our garden."[18] Of greater importance was the acquisition on May 18, 1909, of the previously rented Jason Sprague farm. This gave the monastery a solid holding of property on both sides of the bog. More acquisitions would be made beginning in 1923.[19]

In 1911 the community received two new members who were to play important roles in the history of the Valley. Brother Dominic O'Leary, who made his first profession as a laybrother on August 15, was to render many years of service as the monastery's infirmarian. After the suppression of the monastery of Jordan in Oregon, the choir brother Benoît Barré transferred to the Valley. He was destined to serve one day as its novice master.

FIGURE 33. *Dom Edmund Obrecht, abbot of Gethsemani and third Father Immediate of Our Lady of the Valley.*

Chapter Seventeen

Last Years of
Dom John Mary Murphy

B
Y 1910 DOM JOHN MARY's health was growing increasingly poor. As time went on, it became apparent that whatever the precise nature of his physical ailments, there was also an important psychological component. For this reason, from January 1, 1910, a "commission of accounts" was set up to keep an eye on the monastery's finances, and from July 1, the ledger was signed periodically not only by Dom John Mary but by two, or sometimes three, others.[1]

The first clear description of John Mary's condition is found in a letter Dom Oger wrote to the Abbot General after his arrival at the Valley in the spring of 1911 to assess the situation:

Upon arriving here I went to see the dear Rev. Father Prior at St Joseph's Hospital, where the doctors judge it necessary to keep him for observation and for special treatment twice a day. I found him better but not well at all. His condition is altogether a source of great concern. Though he is better from a physical point of view, his head is very mixed up. This poor Father once so very affable, obliging, sensitive has become intractable. The chaplain told me confidentially that he is insufferable. When he realizes this, he becomes disconsolate, and cries like a child. Father Francis, his confessor, who went Friday to see him, told me yesterday that he seems to him to lapse into something of an infantile state.

Here my job is very delicate and difficult, and I do not know how to manage. Rev. Father Prior has always been very authoritarian, but since he is here he has become a real tyrant for some time now, having no other rule than his will, practically speaking ignoring the Constitutions, usages, and Canon Law. They assure me that he will not put up with any observation made to him. Here is a small example among a thousand others. A religious goes to him to tell him that rain is coming in through the roof, and he is received like a dog in a game of ninepins. The choir religious take on jobs of laybrothers and vice versa; for example, a religious cares for the heating during the night and does not assist at any of the regular exercises. The choir religious during the morning work period wash the dishes of the previous evening. While this is going on, a young laybrother, who is very pretentious, fills the job of secretary, comes into the choir of the religious and, when needed, calls them to order.

All is topsy-turvy in the exercises. Thus this morning they arose at 2 and sang nothing. During Prime the laybrothers are in the lower stalls, supposedly doing their [mental] prayer. . . .

Besides this, recruitment is carried out in a lamentable fashion. Only two religious made their profession here. The first, Brother Augustine (who functions as president) still needs to learn Latin grammar, of which he knows little and learns only with difficulty. He has completed his three years of simple profession. Can he be admitted to solemn profession? He is supposed to have done his studies, including his philosophy, but as a matter of fact he knows almost nothing.

The other, Brother Brennan, [Brendan] who came from the Montreal seminary, is not able to read a line in any acceptable way.

They also have a choir oblate, a big heavyset boy, a singer from Boston, who knows almost nothing, neither French, nor English, hardly any Latin and has never taken any courses in Latin; but he has a strong voice and works well! So, he is very good.

There are no records for the Foundation Masses despite remonstrances made over and over again by yourself as well as by me. What should be done about a foundation for a Mass, which was accepted on April 25, 1907, without the consent of the community or the approval of the General Chapter. [It calls for] a Mass that is to be sung each year on March 6 for three deceased. This is a fait accompli, which it is morally impossible to change.

I began this morning and yesterday to remind [the community] in a serious way of respect for the Rule and the Usages. For that matter, I am dealing with religious who are *all* very well-disposed. But what is most difficult is not to offend the Father Prior of whom they stand in mortal fear, and who is excessively sensitive precisely because of his present state.

The financial situation which seemed to be a cause for concern has notably improved, since the Father Prior no longer concerns himself with business affairs. It remains to be seen what the doctors, nurses, and the hospital will prescribe. My intention is to remain here at least several weeks to help, and to encourage and to see how the illness of the Father Prior will turn out.[2]

The outcome was far from clear. During the coming months improvement was followed by relapse, only to give way to some improvement. Despite his condition, John Mary was able to attend the General Chapter in September 1911. It would be his last. Upon his return, he had another relapse, and the direction of the monastery fell more and more to Father John O' Connor.[3] Once again in November Oger went to the Valley to assess the situation.

Towards the beginning of 1912 his doctor recommended that Murphy be permitted to go away for a rest. He went once again to St. Joseph's Hospital in Providence, this time for an extended stay.[4] Murphy's condition occasioned an unparalleled flow of letters between Oger and the General. Sometime after his visit to the Valley at the end of 1911, Oger had called a meeting of his council at Oka and by an almost unanimous vote it was decided "to ask to be completely relieved of the responsibility for this house, which, moreover, cannot be the daughter of a house which is more recent than itself."[5] The decision was motivated by Oka's inability to send more religious to the Valley, and it was suggested that the paternity return to Bellefontaine or Gethsemani. In his letter to the General, Oger recalled the circumstances in which he agreed to assume responsibility for the Valley in the first place:

In 1898 after a difficult session in the Rotonda of Tre Fontane [during the General Chapter held in Rome that year], I accepted to care for the remnants of the former community of Petit Clairvaux. I had no other end in view than to do some good for this poor community and to avoid new difficulties with the Rev. Father Abbot of Bellefontaine [Dom Chouteau] who was putting very strong pressure on me.[6]

Oger also strongly advised that an administrator be appointed to care for the monastery in light of Murphy's condition. He had sent Father Pacôme to visit the Valley to look into the condition of its finances. Pacôme's inspection of the books showed that there was no immediate cause for alarm; with a little care, interest payments could continue to be made. Pacôme urged, however, that if Murphy died he be replaced by someone whose prime concern would be to pay off the debt, and that such a person be found *soon*.[7] Oger went along with this idea and sent Pacôme's letter on to the General. "I feel that the situation is serious and will become very serious should the Reverend Father partially regain his health and try to take over the administration. At all costs, a capable administrator is needed there, one with full powers."[8] Oger felt there was no one at the Valley capable of filling the need, even though Father John O'Connor continued to keep things going on a day-to-day basis.

A few days earlier Oger had sent the General a "bulletin" relating what he had just heard in a letter from Father Alberic:

> There was a consultation of doctors today; Dr. Kenny called in Dr. Gray of Providence. The n[urse] told me that the result of their examination was that he is a very sick man, might remain so for a long time, might recover, might die any moment, and if he lived would probably be a permanent invalid, that he could never occupy himself with any thing that would give him the least excitement; his pulse is normal, but the heart in no way corresponds with it.[9]

On January 30, 1912, Dom Chouteau himself entered the fray, no doubt having heard that Oger was accusing him of having put pressure on Oger to accept the paternity of the Valley. Writing to the General, he denied the allegation and accused Oger in turn of having made use of Mistassini and Petit Clairvaux to improve the financial situation of Oka.[10] Ever prodigal with his advice, Chouteau suggested the General insist that Oger continue as Father Immediate of the Valley and apply himself to the task of seeing the monastery through this difficult period. The General accepted the suggestion and wrote Oger on February 1 to inform him of the decision.[11] He assured Oger of his support for both the community of Oka and that of the Valley. Oger wrote to Murphy to announce this decision, carefully noting the General's precise words:

> It is absolutely necessary that the administration of Our Lady of the Valley be assured and until future order, this is the responsibility of Your Paternity. I ask you therefore to accept this charge and to do what is necessary. . . . I would like to believe that in this connection Your Paternity will meet with no difficulty either on the part of the community of the Valley or of that of N.-D. du Lac.[12]

His letter also indicated that Murphy was to stop trying to reassume responsibility for the affairs of the community, acting against the orders of both his doctors and his major superiors. Indeed, Father John Mary, taking advantage of a slight rebound in his health, retorted with a letter to the General complaining of Oger's interference at the Valley during his visit there![13]

Murphy was still in the hospital in early March. He had apparently written to Oger to ask pardon. Oger decided to return once again to Rhode Island around March 6. He found Murphy considerably improved yet still hypersensitive, crying like a child over nothing. He now seemed willing to obey the counsels of the doctors and not concern himself with material administration.

On the other hand, Oger saw that the community itself was successfully weathering the storm. The materialities were in good shape, though they depended almost exclusively on the income from Mass intentions and the sale of milk. The brethren seemed to be full of good will and hopeful for the future.[14]

Oger kept in touch with the General during his stay at the Valley. One of his letters written after he had been there for eighteen days reflects his considered opinion of the situation. First of all, he offers a concrete picture of Murphy's condition:

> We find in the Reverend Father two persons almost diametrically opposite to one another. He is good, pious, devoted, affectionate, grateful, firm. Alongside that there is the sick man (and this dates back at least two years.) He is hard to deal with, gruff; he takes part in almost none of the religious exercises, and not being able to do so, he seems to relate everything to himself. He is very severe with others, very exigent towards himself, harsh; he does not listen to observations made to him, and lets himself be exploited by one or other layman, yet not accepting anything from his religious. For example, a self-styled master of singing (almost unlettered) was received as a choir oblate, and put in charge of directing the choir.

As for the community itself, he continued to be optimistic:

> The community (which is now composed of twenty-five members, twelve in choir—including the prior who will return God knows when—and twelve laybrothers) seems to me truly very good, very well disposed. Frankly I believe that there is a much better spirit here than at our place or at Mistassini.

I am convinced that it is best to leave things *in statu quo*, with Father John (who seems to give satisfaction to all, even to the Reverend Father) and a cellarer (I recommend Father Benedict who made stability on Thursday), and Father Alberic for finances. Everything should go very well, as long as the prior leaves things alone; it is an abnormal situation, but it seems to me to be the only possible one, and that perhaps for a long time.[15]

The three old diocesan priests were hanging on, still taking care of the garden. Not everything was in order, however. Oger had noted a number of violations of "regularity" that needed to be addressed. One of these involved the old problem of secular presence at the Valley: "On feastdays the house is invaded by women and girls, several of whom [the helpers of Brother Richard] pass the day in the parlor which is transformed into a small store."

The one bright spot on Murphy's horizon was his hope of spending a period of convalescence at Gethsemani or at Oka, but it was never to be. Oger set off for home towards the end of the month, sending the General one last analysis of the situation and revealing his still lingering love for one whom he once called his "dear prior":

> I repeat, Reverend Father, what I have already several times said and written. Father Jean Marie Murphy was a model religious with us and certainly a model prior. I made the very big mistake and caused a great ill both for him and for myself in releasing him in 1898 in order to please the abbot of Bellefontaine, trying to save Petit Clairvaux. As with others placed in a situation for which he was not prepared, he did his best, [but] did *not* succeed and in the process lost his head. At least he always had the esteem (though not full approval) of his religious, of his superiors and of his numerous friends. Personally, despite the remarks that, in conscience, I was obliged to make, I hold him in esteem and love him deeply and am still disposed to do all in my power to spare him pain and worry.[16]

Murphy apparently returned to the Valley from the hospital towards the end of April.[17] Shortly before his return, a young friend of the community of Oka paid a visit to him in the hospital. His description of Father John Mary's behavior suggests the possibility that he was suffering from Alzheimer's disease:

> I found him in fairly good condition physically and mentally, but I found him also very irritable, easily disturbed and confused; he cannot

without great effort say the Divine Office; he gets so easily confused. The least thing causes him to lose control of himself, so that after a slight disturbance or distraction caused accidentally or otherwise, he gets so mixed up that he has to stop; he does not know where to look for the different parts of the Office in [the] breviary."[18]

Malloy describes the state of affairs after Father John Mary's return to the Valley:

Soon after Easter he received the last sacraments, and recuperated somewhat, so as to be able to go about the house and sit on the veranda. On warm summer days he even ventured out to the roadside, and could be seen sitting on a stone trying to say his Office—meanwhile recounting to passersby who approached him, the hardships of the new foundation.[19]

Oger returned to the Valley on May 27 and found that things had not changed a great deal. Concerned about an eventual successor to Murphy, he was of still of the opinion that Father John O'Connor was not the man for the job. He himself still wanted to be relieved of the function of Father Immediate. Chouteau by now had also come around to this point of view. In a letter he wrote to the General on July 9, 1912, after a diatribe with his usual criticisms of Oger's administration, he admitted that Oger was not the person apt to solve the Valley's problems. Nor did he feel that Bellefontaine was in a position to undertake this role once again. Instead he proposed that Dom Edmund Obrecht of Gethsemani be named Father Immediate and that, beforehand, he be sent to informally visit the monastery in order to sound out the feelings of the community and to get an idea of the general situation. Father John Mary should resign as prior for reasons of health alone and a "simple superior" be named for the present.

⧉ A Change of Paternity

Ever attentive to the counsels of Chouteau, the General set in motion a process that began with a visit of Obrecht to the Valley, probably on his trip through the Northeast as he headed for the General Chapter of 1912. Oger himself came to the Valley for the occasion. Obrecht appeared with an official mandate of the General and outlined to the community the plan for the change in Father Immediate. Judging from a letter that Father Remi wrote to the General, the proposal seems to have been acceptable to the community.[20] The General Chapter approved this plan in its decision of September 15:

> The Reverend Father Abbot and the community of Our Lady of the Lake having asked to be relieved of the function of Father Immediate of Our Lady of the Valley, the General Chapter, after having heard the reasons for and against the proposal, decides that this house will provisionally pass over for a year to the paternity of the Reverend Father Abbot of Gethsemani, who will at the same time be administrator of the monastery until the Reverend Father Prior's complete recovery.[21]

Thus, instead of asking for the resignation of Father John Mary and appointing a temporary superior, Obrecht would not only become the new Father Immediate but would also become the administrator of the monastery.[22] Even though nothing is said of this in the chapter's decision, the subprior, Father John O'Connor, would continue to function as Obrecht's representative on a day-to-day basis.

On November 15 Murphy penned his last surviving letter. It was written to his old friend, the contractor Denis Shea, who had written to Murphy to thank him for being present at the funeral services for his wife. Murphy's letter was typed for him, but it is signed in the familiar self-confident hand, only slightly shaken by his illness. "I will never forget you in our prayers and good works as long as I live, and the Community will do likewise for you as long as the Monastery endures."[23]

Obrecht was on hand once again in April 1913, when along with Father John O'Connor he paid a visit to the bishop to announce somewhat belatedly that he had been appointed Father Immediate and acting superior of the monastery and to brief the bishop on conditions at the monastery. In the words of Bishop Harkins: "The Abbot of Gethsemani Obrecht—with Father John, SubPrior of Lonsdale—called about condition of monastery. Said too much exterior life there. Has been appointed to charge on account of Prior Murphy's illness. I took faculties (*ad extram*) away from all the inmates except Father John."

We have no record of the happenings of the ensuing months, until the summer of 1913.[24] On July 6, 1913, at four o'clock in the morning, John Mary Murphy died. His death was recorded in various local newspapers, some of which took the opportunity to recall the general outline of his life, and even to present a summary of the monastery's history in Cumberland.[25]

The funeral took place on July 8. Various priests and religious of the surrounding area were present, along with Monsignor Doran, Vicar General of the diocese.

John Mary Murphy died at the relatively young age of 64. Looking back at his career as superior of Petit Clairvaux and Our Lady of the Valley, one cannot help but marvel at how much he accomplished in the short period from 1898 to 1902: obtaining single-handedly the approbation of the General Chapter for the move to Rhode Island; the actual transfer itself with all the materialities involved, and the building of a temporary monastery, followed very shortly by a wing of a permanent monastery. Unfortunately little is known of the later years of his regime due to the absence of detailed documentation. If his final years accentuated some of his less desirable character traits, much of this can be attributed to his debilitating illness.

On August 1, less than a month after his death, his longtime superior and old friend Dom Antoine Oger also died. He was succeeded by Dom Pacôme Gaboury, whose election was confirmed by the Abbot General on November 7, 1913.

The General Chapter that met in September decided to prolong Dom Obrecht's mandate as administrator of the Valley one year more. Father John O'Connor would continue to function as superior of the house under the close supervision of Obrecht. The chapter also decided to permit the community a number of small departures from the rigors of the regulations.[26]

Father John O'Connor's mild manner must have come as a relief to the community after the long hard months of Murphy's illness, with his alternating fits of temper and depression. Yet years would go by before the regularization of his role as superior by means of a proper election. This was due in large measure to World War I, which made communications with Europe difficult. During those hard years the General Chapter never met. So Dom John would spend the time consolidating the community's strong points and letting peace seep back into the house.[27]

FIGURE 34. *Dom John O'Connor, acting superior and later Titular Prior of Our Lady of the Valley.*

Chapter Eighteen

Increasing Stability under Dom John O'Connor

✑ WORLD WAR I AND ITS AFTERMATH

ON AUGUST 1, 1914, war broke out in Europe, and it became impossible for the General Chapter to convene. This meant that the situation at the Valley could not be settled, and thus Dom Obrecht's "temporary" authority at the Valley was prolonged throughout the years of the conflict. In his role as administrator he kept a close eye on developments there, visiting three times in 1914 alone. Towards the end of February he stopped by for an "unofficial" visit on his return from a series of visitations in the Orient. In June he returned for the regular visitation.[1] Finally, in early October he returned once again. A pattern of semi-annual visits, one a regular visitation and the other an unofficial one, continued over the next few years.[2] On two occasions he brought back with him to Gethsemani a monk of the Valley for a brief visit. (In 1917 this was Dom John O'Connor himself.) In 1916 Obrecht noted with alarm that "several promising choir religious were in an advanced stage of tuberculosis."[3]

We have little information on life in the monastery during the war years. Father Remi writing to Dom Chouteau in France said that, apart from the inflation of prices, the monastery itself suffered little from the war. As far as food supplies went, the harvests these years had been good and were sufficient to provide for the needs of the community. With so many young people going off to war, however, vocations were rare.[4]

The war would have other consequences for the Order in North America. Several of the monks of the new Petit Clairvaux were recalled to France to fight. In addition to the loss of personnel, vocations were rare in Nova Scotia as in Rhode Island, and this inspired a proposal early in 1918 to close the monastery and bring the entire community back to Timadeuc. This motion was accepted by the chapter of Petit Clairvaux, and the community returned to France. On June 16 the property was sold to a lay association of Montreal.[5] Years later, on April 30, 1926, the bodies of the deceased members of the Timadeuc foundation at Petit Clairvaux were exhumed and transferred to the cemetery of Oka. On the occasion, Timadeuc's abbot Dom Dominic Nogues announced in an address to the parish of Tracadie that the bodies of the earlier monks of Petit Clairvaux would be transferred to a common grave in the cemetery of the parish.[6]

As the war headed towards its end in 1918, the Valley's finances took a decided turn for the better. The account books show an increase of almost $11,000 in liquid assets during that year. During his visitation in October Obrecht signed the ledger, as was the custom during visitations, noting: "Seen and approved the above statement which is very consoling."[7] (Obrecht had been similarly pleased with his inspection of the ledger in 1916.) This was but the beginning of a period of increasing stability. Sometime between 1919 and 1920 the liquid assets were for the first time greater than the debts. Until 1926 the assets continued to grow steadily, a fact noted each year with approval by Obrecht's congratulatory remarks in the ledger. In August 1922, Bishop Hickey visited the monastery to discuss "canceling old m[or]t[ga]ge."[8]

Obrecht consequently reduced his visits to the Valley, reverting to a single regular visitation in 1918, during which he announced his satisfaction with the way things were going.[9] Indeed, in 1919 there is no record of any visit at all!

The armistice of November 11, 1918, finally made it possible to plan for a General Chapter in 1919, but it was impossible to make arrangements in time, and the chapter was called off until the following year.[10]

In January of 1920 the Valley received a visit from Dom Chouteau and his traveling companion, Father Antoine Moussion of Bellefontaine. John O'Connor was waiting for them at the boat in New York and brought them to the Valley by train. Father Antoine wrote a delightful account of his visit, along with various impressions of American life. His remarks show clearly that he had a keen eye for the details of the farm operation. Of particular interest is his description of the barn buildings and the dairy operation:

> Built in wood, they are 25 meters long [82 ft.] (a little longer if you count several service areas) and six meters wide [19.7 ft.]. In the middle between the stalls there is a space of two meters, [6.6 ft.] serving as a passage way used for servicing the animals. Drinking water for the animals is supplied by pipes to troughs. These latter are emptied when it is time to feed the animals. They give them corn and cattle-cakes.[11] The corn is kept in large wooden constructions called silos. Everything is clean and well maintained. The livestock consists of fifty milk cows, a bull, and twelve young animals. These are in a separate building adjacent to the cow barn. The milk has a special taste I have not found elsewhere. It is sold as soon as the milking is completed. It is brought each morning to town in bottles of a liter or quarter liter according to the orders they receive.[12]

Father Antoine's overall view of the community was positive: "Regularity seems to reign in this holy house, the enclosure is rigorously observed, and outsiders have no contact with the inside." His account of the monastery's personnel is the first since the 1905 report made by Father John Mary for the Generalate.[13] There were twenty-three religious: fourteen choir monks (of whom two were novices and two oblates) and nine laybrothers (of whom four were novices). Father Antoine also noted that the living conditions for the monks were crowded, the larger portion of the building being given over for the use of guests, one of the first matters John O'Connor would address upon his election as titular prior in 1921.

The General Chapter, postponed from last year, met earlier than usual—from May 28 to June 8, 1920. Although Dom Obrecht arrived only in time for its last two meetings, Dom Pacôme of Oka requested that the Valley be given definitively to Gethsemani as its daughterhouse, a motion that was accepted by the assembly. No doubt the matter had been discussed by the two abbots beforehand. Dom John profited from his trip to the chapter by visiting Mount St. Bernard and Roscrea. According to Malloy, upon his return "he regaled us in chapter with his impressions, and gave us an inkling of the plans he is already forming in his mind for the conventual buildings on this site."[14] Dom John was already dreaming of the building program he would one day implement.

Dom Obrecht made his visitation of the Valley in October 1920. No doubt the question of regularizing the monastery's status by the election of a superior was discussed, but there is no written record of this. Afterwards, Obrecht brought Father Remi back with him to Gethsemani for a brief visit.[15]

✐ ELECTION OF DOM JOHN O'CONNOR AS PRIOR

An election finally took place at the Valley on April 11 of the following year, 1921. There was little doubt about the outcome: Dom John was the obvious choice.[16] Shortly after the election, the monastery lost a long-time friend and supporter when Bishop Harkins died on May 25, 1921. He was succeeded by Bishop Hickey, who had been his coadjutor for just over two years.

The community's statistics sent in to Rome in 1921 show that by that year it had grown to thirty-two members from twenty-seven the preceding year and from fifteen in 1905 (the date of the last official report that has survived), this despite the turmoil of Dom John Mary's last years as well as the experience of the war years. The four years following Dom John O'Connor's election as prior were years of consolidation and slow growth in the number of monks. Later on in 1930 there would be a noteworthy rise in numbers, linked to a new project that was in the air.

Dom John O'Connor, now titular prior of the monastery, would set out to lay the foundations of the monastery's future development. A remark in Malloy's *Annals* for 1919 shows that he was already thinking great thoughts, attempting to do what he could to bring the monastery more closely into the orbit of the entire Order and not just that of the American houses:

> He intends, God willing, to visit a goodly number of our European houses to imbibe their spirit, observe their ceremonies and chant, and especially to study their buildings in view of planning the best possible monastery for Our Lady of the Valley.[17]

John's interest in the architecture of the European monasteries did not go unnoticed by his Father Immediate. Considering certain improvements at Gethsemani itself, in December 1921 Obrecht invited Dom John and Dom Pacôme of Oka for a visit to discuss his own plans.[18] As for the Valley, the question of a building program was high on John's list of priorities, since he saw the desperate need for additional living space for the monks. This plan would be made possible by the increasing financial stability of the monastery. He was thinking of mak-ing the existing building the point of departure for a typical monastic quadrangle. At first the plan was to begin by building a wing perpen-dicular to the original 1902 building at its northern edge, followed by a third wing perpendicular to the north wing and parallel to the old build-ing. The final step would have been the creation of a monastic church on the fourth side.[19]

By 1922, however, a bold new idea emerged: to begin with the con-struction of the church. Dom Obrecht may well have instigated the change by persuading Dom John that the presence of a fine monastic church would stimulate an increase in the number of vocations (he would prove to be correct). On February 18 Father Augustine O'Brien paid a visit to Providence's new bishop, Bishop Hickey, to outline the project for the new church and monastery. Later, on April 4, Augustine returned to ask the bishop's permission to solicit funds in the parishes of the diocese "for the new monastery church at Lonsdale." The bishop agreed to this, "if the monastery agreed to accept Providence clergy as guests when desired by Bishop."[20] By the fall, the project had sufficiently matured in the mind of Father John, and he decided to present a peti-tion to the General Chapter of 1922 for permission to build the church. The chapter agreed: "The community of Our Lady of the Valley is authorized to build the church of its monastery for a sum of $75,000, according to a plan that has been approved."[21]

The General Chapter was also noteworthy for the fact that Dom Augustin Marre, feeling unable to continue as Abbot General, offered his resignation. An extraordinary chapter was convoked to elect his suc-cessor, and the date was set for November 13. In order to be present at this important meeting Dom John probably spent the two intervening months in Europe, since Malloy relates that it was in this year that he visited a number of monasteries, among them Bellefontaine, Melleray, and Timadeuc. On the duly appointed day, the forty-six capitulants elected the abbot of Melleray, Dom Jean-Baptiste Ollitrault de Kéryvallan, as successor to Dom Marre.

The chapter's approval of the plans for the new church was a first step. The actual work on the building would begin only in the spring of 1924. For the moment Father John set his mind to the development of the monastery's farm. Brother Michael Holland was one of his most important aides in the expansion program on the farm. The story was that as a boy he had served in the Northwestern Royal Canadian

Mounted Police before becoming a seminarian.[22] He decided to enter the Valley on January 1, 1914, while still in his philosophy course, going on to simple profession in 1916 and solemn profession on April 21, 1919. Around 1920 he contracted tuberculosis, but eventually his health improved, and by 1921 he had been assigned the important role of cellarer in the monastery. An article in the *Providence Journal* described his many activities in this capacity. [23]

The article noted that he improved the milking herd by introducing new animals to replace older ones, with the result that the monastery was able to sell 250 quarts of milk a day. He also purchased the first tractor in the monastery's history. Since it was a sturdy caterpillar tractor, he boldly used it to plow some of the outer limits of the bog lands, on which he planted crops. Though his first experiments with growing vegetables there produced meager results, the monks continued to make hay on the bog well into the 1940s, the old tractor still going strong.[24] Michael also expanded the poultry operation thanks to the installation of a large incubator, and a section of the woods was cleared and subdivided for a new hennery. Both poultry and eggs were sold.

Another new monk, Brother Hugh Fagan, a native Rhode Islander, would soon begin to play an important role in Dom John's administration. Trained as an engineer, Hugh entered the Valley in 1918, and even before his solemn profession in 1924, Dom John gave him the mission of inspecting prospective sites around Rhode Island for a possible transfer of the monastery.[25] This might seem odd since the decision had already been made to build a full-scale church for the monastery at Lonsdale. Perhaps it was one last check on the possibilities of finding a better location than Cumberland before going ahead with two important projects: the ambitious building program and the acquisition of a series of eight new parcels of land adjacent to the monastery's holdings. In the event, Brother Hugh found nothing more suitable in terms of size or soil quality, so the eight parcels were purchased from various owners in the fall.[26] Dom Obrecht no doubt approved this plan during his visitation in the spring.[27] The parcels formed a compact group and lay along the western boundary of the monastery's existing property. One small additional parcel was acquired in 1926 along the eastern side, the only further enlargement of the property until 1944. Now that they were staying at the Valley, the monks had to face up to the fact that with the increase of motorized traffic along Diamond Hill Road life would not be as tranquil as it had been in earlier years.

Sometime before leaving for the chapter in September, John visited Bishop Hickey to bring up once more the question of collections for the new building, though there are no details of how the meeting went.[28] A somber note was, however, struck by a letter that John received from Cardinal Dougherty complaining of questionable fundraising attempts being made in his archdiocese by certain laymen purporting to be agents for the Valley. They were offering "enrollment certificates" in the monastery's list of benefactors in exchange for an "an enrollment fee" of $3.00.[29] This matter cannot have escaped the attention of Dom Obrecht, who was a friend of Dougherty's, and it would be brought up later at the General Chapter of 1924.

John took the opportunity while in Europe to visit the monasteries of la Trappe, Westmalle, and Tilburg, no doubt still gathering ideas for the building program soon to begin at the Valley.

∽ THE BUILDING OF A NEW CHURCH

The great event of 1924 was the beginning of work on the new church. John had turned once again to the monastery's longstanding friend, the architect Ambrose Murphy. By this time Murphy had become well known in the field of Catholic ecclesiastical architecture, and in March 1923 he had just finished the new headquarters of the diocesan newspaper, *The Providence Visitor*. The groundbreaking took place on April 7 and initiated a long period of digging the foundations. Malloy's account provides more information about the project:

> Plans, drawn in the office of Mr. Ambrose Murphy, largely by his assistant, Samuel Morino (a Jewish convert), reflected beautifully the ideas gathered by Father Prior in the course of his visits to our European monasteries. They show a complete monastery in the Tudor Gothic style, built around a quadrangle in the traditional arrangement. The church will measure 100 x 40 feet, with 7 radiating apsidal chapels and one side aisle, that on the gospel side; the aisle on the epistle side will serve as part of the cloister.
>
> Ground was broken Monday, April 7 (mid-lent) and work on foundations proceeded very slowly, as we had to blast every foot out of the solid rock. The excavations were not even completed at the end of the year. Meantime, classes and much of the other work were suspended, and all hands worked in our fine quarry of blue-gray granite, on the hillside about a quarter of a mile to the north-west of the monastery site. Brother Hugh, a graduate civil engineer, is in charge of

this part of the work, while construction is being supervised by Frater Michael, now apparently completely recovered from tuberculosis.[30]

Once again we find Brothers Hugh and Michael to the fore on two key positions in the building project. We also catch some flavor of the hectic pace of the monks' work program. Apparently the new quarry had already been opened while the monks were still busy on the foundations. To prepare for the quarry work a monk had been sent to quarries in Vermont, New Hampshire, Kentucky and Canada to acquire the skills needed to man the operation.[31] Despite all the energy expended it was impossible to finish the foundations by the coming of what was to prove a severe winter that lingered on until the following April.[32] No doubt the community greeted the interruption of this strenuous activity as a welcome relief.

Not long after the groundbreaking ceremony Father John was invited to the celebrations that took place on May 21, 1924 at Gethsemani in honor of a triple jubilee: the diamond jubilee of the abbey's foundation, the golden jubilee of Obrecht's entrance into the Order, and the silver jubilee of his abbatial blessing. John served with Father Frederic Dunne as assistant to the jubilarian and was granted the privilege of sitting at the abbatial table during the banquet.[33] On May 24, only three days after the celebrations, Gethsemani's visitation began under the direction of its Father Immediate, Dom Ambrose Bec of Melleray, assisted apparently by Dom Arsène Maurel of Bonnecombe. Dom John was put to work again, this time as translator not only for the scrutinies but also for the abbot's chapter talk. He also helped prepare the visitation card.

Father John left Gethsemani on May 30 and was home only a short time before Obrecht came in early June for the Valley's own visitation.[34] Obrecht signed the account books, adding his by now familiar congratulatory remarks. Obrecht apparently deemed it no longer necessary to keep such close tabs on the monastery's financial status: The books were left unsigned for the next several years.

Dom John did not assist at the General Chapter of 1924, but he learned from the *Acts* of the chapter that he had been singled out for steps he had taken to raise funds for the building project:

> The General Chapter . . . finds fault with the Father Prior of Our Lady of the Valley for not having forbidden the sending of circulars

with brochures designed to bring in offerings in exchange for a simple remembrance at the Masses celebrated in the monastery on November 2 . . . . Furthermore the General Chapter learned with displeasure of certain precise details concerning what amounts to setting up a tariff for diplomas of affiliation that the monastery of the Valley sends around, and also concerning the various methods of fundraising used by this house, and finally the use for this purpose of lay agents, even Protestants and Jews, and even what might be called a sale at a fixed rate for participation in the prayers and penances of the community, for which these agents receive a large commission.[35]

He was ordered to see to it that such practices were discontinued and was told to inform the monastery's council of the reprimand. Finally, he was to give an account to his Father Immediate of the steps he had taken to correct the matter.

The chapter struck a more positive note in its decision to extend voting rights to *all* solemnly professed choir monks throughout the entire Order—not limiting the vote to those who were priests, as had been the case earlier on.

When the spring thaw finally arrived at the Valley in April 1925, the digging of the foundations resumed. The original contractor had proved unsatisfactory and a new one was hired,[36] but it turned out to be a bad decision: The new contractor eventually went bankrupt, leaving the monastery with an additional burden of a $40,000 debt.[37] Meanwhile, though, the concrete foundations were finally poured in May, and by July all was in readiness for the laying of the cornerstone, which took place on July 6 with Bishop Hickey officiating.[38] The *Providence Journal* offered ample coverage of the event in four separate articles. Work in the quarry was now stepped up to provide materials for the church walls. The newspaper's reporter paid a visit to the quarry site and wrote:

> The walls of the chapel are steadily mounting, and already 350 loads of granite have been quarried by the contemplative order. The foreman brother and the engineer have averaged 12 to 14 hours a day in the quarry since the work started, and they face about 11 weeks more of strenuous work.
>
> The brothers and the novices, the latter in charge of a priest, work two shifts a day, from 7 to 11 in the morning and from 2 until 6 o'clock in the afternoon.

. . . The foreman runs the compressed air drill, the engineer and an assistant man the windlass, others stand ready with crowbars and levers, while still others load the truck and clean away the rubble.[39]

All of this work was taking its toll on finances, and in August O'Connor managed to get an indult to borrow $30,000 over and above the $75,000 for which permission had already been given. This brought the total sum to more than $100,000. The overall cost would have been even greater had the granite used in the building not been free and the monks not contributed a considerable amount of the labor. The *Providence Journal* reported that a realistic figure would have been more like $200,000.[40]

In September Dom John attended the 1925 General Chapter while work continued on the exterior of the church. By the fall the roof was in place, although a terrible accident occurred in October: An elevator car came crashing to the ground from the top of the construction, killing two men and injuring four others.[41]

By 1926 work was progressing on the interior, with the erection of a false Gothic vault.[42] The church furnishings were also being planned. At Brother Michael's request Oka provided a model of its choir stalls for the carpenters to follow.[43] Work was delayed by a flu epidemic that raged through the community in March and April. According to Malloy's account, at one point thirty monks were confined to bed at the same time. Three died: the guestmaster Brother Joseph Gilmartin, Brother Charles Lavoie, and the ever famous Father Joseph Conaghan, erstwhile Columban of Petit Clairvaux.[44] The *Providence Journal* had this to say in its obituary:

> The dead man was widely known to the community surrounding the monastery as the confessor and corresponding secretary of the Order. In life he was James J. Conaghan. For 40 years he had been a member of the Trappist Order of monks. He was born in Ireland, March 30, 1853. Prior to his joining the Order he was a secular priest and formerly professor of theology at Maynooth College, Ireland, later becoming curate at St. Patrick's Church, Glasgow, Scotland, from which he came to the United States. He came to the Cumberland monastery from the Tracadee, N. S. [sic] community of the Order in 1901.[45]

Thanks to the ministrations of the monastery's infirmarian, the faithful Brother Dominic, the rest of the community pulled through the flu epidemic. Father Bernard Demers, however, was so weakened by his illness that he had to be replaced as novice master by Father Benedict Barré, who had held the position before Father Bernard.

On May 14, 1926, Dom Obrecht left for the visitation of the Valley, where he was able to see the progress on the new building. By August 1 the *Providence Journal* could report that the staging had been completely removed from the outside of the church and that the gilded cross had been placed on the spire, which towered 170 feet above the ground.

Dom John did not attend the General Chapter in 1926, but Dom Obrecht on his return from Europe visited the Valley and decided to bring Dom John to Gethsemani for a rest after what seems to have been a serious illness that began around Easter, as we learn in a letter of O'Connor to Dom Pacôme:

> Since Easter I have been incapable of doing anything. I had a "nervous breakdown." It has now turned into insomnia. I am still in the infirmary. I am not allowed to transact any business, not even to write letters. This is why you do not hear from me. I ask you to make a memento of me in your Mass every day, as I am anxious to return to the Community.[46]

The stress of the great building project was no doubt beginning to take its toll on John. This bout with nerves is the first mention of an illness that would plague him more and more as time went on. The end of the year brought still one more woe—by now a somewhat familiar one for the community. On December 9 a fire broke out in the engine room, disabling the pump that brought water to the house, and thus to answer their everyday needs the monks were forced to "carry water by hand from the seven adjoining springs about 400 yards from the monastery."[47] Brother Michael Holland somehow found enough quiet time in the midst of his concerns for the building project to prepare for his ordination to the priesthood, which took place on December 17, 1927.

With the increasing expenses of construction, Bishop Hickey underwrote a note of $30,000 for the monastery, and according to an article in the *Providence Journal* of March 20, 1927, Father John informed the writer that this was the only outstanding debt for the building.[48] The same article offered its readers a detailed description of what the new building was beginning to look like, pointing out the particularities of the Cistercian tradition not found in parish churches.[49] These included such items as the presence of the spire over the crossing of nave and transept; the *jube*, or as the article calls it, *ambone*, which divided the area of the choir monks from that of the laybrothers; and the general simplicity of the lines of the building. The traditional plan was modified by closing off the north side aisle of the building from the main body of the church so as to form a cloister that would give added space for the monks' use outside the church proper.

Hopes were running high for a dedication of the building around Easter, but this was put off for another year and a half.[50] There is no record of just when the monks began to celebrate services in the new church, if indeed they did so at all before the dedication on November 21, 1928. Dom Obrecht dropped in for a brief visit in April on his way to meet the Abbot General in New York (stopping in as well to visit Cardinal Dougherty in Philadelphia).[51] No doubt he was curious to see the progress on the church.

The record remains quiet for the second half of 1927 and the early months of 1928, but on Memorial Day of 1928 (May 30) a patriotic commemoration was organized in the woods near the monastery at a spot where nine English colonists were massacred by Indians in 1676. A small monument constructed by Father Benedict was dedicated.

The summer of 1928 brought a visit from the new Abbot General, Dom Ollitrault de Kéryvallan, on his way back to Europe after a visit to New Melleray in Iowa. He was accompanied by Dom Obrecht, who had met him in Philadelphia.[52] The visit made enough of a stir to merit an article in the *Providence Journal*, which noted that "the visit is in the form of an official inspection." Indeed this was a true visitation, as is shown by the signature of the Abbot General in the account books. Obrecht probably accompanied the General to the boat in New York and eventually returned to Gethsemani, bringing one of the Valley monks for a brief visit, as by now had become the custom. This time it was Father Benedict's turn.[53]

Chapter Nineteen

A New Church

T HE MOST NOTEWORTHY EVENT of 1928 was the dedication of the new monastery church by Bishop Hickey of Providence on November 21.[1] Attended by many parish priests and religious as well as by the laity, the dedication was covered in a lengthy article in the next day's *Providence Journal,* which provided long lists of guests' names, including local altar boys who, by way of exception, were permitted to serve for the occasion.[2] A series of photos shows various stages in the procession from monastery to church: the bishop flanked by his ministers, visiting clergy, monks and, bringing up the rear, the laity, as they all clamber up the steep steps leading into the new building.

The new church was a conspicuous feature in what was then a rural area. Of generous proportions, it measured 170 feet by 60 feet and was oriented from west to east, with its entrance situated on the east. A flight of ten steps led up to this entrance, which was considerably higher than ground level, since the floor level of the church was planned to be on the same level as the first floor of the older building. The overall effect of its architectural mass was emphasized by the additional stories that lay beneath the church itself. These offered considerable space for other monastic activities, which now could be transferred from the crowded 1902 building.

A first level below the church mirrored the plan of the church itself. Immediately under the western end was the choir novitiate, which was

FIGURE 35. *Our Lady of the Valley. The new church and the 1902 monastery building.*

transferred from the second floor of the old building. This included a reading room, a dormitory, various parlors, and an office for the Father Master. The laybrother novices would now have more space in what had been the old common novitiate.

The community refectory was also transferred from the basement of the old building to an ample space underneath the western end of the church's nave. Farther east, additional dining areas were carved out for the lay workmen of the monastery and for the infirm, who alone were permitted to eat meat. Finally, a section running along the northern side of this level was laid out as a changing room for the choir monks.

The downward slope of the terrain at the western end of the church allowed for another, still lower floor of limited extension, which served for storage and various work-oriented activities.[3]

The facade of the church lay along approximately the same line as the facade of the older building and might have seemed like a prolongation of it, albeit in much finer stonework. Inside the church, the area immediately behind the facade was intended for transient visitors. Although separated from the main body of the church by a grille, it must have seemed a big improvement to those who had experienced the crowded and improvised space in the foyer of the old building, where visitors were separated from the old chapel by another room (the chapter) through which they had to peer in order to assist at the services as best they could.

Above this area was a tribune reserved for retreatants. Here the visitor had a splendid view of the entire building unhampered by a grille. A large lancet window in the facade offered ample illumination. The nave extended seven bays east of the tribune, the whole lit by a series of clerestory windows above, and its vaults supported on four-centered arches below. On the south side these arches opened into a side aisle. On the north side, however, the space normally occupied by a side aisle was walled off from the church to provide a new cloister for the monks' use. Nonetheless, the piers and arches of the south side were mirrored on this wall by blind arches of similar design.[4]

As the *Providence Journal* had noted during the construction, certain features of the new church would surprise those accustomed to the typical layout of a parish church. The nave was divided into two sections by the *jube*, which looked like a bridge extending from one side to the other, separating the area of the choir monks from that of the laybrothers, in keeping with the traditional Cistercian plan. (Fig. 37) It served as an elevated platform from which lessons were read during certain services.[5] A large crucifix was eventually set up on top of the platform, facing the tribune of the guests.[6] (Fig. 38)

The laybrothers' choir, which was situated immediately adjacent to the visitor's chapel near the entrance of the church, occupied only two bays of the church, given the relatively small number of brothers. Their stalls were consequently arranged in short rows facing the altar and were divided by a central aisle into two blocks of twenty stalls each. There were thus more than enough places for the sixteen brothers on hand at the time.[7] (Fig. 37)

In the monks' choir, west of the jube, the monks' seats, or stalls, were arranged not in rows facing the altar as in parish churches but in two parallel lines on each side of the church, the two choirs facing each other.

At the end of this visual sequence lay the sanctuary, its altar framed by a semicircular series of arches similar to those in the nave. Above the altar at the clerestory level, a central niche held a statue of Our Lady of Victories, which served as a focal point for the "Salve Regina" sung solemnly each evening at the end of Compline. (Fig. 39) Six large windows, three on each side of the niche, provided ample light for the sanctuary.

Between the semicircle of arches and the rear wall was one of the

FIGURE 36. *Our Lady of the Valley. Abbey church. Nave seen from the north transept.*

church's most distinctive features. In the great pilgrimage churches of Europe, this area, known as the ambulatory, served as a passageway around the back of the altar for pilgrims who had come to venerate the relics incorporated into the altar. It typically connected with the side aisles, permitting an orderly flow of pious traffic without disturbing the tranquillity of any ongoing services in these churches, which were often part of monastic establishments. The ambulatory not only provided a "cushion" of space behind the sanctuary but also offered an alluring vista into an area the shape of which could only be partially deciphered by observers in the nave of the church itself.

This plan was not uncommon in some of the larger Cistercian abbeys. From a practical point of view it enabled the placement of additional altars for the daily private Masses celebrated by the often numerous priests of monastic communities during the Middle Ages. In this space at the Valley there were seven altars in addition to the main altar and others in various parts of the church.

FIGURE 37. *(above) Our Lady of the Valley. Abbey church. The choir of the laybrothers with the two altars for the celebration of Masses for living and dead relatives, friends, and benefactors.*

FIGURE 38. *(left) Our Lady of the Valley. Abbey church. Nave seen from the tribune of the retreatants. The jube is in the foreground.*

FIGURE 39. *(left) Our Lady of the Valley. Abbey church. Sanctuary, with the new altar installed in 1945.*

FIGURE 40. *(below) Our Lady of the Valley. Abbey Church. The choir of the monks and the sanctuary seen from the jube. The altar shown is the original one. To the right, the tribune of the infirm.*

Though not so much in evidence from the nave, another important zone of the church was the transept, which intersected the main axis of the nave between the monks' choir and the sanctuary. The bell tower was placed over this point of crossing, a feature that was common, though not universal in the Cistercian tradition. The prominent point in the middle of the church where the bell ropes came down was the scene of a picturesque, albeit unintentional, "dance" by the two monks who rang the bells at the beginning of Offices.(Fig. 40)

The transept was perhaps most in evidence because it interrupted the otherwise continuous flow of arches in the nave and the sanctuary area. More subtly, however, it functioned as something of a buffer zone of empty space between the choir and the sanctuary. There was a special quality to the light here, coming in from a large lancet window on the south wall. Although otherwise largely devoid of objects, the transept housed two altars that further served the needs of the priests, one dedicated to St. Joseph beneath the south window, and another to St. Michael beneath the infirmary tribune on the north.

A unique feature of the transept was the tribune on its north side. This was designed to link up with a projected west wing of the monastery itself, whose second floor would contain rooms for the infirm and the aged monks. The tribune, which was situated on the same level as these rooms, would be easily accessible to these monks and enable them to assist at the liturgical services in church.[8]

For all its architectural splendor, the new church would only gradually receive appropriate furnishings. Although a new main altar was constructed for the building, various older altars, some from the earlier church but most from Petit Clairvaux, were brought in for the ambulatory, transepts, and brothers' choir—where two were needed for the daily Masses for living and dead benefactors, relatives, and friends of the community. (Fig. 37) Other liturgical items from the venerable old Nova Scotia monastery also found their way into the new building, many of them still in use today at Spencer.

Less auspicious was the placement of a large crucifix directly on the tabernacle of the main altar.[9] Bishop Hickey, visiting the monastery before the blessing of the new church in 1928, had seen this arrangement and noted his displeasure. So the crucifix was moved to the southwest corner of the south transept, and totally new fittings were created for the altar. These included, along with new candlesticks, a new crucifix of more modest size and a throne for exposition of the Blessed

Sacrament surmounted by a baldachino.

Adding to the overall modesty of the furnishings, the many windows were, for the time being, filled with plain glass. It would be for the coming generations of young monks to deploy their talents in providing more suitable fittings for their new church.

Nevertheless, Dom John O'Connor could take satisfaction in the new building. Apart from its architectural merits, as well as the alleviation it provided from the crowded living conditions in the old building, its construction was something of a watershed in the history of the Valley. The symbolic value of its sheer architectural mass towering above the Cumberland landscape was a message sent to the world that, after long hard years of struggle, the monastery had finally settled down to a period of stability—with its own elected superior, a good measure of economic security, and, as figures would soon show, an increasing appeal to the youth not only of Rhode Island but of the entire northeast of the United States and beyond.

The personnel lists show a gradual increase for the next few years. While the number of professed monks remained rather stable between 1928 and 1932, there was a notable increase in the number of novices. Most of these newcomers were choir novices: between six and twelve during these years, while the brother novices were only between one and three. On the other hand, those who chose the life of oblates tended to be more numerous among the laybrothers than among the choir monks.

In April, with the work on the church behind them, the monks set out on the construction of a new road that would offer better access to the important area of the barns.[10] (Fig. 29) Beginning where one day the porter's lodge would be built, it branched off from the access road to the monastery, tracing a wide arc to the north that gave the monastic buildings ample berth. The new road was built at the monks' expense, and the two heroes of the operation were Brother Hugh and an old steam shovel donated by Frederick J. Quinn. (This shovel would be the trademark of Brother Hugh throughout his entire career; it even accompanied him to Spencer.) (Fig. 46)

On January 1, 1929, we find once again a group of signatures in the account books: Father John, Father Benedict and, for the first time, Father Michael Holland. In February the Order's Abbot General, Dom Ollitrault de Kéryvallan, died, and the General Chapter met earlier than usual to elect his successor. Dom John attended this extraordinary session, which took place on July 15–20. The man chosen as the new

General was Dom Herman-Joseph Smets.

This change in date for the General Chapter made it possible for Gethsemani to host still another Golden Jubilee, this time that of the priestly ordination of its abbot, Dom Obrecht, on September 19. Dom John naturally attended and is singled out in the Gethsemani Annals as having "delivered the occasional sermon."[11] Not very long after, Dom Obrecht came to the Valley for the yearly visitation in November, once again visiting Cardinal Dougherty, who was preparing to leave for Rome for the celebration of the Golden Jubilee of the Pope.[12]

Obrecht's visitation report sent to the General in Rome shows that though the monastery no longer had any significant debts, it still needed to make improvements in a number of areas. The program of studies for the priesthood left much to be desired. Certain of the monks were still going out to serve in parishes on Sundays. Family visits to the monks were frequent and protracted. The guesthouse too was a source of concern; there was insufficient separation of the guests from the community, and the guestmaster was described as being too talkative.[13]

From the time of this visitation, reports by the visitor begin to appear in the archives of the Order's Generalate. These are of special interest since they offer a fuller insight into the monastery's situation than one finds in the visitation cards given to the community itself. For one thing, the answers to a series of questions on a form sheet provide a kind of check on the monastery's fidelity to observances and the general spiritual condition of the members. Further interesting remarks, such as those noted above for 1929, are sometimes recorded in a space for "Observations." Later on, the visitor would frequently append an additional document pinpointing still further the state of the community.

The 1929 report also included the first mention of a plan to begin construction of a third wing of the monastic quadrangle. In light of the monastery's economic stability Obrecht was happy to lend the project his support. In fact, plans had already been drawn up and approved by the General Chapter.

Chapter Twenty

The 1930s: Enter Malloy

O N OCTOBER 19, 1930, Father John F. Malloy, member of the Congregation of the Holy Spirit, exchanged his black robe for the white habit of a Cistercian novice. The oldest among seven other choir novices, he brought with him many years of experience as a priest and an educator. He had been a professor and prefect of discipline at Duquesne University High School between 1912 and 1925. Such a person would be a great boon to a community that after many years' existence was still trying to set afoot a viable program of studies for its prospective priests.

For us his special importance lies in the fact that, throughout his religious life, he kept a journal in which he recorded almost daily the events of the community. Thus, for the first time in the history of Petit Clairvaux and the Valley, we get a day-by-day account of life in the monastery, from the point of view of a novice but one who had long experience of religious life before entering the monastery.

After six weeks of relative euphoria, loneliness struck as he was preparing for the day of his reception of the habit:

> I had my "agony in the garden"; for several hours as I strove in vain to meditate, an ill-defined unrest seemed to be gathering force. I went into the orchard to say, in spite of it, the Rosary (with the sorrowful mysteries) and had a terrible cry; it must have been caused by loneliness—away so long from all the people and things I have been busy

with, among total strangers, never hearing a word, cheerful or otherwise. I had not expected solitude to have this effect on me. My answer to this temptation, these foolish sobs of self-pity, was to keep right on praying for help to persevere. Before the evening was over serenity and resignation had returned. . . .[1]

The big day of his entrance into the novitiate came and went, and the next day Father Maurice (the new name Malloy received as a monk) managed to catch a surreptitious glimpse of himself in the mirrorless world of the Valley:

Quite unexpectedly, as I experimented at walking outside in the habit, I caught the full-length reflection of Brother Maurice in the low windows of the courtyard side of the new building. The disguise is complete! *I hope the inner transformation is.*[2]

Father Maurice's priestly prerogative would not excuse him from the rough life of the other novices. He partook fully in the work of the farm, the orchard and the vineyard and had to face washing up with a large bar of yellow laundry soap and a "common towel" after coming in from the fields.

Father Maurice would be an astute observer of life in the monastery. As time went on, added responsibilities would bring him into closer contact with the running of the house, and his observations would become even more well informed. His acute power of observation also focused on the person of his superior. Shortly after his arrival he recorded:

I came face to face with Father John the prior, just returned from the General Chapter in Europe. He is taller and milder than I remembered him. After Prime he prostrated and was prayed over; this brought tears to my eyes. At Chapter he spoke ramblingly but graciously of his trip, revealing a very human person and a saintly one. We happened to meet outside the refectory before breakfast, and he called me by name and gave me a memorable welcome.[3]

From 1933 on Malloy offers brief excerpts of John's chapter talks, as when he told Brother Francis on the occasion of his receiving the habit: "You ought to be a proud man today, brother, making your entrance into the grand old Order of Cîteaux, that has been a beacon light to the Church and the world through so many centuries."[4]

✐ New Buildings for the Monastery

Malloy's arrival was well timed to enable him to witness and to document the movement for renewal that was gradually unfolding at the monastery. For one thing, the building program was well under way. When the church was constructed in 1928, plans already called for a new wing that would link up with its transept. The window of the "new building" in which he saw a reflection of himself was in this new wing, which was quickly going up. In April 1930 an indult from Rome had been obtained to borrow $50,000 for its construction.[5] Once again Ambrose Murphy was called in, and after the plans were drawn up the work seems to have begun immediately.[6] By the end of September the outer walls were complete, and work on the interior continued throughout the winter. By June 1931 it was in full use. Parallel to the original 1902 building and perpendicular to the church, it formed the third side of the proposed quadrangle and helped—along with the new rooms beneath the church—to relieve the crowding in the original 1902 wing of the monastery.

Plans were also in process for the creation of a porter's lodge to the east of the old 1902 building and parallel to its facade. More ambitiously, by the end of 1932 there was some kind of master plan initiated by Dom John for a remaining group of buildings.[7] A booklet detailing these plans was published in January 1933, undoubtedly with the intent of stirring up interest that would be translated into contributions for the new venture.[8] The plans called for the construction of a large north wing of the proposed quadrangle containing novitiate, library, refectory, scriptorium, and extensive dormitory space on a third floor. The old 1902 guesthouse was to be destroyed and a splendid new one with accommodations for forty-five guests constructed about twelve yards farther to the east. The church would be extended farther to the east, and a highly elaborate new facade would be built to replace the old one, lining up with the facade of the new guesthouse.

Bishop Hickey was almost certainly one of the driving forces behind these plans. In response to appeals made by Pius XI in his encyclicals for the promotion of retreats for laymen, the bishop had taken up the cause, and it became a frequent theme both in his discourses and in his planning.[9] The generous accommodations for forty-five men in the new wing would have been very much in line with his thinking.

Nothing came of these bold plans for some time, however. On January 24, 1934, we find Malloy busy making revisions to the plan for

FIGURE 41. *(top) Our Lady of the Valley. West wing of the monastery, 1931. Cloister.*
FIGURE 42. *(bottom) Our Lady of the Valley. West wing of the monastery. Chapter room.*

the north wing. Things were going well for the monastery financially. On the occasion of a proposal to purchase material recuperated from the demolition of nearby mills, Malloy noted:

> We were told that the community borrowed $35,000 in 1930 to pay for the 'infirmary wing' and that we have already (in three years) paid off $32,500, though we were given ten years to pay it. Rev. Father said he doesn't know where the money comes from; God is surely with us![10]

Little wonder, then, that by October 24, 1935, the monastery had obtained permission to borrow *another* $50,000 for the construction of the novitiate portion of the plan.[11] Groundbreaking for the new building took place on March 25, 1936, and by the fall the roof was on, and work could continue on the interior. (The choir novices would move in on April 5, 1937.) Since the rest of the north wing was never constructed, it is difficult to picture how this novitiate portion fit in with the overall plan to complete the quadrangle.[12]

That same fall of 1936 Malloy noticed that the old steam shovel was bringing stones to a site a short distance to the east of the 1902 building. These were destined for a new porter's lodge. Digging for the foundations began on November 3 and continued until the weather made further work impossible, and the building site was closed for the winter.

The completion of all these new buildings was beginning to have its effect in attracting vocations to the Valley. By 1930, just a year after the completion of the church, the community statistics show that numbers had risen to forty-six, confirming Dom Obrecht's intuition that a fine new church would be a source of inspiration to potential candidates.

Towards the beginning of this busy period of expansion, the monastery received an official visitation from the Abbot General, Dom Herman Joseph Smets. He arrived in July 1931 at the end of his tour of other American monasteries of the Order. The visitation card he left behind is generally complimentary in tone, not only toward the Valley but toward the other houses he visited. Among the concrete remarks he makes about the observances at the Valley, we find the ever recurring themes of silence, separation from the world, and respect for the superior.

✑ Life in the Monastery

Although Malloy's comments on this period concentrate mainly on the life of the choir monks, he does mention some of the essential events in the life of the farm. The *Annals* report the intensity of the seasons. A drought in 1932 brought with it drastic losses of summer crops, but the yield of apples in the autumn was exceptional. This was followed by the winter of 1932–33, which was the most severe in recorded history, when "horse drawn sleds worked about the farm and woods." Malloy also notes that the monastery regularly shared its produce with various institutions in the diocese. The convent of the Little Sisters of the Poor in Pawtucket was specially cared for throughout the history of the Valley. He also writes of a gypsy moth caterpillar infestation that plagued the countryside between May 10 and June 30 of 1933 and required considerable work that winter to destroy the nests.

Throughout the busy years of 1934 to 1937 that were so filled with building projects, Brother Hugh continued to occupy an important place in the monastery's material affairs. While his name appears on the community roster only as sub-cellarer, he did in fact function as cellarer.[13] Besides being involved in the major building efforts, he was also later responsible for the construction of a new garage and a new hay barn. The entire farm operation, including the milk industry, was also under his supervision.

A special area of concern in the monastery was the program of studies for the priesthood, given the fact that the choir monks were normally destined for priestly ordination. In February 1930 Fraters Aelred Walsh and Robert Egan were sent to complete their theological studies at Gethsemani, a move prompted no doubt by the greater facilities available there. Robert returned later that year and was ordained to the priesthood on December 20. Aelred's stay at Gethsemani was also relatively brief: He returned in March 1931 and completed his studies at the Valley.

Aelred's return might have been prompted by the fact that the Valley now had two new professors of its own, Father Columban Hawkins and Father Maurice Malloy, both of whom entered as priests with considerable experience behind them.[14] Both marveled that until then there had been no clearly defined course of studies at the Valley. But in August 1931, before the school year began, Malloy was appointed prefect of studies, with Columban as professor of theology, Father Philip as professor of philosophy, and Malloy himself in charge of humanities.[15] These assignments would frequently change over the years, the various professors swapping roles. Father Maurice's contribution remained principally in the area of humanities, particularly Latin and to a lesser extent Greek.

In the area of liturgy also there was a gradual regularization of the services, bringing them more in line with the practice of the Order. Thus Malloy could announce in his entry for January 18, 1931, that the conventual Mass and the festal Offices of Vigils and Lauds would henceforth be celebrated with due regard to the different liturgical grades.[16] On May 26, 1932, for the first time in the history of the monastery Vigils and Lauds were both chanted, with the exception of the responsories at Vigils. Previously they had been recited in a monotone, in a style known as *recto tono*. On August 15, 1932, the responsories also were chanted.[17] And in November 1935 the practice of singing Vigils and Lauds (with the exception of the responsories) was extended to Sundays.[18]

More and more care was taken with regard to Gregorian chant. During the early years at the Valley Dom John Mary Murphy had constantly pestered Dom Oger to send Father Guillaume of Oka to help the Valley with its chant, and he had finally come for a chant session in late August of 1905. In January 1933, Dom John O'Connor—on his way to Gethsemani—visited the Pius X School of Liturgical Music, which had been set up at the Manhattanville College of the Sacred Heart in New York. While there he discussed the chant with Mother Georgia Stevens, who at his request sent four books to the Valley, which arrived promptly several days later.[19] Beginning later that year he had Brother Bernard Bailey give voice lessons to the community on a regular basis. Brother Bernard also provided organ accompaniment to the Offices. Another organist who was to serve the community for many years was Father Laurence Bourget, who entered in 1933. Some years later, Father Van de Putte of the Holy Ghost fathers came to the Valley for a four-day session of chant.[20]

The furnishings used in the church services were also being improved. On the occasion of his ordination to the priesthood in 1930, Father Robert Egan received from the atelier of the Sisters of the Atonement in Graymoor, New York, sets of modified Gothic vestments, which were becoming popular at the time. Later on Father Aelred received even more prestigious vestments from the firm of Grossé in Belgium. The first were made of silk, but eventually the monks prevailed upon Grossé to provide vestments in wool, in line with Cistercian tradition. Appareled albs were beginning to make their appearance by the spring of 1933.[21] Much later, in 1939, Father Maurice designed other vestments as well as a full set of altar frontals to round out the monastery's already considerable collection of liturgical vesture and furnishings. These were executed by the Franciscan Missionaries of Mary.

Father Maurice wasn't the only one contributing to the literary production of the monastery. Dom John was working on the Annals of the monastery as well as on descriptions of his travels to Cistercian monasteries in Europe. Both of these projects were given to Father Maurice for polishing, as he himself relates.[22] By October 13, 1934, the "Cistercian Travelogue" was ready and approved for refectory reading.[23] It recounted O'Connor's visits to European shrines and monasteries over the years: Mount St. Bernard, Roscrea, Mount Melleray, Bellefontaine, Melleray, Timadeuc, La Grande Trappe, Tilburg, Westmalle, Cîteaux. A visit to the small Cistercian convent of Notre-Dame de Bonne Garde near the famous shrine of Ste.-Anne d'Auray in Brittany made a special impression on him for the singing of its nuns. Maurice would continue to receive this type of work from Dom John, and eventually was asked to participate in design work on various artifacts as well as architectural projects, for which he also served as draftsman.

During these years a new man was coming up from the ranks to a position of prominence in Dom John's administration, alongside Brothers Hugh and Michael: Father Aelred Walsh. Even before his ordination as a priest, Aelred was named to the important position of secretary to the abbot during the visitation by the Abbot General in July 1931.[24] The office of secretary at that time included not only normal secretarial duties but also those of treasurer. On March 12 of the following year he became cantor. During the visitation of 1933 he was made sacristan and was chosen to accompany Gethsemani's Father Immediate, Dom Corentin le Guyader, to Gethsemani for its visitation.[25] All of this shows that he was held in esteem not only by Dom John but also by Dom Obrecht. The monastery received a number of gifts from Aelred's sister, who lived in England. These included the fine vestments from Grossé and an Orgatron organ, which replaced the Estey harmonium that had been used until then.

Another figure singled out by Dom Obrecht for promotion was Frater Edmund Futterer. While still in Minor Orders he was made third superior at Obrecht's behest during the 1933 visitation. Obrecht also urged that Edmund be ordained as soon as possible. The urgency was perhaps the result of a new source of concern that had arisen.

On July 1, 1934, Dom John went to the hospital of Milford, Massachusetts, for an operation, the exact nature of which is not known. He returned at the end of the month exhausted. Malloy noted that his "speech was thick."[26] On August 1 Malloy records:

> Rev. Father came to chapter and told us of the noisy hospital; of his queer complaint, a nervous depression which prevents him from taking interest in anything—"like the pain of damnation!" We began making one novena after another for him.

From now on there is frequent mention of Dom John's illness, particularly during the early months of 1935. In June, however, he was able to return to the daily, early morning Vigil service. He managed to attend the General Chapter in September and seemed none the worse for it, but his health continued to be a preoccupation for the community. In addition to nervous problems, he suffered greatly from his feet, which increasingly impaired his mobility.

On October 4, 1933, Bishop Hickey died, and on February 12, 1934, Father Francis P. Keough, a priest of the Archdiocese of Hartford, was appointed as his successor. On June 19, 1934, the monastery received a first visit from Dom Celsus O'Connell, abbot of Mount Melleray in Ireland. He was to become a fast friend of the community and particularly of Dom John O'Connor, who had been a frequent visitor to Mount Melleray during his trips to Europe. Malloy offers us his own impressions:

> I found him a very unpretentious approachable Irishman; just my age, but I think he looks older tho' fresh and strong. He kept me for a whole hour, visiting the library, and discoursing like a practical man on such things as concrete tracery for the cloister windows, cheese and butter as stamina producers, fresh air (where walls are not dusty), English Grammar as a foundation for studies, soft and briskly-moving chant (loud singers don't hear the rest of the choir). He much prefers our choir to that of Gethsemani.

∽ DOM EDMUND OBRECHT'S LAST VISITATION

On September 28, 1934, Dom Edmund Obrecht arrived for what would be his last visitation. Malloy has left us a delightful vignette of his reception by the community:

> Almost the whole community went out to greet the Abbot. Stopping in the doorway, he looked incredibly old and decrepit beside a straight young man in street clothes—our Rev. Father—who had marvelously pulled himself together for the occasion. "I'm the sickest man here," said the Abbot, "twice in the hospital in Louisville this year, but I said Mass every day." "Give them your blessing, Rev. Father," urged our superior, anxious to cut the reception short (for his own sake too, I strongly suspect, God love him!). We knelt down to receive the blessing. On the way to his room he let three of us kiss his ring, Father Alfred, Father Augustine ("Hello, old man") and me. "And you, young man, how are you?" He is almost carried around by his young secretary, Father James Fox (of Boston) who is his new subprior.[27]

The visitation was to prove trying for poor Malloy. Only the day before, during the chant class he was giving to the community, he had made a disparaging remark about Gethsemani's singing, little knowing that almost immediately afterwards a telegram would arrive announcing that Obrecht was on his way to make an unscheduled visitation! The worst happened, and the remark was reported to Obrecht during the visitation. Although he let his displeasure be known in veiled words, he accepted Malloy's written apology and generously made an offering towards the upkeep of Malloy's parents, who were going through hard times.

One would like to know what prompted this visitation by a man so advanced in age and, as it turned out, close to death. There is only this in the Gethsemani Annals: "In September news from OL of the Valley was so disquieting to his heart that Dom Edmond . . . resolved to go to the Valley and try to adjust matters." He returned home on October 6, and a bare three months later died, on January 4, 1935. Dom John and Father Columban attended his funeral, which was officiated by his old friend Cardinal Dougherty. On February 6, Dom Frederic Dunne was elected as his successor.

On October 16, 1935, the Valley lost one of its most important figures with the passing of Father Alberic Crotty in his ninetieth year. Thanks to Dom John Mary Murphy's insight (as well as his insistence) Alberic had been generously given to the community by Dom Oger in 1901. There is little doubt that his careful management of the monastery's funds was responsible for seeing the community through the difficult years of Murphy's illness and ensuring its increasing financial stability following the end of World War I.

The death of Dom Obrecht marked an important turning point in the history of the Valley. While he kept tight control over his daughterhouse (as indeed he did over his own monastery), he recognized the progress it had made over the years in achieving financial stability, and he was appreciative of the qualities of its superior, Dom John O'Connor. Indeed, he had been the encouraging force behind Dom John's extensive building campaign, one that he saw only partially completed.

✍ A VISIT OF THE NEW FATHER IMMEDIATE

After his election, Dom Frederic Dunne had visited the Valley informally, on November 16, 1935, on his way from the blessing of the new abbot of Mistassini, Dom François-Xavier Huet. His first official visitation wasn't until the following May, and there is little to relate about it. Like Malloy, he was an astronomy enthusiast and showed Father

Maurice how to locate Mercury. Malloy also offers the sober comment: "We found him deeply spiritual, mild, persuasive rather than forceful."[28] Time would show, however, that he could be forceful in making demands on the community concerning its observance. Dom John commented briefly as well in a letter to Dom Pacôme: "Dom Frederic has just made the regular visitation of the Valley. The monastery remains in statu quo." The remark seems innocuous enough, but it might refer to an unrealized hope that the new Father Immediate would consider reestablishing the Valley's abbatial status. In any case, some waters seem to have been stirred up just before the following year's visitation. In a letter to the English language definitor in Rome, Dom Anthony Daly, Dom John noted:

> When the Monastery began to show signs of prospering, Dom Edmond of Gethsemani presiding decided we should elect a Titular Prior: Why not an Abbot, since this was the Abbey of Petit Clairvaux transferred? This is something I could never understand. Perhaps you can enlighten me![29]

Malloy also makes first mention in 1936 of a situation that would trouble the community for several years to come: One of the monks began to show signs of psychological imbalance. In this particular case, the person in question was briefly hospitalized, then asked to return home. Over the next three years, however, at least five new cases appeared, and a meeting of the professors of the monastery in 1938 revealed that "four or five of our students are 'touched.' "[30] During the 1939 visitation Malloy consulted Dunne concerning this, and Dunne answered quite rightly that there needed to be better screening of candidates.[31]

The monastery lost a promising young monk on June 6, 1937, when Brother Leo Beale, a simply professed laybrother, died suddenly of a heart attack. Malloy recalls:

> Always ready to serve, always ready to oblige, by his genuine piety and his smiling gaiety he was like a ray of sunshine to the whole community; he was grinning through his black beard all the time, with a sort of elfin merriment in his eye.[32]

On the day after Brother Leo's death Dom John reflected on his life in a chapter talk:

Though constantly suffering he never thought of going elsewhere for an easier life. He skipped about like a squirrel, making himself extremely useful—in the wardrobe, the laundry, the infirmary. Who will take care of my poor feet now? . . .[33]

Work continued on the interior of the new novitiate throughout the winter of 1936–1937, and by April 5 all was ready for the blessing of the new building. A procession of the entire community wended its way there, and after two brief prayers Dom John invited those who wished to do so to give a speech. The novice master, Father Benedict, spoke briefly albeit with some emotion on the text: "Behold I make all things new!" (Rev. 21:5). The novices, not expecting this invitation to speak, were somewhat taken aback. Brother Nicholas ventured the modest remark that all seemed in order. In his thick French accent Brother Paul made some comments that were largely unintelligible, which prompted Malloy to remark that he seemed to be speaking in Greek or Arabic.[34]

The new building provided ample facilities. The ground floor contained washing and changing rooms along with various service areas. The second floor had a common room for the novices, which offered space for reading and for conferences, an office for the Father Master, and a small chapel. The third floor housed the dormitory.

Even though the new building was for the exclusive use of the choir novices, the entire monastery profited from the space vacated by them under the church. The laybrother novices could now use the dormitory section of the old choir novitiate under the church, and the wardrobe department moved its operation into the space under the apse that had also been used by the choir novices. The laybrother novices in turn moved into the room on the second floor of the 1902 building vacated by the wardrobe. This room was remodeled to provide a common room and Father Master's room for the lay novices.

Throughout his years in the monastery, Malloy—with what was perhaps a tacit permission from O'Connor—indulged in sunbathing, timidly at first, but with increasing freedom as time went on. On more than one occasion O'Connor urged him to be careful, since several workmen had seen him! He was also not adverse to taking the occasional dip in the monastery stream, as he records on June 2, 1937 (carefully abbreviating the naughty words):

FIGURE 43. *Our Lady of the Valley. Novitiate building, 1937. This photo taken after the restoration of the buildings following the 1950 fire shows (from left to right) the 1938 novitiate, the chapter room building, the remains of the transept, and the base of the church's apse.*

> Reconnoitering for flowers, I took a 10-yard float in brook at S. end of property—foolish! I am going out of my way to seek health. Father A. called me aside very kindly to tell me I was seen last year by a workman at one of my "s-b," and should be more cautious.[35]

Dom John's health became increasingly poor as the years went by. He was keeping more and more to himself. His trips to the General Chapter provided some distraction from his problems. He left on August 4 for the 1937 chapter—the last one he would attend—and returned only on October 9. While Dom John was away, final touches were put on the new porter's lodge, and Brother Vincent moved in as the porter shortly after the feast of the Assumption on August 15. John must have been gratified to find the entire community assembled near the archway of the new building to welcome him back home in October.

After the completion of the new porter's lodge, a garden-like enclosure was laid out between it and the 1902 building, providing guests space for a quiet stroll and serving as an entrance court to the monastery itself. Three new statues were also set up: one of St. Bernard in the new garden area, another of St. Benedict in a niche above the welcoming archway of the new porter's lodge, and a third of St. Michael Archangel on top of a boulder near the front of the porter's lodge. All three survived and made their way to Spencer. St. Bernard stands in front of the

FIGURE 44. *Novices and junior professed at Our Lady of the Valley, April 1937. Left to right: Fraters William O'Connor, Aloysius Zemanick, Paulinus Fitzgerald, Bernard Brûlé, Anthony O'Toole, Stanislaus Watson, Laurence Bourget, Peter Rogers, Father Benedict Barré, Novice Master, Fraters Nicholas Cappon, Stephen King, Alberic Hill, Felix Vecchione, Patrick Cannon, Christopher Benton, Bede O'Leary, Ephrem Honan, Father Gabriel O'Connell. This photograph was taken shortly after the new novitiate building was occupied on April 5, 1937.*

new infirmary enjoying the splendid view out over Manning Hill; St. Benedict occupies a spot near the original buildings of the Alta Crest Farms; and St. Michael, shorn of his wings in transit, adorns the garden of the Energy Center.

The old porter's lodge still stands at the Valley, where it continues to welcome visitors coming down the old access road on their way to the town library and other facilities now located on the old monastic property. In St. Benedict's niche, a low relief now depicts old Brother Hugh and his faithful dog Rex, both facing south, as though they might have caught sight of Malloy on one of his "10-yard floats."

With the completion of the porter's lodge, John's building program was suspended because of "insufficiency of means," as he confided to Dom Celsus O'Connell.[36] He probably thought of this as a temporary pause in his great plan for a full quadrangle and a larger guesthouse, but the porter's lodge would be the last building put up by Dom John.

The community had grown with the new buildings, from forty-six in 1930 to sixty-nine. And the number of solemnly professed monks had almost doubled, from eleven to twenty-one. This core group in a monastery can only be built up slowly since candidates must pass through a five-year period of formation: two in the novitiate and three as simply professed monks. This solid core ensured a firm base for growth for the future.

The major event in 1938 both for the Valley and for all of Southern New England was the great hurricane that crashed ashore at Long Island on September 21. The Providence area experienced sustained winds of 100 mph, gusting up to 125 mph. Storm tides mounted along the entire New England coast from Connecticut to Massachusetts and were highest of all in Rhode Island. Downtown Providence was inundated by a twenty-foot tidal wave; 564 people lost their lives, 8,900 buildings were destroyed, and 15,000 structures were damaged.

The storm hit the Valley area in the afternoon, as Malloy reported:

> The rattle on the church windows during Vespers drowned the hebdomadary's voice. Compline, collation, night office were by candle-light, and this continued all through the next eight days. A clear morning disclosed the immense damage done by the storm. The enclosure fence was down in ten places; copper flashing was torn off the ridge of the church roof; many shingles were ripped off the guest house roof; the old pump-house was moved off its foundations. The whole apple crop (as well as grapes and pears) was on the ground. Worst of all, hundreds of trees were either uprooted or broken irreparably.
>
> Of the five century-old ash trees opposite the cow barn only two were standing; one of the "twins" was broken from its twin at the ground. The great spreading maple by the brook below the milk house was gashed into a shapeless thing; near it, the upturned root of a hundred-foot hickory had made a new pool beside the stream. The double row of poplars flanking the front road suffered most: two-thirds of them were prostrate, and the rest terribly lopped and mangled. Everywhere in the woods were white streaks showing where great limbs had been wrenched away; half the leaves were gone and the remainder torn, dried, *burned* by the terrible wind. In the moist south woods, seven great oaks, uprooted, were piled up on top of one another; west and north on succeeding days, investigators making their toilsome way found like devastation; to clear it all up, two years' work at least will be required. From the spindrift there was salt on the windows, salt on the church tower, salt everywhere; the grapes were covered with salt and had to be washed before they could be served in the refectory.[37]

Dom John's new buildings were put to the test by the high winds, and they stood up rather well. The major damage was to the monastery's forests. Cleaning them up took much of the community's time during the coming winter; some crews went in to saw the fallen trees into manageable pieces, while others carted them away on sleds. Dom John announced to the community that damage at the Valley was estimated at $10,000.

An aerial survey of Rhode Island carried out in 1939 gives a good idea of the overall layout of the property. All of the old and new buildings appear in the photographs of the area around the Valley, including the most recent, Brother Hugh's "garage." The original access road is still visible almost in its entirety. Along its course on the north is the temporary monastery built in 1900–1901, and at its end lies the group of farm buildings that served the monastery over the years. (Fig. 29)

Some nine months before the hurricane, on an evening in January of 1938, a young man appeared at the gate of the porter's lodge after the monastery had closed down for the night. Undaunted, he climbed over the wooden fence of the guesthouse's forecourt and rang the bell. Eventually an irate Father Michael, then functioning as guestmaster, opened the door. After receiving an appropriate scolding, Roderick Gregory was shown to a room. Not very certain exactly why he had come, he realized after a while spent in the monastery that he had found what he was looking for and became first an oblate, then a lay novice. He received the name Brother Leo. On September 3, 1940, he made his first profession and only two weeks later was made submaster of the lay novices.

Work was an important factor in the life of the laybrothers, and Brother Leo's new job involved assigning the novices to specific tasks. In this he worked in close collaboration with Brother Hugh, whom he came to admire more and more not only for his dedication to and competence in his work, but also for what Leo describes today as his gentlemanly qualities. Each evening as the monks filed into church for Compline, the last Office of the day, Brother Hugh would take Leo aside to tell him what work was planned for the brother novices on the following day.

Brother Leo's responsibilities would increase under Dom John's successor. For the moment, he devoted himself to his work with the novices during the difficult years that lay ahead.

The Decline of Dom John

URING 1939 DOM JOHN retired more and more to his room. It was slowly becoming impossible for him to stand or even to sit for extended periods. When he appeared for one of the services on the Feast of Sts. Peter and Paul that year, splendid in a red silk cope, Malloy noted: "We hardly heard a word he said."[1] By March of the following year, he was talking about going into retirement.[2]

Things came to a head on April 12, 1940, when his nervous condition reached such a pitch that an ambulance had to be called to take him to St. Joseph's hospital in Providence. Dom Frederic Dunne came in haste to the Valley and appointed the subprior, Father Alfred Vezina, superior for three months; the doctors had judged that Dom John would need a month's rest in the hospital followed by another two months away from the monastery for further recuperation. He spent that latter time at Gethsemani, Frater Placid Grimes (later to become a laybrother taking the name Brother Alfred) accompanying him as nurse and companion. Near the end of his stay, Dom Frederic had to report to the General:

> Dom John has been with us since May 14th but has not improved. We put him under the care of a new physician last Monday and hope for the best whilst dreading the worst. Father Alfred, former Sub-Prior and present acting Superior, is not giving satisfaction but we must be patient until D. John improves or fails altogether.[3]

John returned home with Brother Placid on July 20, but he was not much better. By this time Father Alfred was all too ready to forego the role of main superior. Indeed he was even relieved of his office as subprior. Father Edmund was chosen to replace him in this office. He had won the esteem of Dom Frederic, who wrote to the General: "This young man will, I hope, be of great assistance to him [John], and at the same time be receiving training for future superiority, for I think him the best they have to succeed Dom John, when that becomes necessary."[4]

Little by little Dom John O'Connor regained strength, and by late August he was able to come to speak to the community in chapter three times a week. By November he was back at his place in choir as well as in the refectory.[5] Dom Frederic was gratified by this, and it must be said to his credit that throughout this entire difficult period, he supported Dom John in his role as superior and did all he could to keep him in this office as long as was possible.

As Dom John improved he apparently began thinking again about further construction. On more than one occasion he asked Father Maurice as well as Brother Clement to work on copies of floor plans.[6] Dom Frederic seems to have put a stop to this, reminding Malloy, for one, of the impossibility of such a project with the country on the brink of becoming involved in the growing global conflict.

John did manage to carry out two small projects. The cellarer, Brother Hugh, was authorized to build a new hay barn slightly west of the old cow barn, the plans for which were in place by August 1941. And important improvements were made in the processing of the milk, as Malloy relates:

> I took a look at the new barn; Brother Hugh told me by signs that it is to be a hay barn of 2 stories; it is as large as the cow barn or a little larger. On Brother's invitation I went down into the new milk house, and was surprised to see the scientific appliances in use—filters, a big cooler worked by Frigidaire, electrically worked brushes to clean bottles, a bottle filler worked with a spring, hot water vats, convenient racks for milk cans, etc.[7]

A couple of years earlier, with help from funds received from the WPA, Brother Hugh had begun to erect a building designed to serve as a garage. Work on the interior was never really completed, and little use was made of it save for the storage of aging farm equipment. It would be turned into a cow barn in 1944.[8]

❧ The Resignation of Dom John O'Connor

By December 2, 1941, Dom Frederic felt that the time had finally come for Dom John to resign and wrote to the General to say that if John made the request, it should be accepted.[9] Soon after, perhaps at Frederic's suggestion, Dom John himself wrote to the General, Dom Herman-Joseph Smets, on January 21, 1942, asking to resign for reasons of health.

Processing such a request, which normally required the approval of the General Chapter, was problematic during the war years. Because the chapter was not able to meet, the Order's definitory, acting in connection with the General, was given the power to make decisions regarding urgent matters. Despite the position taken by Dom Frederic, on April 17, 1942, the definitory decided against granting Dom John's request.

By the time Dom Frederic began the 1942 visitation at the Valley in early July, news of this decision had not yet reached America. Judging from Malloy's report the visitation raised no significant issues—Frederic and John would have still been waiting for a decision from the Generalate. News of the decision arrived a few weeks after the visitation was over but Frederic seems to have made no move to contest it.[10] Later, however, he must have written to the definitory again since on September 12, Dom Daly wrote explaining that the definitory wished O'Connor to remain "on account of the great good he was doing."[11]

The following year, Dunne made his visitation on May 19-23. Once again Malloy had nothing significant to note. But after returning home, Dunne wrote to the General:

> I have just returned from the Regular Visitation at Our Lady of the Valley. Dom John dictated two letters to different members of the community, for Your Paternity, asking that his resignation be accepted. I was told that these letters were found in the waste basket, so that he was possibly expecting a demotion and was preparing the way for it. However, if a letter to this effect should reach Your Paternity, I beg you to accept his resignation. I do not feel Myself obliged to ask him to write such a letter, but I know that it would help the community, if he were to resign especially as now we have there Father Edmund Futterer, who has been second Superior for more than two years and has proved himself a "persona grata" to the majority of the community.[12]

In early July Dunne wrote Dom Anthony Daly, the definitor for the English language, in order to press his point:

Today, I am writing to you about Dom John, of The Valley. He is growing weaker all the time and, according to a letter just received, he has a bed in his office and is now receiving those members of the community, who want to see him, in bed. So, I think we are going too far in allowing him to remain at the head of the community and, much as I regret it, I think it is imperative that the resignation which he handed in last year should be accepted. He is suffering much and his community is suffering very much more. . . . please write to us, or to Dom John, that his last year's resignation has been accepted and that we may proceed to take care of the house.[13]

Still no word came from the Generalate, and as matters worsened at the Valley Dom Frederic decided to approach Cardinal Cicognani, the Apostolic Delegate to the United States, as he later related to Dom Barbaroux, the Order's Procurator General. Overriding the definitory's decision, Cicognani authorized Frederic to insist on John's resignation.[14] Armed with this new mandate, Frederic proceeded to the Valley on September 1 for a whirlwind visit. Malloy relates what happened:

Abbot Frederic arrived early, said Mass at 8 o'clock, held chapter after none. Said this community was "suffering," that great irregularities went uncorrected, that there was lack of union. He proposed a vote as to whether our V. Rev. Father Prior should resign (not be deposed): He was met with a storm of protest. At least half the religious spoke, and he could not settle on a proposition that we were willing to vote upon.

[The next morning] After regular chapter the Abbot had to admit some indiscretions. (Fr. M[ichael] and Fr. Gab[riel] have heard 2 priests quote him, on the difficulty of managing this community while the present Prior remains.) He also was constrained to say that this extraordinary visit (which looked uncanonical) was authorized by the Apostolic Delegate. Finally he proposed a vote thus: "Those who think it opportune that Rev. Fr. should resign now, vote black; contrary minded, white." The 2 Rev. Fr. and Fra. Paulinus abstained from voting. Fr. Charles was absent. The Abbot quickly counted the votes, but did not announce the result. I had the impression of an overwhelming majority of whites. If the vote had been unfavorable, I'm sure he would have called for the election of a new Prior. He left about 9 o'clock.[15]

The indiscretions referred to have to do with the fact that Dom Frederic had inappropriately revealed community matters to two visiting priests, who reported the matter to two of the monks. In any case

Malloy was wrong about his guess, as we learn from Dom Frederic's letter to Dom Barbaroux already cited:

> 17 voted in favor of Dom John's resignation, whilst 9 were in favor of leaving things as they are. No doubt, these 9 religious are just those who are causing so much trouble in the community at present. At any rate, Dom John still refuses to resign. So, for the moment, I left things as they are and returned to Gethsemani.[16]

Malloy's account of the "storm of protest" gives us a good idea of the state of the community as a result of these happenings. Dom John's own spirits must have also been at low ebb. The early reported story of two letters of resignation that made their way into the wastebasket probably reflect his indecision. Earlier on, it was easy for him to offer his resignation of his own will. Now that he sensed pressure, he reacted strongly. Father Laurence recounts that on still another occasion, after having written and sent a further letter of resignation, Dom John sent one of the monks to retrieve it from the post office! On top of all this there was the question of John's favorites who were known to strongly oppose his resignation. While this was based no doubt on their esteem and affection for him, there was also the consideration of the influence that they stood to lose if he should indeed resign. It seems likely that the active "troublemakers" alluded to in the letter just cited were relatively few in number and that they coincided with these favorites of Dom John. In his distress Dom John himself seems to been making imprudent remarks, as we learn from a letter of Father Edmund to Dom Frederic. The abbot had asked Edmund to give a chapter talk to the community from time to time. Edmund responded:

> How can I enunciate principles of the supernatural order when these are in circuitous ways held up to scorn in public and in private by the one for whom I am substituting? As you said in your chapter here "the Prior's state of mind is not isolated but is shared by a definite portion of the community who resent a supernatural approach to life's problems."[17]

This letter sums up well the confusion in the community during these days of waiting. The end was in sight, however, for three days before Edmund wrote his letter the matter had been brought to the attention of Pope Pius XII, who decided that Dom John's resignation should indeed be accepted. On November 9 the Congregation of

Religious commissioned the Apostolic Delegate to accept Dom John's resignation. The following day, the Apostolic Delegate sent word to Dom Frederic, authorizing him to go to the Valley to accept the resignation and to appoint an administrator.[18] On November 23, Father Edmund as subprior read to the chapter two letters from Dom Frederic, the first announcing the resignation of Dom John, and the second announcing his own arrival at the Valley on the following day.

✍ Dom Edmund Futterer Appointed Superior of the Valley

On Thanksgiving Day, November 25, Dom Frederic met with the community in chapter and appointed Father Edmund superior ad nutum until such a time as a General Chapter could once again convene and authorize an election. Apparently, Dom Frederic had some difficulty transmitting the news to the Procurator General and had recourse to Cardinal Fumasoni-Biondi, Prefect of the Congregation of Propaganda Fide, himself a former Apostolic Delegate to the United States, requesting that the news be communicated to the Order directly by the Vatican. No doubt this move was the suggestion of Cicognani, who probably offered to have the letter forwarded in the diplomatic pouch.

FIGURE 45. *Dom Edmund Futterer, Superior ad nutum of Our Lady of the Valley, later abbot of Our Lady of the Valley and Spencer.*

The choice of Father Edmund came as no surprise to the community. He had long been admired and respected, and his experience as subprior since the summer of 1940 had shown, albeit in a limited way, his capacity for leadership.

Significant changes were also made among the other officers. Father Owen was confirmed as subprior. Father Ambrose was appointed secretary in place of Father Aelred, who had held this important position for a number of years, and on December 19 Father Michael was replaced as guestmaster by Brother Leo. Finally, Frater Paulinus Fitzgerald was appointed cellarer in place of Brother Hugh, who had for many years been doing the work of cellarer without enjoying the title. Brother Hugh continued to have an important role in managing certain activities traditionally linked with the cellarer, in particular the care of the cows and the dairy operation. In subsequent community lists his new title appears as "assistant to the cellarer."[19] Edmund's intention was to assign to the new cellarer the overall supervision of the monastery's temporalities.[20]

The best proof of Brother Hugh's continuing influence on the running of the farm was Paulinus' decision to pursue its mechanization. They purchased an International Harvester Farmall H tractor, along with equipment to work with it: a two-way plow, corn planter, and disc harrow.[21] Notwithstanding this nod to current technology, the monastery's work horses and mules continued to take part in agricultural activities, providing moving power for raking, plowing, spreading manure, and hauling firewood, not to mention the role of horses in the delivery of milk around the area. The mules were especially appreciated for work on the vegetable gardens, where their small feet did not trample the plants. One of the mules, Red, survived into the 1950s, accompanying his master Brother Stephen to the foundation at Berryville.[22]

There is little doubt that the new appointments reflected the views of the new administration concerning monastic values. The lifestyles of Michael and Aelred, for instance, were not in accord with Dom Edmund's ideas on monastic observance, nor with those of Dom Frederic for that matter. These two veterans eventually decided to leave the community.

Father Aelred took the changes with good grace but was soon expressing a desire to leave monastic life for work in the army.[23] By June 24, 1944, he had made the decision to leave and was assigned work in New York as a priest of the Military Ordinariate. According to Malloy, he had been considering transferring to Mt. St. Bernard, but for some reason this did not come to pass.[24] After spending about two years in the

Military Ordinariate, he decided to return to monastic life and applied to Rome for a transfer to the English Congregation of Benedictines. On July 1, 1947, he received a definitive *transitus* and entered the Benedictine Abbey of St. Anselm's in Washington, D.C., where he remained until his death on June 13, 1970. Those who knew him recall his great devotion to the community over many years, functioning with great competence as secretary-treasurer and lending his expertise and good taste to the evolving program of liturgical and architectural reform at the monastery.

Father Michael went to New Melleray in the second half of 1945 to share his expertise with those engaged in the construction of the new monastery there. Though the initial agreement was for a stay of only six months, Michael eventually transferred definitively to this community, where he died on January 14, 1967.

In February 1944 the new cellarer, Father Paulinus, turned his attention to improving the food services of the monastery. This involved extensive renovations in the basement of the old 1902 building. The kitchen that prepared the food for the monks was relocated to a position near the guest kitchen, and the scullery for the preparation of vegetables was enlarged. To make space for all this on the basement level, Paulinus removed the original staircase between the basement and the first floor, and in the space gained on the first floor a small confessional was installed. Father Paulinus' tenure, however, did not last long. On March 5, 1944, he was replaced by Brother Leo, who held the office for only a year and some months.

✆ IMPROVEMENTS ON THE FARM

At the time Brother Leo was appointed, the old red cow barn was showing its age. The floor was beginning to decay and the hooves of some of the cows had started going through the boards. So the move was made to convert Brother Hugh's essentially unused "garage." It had the advantage of being closer to the monastery and could provide space under one roof for housing the cattle, storing the hay, and processing the milk, which henceforth would be extracted by machines. The stanchions were designed so that the cows would face away from one another and a manure spreader or tip cart could be driven down a central path and loaded directly from the gutters. This concentration of the milk production in one building would lead to the gradual abandonment of the old buildings around the farmyard.[25]

It was also decided to change the herd. By April 14, Maurice Malloy could report that "our 35 nondescript cows are to be replaced by a herd of nine Holsteins, a bull and 5 calves. They are unbelievably fine looking animals." The animals were purchased through a local livestock dealer, Abe Spungeon. Also part of the deal was the famous "Baker Farm bull" from the Gammino farm in Peacedale, Rhode Island. It would serve as breeder of the herd for some time to come. While the garage was being converted, these new animals were housed in stanchions temporarily set up in Brother Hugh's hay barn, as was a DeLaval milking machine by way of experiment. By September 9 they had been moved to the new barn, with the famous bull lodged in the first pen.[26]

Thanks to new connections with the monastery of Prairies in Canada, several months later the Valley purchased thirteen more purebred cows from the Canadian monks. The animals arrived at the Valley Falls train station in freight cars. From there they were led up Diamond Hill Road in picturesque procession all the way to the monastery. Also part of the retinue was a huge bull that had been purchased not for breeding but to be sold for meat. The new animals took their places in the barn, the great bull next to the Baker bull until it was sold several weeks later. The dairy operation was further improved the next year with the installation of a Damrow milk pasteurizer.[27]

Leo's appointment as cellarer also saw the beginnings of another imposing project: draining the bog that had plagued the monastery's farm operation since its earliest days. Brothers Dominic Mihm and Philip Friel, who had entered as novices within days of each other in July 1942, were assigned to work with Brother Leo. The backbreaking labor took its toll on them all. Apart from the sheer fatigue, they experienced terrible headaches at night from handling the dynamite used to blast through the rock that impeded the flow of water. Eventually Mr. Quinn, owner of a nearby quarry, kindly provided a motorized crane manned by one of his own workmen to put the finishing touches on the operation, which overall took nearly a year. This would be the last of the megaprojects in which Brother Hugh and his steam shovel played a role. (Fig. 46)

The Valley's contacts with the monastery of Prairies were reinforced when Brother Dominic was sent there after his simple profession in 1945 to study animal husbandry. He also went to the Scientific Breeding School at St. Paul's, Minnesota, for an intensive one-week course. Dominic returned to the Valley after about six months but continued his training by assisting at workshops at a number of nearby universities.

Leo had given Dominic considerable responsibility for the barn operation while he was still a novice, and when he returned from the Prairies he was put in charge of the barn in an official way. He also managed to hold down other jobs, such as delivering milk three times a week to the Little Sisters of the Poor and driving monks to their medical appointments, a task he inherited from Brother Hugh.

The hectic pace of Brother Leo's term as cellarer ruffled more than one contemplative spirit. As he himself once put it, "I combed a lot of people's hair backwards." Two of his own architectural ventures were a machine shop and a new building to house the laundry. While digging a trench for the pipes leading to the new laundry, an injudicious amount of dynamite was used to blast away a particularly rocky spot. The resulting explosion broke the outer glass of the church's windows as the monks were chanting Vespers, to the consternation of Dom Edmund and the monks, who came running out to see what had happened.

To spare expenses the laundry was built of cinder blocks and was put up without the help of a proper architectural drawing, in what seemed to Malloy a rather slipshod way:

> I saw a sketch for the Laundry in the hands of Fra[ter] Alberic [Gainer], our wardrobe keeper, but no architect's drawing. I was not asked to make any. The cellarer, Bro Leo, and Brother Louis inspect the work now and then, but I really do not see anyone in full charge. Fra. Stephen showed me rather bad leveling in the brickwork.[28]

The increasing urbanization of the area near the monastery was a source of concern to Edmund, threatening as it did the community's solitude. As a kind of buffer, the monastery had purchased four adjacent properties between May and August 1944,[29] the most important of which, the forty-seven-acre Angell property, contained a well-maintained apple orchard that promised to be an added source of income. Both Dom Frederic and the Apostolic Delegate approved the expansion, and when Dom John O'Connor in his infirmary room heard of it, he remarked to Malloy, "We should have had a thousand acres here years ago, if the old Abbot [Edmond Obrecht] had not put his foot down, saying 'You have enough land.'"[30]

Sometime before October, Edmund sent Dom Frederic a detailed report concerning the monastery and its activities.[31] In addition to the acquisition of new parcels of land, Edmund's concerns were directed

FIGURE 46. *Our Lady of the Valley. Blasting a drainage outlet for the bog. Brother Hugh is seen at the controls of his steam shovel, Father Alberic looking on.*

principally to the improvement of the farm and dairy operations as crucial means of support. The need for a new laundry is also mentioned, as well as a plan for the renovation of the church's sanctuary. The financial statement he included shows that despite the recent expenditures on land acquisition the financial situation was increasingly promising.[32] The report demonstrates Edmund's determination to improve the material situation of the monastery.

Dom Frederic seemed gratified and wrote on December 8 to the definitory in Rome expressing his approval of Dom Edmund's administration and urging for the first time that the monastery be elevated to the status of abbey.

Dom Celsus of Mount Melleray stopped at the Valley in early January 1945 on his way to the election of a new abbot at New Melleray. It was his first visit since 1938, and he expressed satisfaction with the Order's flowering in America. He raised the possibility of a monastery for nuns, suggesting that prospective vocations be sent to Glencairn in Ireland for their novitiate. This turned out to be his last visit with his old friend, Dom John O'Connor, and Celsus did not hide his pique concerning Dom John's removal from office, as was dutifully reported to Dom Frederic by Father Bede O'Leary.[33] Celsus also visited Father Aelred in New York and apparently tried to get more inside information about what was happening at the Valley.

∽ Liturgical Concerns

In addition to his concerns for the farm, Edmund had since his appointment shown an interest in improving the architecture and the furnishings of the church. As early as March 7, 1944, he had instituted minor alterations to the church's altars in an effort to simplify their decoration. Plans were also afoot to relocate six of the other altars deemed too large for the space they occupied.

In February 1945 fuller plans for the renovation of the church began to take shape when Harold Rambusch, head of a renowned New York design firm, visited the monastery to discuss plans with members of the architectural commission. The first phase consisted of a simplification of the main altar, which received more sober furnishings. A more subtle painted decoration was provided for the walls in the style of "Caen stone."[34] In April, stained glass windows were discussed, and by August 14, three had been installed in the ambulatory.

In the spring Dom Edmund also announced plans for further improvements in the physical plant of the monastery: a pasteurizing unit, a new machine repair shop and garage, a poultry house, and a cold storage room. The total cost would be $30,000, which, he reported, the monastery had on hand.

∽ Preparations for an Election

Despite all of the improvements he had made, Dom Edmund was meeting opposition from certain members of the community, and it was beginning to take its toll on his spirits. He had kept silent himself, but when one of his erstwhile supporters turned against him, protesting that Dom John had been forced to resign, Edmund wrote to Frederic to complain of the situation.[35] The person in question was Father Bede, whom Edmund had named third superior. In effect, Edmund demanded that unless something was done, he would be forced to turn in his own resignation as superior ad nutum. In the meantime, Bede apologized for his behavior, and Edmund decided not to remove him from office, although he was determined to take action should there be trouble in the future.

Nonetheless, Dom Frederic seems to have taken Edmund's letter seriously. Reflecting on this latest state of affairs as well as on the opposition that Edmund had experienced from a small group of monks ever since Dom John's resignation, Frederic decided that the time had finally come for an election. Edmund's performance over the preceding fifteen months had been impressive, not only for his spiritual leadership, but also for the important improvements he had made in the material life of the community.

Making arrangements for an election during wartime was no easy matter, but Dom Frederic was aiming even higher than simply an election. He felt that the time had come to implement his plan for raising the monastery to the rank of an abbey. With an elected superior who would also be an abbot, further opposition to Edmund's regime would certainly be lessened.

Dom Frederic decided to set the plan in motion by making a visitation at the Valley in May. Not knowing what was at stake, Edmund tried to have him postpone it until some of the new buildings would be ready for his inspection.[36] The visitation itself seemed to go well; Dom Frederic wrote to the Generalate to register his satisfaction with the community. He also let the community know of his hopes to elevate the monastery's status. While the proposal was received with great enthusiasm by the majority, some members of the opposition complained that since Dom Edmund had been named as a temporary superior directly by the Holy See (*ad nutum Sanctae Sedis*), the present proposal went beyond the competency of Dom Frederic as Father Immediate. However, upon hearing that the overwhelming majority of the community was in favor, the definitory formally approved the petition on May 19.

The definitory's own petition to the Holy See reflected the reason offered by Dom Frederic himself: "There exists in the Community of Our Lady of the Valley a small group of religious, who, discontented with the retirement of the Very Rev. Father John Mary O'Connor as First Superior of the House, endeavor to thwart the government of the new Superior, nominated ad nutum Sanctae Sedis. To cut short this baneful activity the definitory unanimously decided . . . that the request of the Father Immediate be complied with. . . ." By May 24 the approval of the Holy See had been obtained, thus removing any doubts about the legality of the procedure.[37]

The good news was officially communicated to the community on June 15.[38] Dom Frederic arrived on July 31, and that evening the community gathered in chapter to listen to the reading of the Abbot General's mandate concerning the erection of the monastery to the status of abbey. The election itself was held the next day. One wonders if it was with a playful sense of irony that Dom Frederic recommended as scrutators three of Edmund's critics. Dom Edmund was elected with 21 out of 30 votes.[39] On August 5 the Abbot General, Dom Dominic Nogues, a longtime friend of the Valley, wrote to congratulate Frederic on the event.[40]

∽ The Blessing of the new Abbot

Before the blessing of the new abbot, Rambusch's crew set to work once again in the sanctuary in preparation for the great event. The old altar was dismantled and sent as a gift to the Monastery of the Holy Spirit in Conyers, and a new marble altar of simpler design was installed, along with a new tabernacle. Though the tabernacle underwent some reworking after the blessing of the abbot, this altar and tabernacle were destined to make their way to Spencer after the tragic fire of 1950 and find a new home in the converted hay barn chapel of the new monastery, where they still stand in what has become known as the "barn chapel."

The blessing of the new abbot took place on October 2, the Feast of the Guardian Angels, as people around the world were still celebrating the end of war. Bishop Keough of Providence was assisted by Dom Frederic and Dom Albert of New Melleray. Among those present were Dom James Fox, then abbot of Conyers; Father Eugene, subprior of New Melleray; and a Father Louis representing Dom Cherubim of Calvaire, who was not able to assist. The Valley's longstanding friend Dom Pacôme of Oka was also hindered from coming. A great number of clergy from the surrounding area assisted, including several Protestant ministers. The only discordant note was that the new arrangements in the sanctuary were not to Dom Frederic's liking. Quite the opposite reaction was registered by the visitors from New Melleray, who were impressed with the church and its furnishings—prompting their request that Father Michael be permitted to come and help with the building of their own new church.

∾ THE DEATH OF DOM JOHN

Less than two weeks after the ceremony, Dom John O'Connor died of cancer on October 13. He had fallen during the summer and fractured his pelvis and continued to decline thereafter. During his last days he was well cared for by the monastery's doctor and infirmarian, Father Raphael Simon, as well as by Brother Philip Friel and Brother Leo, who was in the room next to him suffering from an ulcer.

Dom John was not given the luxury of dying in office, with the knowledge that his service to the community had held out until the very end. After his resignation in 1943, he lived for almost two painful years in an infirmary room, observing from the sidelines the changes set afoot by the new regime, changes that included the setting aside of a group of men who had unfailingly supported him during his own tenure of office.

Paradoxically, our first glimpse of John O'Connor was as a young monk at Petit Clairvaux concerned for the future of the community, strongly convinced that Dom Dominique Schietecatte had to be replaced. It must have been hard for him, in his own turn, to see a younger man rising to prominence in the community and to be forced to resign in his favor. Yet there seemed to be no bitterness at the end. Brother Philip, among those who cared for him during his last days, testifies to his patient endurance of suffering in the terminal stages of his disease. 🙞

FIGURE 47. *Abbatial blessing of Dom Edmund by Bishop Keough of Providence on October 2, 1945. Dom Edmund is shown in the middle of the three kneeling abbots. On his right is Dom Frederic Dunne of Gethsemani, on his left Dom Albert Beston of New Melleray.*

Dom Edmund Futterer, Abbot

ORK ON THE CHURCH continued after the blessing. A new oak floor was laid in the sanctuary, and on the feast of All Saints Mass was celebrated with the new floor in place for the first time. In a letter to the Abbot General, Dom Dominique Nogues, Dom Edmund confided that all of the renovations had been completely financed by benefactors without any expense on the part of the new abbey.[1] Before the year was out the new tabernacle that had been installed before the blessing had finally been remodeled to everyone's satisfaction. Little by little, stained glass panels were fitted into the church's windows. By September 1947 panels had been installed into the remaining ambulatory windows, as well as those in the clerestories of the apse and of the transepts. Stained glass was never provided for the clerestory windows of the nave or the two large perpendicular lancet windows in the south transept and the east facade.

In his letter to the Abbot General, Dom Edmund reflected on the personnel situation at the Valley:

> We are now close to ninety in the Community, about twenty-five of whom are novices or postulants; the Lay-Brothers are especially flourishing; a good dozen of postulants are waiting to be admitted. Due to the fact that the original founders have all disappeared and that, of the "intermediate" generation, to which I belong, the majority have not been faithful, it now happens that the government of the house, i.e. all

the important charges, are in the hands of younger Fathers, upon whom I can rely having trained them myself, if I may so speak, in the spiritual life. They are supernatural men, with their faults, of course, but who are "led by the Spirit."[2]

The dynamism that characterized Dom Edmund's administration as a temporary superior did not slacken after his election as abbot. Towards the end of November, Malloy could report that progress was being made in the modest vestment industry headed by Frater Alberic Gainer.[3] In February 1946 the possibility of constructing a new guesthouse was raised, and Sam Morino prepared a set of sketch plans for a ninety-room facility to be situated south of the church.[4] And work on a new, enlarged chicken house—begun by a group of lay workmen without proper organization—was taken over in November 1946 by a group under the supervision of Frater Stephen King; by May 10, 1947, the building was in working condition.

The area of liturgical chant was a concern for Edmund as it had been for Dom John, and on June 27, 1946, Father Andrew Klarmann of Brooklyn's minor seminary, Cathedral College of the Immaculate Conception, came to the abbey to give lessons to the community, introducing them for the first time in a systematic way to the so-called Solesmes method of chant. Father Klarmann would be a frequent visitor at the Valley over the coming years, and much later, in 1953, he came to Spencer to help the community prepare for its first Mass in the new church.

⁀ THE FIRST GENERAL CHAPTER AFTER THE WAR

The first General Chapter after the war took place on May 1–7, 1946. The General and definitory would have to report on all decisions made during the interim period, which would have to be approved by the assembly. For Edmund, it was even more significant for being the first chapter he would attend. He left on April 21 "in one of those great transatlantic airplanes that make the trip in 24 hours."[5] During the chapter he requested permission to buy land near the monastery for $10,000. The permission was granted.[6]

Before coming to the chapter, Dom Edmund had contacted Archbishop Cushing of Boston about establishing in his archdiocese the first Trappistine convent in the United States, the idea that had been suggested by Dom Celsus O'Connell of Mount Melleray during his visit to the Valley the year before. Dom Edmund's thought was that this would be founded by the nuns of the monastery of Igny in France. The Archbishop showed great interest in the project but was very insistent that the foundresses be Irish—which, in fact, is what Dom Celsus, who was Father Immediate of the Irish convent of Glencairn, had originally proposed. When Edmund got to the chapter he spoke to Dom Celsus with this in mind, assuming he would meet with an enthusiastic response. Now that the American convent was on the horizon, though, Celsus became reticent. The subject never made its way onto the floor of the chapter meetings even though the Abbot General himself seemed favorably disposed. Because Dom Celsus had not categorically rejected the plan, Edmund asked his Father Immediate, Dom Frederic, to visit Glencairn after the chapter in his stead to lay the matter before the Mother Abbess. As Dom Edmund later wrote to Dom Frederic:

> Glencairn would make the foundation if Dom Celsus allowed them; the Lady Abbess delayed her answer to you because she waited until he returned from Rome. The thing that disconcerts us is that it was Dom Celsus himself who in our Chapter [at the Valley] spoke so encouragingly of our efforts to have nuns; if he could remain their Father Immediate he would consent; I was much hurt at his unsympathetic and almost rude and mean manner towards me at the Chapter.[7]

Dom Frederic went to Glencairn and later received a favorable answer from the abbess by letter. But he complicated the whole matter himself by subsequently contacting Dom Pacôme of Oka about sending Canadian nuns to staff the foundation—without consulting Edmund. The upshot would be an unfortunate misunderstanding between the two houses.

It was probably due to a shy streak that after the chapter Edmund did not go to Glencairn himself, and his difficulty with foreign languages may have kept him from visiting any other monasteries in Europe as his predecessor had frequently done. In any event, he was back home by May 13. But the experience of Dom Frederic's involvement at Glencairn would prove a lesson to him, and for future chapters he brought along a monk or a brother to serve as intermediary or interpreter.

Back at the Valley a prospective property for the convent turned up in a curious way. Brother Dominic had found himself short of milk for his customers and approached the nearby Garelick Dairy in Franklin,

Massachusetts, for an extra supply to meet the emergency. The two brothers who were proprietors of this farm owned eight or nine other farms in the vicinity. When they heard that the Cistercians were looking for a property for the future convent of nuns, they offered Dominic the Mount Farm situated partly in Franklin and partly in the adjacent town of Wrentham.

Even though the foundation was by no means certain, Edmund decided to take out an option on the Franklin and Wrentham land by means of a binder for $500, and a request was sent to the definitory for permission to borrow $40,000 to purchase the land. Permission was granted on July 29.[8]

Edmund's conversations with his fellow abbots at the General Chapter had enabled him to get a broader view of life in the Order than he had received from Dom Frederic. Upon his return he lost no time in implementing one important change, as Malloy reports: "After careful inquiries among abbots on matters of cleanliness, Rev. Father states that it is his will that we shave twice a week, and bathe oftener."[9] By the following year the renovated washroom was in working order, and Malloy could note: "New showers open to public even daily, in hot weather."[10] (Malloy is clearly referring here to the monastic "public"!)

The early summer brought news of a serious accident involving Father Michael Holland at New Melleray: He had been crushed by a wall that fell against him as he was helping to direct the building operations. There was fear for his life at first, but fortunately he recovered.

Not long after his return from chapter Dom Edmund outlined a plan for expansion motivated by the fact that there were now 110 persons in the community, twenty-five in the lay novitiate alone:

> Impressed by the influx of solid vocations, Rev. Father said in chapter, "We must build!" No community of our size in the Order is without a completed monastery. The bishop (whom Reverend Father visited yesterday) says we ought to build now with second hand materials before the Great Depression comes. (It is due about 2 years hence). Make a campaign for funds by means of letters and contact through influential friends. . . .[11]

On July 24, 1946, Edmund had written to Dom Pacôme to negotiate a loan of $100,000 (Pacôme had initially offered $50,000).[12] Several days later the definitory of the Order authorized the loan "in order to continue the construction of the monastery, which has become too small as a result of the abundance of novices."[13]

The proposed program for expansion called for the creation of a guesthouse and the enlargement of the existing church. The person chosen as architect was Monsignor John C. Hawes. Trained as an architect in England, Hawes was later ordained to the priesthood in the Anglican Church and eventually moved to Australia, where he designed a number of churches. He became a Roman Catholic in 1911, and in 1912 he was received into the Franciscan Third Order at the Basilica of St. Francis in Assisi. In 1939 he left for Nassau in the Bahamas, eventually settling on Cat Island, where he lived as a hermit, taking the name of Fra Jerome.

A first contact with Hawes was made during the early summer, asking if he would be willing to undertake the work at the Valley.[14] He soon agreed, proposing a grandiose project to reverse the plan of the existing church and extend it to the east, and to build an entirely new monastery south of the old one, which itself would now become the guesthouse.[15] Though impressed, the committee agreed that the plans were beyond the monastery's means. The matter was put on hold for several months.

Sometime after the feast of the Assumption in August 1946, a young man appeared at the Valley and announced that he had a gift for the monastery. Dom Edmund came out to receive him. He was Harry John of Milwaukee, heir to the Miller fortune. His gift was a check for $5,000. Brother Leo was called in from the fields to meet him. In the course of their conversation Harry suggested that the monks contact Michael Grace, a prominent Catholic of the New York area.

It comes as no surprise that Dom Edmund invited Brother Leo to be present at the meeting with Harry John. Early on, he had come to appreciate Leo's talents. Shortly after his appointment as superior, he had assigned him to the important job of guestmaster, a position in which Leo got to know a number of prominent visitors to the abbey, and when some months later he became the monastery's cellarer, he became well acquainted with the monastery's material needs. Now with the prospect of new contacts opening up, he seemed to be the right man to follow up the suggestion of Harry John.

As Michael Grace was in Boston at the time, Brother Leo was sent to meet him. Michael in turn invited Leo to come to visit the whole Grace family, which soon would be gathering at their summer home on Mount Desert Island in Maine. At Dom Edmund's bidding Leo accepted the invitation and set off two weeks later. At the family home, he met Michael's father, the patriarch of the family, Joseph Grace (who would soon visit the Valley for an overnight stay), and more importantly his son Peter, who was destined to become one of the monastery's benefactors and closest friends. Although in terms of financial assistance Peter was heavily committed to a wide range of charities throughout the Church, he would nevertheless contribute generously to the abbey, and it was at his prompting that over a period of time his friends and relatives made significant monetary gifts to the monastery. Furthermore, as time went by Peter would be more and more called upon to offer his support and counsel with the many projects that the phenomenal growth of the community would necessitate over the coming years.

✑ The Possibility of a Transfer of the Valley

Shortly after Hawes submitted his first plans, Archbishop Cushing came to the abbey to ordain three of its monks to the diaconate: Fathers Alberic Gainer, John Holohan, and Tarcisius Quirk. The next day he returned to ordain them to the priesthood.

During his visits, the prelate learned of the property that had been found in his own archdiocese for the proposed Trappistine foundation, and shortly after he left he received a letter from the Valley formally requesting permission to purchase the land, a permission that was granted within a week.[16] The land was purchased on September 13, 1946, for $37,500 with the help of funds donated by Michael Grace. The herd of fifty cows at Mount Farm were not included in the sale, and the Garelicks were permitted to continue their dairy operation on the premises for the time being.

The abbess of Glencairn was once again contacted and reported that her nuns were unanimously in favor of the foundation. But Dom Celsus was apparently still hesitant; he wrote to Archbishop Cushing expressing his desire to meet with him on his next trip to America and intimating that there was more to say on the matter.[17] Nonetheless, on November 10 Dom Edmund formally announced to the community his plans for the foundation. Three years would go by before the actual arrival of the nuns.

Archbishop Cushing had himself brought up another important matter during his visit for the ordinations when he boldly suggested the possibility of transferring the monastery to his own archdiocese. He even went so far as to propose that the monks contact the archdiocese's real estate agent in Framingham for help in locating a suitable property.

The reasons for such a move were daily apparent. In addition to the property's agricultural limitations, increasing settlement around the monastery was making for considerable noise and chaos. Not only were houses beginning to appear here and there, but over the next few years several recreational facilities were built nearby, all well within earshot. About a mile and a half away in a bend of the Blackstone, loudspeakers at a racetrack for automobiles blared out the results of the noisy races. The speakers were high above the spectator seats and could be heard at the abbey, although Brother Dominic Mihm had at least convinced the owner to point the speakers away from the monastery.[18] Even closer to home, a barroom had opened just up Diamond Hill Road from the monastery entrance. Its jukebox played loud and long into the night, disturbing the monks who were already in bed by 7:00 p.m. On Saturday nights there was the added attraction of a polka parlor down Diamond Hill Road in the opposite direction. Thus on the night before Sunday, when the community had to rise even earlier than usual, they were serenaded on one side by the latest popular hits and on the other by the strongly marked beats of polka rhythms.

These drawbacks were actually less significant than the fact that transferring the monastery would give the planners a freer hand in providing realistically for a growing community. So Edmund readily agreed to consider the archbishop's offer and sent three monks to speak with the real estate agent and inspect some of the properties he proposed. Though nothing was to come of this plan to move to the Boston area, the idea of a move remained in Edmund's mind and would soon receive new impetus from contacts Brother Leo was making through the kindness of both Michael Grace and Harry John.

Encouraged by the interest of these benefactors Dom Edmund decided to consider other possible locations and even sent Brother Leo to inspect properties in California. One in the Stag's Leap area proved especially appealing, and although nothing immediate resulted, it would factor in the community's plans for a number of years to come.

In a year filled with so many different options, yet another emerged in the fall when Archbishop Byrne of Santa Fe, New Mexico, came to the Valley for a retreat and broached the subject of a possible foundation of Cistercians in his own archdiocese. The idea went no further for the moment, but Edmund filed it away in his mind as one more interesting approach to the problem of crowding at the Valley.

FIGURE 48. *Our Lady of the Valley. Proposal of John C. Hawes for a guesthouse and enlarged church.*

Amazingly enough, notwithstanding all these plans—for the Trappistines, for a foundation in New Mexico, and for a transfer of the Valley itself—Edmund announced on November 11, the day after his presentation of the Wrentham project, that "we now have funds (or sure promises) sufficient to warrant undertaking the building of our guest-house and the completion of our church, and prospects of more, to complete our whole monastery."[19] The notion of staying put was clearly still a good possibility.

Indeed, in a somewhat impetuous move, he had set out for the Bahamas with the newly ordained Father Alberic towards the end of October to discuss the whole massive building scheme with Hawes in person—without, apparently, warning Hawes of his arrival! Hawes happened to be away on another island at the time, but when he found out by telegram that he had two visitors waiting for him in Nassau, he took the next mail boat back. Edmund and Alberic spent a week with him, during which time he produced several revised sketches and plans. From a letter that Hawes wrote to a monk of Prinknash Abbey in England we learn that there had been a change in plan for the Valley building project. Instead of a new church a sixty-room guesthouse would be built to the south of the church. This would be linked to the church by a cloister-like area. The church itself would be lengthened to 200 feet, providing stalls for 130 monks and sixty-five laybrothers.[20]

The extensive renovation of the church still involved reversing its existing plan. The monks' choir would become the space for visitors, the laybrothers' choir would occupy the remaining portion of the church, and a new, elevated choir for the monks would be constructed beyond the existing eastern end of the church, which itself would receive a splendid new facade. The new interior was to be provided with "eleven side altars, five of them around an ambulatory behind the high altar. . . ."[21]

After Dom Edmund and Father Alberic left, Hawes set to work on more complete plans and by November he was able to send the drawings off to the Valley. Unfortunately the only item of this documentation that has survived is a sketch of the entire project, perhaps the one brought back to the monastery from Nassau by Dom Edmund after his trip to the Bahamas.[22] (Fig. 48)

After Dom Edmund returned with the new plans, the architectural commission met on November 26, but opinions were divided.[23] The ever-faithful Sam Morino was contacted, and although his remarks were generally favorable, in several areas he recommended changes based on practical considerations. By January 1947 he would provide the commission with plans incorporating these changes—which in turn would come in for some criticism. Ever modest, Morino would produce still new plans incorporating the committee's latest suggestions.

In the interim, a familiar nemesis struck. In the early hours of Christmas Eve, the old building that had housed the first members of the community prior to the construction of the 1902 building caught fire. Fanned by a brisk wind, the flames continued unabated until the entire building was consumed. Malloy, who climbed onto the roof of the monastery with a pair of binoculars, was able to look down into its cellar, where a recently replenished supply of potatoes and other vegetables was being stored. The ground floor had been serving as a machine shop, the upper floor as a dormitory for some of the transient workers. Fortunately no one had been injured, and a new machine shop was already being built. The greatest loss was the large store of foodstuffs in the cellar, and there was no insurance either on the building itself or its contents.

Throughout January the architectural committee continued to take seriously the great new building project, and Sam Morino kept obediently producing revised graphics, occasionally offering a suggestion.[24] This is, however, the last we hear of the project, which apparently was finally put to rest around this time. And it is also the last we hear of Samuel Morino, who had rendered such notable services to the abbey over a number of years by his architectural drawings and designs, and by the self-effacing spirit in which he tried to carry out the sometimes discordant suggestions of the architectural commission, one member of which still remembers him with affection.[25]

∽ A Visit from the Abbot General

On March 20, 1947, the new Abbot General, Dom Dominique Nogues, arrived by boat in New York for a two-month stay in the United States. He had come to carry out a series of visitations, the first of which was to be at Gethsemani. Though he would be spirited off almost immediately by Gethsemani's prior, Father Robert McGann, Dom Edmund was also on hand at the dock to welcome him. After this brief encounter, Dom Edmund went to Peter Grace's mansion on Long Island for a night's rest before returning to the Valley the next day in a plane provided by Peter. Malloy was on hand to witness his arrival at the Valley:

> After Benediction, saying the Rosary in the orchard behind the Church, I saw a beautiful silver plane circle our property three times— Rev. Father Abbot was in it, returning from N.Y. The plane is one of many belonging to the wealthy Grace family, who entertained R[everend] F[ather].[26]

After making several other visitations, the Abbot General arrived at the Valley on April 11, but his first days there were mostly spent in preparation for eye surgery at St. Elizabeth's hospital in Boston on May 3. By May 10 he was back at the Valley, and the visitation took place on May 19–23. On the last day a group of twenty religious were invited to come to his room to discuss the issue of a move.[27] According to Malloy, the Abbot General gave his firm support to the plan of transferring the monastery "to a more secluded and fertile site."[28] His endorsement gave focus to the abbey's plans for future development and may help account for why the building program for the Valley waned.

It seems likely that among the subjects Edmund and the General discussed in private was the question of a possible change of mother-house for the Valley—specifically, reverting to Bellefontaine. A slowly growing tension between Gethsemani and the Valley may very well have been the motivating force.

ᴂ A Misunderstanding with Gethsemani

That tension, which traced in part to differences between the two communities regarding the observance of the Rule, was exacerbated by an exchange of letters occasioned by the chronicle of Gethsemani that had appeared in the April issue of the Order's periodical, *Collectanea*:

> Not content with his three hundred Trappists at Gethsemani and his two daughterhouses, Our Lady of the Valley and Our Lady of the Holy Spirit, our dear Reverend Father Abbot wants to establish the Trappistines in the United States and has accepted the paternity of a monastery of Cistercians in the Archdiocese of Boston; many difficulties lie ahead, but they do not diminish his courage, for the Cross increases his confidence; already postulants are presenting themselves for the foundation of Trappistines.[29]

Similar affirmations giving the impression that Gethsemani was responsible for the Wrentham foundation appeared in a proposed second edition of Father Raymond Flanagan's book, *Burnt Out Incense*. The Valley learned of this because the text had been sent for approval to one of the Order's censors, Father Gabriel O'Connell, a monk at the Valley. All of this surfaced while Dom Edmund was away at the 1947 General Chapter. In his absence the prior, Father Owen, acting in the name of the abbot's council, wrote a letter of objection to Dom Frederic, who replied:

> In the first place, I have not read one word of *Burnt Out Incense*, or of any other MS that we send out for censorship. I simply have no time to spare. Nor do I have any time to read the *Collectanea*. ... Secondly, after reading carefully the quotations you sent me, I must say that, although not absolutely true as a whole, yet there is a great deal of truth in them and many of the statements made therein are perfectly correct.[30]

Predictably enough, this equivocating answer did not satisfy the Valley's council, so Father Owen wrote again. While admitting that Gethsemani had at one time fostered the idea of such a foundation and had indeed supported the Valley's own efforts, he asserted in no uncertain terms that the specific project originated at the Valley, that it was being carried out there step by step under the auspices of Archbishop Cushing, and—perhaps most telling of all—that the land for the new convent was purchased with Valley funds. The tone of the letter is well reflected in the following points that were singled out:

3. The manner in which you state, "There is no doubt that your good Reverend Father has done very much, and is still doing so, for this proposed foundation," is somewhat provoking because our Reverend Father and our Community has [sic] done everything save what was pointed out above: your going to Glencairn, your approaching Dom Pacôme, and your receiving applications. Our Reverend Father has had all the worry, which is increasing daily, of securing the estate, of footing the bills (it is a truth that Gethsemani has not advanced anything financially), of providing for the upkeep of the estate until nuns arrive.

4. You give a wrong impression re the estate. You seem to imply that our Reverend Father was your delegate even in obtaining it. The truth is simply that if he brought the matter to your attention at successive stages it was principally through courtesy. Bear in mind that all active steps have been taken since his election as local Superior. He took the option, not at your suggestion but on his own and the Archbishop's initiative. Apart from the "Dom Pacôme incident" we were not aware that you had done any negotiating with the Archbishop, and re the celebrated incident, the Archbishop was not a little provoked at the uncalled for interference: [Dunne had written to Cushing, who then sent a copy of the letter to Dom Edmund:] "The enclosed (your letter to him of September 7, 1946) came today. I don't think it deserves an answer. This good Abbot [Dom Frederic] is certainly unfamiliar with this part of the country. . . ." Finally, The Archbishop wrote to Dom Celsus and to the Bishop of Waterford on our suggestion August 20, 1946—we even furnished the addresses.

5. Finally, the Paternity. Let me quote from our *Memoire* to the General Chapter: "The April no. of the *Collectanea* states more or less officially on the part of N.D. de Gethsemani, that the Father Abbot of that Abbey had accepted the paternity of the new Foundation." This statement was corrected by the RRme [Abbot General] on June 7, 1947: the paternity was refused to Dom Frederic last November [1946]. The RRme wrote, through Dom Benedict: "The paternity of the foundation of the Trappistines was never offered to Rt. Rev. Dom Frederic. I may add that when he inquired on that topic I replied myself in the name of our RRme and told him that the Rt. Rev. Dom Edmund would very likely be the Father Immediate of the new foundation, that he would have to take care of the Sisters and furnish them with the chaplains. . . . Dom Frederic knows allright (at least since last November when I wrote the reply above-mentioned) that he will not be the Immediate Father [sic] of the Sisters."[31]

Dom Frederic did not reply to this letter, but upon Dom Edmund's return from the chapter sent him a copy with a covering letter, which in part reads:

> [Father Owen] wrote another letter, which you will find enclosed herewith, and which shows that much of the old spirit of the House, a spirit which I thought was entirely extinguished, still lives. I had hoped that when you were elected and blessed as Abbot that spirit was completely crushed. . . . If you read the enclosed letter, you will see what I refer to. . . . I am sure, Reverend Father, that there is no quarrel existing between you and I [sic] and no quarrels in the communities either, unless created by some the members thereof.[32]

Thus without addressing the issues at hand, Dom Frederic characterizes the whole affair as proof that the Valley was up to its old ways. Admittedly, the bold tone of the Valley's missive must have come as a great surprise, but no excuse is offered for his own lack of vigilance on what was being written by his monks. In any case, things were smoothed out concerning the truth of the Trappistine foundation, and the text of the second edition of *Burnt Out Incense* was emended accordingly. The new version posits an imaginary conversation between the General, Dom Dominique Nogues, and Dom Frederic:

> Dom Frederic hurriedly added, "I've been hoping and praying they would come for longer than I care to remember. I've sent postulants to Canada, grieving that the United States did not have a house of our nuns; but now my grief is at an end. Coming back from the General Chapter I stopped at Mount Melleray to talk with Dom Celsus and the Trappistines at Glencairn. I was acting as delegate for my daughterhouse at the Valley. Dom Edmund has property in the Archdiocese of Boston, and zealous Archbishop Cushing wants Irish Trappistines to make the foundation. But Dom Celsus had better hurry. I have received forty-nine applications already."
> "What exactly did Dom Celsus promise?" inquired Nogues.
> "They will be here by 1950," replied Frederic.[33]

More important than the disagreement itself, this incident demonstrates the Valley's growing sense of independence from Gethsemani—an independence that would become a reality when Bellefontaine replaced Gethsemani as Spencer's motherhouse in 1952. As the years went by, the two houses came more and more to represent two different ways of envisaging the Cistercian life. However, looking back on these differences at a distance of more than fifty years, from the perspective of a closely united region of American Cistercian monasteries, one cannot help but wonder what substance there was to it all.

All of this was happening while Edmund was away at the General Chapter! After the conclusion of the meeting, he decided to visit some of the European houses of the Order and to take Brother Leo along as companion and trail blazer, a role for which Leo was well suited. In order to have sufficient time they set out on July 24. Starting out in Portugal, they traveled through Spain (where they visited Dom Thomas Verner Moore at the Miraflores Charterhouse), France, the Low Countries, Germany, and Belgium. Dom Edmund was much taken with Orval.

They arrived at Cîteaux for the opening of the chapter on September 12. Edmund was able to relate to the capitulants the steps that had been taken for the foundation of a new convent of Trappistines: the purchase of the property and the agreement made with the archbishop of Boston. The chapter voted unanimously in favor of the foundation, and Dom Edmund was named its Father Immediate, his powers beginning with the foundation itself (which eventually took place in the fall of 1949), thus obviating any further discussion about the relationship of the foundation to Mount Melleray or Gethsemani.

After the chapter Edmund and Leo continued their travels, in the Holy Land, Rome, and finally Ireland, where Edmund was at last able to visit Glencairn and meet its abbess, Mother Margaret Shaw, who graciously agreed to receive American candidates as novices in view of the future foundation. Over the next two years ten Americans received their monastic formation at Glencairn, seven of whom would return as foundresses along with seven Irish nuns.

The possibility of the Valley returning to Bellefontaine as its motherhouse seems to have been discussed privately at the chapter (it does not appear in the minutes). Apparently some kind of unofficial agreement must have been reached, since on October 28, after his return, Edmund told Malloy that this would be happening.[34]

Back home, the search for a suitable property for the transfer of the Valley continued. And the Valley's architectural commission, in conjunction with the archbishop's building representative, was also looking for a favorable spot on the Wrentham property for the nuns' new monastery building.

During the summer months Brother Leo had managed to acquire war surplus materials from the government at the specially reduced prices offered to charitable organizations. Included were a truck lift, a tractor, a jeep (which several members of the architectural committee used in their survey of the Wrentham property), a variety of trucks and even an old ambulance, which was eventually inherited by the brothers sent to live at the Wrentham "grange."

Another piece was added to this collection when in October the Johnston, Rhode Island, fire department donated their thirty-four-year-old fire engine to the monastery. Proudly marked "Johnston Hose Co. No. 3," the old "pumper" joined another engine donated earlier by the Valley Falls fire department. The monks were more than happy to receive these gifts given the community's history, and a monastery fire department was organized by Father Peter. The *Providence Journal* reported that one item was still unresolved: "What signal will be used to summon the monastic firemen is still a question. The siren and bell have been removed for use on the new truck; they would be out of place in the peace and quiet of the monastery."[35] The engines would be put to the test in the following spring, when brush fires ignited a pile of old lumber near the saw mill. The fire crew set to work, but just to be sure other fire departments were called in to help. No significant damage was reported.[36]

✍ THE VALLEY'S FIRST FOUNDATION

On September 1, 1946, a year after the end of World War II, the Valley had numbered ninety-two members. Incoming vocations that year had shown no significant increase over the preceding four years. In 1947, however, there was a marked increase in the number of novices, which rose from nine to nineteen among the choir novices and from six to twenty-four among the lay novices, all of this bringing the community total to 123. The immediate consequence of this happy influx was lack of sufficient space to accommodate the newcomers.

Back from the General Chapter, Edmund wrote to Dom Pacôme on October 21 that he was seriously considering moving forward with a foundation to ease this crowding of the Valley community, which by then had risen to 130 members.[37] Archbishop Byrne, who had earlier invited Edmund to make a foundation in his Archdiocese of Santa Fe, informed him around this time that a promising property, the "Valley Ranch," had recently come up for sale in a secluded valley in the Sangre de Cristo mountains at Pecos, New Mexico. Edmund promptly set out to visit the archbishop and to inspect the property.[38] He liked what he saw but decided to send for Fathers Columban and Christopher so he could garner other opinions. Back home, they gave a report to a small group at the Valley on November 12. The very next day the abbot outlined his plan for the foundation, and in the afternoon the community voted unanimously in favor of purchasing the property for $150,000. The Father Immediate was informed and himself wrote to the Abbot General to give his enthusiastic support and to formally ask for the consent of the General and of the definitory.[39]

Careful consideration has to be given to such a project. A monastic community cannot be simply divided into two segments without further ado. Apart from the material considerations of property and buildings, it is necessary to have a group of officers, including not only monks able to manage material affairs, but also formators for young monks in the monastic life, priests to serve as confessors, and most of all a superior capable of leading the group into the new reality of a foundation. Sheer numbers are not enough. By this time, however, the core group of the Valley, the solemnly professed, numbered thirty-two, among them thirty priests. Two more priests among the novices brought the total to thirty-two. These numbers seemed sufficient for making a new foundation, and it was decided to send thirty-seven founders, chosen from all the various categories of monks.

	Choir monks	Laybrothers
Solemnly professed	10	3
Simply professed	4	5
Novices	5	8
Oblates	2	

The group included nine priests.

By November 26, permission for the foundation had been received from the definitory, and Edmund asked Malloy and Father Christopher to go New Mexico "to carry on the arrangements for the coming of the founders."[40] The gift of a large red stake truck arrived at the Valley just in time to carry a first group of religious to New Mexico. (They managed to get a traffic ticket along the way in Indiana).[41] During his stay Malloy drew up a proposal as to how the existing buildings on the ranch might be adapted for monastic use.[42] Upon his return, he gave a report to the community on his experiences, and about a month later, on February 25, 1948, the Holy See gave its formal approval for the foundation.[43]

By early April all was in readiness at the Valley Ranch in New Mexico to receive the founders, and after None on April 18, a farewell party took place in chapter, at which the founders appeared with bandanna handkerchiefs tied around their necks. Nine brothers trained by Brother Luke Roberts provided the music. The next day general permission was given to speak with the departing brethren, and at 4:30 p.m. they headed off for Union Station in Providence, where a specially fitted Pullman car at the end of the "Gilt Edge" train awaited them. Despite the monastery's plea for privacy, the departing founders received a rousing send-off at the station. Among the well-wishers was the brother of Dom James Fox, who just happened to be in the station.[44] A newspaper account added some concrete details:

> There were dozens of well-wishers and a battery of cameramen on hand when the monks reached Union Station.
>
> The priests, novices and laybrothers in their brown, black or white habits, graciously forgot their desire for privacy. They chatted with friends and posed informally as dozens of flash bulbs blazed from cameras.
>
> When the Gilt Edge pulled in, there was an exchange of kisses on both cheeks between the monks and well-wishing priests, former members of the order and friends.
>
> Through the windows of the Pullman Wilbur Wright, they blew kisses and offered blessings in the sign of the cross.
>
> One member carried a white wooden cross, about three feet long, bearing the inscription, "Our Lady of Guadalupe," the name of the new community.[45]

After changes of train in New York and Chicago, they arrived at their final destination in Glorieta, New Mexico, at 8:16 a.m. on April 22. Father Columban, appointed as superior of the community, awaited them. Dom Edmund, who had accompanied them, was back home at the Valley three days later.

✐ The Wrentham Building Rises

After examinations of the Wrentham property back in the late summer and fall of 1947, a site for the convent building had been chosen and its architectural plan was being discussed. But in late February 1948 Archbishop Cushing showed some reticence about immediately going ahead with the project. Undaunted, Dom Edmund headed out in the rain on March 19, the feast of St. Joseph, with two religious to the spot chosen for the building. He then proceeded to bless the site, carefully burying medals of St. Joseph and St. Benedict beneath a wild hawthorn bush around which the first two wings of the building would rise. This bush eventually grew to a considerable size and witnessed the completion of all four wings of the monastery.[46]

By early April the Valley had purchased the Garelick cows on the Wrentham property, and Brothers Philip, Justin and Paul were sent right away to take over the milking; they commuted for several weeks, then took up residence at the farmhouse. Earlier, Edmund had informed Malloy that, instead of going to New Mexico as part of the founding group, he would serve as chaplain for the brothers who would live at Wrentham,[47] but when it came time to send someone, it was the ailing Father Francis Dougherty who was chosen instead of Malloy.[48] During the summer Father Paulinus would replace Father Francis, but Malloy would ultimately get his chance as well. With the arrival of the Brothers and a priest to serve their needs, the little community was now considered a "grange" of the Valley.

Dom Edmund's confidence was rewarded in May when the archbishop finally decided to provide the funds he had promised, and to give permission for construction to begin. By the beginning of June a plan had finally been agreed upon, and on June 6 excavations for the foundations got under way despite heavy rains. By October, things were moving along, and the monks were able to make use of building materials acquired from the dismantling of a mansion in Newport, Rhode Island. Overlooking the entrance to Narragansett Bay, "Bleak House" had been built around 1870 and was acquired by Marsden J. Perry towards the turn of the century. In 1948 his son decided to have it demolished because of taxes. The monks purchased the rights to cart off the stone, which they used in the construction of the chimney and the entranceway to the monastery.[49]

At the Valley itself, despite the firm plans for a transfer Dom Edmund decided to institute at least one further improvement by enlarging the space within the monastic enclosure. The area available to the monks for a bit of contemplative leisure out in the open had always been extremely limited, and was even more so now that the community's numbers had swelled. So on June 14 the old wooden enclosure wall was torn down and replaced with a metal "cyclone fence" that allowed for four times as much room.[50]

Spencer on the Horizon

✍ THE PROJECT OF A TRANSFER

SINCE THE ABBOT General's visitation in 1947, it had been virtually certain that the Valley community would transfer to a new location—but where? Sporadic efforts to find something suitable had turned up nothing. Finally, however, in the spring of 1948 Brother Leo learned from the real estate publication *Previews* that an interesting property in Spencer, Massachusetts, was up for sale: the 700-acre Alta Crest dairy farm, owned by Richard Sagendorph.[1] Bypassing the *Previews* agents, Leo went directly to the home of the owner to make inquiries. To his surprise he learned that he was not the first Trappist to visit Alta Crest. Sometime earlier, monks from Oka had come to inspect Sagendorph's fine herd of Ayrshire cattle. The Sagendorphs were happy to hear of the monastery's interest in their property, for it was getting hard to make ends meet. In the words of Malloy, "The owner wants to sell, as income tax and the cost of labor make dairying unprofitable now."[2]

Dom Edmund went out with Leo to see the property and was impressed. On May 28 he wrote to Bishop O'Leary of Springfield, Massachusetts, in whose diocese the property was located, outlining all the reasons for a transfer; he wanted to know, before considering the purchase of Alta Crest, if the bishop would be willing to welcome the community. The bishop responded enthusiastically.[3]

When Dom Frederic came for the Valley's next visitation in July, Dom Edmund and Leo took him to inspect the prospective property, and he also seemed very pleased. They later recalled his genial mood that day, as he played with the lambs, little realizing that this glimpse into Spencer's future would be his farewell to the Valley community. Less than two weeks later he died on the train that was carrying him to Georgia for the visitation of his foundation at Conyers.

Notwithstanding a certain tension that arose between himself and the Valley towards the end of his life, over the years Dom Frederic had shown himself a true friend. He had been the first one to appreciate Edmund's qualities, in particular his capacity for leadership. Then, relatively soon after Edmund's appointment as superior ad nutum, Frederic moved toward resolving the longstanding anomaly of the Valley's status as priory, by proposing its erection to the status of abbey, which it had acquired in 1876.

Dom Frederic's successor, Dom James Fox, was elected by the community of Gethsemani on August 23, 1948, and thus also became the Valley's new Father Immediate.

It was one thing to have found an ideal property, but now Dom Edmund faced the problem of financing. The asking price was $175,000, a figure beyond the Valley's means. Selling the Valley was one possibility, but whereas homeowners routinely buy a new house contingent on the sale of their old one, it wasn't quite that simple in the monastery's case. For one thing, it would not be possible to give a prospective buyer a realistic date for eventual occupancy. And even if an interested buyer were found, where could 115 monks be housed while a new monastery was being built at Spencer?

Edmund's thoughts naturally turned to the community's benefactors and specifically to Peter Grace. Though we have no details about the first steps taken to contact him, Dom Edmund went to New York on August 28 for a conference with Grace that lasted until late in the night. He returned to the Valley in the early hours of the morning with what he believed to be an extremely attractive offer from Peter, and after None on August 29 he broached the subject of the transfer to all the professed members of the community, outlining Grace's presumed offer:

> Whereas it would be impossible of ourselves to undertake such a project at a time when we are occupied with two foundations, yet owing to the offer of a generous benefactor we are convinced that this trans-

fer is entirely workable. 1) Our benefactor has offered himself to purchase the property and to donate the same to us. 2) Provided we dispose of our present monastic buildings, this friend has promised to complement the funds thereby secured with whatever further funds are required to erect a new monastery.[4]

The following day another meeting was called to permit the community to ask questions and to make further observations. Finally, on August 31, a vote of the solemnly professed was taken. Out of twenty-four votes cast, eighteen were in favor and six opposed.

A document was then drawn up outlining the steps that had led to the vote and expressing a desire for the General Chapter to authorize the transfer—namely, for the benefactor to purchase the property and for the community to sell the Valley and "with the capital received from this sale, complemented by funds which our friend has offered us, erect a monastic cloister according to true Cistercian lines."[5]

Though this particular document apparently never reached the Generalate, the matter was proposed at the next General Chapter, and on September 15 the petition was received favorably:

> The Reverend Father Abbot of Our Lady of the Valley asks for the authorization to transfer his monastery to another place for the following reasons. The present monastery's property is not sufficiently extensive, and is not fertile enough. It is also not sufficiently secluded. There is now an opportunity to buy with the help of a benefactor a fertile and solitary tract of land. The General Chapter approves of the transfer in principle, namely 1) the purchase of the property in question by the benefactor, 2) the sale of the present monastery, and 3) the construction of the new monastery.[6]

Now that the transfer had been approved in principle, the actual purchase of Alta Crest would have to wait at least until January or February, when Peter Grace hoped to have the necessary funds available.[7] Dom Edmund meanwhile turned his attention to selling the Valley property. Brother Leo set to work on this project and contacted the New York firm of John J. Reynolds, Inc. No offers were forthcoming, and in early January 1949 Dom Edmund wrote to Dom James Fox, "So far we have found no purchaser for the Valley property, and if we are to do anything in the way of building this year, we must raise funds in some other way."[8] To this end, he made two trips to Texas to visit friends of the monastery's benefactors in the hope of interesting them in the project—all to no avail.[9]

✎ DISTRESSING NEWS

Around the beginning of February a serious misunderstanding surfaced concerning the Valley's project to buy the Alta Crest farm. A meeting of the monastic council was called, to which Brother Leo was also invited. From the minutes of the meeting we learn:

> At the outset of the meeting, Reverend Father asked Father Alberic to repeat a conversation he (Father Alberic) had had two evenings ago, with Brother Leo. The latter had stated that we would soon find ourselves in a very embarrassing financial position if the Reverend Father went through with the disposal of this Monastery at the "low figure" which was the only way we could sell out (this in connection with the Holy Cross Fathers who are interested, but have so far desisted from naming any figure). Bro. Leo had then gone on to divulge that at the meeting held in New York with Peter Grace on the evening of August 29 of last year Reverend Father had been made to receive an inaccurate idea of the extent to which Mr. Grace would help us effect the transfer, and also of the means which would be taken to raise the funds for the purchase of Spencer and for the construction of the new Abbey there. It would seem that the assurances, upon which the Reverend Father had based his whole presentation of the project to the Conventual Chapter, were not to be taken strictly according to the words used by Mr. Grace to Reverend Father and which Reverend Father repeated verbatim to the Conventual Chapter the following day, but in the light of a previous agreement with Brother Leo.[10]

The gravity of the situation consisted in the fact that both the vote of the Spencer chapter in favor of the transfer and the approval of the General Chapter of 1948 were based on a false premise. The council suggested that someone other than Reverend Father or Brother Leo go to New York to see Peter Grace in order to clarify matters. The person chosen was the prior, Father John Holohan. The council met again on February 17 to hear a report Father John had telephoned to the monastery about his meeting with Mr. Grace:

> Father John had been interviewed by Mr. Grace yesterday morning and our friend was kind and understanding; in fact, the conversation

had not progressed very far before Mr. Grace sized up the situation and whilst undeceived was not thereby losing interest in our Community. It would seem that he had been made to believe that the Spencer purchase would be carried in the main by a one hundred thousand dollar donation by Mr. Duggan of Springfield; this is the first time the fact has ever been mentioned and our letters to Mr. Grace re the purchase made of course no reference whatsoever to any other donation besides Mr. Grace's own. Father John also stated that with his innumerable commitments to other charities, Mr. Grace was not in a position to raise funds without our very active cooperation.[11]

In the course of the ensuing discussion it became clear that the transfer could not go forward as planned since the entire project as presented to the community was based on inaccurate information. But towards the end of the meeting someone suggested that it might be possible to consider only the *purchase* of the Spencer property without an immediate transfer of the community. The report continued: "We have some $55,000 on hand for this purpose and the rest would have to be raised somehow." Grace had agreed to accompany Father John back to the monastery that same evening, and they met with Dom Edmund and Fathers Alberic Gainer, Laurence Bourget and Hugh McKiernan, all council members. The meeting lasted until almost midnight. The next day the abbot's council reported the following:

> Mr. Grace has shared our misunderstanding of the original terms of the part he was to play in our transfer to Spencer; Mr. Grace's mind was perfectly known to Brother Leo, but not to us, and we were allowed to proceed until very recently on false assumptions; Mr. Grace whilst being utterly devoted to us, is unable to sponsor, financially speaking, the transfer project.[12]

The meeting then arrived at the following resolutions, taking up the idea that had surfaced the preceding day:

> 1. We shall proceed with the purchase of Spencer if this can be done independently of our "treasury."
>
> 2. The transfer cannot take place, but a Grange (or Annex) can be set up at Spencer with some 20 Brothers and one or two Fathers (all professed of course).
>
> 3. If a good price (around $400,000) is offered for this property, we "might" consider selling and going through with the transfer, *if* other

donations are forthcoming for the new buildings, which latter might be minus the Church originally planned.[13]

In late March there was still no sign of a buyer for the Valley, and Edmund was coming to realize another aspect of the whole question: the real need of another foundation:

> We shall have to think of a Foundation, because the transfer, if and when it goes through, will be only a partial solution to our problem. In fact, if the property comes to us soon, we shall have to open an "Annex" in Spencer, pending a Foundation.[14]

✍ HOPE FOR A RESOLUTION

New impetus was given to the process in late April as a result of a visit by Stephen Breen, editor of the *Scapular Magazine*. Dom Edmund had discussed Spencer with him and he in turn put Edmund in touch with his friend William Haffert, publisher of a farming magazine. At Edmund's request Haffert visited the Alta Crest property to make an informal appraisal of its value. His reaction was very positive: "As a farm magazine editor, whose work takes him to many farms in the course of a year, I must admit that the particular piece of property is one of the finest of its kind I have ever seen. . . ."[15]

Not only did Haffert visit the property, but he also spoke to Sagendorph as though he himself were interested in the property. He came away with the impression that the owner might be willing to sell for $85,000, well below the asking price, which by now had been lowered to $120,000.[16] Haffert promised to give Sagendorph an answer by morning.

Surprised but inspired by this, Dom Edmund resolved to turn to Harry John for help. On April 29 Haffert wrote to Harry John—no doubt at Edmund's request—singing the praises of the property. Edmund telephoned Harry himself to discuss the situation, explaining that the abbey had $50,000 available but needed about $40,000 more. He hoped that Harry would be willing to come out to the Valley to negotiate the whole sale in his own name.[17] Things were moving quickly, and Harry must have come to the Valley sometime early in May. Just what transpired at that point is not recorded, but there was almost certainly a period of negotiation before a plan of action was decided upon.

❧ THE ABBOT GENERAL VISITS AGAIN

In the midst of all these negotiations Dom Dominique Nogues once again arrived at the Valley for a visitation, which took place on May 23-29. The Abbot General's own private notes reveal his confidential view of the situation of the monastery and—of particular interest—his impressions of the superior's personality: "The Father Abbot is nervous and lets it be seen when he is contradicted; he has difficulty in carrying out his responsibilities, and his health is poor." In an earlier redaction of the document he notes: "Superior nervous—sickly—touchy, but very devoted to his community." He also adds: "The community is certainly fervent. There is too much noise in the guesthouse; those on retreat are too mixed in with the religious. There are women all about."[18]

By the time of Nogues' visitation, plans for the purchase of Spencer must have been very near completion. However, a small group of important office holders in the abbey were not at peace about the situation and presented the General a report drawn up on the very day the visitation opened. It spelled out the history of the project, paying special attention to the controversial events of mid-February, and even included copies of the four meetings of the abbot's council. But it all failed to produce the desired effect: The General made little of the affair. His notes make as much clear and also reveal an important new detail not previously mentioned:

> The great question is the transfer from Valley Falls to Spencer. The community is hesitant, above all the officers; however, when the vote was taken, there were 16 in favor, which is a sufficient majority. But they are asking for a loan of $400,000 in installments of about $50,000. They could pay it back in twenty years. The banks willingly offer loans for this sum; benefactors would help. The present monastery is surrounded by nearby villages, houses of pleasure.[19]

Other sources indicate that the idea of borrowing $400,000 had been suggested to Dom Edmund by the legal counsel of the Grace firm as a practical way to provide funds to get the building program under way once the property was purchased.[20] The conventual chapter of Spencer voted favorably on the loan on May 28, the day before the visitation ended; the General himself had proposed spacing the loan installments. A final point concerned the fate of the Valley property itself. If it could not be sold for $400,000 at least, the plan would be to keep it "as a merely temporary foundation."[21]

In the short space of just over three months, a move to Spencer was once again being seriously considered, along with a building program for a new monastery. One cannot help but get a sense of inevitability about where the community was heading.

On May 27, while the visitation was still going on, an agreement to purchase was drawn up between the Sagendorphs and the Valley in partnership with Michael Grace and Harry John, with the abbey holding 5/9 of the property and the two benefactors 2/9 each. The purchase price was set at $90,000. By July things were ready for the final step and on July 15 the act of sale was concluded. In due time the two lay partners contributed their portions of the property to the abbey as a gift, Harry John on December 9, 1949, and Michael Grace on March 16, 1950.[22] Thus, as things turned out, the ones who came to the rescue were Harry John, the man who came to the Valley with his $5,000 check in the summer of 1946, and Michael Grace, whom Harry had recommended to Brother Leo in the first place.

The New Home: A First Move

✍ THE SAGENDORPH FARM

WITH THE ACQUISITION of the Sagendorph holdings, the abbey found itself in possession of one of the most prestigious farming properties in Massachusetts. Noah Sagendorph had come to Spencer in 1863 and married into the prominent Sugden family. In addition to his interest in the local mills he turned his attention to dairy farming, and in 1898 built up a Guernsey herd at a farm on Pleasant Street, not far from the center of town. His son Arthur was sent to study at Cornell's School of Agriculture and probably soon after his graduation in 1901 was able to purchase the Henry Knowlton farm in North Spencer thanks to a considerable inheritance from his grandfather Richard Sugden.[1]

This property was about five miles from the center of town on a lesser road leading off what is today Route 31. Arthur eventually expanded his holdings along this road by purchasing a number of smaller adjacent farms. One of these, on a hilltop immediately to the south, was owned by David Manning (the hill is still known as Manning Hill); another, farther south on the slopes of this same hill, had been in the Allen family at least from the time of an 1834 map.[2] The top of Manning Hill commanded an imposing view east to the Sevenmile River valley and west to the Fivemile River valley. Early on, Sagendorph's property became known as the Alta Crest Farms and the road eventually became Alta Crest Road.[3]

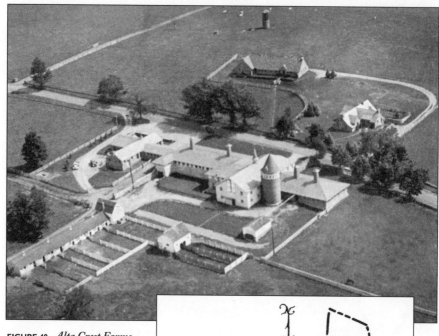

FIGURE 49. *Alta Crest Farms around 1939. Aerial view from southwest.*

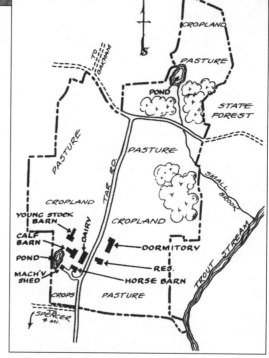

FIGURE 50. *Alta Crest Farms. Plan. The road shown as Tar Road is the Alta Crest Road.*

Sagendorph made the Knowlton property the center of his holdings and built an eighteen-room house for the farm manager on the other side of the road from the main barn. A "private stable" erected around 1903 survives to the present day as the cellarer's building. Over the years this building would be reserved for animals other than cows and eventually came to be known as the horse barn. Plans for this building were drawn up by the firm of Cutting, Carleton, and Cutting of Worcester, and though no architectural drawings survive for the farm manager's home, it is quite possible that it too was the work of this firm. By 1909 Sagendorph had begun to specialize in Ayrshire cows, and he built a large barn for them about half a mile south of the old main barn. The refinements of this structure betray Sagendorph's dedication to his herd, for which he was to become famous among the foremost breeders of Ayrshires. It was said to be the largest barn in Massachusetts.

In the course of time he began raising a variety of other types of animals and fowl:

> Sagendorph's agricultural interests were not limited to cattle. The newspaper reported that not only did he raise angora goats, white China geese, Toulouse geese, Rouen ducks, Plymouth Rock chickens, Guinea hens, English sheep dogs, French bull dogs, Shire draft horses, Morgan horses, Scotch highland sheep, Toggenburg goats, pedigreed Jersey pigs, Scotch Highland cattle, and Sicilian donkeys, but they often won prizes at fairs throughout New England.[4]

In 1918 the main barn burned down and once again the firm of Cutting, Carleton, and Cutting was called in the following year to replace it with a handsome masonry structure using cobblestones gathered from local fields for the exterior walls. This would one day be transformed into the first monastery at Spencer.

Two large fires in the 1930s would occasion the rebuilding of other nearby structures in the same style of masonry. In 1933 after a fire destroyed the old house that Sagendorph had built in 1902 for the farm manager, the same architects constructed a smaller cottage on the site using the same masonry as the new barn opposite it. It would become the residence of Arthur's son, Richard, who by this time had taken over the supervision of crop production on the farm. In 1938 the firm of Harry L. Meacham was engaged to construct an attractive addition to the main barn itself, in the form of a milk processing plant and a milking parlor with large picture windows, where visitors could watch as the prize animals of the herd were milked.

Such a large farm required considerable numbers of workers, and sometime prior to 1907 a building "of stucco construction" had been erected as a boarding house for those who were unmarried. This was situated on the other side of the Alta Crest Road from the main barn at a distance of about a hundred yards from the road itself.[5] Fire struck again, destroying this building on the afternoon of March 12, 1933. It was replaced two years later by a fieldstone structure of similar dimensions. The new version included, in addition to a dining room and small bedrooms for the workers, an apartment at its north end for the family that managed the building and provided meals.[6] Together, the new boarding house, barn and cottage, all in the same style, formed a central cluster of buildings that blended into a harmonious whole.

The buildings of the former Allen and Manning farms to the south of the main complex housed families of workers.[7] The family at the former Allen farm cared for livestock that were housed in the barn across the road from the house, and for fowl in a cluster of henhouses nearby. The farm manager and his family now lived in a duplex near the Ayrshire barn on a road leading west from the Alta Crest Road.

Other, smaller buildings that would ultimately find use in the new monastery included two barns for younger cows to the west and a machine shop to the south.

On December 14, 1945, the famous Ayrshire barn became the latest victim of fire, which must have pained the aging Arthur Sagendorph more than any of the other losses. There was also the practical consideration of having to find space to house the herd of thirty cows and two bulls, which fortunately were saved from the fire. Less than six months later, on June 3, 1946 Arthur died.

The overall responsibility for the farm now fell to his son Richard. The farm was proving more and more difficult to maintain, a situation that would grow increasingly acute with the burden of income tax and the cost of labor, as Malloy was later to note.[8] In fact, on September 22, 1947, an auction was organized for the "dispersal of the milking herd."[9] Ninety-three animals were put up for sale, but a small number were kept aside, it being Richard's intention to continue the dairy operation on a reduced scale. After the farm was sold, these were transferred to a property in North Brookfield, where the old name of Alta Crest lived on.

It is not known exactly when the property was put on the market, but it must have been not too long after the auction. In any event, the advertisement appeared in *Previews* by the spring of 1948, when Brother Leo saw it and the wheels of change began to turn more quickly for the monks of the Valley.[10]

✑ PLANS FOR A NEW MONASTERY BUILDING

Boldly anticipating the permission to borrow $400,000, which he intended to ask of the General Chapter in September, Dom Edmund began making arrangements for the construction of a permanent monastery on the newly acquired property. In fact, a mere four days after the final closure of the sale on July 15, the firm of Eggers and Higgins in New York City had already drawn up plans for "Our Lady of the Valley, Spencer, Massachusetts." These include a site plan and a set of more detailed drawings for a monastic quadrangle to be situated on a hilltop approximately 150 yards north of the old workmen's dormitory. The church is oriented in traditional fashion—unlike the church at the Valley—with the apse to the east. An octagonal chapter house sits off the eastern range of the cloister. These few drawings are the only existing documentation of this initial plan for Spencer.

Edmund was also in touch with Charles D. Maginnis of the firm of Maginnis and Walsh in Boston, and on September 19 he furnished Maginnis with a detailed site plan and a lengthy description of the architectural spaces the main monastery building should contain. By November 3 Maginnis had prepared a series of drawings for "St. Mary's Abbey, Spencer, Massachusetts." The name had changed to "Holy Cross Abbey" by the time Maginnis finished fine-tuning these plans in December. Unfortunately, the site plan sent by Edmund has not been preserved, although a section drawing by the architects make it clear that the building was to be situated on a hill.[11] The two plans did share the same orientation of the buildings, a chapter house that was octagonal, and a refectory in the traditional Cistercian position, perpendicular to the south wing of the quadrangle. The Maginnis and Walsh plan was more elaborate, with additional structures beyond the south wing.

Despite the ambitious character of both of these proposals, it seems clear that Edmund intended only a portion of the full plan to be constructed as a first stage of the building program.[12] The *Supplemental Report* drawn up for the definitory on October 31 notes that the plan was:

. . . to complete three units of the proposed monastery at Spencer. Probably, these will consist of a Church and two permanent wings. These three wings of the building will enable us to house ninety religious in permanent quarters with all regular places. Nothing more will be absolutely necessary to enable the community sent there to lead a life regular in all details.[13]

✑ WAITING FOR THE PASSING OF THE DEEDS

The original purchase agreement of May 27 had stipulated that the deeds would be passed one month after the signing of this agreement (June 27) "unless otherwise mutually agreed" and that the Sagendorphs would have continuing use of the property until July 15, 1950, exactly a year after the final settlement.[14] But the workmen's dormitory was to be given over to the monks as a dwelling place, and they could choose a plot of approximately four acres "for the purpose of commencing thereon the building operations."[15] It was further stipulated that the monks could require the sellers to vacate their cottage and move to "premises south of the road on which the duplex was situated," a reference no doubt to the house on the former Allen farm. The dairy operation in the main barn was to continue unhindered. The Sagendorph herd was by now much reduced, and by the time the family moved to their new farm in North Brookfield, they had only twenty or thirty heifers.

Another important stipulation was that from the time of the actual purchase and the passing of the deeds, the purchasers would have the right "to institute and prosecute before the proper Town authorities any and all proceedings to abandon and close all public roads adjacent to the premises described in this Agreement." From early on in the negotiations, the monks had seen the importance of closing to traffic the two public roads entering the property. One of these was a road leading west from the property to another road parallel to the Alta Crest. (Fig.50) Of even greater importance was the closure of the Alta Crest Road itself. This old road lay at the heart of the Sagendorph property, and if it were not closed it would be impossible to assure the seclusion needed for the new monastery. The lessons learned at Cumberland had made their impression on the community.

Dom Edmund had hoped things could be settled "before signing any papers,"[16] and he had discussed the matter with Bishop O'Leary during the negotiations. The bishop was sensitive to the problem and, according to verbal reports, personally charged the pastors of the two

Catholic churches in Spencer to get their parishioners out in force to attend the appropriate town meeting and vote in favor of the monks. The bishop died on October 10, 1949, however, not living to see the successful outcome of his strategy when the town meeting that settled the issue finally took place on March 9, 1950.

✎ The General Chapter Gives Permission for the Loan

By the middle of August it was getting close to the time for the General Chapter, which would have to give its approval for the $400,000 loan on which the building program at Spencer now depended. Edmund wrote to the Abbot General at Cîteaux, where the chapter was to meet, and proposed asking the chapter to give permission for the loan, echoing the General's own suggestion that the whole amount would not be "borrowed at once but only inasmuch as the funds are needed to continue construction at Spencer." He also told Dom Dominique about the plans being drawn up for the buildings:

> We have engaged an architect after serious and prolonged consideration; this architect is now in the process of drawing up the plans and designs for our new monastery. The plans however will not have been sufficiently elaborated to enable me to present them at the next General Chapter.[17]

The General replied that more detailed information on the financial status of Spencer would certainly be requested by the chapter. Since Edmund was not planning to attend, the General asked him to send a report,[18] which Edmund did at the beginning of September.[19]

When the chapter met on September 12-15, a commission was set up to study Spencer's loan request. Looking beyond the $400,000 to begin the construction, the commission saw that Spencer's financial report indicated the final figure needed to complete the project would approach $1,250,000. The commissioners decided to request further information from Dom James, the Valley's Father Immediate.[20]

Somewhat embarrassed, Dom James had to admit that he knew nothing of the proposed loan, since Dom Edmund had failed to mention anything about it. Nonetheless, the chapter decided that upon submission of a satisfactory report, the definitory would be commissioned to grant the request. Dom James wrote in haste to Edmund asking that such a report be drawn up and sent to him at Gethsemani. He duly received it and forwarded it to the definitory in Rome.[21] The definitory replied favorably on November 17, and permission to seek the loan was finally granted.

But there were still problems. The estimates of expenses provided by Eggers and Higgins and by Maginnis and Walsh for the existing plans made it clear that even constructing three wings of such a monastery was beyond the combination of any donations from benefactors and the loans contemplated by the Valley.

These economic constraints no doubt led Maginnis and Walsh to revise their plans. A new version was ready by February. Among other things the cluster of additional buildings and open courts to the south of the south wing were eliminated and the chapter house now appears as a circular rather than octagonal structure.[22]

A further measure was taken to meet the economic challenge. Instead of proceeding immediately to build a permanent monastery, the existing farm buildings would be converted into a *temporary* monastery for the monks. A petition was sent to the definitory on February 15, 1950, along with a plan and a detailed description of where each of the regular monastic places would be situated in the reworked buildings.[23]

The definitory wrote back on February 28 approving the decision albeit with some hesitation, questioning the prudence of moving the community before more permanent buildings had been constructed. In any case, the last step in the process would be the approval of the Holy See, which required a letter from the local bishop.

✍ THE FIRST MONASTIC SETTLERS

Even before the definitory's permission was granted, Father Paulinus Fitzgerald and Frater Paul Shiebler were sent to Spencer to supervise the conversion of the barn buildings across the road from the Sagendorph residence into a temporary monastery.[24] They left the Valley at 10:30 a.m. on February 2 in the monastery's Chevy, stopping on the way to pay their respects to Father Leon McGraw, the pastor of Holy Rosary parish in Spencer. Throughout these early days Father McGraw proved to be a good friend to the monks in their various needs. That first evening he invited them to dine at the rectory, after which they moved on to Alta Crest. A truck had been sent ahead with the necessary furnishings, so they were able to settle down for their first night in their new home in the "dormitory" building. The next day they offered Mass at Holy Rosary parish, but in the course of that same day they adapted one of the rooms in the dormitory as a chapel and installed an altar. On February 4, Mass was offered for the first time on the property. The Martel family who had been caring for the dormitory was still living in the apartment at its north end; they would move to a duplex on the property on the tenth. Until then, the monks were the guests of the Sagendorph family for meals at their home. The installation of the monastery's first telephone with the number Spencer 3011 put the finishing touch on their moving in.

Relations with the Sagendorphs were warm and grew even closer with the arrival of the monks' own cook, Brother Bernardine O'Shea, on February 9. He would be a frequent visitor to the Sagendorph home. Paul Sagendorph, one of Richard's sons, has fond memories of many Ping-Pong games played with him in the attic of the house. On at least one occasion the Sagendorphs attended Benediction in the new little chapel.[25]

In the first fervor of those early days Paulinus and Paul gathered in the little chapel each morning to chant Vigils and Lauds with the temperature at ten degrees Fahrenheit, an experience that eventually led to the installation of baseboard heating.

Even with all they had to do—and the ongoing concerns about finances—Frater Paul Shiebler gave some thought to the question of which parcels of land adjacent to the property were worth purchasing in order to ensure the tranquillity of the future monastery. Two properties to the west could be crucial in connection with the closing of the public roads, so he made initial contacts with the owners.[26]

∾ RESTRUCTURING THE BARNS

The cluster of adjacent barns at the heart of the farm would provide space for the core structures of the new monastery. The hay barn was flanked on the north by a large cow barn on the same level as itself. On the south it was flanked by a smaller cow barn constructed at a lower level. (See Fig. 51 where the hay barn appears as "church.") Plans called for the transformation of the hay barn into the monastery's church, the adjacent silo serving as bell tower. The lower barn was to become the dormitory. The larger cow barn would be divided into a large central passageway flanked on the west by a chapter room and on the east by a series of offices. The 1938 milking parlor for prize animals would become the library-scriptorium, and the milk processing plant was to be

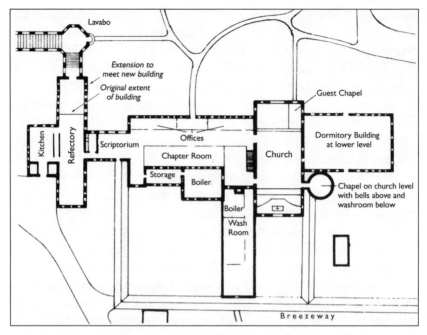

FIGURE 51. *St. Joseph's Abbey. Sagendorph buildings converted into the temporary monastery. This also shows the Lavabo building of the new monastery and the link to the temporary monastery.*

transformed into a refectory with adjacent kitchen.

By February 24 preparations were under way for the conversion of these buildings. Frater Paul had begun to purchase building supplies, and 3,000 feet of planed spruce was brought from the Valley and stored in the horse barn. On March 5 both Paul and Paulinus returned to the Valley to take part in a meeting of the architectural committee. On March 13 Dom Edmund came to Spencer with Brother Blaise Drayton, and the Antell brothers of Spencer were contracted to perform the work for a fixed fee of $17,000.[27] Work began in earnest a week later with the tearing down of the stanchions in the lower cow barn.

There was talk of building a large new barn at Spencer; Brother Bernard Matthews recalls overhearing such a conversation while he was dusting along a corridor at the Valley. Brothers Dominic and Philip visited Spencer to get an idea of what would be possible, and it was soon decided to erect the new barn on the site of the old Ayrshire barn that had been destroyed by fire in 1945.[28] The wing of the old barn that had housed the Ayrshire calves had partially survived. This was restored and incorporated into the new structure. Once again Antell supervised the construction.

∽ A New Diocese and a Meeting with Its First Bishop

Until 1950, Spencer had been part of the Diocese of Springfield, but on January 14, Rome had created the new Diocese of Worcester, coinciding with the county of the same name and including the town of Spencer and its environs. On March 7, Dom Edmund and a contingent of eleven monks from the Valley (including Paul and Paulinus) assisted at the installation of Bishop John Wright as Worcester's first bishop, rounding off the event with a meal at the home of Frater Ignatius Sullivan's parents.[29]

Two days later, the long-awaited town meeting about closing the two public roads took place. As Bishop O'Leary had urged, the town's Catholics turned out in great numbers. Paul's diary entry for March 9 lingered longer than usual on the event:

> Annual town meeting in Spencer.
>
> Art 36 and 37 re abandoning town road thru our property . . . Discussion on article lasted over an hour. Our article sponsored by Howard Hurley. [Unintelligible words] The State auditor took floor in our behalf against the principal opponents, Mr. Liedwell [?] and Mr. Kerlin and his son. Father McGraw had spoken in church last Sunday, as had also Father Durocher who is administrator of the French church.

The town's official record of votes reads:

> Article. 36. Voted that the Town abandon as a town road, the so-called Alta Crest Farm Road, from the point where this road enters the limits of the so-called Alta Crest Farm property, to the point where it joins the so-called Oakham Road to the west. YES 508 NO 39
>
> Article 37. Voted that the Town abandon as a town road, the cross road running east and west between the so-called Alta Crest Farm Road, and the boundary line of the so-called Parker and Eddy land, or act thereon. YES 485 NO 27

On March 15 Paulinus and Paul joined Dom Edmund for an interview with Bishop Wright. Paul's diary has preserved an account of the visit:

Rev. Father, Father Paulinus and Paul interview with Bp. Wright
at 2:30 PM. Bp. okayed erection of Abbey

- opposed to expensive structure as not being in conformity with
our spirit.

- opposed to name of Holy Cross due to possible conflict with
name of Holy Cross College

- agreed to let us make personal contacts with not more than
12 individuals to seek aid

- He stated that people suffered greatly in this country during
depression and wanted to count on our *material* aid in way of
milk, if necessary, in a future depression.[30]

The bishop's objection to the proposed name for the new monastery
led Dom Edmund and the community to rethink the matter for what
was apparently the third time. "Our Lady of the Valley" (July 1949),
then "St. Mary's Abbey" (November 1949), then "Holy Cross Abbey"
(December 1949) finally became "St. Joseph's Abbey" on a revised plan
dated July 28, 1950.[31]

The *Worcester Daily Telegram* reported on the meeting between the
monks and the bishop and offered a description of the latest plans for
the adaptation of the property for monastic uses:

Original plans for the monastery called for construction of an entirely
new set of buildings on the hilltop overlooking Route 31. These were
ruled out some time ago.

Changes include the conversion of the residence of Richard S.
Sagendorph, former manager and treasurer of the farms, into the
abbot's home with rooms for visiting prelates.

The hay barn will be made into a church; the lower barn into a dormitory for 50 religious, and the upper cow barn into living quarters.

The pasteurizing room will become a dining hall and the bottling
room, a kitchen.

The calf shed will be altered to house the laundry, wardrobe room,
shoe shop and book binding shop.

The horse barn will be made into a novitiate, with living quarters
and locker rooms on the first floor, a dormitory for 25 or 30 persons
on the second floor, and a chapel. . . .

Father Paulinus said that a cloister or covered passage would connect
the main cow barn with the out-buildings.

The infirmary will stand alone near the abbot's house. Dairy workmen lived in the structure until a short time after the sale of the farms. . . .

A guest house for retreatants will be established on the farm unit several hundred yards from the main buildings. This is the portion of the Trappist territory on Alta Crest crossroad.

The old barn there will be made into a porter's lodge, and the crumbling cow barn will be reconstructed to provide tie-up for 30-head of pure-bred cows. . . .

A permanent church and permanent living quarters for professed members of the community however, will be erected. Drawings are now being prepared by Maginnis & Walsh, architects in Boston.

The drawings are not expected to be ready before Spring and it will be perhaps another year before construction is started.[32]

Edmund wrote to the definitory on March 19 to thank its members somewhat belatedly for the permission given on February 28 for the transfer. Included was a document the definitory had requested: Bishop Wright's written approval of the establishment of the monastery in his diocese. Edmund also passed on the amazing news that a foundation was in sight, thus making it feasible to vacate the premises of the Valley and facilitate its sale. No doubt he hoped this would calm the definitory's lingering fears. Brother Leo was already in Virginia looking for a property, and by June a property would already have been purchased.

ᴖ The Nuns Arrive

All this time since Spencer was discovered, the building program at Wrentham had been moving forward. On March 1, 1949, Edmund told Malloy privately that he was to be grange master at Wrentham. This time he held true to his promise. Five days later Malloy packed his things and set off with the grange brothers in the "Wrentham ambulance" for his new home. His confreres were Brothers Justin Cunningham (who would be in charge of the milking), Paul Heide, John Gore, Kenneth Hartley, Martin DeMarco, and Bernardine O'Shea (who served as cook until he moved to Spencer less than a year later). Brother Arthur Beaudry and Brother Xavier Gileesse also resided there temporarily to prepare the fields.

Two wings of the Wrentham convent and the cloister were completed in March, and Malloy's first great experience as grange chaplain was witnessing Archbishop Cushing's fitting of the cornerstone into the newly completed building:

> Very soon after None priests and lay people began arriving to inspect the convent (as the Archbishop had announced that it could be visited), and I was kept busy entertaining them and directing them, whilst remaining at my post. About 4 PM three school busses [sic] brought the whole community of 130 from Valley Falls (first time in history they left the monastery in a body). Archbishop Cushing arrived promptly at 4:30 and the ceremony began. About 2000 people witnessed it. . . . I merely kissed the Archbishop's ring and shook hands with Mr. John McMahon[33] [former owner of part of the land purchased for the convent] and went over to the chaplain's house. . . . Many of the religious went thru' the [chaplain's] house before the ceremony, and all were pleased.[34]

Though the buildings were now complete, there were the furnishings to think of, and the summer months would be taken up with landscaping and constructing a new access road to the convent building.[35]

During his time at Wrentham, Malloy paid occasional visits to Mr. McMahon at his home across the road from the chaplain's house:

> This afternoon I made the visit Rev. Father had advised to Mr. McMahon's home, across the way. He was extremely cordial, showed me his house and some of its treasures—gold vestments on the wall; the be-outiful [sic] views from the third floor porch; the rock garden and flower beds where "something new comes up every day or 2"; the "bird sanctuary." I told him of my love of birds, similar to his; he showed me his bird books. An old friend, Mr. McGowan was there.[36]
> . . . visited Mr. McMahon for the second time, saw his lovely rock garden, tulip garden, exotic trees. He gave me a fine pair of binoculars (for use). I watched scenes in EGYPT, via his TELEVISION cabinet![37]

Malloy's stay at Wrentham was to be a brief one. On June 18, Dom Edmund told him that Father Anselm Fitzgerald would be returning from the Guadalupe foundation because of poor health and asked Malloy if he would be willing to take his place. He accepted and on June 28 wrote in his *Journal*: "Spent last day in New England at home in my monastery of Our Lady of the Valley." In the afternoon he was driven to the Boston airport to board a plane for New Mexico.[38]

After years of preparation, all was finally in readiness for the first American foundation of Trappistines. There were six choir nuns, six novices, and two professed laysisters. Six of these were Irish: Mother Bernard O'Donnell, the superior; the choir sisters Mothers Agnes Fahey and Imelda Power (in perpetual vows) and Sister Patrick Heraghty (in temporary vows); and the laysisters Francis Fitzgerald and Veronica Griffin. One was English, Mother St. John Tighe (in perpetual vows). The others, all choir sisters, were North Americans: from the United States Mother Michael Howe (in perpetual vows), Sister Paul Reilly (in temporary vows), and Sisters Stephen Vigilante, Celsus Payant, Andrew Forster, and Edmund Faglio, (novices); and from Canada Sister Emmanuel Holohan (novice).[39]

They left the Abbey of Glencairn on the afternoon of September 23 and went to Cobh to spend the night in a hotel in order to be ready for the departure of the ship *Britannica* the next morning. Archbishop Cushing happened to be in Ireland at the time leading a pilgrimage to the Emerald Isle; Bishop John Wright, soon to become bishop of the new Diocese of Worcester, was along as his Auxiliary. The archbishop and his group were also returning on the *Britannica;* as a special send-off the bells of the cathedral were rung late into the night of the twenty-third, and in the morning the dock was lined with children and other wellwishers, singing "Come Back to Erin!" The sisters liked to think that part of this festive send-off was for themselves, little realizing that the Irish sisters in the group would in 1955 follow the call of the song and indeed come back to Erin to help out at Glencairn, which was by then going through difficult times.[40]

The sisters, escorted by Dom Celsus as well as the archbishop and Bishop Wright, arrived in the United States on October 1. They were welcomed at the doors of their new home by a battery of abbots: Dom Edmund, Dom James Fox of Gethsemani, and Dom Eugene Martin of New Melleray. Though they would start living in their new quarters right away, the enclosure was not yet in force since the brothers still had a certain amount of work to complete in the building. The sisters put this time to good use, getting to know their new property.[41]

A pleasant surprise was arranged for them two days after their arrival: They were brought to Our Lady of the Valley for a visit and a buffet lunch with the monks in the courtyard in front of the 1902 building. They assisted at Vespers and Benediction that evening from the tribune of the guests and were even invited to sing a Gregorian chant at the latter service.[42]

Finally, on November 21 Archbishop Cushing came to bless the convent and to officially declare the enclosure in force. Father Anselm Fitzgerald, whom Malloy had replaced in New Mexico, took Malloy's place in turn and was assigned as their first chaplain.

On December 17, the day on which the first of the Advent "O Antiphons" is sung, the sisters were joined by four others who had previously entered the convent of N.-D. du Bon Conseil (popularly known as St. Romuald's) in the province of Quebec. Two of these, Sisters Julia Haigh and Pia Casteletti, would leave the monastery; the two others, Sisters Angela Norton and Bernadette Saia, would remain. (Both were religious in perpetual vows; Sister Angela had belonged to the Dominicans, and Sister Bernadette to the Missionary Sisters of the Divine Child.) All four were met at the station in Boston and were treated to a visit to the Valley before going to Wrentham.

By this time monastic life at the convent had begun in earnest. A document released by the definitory in Rome on January 14, 1950, gives some idea of Wrentham's first steps toward self-identity. In an obvious attempt to resolve what seemed to be a clash of interests, the document purports to "define the authority of the undernamed superiors" involved in the foundation. Dom Celsus is to "persevere in an attitude of non-interference." For his part Dom Edmund is reminded that:

> he must remember that he is not to interfere too often, that he is not to put himself in the place of the local superioress, in particular that he cannot, by his own authority alone, change an official nor send a religious back to Glencairn. Nay breathing the spirit of St. Benedict, let him see to it that vices are uprooted "with prudence and charity" and making his own the spirit of Cistercian legislation, let him do all in his power to keep peace in the Community and to foster therein respect for the local superioress and for the Abbess of Glencairn.
>
> He has to do with a new community, a seedling from Ireland. Let him not wonder if, in points of local usage, he find in it traces of its parent house, and let him not forbid anything save what is directly opposed to the Holy Rule, to our Constitutions or to our Regulations. To make any important change he must await the regular visitation and take the advice of the Father Visitor.[43]

As the definitory document expressed it, the Abbess of Glencairn continues to hold authority over the sisters of Wrentham and alone has the right to delegate her authority to their superior, but she is reminded: "she will have the prudence not to restrict overmuch this delegation for affairs of ordinary administration. If already this delegation has not been given let it be so without delay." Even more significantly: "Moreover, let her keep well before her mind that this foundation is made in America, that its members are to be Americans, that in the near future it ought to become 'sui juris' and be able to manage its own affairs. Hence her aim ought to be to make it gradually self-sufficient as a Cistercian community of nuns in America."

The words of counsel to the local superior are few, suggesting that she "take account of the directions of her Mother Abbess, whom she can freely consult, and those of her Father Immediate. Let her arrange details regarding the Regulations with her Father Immediate." In other words she is to do her best to maintain some kind of balance between the abbess of Glencairn and her Father Immediate—perhaps not the easiest of tasks.

What is most significant here is that after little more than three months the definitory is thinking in terms of Wrentham's independence in "the near future."

On March 21, 1950, as the monks of Our Lady of the Valley celebrated the feast of St. Benedict, all seemed poised for the great project of transfer to Spencer, But shortly after the community retired, an event occurred that would considerably change the way that transfer would take place.

FIGURE 52. *Our Lady of the Valley. Second monastery, 1902. Foyer. The stairs in the background led to the guestrooms on the second floor. A display case to the left of the stairs contained samples of the monastery's production of vestments. Smoke coming from under these stairs alerted a guest to the fire, which broke out on the night of March 21, 1950. To the extreme left (not visible) is the corridor leading to the confessional in which the fire probably started.*

The Fire

A T 10:15 P.M. ON MARCH 21, 1950, an urgent call came in to the switchboard at the Pawtucket telephone exchange: A fire had broken out at the monastery of Our Lady of the Valley. The alarm went out immediately to the local Valley Falls fire station and to ten others in the vicinity.[1]

The fire was discovered by one of the guests on retreat. Waking up and smelling smoke, he came down to the foyer from the second floor guests' wing and discovered flames coming out from under the stairs he had just come down. After a vain attempt to bring the flames under control with a fire extinguisher, he rushed back up to the second floor to warn the other guests, and together they safely left the building—in their pajamas.

The cellarer, Brother Michael Desilets, who was sleeping in one of the dormitories on the third floor, had also smelled smoke and come down to the foyer. Rushing down to get a fire hose from the basement, he discovered that there were no flames on that level and decided instead to go back to the dormitories to warn the monks, who were sleeping in what was effectively a firetrap on the third floor. Instead of crying out an alarm, he roused the prior, Father John (the abbot was sleeping that evening in the infirmary wing), and urged him to wake the others. Instead, Father John followed Brother Michael back down to evaluate the situation—a move he later regretted. Fortunately others nearby had heard the news and began making the rounds of the cells to waken the rest of the monks. Characteristically reluctant to break silence, some tried to communicate in sign language or in a subdued whisper!

There were two stairways leading down from the third level dormitories. The one at the north end was normally used by the monks since it gave access to the monastic areas of the building; on the first floor it came out into the cloister at the rear of the building. The other staircase, which was in a small corridor separating the two third floor dormitory areas, led down to the corridor of the guest rooms on the second floor and then to the foyer on the first floor. Normally locked, it was by chance open on the fateful evening.

Among the first to leave the dormitory was Father Laurence Bourget, who came all the way down the north stairs to the cloister. There was still no smoke there, but the lack of oxygen was becoming increasingly noticeable. Father John, who had gone back upstairs and was leading a group down the same stairs, insisted that Father Laurence and the others follow him through a door into the laybrothers' common room on the front side of the building. From there they were able to safely jump about ten feet to the ground.

Running around to the church and into the shorter cloister that flanked it, Father Laurence saw that the vestments and sacred vessels stored in the sacristy were being passed out of a window and handed to someone on a ladder outside. From there they were taken to a nearby field at a safe distance from the burning building. All of the sacristy's sacred materials were removed, and amazingly enough the operation only took about fifteen minutes.[2] Father Laurence proceeded to the church and organized a group of laybrother novices to remove some of the large choir books and bring them to the choir novitiate building. Father Alberic Gainer was able to save the tabernacle with the Blessed Sacrament, carrying it out in his arms. Meanwhile, smoke had forced all who had been attempting to salvage things from the monastery building's first floor to leave.

Brother Philip almost met with disaster. Before leaving the dormitory, he decided to freshen up in the lavatory, then headed for the middle stairs to warn guests on the second floor. When he opened the door to the stairway, a blast of black smoke almost engulfed him. Hastily closing the door, he made his way to the other stairs and forced his way down to the cloister through the blinding and choking smoke now filling the stairway. Not knowing which way to turn from there, he heard

FIGURE 53. *Our Lady of the Valley. Facade of the church and of the 1902 building after the fire.*

the voice of Father Hilarion calling to him from the same window on the front side of the building through which Father John's group had jumped. Unable to see anything, he followed the sound and was probably the last one to escape along this path.

Earlier on, Brother Dominic and another group had managed to come down the central stairway to the second floor and make their way into the laybrothers' novitiate at the front of the building, where they were able to avoid some of the smoke by crawling along close to the floor. Hastening over to a window that gave easy access to the roof of the front porch of the building, the group began to climb out.

Father Thomas Keating had his cell at the southern end of the third floor dormitories. By the time he got moving, thick smoke had begun to fill the dormitories, and he and a group of others decided to go down the stairs nearest their cells—those leading to the guest quarters. They managed to get to the second floor but were unable to go farther: The flight leading down to the foyer had already collapsed in the flames. With the smoke and heat increasing in the corridor, he began to despair, when all of a sudden he heard Brother Dominic crying out from the laybrothers' novitiate: "Stay low and come this way!" Following the sound of his voice, the group headed over to Dominic. Some of Thomas's group followed the others out of the window onto the roof, from where they reached the ground by means of a ladder that, providentially, had been left resting against the roof's edge.

Somehow, though, the word did not get through to everyone in Thomas's group. He and some of the others returned to the guests' corridor and headed for the north stairs leading to the first floor cloister. But when Thomas opened the stairway door, a wall of flames confronted them. His companions retraced their steps and eventually made it to the porch roof. Father Thomas took the harder road. In desperation he rushed through the flames and down the stairs, then fought through to the laybrothers' common room, unknowingly following the path of those who had escaped with Father John. Throwing open the first window he could find, he too jumped ten feet to safety, landing in the shallow snow.

Compared to those who escaped from the third floor dormitories, the novices evacuated their own dormitories with no difficulty. The choir novitiate's dormitory was in the building that was farthest from the scene of the fire, and the laybrother novices were housed in the basement of the church building, which was less affected by the fire. In any case, they were able to leave before the church itself was fully in flames, thanks to Brother Arthur who had called out an alarm to them in the fire's early stages.

There seems to be little doubt that the fire originated on the first floor of the building somewhere in the vicinity of the dumbwaiter that ran from the basement kitchens all the way up to the third floor.[3] (Fig. 52) One theory has it that the fire started in the pantry under the stairs leading up from the foyer to the second floor guest rooms; the other, more widely accepted, holds that it was in the small confessional farther down the corridor leading to the guests' refectory. In this confessional a small vigil light was always burning in front of a statue of St. Agnes, who was much venerated by the confessor of the guests, Father Raymond.

The possibility of faulty wiring seemed highly unlikely due to the fact that the entire system of wiring had recently been brought up to date by the monastery's electrician, Brother Leonard O'Dowd, an electrical engineer.

Whatever the fire's origin, the shaft of the dumbwaiter clearly played an important role in propagating it, leading the flames all the way up to the crawlspace under the roof of the third floor and more importantly into the one above the church itself. From here the flames were

FIGURE 54. *Our Lady of the Valley. Interior of the church after the fire. The twisted remains of the steeple are seen hanging down into the building.*

drawn up into the open bell tower above the crossing of nave and transept. Functioning like a chimney, the tower intensified the power of the blaze, which eventually melted the bells and caused the tower to topple over into the nave. This final dramatic event occurred around midnight, about two hours after the fire began.

The abbey did have its own fire engines, manned by a sort of monastic fire brigade. Indeed, at the time of the fire, efforts were being made to better organize the community's firefighting and fire prevention program at the behest of their friend A. J. Coté, the fire chief of Woonsocket, who himself arrived on the scene not long after the call for help. After rousing the brother novices, Brother Arthur had gone down to the pond to start up a pump that was designed to provide water for just such an emergency—but he could not get it started.

A good number of the monks after safely clambering out of the burning building were standing around watching the blaze at a safe distance, but according to one of the brothers who was a novice at the time, Dom Edmund in his concern made some of them gather inside the safety of the choir novitiate building.

Several eyewitnesses also noted that despite the heroic efforts of the firemen, the overall operation was hindered by a lack of organization among the ten or so fire departments that answered the call. Special honors go to the Ashton fire department, which was one of the first to arrive and was the last to leave the next day at 3:30 p.m. They also came back later that day to extinguish a small fire that had broken out in the debris.

Though the devastation was extensive, there were many things to be thankful for, most of all that no one had fallen victim to the flames. Among other things, the huge fuel oil tank under the porch of the destroyed building had not ignited. And the west wing of the monastery, which housed the chapter house and infirmary, suffered only minor damage. Patients in the infirmary were nonetheless eventually evacuated, some to St. Joseph's hospital in Providence, others to the care of the Little Sisters of the Poor in Pawtucket, and still others to the residence of a friendly neighbor, where they were joined by the abbot and several others.

Most of the community went in buses around 1:30 in the morning to Mount St. Charles Academy in Woonsocket, where the Brothers of the Sacred Heart who operated the school generously offered them hospitality. The next morning the brothers sent their 132 boarders home, thus making the west wing of the school available for the exclusive use of their guests.

Although no one was lost in the fire, this was not known until some days later. The monastery's archives had been destroyed, and there was no readily available list of guests and prospective candidates present. One indirect victim of the fire was the Valley's old friend Dr. Cormier, who had rushed to the monastery the night of the fire, suffered a stroke at the sight of the flames, and died a short time after.

Amazingly enough, early photographs of the facade of the old guesthouse show a fire escape leading from the third floor dormitories down to the roof of the porch. Had this not been properly maintained? For some reason did it no longer figure among the escape patterns established by the fire committee? Or was it simply forgotten about in the confusion that surrounded the monks' hasty escape? (Fig. 31)

✑ FINDING A REFUGE

The day after the fire was to prove a busy one for Dom Edmund. In the morning he went to the convent at Wrentham to share with the nuns the experience of the previous evening. While there he offered Mass and confided to the sisters' care the monastery's sacred vessels.

Back at the Valley the abbot received Bishop McVinney of Providence and Father Joseph F. Bracq, the editor of the diocesan newspaper, the *Providence Visitor*. The state's governor, John Pastore, had set up in record time a committee to assist the now homeless monks, and Bracq had been assigned by the bishop as contact person. Even in such a short space of time, the committee had already come up with a plan to offer the monks the use of the former George Washington Civilian Conservation Corps (CCC) camp on the Bowdish Reservoir in Glocester, Rhode Island, near the Connecticut border. Dom Edmund was invited to visit the property that very afternoon along with Father Bracq and John E. Duffy, the superintendent of the Divisions of Forests and Parks.

In the context of the Great Depression, the Civilian Conservation Corps had been established by President Roosevelt in 1933 to provide work for young men in a variety of conservation and reforestation programs. Camps were set up around the country to house them; in Rhode Island alone there were eight. The program had come to an end in 1942 and only the barracks of the George Washington camp were in use during World War II. Since the end of the war, however, all of the buildings on the property had been unoccupied. At the time of the fire the Glocester camp had only recently passed to the authority of the Divisions of Forests and Parks of Rhode Island and was known as the George Washington Reservation.

It was a gray afternoon, and the long-unoccupied one-story wooden buildings that Edmund found there seemed depressing. Yet there were fifteen of them, some as long as a hundred feet. So the camp seemed like a reasonable solution until Spencer could be readied for occupancy.

Father Paulinus Fitzgerald was called from Spencer to oversee the adaptation of the buildings for monastic use. This turned out to be a daunting task, despite the help he received from workmen provided by the state. He was replaced at Spencer by Father Thomas Aquinas, who had suffered more than others from inhalation of smoke during his escape from the burning building. The quiet of Spencer seemed a suitable place for his recovery.

Apart from the challenge of converting existing buildings for new purposes, there was the question of furnishing them. As much material as could be salvaged from the Valley was brought over, and the governor also saw to it that bedding and a variety of utensils were provided for the monks. Managing the whole operation took its toll on Paulinus' health, and after it was over he came down with a serious case of pneumonia.

After his visit to the CCC camp Edmund returned to the Valley, and this first day after the fire drew to a close with a new outburst of flames in the ruins of the guesthouse wing, which the Ashton firefighters promptly dealt with.

The excitement was not over. The following morning at about 4:30 a.m., Brother Philip was coming home after milking the herd when he noticed a strange emission coming from the chimney of the laundry building. As he drew nearer he detected an increasingly strong metallic smell and sensed that something was malfunctioning. Inside the building he found Brother Placid sleeping on his bed outside the boiler room. He walked into the boiler room and saw that the boiler was white with heat. Quickly throwing the switch, he awoke Brother Placid and headed out to get the electrician, Brother Leonard, to cut off the current to the building. As it turned out, there had been a malfunction in the low-water cutoff mechanism and the boiler had continued to fire despite the absence of an appropriate amount of water in the tank. Thanks to his intervention further destruction was averted.

While the CCC camp was being readied, Dom Gregory Borgstedt, the prior of Portsmouth Priory, offered the Valley community hospitality at their monastery.[4] The students of the priory school were sent home early for their Easter vacation, and a first group of monks consisting of the Valley's novices arrived on the evening of March 22, the rest following the next day. Father Hugh McKiernan was appointed superior of the group, and as best as was possible monastic life was taken up once again. The monks made a contribution to their hosts by doing a certain amount of work around the grounds. Others set themselves to sewing replacement habits for those that were lost in the fire. (Sewing machines were among the items salvaged.)

A core group remained at the Valley to act as guardians, receive such visitors as might come, and continue caring for the cows, the poultry, and the vegetable gardens. The porter's lodge, which had survived the fire intact, became an important center of operations. Father Anthony as guestmaster was stationed here to greet visitors, and in the adjoining rooms the secretaries began the arduous task of reconstituting such essential archival material as the community's personnel cards. Dom Edmund made the Valley his base, though he was naturally required to travel frequently to various locations in the challenging operation of getting the community settled.

Father Owen was placed in charge of the group of twenty-eight monks and brothers remaining at the Valley; they took up residence in the novitiate building, its little chapel becoming the monastic church.[5] The Rhode Island branch of the National Guard set up a kitchen in the basement of the monastery's surviving wing. The Red Cross provided meals during the first week until the monks were able to organize the preparation of meals themselves.

In Dom Edmund's thinking, the Valley would for the present remain the seat of a little community:

> A sufficient number of religious, mainly Brothers, will occupy La Vallée to attend to the farm, dairy, and poultry. . . . the novitiate building will suffice for about 40; if and when the Infirmary building is restored these accommodations will be ample for such a small community.[6]

He was counting on it as one of several locations in which the numerous members of the community could be housed until it became clear just how many people could be brought to the reconditioned farm buildings at Spencer.

✍ CLEANING UP

The next major task was to begin cleaning up the debris left by the fire and repairing the damage in the surviving buildings. A local contractor who had worked on the Wrentham project was hired and put under the direction of Brother Blaise Drayton, who would become increasingly involved in the many building projects that lay ahead. Though still a novice, he was nearing the time of his profession and was well suited for the task. Once the community was settled in the CCC camp, the lay-brother novices would serve as workmen on the project.

Already on March 25 the work of restoring the monastery's western wing had begun. The main damage was on the facade opposite the burnt east wing. The wooden frames of the windows had been charred and needed to be replaced, and there was considerable smoke and water damage inside the building.

By March 26 the two chimneys and the surviving walls of the old guesthouse building had been demolished. Even though the walls of the church were still standing all the way up to the roof line, the effect of the fire on the stones and mortar was such that they too were judged unsafe. But the walls of the ambulatory, which were considerably lower than those of the main structure, were left standing up to the roof line. The main altar and the stained glass windows were removed and sent to Spencer for safekeeping.[7] The demolition of the church walls was completed by April 7. The rooms that lay beneath the floor of the church were saved, except for the area at its eastern end, where the tribune of the guests had collapsed, breaking through the floor of the church into the lower level. Some of the vast amount of debris was carted off to the city dump, and some was used for highway construction.[8]

One big question hung in the air. Would the monks be leaving Rhode Island entirely? Dom Edmund let it be known that plans for the future were undecided, even intimating that a group of monks might remain at the Valley site while a larger segment of the community moved to Spencer. On March 26, the first Sunday after the fire, Rhode Islanders turned out in great numbers to visit the ruins, causing serious problems for traffic along Diamond Hill road. On the following Sunday also, though diminished in numbers, many came to see what remained. ❧

Our Lady of Refuge: The CCC Camp

O N APRIL 5—WEDNESDAY of Holy Week—all was in readiness at Glocester. Grateful for the two weeks with the Benedictines, the community left for their temporary new home, which had been renamed "Our Lady of Refuge." The next day the solemn celebrations of the last three days of Holy Week began around 2 a.m. with sung Vigils of Holy Thursday and concluded on Sunday with the celebration of Easter. After the demanding Services of these days the community had somewhat more leisure to appreciate their new surroundings. At the Valley, available outdoors strolling space had consisted of little more than an acre. Now the monks found themselves in the unfolding springtime of the year on a 3000-acre property situated in a secluded corner of Rhode Island—far from the noise of Diamond Hill Road and the nearby race track and bar, not to mention the polka parlor.

The various buildings had been adapted for monastic uses, one each for church, refectory, infirmary, toilets and showers. Three were laid out as dormitories, each containing twenty cots lined up in army fashion, without the partitions of the old dormitories of the Valley. There was even a "lodge" near the reservoir with room for four or five guests, most of whom were aspirants. Quite a few of these entered monastic life at the camp. Occasionally diocesan priests came for a retreat.

This partitioning of the monastic life into totally separate buildings

FIGURE 55. *Glocester, Rhode Island. The CCC Camp. Aerial view.*

had its disadvantages. For one thing, it was necessary to venture out in the springtime snow and rain to get from one place to another; this was especially bothersome in the early hours of the morning as one headed from the dormitories to the rather distant church. Little wonder that by Holy Saturday there was a severe epidemic of colds.

Thanks to the great number of items that had been salvaged from the fire, the community was able to take up the liturgical life of the monastery with relative ease. A good number of the large folio choir books had survived, along with the altars and their appurtenances. Vestments and sacred vessels had also been rescued from the sacristy by Father Edward and his crew.

One of the things that comes out most forcefully from the oral testimonies of those who lived at the CCC camp was the supreme importance of the experience in reshaping the spirit of the community and orienting it to meet the challenges of the future. In the words of Brother Bernard:

There was a sense of increased space when we went to the camp. It was like being in a community without walls, even though there was an official conceptual enclosure. That space was magnified a hundred-fold when we came to Spencer, which offered a sense of scope, like a symbol of the width and breadth of the service of God. These were also times of expansion in the nation itself after the war.

The ambiance at the camp was welcoming: the rustic setting on the lake, the early spring weather, the simple government barrack-style buildings well suited to the environment and to the uses to which we put them.

All this had a bearing on our psyches. There was a spirit of camaraderie there. The brothers were seen in a different setting with much less formalism than at the Valley. Who could say that it would be any better elsewhere?[1]

Among those forming the community at the camp was a group of World War II veterans, many of whom had decided to enter the monastic life precisely because of their experiences in the war. These men had learned endurance in the war that helped them to persevere in their new life, and the spirit of camaraderie they had experienced with their fellow servicemen helped foster a strong sense of community during their lives as monks. But perhaps most important of all, the capacity to distinguish between what was essential and what was secondary that combat had bred in them made them open to the process of renewal that would characterize the Order in the next years.

✑ THE WORK PROGRAM AT THE CCC CAMP

The work program of the community at Our Lady of Refuge, was at first largely dedicated to cleaning up the property at the Valley. In addition to the skilled laborers who worked under the contractor, the main monastic contribution was provided by the laybrother novices, who each morning were piled into the cramped seats of an old school bus and carried off to their old home. The day was wholly devoted to work, during which, in the words of one of their number, they "raked, dug, carted materials, etc." There was a break at noon, when dinner was served, and at 4 p.m. the bus returned to the camp.

The choir novices were given time in the morning for their studies, but after dinner they too were brought to the Valley in a truck for an afternoon's work. In general, they were more involved in the upkeep of

347

the camp, as were other professed members of the community. During the late summer a group of fifteen choir novices took up temporary residence at Spencer for one or two months to help out on the farm. They lived in the duplex under the care of Father John. In November they returned to the camp.[2]

The vestment-making industry that had been in operation at the Valley since at least the autumn of 1945 continued at the CCC camp, with six brothers and two choir novices assigned to the work.[3]

The monks also helped with the ongoing cleaning of the forest, thus carrying on in a modest way one of the original aims of the CCC camps.

Meals at the camp were prepared by Brother Bernardine, who had been called back from Spencer. Two of the more fortunate laybrother novices took turns helping him with the wood-burning stove instead of going to the Valley to work.

∾ FINAL PLANS FOR A PERMANENT MONASTERY

During the early days at the camp Dom Edmund's concerns were many: helping the community settle down into the new surroundings, keeping an eye on the clean-up operation at the Valley, and intensifying the preparation of the buildings at Spencer. Thoughts of what the permanent monastery might some day look like were not uppermost in his mind. Yet something happened soon after his arrival at the camp that would turn his thoughts in that direction. After the fire Charles Maginnis had sent a letter of condolence and, as a gesture of largesse, dismissed the debt for the work his company had done on the project up to that time. But he was nonetheless concerned to have something set down in writing about what his relationship to the project would be in the future. So he drew up a contract and sent it to Dom Edmund on May 3. It arrived after the community had been there for little over a month.

With a contract in hand Edmund could hardly put off a decision. Yet there were new financial pressures weighing on the community, and he was hesitant to make a definitive commitment to Maginnis's proposal. Besides, since the time Maginnis was first called in, new possibilities were opening up. The abbot had come more and more to appreciate local artistic talent. He recognized the high quality of Blaise's restoration of the Valley buildings as well as his genial plans for creating a temporary monastery out of farm buildings evacuated not long before by a herd of cows. Not only this, but he was now in the process of seeing to it that these plans were being efficiently carried out in a way that won the respect of those working under him. Nothing seemed to stand in his way; his gift of improvisation helped him find a solution for almost any problem that arose.

Father Laurence's longstanding familiarity with Cistercian architecture and his contacts with European houses of the Order made him an ideal collaborator for Brother Blaise. Working together, might they not be able to produce the plan they were looking for? Yet, however real these talents might be, the services of a professional architect would still be needed in the areas of engineering and in the drafting of final working plans. With this in mind Dom Edmund sent Frater Paul to discuss with Maginnis the possibility of changing his role in the project to that of consultant architect. Maginnis described the interview to Dom Edmund in his letter of June 2, 1950:

> Frater Paul revealed to me clearly the financial predicament, in consequence of which it had been necessary to take grave account of the expenditures represented by the professional service, and the community had concluded to depend instead upon the latent capacity of certain individuals in the Order to deal with the artistic phase of the building problem. Frater Paul was, however, sympathetic with that Maginnis and Walsh should hold, however slight, a contact with the work in the interest of avoiding a public apprehension that it had somehow or other been found wanting, and that this could be fairly accomplished through the identification of an engineer rather than an architect in the development of the working drawings. The association of Maginnis and Walsh would then be limited to an endorsement of your design, by virtue of which they might more or less questionably qualify as consulting architects, and thus, as it were, protect their professional pride.
>
> The interview was an unfamiliar experience for me, and I have since wondered whether the advice I gave Frater Paul was as wise as I thought it at the time. I was at pains to assure him that he could limit our service to the vanishing point in this interest and compensate us on the basis of actual service, which would be narrowly confined to the stage when your preliminary sketches would have been completed, and we would be expected to give it our formal sanction or withhold our approval. It had not occurred to me that this was bound to be a moment of most exquisite embarrassment to ourselves and to the authors of your Community. I wonder whether you do not agree with me in thinking it would be best to avoid it if possible. It is hardly likely that, especially at a time of such conflicting architectural philosophies,

your study of the problem would bring forth a solution with which we could be in completely sympathetic agreement.

As the result of my reflection on this matter, I am writing to invite you to consider the idea of proceeding without taking account of us at all, and assuming for the Community the complete authorship of the design. In making the suggestion, I feel sure that the independence of such a proceeding will seem quite agreeable to the Cistercian tradition. I hope you will appreciate how much I sense the disappointment to my hopes in having to relinquish so interesting a project, and I sincerely pray that the Monastery will, under the conditions we have been discussing, come to a convincing and happy accomplishment that will embody the finest thought of the Community.[4]

After this there is no mention in the sources about further plans, until two months later, when an entirely new set of plans was drawn up on July 28, bearing the title "Alterations and Proposed Construction, St. Joseph's Abbey, Spencer, Massachusetts." They include an extensive site plan extending from a proposed guesthouse on the north to the new cow barn on the south. Nowhere in the Spencer archives is there any indication of deliberations that led to this new plan, nor do the names of the architects appear on the drawings themselves. However, given the fact that Maginnis had retired from the scene on June 2, it seems likely that these professionally drawn plans were the work of Eggers and Higgins and represented alterations to the drawings these architects had produced in July 1949. Why this would happen at a time when Dom Edmund had already decided to use local talent is a mystery. Possibly the new Eggers and Higgins plans had been in the works for some time and were only delivered in late July, or, alternatively, these plans might be the result of a first attempt of the monks to collaborate with an architectural firm, in the way Edmund had proposed to Maginnis.

In any event, on this plan the proposed monastery has been shifted to a new position, close to the existing Alta Crest buildings, which are also shown and identified by their new functions in the temporary monastery. Furthermore, the proposed new building is here linked to the existing building by a passageway leading from the southeast of the new cloister to the existing refectory in the Alta Crest building. Though this plan would never be executed, clearly the monks had decided that some of the structures of the provisional monastery would continue to serve as integral parts of the "permanent" monastery—the refectory, for example, and the kitchen—and this would obviate the need to construct certain components of the traditional monastic quadrangle. Thus there is no refectory in the traditional place, perpendicular to the south cloister gallery. Beyond this plan no further information surfaces about the project for another fifteen months.

✐ ANOTHER FOUNDATION

Even before the fire Dom Edmund had realized that the accommodations at Spencer would not be sufficient for the number of people he had to care for. Clearly another foundation must be considered. This might seem like a bold move, considering that another foundation had been made only two years earlier, reducing the community's pool of priests to twenty-six. Yet vocations continued to come, a trend witnessed by the increase in numbers at the camp over the coming months: 151 by July and 166 at the end of the year.

Even before the fire, the growing numbers in the community had led Dom Edmund to send Brother Leo off again to look for a prospective site, this time in the state of Virginia, and on March 19 in a letter to the definitory the abbot could announce that negotiations for a property had already begun.[5] This first prospect came to nothing, and Leo returned to the Valley on March 20—the night before the fire. Dom Edmund realized that now the search had to be intensified and sent Brother Leo off to Virginia once again on the very day after the fire, while the firemen were still at work.

Ever concerned with the demands of dairy and agricultural work, Dom Edmund was looking for a site of about 1,000 acres able to support 300 head of cattle. The first recorded "find" in Virginia was one proposed by a real estate agent in Charlottesville. It was a large tract in the heart of the George Washington National Forest in the southwest portion of the state. Brother Leo offers a more detailed description:

> It was called Hidden Valley and in all had 8734 acres of woodlands that enclosed a very fertile 450 acre valley through the middle of which flowed the Jackson River. This same river wound its way through seven miles of the property as a whole. There was a large frame two-story home with out-buildings and barns and a fresh spring of pure water that bubbled out of the limestone at a great rate. The seclusion was admirable, and yet the site wasn't too inaccessible from markets. . . . There was only one road into Hidden Valley, and this could be secured by a gate at the front from which the valley itself and its buildings couldn't be seen.[6]

The house in question was a mansion built around the middle of the nineteenth century by Judge James Woods Warwick. Unfortunately, due to divorce proceedings that were in process, the current owners were not in a position to proceed with the sale. But an agreement was drawn up that gave the monastery first option on the property if it were to become available within ten years. Constrained by the needs of the moment, though, Leo continued to look elsewhere. The same agent then proposed several properties, among them one in Culpeper, but here too an agreement could not be reached. Finally in June another real estate agent showed Leo a property near the town of Berryville, about fifty-five miles west and slightly north of Washington. At its heart was an impressive fieldstone house built in 1784 by William Wormeley, an English friend of George Washington's, on what was originally a tract of more than 11,000 acres along the Shenandoah River.[7] The sale included a cluster of smaller farms, each with a farmhouse that would be able in one way or another to serve the needs of the future community.

Already in April Dom Edmund had made contact with Bishop Peter Ireton of Richmond concerning the possibility of such a foundation in his diocese. The bishop expressed his personal satisfaction with the project and on April 28 was able to report that his diocesan consultors were unanimously in agreement. Dom Edmund kept the bishop abreast of developments throughout the difficult negotiations with Hidden Valley and Culpeper and sent a group of monks down to confer with him; he himself was unable to go, having come down with pneumonia.

The Valley's conventual chapter was consulted on May 21, while negotiations were still under way for the Culpeper property. A petition was made for the foundation, along with a further request for permission to spend a total of $200,000, which would include not only the purchase of land, but necessary constructions and the procurement of cattle, etc. The proposal passed by a vote of twenty-three to three. On the same day Edmund wrote a petition to the Abbot General and definitory explaining his reasons for the foundation and asking their permission. Ten days later the definitory voted to accept the project, limiting the expense to the proposed $200,000 and indicating that there was no need to consult the Holy See.

Things moved quickly thereafter. By the end of June the Culpeper deal had fallen through and the Berryville property had been purchased for $150,000, with $50,000 set aside for building purposes.[8] On July 12, the deed was recorded in the name of the abbey's corporation and sent to Dom Edmund.

On June 29 Frater Paul was ordained to the priesthood by Bishop Wright along with Frater Ignatius Sullivan and Deacon John Cardullo of the Worcester Diocese. After the deed to Berryville was received, Paul—now *Father* Paul—free from other obligations, was assigned to take charge of the renovation of the existing buildings there, and to lay plans for the creation of new ones that would be needed by the monastic community, which was to arrive in November. He also looked into the important question of the purchase of the herd of cows that would be important to keep the monastery self-supporting. Once the work program had begun, Father Peter Rogers was sent down and remained throughout the renovation. He was on hand to welcome the founders when they arrived.

✑ A SUMMERTIME VISITATION

Dom James Fox came to the camp for a five-day visitation in July. In his visitation card he encouraged the community to remain as faithful as possible to the Cistercian life in the unusual circumstances in which they were living.

One of Dom James's remarks strikes a note hitherto unheard in Gethsemani's relations with the Valley:

> Technically, indeed, Gethsemani is listed as Mother-House and Our Lady of the Valley as Daughter-house but we always look upon Our Lady of the Valley as a Sister-house, working side by side in the great work that Jesus has to do through both our houses in this great American world. We are very proud to have such a wonderful sister as Our Lady of the Valley. May the beautiful cooperative and loving spirit that now exists between our two monasteries ever remain.[9]

Apparently Dom Edmund's efforts in the matter of chant had begun to show results since Dom James also complimented the community on its singing.

In his report to the General, he noted the danger of too much travel in connection with fundraising, but praised the community for its spirit during these difficult times:

However, the spirit of the community is beautiful. All are generous, most cooperative, fervent for the observances—as far as possible under the circumstances. The future of all these various ventures seems very bright.[10]

The visitation card notes the following statistics:

Choir	28	Solemnly professed choir religious
	10	Simply professed
	32	Novices
	8	Postulants
	78	Total
Lay	22	Solemnly professed brothers
	24	Simply professed
	16	Novices
	10	Postulants
	1	Oblate
	73	Total
Total	**151**	

The numbers are, in their own way, even more impressive than Dom James's report and comments. They show that despite the incredible hardships of the preceding months, the community had not only not diminished but had actually grown, from somewhat fewer than 140 to 151 members, and many of the eighteen postulants had entered the community at the CCC camp. Edmund frequently mentioned this in answering the letters of sympathy he received from other communities. Writing just more than a month after the fire to Dom Celsus O'Connell he said:

> No one among the novices and postulants has asked to leave; in fact, we have taken in four new postulants, given the habit to three, had two simple professions and two solemn, and four more professions are scheduled for next month.[11]

Slightly earlier, Dom Pacôme had responded to a similar missive from Edmund with an appreciation based on his own experience:

> Thanks for the details you gave concerning the fire and the community. Our best vocations came to us immediately after our fire and while we were poorly lodged. So I congratulate your fervent religious for their abnegation and their courage, and I have confidence that

God will increase their numbers. The virtues which your religious will have to practice during this time of trial will make a deep impression on the postulants, and they will themselves become fervent religious.[12]

Not long after the visitation, the monastery got an unwelcome surprise when they were informed by the National Guard that the 300 blankets and 100 mattresses and bedsteads lent to the monks had to be returned! Appeals for blankets launched over the radio and in the local newspapers brought in the needed supply. The old straw mattress maker was rolled out and hastily put to use, and the carpenters set to work to make simple bedsteads.

∾ Wrentham's Autonomy

In addition to everything else he was attending to, Edmund was busy through the summer with plans for Wrentham's autonomy. He mentioned the project in a letter to Dom James Fox:

Along with Guadalupe's autonomy, I am obliged to ask for Wrentham's. . . . The nuns at Wrentham want their autonomy (at least they say they do, when questioned), but I know that Dom Celsus and Glencairn might not possibly see things in the same light.[13]

A letter from the abbess of Glencairn to Dom Edmund two weeks later indicated that this was indeed the case.[14] Nevertheless, the matter was placed on the agenda of the General Chapter, which was to meet on September 12–16. Dom Edmund drew up an official request, prefaced by a lengthy report on the history and current status of the monastery, to which he appended copies of the documents he had received from the archbishop as well as from the abbess of Glencairn.

Given the importance of the vote concerning Wrentham, Edmund made a point of assisting at the chapter despite all he had to do to prepare for the move to Spencer. He reported on the complex situation of the community. Current plans called for a transfer of eighty persons to Spencer. Thirty-five more would go to the new foundation in Berryville and three would remain at Wrentham. All of the others would have to spend the winter in some refuge or annex. Vermont and Long Island were mentioned as possibilities.[15]

To Edmund's great satisfaction, on September 14 the chapter voted in favor of the erection of both Guadalupe and Wrentham as abbeys. The results were communicated to the CCC camp, and Father Owen sent the good news concerning Wrentham to Archbishop Cushing, who answered:

> I will send this info to Mother Bernard, even though I think it is her mind and the Superiors in Ireland to delay this matter. We have the decision. I presume it can be put into effect just as soon as the sisters are satisfied.[16]

The Trappistines, however, were not ones to object to a decision of the General Chapter, and things were soon in readiness for the election of an abbess. On November 11 Mother Bernard received a majority of the vote, but she refused the charge. A second ballot was inconclusive, and on the third Mother Margaret Shaw, former abbess of Glencairn, obtained a majority. The chapter meeting was adjourned while she was contacted at Glencairn for her consent. But she also refused. The chapter was reconvened on November 13, and on this fourth ballot Mother Bernard was once again chosen. This time she accepted.[17]

On November 23 Dom Columban Hawkins was elected Guadalupe's first abbot, and on January 24, 1954, received the abbatial blessing.

✌ CARING FOR THE HERD

Even with all these other matters at hand, Dom Edmund's central focus throughout the time spent at the camp had remained on Spencer, where the program of transforming the existing buildings into a temporary monastery had been stepped up in the aftermath of the fire. At first, however, the monastic presence had been limited to the small group living at the former workers' dormitory.[18] In July, however, Father Thomas, who had returned to the camp, returned to Spencer as Father Master of a group of some twenty professed laybrothers who had come to start up the dairy operation. The splendid new barn was in place on the site of Sagendorph's Ayrshire barn; the final cost had been $40,000. By August the old herd had all been transferred from the Valley and installed in their magnificent new home. Their tenure would be brief: A new herd would be acquired in April 1951 and the old animals auctioned off.[19]

This new herd had been in the works as early as May 8, 1950, when Dom Edmund had received a "confidential memo" reporting an offer by Michael Gamino of Rhode Island to sell the monastery his family's prestigious Broad Rock herd of Holstein cattle. As noted by the unidentified author of the memo, "This is a very rare opportunity to get into Holstein first-class breeding, starting in the middle of an established breeding program, for the cost of an ordinary mongrel herd." Determined as he was to favor the dairy and farming orientation of the monastery, Edmund could not fail to find the offer appealing. Indeed, it is very likely that the prospect of obtaining this fine herd had played a significant role in the layout and high quality of the appointments in the new barn.[20]

The brothers who had come to run the dairy operation took up residence in a building that became known as "the Grange." It was on Browning Pond Road in Oakham, near the border with Spencer, and was part of a farm that had been owned by several different families since the land was originally acquired in 1769. A cemetery that served the Boyd family, who were the owners from 1787 to 1826, is still preserved near one of the fields to the rear of the property. The present house was built in 1895.

The farm had been purchased by the abbey on July 25, 1950, and the house was ready for the laybrothers by the end of the month. Their dormitory occupied the greater part of the upper floor, and a chapel was laid out in one of the ground floor rooms. An informal breakfast was served in the house, but the brothers took their main meals in a dining area that had been set up in the old horse barn on the main property, along with a refectory and small kitchen. Father Thomas was ferried back and forth to the Grange in an old vehicle known affectionately as the Green Hornet. He looks back with pleasure on this period, which he considered idyllic in its simplicity.

With the approaching transfer of the community, the Sagendorph family moved in August to their new farm in nearby North Brookfield. Their livestock remained in the barn but were scheduled to be moved to their new farm soon.[21]

∾ The Arrival of the Lay Novices

On October 7 a new phase in the "occupation" of Spencer took place when the laybrother novices were sent en masse to take up residence in the horse barn.[22] They had finished the work of cleaning up the Valley and had started to commute to Spencer each day to lend a hand in the preparations that were now being stepped up in view of the final transfer of the community.

A dormitory was created for these novices in the hay storage area on the barn's upper level, as well as a chapel in the space where there had once been a small apartment for a family of workers. A refectory and small kitchen had already been created on the ground floor for the use of the professed brothers who had come to the Grange in July. Now a room for Father Tarcisius, the novice master, and a common room for the novices were created, and a Bradley fountain and two shower rooms were installed as well. Father Tarcisius moved into his new room along with his St. Bernard dog, Bruno, for whom a window was always left open night and day.

There would be scant rest for these novices after their hard work cleaning up the Valley. Now they had to help finish the renovations on the old barn, the horse barn, and other buildings that were to serve as temporary monastery. The work was rather well advanced and was now under the supervision of Brother Blaise, who had made his simple profession at Our Lady of Refuge on April 16. The main section of the barn, which was to house the various offices of the monastery along with its chapter room, had already been gutted, and the novices were put to the task of stripping away the plaster that lined its inner walls. In September, the MacDonald company of Boston provided a revised plan for the transformation of the dairy into the monastery's kitchen, updating their earlier proposal of May 8.[23]

Two months of hard work lay ahead assisting the professional laborers in various capacities. One such project was the building of the "breezeway," which would link the horse barn with the main part of the new monastery. This involved laying foundations, pouring cement for the walkway, and roofing over the completed structure. There was also much to do in the hayloft of the barn that would become the monastery church: installing the subfloor, putting in the new ceiling, boxing in the beams. In the haste of those days, the new oak floor was laid too soon on top of a concrete base that had not sufficiently dried. When the radiant heating system embedded in the concrete was turned on, the boards buckled and the operation had to be repeated. By October 30, it had become clear that the community could not hope to take over the buildings at Spencer until around Christmas.[24]

By this time the Berryville project was close to completion. On November 6 Dom Edmund informed Bishop Ireton that a name had been decided upon for the new monastery; it would be known as Our Lady of the Holy Cross. As the monastery faced its second foundation a little more than two years after its first one, a new problem emerged. Dom Edmund began to realize that while it was easy to find monks to send to the new monastery, it was becoming increasingly difficult to come up with a sufficient number of persons capable of filling positions of leadership. Since ordination to the priesthood was at that time considered a basic prerequisite for such jobs, Edmund requested permission of the definitory to waive certain requirements for four candidates who had completed their studies but were below the required age or who had not been in the monastery for a sufficiently long period of time. The General and the definitory were adamant, however, and this led to some heated correspondence between the CCC camp and Rome.[25] It would be an ongoing problem as Spencer continued to grow:

> Our great lacuna is that of priests. We have about 30 in theology and several are ready for Major Orders from which they are debarred because they are not yet solemnly professed. I must discuss this problem with the Reverendissime at his coming visit.[26]

Two days before the departure of the founders for Berryville, Brother Blaise and Fraters Gregory and Columban were involved in an automobile accident as they were returning to the CCC camp from Spencer. Columban and Gregory were seriously injured, and Columban remained on the critical list at St. Vincent's hospital in Worcester for a number of days. But the thirty founders had to carry on, and on November 18 they set out as planned in a bus owned by Tony Sansone, the uncle of Brother Simon Sansone. He was to become a longtime benefactor of the community and the faithful supplier of buses for the various needs of both Wrentham and Spencer.

Two months before the final move to Spencer, Peter Grace had expressed to Dom Edmund his concern over the fact that sufficient care was not being taken to remain within the limits of the budgets set for both the Valley restoration and the preparations at Spencer. The Valley work had cost $190,000 even though the projected expenses had been set at $60,000. More dramatically, $390,000 had already been spent on the transformation of Spencer, well over the projected $140,000.[27] The monks seemed to take this advice to heart, for, once the building of the permanent monastery began in 1952, individual contracts for each section of the building were signed only when current finances seemed to warrant further construction.

The big day for the transfer finally arrived. On December 23 the combined forces of those living at the CCC camp and those still at the Valley headed for their new home. Vespers were sung that day for the first time at Spencer. It turned out there was not enough room for the lay novices, who had to be content to remain in their own little chapel in the horse barn. No room in the inn!

The unfortunate reality was that Spencer simply could not yet accommodate all those who now made up the community. There was no choice but to send the first-year novices back to the camp until sufficient living space was constructed. This turned out to be more than just an inconvenience. The novices ended up facing the full brunt of a humid winter in poorly heated buildings without any mitigation in their diet. The result was that a number of them came down with tuberculosis. So many things were facing the community as it worked hard to settle down into its new nest!

A New Beginning

✑ Settling in at Spencer

AFTER THE EXCITEMENT of the Christmas celebrations the community could settle down for the winter into a period of relative quiet after all the activity of the preceding months. It was a time to reflect on the great changes that had taken place in their lives since March 21, 1950. Father Thomas Keating recalls the thoughts that came to him as he sat in the snow after jumping from a window at the Valley on the fateful night of the fire. "As I sat there the insight came to me, 'Well that's the end of the Valley, and maybe God isn't as interested as I am in the Strict Observance.'"[1]

The fact that a phase of the community's existence had come to an end must have occurred to many of the monks that night as they watched the monastery burn, and now during this period of winter seclusion in their new home, they no doubt continued to ponder what the consequences would ultimately be. In the words of one of the other brothers:

> The Valley was about as austere as you could possibly get. In one sense, the fire was a pleasant interlude; there was a sense of excitement, something new. We never thought it was going to be so disastrous; there wasn't a sense of sadness or foreboding. There was rather a sense of euphoria, the sense that we were going to make good, do something, overcome the loss. It wasn't a heartbreaking thing, the fire, at least I didn't feel that way. People had a sense of beginning something new.

Spencer was a new beginning; the fire was all forgotten when we came up here. We just wanted to work and get the place built.[2]

By January 1951 a buyer had been found for the Valley. The Franciscan Friars of the Atonement of Graymoor, New York, had been looking for a property to house their novitiate, and through the realtor John J. Reynolds of New York they had learned of the Valley. An agreement was reached that included all of the land owned by the monastery except the so-called Connolly tract, which the Cistercians sold to a neighbor. The latter part of January was filled with ongoing discussions about just how much the realtor's fee would be. But the papers were signed on February 15, and on April 19 the property was handed over to the friars. The price was $462,000.

The disagreement concerning the realtor's fee dragged on into the summer. By this time Cardinal Spellman had entered the fray (perhaps at the realtor's request), and Dom Edmund agreed to abide by his judgment. He found in favor of Reynolds, who was asking for $12,000, a figure that he claimed was his due.[3]

Not long after Christmas, things at Spencer were sufficiently settled for the monastery to open a temporary guesthouse. The little Allen farmhouse, south of the monastery along the Alta Crest Road, was chosen. The venerable Brother Vincent was installed as porter in the old milk processing room of the nearby barn, and next to it a gate was set up as the entrance to the new monastery. By early spring the monastery had plans to purchase as a guesthouse "Allenacres," an estate about a mile away on Route 31. In the interim the guesthouse was transferred from the Allen farmhouse to the more ample facilities of the Grange.

With the arrival of spring the community shifted into a rhythm of greater activity. The need for more workspace for various activities led to the construction of a new building to the west of the breezeway. This one-story "shops building" was erected under the direction of Brother Blaise, working once again with the Antell construction company.

The laybrother novices assisted extensively on this job, which served as a training ground for their work on the construction of the permanent monastery a year later. Brother Paul Forster, already experienced in electrical work, helped a professional electrician install the electrical system of the new building (he would ultimately earn a journeyman's license as an electrician). Brother Jerome Collins was entrusted with the care of the stock of plumbing materials, which helped prepare him for his later work installing the radiant heating system of the new monastery.

✑ The New Guesthouse Opens

On May 8, 1951, Allenacres was purchased by the abbey in partnership with Peter Grace, who acted as principal partner. Over a period of several years the abbey purchased additional shares from him until it finally acquired full ownership on August 2, 1954. The centerpiece of the estate was an elegant mansion atop a hill between Route 31 and the Sevenmile River, which ran through the property. Its many rooms offered ample accommodations for as many as thirty-six guests, and a kitchen and dining room meant meals could be prepared and served to the guests without resorting to the monastery's own facilities. A small library was set up in one of the sitting rooms, and a large living room provided additional reading space for the retreatants. A chapel was fitted out in one of the basement rooms, with a confessional in an adjacent room.

Although the new property was only a mile from the monastery as the crow flies, there was no direct road leading to it, the only access being by a roundabout route of almost three miles. To remedy this situation, late in May construction was begun on a new paved road leading from the new guesthouse directly to the monastery. This road first crossed the Sevenmile River, then made its way up the hill to join the old Alta Crest Road at a point near the temporary monastery, where space was reserved for visitors in the southeast corner of the former hay barn, newly converted into the monastic church.

A smaller building on the Allen property near Route 31 that had originally served as a stable for horses was transformed into the abbey's porter's lodge and gift shop. Access to the monastery by Route 31 thus became the main entrance, and the original entrance along the Alta Crest Road was eventually closed to the general public.

The guesthouse was opened to the public on May 31, and the Grange was reserved for priest guests on extended stays at the abbey. This latter arrangement lasted little more than a year, however.[4]

The abbey's vestment-making department, the Holy Rood Guild, which had managed to continue its work on a modest scale at the CCC camp, had to suspend operations altogether at Spencer until the new shops building was completed. The Guild took up again during the course of 1952 with five or six monks under the direction of Father Alberic, but production was still limited because of reduced working space. So they experimented with giving out assignments to lay associates—mostly groups of women working in private homes. One such group organized by Arnold Amadon made albs according to the Guild's specifications. Associating women with its operations became a lasting feature of the Guild.

℘ Toward a New Foundation

New dormitory space was finally ready for the entire choir novitiate, and the thirty novices who had remained at the CCC camp finally arrived on May 17. Even though everyone had a bed to sleep in, the overcrowding at Spencer was all too evident. And so yet again the idea of still another foundation was in the air, despite the fact that the abbey had already made three foundations over the past three years—Guadalupe in 1948, Wrentham in 1949, and Berryville in 1950. By the end of May, Brother Leo went forth once again in search of a property. This time he found one near Albany, New York, in the village of Kinderhook, and the bishop of Albany was quick to welcome the possibility. With this in mind, Edmund outlined the plan in a letter to the definitory, reporting the favorable vote of the community.[5] For the present, though, he cautiously asked only for permission to purchase the property *in view of* a foundation, and not to establish the foundation itself. The request was granted, and on June 5 permission was also given to borrow $200,000 for this purpose.[6]

Over the summer, however, the Kinderhook sale fell through, and Dom Edmund found himself reconsidering the wisdom of making a new foundation while at the same time pursuing construction at Spencer. By late August he decided to postpone the foundation project in favor of an all-out effort to provide Spencer with a suitable home. In a report drawn up for presentation to the General Chapter of 1951, Edmund asked that permission be granted to negotiate a loan of $300,000 and that the $200,000 loan already approved for the purchase of land for a new foundation be redirected towards the construction of a permanent monastery at Spencer.[7]

Although immediate plans for a new foundation had been abandoned, the abbey apparently still had an interest in the Hidden Valley property in Virginia, which had once again come on the market. On August 22, Brother Leo wrote to Charles Grace: "I just heard from Peter that you and he are going to help us obtain 'Hidden Valley,' which will be set up as a family memorial. I cannot tell you how much we appreciate this!"[8] The plan that eventually emerged was that Charles Grace would purchase and care for the Hidden Valley property until Spencer was in a position to make a foundation there. As it turned out, the property was purchased late in 1952 with funds from a financial foundation that was especially set up for this purpose, and Charles Grace ultimately became the owner. Spencer never did establish a foundation there, and Grace ended up selling it to the George Washington National Forest in 1965.[9]

Properties and building plans were far from Dom Edmund's only concerns. Among those who had contracted tuberculosis during their extended winter stay at the CCC camp, four were still under treatment in two different sanatoria and would not return to the community until February of 1952. Another case would surface in June of that year, and two more in 1954.

✑ The Regular Visitation of 1951

Dom James Fox made his first visitation at Spencer from July 31 to August 5, 1951. He showed concern for the state of Dom Edmund's own health, but his official report to the General about the community's well-being was enthusiastic:

> The financial state of the abbey is in most excellent condition. The abbey has also an excellent future, through the wonderful dairy herd, the marketing of milk and breeding of cattle.... Considering the most extraordinary circumstances between the fire in March of last year, the making of a foundation in Berryville, living in the Army barracks, the transfer to an entirely new site in the middle of winter, the community has maintained a good spirit and love for the Divine Office.[10]

In a more private letter to the General, however, he expressed some reservations about the "tone" of the monastery:

> The impression now of their monastery is one of over-ornateness. This, together with the tremendous improvements in the farm, both in machinery and in buildings, gives an overall impression of wealth.
>
> I mentioned this to Brother Blaise. He told Dom Edmund and the latter was tremendously upset—so much so that his stomach reacted. He suffered pains so severe that he was forced to lie down. . . he was unable to come to the chapter for the closing of the Visitation.[11]

It was not the last time that Edmund's strong reaction to criticism would be noted in such reports.

✎ A New Abbot General

Throughout the summer the community was busy with the construction of the shops building and work in the new vegetable garden. It was probably early in September that Dom Edmund headed to Europe for the General Chapter at Cîteaux, accompanied this time by Brother Blaise. While visiting Lourdes on the way, he had a severe abdominal attack and was hospitalized—and was thus unable to assist at the chapter. When the question of Edmund's proposed loan came up, the assembly asked that further information concerning Spencer's finances be provided by Dom James, the abbey's Father Immediate.[12] But since neither Dom Edmund nor Dom James was present at this chapter, the issue was put temporarily on hold.

The most important matter taken up at that chapter, however, was the acceptance of the resignation of the Abbot General, Dom Dominic Nogues, who had served since 1943. An additional chapter was scheduled on November 7 for the election of his successor. Dom Gabriel Sortais, the abbot of Bellefontaine then also serving as Abbot Vicar of the Order, informed Edmund by letter that the question of his loan would be taken up once again at this special chapter.[13]

By September 15 Dom Edmund's health had improved enough for him to be able to return to the United States. The next day he was admitted to St. Joseph's hospital in Providence and on September 21 underwent surgery for the removal of gallstones. As was typical at the time, his recuperation was slow.

Dom Sortais' letter announcing the special chapter must have reached Edmund while he was still in the hospital, or soon after his return to Spencer, where he continued his recuperation in the Sagendorph cottage, which had become the abbatiale or abbot's quarters.

✎ Finalizing Plans for the New Building

In addition to sending the news that Edmund's request for a loan would be taken up at the special chapter, Dom Gabriel—who also served as president of the architectural commission of the Order—requested plans of the proposed permanent monastery at Spencer that were more complete than the summary ones the commission had received from Edmund earlier.[14] Dom Edmund realized that if such plans could be ready on time, they might be approved right away by the special chapter and the building project could be launched without further delay.

The summary plans that were already in the hands of the commission by September 15 are the first ones we hear of since the July 28, 1950, plans. It seems likely that during this period of well over a year Brother Blaise and Father Laurence had been at work, at least discussing possibilities, and that the plans in question were the fruit of these discussions. As a matter of fact, Father Laurence recalls that it was in September when he visited Dom Edmund during his convalescence that he was asked to draw up a general plan for the new monastic quadrangle, with some basic measurements. It was no doubt these plans that were then in Dom Gabriel's hands. Now that more detailed plans had been requested, the monks turned to Harry Meacham, the same architect who had built the 1935 addition to the Sagendorph dairy, which had the same type of fieldstone masonry that the monks planned to use for the new monastery's exterior walls. Their discussions concerning the terms of the work were successful, and on October 13 Meacham wrote to Dom Edmund to finalize the arrangements:

> Thank for your great kindness in selecting me as the ... architect for the new Monastery to be erected at Spencer. I wish to confirm the verbal agreements which the writer has previously made with Father Lawrence and Brother Blaise in regard to the professional services to be rendered by the writer and also as to the fees to be paid for the same. ... My compensation is to be at the rate of $3 per hour for the time spent on the project by the writer, or any assistants.[15]

Meacham must have set to work immediately, for by November 1 a set of reasonably detailed plans were already in Edmund's hands.[16] Edmund had hoped to attend the chapter of November 7 but finally decided that it would be imprudent to do so because of his recent operation. In his stead, Dom Columban Hawkins of Guadalupe, who was already planning to attend, offered to take the plans to the architectural commission.

The prime order of business was the election of Dom Gabriel Sortais as the Order's sixth Abbot General. Son of an architect, he himself had spent two years in preparation for the entrance examinations at the École des Beaux-Arts in Paris. Though he was among the candidates admitted, he decided not to follow in his father's footsteps but

FIGURE 56. *Dom Gabriel Sortais, Abbot General of the Order of the Cistercians of the Strict Observance.*

rather to enter the monastery of Bellefontaine, which he did on August 4, 1924. Twelve years later he was chosen as abbot while still only thirty-three years of age and went on to become a highly respected figure in the Order as his various offices attest. Throughout his very active monastic career, however, he never lost his interest in architecture.

Dom Gabriel proved to be a staunch supporter of the reforms that brought the Order fully out of its "Trappist" period. One of his most important contributions was the reduction of the excessive number of liturgical Offices that had accrued in the Order over the ages. At the same time, he insisted on a renewal of the spiritual values of Cîteaux, such as silence, enclosure, and prayer, themes that would frequently recur in his yearly letters to the monasteries.

After the election, the new Abbot General wrote a friendly letter to Edmund informing him that his plans for the new monastery had been unanimously approved by the architectural commission, with the proviso that some attention be given to the proportions of the bell tower, which seemed to some of its members to be too wide. The loan of an additional $300,000 that had been brought up at the September chapter was also approved.[17]

Meacham's initial graphics, which were brought to Rome by Dom Columban, have survived in Spencer's archives as a series of fifteen drawings numbered P-1 to P-15.[18] They show that the location chosen for the new monastery was not very different from the one on the plan of July 28, 1950, though the link provided between the old buildings and the new is worked out in a more organic and pleasing manner in Meacham's rendering.

The overall plan was fine-tuned in such a way as to incorporate into the cloister garth of the new monastery two venerable elm trees that had stood beside the old Alta Crest Road. The section of the road that ran to the west of the trees was itself covered by the west cloister of the new monastery.

Meacham's early drawings are of interest in that they illustrate certain features of the new buildings that were never actually carried out.[19] These may best be seen on two renderings of the proposed buildings made by the famous Worcester artist Leon Hovsepian.

The exterior view shows the complex from the northwest. Along the north roof of the church's nave are nine dormer windows. Meacham's drawings indicate that a similar row was planned for the south roof. These, however, were never constructed.

In Hovsepian's interior view of the church, the sanctuary is two steps lower than in the final construction. Also, the stained glass window in the east wall in honor of the Madonna is in the form of a wheel window instead of the tripartite composition in three separate lights that was eventually adopted. By the time the working drawings for the church appeared in June 1952 all of these features had disappeared or been altered.

By a happy chance, in studying Meacham's early plans in order to carry out his own rendering, Hovsepian noticed that the sets of purlins or horizontal beams that supported the rafters of the roofs were set at different heights in the transept and in the nave, and consequently would not match up at the point where they were supposed to meet at the crossing. He traced the cause to the exaggerated pitch of the transept roofs. It took some convincing, but eventually Meacham was forced to admit the error and consequently redrew the plans so that the roofs of transepts and nave would be of equal height and pitch.

Another point that emerged from Hovsepian's drawings was that the bell tower as planned would not be tall enough to be clearly visible from all parts of the building's exterior. This too was modified.

All through the planning, there seems to have been much discussion among the abbey's designers about providing space in the new church for guests and retreatants—and also about the important matter of precisely how such visitors would approach the new buildings. It was essential to safeguard the integrity of the monastic enclosure, and since the various monastic buildings would form a tightly organized unit, the only feasible arrival point for guests coming to assist at the services would be near its eastern facade, behind which the sanctuary and altar would be located. In order to make this accessible, a new road was constructed

FIGURE 57. *Drawing of the proposed monastery by Leon Hovsepian on the basis of the first plans of Meacham. Exterior view from northwest.*

from the eastern end of the church to meet the road that had recently been built from Route 31 up to the old Alta Crest Road.

More difficult was the choice of a location within the church for the guests. In the Maginnis plan the north transept had been extended outward to provide sufficient space for guests (who would be led around the eastern facade to an entrance in this extension). But this solution meant that the main altar had to be positioned in the middle of the transept in order to be visible to the guests, and thus the sanctuary practically dis-

FIGURE 58. *Drawing of the proposed church by same. Interior view.*

371

appeared or was rather transferred into the transept.

The planners decided instead to retain a true sanctuary, to be flanked on either side by two areas for guests. Two doors in the eastern facade of the church would give access to these north and south spaces. To the west of these guest areas were four chapels (two on each side) opening out into the transepts; these would provide altars for the private Masses of the priests. (Fig. 61)

This plan, however, generated a new problem. In Cistercian churches the roof of the sanctuary is often lower than that of the nave. Such a low roof could not be extended at the same pitch over the proposed areas for the guests without severely cramping the space. Rather than altering the roof's pitch just over the guest areas, the designers chose to modify the pitch of the entire roof of the sanctuary.

To complicate matters further, when Dom Edmund saw Hovsepian's drawing of the interior of the church he did not like the fact that the sanctuary was raised only two steps above the nave, and he insisted that two more steps be added. This had the effect of placing the guests in a somewhat sunken area.

With the acceptance of the final Meacham plan, the community could look forward to the springtime when work on the great building would begin.

Building a Monastery

A MONG THE MOST SIGNIFICANT events of what would be a busy year was the first celebration at the abbey of the restored Easter Vigil, on April 12–13. The Roman decree that promulgated the new rite had been published on January 11, 1952, and the Vigil was celebrated that same year in churches around the world. By restoring the Vigil to the Universal Church Rome showed its commitment to restoring its Liturgy to earlier and more authentic forms. Among the various revivals of interest in liturgical prayer that took place throughout the history of the Church, the work of Dom Guéranger of Solesmes in the first half of the nineteenth century was of particular importance for the Church in modern times. New impetus was given to the movement by various churchmen towards the beginning of the twentieth century. This movement had important, albeit limited, effects on the liturgical life of the Valley, most particularly in the areas of the liturgical arts, such as vesture and furnishings, and in music. Each of its superiors had in one way or another fostered an improvement in the execution of Gregorian chant, the only form of vocal music used—with rare exceptions—in the services at the abbey until the 1960s. Dom Edmund was particularly active in this regard, inviting Father Andrew Klarmann to help form the choir at the Valley, and later on at Spencer, Dom Ludovic Baron of St. Anne de Kergonan, Dom Desrocquettes of Quarr Abbey, and most important of all, Dom Joseph

Gajard, the choirmaster of Solesmes, who would come for two successive summer sessions of work with the choir in 1959 and 1960.

✑ Work on the New Monastery Begins

The early months of 1952 were fairly quiet ones. Meacham's final working plans were being readied, and construction was set to begin in the spring. The plans for the foundations and other substructures came off the drawing board in March, and the great project was finally launched on March 19, the Feast of St. Joseph, with a groundbreaking ceremony on the hill where the monastery was to be built. On April 15 a contract was signed with the Granger Contracting Company of Worcester to lay the foundations of the monastic quadrangle, and on the very same day a benchmark was established that signaled the beginning of the actual work. This auspicious start was followed by many rainy days, which slowed down the work that had been begun with such enthusiasm.[1]

In a letter to Harry John, Dom Edmund gave a hint as to why the abbey's first contract with Granger was limited to the foundations:

> After many delays, work finally began yesterday [April 22] on our new Abbey here in Spencer. Prudence dictated that we obtain bids only on the foundations. . . . Work on the superstructure of the Church should commence around mid-June; from then on we shall have to rely very much on Divine Providence, for our many projects of expansion make us live very much from day to day.[2]

The plan was to negotiate with Granger for a series of separate contracts for successive phases of the construction. In this way each contract could be negotiated only when sufficient funds were available to finance the work involved. The list of the contracts serves as a guide to the order in which the various parts of the building were constructed.

1952, June 25	Contract for church and bell tower
1952, August 9	Contract for east wing and chapter house
1952, December 2	Contract for laybrothers' dormitory and west cloister
1953, January 19	Contract for library and south cloister
1953, January 19	Contract for lavabo and addition to refectory

All of these contracts with Granger contained the proviso that a dozen or so of the monks and brothers would be hired as workers, a move that would lessen the financial burden. For his part Meacham had accepted Brother Leonard O'Dowd, an electrical engineer, as collaborator on the project and had given him the responsibility of drawing up the electrical plans for the entire monastery. Several times a week Brother Leonard would be taken to Meacham's studio in Millbury, where he set to work at a drafting table.

The first of the brothers to work on the construction was Brother Gerard Bourke. His first job was to bulldoze the earth excavated from the western side of the building site, fashioning a mound farther to the west that would eventually be planted with shrubs and trees. Joseph Granger, who was the main overseer of the project, came to appreciate Gerard's talents and used him also as an assistant in surveying work. More brothers joined Granger's crew as the digging of the foundations began.

✑ A Visit from the New Abbot General

An event of prime importance in the life of the community was the first visitation of the abbey by the Order's new Abbot General, Dom Gabriel Sortais, from April 27 to May 2, 1952. During this first visit there was little for him to see of the new building save the pouring of the foundations. What did impress him, however, was the converted barn monastery the monks were living in. In a talk given to the community on May 1 he described it as "well built, in a rather rustic style, without architectural pretension, [with] very simple lines. I would be rather pleased if the new monastery matched the present one."[3] He apparently told Dom Edmund privately that, had he known how beautiful and functional the temporary monastery was, he might not have given permission to build the new one!

Dom Gabriel spoke to the community several times during the visitation, touching on various points related to the spiritual life of the monastery, in particular the important practice of *lectio divina*, or meditative reading. Central to his outlook on monastic life was the importance of simplicity and poverty in the lifestyle of the monks and in the appointments of the monastery—an issue that would come to the fore during his next visit to Spencer in 1953. In his visitation card he praised the solitude he found at Spencer, as well as the performance of the Divine Office.[4] More importantly he noted the community's unity around its abbot.

In the summary of his visitation report the General was enthusiastic:

Community rapidly growing. Novitiate of 47 young persons, of whom 28 are laybrothers. A young community, full of vitality, joyful.

Almost perfect solitude, thanks to an immense property, thanks also to the exclusion of seculars. Only one salaried employee who does the shopping outside. That is all. And the guesthouse is situated a good mile away from the monastery.

The Father Abbot is a very supernatural man, constantly insisting on the interior life.

To sum up: Spencer made an excellent impression on me.[5]

Under the heading of "Superiors" he added that the abbot "is much loved by almost all of the religious. His health is truly in jeopardy and should take care of himself." He also noted:

The novices are very numerous but form an excellent group. Their joy, their regularity and their mutual charity is noticeable. [Monastic] formation seems a bit hurried due to the lack of space in the novitiate and the small number of priests. Studies are begun a bit too soon, and those who are able-bodied are taken up with construction work. [The reference here is to studies in preparation for the priesthood.]

But he did sound a significant note of warning that would be an ongoing concern of his about Spencer:

They must take care that art (which is in honor at Spencer) does not endanger poverty. Up until now there is nothing to note, but concern must be shown in furnishing the new buildings. The Father Abbot must pay close attention to this himself.

Afterwards, the Abbot General went to Wrentham for his first visit. Towards the end of his interviews with each of the sisters, he called Dom Edmund over to Wrentham to confer. It turned out they both felt that there was need for a change of superior. The person recommended by Dom Edmund was Mother Angela Norton, who had begun her religious life as a Dominican sister but in 1947 had entered the Trappistine monastery of N.-D. du Bon Conseil, near Quebec City. After her profession she had come to Wrentham in December 1949 to join the new foundation. Sister Angela was now 40 years old and had been functioning as housekeeper and secretary to the abbess, Mother Bernard. She was called in to meet with the General and Dom Edmund, and when the office was proposed to her, after some reflection she expressed her willingness.

Given the importance of the move, the two men decided to consult with Archbishop Cushing. On the following day, an evening visit with the archbishop was scheduled. When the visitors arrived at the archbishop's home, they were shown into a room and then were somewhat hurriedly received by him as he made his way to his nightly broadcast of the Rosary Hour. When they explained the situation and proposed Sister Angela as superior, he gave his consent but asked that they write him a letter regarding the matter. The very next morning the change was announced. Mother Bernard tendered her resignation and graciously returned her pectoral cross and ring to Dom Gabriel. Mother Angela was then appointed superior ad nutum until the change could be fully implemented by a decision from Rome.

The General moved on to visit the other monasteries in the United States. In the meantime Edmund made plans for seeing the General off to Europe from New York at the end of his tour; he was hoping to introduce him to Peter Grace, who had graciously invited the party to his Long Island home for an overnight stay. Late in May, however, Edmund received a letter from Dom James saying that he had arranged to chaperone the General to New York himself.[6]

After his visit to Gethsemani, Dom Sortais wrote to Dom Edmund, saying that he had taken up with Dom James the delicate question that Edmund himself had raised of changing Spencer's paternity to Bellefontaine; he felt that New York would be an ideal place to settle the matter. The letter is an excellent example of Dom Gabriel's tact:

> Dom James spoke to me himself of the matter [the change of paternity], noting that the monasteries did not have the same spirit and that the houses were sisters rather than mother and daughter. I told him that it would be best to speak of the matter together in New York, for the Reverend Father intends to bring me there on June 27. He will come to Mepkin with me and plans to accompany me also to Berryville because he wants to see you in New York on the twenty-eighth.
>
> I wrote to the Procurator to have him do a historical outline [of the question] and to get his personal opinion without revealing the project to the other definitors. He sent me the two enclosed sheets. I believe that James will accept, I imagine that Bellefontaine will also accept, but I fear Dom Pacôme of N.-D. du Lac, who on several occasions said that, though the foundation of Petit Clairvaux was made from Bellefontaine, that of the Valley was made from Lac. But one could answer him by saying that if he thought that the paternity of Bellefontaine was lost by a transfer from one place to another, (from

Petit Clairvaux to the Valley), the paternity of Lac was lost in the same way when the Valley was transferred to Spencer.

I think, that if you wish to succeed, you must be very discreet and for the moment say nothing to anyone in America. We will speak of this to Dom James. Then, if he accepts in principle, I will speak of the matter to Bellefontaine. Only then should you speak to the whole community, and if things work out, to the General Chapter. Such matters require prudence if they are to succeed.[7]

He returned to the same theme two weeks later:

We will meet in New York as agreed and in the evening I will leave Dom James and go with you to your friends. He will leave, I think, for Notre Dame du Lac with Father Bernard, my interpreter, whose services I will no longer need, provided you bring along someone who speaks French. As a matter of fact, I would prefer that this matter of the change of paternity not be treated in the presence of someone who is from Notre Dame du Lac. See if you can bring Father Laurence or someone else who speaks French.

I think it better that this question . . . be treated in the presence of a third person such as myself. Dom James knows that you would be happy with this change. You will always find yourself in a difficult situation in his presence and would risk (as you told me) saying things that would be painful for him.

In my presence it would be different. I will direct the conversation, smoothing out the rough spots. I will bring the matter to a conclusion in charity, since I am not on the side of either of you. Then, when you meet Dom James once again, the question will have been treated and settled. If you want to avoid this first encounter, one day or other there will be another that might not be so easy. . . . [Besides,] since I will be coming with Dom James, I will have prepared him for the meeting.[8]

These further remarks convinced Dom Edmund to agree to the meeting in New York.[9]

In his letter of May 23 Dom Gabriel had also reported that Dom Celsus seemed to feel an injustice had been done to the Irish sisters in replacing Mother Bernard, and that they should have the option of returning to Ireland. Gabriel offered the following suggestions:

I think that if the Irish sisters would write a letter to Glencairn saying that the move was a wise one and that they have only praise for Mother Angela, this would smooth things over nicely.

As for Mother Angela herself, I will look into the matter when I arrive in Rome. I am not writing about this now [to the definitory], because Dom Colman might inform Dom Celsus and take up the matter with the Congregation, where he has very powerful friends. When I return to Rome I will do all I can to see that the proposal be accepted by the council [of definitors], then try to obtain what we want from the Congregation. [Dom Colman Foley, a monk of Mount Melleray, was the English language definitor at the time.][10]

A somewhat cool letter that Archbishop Cushing sent to Mother Angela seems to suggest that Dom Celsus' concerns had begun to spread to other quarters. Edmund himself received a letter from the archbishop and wrote to Dom Gabriel about it:

It is very evident that someone has written to His Excellency, creating doubts and other misgivings in his mind. At any rate, the tone of the Archbishop's latest letter differs very much from that of his letter to Your Paternity of May 16.[11]

Indeed the whole matter continued to smolder until July, when the Holy See itself would take matters in hand.

∽ A BRUSH WITH DISASTER

As Edmund was planning the New York trip, he wrote to Dom Gabriel suggesting that he might show him the Hidden Valley property, which was being "nursed" for Spencer by Charles Grace.[12] Fitting this in would be something of a challenge, since Dom Gabriel was scheduled to fly to Paris on June 29, and the famous meeting with James about the change of paternity had to be given pride of place.

Dom Edmund set off for New York with Father Laurence on June 27, and they were met at the airport by Dom Gabriel and Dom James. The much feared encounter took place over lunch in a restaurant at Oyster Bay, and the discussion lasted all of five minutes. Dom Gabriel had obviously done his work: James had no objections to make. Both parties immediately agreed to the proposal. With this out of the way, Dom James and Father Bernard of Oka returned to the airport to catch their plane, and Dom Edmund, Dom Gabriel and Father Laurence headed for Peter Grace's home on Long Island where they spent the evening.

While they were there, they found out that Dom Gabriel's flight was delayed for a day, so Peter chartered a plane from La Guardia for a brief afternoon visit to Hidden Valley the next day. The party was to include Dom Edmund, Father Laurence, Brother Leo, Peter and his wife, Margie, and three of their sons. Dom Edmund later related the rest of the story in a letter to the monastery's old friend Monsignor Oechsler:

> We chartered a plane on the twenty-eighth hoping to return the same day to New York; that evening we made a forced landing which was bad enough; we had to motor to the site the next day, Sunday; when we tried to take off our plane got out of control, plunged into brush land, knocked down small trees, and finally came to a standstill with the fuselage knocked in, the tail and part of the body (eight inches behind my head) ripped off. I was thrown around a good deal and for a few moments my companions thought that I would die, but I came to; I was hospitalized and came home by easy stages after it was ascertained that I had no fractures or concussions or lesions. I am now getting rid of my sore back and neck, and the bruises are healing.[13]

Fortunately, no one else was hurt in the crash. The General was spirited off in a taxi to Washington, DC, accompanied by Peter and Father Laurence. A car was waiting at the station to take them to the airport for the General's flight to Paris. Margie and the others remained behind with Dom Edmund. They took him to the nearby town of Hot Springs where they stayed until Monday evening, when they all returned to New York. He rested for a few days at the Graces' home before returning to Spencer on Wednesday, July 2.

Not long after his return Edmund learned from Dom Gabriel that Rome had officially appointed Mother Angela superior of Wrentham for a period of three years. When the indult arrived, however, Edmund was somewhat put out to learn that he had been named as the one responsible for the appointment, as though the request had stemmed from him alone. His hope had been that the request would have been made by the Order itself. He wrote to Dom Gabriel, saying he felt that this would not sit well with Archbishop Cushing.[14]

In response, Sortais once again took up the matter with the Holy See, framing the request in his own name in virtue of his role as official visitor of all the monasteries of the nuns of the Order. The Holy See responded by taking the appointment upon itself, and further stipulated that Mother Angela would be appointed as *abbess* and not simply as superior.[15] She was duly installed as abbess on September 14, 1952.

✑ The Walls of the New Building Begin to Rise

Shortly before Dom Edmund left for New York, the building project moved forward into another significant stage: The contract was signed with Granger for the construction of the church and the adjacent bell tower on June 25. Stepping up from the somewhat uninspiring work of pouring foundations, the workmen and their monastic helpers now turned to building above ground level.[16]

As the walls began to rise the brothers were assigned to different jobs, such as tenders to the stonemasons or brick cutters. Some were given more significant duties. Brother Paul Forster had by now become very involved with the electrical work, first as assistant to a professional electrician, then with full responsibility for the job. Reading Brother Leonard's blueprints, he took on the daunting task of laying the wiring in the new church, often adapting the layout to unforeseeable changes made as the masonry structures began to rise. On days when Brother Leonard was not working at Meacham's, he made the rounds at the site inspecting the progress Brother Paul was making with the actual installation.

Though some choir religious worked on the site, their major contribution was finding suitable fieldstones for the exterior walls. The masons

FIGURE 59. *St. Joseph's Abbey. Monks unloading fieldstones. The chapterhouse is seen in the background.*

often made very specific requests, explaining just what shape of stone was needed for an exact spot. It is said that the choir monks who directed the stone gathering became experts in ferreting out the perfect piece. Others, professed as well as novices, joined in the search for suitable stones in the old dry stone walls that criss-crossed the woods on the monastic property, loading them onto flatbed trailers that then carried them to the building site.

As time went on, Granger and his workmen came to respect the brothers and appreciate the work they did more and more. The bond that developed often led to workmen sharing the secrets of their trade. Brother Gerard seemed to make the most of this, little by little getting a firm grasp on a variety of building techniques. He eventually assumed a special role, working with individual brothers on a personal level, finding out where their talents lay, encouraging them when they made mistakes and gradually turning them into professionals in their own right.

Among those who worked on the site were: Brothers Peter Larrowe, Edmund Deignan, Bonaventure Crocker, Stephen Brown, Alan Hudon, Anthony O'Connor, Richard Ross, Brendan Kelly, George Meisenzahl, Alphonsus (later Patrick) Brown, and Emmanuel Lachance; and among the choir religious, Fraters Damian Dowdell and Alphonsus Chruma.

The next contract in place was for the monastery's east wing—including the sacristy and scriptorium on the ground floor and the dormitory of the choir monks on the second—and for the chapter house, which would be built perpendicular to the east wing of the cloister.

Although the church had risen only to the height of the windows of the side aisle, work began on the east wing soon after the contract was signed on August 9. There were now several work sites under way at the same time, as the foundations continued to be laid for other parts of the building as well. This helped expedite the work. Dom Edmund described the status of the whole project in a letter to Dom Robert McGann of Conyers:

> All the foundations for the entire quadrangle are now complete. The stone exterior and brick interior on the Church is now above the windows of the aisles, with the piers of the nave even higher. The contract has been awarded on the sacristy-chapter-scriptorium wing, and work should begin this week or next.[17]

Meacham's plans for the east wing had been ready since March, but a revision was made on June 28. Originally the outer masonry on the second floor was to be in half-timbering; now it was replaced with walls of irregular "swell-belly" bricks, a type of masonry that would become popular in later constructions at the abbey.

By August Brother Jerome Collins and Brother Bonaventure Crocker were at work on the plumbing and the radiant heating installation. First of all, each section of copper pipe had to be bent into shape *by hand* on a wooden form. These were then soldered together and laid in place. Finally, concrete was poured over them and the tiles laid.

As the building progressed the whole work site became more and more the scene of intense activity, a sense of which we catch in the following remarks of one of the brothers who was in the heat of it all:

> At the height of construction there were on the job two brick foremen, a stone mason foreman, a carpenter foreman and a supervisory foreman, Hank Stintson; "Hollering Hank" they called him. His voice could be heard from one end of construction site to other. Although he could strip the skin off the lay workers for mistakes they made, he never did this to any of the brothers.
>
> It was a busy place. Each of those foremen had twenty people reporting to him.[18]

By August 13, the foundations for the entire building were finally complete, and two days later, on the Feast of the Assumption, the community went in procession to the spot near the main (west) entrance to the church for the ceremony of laying into the northwest corner of the building the old cornerstone, which had been removed from the ruins of the Valley church. As Dom Edmund related to Dom Robert of Conyers before the event:

> The stone itself is that of the Valley church which we saved from the ruins. The original date (1925) has been retained on one face, and the new date (1952) carved on the other with a beautiful inscription: LAPIS ISTE * QUEM EREXI IN TITULUM * VOCABITUR DOMUS DEI. [This stone that I have set up as a pillar will be called the house of God.] In the stone itself we intend to insert the list of all the religious of the Abbey "ad perpetuam rei memoriam." [for eternal remembrance of the fact.] For we trust in God that this church will stand more permanently than that of the Valley; however, its fate, like ours, is in His Hands.[19]

The stone was set in such a way that both dates are visible. This important symbol of the community's continuity had been hewn from Cumberland granite quarried by the Valley monks themselves. From it Spencer's fieldstone walls would "grow," as each stone was set in place by this new generation of monks. The cornerstone's new blessing in 1952 affirmed that the worship of God established by the 1925 blessing would be taken up in the new church.

On another front, the question of the transfer of Spencer's paternity would be coming up at the General Chapter in September. By that time the local chapters of both Spencer and Gethsemani had voted on the matter, and the positive results in both cases had been transmitted to Bellefontaine, where its chapter also voted in favor of the change. The General Chapter met September 12–16, 1952. With all the concerns of the ongoing building project at Spencer, Dom Edmund was not able to attend, but the proposal was accepted unanimously in any case. Another decision of the chapter dealt with Spencer's first daughterhouse, Guadalupe. Dom Columban had come to the conclusion that the monastery's property was insufficient to support a dedicated program of agriculture. He thus requested permission to move. The chapter unanimously approved the proposal, even though no new site had been proposed as a possibility.[20]

Profiting from a fine spell of weather in November, the builders were able to complete the roofing of the new church as well as most of the east wing. Then, on December 2, the contract was signed for the monastery's west cloister and the related structures of the brothers' dormitory and chapter room.[21]

Around the same time, plans for a new unit of the future monastery were completed: a small guesthouse for the exclusive use of priest visitors, to be situated near the southeast corner of the quadrangle. In order to permit Meacham to keep his attention focused on the main part of the monastery, the plans had been entrusted to another architect, Albert Roy. Details of the early phases of the construction of this building are wanting. In all probability the Granger company was responsible for the foundations and a certain amount of aboveground construction.

Throughout this period the area later occupied by the south cloister was left open so that soil for future garden beds could be hauled into the space of the open cloister garth. A rather large beech tree, which has survived to this day, was also brought in by truck.

On January 19, 1953, the final contracts were signed—for the south cloister, the library, the lavabo and the link to the refectory. This required a rather large financial outlay all at one time, but opening several new sites meant that workmen could begin there—weather permitting—at the same time as others completed what remained to be done in areas that were roofed over.

With this added financial strain, Spencer's chapter voted unanimously on February 1 to propose refinancing the loan of $500,000, pledging the monastic property as collateral. A letter was sent to the definitory to obtain its permission. An added appeal was made to Harry John, but he turned out not to be in a position to help.[22]

✑ Windows for the New Church

While all this work was going on, Brother Blaise—in addition to his busy occupation as clerk of works on the building site—was negotiating for the planned stained glass window of the Madonna for the apse of the church, as well as for other artifacts.[23] The person chosen for the work was the Dutch artist Joep Nicolas, who had made important artistic contributions to the Abbey of Orval in Belgium that had impressed both Dom Edmund and Brother Blaise during visits to the abbey. Joep had come to live in New York in 1939 and had received commissions from Harold Rambusch, with whom Edmund had been in contact since the time of the restoration work at Our Lady of the Valley in 1945.

An undated letter that seems to have been written fairly early in the design process discusses an early plan for the iconography of the window, which had been altered from the original circle to three round-headed windows. According to this letter the central window was to depict Mary with the child Jesus. The two flanking windows were to be divided into two registers: above, Adam and Eve (left panel) and the Annunciation (right panel); below, four major prophets (left) and evangelists (right).[24] This plan for the side panels was eventually abandoned in favor of a simple pattern of rectangles with occasional fleur-de-lis, which also served as background in the limited space around the figure of the Madonna and Child in the central panel.[25] Joep's wife, Suzanne, would also make a contribution to the furnishings of the church in the form of a series of bas-relief crucifixes for the private altars. These were copies of a model she had originally created for Orval.

✐ THE ABBOT GENERAL RETURNS TO NORTH AMERICA

Sometime after the General Chapter of 1952 Dom Gabriel set out on another visitation tour of the houses of the Order. While in Japan he received a letter from Dom Edmund informing him about further developments in Guadalupe's plans for transferring its location: Dom Columban was enthusiastic about a property he had discovered in Oregon. Edmund also offered the curious suggestion that since the community of Prairies in Canada was coming upon hard times, Guadalupe might simply be transferred there to save the situation! As a matter of fact, Dom Gabriel himself showed great concern about the situation at Prairies. He answered Edmund from Our Lady of Lourdes convent in Japan:

> The Reverend Father [Dom Columban] has not written to me about his projects in Oregon. . . . Your idea is interesting and I will speak of it to him. This will be even easier after my visit to Prairies where I will be on the fifteenth of this month. I foresee great difficulties there, more serious even than those that you mention in your letter. On the other hand, I strongly desire to have an English-speaking community in Canada, and I spoke of this to Dom Pacôme once again this year at the General Chapter. Might the solution to these two difficulties (crisis in the community of Prairies and absence of an English-speaking house in Canada) consist in the establishment of the community of Guadalupe on the property of Prairies? It is possible, and I will speak to Dom Columban of this as coming from myself, whether or not he judges it appropriate at the present time to bring me up to date on his plans in Oregon.[26]

This plan was soon filed away in the archives of "what might have been," for when the General landed in Canada at the Vancouver airport on his way to Prairies, Dom Columban was there waiting for him, begging him to come immediately to see the Oregon property, which his community had already voted to purchase![27] The General agreed, and the next day they flew to Portland and went to inspect the property at Lafayette. The General found the site attractive and the land fertile, and felt that Dom Edmund would also be impressed when he saw it. And so no mention was made of a possible transfer of Guadalupe to Prairies. On January 20 the definitory approved Guadalupe's move to the new site, giving permission for the sale of the New Mexico property as well as for a loan to purchase the new one in Oregon.[28]

Dom Gabriel's prime intention in coming to North America this time was to visit the Canadian houses, so he continued his journey to Prairies. But he had other plans as well, as he had written to Peter Grace back on August 26:

> I intend to pay a six weeks' visit to our Canadian monasteries. . . . After my visit to New Brunswick I would come down to Spencer to see Dom Edmund and from then on be entirely at your disposition for our journey to South America. . . . I could plan on being at Spencer towards the end of January so as to leave for South America in early February, 1953.[29]

He proceeded to Oka as scheduled on January 20, 1953, and opened the visitation but five days later he became ill and was taken to the hospital of Notre Dame de l'Espérance in Ville St. Laurent. He was diagnosed with a serious kidney disorder, and twice underwent surgery; on February 19, in the second procedure, one of his kidneys was removed. Edmund sent his condolences and suggested that he come to Spencer to convalesce before returning home to Europe, adding that Peter Grace had offered to drive the General to New York for his return flight.[30] The General was finally able to return to Oka from the hospital on March 20. Though he thought he would have to cancel his trip to the United States, his condition improved, and several weeks later he was able to set out for Spencer by plane for an informal visit of one week. The regular visitation that year was delegated to Dom Louis de Gonzague Le Pennuen, who arrived shortly after Dom Gabriel's departure.[31]

When the General had last visited Spencer, there had been little to see at the building site. Now the basic structure was complete, as Edmund reported to Dom James on April 1, 1953:

> Our church and abbey are about 4/5[ths] completed. Just now we (the Brothers, that is) are about half finished installing the radiant-heating coils in the floors of all the Regular Places and pouring in the cement sub-floors. In the church, the quarry-tile floor has been installed in the entire body of the church and the workmen are now doing the sanctuary steps and the presbytery. . . . All the windows, except the great triple lancets in the apse, have been filled with the geometric glass saved from the ruins of the Valley, which gives us a blue-tinted interior. We hope to have the Madonna window by Joep Nicolas before our Reverendissime arrives on the thirteenth from Oka. [With a little prodding from Brother Blaise, Joep was able to deliver at least the central panel of the Salve window in time for the visit.][32]

Dom Gabriel's impressions of the central portion of the new monastery have not been preserved in letters or other documents, but an unsigned memorandum—most likely by Brother Blaise—in the Spencer archives throws some light on the subject.[33] It relates in some detail Dom Gabriel's feelings about the project of the small retreat house for visiting priests. By this time the foundations of the building had been completed, but the only structures showing aboveground were a series of reinforced concrete posts.

The author cites a series of remarks made by the General over breakfast, in which he expressed his concern that the guesthouse might intrude on the quiet and general privacy of the properly monastic parts of the building, in particular the infirmary. He apparently offered some suggestions as to how to remedy the situation without, of course, changing the location of the building.

In what the author describes as a second visit with the General, Dom Gabriel turned to finances:

> If there was question of [continuing] building and thus jeopardizing our chances of getting sufficient funds to finish the guesthouse and pay against the debt on the monastic quadrangle he felt it far better that it be left standing thus for seculars to see we don't have all the money that a finished product would suggest that we have. In doing what we have done, he said, he knew Dom Edmund has only been seeking to provide the best for a community that he loves very much. There has been no self-seeking in this work and he felt that Dom Edmund would take it all in a truly supernatural spirit. . . .
>
> Reverendissime did not make his judgment to stop the guest-house on [the basis of the] monies involved because he was certainly under the impression at that time that we had sufficient funds. It was his fear that a false impression would be given by its completion. This was proven by the fact of his recommendation that the polish be removed from the altars even though it cost money for the finished effect. . . . In no way did our financial position color his decision other than he felt if we completed everything in one swoop it would jeopardize our chances for benefactors to assist in defraying our debts which were incurred with Rome's placet [assent].
>
> All these quotations are, of course, of individuals involved [and] are to be read with the understanding that they are repeated a week after the conversation took place, and that they are retold in the language of Brother Blaise.[34]

From the pen of Brother Leo (writing many years later, in 1993) we get a somewhat different picture:

> As regards his own person he [Dom Edmund] observed the sense of poverty more than I've ever known it in any other monk, but when it came to the Lord's buildings, nothing was too good for Him! And hence it is that he and I clashed on more than one occasion about the costs of Blaise's constructions. They were very high. . . . When it [the priests' retreat house] was finished, over a bottle of champagne we split together as a peace offering in that building, he admitted with a certain satisfaction that it was the most expensive construction per cubic foot that had been built that year in New England for a one story affair, and he may well have been correct. My only comment was to take another sip of champagne.
>
> If the economic cube is the cheapest thing to build, what he had done was just the opposite. That little affair with its more or less ten rooms and baths cost more than the entire new monastery at Miraflores in Chile, a monastery which includes a guest house. For me it was too costly, and Dom Gabriel agreed with me when he as an architect made the nice distinction between "the style of simplicity" which was Blaise's and "simplicity of style" that for example belongs to Miraflores. . . .[35]
>
> I was also often during those years weighed down by my long absences from the regular life, and on this occasion the priests' retreat house was like a last straw. I knocked on the Abbot's door and when he signaled me to come in I knelt down before him as was the custom, to get his blessing. I reported on my trip and then after small talk, came to the point, "Reverend Father I've just seen the plans on the new priests' retreat house, and I've got to admit I think this affair is going to cost too much money. I don't feel I can raise funds for a construction like this when there are so many more pressing needs in other areas." The Abbot was silent and I could see he was hurt. He didn't say anything more, and I rose, made the prescribed bows and left. For some reason the General came to Spencer [this refers to the 1953 visit] and recognizing that I had displeased my Abbot (something the Rule heartily damns), I discussed the matter with him and was a little surprised when he wholeheartedly agreed with me, with the very noticeable result that construction stopped on the priests' retreat house, leaving the desolate up-right corner posts standing in the winter snow. I had wounded the Abbot's sensitivity and felt his displeasure, spending the next months at home working over my shoes in the cobbler's shop.[36]

Wherever the truth lies in this tug of war concerning the new guest-house, the General convinced Dom Edmund to bring its construction to a halt for the moment.

✺ A Visitation by Dom Louis de Gonzague Le Pennuen

Following hard upon Dom Gabriel's friendly visit, which ended with a brief trip to Wrentham, Dom Louis de Gonzague of Melleray arrived at Spencer on May 2 for the official visitation. One might have expected Spencer's new Father Immediate, Dom Emmanuel Coutant of Bellefontaine, to take this opportunity to make his first visitation to his new daughterhouse. But apparently in an effort to cut down on the costs of transatlantic voyages, it had been decided that Dom Louis, Father Immediate of Gethsemani, would make the visitations at both Gethsemani and Spencer this time, and that Dom Emmanuel would do the same the next time. In any case, Dom Louis also made visitations at Gethsemani's foundations at Mepkin and Genesee, neither of which was yet independent, as well as an informal visit to Conyers, which had already achieved autonomy.

Dom Louis de Gonzague Le Pennuen had been definitor in Rome from 1946 until 1949, when he was elected abbot of Melleray. He was well versed in the material workings of the Order and its finances and had even offered a certain amount of encouragement to the Valley when it was preparing to ask for a $400,000 loan in 1949.[37]

While his lengthy, four-page visitation report to the General betrays something of the rougher side of his character, it contains interesting observations about the abbot and the community. His judgment of the community itself was balanced:

> Spirit of the Community. Very good community in general; a bit young as are all our communities in the United States. Different mentality from that of Gethsemani, which they consider as "de Rancé" and too observant of the usages. Here, they are "Cistercian" and not Trappist. There is a real difference, although much less pronounced than is imagined in the two houses themselves. What is unfortunate is that both houses imagine themselves to be the "model house." Nonetheless, Spencer is a good community, considerate and sometimes hypersensitive with regard to its abbot.[38]

His concern with the abbot centered on Dom Edmund's temperament and on what seemed to be his restriction of access to the community confessors:

> His good will is evident. Yet, nervous, due in part to sickness and to his preoccupations; for this reason it is not good to go against his ideas; he is given to making sudden grimaces.
>
> A tendency to reserve for the external forum (Abbot and Father Masters) that which belongs to the internal one. For this reason there is a general remark on this in the visitation card. On several occasions he let it be understood that the Father Masters alone were the spiritual directors of the novices and asked that confessions be brief (4 or 5 minutes).

The first point is one that would continue to surface in later reports drawn up by other visitors. Also, like Dom Gabriel, Dom Louis was concerned with the question of poverty in the appointments of the monastery and called this to Edmund's attention in no uncertain terms. A further issue was the quality of priestly studies at Spencer: lack of preparation of the professors, and the absence of courses in canon law and liturgy. It was a problem he noted at other American monasteries, and in each case he strongly urged that some students be sent to Rome to answer this need. But he met with resistance, and not only at Spencer.

Surely no one would disagree with his assessment of Father Owen: "The Father Prior. Must be very good, for no one has a word to say about him. A bit deaf."

Perhaps of greatest interest is his sober, informative report on the financial situation at Spencer at this crucial moment when construction was approaching completion. His report shows that at the time of the visitation two loans were in course: the $300,000 mortgage with L'Union Saint-Jean Baptiste, and a five-year loan of $275,000 from a bank. The estimated cost to complete the construction (exclusive of the priests' retreat house) and to furnish the buildings was $273,000. Under the heading "sources of revenue," he notes that, realistically speaking, the money coming in from ordinary activities was about $26,120, and that for the rest, the monastery depended on Mass stipends, various offerings, and education funds from the GI Bill.

From the community's perspective, what was particularly vexing was the visitor's manner, which was often lacking in tact. To take one example (perhaps the most telling), prior to the visitation Dom Edmund had reminded the community that it was important to point out not only faults with the administration but also its positive aspects. Indeed, it seems that he even offered some concrete examples that might be mentioned. The result was that the first interviews between Dom Louis and the monks sounded a somewhat repetitive note: They always began with several concrete positive points about Dom Edmund's administration. After hearing several interviews of this kind, Louis came out of his room after one of the interviews and announced to those waiting to see him that he did not wish to hear any further enumerations of the abbot's strong points, but only of his weak ones![39]

In all fairness it must be admitted that his visitation card was generally positive in tone. His closing remark for Edmund needs no translation: "*Bon courage! Excellente communauté.*"

Nonetheless, the community reacted strongly.[40] Two of the monks wrote in complaint to Dom Gabriel. He replied to Edmund and offered some excuse for Dom Louis by pointing to his poor health and the many visitations he was called upon to make in America. He put to rest the idea that Louis and Emmanuel would take turns coming to America to make the yearly visitations of Gethsemani and Spencer.[41]

℘ COMPLETING THE WORK

As summer approached, another important addition was made to the abbey's holdings: a small house owned by Edna Parker on Route 31 near the porter's lodge, acquired in partnership with Peter Grace. Once again, as in the purchase of Allenacres, it was Peter who assumed the major portion of the financing, the understanding being that the abbey would year by year purchase additional shares from him. By August 2, 1954, the monastery was able to settle affairs with Peter and become full proprietor of both properties.

The Parker house, which was known first as the "Red House" and then became the "Green House" when it got a new coat of paint, was one of the places where monks could receive their families and close friends. So was the Grange, which had finally been closed as a guesthouse.

On June 5, 1953, Granger closed down his own operation, a sure sign that the construction was almost complete. The exteriors of all the buildings were finished, with of course the exception of the visiting priests' retreat house.[42] Work on the interiors was being continued by the monks themselves, as Dom Edmund reported to Monsignor Oechsler:

Our Brothers have gradually learned many of the tricks of the trade and can get along without paid labor. So we have continued the electrical installation, the painting, and the laying down of the tile floors throughout the house, with the result that more slowly, but just as surely we are coming along.[43]

The brothers involved in the finishing work functioned as a team under Brother Gerard and were ultimately responsible to Brother Blaise. Among the first jobs they carried out was the laying of the tile floor in the brothers' chapter room and in the porch on the east facade of the church. They also worked on the construction of the reception room. A later note from Brother Blaise describes the provenance of its wall paneling:

It was originally in an octagonal dining room. The house that it was part of burned one demented winter night and this room was all that was saved. This home was possibly located in Warwick or Bristol, RI. The deeply undercut carving around and above the fireplace, in two cupboards, and over the double door and windows, is very fine.[44]

For its floor, white marble plaques were obtained from still another building, and supplemented by black slate.

By the end of the month Dom Edmund could see his way to planning for a grand entrance into the new building on August 15, the Feast of the Assumption. Mass would be celebrated for the first time in the abbey church:

I have decided, as a gesture of faith, to take possession of the Church, sacristy, cloisters, and two chapter houses on August 15th. The stalls for the Church and the sacristy cases are being installed next Tuesday (although not yet paid for!); all the altars are in now, and the marble tabernacle is to be ready within another week or ten days.[45]

FIGURE 60. *St. Joseph's Abbey. Aerial view from the southwest. To the north, church and bell tower. The east wing: dormitory of the choir monks on the second floor. The west wing: laybrothers' chapter, cloister walk with laybrothers' dormitory below. To the south, the cemetery flanked by the library to the east, abbatiale and lavabo to the west. In the foreground, the remodeled Alta Crest buildings.*

Settling In to the New Home

B Y THE SECOND WEEK of August work on the monastery was still not complete. The two large dormitories were not yet ready for occupancy, and the timbering of the church's ceiling had not yet been stained. Nonetheless Dom Edmund decided to plan for the inauguration of the church on August 15, the Feast of the Assumption, and the monastery's old friend, Father Andrew Klarmann, was called in to help the choir prepare for the great event. Since the enclosure would go into effect after the ceremony, the abbot invited several important guests to visit the new buildings on the fourteenth.

Thanks to careful study of source material on Cistercian architecture and a well-organized construction program, the community had as its new home a monastery that, with adaptations to local needs, reflected the traditional Cistercian plan: the church situated to the north, a wing for the choir monks to the east, and one for the laybrothers on the west.

The east wing follows the usual layout of a Cistercian monastery. The monks' dormitory occupies its entire upper floor, with stairs at its northern end leading down to the church and at its southern end to the cloister. At ground level the sacristy is to the north and the scriptorium to the south. The chapter house lies perpendicular to this wing, its western extremity occupying the ground level space between sacristy and scriptorium.

The west wing departs more radically from the typical plan. During the Order's first centuries, the western range normally consisted of a

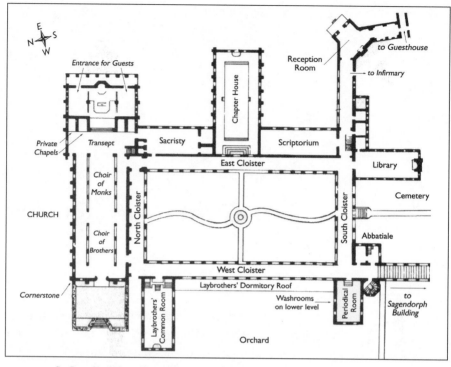

FIGURE 61. *St. Joseph's Abbey. Plan of the central building.*

two-storied building with the brothers' dormitory on the second floor and their refectory and other rooms below. Though often built close to the west cloister gallery, this structure was usually separated from it by a corridor (the "laybrothers' lane") that facilitated comings and goings within the building itself and also served as a passageway to the church for the laybrothers. The outer wall of the west cloister gallery itself was normally interrupted only by a door offering access to the "lane" on the main floor of the brothers' building, thus giving this cloister gallery the character of a passageway.

This physical separation between cloister and laybrothers' building was based on the laybrothers' status in those early years, when their interaction with the choir monks was strictly limited. As the laybrother vocation evolved during the nineteenth century revival of the Order in France and there was increasing contact between monks and laybrothers, the physical separation of the two groups became less marked. For one thing, the entire community—choir monks and laybrothers— henceforth shared a common refectory.

This evolution influenced the way the west wing at Spencer was constructed. The laybrothers' dormitory occupies the space immediately *below* the west cloister but extends outwards beyond the line of the cloister walk above, recalling in miniature the laybrothers' building of earlier times. At the northern end of the wing, a separate building houses a room—one of the most attractive in the monastery—for the general use of the laybrothers, in particular for the regular conferences given by their Father Master. Such a room was conspicuously absent from the medieval layout; the brothers' refectory was apparently used for these conferences.[1] A two-storied building at the southern end of the wing houses the monastery's main washrooms on the ground level. Above, a large room has served various purposes and is used today as a periodical room. This new and simpler arrangement of the laybrothers' area without a second story on the cloister level made it possible to open the solid wall of the west cloister into an arcade, thus providing views not only into the cloister garth but out over what was originally one of the monastery's orchards. (Figs. 60 and 61)

This same feature would be taken up in the south wing of the cloister, where once again there was a departure from the typical Cistercian plan. Since the refectory in the Alta Crest building would continue to serve the new monastery, there was no need to construct a new refectory perpendicular to this wing, as was typical of the medieval plan. Thus once again open arcades run along both sides of the south cloister gallery. From here there is a view south to the cemetery and the old Sagendorph cottage, with even a glimpse of the countryside beyond.

This view from the south cloister is framed by two important buildings. To the east, the imposing structure of the library, which matches the height of the dormitory off its northeast corner, consists of a single room of full height directly to the south of the east cloister. A fireplace against its rear wall serves as a point of focus for one coming down this cloister. The library stacks are situated in the large room below ground.

Opposite the library on the west lies the abbatiale, or abbot's quarters. Entered from an extension of the west cloister, this two-storied building contains an office as well as private space for the abbot on the upper floor, with waiting room and meeting room on the lower floor and a basement below. On the opposite side of the extension of the west cloister sits the stair tower. Slightly higher than the abbatiale, its upper story contains a chapel for the abbot, accessible from the second floor of his office. The stairs themselves lead down to the level of the laybroth-

FIGURE 62. *St. Joseph's Abbey. Church. View from laybrothers' choir.*

ers' dormitory and the monastery's main washroom.

The extension leading past the abbatiale continues down a set of broad steps to the lavabo building, which houses a fountain formerly used by the monks to wash their hands before meals. From here stairs leading off to the west connect to the refectory. To the east, the axis of the south cloister is prolonged in another corridor in which the offices of the subordinate superiors are located and which leads further on to the reception room of the monastery and to the guesthouse.

FIGURE 63. *(above) St. Joseph's Abbey. The library.*

FIGURE 64. *(left) St. Joseph's Abbey. Monks in procession along the east cloister. The window and door into the chapterhouse are partially visible on the left wall. The library is seen in the distance.*

The crown of the abbey is, of course, the church. The main body is divided into a nave and two side aisles by twin arcades of simple design that support a broad roof of open timbering. The nave itself is divided by a low wall—rather than the bridge-like "jube" at the Valley—into the choir of the monks and that of the laybrothers.[2] The division between the two choirs is further marked by a "rood beam" extending across the nave overhead. The rood in medieval churches was a representation of Christ on the cross, flanked by the figures of John and Mary in mourning.[3] There were plans for three sculpted figures for the beam in Spencer's church, but these never materialized. Two elevated platforms, or ambos, situated in an arch on either side of the nave originally provided lecterns for the readings. (The ambo on the northern side of the church was later removed to make space for a new organ.)

The decision not to install dormer windows along the church's roof led to a considerable darkening of the nave, an effect heightened by the dark blue windows of the north aisle, which were originally designed for the over-bright western end of the Valley church.[4]

The transepts offer an intermediate space between nave and sanctuary. From the south transept the traditional Cistercian "night stairs" lead up to the choir monks' dormitory, providing easy access to the church for the early morning Vigil service. A large lancet window in the north transept offers more light to this area of the church, setting it off from the darker nave.[5] This is supplemented by the light from five smaller windows placed above the arch leading up to the sanctuary, a feature inspired by a similar arrangement at the famous abbey of Fontenay in Burgundy.

To the west of the night stairs lies the bell tower, housing three bells that ring out over the countryside through tall slender arches on its eastern and western sides. Below the level of the bells there are two chambers that originally housed the pipes of the church's first organ.

Altering the original plan for a relatively low sanctuary area, four steps now lead up to the "presbytery," beyond which a single step gives access to the sanctuary proper, with a final step leading up to the predella on which the altar is placed. The altar itself consists of a single block of Champlain Black marble quarried in Vermont. Because of its size and weight it had to be set in place by a crane, before the roof of the church was built. A smaller altar with tabernacle sits in an absidiole built into the rear wall of the sanctuary, flanked by two blind arches. Above these are the three large lancet windows by Joep Nicolas, the central one depicting the Madonna and Child.

In addition to the main altar and the tabernacle altar in the sanctuary, there are a number of other altars throughout the church: four in the chapels flanking the sanctuary, one in each of the transepts, two in the choir of the laybrothers, and two in the northwest and southwest corners of the church, making a total of twelve. Together with the twelve others in the Alta Crest complex, these altars served the needs of the individual priests of the monastery—by the summer of 1953 there were twenty-five—who, in addition to assisting at the community Mass, still offered individual Masses each day. The two altars in the laybrothers' choir were of particular importance. Each day Mass was offered for the friends, benefactors, and relatives of the community: on the altar of the

Blessed Virgin for those living, and on the "Pro Defunctis" altar for those who had died.

The light from the three great windows in the sanctuary make this the brightest part of the church by far, dramatically so at sunrise and during the early morning hours. At the opposite end, a wheel window set high up in the western facade shines with a diffuse brightness throughout the first part of the day, but towards the late afternoon it sends a slowly moving projection of its patterned color onto the area of the laybrothers' choir and beyond.

This window is one of the elements in the church that serve as a link between past and present. Sections of red and blue glass from the narrower panels of the large perpendicular-style windows of the Valley's clerestory were recomposed to create it, the linear elements in red ingeniously set into a ray-like pattern against a background of blue.[6]

The use of stained glass in the church represents another departure from early Cistercian practice, which forbade it. There is, however, a reference to tradition in the use of floral themes inspired by the grisaille windows of the French monastery of Obazine, some of which have survived.

Color plays an important role in other areas of the monastery, thanks to the variety of bricks used in its construction. The basic type in the church, cloisters, sacristy, and scriptorium is a thin (about one and half inches) brick in a rather narrow range of beige tones. The library, chapter house, and refectory have thicker (about two and a quarter inches) rose-colored bricks with a greater variation in tones. The laybrothers' common room has thin, dark red bricks of somewhat irregular dimensions, with added texture supplied by deeply raked mortar beds.

Seen from outside, the church is reminiscent of another type of building found in medieval Cistercian architecture: the barn. One typical form was a large rectangular building with low side walls, covered by a high-pitched roof supported on the interior by a timber frame resting on two rows of posts. Window openings were originally small, and doorways were usually paired on opposite sides of the building to permit the entrance and exit of carts or animals along a single path.

The exterior of Spencer's nave presents a similar arrangement, with its pitched roof extending down to low side walls. Spencer's church recalls the barn at Great Coxwell in Britain, where there are two transepts on the long sides of the building marking entranceways into the barn itself. A view from the southwest side of the barn is strikingly similar to the view from the northwest of Spencer's church, even though the proportions of the two buildings differ greatly. Even the interior double-rowed support system of the roof is similar, although the materials used were different.

The two monks involved in the design of the Spencer buildings denied that there was a conscious, formal intention to imitate a Cistercian barn. Yet they were certainly aware of the building type and had seen illustrations of it. Inspiration came perhaps in an indirect way. Furthermore, in a building project based on limited funds, interior vaulting for the church must have seemed implausible, and the idea of a fairly simple roof with open timbering on the interior presented an attractive solution.

✐ The Aftermath of the Inauguration

With the community settling in at last to its new home, Dom Edmund decided to attend the General Chapter of 1953, even though he was at first hesitant to do so, perhaps due to his experience of illness in Europe the preceding year. He left for Paris on August 22, accompanied once again by Brother Blaise. Their exact itinerary is not known; they may have visited some monasteries. But when they arrived at Fatima in Portugal, Dom Edmund realized that he was heading for another attack of illness similar to the one he had suffered the last time, and he decided to head home immediately, arriving on August 30.[7] He was out of circulation for almost two months, part of the time spent at a small house not far from the abbey. He returned towards the end of October.[8]

The debilitating attacks that Dom Edmund suffered throughout his career as abbot of Spencer were an ongoing concern for the community, as well as for the General and the Father Immediate. In this case, subsequent tests showed that his present condition was under control, but they also revealed a more serious problem:

> However, the x-rays showed a pronounced hardening of the aorta, which can be considered incipient arterio-sclerosis. The Doctor insists that R[everend]F[ather] should not overtax himself when he feels fatigue coming on.[9]

✐ The Order Updates

The General Chapter of 1953 turned out to be among the most important for the Order in modern times. Inspired by the contemplative ideal that had slowly begun to re-emerge during the first half of the twentieth century, the chapter took matters in hand and addressed two crucial defects in the basic horarium found in the usages: the exaggerated amount of vocal prayer and the insufficiency of sleep available to the monks and nuns. Over the centuries, the amount of liturgical services demanded of monks had grown to such an extent that the delicate balance between liturgical services, *lectio divina*, and work had been upset. The ancient liturgical Offices of Vigils, Lauds, and Vespers were not only doubled by an additional devotional "Office of the Blessed Virgin," but on some days *tripled* by the further addition of an Office for the dead. These Offices were lined up one after the other, so that certain psalms were sung three successive times in the course of a single service.

Dom Gabriel drew up a proposal to reduce the number of these additional Offices and, before the chapter began, wrote to all the superiors of the Order to solicit their opinions. The results showed that the subject merited a place on the agenda of the 1953 chapter. After much discussion at the chapter itself, it was decided that the Office of the Dead would be recited only once a month, on a day specially set aside for this purpose. And four times a year this monthly commemoration was to take on a more solemn character.

The question of the Office of the Blessed Virgin was more delicate, given the importance of the Order's traditional devotion to Mary. As a first step, it was decided that during the coming year this devotional Office would not be celebrated on days when the main liturgical Office was in her honor.

Another liturgical decision involved the second Mass that the monks were currently obliged to attend on certain feast days. The chapter decided that this should, in effect, be reduced to the status of a private Mass offered after Vigils at the same time as the priest monks were celebrating their own "private" Masses. Attendance at this service by other monks was to be optional.

These changes and others that would be made at later chapters went far in alleviating the overloaded schedule that earlier generations had to follow. An extreme case was the timetable for weekdays throughout Lent, as presented in the usages of 1926, which in 1953 were still in force. In the following list of activities for each weekday, there is no break in time between the items shown unless otherwise indicated. The "brief intervals" are less than a half hour in length. (The Canonical Office referred to here is the traditional Office of the Church as opposed to the devotional Office of the Blessed Virgin.)

2:00 A.M.	rise; Vigils and Lauds of the Office of the Blessed Virgin	
2:30	"Mental Prayer" in common	
3:00	Vigils and Lauds of the Canonical Office	

2:00 A.M. rise; Vigils and Lauds of the Office of the Blessed Virgin
2:30 "Mental Prayer" in common
3:00 Vigils and Lauds of the Canonical Office
prayer of the "Angelus"
(on Fridays: the "discipline" in the dormitory cells)[10]
private Masses of priests, at which servers receive Holy Communion
brief interval

5:30 Prime of the Office of the Blessed Virgin
Prime of the Canonical Office
gathering in chapter house for a conference by the abbot
(on Fridays: a procession through the cloisters chanting seven penitential psalms)
bed making
"frustulum" consisting of coffee and a slice of dry bread as breakfast
brief interval

7:00 Tierce of Office of the Blessed Virgin
Tierce of the Canonical Office
Sext of the Office of the Blessed Virgin
Sext of the Canonical Office
brief interval

8:00 None of the Office of the Blessed Virgin
None of the Canonical Office
High Mass (at which only the celebrant receives Communion)
assigned work
10:30 end of work and change into house clothes
brief interval

11:00 *(about)* Vespers, examination of conscience on a particular point
12:00 dinner followed by an interval (about an hour and a half)
2:00 P.M. assigned work
4:00 end of work and change into house clothes
brief interval

4:30 "Lenten reading" (reading in common of a book distributed to each monk at the beginning of Lent)
5:15 "Mental Prayer" in common (in church)
5:30 Collation (light supper, more like a snack)
brief interval

6:10 public reading by a monk in the reading cloister or in the chapter room
Compline of the Canonical Office
Compline of Office of the Blessed Virgin
prayer of the "Angelus"
7:00 *(about)* retire

Thus the entire day consisted of an almost nonstop series of community activities carried out in the church, the cloisters, the chapter house, and the refectory. Indeed, in five cases the transfer from one place to another took the solemn form of a slow procession headed by the abbot with monks following according to their seniority—with their hoods up. Only on one occasion did the monk find himself with an hour and a half of continuous time at his disposal for either reading or private prayer.

One cannot help but notice that the midafternoon prayer of None and the evening Office of Vespers both take place in the morning. There is a reason for this apparent anomaly. St. Benedict in chapter 41 of the Rule prescribed that what was in his time the single meal of the Lenten day be put off until the evening. Not wanting to push matters quite that far, the authors of the timetable nonetheless respected the letter of the law and "got everything done" before the meal took place more or less at the usual time, around noon. Apart from revealing a bent toward legalistic thinking, this arrangement showed no concern for upsetting the important balance of the monastic day.

The traditional laybrothers' timetable was more reasonable since they did not participate in the activities of the choir, even though they too completed their own day Offices of Our Fathers and Hail Marys before lunch. Furthermore, since their vocation centered on their work—manual or otherwise—it was easier for them to achieve a healthier balance between activity and contemplation. More than one person attracted to the monastic life because of the time they assumed it provided for quiet prayer were surprised when they found what they were really getting in for. This was one of the reasons why, at certain periods, a significant number of candidates chose the laybrother vocation over that of the choir monks.

Granted, the case of Lenten weekdays—and Fridays in particular—represents an extreme. A normal day (apart from Sunday) included a "free hour" three times in the course of the day: at 6:45 in the morning and at 12:30 and 3:30 in the afternoon. Nonetheless, if special needs arose, these were the hours that suffered. The term "interval" employed in the usages to describe these moments of pause betrays a point of view about their relative importance: They were secondary to the various forms of pious activity and work specified in the timetable.

To further address these problems with the basic horarium, the General Chapter of 1953 also considered the question of the amount of sleep permitted to members of the community. Prior to this chapter, during the summer months one of the hours of sleep during the night was replaced by an obligatory siesta during the heat of the day after the noon meal. Apart from the complications this created for the work schedule, the siesta did not adequately make up for the lost nighttime sleep. The chapter decided that the monks would be assured of seven hours' sleep each night throughout the year, and that they would also have the option of a siesta. The nuns were given eight hours of sleep. On November 9 Rome approved these changes on an experimental basis until the General Chapter of 1955.[11]

The 1953 chapter also addressed the role of the laybrothers in the life of the community—especially its liturgical life. First, the rites of simple and solemn profession of laybrothers were brought into closer conformity with those of the choir monks. And the brothers would henceforth participate more fully in the installation of a new abbot. Finally, when assisting at High Mass they were now permitted to come to the choir of the monks (space permitting) and to sing certain of the Mass chants with the choir. The chapter also heard reports that a number of abbots had been fostering a program of translating portions of the Latin liturgical books and that efforts were being coordinated to produce a book with the Day Hours of the Cistercian Office for use by the brothers.[12] When the *Cistercian Day Hours* appeared (the English edition was published at Gethsemani in 1961) it was offered as an alternative to their traditional Office consisting of the recitation of specified numbers of the prayers "Our Father," "Hail Mary," and "Glory Be." This offered the brothers the option of praying together at least part of the Divine Office in the vernacular. More would come of this during the chapter of 1957, but we can see here the beginnings of a movement that would eventually lead to the unification of choir religious and laybrothers who so wished into one monastic body.

As for general life at the new abbey, things had finally returned to relative normality. During the months after the completion of the church there must have been something of a sense of repose after all the activity of construction, not unlike the feeling the monks had after Christmas 1950, when after months of preparation for the great move they finally found themselves in their new home. Cells still had to be installed in the dormitories, and suitable furnishings provided for the scriptorium and library, but most of this work was complete by the end of 1953.[13]

✏ Work on the Priests' Retreat House

During the festivities of August 15, guests entering the church for the first Mass must have been struck by the stark, ruin-like structure of the unfinished priests' retreat house. Peter Grace, who was among the notables present on this occasion, brought the matter up with Dom Edmund and gave his support to a new plan that was taking shape. Dom Edmund wrote to the General about it shortly after his return from Europe:

> Mr. Grace was thus in complete accord, as he stated to Brother Leo, Brother Blaise, and others, with all that had been accomplished—with the one exception of the Priests' Guest-House. He was frankly distressed by the fact that work had been suspended on that unit. He expressed his regret that at least the exterior walls and roof could not be completed and thus remove the eye-sore presented by the excavations and unfinished walls at the very entrance to the abbey.
>
> The request that I intended to place before Your Paternity at Cîteaux—a request that would have been supported by Brother Leo and Mr. Grace—was that we be permitted to erect the exterior walls and the roof of the Priests' Guest-House before winter sets in, and this at the estimated cost of about $25,000. As to the interior, we feel that we could gradually complete it with our own local talent, judging from our recent past performance. Mr. Grace was very much in favor of this modus operandi.[14]

He also stressed that the financial situation of the abbey had improved considerably thanks to a refinancing of its loans. Peter even promised to visit the General to discuss the issue. The General answered Dom Edmund's letter within the week, giving his approval for the plan.[15]

So, before the coldest weather arrived, Granger came back to complete the walls of the building, and the timber structure of the roof was put on. The brothers took over from here, under the direction of Brother Blaise and Brother Gerard, who now really came into his own as master builder. Through the winter they laid brick for the interior walls, worked on the wiring, and started installing the heating system.[16] Brother Gerard was genuinely able to congratulate them on the high quality of their work, but once he did have to point out to one of his over-fervent bricklayers that he had just walled up the entrance to two of the guest rooms.

The rest of the work proceeded sporadically, as funds became available. There seems, for instance, to have been a lengthy interruption during most of the summer of 1954.[17] Tiles were being laid on the roof by late fall of 1954. The whole thing was not finished until the following summer, and the new facility finally opened around the beginning of August 1955.[18]

By the fall of 1953 Wrentham was showing signs of growth and was considering making a first foundation of its own. Dom Vincent Daly of New Melleray had offered to sponsor a convent of Cistercian Nuns. However, upon consultation with Mother Angela, Dom Edmund decided that it was still too early for such a plan and reported as much to Dom Vincent in November.[19]

At Spencer itself Dom Ludovic Baron, O.S.B. of Kergonan Abbey in France, arrived for a visit of two and a half months, during which he gave lessons in Gregorian chant to the community. In his early days as a seminarian, Dom Louis de Gonzague had been a student of Dom Baron's and had recommended him to Dom Edmund during the 1953 visitation. During his stay at Spencer Dom Baron was treated to some stormy New England weather, when on November 6 a seasonal hurricane did severe damage to the roof of the church.

Early in 1954 a new project was in progress at Wrentham. Archbishop Cushing had offered to finance a new church for the abbey along with a fourth wing for the monastic quadrangle. By January the new building was already going up. After its completion, on November 23, 1954, the archbishop himself arrived for the blessing with a group of seminarians from St. John's in Brighton. When Mother Angela welcomed him before the ceremony, the archbishop informed her in vintage Cushing style: "The seminarians will do the singing. You can take a rest!"

Suzanne Nicolas, who had made the crucifixes for the private altars of Spencer's new church, was commissioned to make a set of Stations of the Cross in cast stone. These were set up in the east cloister in the summer of 1954.[20] And in 1955, after the completion of the priests' retreat house, the abbey acquired from her a series of ceramic figures of saints that were installed on the walls of the retreatants' rooms. Each room was then named after the saint whose likeness it housed.[21]

∽ THE FIRST VISITATION BY SPENCER'S NEW FATHER IMMEDIATE

The spring and summer of 1954 brought two last cases of tuberculosis. Two of the solemnly professed choir monks who were priests were hospitalized but were eventually cured.[22] On a more positive note, from

June 2 to 11 Spencer's new Father Immediate, Dom Emmanuel Coutant of Bellefontaine, made his first regular visitation of his new daughter-house. Elected abbot of Bellefontaine at the exceptionally young age of 27 after Dom Gabriel Sortais' own election as Abbot General, Dom Emmanuel was only thirty when he first visited Spencer.

Memories of the last official visitation by Dom Louis de Gonzague were still lingering in the minds of the monks. Dom Emmanuel made it a point to strike a cordial note and establish an atmosphere of mutual confidence. The visitation card was thus basically complimentary, underlining only two points that were common refrains in such documents throughout the Order at the time: silence and punctuality.

Even in his more confidential report to the Abbot General Dom Emmanuel's remarks were mostly positive. He expressed his amazement at how much had been accomplished since the transfer from Rhode Island, from the construction of the new monastery to the acquisition of a fine herd of cattle and the flourishing atelier of ecclesiastical vesture.

His assessment of Dom Edmund's character differs little from those of Dom Gabriel himself and Dom Louis de Gonzague:

> The Reverend Father is a very supernatural man and is as regular as possible given his concerns for the recent foundation as well as his poor health. Being very sensitive and having a nervous temperament, the Reverend Father sometimes makes rather hasty decisions and changes his officers too often. The community suffers somewhat from this state of affairs, as it does also from the Reverend Father's absence (albeit justified) from certain community exercises. However, the majority of the religious seem very attached to their Reverend Father and appreciate his fatherly and supernatural direction.[23]

Concerning the community, he remarked:

> [The supernatural level of the community] . . . could improve even more if a more serious intellectual formation were offered to the young students, and if the library were better supplied with studies on Sacred Scripture and spirituality. I have spoken to the Reverend Father concerning this.
>
> Yet at Spencer there is much enthusiasm and generosity in the service of God.

This observation turned out to be the most important one made during the visitation—it led to a resolution to improve the level of clerical studies. Though these had never been interrupted by the program of construction, now that this was tapering off, the general atmosphere of the house was more conducive to such pursuits. Before the beginning of the school year Dom Edmund obtained from the eastern province of the Dominican Order in the United States the services of Father J. B. Mulgrew, O. P., as professor of theology. He began classes in September. As a result of this not only did the general tone of theological training improve, but Father Mulgrew inaugurated as the matrix for the abbey's theological curriculum a textual study of St. Thomas Aquinas's *Summa Theologica* with an ongoing commentary that pro-

FIGURE 65. *Dom Emmanuel Coutant, abbot of Bellefontaine and Father Immediate of Spencer.*

vided appropriate updating where this was necessary.

✑ GROWING INTEREST IN INTELLECTUAL PURSUITS

Trappist tradition had from the beginning downplayed intellectual interests. After the reunion of the three Trappist Congregations in 1892, however, there was a slow change towards greater openness in this regard. During the first quarter of the twentieth century Dom Vital Lehodey of Bricquebec, Dom Chautard of Sept-Fons, and Dom Anselme Le Bail of Scourmont had stressed in their writings the primacy of contemplation in the life of the Order. Then, in 1933 the General Chapter decided to create a periodical dedicated to Cistercian studies, *Collectanea Ordinis Cisterciensium Reformatorum,* and Father Joseph Canivez began the monumental publication of the statutes of the General Chapters from the beginnings of the Order, its eighth and final volume appearing only in 1941. More important, after World War II translations of early Cistercian writers little known to most Cistercians began to appear. Eventually new studies on early monasticism prompted the translation of documents from an even wider range of monastic literature. Prominent also was a renewed interest in patristic writings. This new trend not only affected clerical studies in preparation for the priesthood but extended also into the area of basic monastic formation.

Little of this new ferment had filtered across the ocean to Our Lady of the Valley. Dom Edmund's own training at the Valley was not untypical of what was commonly offered in the American houses of the Order at that time. It stressed monastic values based mostly on the Gospels and the Rule of St. Benedict, supplemented by more recent works such as those of Dom Columba Marmion and others in the general field of spiritual theology that were popular among religious of all Orders in English-speaking countries. While the writings of St. Bernard were available, for instance, they were not widely read or promoted in the formation of young monks.

Now that some of his young religious were beginning to show an interest in the sort of monastic and patristic writings that were appearing both in and outside the Order, the abbot did not feel at ease with the situation, since he himself had not been formed in this mold and was unfamiliar with the new literature. On the other hand, even before the arrival of Father Mulgrew, a new figure who had been appointed to the faculty at the abbey had begun to exercise an influence on the young monks, Father Hugh McKiernan.

Father Hugh had entered the Valley on September 29, 1945, as a young religious of the Passionist Order, to which Dom Edmund himself had once belonged. He had been ordained to the priesthood only five months earlier, and after a novitiate at the Valley of only two years, he made his solemn profession on December 10, 1947, and soon became an important figure in the life of the community. The theological training he had received with the Passionists and his own intellectual bent made him a popular figure with some of Spencer's up-and-coming intellectuals. This, added to Hugh's personal appeal, must have posed something of a threat to Edmund in his role as superior, and helps in part to explain the friction that eventually developed between them.

Nonetheless, Edmund was dedicated to the training of priests, cost what it may. They would be much needed, both at Spencer and at a new foundation that was already on the horizon.

Chapter-Thirty

A New Foundation

A T SPENCER THE IDEA of another foundation had long been in the air. Berryville had only partially alleviated the problem caused by the incredible influx of vocations that had continued even during the hard months at the CCC camp, and in August 1951 the possibility of a foundation at Hidden Valley had been set aside in favor of an all-out effort to finish constructing the new monastery at Spencer. By the end of 1953, however, Spencer's main monastic buildings were complete, and it became possible to return to the project of a new foundation.

From December 19, 1953, to December 21, 1954, fourteen monks had been ordained to the priesthood—truly an *annus mirabilis* in the community's history. The choir vocations that had come to the Valley in the late 1940s were now reaching full maturity. Dom Edmund finally had at his disposal enough qualified persons to fill positions of leadership in a new foundation.

Dom Edmund had been in contact with Archbishop Vehr of Denver about a possible location south of Denver,[1] and in March 1954 he had returned once again to Colorado, this time with Fathers John, Paul, Xavier and James, to inspect several properties on the western slopes of the Great Divide. Though somewhat daunted by the amount of snow they encountered, they eventually found a property that seemed suitable, but as luck would have it, it had already been sold. Edmund also took opportunities during his 1954 visitations at Berryville and Guadalupe to continue the search even as far afield as the Southwest and Wyoming.[2]

By March 1955, however, the Stag's Leap property in California had once again become a viable option as the site of the proposed foundation. On March 21 Edmund wrote to Archbishop Mitty of San Francisco to outline the project:

> Stag's Leap Ranch is located in the Napa Valley about 9 miles NE of Napa; it is 3 miles from Yountville, 9 miles from St. Helena and 50 from San Fran[cisco]. There are about 539 acres of which 115 are vineyards. To ensure privacy it would be necessary to buy three adjoining properties, making in all a total of about 1000 acres. The buildings are adaptable to monastic requirements; within a few months the main house could be made into a temporary monastery for about 50 monks. . . . The bulk of the income would stem from the vineyards; the balance of the land could be made productive as a dairy or cattle-raising operation.[3]

Edmund was obviously eager. He had also contacted the Abbot General for permission to acquire Stag's Leap. But yet again there were frustrations. Within a month of first writing to Archbishop Mitty, Edmund had to report to him that negotiations on one of the parcels of land could not be finalized and that the project was in abeyance.[4]

There was good reason for Edmund to be anxious to get the matter settled. Dom James Fox also had his eye on a California property for a Gethsemani foundation, in the town of Vina. Dom Edmund contended that the properties were sufficiently far apart to ensure that there would be no competition for vocations, given the size of California's Catholic population. But Dom James strenuously objected to this point of view. The General had heard from both parties and felt that getting the two of them together—just as he had done over Spencer's paternity—would be the best way to resolve the issue. He wrote to Dom Edmund in August urging him to put off the question until the General Chapter in September.[5]

By August negotiations for Stag's Leap were under way once again, and Edmund returned with Fathers John, Paul, James, and Xavier to see once again the property that had so impressed him in the 1940s. And in September, with Dom Edmund at the General Chapter, Spencer's prior, Father Owen, sent Father Xavier McInerney and Father James Shine to discuss the foundation with Archbishop Mitty.[6]

✍ Wrentham's Irish Foundresses Return to Glencairn

Closer to home, there was sad news about the situation at Wrentham. The story is told by Sister Gertrude Kelly, Glencairn's archivist:

On 22nd May 1955, the Abbot General, Dom Gabriel Sortais, opened the Visitation in Glencairn. The Annals record his "deep fatherly concern for our best interests" and the response from the community of "the openhearted confidence due to a father." At the beginning of the Visitation the Prioress, M. Margaret, became ill and it was obvious that she would not be able to continue her duties for the immediate future. The Abbess, M. Gertrude, then 81, had been in very poor health for about a year prior to the Visitation. It was decided during the Visitation that, because of the work situation and the sickness in the house, the Irish Foundresses in Wrentham should be recalled. This decision was taken by the Abbot General, Dom Gabriel Sortais. It was probably Dom Gabriel too who said that a Superior and a Prioress were needed in Glencairn.

When Dom Edmund Futterer was informed that the Irish Foundresses were to return to Glencairn, he called them into the Secretary's room and told them the news. He said Glencairn needed an Abbess and a Prioress and he thought it unnecessary for all six Sisters to return; he thought that if two went back to fill these offices, it would be enough. He therefore contacted the Abbot General, requesting that four of the six remain in Wrentham. However the immediate reply was "Six Irish." The Sisters were told not to let anyone else know about this. The same secrecy applied in Glencairn where the community were not informed until the last moment about the return of the Irish Foundresses. Dom Celsus, evidently with the Council in Glencairn, agreed, before the departure from Wrentham, that M. Agnes Fahey would be Superior in Glencairn.[7]

There is a longstanding tradition that the plan to bring the Irish nuns back to Glencairn was instigated by Dom Celsus O'Connell, who was supposedly still smarting about the removal of Mother Bernard as abbess of Wrentham. But Sister Gertrude's account—and the absence of any contrary evidence—should put this hypothesis to rest. The decision to recall the nuns was made by Dom Gabriel himself.

On June 15, 1955, the nuns set out with Dom Edmund for Peter Grace's home on Long Island, where they spent the night. The next day they left by plane for London and arrived in Ireland on June 17 where they were met by Brother Lachteen of Mt. Melleray, who drove them to Glencairn.

✍ A New Industry

Over the preceding year Spencer's industries had been moving forward, and on June 2, 1955, a request was submitted to the definitory for permission to spend $10,000 to acquire equipment for a new venture. Back in the summer of 1954 the monastery's cook, Brother Berchmans Risi, had experimented making mint jelly with plants he had grown outside the kitchen. After a trial batch that turned out well, he made sixty more jars, which were put on sale at the porter's lodge. It was not long before visitors had emptied the shelves, and Brother Berchmans was soon trying his hand at other products, first a cranberry conserve made with fruit harvested from a bog near the Grange, then wine jelly from wine that had been donated by a Worcester restaurant.

The whole operation was soon transferred to more spacious quarters at the northern end of the shops building, but the equipment rounded up for the new installation was little better than domestic cooking materials. More professional facilities would be required if the new industry was to produce significant income for the abbey. Thus it was decided to put the operation on a more secure footing by mechanizing production, and for this purpose remodeling the space at the north end of the shops building, and expanding into an adjacent part of the same building. On June 21 the definitory granted permission for the loan that had been requested, and Trappist Preserves were on their way to fame.

Around the same time the abbey hired Ditzler Jones—known affectionately as "Ditz"—to work as a sales representative and extend the customer base. He began by soliciting accounts from various department stores throughout New England and eventually set up a network of brokers to sell the products of Trappist Preserves along the northeast corridor of the country.

By the beginning of August work on the new priests' retreat house had been completed, and the first guests were received almost immediately. The first sizable group included thirty-five prelates and priests who had recently attended a "Liturgical Week" in Worcester and became the monastery's guests from August 25 to August 28. The relatively small, eleven-room facility was destined to become Spencer's only guesthouse, when in 1965 the Allenacres guesthouse was closed due to decreasing personnel.

✍ The General Chapter Continues Its Reforms

The General Chapter of 1955, which met from September 12 to 16, completed the work begun at the chapter of 1953 to free the Divine Office from the accretions that had grown up over the centuries. After the earlier chapter, questionnaires had been sent around to the superiors of the Order to ascertain how far they thought the process of reform should go. The tenor of their responses would become evident in the voting that took place in the 1955 chapter.

There was, first of all, some fine-tuning of the decisions that had been made concerning the Office of the Dead.[8] And the second ("Matutinal") Mass, which the earlier chapter had reduced in status, would now take the form of a simple "private" Mass offered by one of the priests. The most important decision, however, was that the Office of the Blessed Virgin would be totally suppressed. Though there was discussion about the possible inclusion of a chant in honor of Mary during each of the Offices, this idea was rejected. Since these decisions touched upon points of the Order's Constitutions, permission was once again requested of the Holy See after the conclusion of the chapter.

Next the assembly took up the more general question of the daily timetable of the monks and nuns. The reduction of the time spent in vocal prayers had already made for a greater sense of balance in the monastic day. But the official daily timetable imposed on all the houses of the Order still divided the day into bits and pieces that were, practically speaking, unsuitable for anything like serious reading or private prayer.

Realizing that a substantive revision was impossible within the limits of the chapter's relatively brief duration, Dom Gabriel asked the assembly to express its opinion on a series of general principles that the definitory could use to draw up a new trial timetable. The main results of the deliberations may be summarized as follows:

1. The use of separate summer and winter timetables would be maintained.

2. The half hour devoted to "mental prayer" in community would take place between the Office of Vigils and that of Lauds. Contrary to the old stipulation that the monks must either kneel or stand during this period of prayer, they would henceforth be permitted to sit. It would even be acceptable to spend this prayer time in the cloister instead of in the church itself.

3. Breakfast would be before the Office of Prime.

4. The Office of Sext would always precede the noon meal, and that of None would precede the afternoon work period.

5. The noon meal would always be at 11:30 throughout the year.

6. In drawing up the new timetable, the term *lectio divina* was to be used in place of the expression "interval," which suggested that the moments left to oneself in between the many regular "exercises" of the day were little more than breathing spaces.[9]

Despite what seems today only a dreary list of regulatory points, these resolutions embodied a new spirit in the Order, which had at heart the restoration of personal prayer and reading as integral elements in the monastic day.

The chapter also took up an issue that had been recently discussed by the American superiors. Though the American monasteries—which were becoming larger and more numerous—were growing in importance within the Order, there was no American monk serving on the definitory. According to the Constitutions, the council did include an English-language definitor, but in practice this person had always been chosen from the English-speaking houses of Great Britain or Ireland. So it was decided that henceforth there would be two English-language definitors: one for Europe, and another for America. The man chosen by the chapter to fill this position was Father Augustine Moore of Conyers. As definitor, he would henceforth enjoy the title of "Dom."

Finally, the Abbot General convened a private meeting with Dom James, Dom Edmund, and a few other abbots to discuss the proposed California foundations. Dom James held fast to his position that the area in question was not large enough to supply vocations to two separate monasteries that would be only 110 miles apart. What was more, his plans were further along, so if it was to be one foundation or the other, the choice was clear. Dom Fox's point of view won the day. So Stag's Leap, like Hidden Valley in Virginia, became one of Spencer's fond memories, refreshed from time to time by a case of the area's fine wine sent by friends as a gift to the abbey at Christmastime.

✍ A New Location Proposed for the Foundation

Though Dom Edmund had to return to Spencer without the coveted permission, he was unwilling to give up the idea of another foundation, which he still considered to be of prime importance. He turned once again to Colorado.

At the suggestion of Don Joslyn, an agent in Denver whom Brother Leo had met during the first trip, Brother Leo returned to the Snowmass area to visit the LaMoy ranch, a property he had seen the preceding year under deep snows:

> We drove across the Rockies at Glenwood Springs where we spent the night in an old hotel and on the following morning drove up into the Snowmass basin where we'd been nearly 18 months before, when the snow was still so deep on the ground. This time we had a good look into the LaMoy ranch, with its own little basin up against the back hills of the property. There was the troublesome road we'd seen the previous year, but Don Joslyn pointed out that if we could purchase parts of two adjoining farms, our privacy would be complete, and we agreed with him.[10]

Leo phoned Dom Edmund and convinced him to come out to see the property and bring along the same monks that had accompanied him the previous year. They left by car on October 27 and upon seeing the property, all agreed that, if the additional parcels of land could be purchased, the LaMoy ranch would be the site of the new foundation.[11] Dom Edmund and his companions then returned to Spencer, leaving Brother Leo behind to negotiate the purchase. The monastery's old friend and benefactor Harry John had agreed to help make the purchase possible, and on November 14 Dom Edmund wrote to him to announce that they had settled on the Snowmass property and to thank him for his "magnanimous offer to finance the purchase of this extensive property, and this to the extent of approximately $200,000."[12] By the end of November all had been arranged, including the acquisition of the additional parcels of land.[13]

✑ Dom Emmanuel's Second Visitation

By this time the general plan agreed upon for the administration of the American monasteries called for a visitation every two years. Thus Spencer would have been due for a visit from the Father Immediate in the summer of 1956. However, Dom Emmanuel was scheduled to come to Canada in 1955 to assist at the blessing of the first abbot of the monastery of Prairies in Manitoba. To avoid two transatlantic journeys in a relatively short time, Dom Emmanuel decided that he would make his second visitation to Spencer after the blessing, even though it meant that this would overlap Spencer's yearly retreat. Accordingly, he was on hand at Prairies on November 13 for the blessing of Dom Fulgence Fortier, whom the community had elected as its first abbot. After this Dom Emmanuel went to Oka for their visitation, then finally headed to Spencer on November 24.

Spencer's visitation took place from November 26 to December 9. The official visitation card for the community touched on the same themes as in 1954, but certain new items appear in the report to the General:

> The Reverend Father is a very supernatural man, who always gives primacy to the spiritual with regard to his community. Of a delicate constitution, he does not always care for his health as he should. [In fact, Dom Emmanuel asked him to live in the infirmary for a few weeks after the visitation ended.] The majority of the religious have great love for their Reverend Father and are at ease in their relations with him. Several suffer from his great impressionability or are disturbed by the excessive importance that, in their opinion, his artistic temperament causes him to attribute to certain areas such as the chant or the carrying out of [liturgical] ceremonies. They also criticize him—with some justification—for making decisions too hastily or changing them too easily. Being very sensitive, the Reverend Father accepts contradiction only with difficulty. Nonetheless, the Reverend Father does much good and is very regular despite the multiple concerns he has with the government of a large community, the care of the sisters of Wrentham, the foundation of Berryville, and the project of a foundation in Colorado.[14]

He expresses satisfaction with the improved situation of studies in the monastery, thanks to the efforts of Father Mulgrew. He notes, however, a new problem that had begun to surface:

> But the great problem at the present time . . . is that of perseverance. For two or three years there have been departures of several young priests in solemn vows who enter the diocesan clergy or who are applying to other religious Orders (Benedictine or Carthusian). The Reverend Father believes that this stems from a lack of severity in the admission of candidates; others attribute it to insufficient formation due to the heavy work involved in the construction of the monastery, in which the young priests took part while novices or young professed—also the frequent changes of novice masters. The

Reverend Father hopes to remedy the situation by exercising greater severity than in the past with regards to the reception of the habit or to profession.

Notwithstanding these remarks, the monastery's statistics show that during the year 1955 there were no members of the community absent with a view to entering the Carthusians or the Benedictines. Furthermore, only two priests were absent for the purpose of seeking incardination in a diocese, and one of these was a senior monk who had entered at the Valley. Of course, the attractiveness of the Carthusian vocation, which offered greater solitude, was an ever-present factor in the life of Cistercian monasteries, and the abbot continued to receive requests from monks who wanted to try it out.

Dom Emmanuel's view of the community's "regularity" was positive:

I have the impression that this community is very regular; in particular the intervals are generally well respected. The laybrothers make an even better impression than the choir monks; [they are] regular, supernatural, obedient.

Dom Edmund took the opportunity during the visitation to go over the project of the new foundation with Dom Emmanuel, whose favorable opinion would be important in securing the permission of the General and the definitory. Surviving documents do not reveal just what Dom Emmanuel's reaction was, and as late as February 1956 he had still not communicated his impressions to the General, who was eagerly awaiting them.[15]

In any case, on the day after Christmas 1955 Dom Edmund himself wrote to the General to propose the matter of the foundation, offering him a detailed description of the site and assuring him that the project had received the warm enthusiasm of Archbishop Vehr of Denver:

The purchasing of the property has been financed by Mr. John with the help of Mr. Grace, with the result that the site comes to us as a gift. We plan to acquire title to the land towards the end of January, at which time it is proposed to send a small group of five or six brothers with one or two priests to manage the cattle already on the ranch.

Moreover, if Your Paternity approves of our plan, we would in the spring send out a group of our own experienced builders to begin work on the wing of a permanent monastery. The financial assistance on this phase of the foundation would in all probability derive from a benefactor in a nearby state, Mr. Dudley Dougherty.[16]

As things turned out, the hoped-for assistance from Mr. Dougherty was not immediately forthcoming, and the question of financing the building project remained a problem for Spencer.

Dom Gabriel wrote back on January 3, expressing his reservations about the project. While he sympathized with Edmund concerning the loss of his chance to make a foundation in California, he added:

> I must tell you in all truth that I have a sense of regret seeing you under-take this new foundation. Certainly I know that things are cramped at Spencer with a community that is too numerous, but still I wonder if it is really necessary to make another foundation in order to remedy the situation.
>
> Despite the number of religious whom you have sent to Berryville, I still have the impression that your monastery in Virginia has not yet been properly launched, and that it would have been advantageous for it to receive at least several of those that you have earmarked for positions of responsibility in the Colorado foundation. Perhaps you will say that you are able to provide for the one without neglecting the other. I do not know. I want simply to call your attention to the present state of Berryville and ask you not to forget your older daughter in favor of the youngest.
>
> Another point which makes me uneasy is the question of your finances. No doubt the situation is not growing worse, but neither is it improving. Also, I know that you can count on the support of bene-factors who are as generous as they are well-off, and whose good will towards you has recently once more been in evidence. Finally, you assure me that, thanks to another generous friend, Mr. Dudley Dougherty, you are able to consider without fear building the first wing of the future monastery.
>
> I do not intend to hinder you, or even to advise you against car-rying out these projects, but, here once again, I would like to ask you not to forget your own monastery and to avoid letting yourself become absorbed by the care that will be necessary for this founda-tion. Even though it should not further jeopardize the financial equi-librium of Spencer, since it is offered as a gift, I can't help thinking that the sums that your benefactors will dedicate to it could have served to free the motherhouse of its own debts, at least in great mea-sure. Thus it seems certain that your own house will have to wait even longer to be freed of debt. Do you not think that it would be impru-dent to postpone this indefinitely?
>
> I felt that in all loyalty I had to tell you my thoughts, dear Reverend Father. That having been said, I repeat that I am very happy to see you rewarded for your attitude at the last General Chapter.[17] And if you can set my mind at rest on the two points that I have just

mentioned, I would be altogether happy to see you give the United States still another monastery.[18]

Edmund responded on January 9, reminding the General that he had just sent seven men to Berryville, and that their presence had had the intended effect of improving the situation there. (In actual fact in the course of 1955 *nine* men had been sent there, including Father Edward McCorkell, who was one day to become its abbot.)

Regarding Spencer's finances:

> It might set your mind at ease to know that the legal set-up of the Harry John Trust is such that its funds cannot be given to Saint Joseph's Abbey. In the main, benefactions upon which we will count for Colorado would not be given to us for use at Spencer. The benefactors are interested in founding a new monastery; paying off the debt of an already existing monastery does not appeal to them, nor would it evoke any but scanty support. Local interest plays a large part in this; a monastery in the east would receive little help from benefactors who will outdo themselves in generosity in support of a house in the west.
>
> It is in view of this situation and your own fatherly advice that we have bent every effort to establish a jelly industry here at Spencer. . . . This venture is succeeding in a manner and to a degree beyond all our expectations. The following figures are pertinent and interesting. During the years 1953 and 1954 the net income from our industries alone (excluding alms and other sources) averaged $80,000; for the year 1955 it was $130,000. This represents an increase of 60%. . . . Add to these facts the bright picture of our debt reduction and things become yet more reassuring. During the coming year we expect to pay $80,000 on our debt, while all we are required to pay is $40,000, excluding interest. You can see that we have ample reason to say that our debt will be eliminated in a period of time considerably shorter than the twenty years originally envisaged.[19]

The General found himself in a delicate position. Spencer's own benefactor, Harry John, had been making sizable contributions to Dom Gabriel's program for improving conditions in the Order's Japanese convents. These contributions would now be coming to an end in the form of a final payment, and it was Dom Edmund who was negotiating the transaction with Harry. This fact would certainly give Dom Gabriel pause as he deliberated on the formal request for the Colorado foundation, which Dom Edmund finally sent to him on February 3.

In his letter Dom Edmund reported that he had laid the matter before Spencer's chapter and that of the thirty-five voters, twenty-eight were in favor and seven opposed. Edmund wrote to Dom Emmanuel on the same day, also informing him of the vote and again requesting that he tell the General his own point of view. Edmund insisted on the urgency of the matter:

> In a few days I will have to send five brothers with two priests to Colorado, for title will be passing very soon, and we will need those men there to care for about four hundred head of cattle on the property at present.[20]

But still from Dom Emmanuel there was nothing.

✐ EARLY DAYS AT SNOWMASS

While Dom Edmund's letters were on their way, two groups were sent out to Snowmass as planned, the first on February 6 and the next on February 13. The monks were already able to settle into the existing ranch house even though the deeds for LaMoy and the Gobbo property had not yet been transferred. As their numbers eventually increased, sleeping quarters were created in the old LaMoy house a half mile away. A note in the Spencer archives gives a list of the first two groups to go:

> Brothers Mark Kalin, Bernardine O'Shea, Gerard Bourke, and Timothy Boyle arrived Snowmass on February 9. These were followed by Father Leo Slatterie, Father Terence Kiernan and Brother Peter Larrowe who left on February 13. They had to maintain the 3100 acre ranch with 343 head of cattle.[21]

It is important to realize that the sending of monks and brothers to Snowmass at this time was not the beginning of the foundation as such—permission had not yet been obtained for this. Rather it was something of what today would be called a "pre-foundation," a group sent to the property to prepare the way. Father Leo Slatterie was named its superior, even though Edmund shied away from the use of this name since it might give the impression that the foundation had truly begun.

Around the middle of February the deeds for the LaMoy and Gobbo properties were in the hands of the monks. The Fiou property, which was still being negotiated, would not be finalized until May 15. In the meantime, Dom Gabriel had received Dom Edmund's formal request for the foundation but was still waiting for Dom Emmanuel's assessment of the proposal, which was required before the definitory could act.[22] Finally, on February 10, Dom Emmanuel sent Dom Edmund a copy of the letter of approval he had just sent to the General, and on March 6 the definitory granted the much-desired permission.[23]

Now that final approval had been given, Dom Edmund had to turn his attention to building a new monastery for the founders. He had decided that, as at Spencer, the best solution was to plan for a permanent monastery, even though at Snowmass this would consist of only part of a full monastic quadrangle. On April 12, 1956, he sent a new group of men out to Colorado: Father Daniel Demers and Brothers Arthur Beaudry, Basil Byrne, William James, Blaise Drayton, and Alan Hudon. Three of those present were brothers who had distinguished themselves in the building project at Spencer: Brother Blaise, who had been clerk of works and also responsible for so much of the design, and Brothers Gerard and Alan, both of whom had become highly competent in the actual building operation. Spencer's builders faced a new challenge—to build a monastery in a totally different landscape and under different climatic conditions.

As for the plans themselves, Harry Meacham, who had given such satisfaction at Spencer, had agreed toward the end of February to collaborate with Brother Blaise on the Snowmass project. He had started work but a severe illness hindered him from advancing as quickly as he had hoped.

Nonetheless, on April 12 Dom Edmund wrote to Dom Augustine Moore, the American definitor, to announce that the plans would soon be on their way to Rome for approval, along with a description of the layout of the new building. The east wing and the major part of the south wing of a permanent monastery would be constructed. These would contain the permanent sacristy, scriptorium, chapter, refectory, kitchen, offices and auditorium. The permanent dormitory of the choir monks would be on the second floor of the east wing. Until the construction of the church itself, the chapter house would serve as oratory and the scriptorium as chapter house. He further described how the construction was to be carried out:

> Almost all the work will be done by our own brothers, who have become, from their experience in the construction of Spencer, thoroughly competent in the various skills. We have our own carpenters, plumbers, electrical engineers, plasterers, roofers, and of course, masons.

The plans I am submitting are the work of Brother Blaise and Mr. Meacham, who did the drafting and engineering of the plans of Spencer. The purchase of materials and supervision of the actual construction work will be entrusted to Brother Blaise, who showed himself entirely capable while serving in this same capacity during the construction of Spencer.[24]

Only four days later and perhaps as a result of all the tensions of this new project, Edmund came down with a severe gallbladder attack, and on April 16 he underwent surgery for the removal of both gallbladder and appendix.

By early May the most important drawings of the Snowmass buildings were in the hands of the definitory. Even as he was recovering, Edmund pushed for a speedy approval since work on the foundations needed to begin as soon as possible. It was hoped that the roof could be in place by the end of Colorado's short summer, so that work could continue indoors throughout the winter.

On May 17 the General wrote briefly to express his approval of the plans and to congratulate Dom Edmund on his decision to construct buildings that would be part of the definitive monastery, instead of settling for temporary structures.[25]

Not long after his operation Dom Edmund somewhat imprudently set out by car on a cross-country trip with Father Anthony O'Toole. They arrived at Guadalupe in late May, and the regular visitation took place on May 27–30, with Father Anthony serving as secretary. They stopped in at Snowmass afterwards, but Dom Edmund experienced an adverse reaction to the high altitude, and they were forced to leave sooner than planned. On the way back they made a last stop at Berryville.[26]

On May 21, 1956, a new group left Spencer for Snowmass: Fathers Gregory Norman and Kevin Anderson, Fraters Bonaventure Steriti, Basil Pennington, Alexander Dietzler, Gabriel Bertoniere, and Alphonsus Chruma, and Brothers Paul (then known as Nivard) Forster, Eric Ryan, George Meisenzahl, Columban Hadfield, and Jude Stack. The five young choir monks stayed only for part of the summer and returned to Spencer on August 15 to resume their studies. In addition to two more priests, the new group included several laybrothers who had been important workers on construction at Spencer. Brother Paul, who had carried out the electrical installations, would do the same at Snowmass and would also be in charge of installing the plumbing, sewerage, and heating systems.

Work finally began on July 16. The nature of the land was such that a contractor had to be called in to drill a series of caissons on which the foundations would rest, but the foundations themselves were put in by the monks, who borrowed the necessary equipment from a contractor friend in Denver. On August 19 three more brothers left for Snowmass to lend further help: Brothers Edward McLean, Cyr St. Cyr, and Jerome Collins, who would serve as Brother Paul's assistant. By the time they arrived, the foundations were in place and the walls had begun to rise. Brother Jerome remembers, however, that when they were taken to see "the new building," there was little to show save for three or four courses of brickwork at one corner of the building.

The Order Updates

O N JULY 28, 1956, Dom Edmund made an important decision: He appointed Father Hugh McKiernan, Spencer's
popular professor, to replace Father John Holohan as superior at Berryville; Father John returned to Spencer to become its prior. In
a letter to Dom Emmanuel, Dom Edmund explained his reasoning:

> You will recall that I discussed the possibility of this change with you
> on the occasion of the last Visitation, and told you that I felt Father
> Hugh would be a likely choice if for any reason Father John did not
> continue in office. Things had improved greatly at Berryville, and
> Father John was doing consistently good work, despite the difficul-
> ties presented by a few older religious. It was certainly not with any
> view to correcting abuses at Berryville that I made the change, for
> there were no abuses; it was rather to complete the work already
> begun with the appointment of Father Edward and Father William
> as second and third Superiors, and to enter more fully into what I
> thought was the mind of our Most Reverend Abbot General and
> your own mind. Father John has accepted the change with disposi-
> tions 100% supernatural.[1]

Seeing that Father Hugh had had solid theological training and was
endowed with good judgment, Dom Edmund had over the years
appointed him to a number of important offices: subprior at the Valley,
superior of the monks that stayed at Portsmouth Priory immediately

after the fire, then at Spencer, master of the laybrothers and professor of philosophy. All of this experience made him a promising candidate for the office of superior at Berryville. Furthermore, his popularity and his capacity of inspiring confidence would be a winning quality in a superior. Edmund's willingness to make the sacrifice of giving Hugh to Berryville was a sign of his level of commitment to Berryville's future. But playing beneath the surface perhaps more tellingly, Father Hugh's intellectual approach to the monastic life was something of a threat to Dom Edmund. This parting of the ways might have been an attempt by Edmund to strengthen his own position while at the same time giving Hugh a freer hand to create a monastic community according to his own vision.

Beyond these matters, Dom Edmund also had his own health to think about, and by early fall, he was beginning to feel the effects of the lengthy automobile trip in May. His doctors advised him to take a month's rest outside the monastery. In early October, he reported to Dom Emmanuel:

> As for myself, I am happy to say that the rest which I have been taking has profited me considerably; my heart seems better especially. . . I am staying at a little cottage about an hour's drive from Spencer, and have returned for about a day each week for the purpose of attending to some of the more pressing problems. I hope to be back for good before long, fully recovered from the excessive fatigue which my trip to Oregon and Colorado (made too soon after my operation in the spring) caused me. I am grateful to you for your prayers, and grateful, too, for your kindness in presenting my request for a rest to the Reverendissime.[2]

ᨭ The General Chapter of 1956

During the General Chapter of 1956, from September 12–26, the Abbot General announced that the Holy See had finally responded to the requests that the General Chapter of 1955 had made concerning the reduction of vocal prayer in the Order. All of the requests were accepted—with certain provisos. Most importantly, a brief liturgical Office must substitute for the suppressed Office of the Blessed Virgin. The chapter decided that this would take the form of a simple antiphon in her honor sung before each of the main liturgical Hours each day. (A similar proposition had already surfaced at the 1955 chapter itself.)

Rome had, however, expressed concern that the lessening of the amount of liturgical prayer might be a sign of decline in fervor in the Order and urged that efforts be made to stress the twin commitment to poverty and separation from the world. Accordingly, Dom Gabriel devoted a conference to each of these topics at the chapter, and both were to be recurrent themes in the letters he addressed to the communities of the Order once a year.

As for the amount of sleep, Rome decided that the monks should have seven and a quarter hours each night throughout the year. The brief period of rest after the noonday meal would be available to all during the summer months as an option, but in the winter the superior's permission would be needed. Finally, to the request that the nuns be granted eight hours of sleep, the answer came back that they might have seven hours and three quarters!

∞ SNOWMASS

In November Brother Blaise was still trying to come to grips with Dom Gabriel's ideas on simplicity in monastic architecture. Responding to a letter from the General, he wrote:

> I must admit that I am somewhat at a loss as to the method of always carrying out your injunction *"mais seulement de créer un cadre co[n]venant à des personnes de condition très modeste"* ["but only to create a setting that is suitable for people of very modest circumstances"]. There is first and foremost the problem in my own mind of the "permanency" of the structure being built. It seems to me that by its very nature a monastery should be constructed for withstanding a long number of years. Literally for the Centuries. In America persons of very modest circumstances rarely seem to build for more than a generation or so. Then too the very demands created by a community of eighty or so monks inherently carry with them an aspect that makes the literal fulfillment of this injunction difficult. For example, the most simple room that will serve as a refectory, with no pretense whatsoever of studied architecture, carries in its very proportions, dictated by physical necessity, an element not found in a similar room, say, for a family of five or six of the working class.
>
> Likewise, the cloisters, which the rule would seem to call for, are a type of construction which of their very nature seems to call for a mode of execution which appears to be very difficult to being [sic] within the bounds of comparison to a like situation found in the menage of the family of the working people.

Please do not think that I am being argumentative in this series of reflections. It is only that I am trying to arrive at a modus agendi that will fit within your maxim and do find it difficult.[3]

With the new building project at Snowmass Dom Gabriel was apparently pressing his point.

By November 28, Dom Edmund could report to Dom Emmanuel: "The foundations of both the East and South wings are complete, and considerable work has been done on the walls. A winter in the mountains faces them, but they will have plenty of indoor work."[4] After the foundations were laid, the basement areas were closed over by constructing above them the floor of the next story up, thus enabling work at this lower level to continue with relative ease during the cold months. Some work even continued out of doors when the weather permitted.

While construction was going on, a group of brothers was assigned to work on the cattle ranch, which was being managed by Brother Timothy and Gordon Lamoy, the son of the former owner who had been hired to assist the monks in this work.

✒ SOUTH AMERICA, DID YOU SAY?

Even though the Snowmass buildings were still not complete, Dom Edmund was showing interest in the possibility of future foundations! In late December he wrote to Bishop Larrain of Talca in Chile:

> I was in Peru until a couple of days before Christmas. When I returned Brother Leo showed me your letter of December 8th for which I send you my thanks—it is very inspiring to read of your continued interest in having the Trappists in Chile—I well remember how kind you were to Brother Leo when he was in Chile a few years ago. . . .
>
> I expect to be in Peru in January but only for a few days and I am not certain as yet just when I will be getting back for a general trip through South America.[5]

Furthermore, the bishop's letter to Leo makes it clear that there was some definite hope for a foundation in Chile:

> I am intimately convinced that God does nothing in vain, and that your trip to South America, sooner or later, in the time of God, has to yield fruit.

According to your letter I give notice of the arrival of Mr. Peter Grace to Chile, with one of you at the beginning of the new year. I desire that the foundation be made in Chile. It doesn't matter whether it be in my Diocese or not, but in whatever place that it may be I am sure it will be a fount of blessings for this land.[6]

Edmund's trip in December and the one he would take in 1957 were only soundings, but by 1958 things would begin to take shape.

✐ THE LAYBROTHER QUESTIONNAIRE

In the spring of 1957 Dom Gabriel formally addressed the question of the status of the laybrothers in the Order, since he had been receiving letters from various monasteries on the subject.[7] Several houses had touched on the fact that the laybrothers had no right to cast a vote in official deliberations of the chapter or to be elected to an office in the community when such was the object of a vote. Furthermore, with the burgeoning liturgical movement in the church, the laybrothers in many houses were seeking fuller participation in their communities' liturgical life. On the other hand, many of the brothers—even those who were well educated—preferred the humble quality of the laybrother's life, which they looked upon as a vocation specifically different from that of the choir monk.

In order to get a better idea of where things stood, the General sent around a questionnaire and requested comments from the superiors of the Order. Dom Edmund sent his own report on May 22. Because of the importance of this theme in the Order's development during the 1960s, his comments are worth quoting extensively:

> With regard to the lay brothers, I must admit from the outset that here at Spencer we have not experienced the problems which may have been seen elsewhere, judging from the proposals that have been made. Our lay brothers are markedly content in their status, and envious glances are perhaps more frequently cast in the direction of their ranks than the contrary. Class separation, as you mentioned in one of your letters to me, means little to Americans, and this may be a strong factor. . . .[8]

Taking up specific points on the questionnaire, Dom Edmund continued:

> On the question of the new Office for the lay brothers, again, we think that for every brother who would be happy with the change and would profit by it spiritually, there would be any number who would not be happy and would look back to the good old days. . . . It has been our experience that the lay brothers like their simple and hidden life and prefer to remain in it. An Office such as that proposed, even though in English, would be an unnecessary complication of their life which would neither please them nor profit them spiritually; such, at least, is our opinion. It is based on our brothers here at Spencer and our experience with them.

The proposed "new Office" was a translation of the day hours of the Cistercian breviary that had been discussed at the General Chapter of 1953. The eventual popularity of this new Office with many of Spencer's brothers would show that Dom Edmund's view of the matter was over-simplified. He also appears to take a position of caution on the question of the brothers participating in the Divine Office of the monks in Latin:

> It is our strong opinion that participation in choir by lay brothers should be allowed only in cases where the brothers in question can add something to the choir. To allow them to participate at will would be destructive of all efforts to improve the chant and the execution of the Divine Office. We think that it should be left to the judgment of the Abbot alone whether a picked group of lay brothers can be asked to help with the choir work. As a matter of fact, here at Spencer we have done just that, to the satisfaction of all concerned.
>
> We think that this group of picked brothers should be allowed to sing the entire Mass (i.e. whenever the lay brothers as a group are assisting at the Mass) and should remain in the choir of the religious for Tierce and Sext whenever they are there for Mass.

Another comment by Dom Edmund shows how thoroughgoing some of the proposals being made in the Order at that time were:

> We see no reason for changing the habit of the lay brothers. We do not think that our brothers desire to be dressed like the choir religious or that they have ever resented the difference of habit. Further, if the cowl remains the distinctive habit of the choir religious, the whole purpose of the change is defeated, for not even the external, superficial similarity has been attained.

The entire laybrother question remained a subject of debate until the General Chapter of 1965, when it was resolved in quite a radical way. Legislation was passed that unified the communities of the Order so that there would be only one category of monk, with each monk having voting rights and participating in the Liturgy of the Hours and the work of the monastery as determined in consultation with the abbot. Laybrothers already professed would have the option of remaining a laybrother but with full voting rights.[9] The new legislation was confirmed by the Holy See at the end of the year.

While many of the laybrothers went on to embrace the choir life, Dom Edmund's point of view concerning the charism of the laybrother vocation struck a chord with a considerable number of the other laybrothers. Indeed, we hear an echo of this in the voice of Thomas Merton, as he confided to his journal on February 4, 1964—less than a year before the changes were to take effect:

> In the first place many of the brothers themselves do not want it. And those who do have perhaps a strange reason for wanting it. I do not really know where the idea originated and the reasons for it have never clearly been given, except the cliché about "all one family" which is used to explain anything that does not have a more specific explanation of its own. I have no objection to the "one family" idea. On the contrary I think that in reality the white habit is going to defeat this purpose more than help it. It is simply resorting to blanket uniformity, a kind of totalizing, a reduction of differences, rather than an integration. In point of fact, I think the difference in habit, as the difference in schedule and manner of life between the two groups, had a profound importance for *unity*. Psychologically and spiritually the effect of "complementarity"—of two groups needing one another, completing one another by definite and useful functions, had and has a great deal of meaning both for brothers and choir. It made possible a sense of relationship, of mutual interdependence, which had great significance for unity. It produced an *organic* unity, living. It is being replaced by a juridical unity, a unity on paper. And it certainly seems that the whole thing will go further and that the two lives will be reduced to a uniform observance, with the brothers more and more involved in choir and withdrawn from work. This is what more of them, or more of the real brothers, actually want—quite the contrary. The impression I get is that the serious and very earnest desires of those who have genuine brothers' vocations are being ignored, and that a very beautiful way of life—a very monastic way, perhaps a more authentic monastic vocation than that of the "choir monk"—is being quietly done away with.[10]

✍ A Challenging Decree from Rome

On May 31, 1956, Pius XII issued the Apostolic Constitution *Sedes Sapientiae*, addressed to the various Orders in the Church concerning the priestly formation of their members. To implement this constitution on a practical level, the Vatican followed up with a series of General Statutes on July 7, which established guidelines for drawing up a plan of studies (*ratio studiorum*) specific to the character and needs of each Order. These individual plans would then be submitted to Rome for approval.

Since most of the Orders were organized according to provinces rather than individual religious houses, central novitiates and houses of clerical studies provided formation for all the houses of the Order throughout each province. This type of organization was more or less taken for granted in the "General Principles" of *Sedes Sapientiae* but was a source of concern for the Cistercian Order, where each monastery was a self-contained unit that provided within its own walls both formation for its novices and priestly training for its junior professed. Nor was this just a question of practical organization; each monastery had its own spirit, which was reflected in the training it offered its younger members. Would it now be necessary for them to establish "common" novitiates and houses for clerical study on a provincial basis?

Also challenging in the new decree was the insistence that professors in the major disciplines have graduate degrees in the subjects they taught. At the time the decree appeared, no one at Spencer was so qualified.

The General Chapter of 1956 did not have adequate time to prepare a response. But the definitory agreed to draw up a proposed *ratio* for the whole Order, and this would be sent to the monasteries before the chapter of 1957 to solicit reactions from local superiors. To prepare this document the definitory organized a December meeting at the Generalate to which various members of the Order competent in the matter were invited.

After this meeting the definitory pursued its work and eventually sent to the monasteries a summary of the remarks it had received, along with its own proposal for a study plan. When the chapter of 1957 met in September, a solid majority voted in favor of the following major points:

> 1. In keeping with the Order's tradition, both the novitiate and the training program for the monastic priests should remain in individual monasteries insofar as possible.

2. Training of future professors in the major disciplines should take place in Rome.

3. For this purpose a new Generalate and House of Studies was to be built in Rome to house the many students that were expected.[11]

After the chapter the definitory was to draw up a final version of the *ratio* to be submitted to Rome.

Even before the appearance of *Sedes Sapientiae* Spencer had become increasingly aware of the need to improve the priestly training offered in the monastery, as the remarks of Dom Emmanuel Coutant during his first visitation at Spencer in 1954 made clear. Father Mulgrew had been hired for just this purpose, and he had spent three fruitful years teaching the young monks at the abbey. His time of service came to an end after the spring semester of 1957, and he was replaced by a fellow Dominican, Father Dominic Hughes, who served as professor of theology until the summer of 1959. By that time the abbey's own professors had obtained their degrees and were able to take over.

Before the chapter of 1957 met, Dom Edmund had foreseen the need to provide training for his future professors and resolved to send Father Luke Anderson to Rome to obtain a doctorate in philosophy. As a place of study, the Angelicum University, a Dominican establishment, seemed a natural choice in light of the training the abbey's students had been receiving over the past years. It would remain the school of preference for those sent to Rome during the next years. Dom Edmund took Father Luke with him to the chapter, then sent him to spend some time at Bellefontaine until studies were scheduled to begin in Rome in mid-October. He was also accompanied by Brother Berchmans Risi, who was to serve at the Generalate for three years.

The chapter of 1957 also returned to the question of the laybrothers. The most important decision was the establishment of a format for the brothers' Office, which was to consist of a translation of the day hours of the monks' Office (with a shortened form of Lauds). Brothers could either continue to use their traditional Office or adopt the new one in its place. The English version of this would be prepared at Gethsemani and finally published in 1961.

When he got back from the chapter Dom Edmund decided to send Father Kevin Anderson to Rome as well. He joined Father Luke at Bellefontaine and they traveled together to Rome.

Shortly after the chapter, America lost one of its most beloved and venerable abbots, Dom Robert McGann of Conyers. (Spencer had been privileged to have a brief visit from him earlier in March.) He had been taken ill in Paris after the chapter and died on October 3. The American definitor, Dom Augustine Moore, himself a monk of Conyers, accompanied the body back to the monastery. The election for the new abbot took place on October 22, and Dom Augustine was chosen as the monastery's new spiritual father.

Since someone would have to replace Dom Augustine as American definitor in Rome, Dom Gabriel instructed the American superiors to discuss the matter among themselves when they met at Dom Augustine's blessing in December and to submit the names of three candidates. The matter was quickly settled, and on December 17 the definitory officially chose Spencer's subprior, Father John Holohan. John set off for a five-week tour of all the American houses in the middle of January. At Conyers he got some practical advice from his predecessor, Dom Augustine.

✑ SNOWMASS

The end of the year 1957 brought a temporary halt to the work at Snowmass: Mr. Dougherty had not come through with the necessary funds. Most of those working on the project returned to Spencer. Only four remained, among them Brothers Gerard and William. Fortunately the walls of the building had been largely completed, and the skeleton crew was able to erect most of the roof over the winter. With spring came welcome news: Harry John had provided a substantial gift that made it possible for full-scale construction to begin once again, and the monastic workers returned to Snowmass.[12]

Edmund made another important move in April. He sent Father Thomas Keating, Spencer's master of choir novices, to Colorado to replace Father Leo Slatterie. Later on he wrote to the new definitor, Dom John Holohan, describing where things stood at Snowmass towards the end of the same month:

> Father Thomas, as you know, is in charge of the group there now, and it is my intention to make him the First Superior when the community is finally organized there. Father Leo did excellent work in getting things started, but it had never been my intention to have him as Superior there. In a few days we will be sending out additional men to Snowmass – three theologians and two philosophers with a professor

(Father Hilarion). The latter will fly out, but all the students will drive out with Br. Blaise. This will bring the total residing at Snowmass to 25. The students will continue their studies there, and will be able to help considerably by working afternoons, probably on the ranch, thus freeing Brothers for construction.[13]

ༀ SPENCER IN 1958

At Spencer itself, the first significant event of the new year 1958 was the community retreat, which was held during the second week of February. Dom Eugene Boylan, a monk of Roscrea Abbey in Ireland, who was at the time superior ad nutum of Caldey, served as retreat master. He had visited Spencer in late January 1955 with Dom Camillus Claffey, the abbot of Roscrea, and his books had always been very popular in the community. The retreat was a great success.[14] On a more somber note, during the same month the epidemic of the "Asiatic flu" fell upon the community, and a large number of monks were confined to their beds for a considerable time. Fortunately no one died.

On February 28, 1958, Dom Edmund reported to the definitory that Brother Berchmans had written asking to return to Spencer from the Generalate because of depression and stomach trouble.[15] Dom Edmund sent Brother Gabriel Brochu in his place; he traveled to Rome with Father John Holohan, who was going to take up his new assignment as definitor.[16]

Spencer had not had a regular visitation since Dom Emmanuel's second in November 1955. Dom Gabriel was planning a trip to the United States early in 1958, so he decided to make the visitation himself.[17]

By the end of 1957 Spencer was in the somewhat unique position of being the motherhouse of two non-autonomous foundations that depended on it for financial assistance as well as for personnel: Berryville and Snowmass. Indeed, Snowmass had not even been officially founded. Concern for the financial situation of the motherhouse—still laboring under its own construction debt—was reason enough for Dom Gabriel to make the trip, but he also needed to consult with the surgeon who had operated on him at Ville St. Laurent near Oka in 1953. He set out for Montreal toward the end of November and was present for Dom Augustine's blessing as the new abbot of Conyers on December 12, but soon afterward he had to return to Canada for further surgery. His recuperation was slow, and finally he had no choice but to cancel his plans for the visits to Spencer and its foundations.[18]

Dom Emmanuel decided to delegate Spencer's visitation to Dom Augustine, perhaps at Dom Gabriel's suggestion. Augustine had worked closely with the General as definitor in Rome and was well versed with financial matters in an American context. As a matter of fact, he visited the General in Montreal before heading to Spencer.[19]

Dom Augustine's visitation took place from March 5 to 11, 1958, and was the first evaluation of Spencer by an American since Dom James' final visitation in 1951. The practice of having exclusively European visitors to American monasteries had been less than ideal, particularly during the 1950s when European awareness of the concrete realities of American culture was not yet common.

Dom Augustine's brief assessment of the community in his report to the General was positive:

> I was much edified. During the scrutinies a very supernatural spirit was in evidence. The abbot carries out his duties well and is truly more concerned with spiritual things more [sic] than natural ones.
>
> I found the community flourishing under the able direction of Dom Edmund Futterer. The superiors seem well chosen for their respective duties. However, I heartily approve of the proposed change of the Father Master of the choir novices, in order to appoint him superior of the new foundation in Colorado.[20]

It was traditional in the Order that, in choir, the monks stand in seniority according to the date of their entrance into the monastery. The visitor took exception to the fact that Spencer departed from this practice in order to place additional cantors in key positions. The visitation card for the community also stressed the time-honored themes of regularity and silence.

Most important of all, Dom Augustine was able to assure the General that Spencer's finances were in order, his major point being that the debt was gradually being paid off by income from the industries and by various pledges from benefactors. He projected that the debt would be fully paid in three years, a calculation that would prove incorrect.

He also expressed his satisfaction with the Spencer community in a letter he wrote to Dom Emmanuel during the visitation:

> You mentioned in your letter that you felt some pain at having to relinquish your visit to Spencer due to your fondness for the community here. Having now come to know them better myself, I can appre-

ciate your sentiments. There is a genuine family spirit here, which manifests itself in true supernatural joy and peace. My stay here at Spencer is proving to be a most enjoyable one.[21]

Dom Augustine went next to Wrentham to carry out the visitation there, by delegation of the Abbot General, and after a brief visit home to Conyers completed his round of visitations at Berryville.[22] While he was there, Dom Edmund was able to win his support for Berryville's autonomy, as Edmund noted in a later letter to Dom Gabriel:

> It is my understanding that you have already received "unofficial" word of our desire to petition the coming General Chapter for the autonomy of Berryville. Working in collaboration with Dom Augustine during the recent Visitation there [i.e. at Berryville] and taking into consideration all the factors involved, it seemed that the time for such a petition had come.[23]

After his return to Rome from Montreal in March, the General confessed to Dom Edmund that he had wanted to make the visitation to Spencer and the two non-autonomous foundations himself specifically to check on their financial situation, and when he couldn't, he had decided to consult Peter Grace, whom he had come to respect more and more. He went on to describe his satisfaction with Peter's response:

> He [Grace] took the opportunity to give me a detailed report on your financial situation and the help that he gave you. I am very happy to see that thanks to his generosity, by the end of 1960 you will have a perfectly balanced budget. As a matter of fact, I was worried about your debts, which I knew were considerable. I also knew that you could count on Mr. Grace, but nonetheless I wanted a clarification concerning your situation as soon as possible. The news that I received from your generous benefactor now gives me this assurance, and I must tell you that I am very satisfied.[24]

On the same day, Edmund himself was writing to the General, informing him that Dom Augustine had looked carefully at Spencer's finances and would be forwarding his observations to the General. He also offered further assurances:

> The industries last year gave us a cash surplus after operating expenses and mortgage payments of over $75,000. (This figure includes returns from our guesthouses, but is exclusive of all benefactions. . . .) Hence I believe that we would be in a position to meet our debt even inde-

pendently of Mr. Grace's help, although his generosity and charity are making it possible for us to meet it much more quickly.[25]

✐ GROWTH OF SPENCER'S INDUSTRIES

The success of Spencer's industries was showing that more and more they were the future hope for the community's financial health. The income from the farm and dairy operations was proving increasingly undependable and even illusory despite the presence of the splendid herd of Holsteins conscientiously managed by Bert Henman with the assistance of the brothers working in the dairy. Large commercial dairies were presenting a greater challenge to the ability of smaller producers to make a livelihood.

Beyond this, serious difficulties had always faced New England farmers. They had to deal with rocky soils and short growing seasons, and the inconstant weather made it next to impossible to count on sufficient drying time for newly cut hay before baling.

Dom Edmund realized something had to be done, and so he made an important decision: The famous Broad Rock herd would be sold. In a last attempt to make something of the farm, the raising of pigs would be introduced.[26] Dom Edmund summed up his vision on moving forward with the farm in a letter to the new American definitor, Dom John Holohan:

> We think that by the sale of the hay from the farm, we can actually realize almost as much as has been realized from the barn in the past. We plan to obtain a sufficient number of grade cows to care for our own domestic needs. The work heretofore put into the barn can be diverted to the garden, which should be built up, and other agricultural pursuits—the hogs, some chickens, and perhaps even a few sheep. Hence we will actually be going even further "back to the soil" by the sale of the herd, and the move in no way represents a withdrawing from agriculture. But we know that it will remain true that we will get the bulk of our income from our industries—Trappist Preserves, the Holy Rood Guild, etc.[27]

Edmund's attempt to convince the community of the feasibility of increasing hay production called forth some secret laughs from those who knew better. Father Richard Gans, who had played an important role on the farm, narrates:

I remember the Cody brothers laughing one day as we came out of a chapter meeting during which Dom Edmund announced to the community that we had fine, top-class hay in our barns. Those of us who worked on the farm knew that it was all moldy! Such was our "High Class Cattle Hay." We simply had great difficulty baling hay. New England weather didn't favor it.[28]

In any case, the sale of the herd would go through. On the same day that Edmund wrote to the definitory the Spencer chapter approved the move, but selling off such a considerable asset as the herd would require the consent of the Holy See as well as of the definitory. Official application was made to the definitory, which gave its consent and then forwarded the request to the Vatican. On June 16 Rome gave its approval, and the auction took place on July 12. The immediate monetary results were disappointing: The sale brought in much less than Edmund had been led to expect.

For all the promise of the industries, the fact of the matter was that their contribution to the abbey's support was slow in coming. The income most responsible for the support of the house still came from Mass stipends, benefactions, and receipts from the guesthouse and the small store in the porter's lodge. Trappist Preserves required a considerable outlay over a long period of time to improve production. The Holy Rood Guild, however, was able to help defray the running expenses of the house, albeit in a modest way. Indeed, by 1962 the Holy Rood Guild was providing 23 percent of the total income, while Trappist Preserves was still unable to contribute anything at all.

South America Looms

OM edmund's interest in South America dated back to 1948, when he had received an invitation from the bishop of Tingo Maria in Chile to make a foundation in this recently created diocese. He sent Brother Leo to make an exploratory trip with Peter Grace, who was going there on business. On his own, Leo crossed over into Argentina in early 1949. Although he made some interesting contacts, he realized there was no realistic hope of a foundation in either of these countries at the time.

In 1952, Dom Gabriel himself had shown interest in the possibility of a foundation in South America and had even agreed to go there with Peter Grace, but illness prevented him.

In December 1956 Edmund had visited Peru and the following year Brother Leo convinced him to join him for a longer exploratory trip. They left New York on March 4 and over the course of the next four weeks visited Venezuela, Brazil, Uruguay, Argentina, and Chile.[1] Nothing specific resulted from this trip. But in 1958 through Ricardo O'Farrell, a Jesuit scholastic in Argentina, Leo had come to know of Don Pablo Acosta, whose estancia "Los Angeles" was located between the towns of Azul and Tandil. Earlier on, Don Pablo had offered land to the Salesians for a school, but they had declined the invitation. Having heard of this, Brother Leo sought permission to go back to Argentina and investigate.

He arrived in Buenos Aires on March 15, 1958, and the next day he and Brother Ricardo were driven out to the estancia by the O'Grady brothers from Iowa, one of whom, Francis, was living in Argentina. Brother Leo continues the story:

> Since the Acostas had no phone, they were unaware of our coming until the four of us knocked at their front door. It was promptly opened by a dignified porter in white jacket wearing gloves to match, and we were escorted into the parlor. Soon Don Pablo presented himself, accompanied by Doña Carmen, and we were cordially welcomed by our somewhat surprised hosts. Frater Richard and I were dressed in black suits with clerical collars and so they must have sensed our visit wasn't a social one. We were taken into their living room and asked to sit down. When we explained our reason for coming, Don Pablo was obviously taken aback since his offer to the Salesians had been made long ago and forgotten. He asked if we Trappists wanted to organize a boy's school, and we explained that our work was different, briefly outlining the nature and goals of a contemplative community. I wasn't too successful, but when I said we were also farmers and raised cattle, this was more to his understanding. Doña Carmen however, grasped clearly what I was trying to say and was obviously sympathetic in her discreet way that would leave the decision to her husband. He stood up and suggested we drive down to Pablo Acosta where he would show us the plot of land, less than half an hectare, he had offered to the Salesians, and we set off in two cars. We soon reached the railroad that forms a boundary line between "Los Angeles" and the adjoining estancia and here we came to a small group of humble dwellings that constituted Pablo Acosta with its miniscule population. It was here, he told us, he wanted a school built, pointing out the bare plot of land he had earmarked for this purpose. But of course this wasn't what we were looking for. However it was a seed that might grow and become something bigger.
>
> As we drove back to the estancia-house, this time we accompanied Don Pablo and Doña Carmen and tried to better explain all that was needed for a Trappist foundation in the way of privacy and productivity. To become self-supporting we would require at least 600 hectares of land and instead of being on the railroad track, this land should be situated back in the hills with a view comparable to what Don Pablo's own home enjoyed. His reaction was grim silence, and Doña Carmen who sat beside him, was also quiet. She well knew her husband's character, and held her peace, although I'm sure inwardly she was delighted at the possibility of having a monastery nearby. Had we asked for Don Pablo's right arm, he might not have been more sur-

prised. His land meant a great deal to him; it was as it were a part of himself, and he didn't intend to part with a sizeable piece of it without first being convinced he should do so.[2]

The monks were then invited for tea at the Acosta home, during which the conversation turned once again to the subject of the contemplative nature of the proposed monastery. Towards the end of the tea Don Pablo announced that he would consider the request and let them know. Brother Leo then asked if Dom Edmund himself might come to meet them, which was considered a good idea all around. Back in Buenos Aires Leo phoned Dom Edmund, and he agreed to come, along with Fathers John, Paul and Xavier. Peter Grace kindly offered to provide funds for the trip. Just a couple of days later, on the morning of March 19, they arrived in Rio de Janeiro, where Leo met them. After a brief stay in Brazil, they headed for Argentina on March 21. Leo's account continues:

On the following day we drove down to "Los Angeles" where the Abbot and his companions were introduced to Don Pablo and Doña Carmen. They were happy to see us, and by this time Don Pablo had decided to try to work along with us in our desire to establish ourselves in Argentina. He told us he had picked out a 640 hectare section of land that he would give us as a gift, but it was located immediately to the south of his home, and studded with outcroppings of limestone. We were very disappointed when we saw it, but we concealed our feelings as best we could. Between this land and Pablo's home was his densely planted park of trees and the thought came to us that he had chosen this site so that no matter what we might build on it in the future, would be discreetly out of sight. After a moment's reflection, Dom Edmund asked him if we could look around on our own, and then come back and discuss the matter with him. Pablo willingly agreed, and off we went. With the instinct of a homing pigeon the Abbot led us directly to the top of the hill that lay directly across the road from Pablo's home; this was where the monastery would be if it were to become an Argentine reality. There were two piles of stone overgrown with brush, and in the southern pile Dom Edmund planted a medal of St. Benedict and then we all said a little prayer to Our Lady and Benedict that if it were God's will, a monastery might one day be built between those two piles of stones, and 12 months later that is what began to happen.

We returned to the home of the Acostas, and Dom Edmund with much meekness and strength told Dom Pablo that the other 640 hectares would not do, but that if we could have the same amount of land directly across the road from his house, then we would gladly come. It would be necessary to know Don Pablo better than any of us did to appreciate what impact these words had upon him, but one thing that I'm sure of is that the silent prayers of Doña Carmen helped him not to explode. He listened quietly to all that Dom Edmund said to him and then after a pause told the Abbot he would consider the matter and let him know his decision. With this we said our good-byes to both of them. We knew very well that Doña Carmen was completely on our side, and this gave us hope. They were both most cordial in sending us off, saying they hoped to see us again soon. And so we parted. That night we stayed in Azul and early the next morning after Masses in the Cathedral with its encouraging statue of [St.] Bernard, we drove back to Buenos Aires. . . .[3]

Since the group had come so far, Leo decided it would be well to show Dom Edmund and his companions one more site of great potential for a South American foundation. And so on March 25 the party set out by plane for Santiago, Chile:

The following afternoon, an hour deliberately chosen by us, we arrived at Pepe's [Pepe Fuenzalida] home in La Dehesa, and were escorted out to his porch with its truly spectacular view of the bottom lands with the Andes in back. The setting sun has a way of making the Andes blush at this hour, and the effect was striking, with the alfalfa fields directly below us, and the mountains tinged a rose color rising tier upon tier behind, and finally the snow-capped higher peaks in the distant background. Dom Edmund took it all in, saying nothing, and then he turned to us and dryly remarked, "You've kept the best wine till the last!" No property he ever knew during those years of his foundations ever moved him more, except perhaps Stag's Leap.[4]

The group agreed that both Azul and La Dehesa would indeed be ideal locations for a monastic foundation, and, as things turned out, both were destined to receive a monastery. Thus in less than a week the sites of South America's first two Trappist monasteries had been found.

ᗱ Dealing With Higher Authorities

In April Don Pablo, who was still considering Dom Edmund's request for a choice piece of his land, expressed a desire to visit Spencer in order to see a contemplative monastery at first hand. This augured well for Spencer's project, and Dom Edmund felt that the time had come to inform the General of his plan, all the more so since he could now point to Spencer's greatly improved financial condition.

It would also be crucial for him to show the General that he was not neglecting his two other foundations, so on April 30 he wrote to Dom John Holohan announcing that he was planning to launch the Snowmass foundation in an official way, would appoint Father Thomas Aquinas Keating as its superior and bring the roster of monks up to twenty-five. And he would apply for Berryville's full autonomy.

Finally on May 24 Edmund composed a letter to the General himself about the Argentinian project, stressing that the land would be a gift and that the expenses of construction would be covered by benefactors.[5] He also noted that Don Pablo Acosta would be arriving at Spencer in a matter of days. (As it turned out, he didn't arrive until August.) As far as the other foundations were concerned, he expressed the hope that there would be forty monks at Snowmass by the end of the year and indicated his intention of proposing the autonomy of Berryville at the next General Chapter.[6]

Dom Edmund cleverly asked Peter Grace, who was going to Paris on business, to deliver the letter to the General by hand; he had mentioned in the letter that Peter would tell him more about the whole thing in person. When they met in Paris, Peter not only discussed the proposed foundation at Azul but also revealed Dom Edmund's interest in La Dehesa in Chile as a possible foundation in the future.

Apparently the strategy worked. Dom Gabriel wrote to Dom Edmund saying that he was in favor of the move and reminding him: "As you know, I have been wanting a foundation in South America for a long time now."[7]

Early in June Dom Edmund presented the Azul project to Spencer's chapter, announcing that, although Don Pablo's trip to Spencer would be delayed, he had received a telephone message from him announcing that he had definitively accepted the abbot's request for the specific land he wanted and would also give the monks the first option on his house, as well as on the land between it and the public road in front of it.[8]

At this point, notwithstanding his enthusiasm for the project, the General felt it was imperative for Dom Emmanuel to assess at first hand the twin projects of Berryville's autonomy and the foundation at Azul, and to verify the improved conditions at Snowmass. So Dom Edmund sent Dom Emmanuel an urgent request:

In the hope that you will be able to comply with our request that you come to Spencer sooner than you had planned, and against the possibility that you may need some document from us to present to the American authorities, I am hastening to send on to you the enclosed statements.[9] Each is identical to the other except for the salutation; you can use whichever one you prefer.

As I mentioned in my cable, the gentleman who owns the property in Argentina has made formal offer of it to us. Originally he had expected to visit us before the first of this month, but his plans changed, and he will not be arriving until June 20th. Since he is coming in the hope that matters can be finalized, I most sincerely hope that you will be able to come to Spencer within the week, so that some definite word can be given him. The property which he is offering us leaves nothing to be desired for a monastery of our Order. . . .

I shall be anxious to discuss with you not only the Argentine proposition, but also the important question of the autonomy of Berryville. I think that you will find the condition of the community there quite satisfactory.

Once again I express my own and the community's sincere hope that you will be able to make your visit prior to Mr. Acosta's visit in order that we may have some definite word to give to him. He is, as you will see, showing keen interest in the matter by making such a long journey by plane at his age (seventy-two).[10]

∞ Dom Emmanuel's Visit

Dom Emmanuel agreed to the proposal and arrived at Spencer in record time, on June 14, less than a week after Edmund sent his letter. The same afternoon both men left for Colorado.

The events of this whirlwind visit—which was not an official "visitation"—and Dom Emmanuel's own reactions to it have been chronicled in his lengthy correspondence with Dom Gabriel, which is preserved in the archives of the Generalate of the Order.[11]

His first letter was written on June 20:

My long silence must have surprised you. The fact of the matter is that since my arrival in America I have truly not been able to catch my breath. Dom Edmund and I have had to cover much territory in a short time. On Sunday afternoon [June 15] in company with Brother Leo we left for Colorado by plane, stopping down at Chicago and arriving in Denver that night. Early on Monday we left for Snowmass where we arrived around 11:00. During the afternoon we visited the property and the buildings that are going up, and I had the time to have two rather long conversations with the two superiors, Father Thomas Aquinas and Father Hilarion.

We left by car that evening and spent the night in a small motel two or three hours from Denver. Late the next morning we caught a plane at Denver for Washington, and we arrived at Berryville on Tuesday at ten in the evening. On Wednesday, I had the time to interview each of the religious and to have a rather long meeting with Dom Hugh. We left Berryville late in the morning yesterday (Tuesday) and flew to Boston, arriving here at Spencer last evening around ten.

You are no doubt wondering what the reason was for all this rush! The reason is that, for one thing, Dom Edmund wanted me to send you my report without delay so that, if need be, the definitory could give its opinion [on the matter] before most of the definitors leave Rome [for the summer]. In any case, we had to be back to Spencer for this morning (Friday) since Archbishop Cushing of Boston was coming to ordain four deacons and one priest.

Dom Edmund has been extremely kind and considerate towards me. When we began to discuss matters, [it became clear that while he was willing][12] to bring me to see Snowmass, he did not think a visit to Berryville was necessary, the question of the autonomy of this latter being altogether secondary in relation to that of the foundation in Argentina. I told him that as I saw it, it would be difficult to give a favorable opinion about a new foundation without taking stock of how things were going at Berryville after two and a half years. Besides, the erection of a house to the status of autonomous monastery requires a special visit in connection with it. The Reverend Father then willingly arranged things so that we could visit both houses before the twentieth. Despite the rapidity of these visits, I think that I can say that I am able to send you a report today touching both the question of the foundation in Argentina and the autonomy of Berryville.[13]

Dom Edmund's agreement to the Father Immediate's proposition was well advised, for, as a result of these admittedly hasty visits, Dom Emmanuel was won over to the idea of the Argentine project and told the General so. He saw that a new foundation was necessary because Spencer was indeed growing, and in three years there would be sufficient personnel to fill positions of responsibility at such a foundation. Furthermore, he felt Berryville was ready for autonomy and Snowmass was developing well.

He dwelt at some length on the question of Berryville:

For the past two years, Berryville has received little from Spencer. Two years ago, Dom Edmund made a great sacrifice in sending there three new superiors: a prior (Dom Hugh), a subprior (Father Edward) and a novice master (Father William). The three superiors are very supernatural and very united among themselves. Father Hugh, who is exceptionally gifted, is much esteemed and would, I believe, make an excellent abbot. I had an excellent impression of the community itself. Everyone is in favor of autonomy, save for one, Father Joseph, who thinks that this could wait. . . .

The financial situation is healthy. . . .

Dom Emmanuel later gives a glimpse of the difficult relations between Hugh and Edmund:

I would have liked to obtain certain benefits for Dom Hugh, both in terms of personnel as well as of finances. But here, once again, Dom Edmund was very reluctant. As I already pointed out to you in December 1955, Dom Hugh has a very strong personality, [and] Dom Edmund seemed to find it difficult when he [Hugh] was at Spencer. Relations have never been cordial between them. They needed a great spirit of faith in order to work together for the past two years, but the going was not easy. Furthermore, Berryville was never the beloved child of Dom Edmund in a way that Snowmass is at the present moment, for instance. The religious are well aware of this.[14]

Despite Edmund's reluctance to help Hugh with personnel and some financial support, Emmanuel felt that Berryville could make its own way:

Dom Hugh himself thinks that he will be able to manage by himself, and I agree with him. . . . Several religious mentioned how difficult mutual comprehension and collaboration are between the two superiors. One of these religious told me: "At least, instead of four or five 'regular visitations' each year, we will have only one, and there will be more peace for everyone in the house." Although I am aware of some exaggeration in this remark, I can't help thinking that there is some truth in it.[15]

In his remarks on Snowmass, after dwelling on the stunning beauty of the site and its solitude, he describes the situation of the community itself:

This house that was begun around two years ago is doing well. Two wings of the definitive monastery are already far advanced; it seems very likely that they will be completed by next Christmas; there will be ample space for 60 to 70 monks. The community is now composed of twenty-five religious; it is thought that by Christmas the buildings will be ready for occupancy, and at such time the number of monks will be brought up to forty.

The superior is Father Thomas Aquinas, former master of choir novices, who has been there [at Snowmass] for only two months, but seems altogether gifted. . . .

Father Thomas Aquinas assured me that in December after the arrival of the fifteen religious whom Dom Edmund promised to send, there will be a sufficient number of confessors (4 to 5) and of professors. Father Hilarion gives satisfaction as second superior and professor. Father Leo would return to Snowmass in December as master of novices, if the General Chapter permits the house to open a novitiate—which is certainly desirable.

From the point of view of finances, half of the debts contracted up until now have been paid. For the other half, several firm promises have been made by a dozen benefactors. And if one or other of these should fall through, Mr. Grace would step in; he has given assurance of this. The community could live on the income from the raising of beef cattle, which is already doing very well; it could also be supported by a small candy industry that will soon be set up. The land is very fertile and irrigation is easy; there should be ample revenue from this immense property: 3,000 acres of which 1,100 are cultivated.[16]

With Berryville and Snowmass as they were, he expressed his conviction that the foundation at Azul was indeed possible, provided the land be accepted with the understanding that a true foundation would take place only after three years. For the present a group of two or three priests and four or five brothers would be sent down to care for the property and to begin construction. Dom Emmanuel went further: He considered the project not only possible, but also worthy of recommendation. Among other things, the Holy Father had urged the North American Church to play a key role in the development of the Church in South America. Striking a more personal note:

[There is] . . . the favorable opinion of Brother Leo, whom you know well and who seems to me one of the best religious of Spencer—very supernatural, thoughtful, measured in his judgments. He judges this foundation to be possible and desirable.

The second of Dom Emmanuel's letters sent only three days later—one senses Dom Edmund's prodding—returns to the theme of the urgency of having a decision from the definitory. He concludes with the following observation: "Consider then what it would be best to do; you now have, I believe, the basic information, and you know dear Reverend Father [Edmund]. . . ."[17]

The very day after Emmanuel arrived at Spencer, Edmund wrote to the General making a formal petition to accept the land offered by Don Pablo, reiterating his desire to have things settled by the time the donor was due to arrive at Spencer, on June 20.[18] The letter reached Dom Gabriel while he was away from Rome, and he wrote back explaining that it was imperative that he himself be present at the definitory's deliberations on the matter, adding:

> You are aware how favorable I was to your project as soon as Mr. Grace spoke to me of it in Paris. . . . My enthusiasm has in no way diminished. Nonetheless, serious matters must be treated with all the attention they merit. Since with the help of my council I must assume the responsibility for authorizing this foundation, I would feel that I was unfaithful to the duties of my office if I did not wait to hear the opinion of the definitors.[19]

Dom Edmund had still some time to wait for a decision, which would be given only on July 15:

> Spencer is authorized to accept land in Argentina and to make preparations for a foundation that would be realized in three years.[20]

In any case, the delay in a decision had no negative consequences because of Don Pablo's own delayed arrival at Spencer. When he finally arrived in August, all the necessary approvals were in place.

As the summer of 1958 moved on, negotiations concerning the proposed autonomy of Berryville came more to the fore. In his letter announcing the approval of Azul, the General took the opportunity to return to the question of Berryville's standing debt, presumably hoping to profit from Edmund's undoubted contentment over the good news. Would it not be proper for Spencer to alleviate this debt before the granting of autonomy? Dom Edmund vigorously rejected this proposal, however, going so far as to affirm that he would cancel his request for the autonomy if this were to be an essential condition. But he did add:

Here at Spencer we have pledged ourselves to loan them the necessary money should they at one time or another find themselves unable to make the payments; but that is as far as I think we can go . . . .[21]

This seemed to appease the General, for the General Chapter of 1958 would not only grant autonomy to Berryville but also raise it to the status of abbey.

Having received the good news concerning Azul's approval, Dom Edmund was no doubt in proper spirits to welcome Don Pablo Acosta, who finally arrived in the United States on August 24. The first phase of his visit was a trip to Snowmass, accompanied by Brother Leo. They both then headed for Spencer, and as Brother Leo reports:

Dom Edmund himself met us [at the Boston airport] and drove us back to Spencer. Don Pablo passed several days with us, staying in the new bishop's suite of the Priests' guesthouse. It was obvious [that] he was surprised by all he saw, and impressed.[22]

Don Pablo was anxious to proceed with the donation and had been pressing the matter since June. He was concerned because some land near his own was being developed by the military.[23] Shortly after his visit, Spencer hosted a certain Mr. Massey, an Argentinian contractor who was being hired for the Azul project.[24] At this stage the plan was for a building "designed as a diminutive monastery for a group of ten Fathers and brothers" that would take eight months to build and cost $40,000; it would then one day become part of the final building. As at Spencer and Snowmass, Dom Edmund was determined to avoid erecting temporary buildings.[25]

Father Benedict Twaddell, who had been serving as Spencer's choir-master, was, according to Brother Leo, "given full authority to finance and build the monastery."[26] His exact role in the design process is not clear, but he did draw up a somewhat detailed proposal for a monastery to be built at Azul, which may have been the aforementioned "diminutive monastery."[27] In any event, the small monastery idea—or whatever other plans Father Benedict had created—was eventually discarded, no doubt because it was deemed impractical to spend $40,000 to house only ten monks in a structure that would take eight months to build.

∽ Berryville and Snowmass Advance to New Status

After the General Chapter of 1958's decision on Berryville, an indult was obtained from Rome, and on September 24 Dom Edmund officially declared Berryville an abbey. The abbatial election was held the very next day, and the community chose Dom Hugh McKiernan. His election was confirmed by Dom Gabriel on September 27, and his blessing and installation took place on November 18 at Saint James Church in Falls Church, Virginia, since there was not sufficient space to accommodate guests in the monastery's small chapel.

In the fall Snowmass also moved on to a new phase in its existence—but not without a preliminary setback. Late in the summer Dom Edmund called Father Thomas Keating back to Spencer and informed him that due to Spencer's commitments to the proposed foundation of Azul there were not sufficient funds to continue with the buildings at Snowmass. Thomas asked for a week's grace to see what funds he himself might be able to find. A generous gift of $20,000 from his father, along with additional funds of $4,000 from others, saved the day and the work was able to continue.[28]

On September 25 Rome gave permission for the opening of a novitiate at Snowmass, and in October Dom Edmund raised the monastery to the status of a true foundation with Dom Thomas Keating as its superior. All involved put in their best efforts, and by the middle of November the buildings were nearing completion. Hopes were high that the community might be able to enter the new monastery on the November 21 feast of the Presentation of Our Lady, but the great moment had to be deferred to the next day, November 22, the feast of St. Cecilia. The day after that, which was a Sunday, Dom Edmund celebrated the first Mass in the chapel. By that time, as Dom Edmund had promised the General, nearly forty monks were in residence.

With a South American foundation on the horizon and Snowmass still dependent on the motherhouse, Dom Edmund realized there was an urgent need to provide sufficient professors for all three communities, Spencer included, so he decided to send a large group of students to Rome for training over the course of the next year. For the 1958–1959 school year, Father Luke went back to Rome to finish his doctorate in philosophy and was joined by Fathers Joachim, Francis, and Basil, who along with Father Cyril of Berryville began studies for the licentiate in theology at the Angelicum. They returned with their degrees during the summer of 1959, ready to assume positions on the faculty at Spencer for the 1959–1960 school year. Fathers Basil and Joachim taught theology, while Father Luke taught philosophy. Father Joachim was also appointed Father Master of the laybrothers.

In late June 1958 Dom Edmund pursued his program of improvement of the abbey choir by sending the author and Father Placid McSweeney to the abbey of Solesmes for two months' study with its choir director, Dom Joseph Gajard, and its accompanist, Dom Jean Claire. This would be the beginning of a close contact between Spencer and Dom Gajard, who would come to Spencer for a chant session twice during the next years.

As for the new foundation in Azul, Dom Edmund, who had not attended the chapter, lost no time in getting the project fully under way. On September 15 Father Benedict Twaddell left for Argentina to take up residence and get things in readiness for the arrival of the first group of monks on October 28. Until accommodations could be arranged for them, they lived in the house of Don Pablo's major-domo.

According to Dom Edmund's overall plan for the construction, key monastic workmen who were just now completing the work on Snowmass's buildings would be sent to Azul. The crucial figure in this group, Brother Gerard Bourke, arrived on December 8 to serve as the director of building operations. His first task was to arrange for more adequate temporary quarters. What would eventually develop into a cluster of small buildings began with a modest, somewhat elongated structure that had been the home of the *puestero* and his family who had cared for this section of the Acosta estate. After some initial modifications the community was able to move in on December 14, and shortly afterwards work started on another building of similar size. Then another small wooden building was erected between these two larger ones. This first cluster of Azul's monastic buildings came to be known as the *casita*.

As 1958 drew to a close Dom Edmund could look back on the year as a crucial one in Spencer's history. *All* of Spencer's foundations were in place or in sight. Guadalupe and Berryville were both autonomous abbeys; Snowmass had been officially established. Azul already had its first contingent of monks, and its first buildings were rising. Chile was still a well-guarded secret, although Peter Grace had broached the subject with the General and Dom Edmund had again visited the site he had come to love.

By 1958 Spencer was firmly committed to the process of educating its future professors and without completely abandoning its agricultural interests had also committed itself to what would remain up to the present day its major sources of income: Trappist Preserves, the Holy Rood Guild, its gift shop and its guesthouse.

And beyond the relatively small world of Spencer and its foundations, 1958 was also destined to become a turning point in the history of the Universal Church. Pope John XXIII was elected on October 20, and less than three months later he announced plans to convoke an ecumenical council. Although the council would open only in 1962, the change in tone that his papacy initiated made the Vatican an increasingly different place, and the Cistercian students from the American monasteries studying in Rome would have ample opportunity to experience the changed atmosphere.

Retrospect

THE FOREGOING ACCOUNT of Spencer's first eight years—brimful as it is with activity on all sorts of fronts—might give a misleading impression. The fact of the matter is that all of this activity took place against the background of the day-to-day monastic life of the community, punctuated as it was by the daily celebration of the liturgy and the private prayer and spiritual reading of the monks. The secret of the dynamism that nourished this deeper level of life in the monastery during these years lay in the personality of its abbot, Dom Edmund Futterer.

From his first day at the Valley—January 10, 1927—Joseph Spensley Futterer had made an impact on the community. Father Malloy, who had entered fairly early in Edmund's monastic career, did not hesitate to use the word "saintly" to describe him. By the time of his ordination to the priesthood in 1934, he had long been admired as a man of contemplation who, whenever he could, retired to a favorite spot in the church's side aisle to devote himself to prayer. Early on, both Obrecht and Dunne had appreciated his qualities and eventually urged that he be given more responsibility, setting the stage for his gradual appointment to a series of increasingly important offices.

Father Laurence remembers the impression he had of Father Edmund when he himself entered the Valley in 1933:

I came into the community and I saw this professed who was next to the superior, tall, extremely silent and who never spoke, ate practically nothing. . . . He would rush from work, and within three minutes after coming into the house he would have changed . . . and was in church in the same place, in the side aisle hidden away without books or anything else, and oftentimes with the most beatific light on his face; something just shone out, a numinous presence surrounded him.[1]

That impression of austerity was tempered when after Father Edmund's ordination to the priesthood on September 22, 1934, he was made confessor to the novices. Father Laurence recalls his own first encounter with Edmund in confession while still a novice:

I went with fear and trembling to where he was, behind the High Altar, and I found a completely different man. Dom E had a tremendously loving heart. . . . [It was as confessor to the novices that] his real apostolate began, because in the confessional he was always spurring one on to greater things.[2]

This first priestly assignment brought out something new in Edmund, or at least revealed to those that approached him something that had been hidden: a capacity for welcoming and caring for others and a desire to help them move forward in their spiritual development. As time went on, the engaging quality of his personality became more and more apparent and even touched people who were not themselves particularly religious or even believers. Dom Augustine Roberts recalls the effect his mere presence had on many—diocesan priests on retreat at the abbey, young aspirants to the monastic life, healthcare personnel in hospitals—who observed him without even being able to converse with him. His dignified bearing, particularly evident when he celebrated pontifical ceremonies, only enhanced the effect.

After his appointment as superior in 1943, another quality emerged: his determination to follow through on projects he saw as important. Working hand in hand with this was his ability to ferret out and use the talents of those around him. Indeed, among his first moves as superior was placing just such men in key positions.

This sense of determination became even more apparent after his blessing as abbot, when he set himself to finding a solution to the problem of the inadequacy of the Valley's facilities. Yet what was demanded of Edmund after the acquisition of Spencer seemed to make his earlier efforts pale into insignificance: dealing with the fire and its aftermath, the CCC camp, the foundation of Berryville, the relocation at Spencer, and the construction of an entire monastery within a period of fifteen months.

The planning and construction of the new abbey at Spencer brought all his qualities into play in an extraordinary way. That he was able to accomplish all that he did was due, first of all, to his outstanding capacity for inspiring and fostering in his monks not only a deep spiritual life but also a sense of the profound importance of their new venture. Though many members of the community helped bring Spencer into being, the material realization of the project would rest largely on the shoulders of a small group of men. In the words of Alan Hudon, who as a laybrother worked on the construction and later held the important office of treasurer of the monastery:

I occasionally think over the battle days and the part that people like myself and Father James, Father Xavier, Father Paul, and Brother Nivard [Paul] played in this. And without trying to disparage their talents and virtue, we were all second-tier players, supernumeraries carrying spears. We could have been replaced by others very easily.

[There were] four people who could not have been replaced. If any one of them had been pulled out or dropped dead from a bolt of lightning, the whole structure would not be what it is today. And starting with the easiest one of the four people, this was Brother Gerard.

Brother Gerard's quite different from the other three because he never held an overt position of responsibility with his head above the horizon. He kept his head below the horizon all the time and focused on becoming and staying a master builder. He acquired skills, he acquired people management, he acquired everything he needed to do his job, spent whatever energy he had left, not getting engaged in politics, not getting engaged in financing. . . . The monastery would not exist without him.

Above him, still at the first rank there were three others. Brother Leo, Brother Blaise, and Dom Edmund. Brother Leo was a man of formidable talent. . . . He could do things I couldn't imagine others doing. But he was a very difficult personality. He had all the concomitant weaknesses that go with his strengths. He was impossible.

Sitting right beside him was Brother Blaise Drayton, a man of formidable talents and—impossible to deal with. Guess what? They didn't like each other. They couldn't get along. They were hardly ever in the same room. If they were, one of them was mad at the other. It took the genius of Dom Edmund to use both of these people to the

461

fullness of their abilities to accomplish what was accomplished. I can't think of any other monk I ever met who could have managed *one* of these guys by himself and get that person to accomplish what he accomplished by himself. But Dom Edmund managed it with both of them. Brother Gerard was not hard to manage; he just made a tremendous contribution. Dom Edmund managed this triumvirate with extraordinary skill and with a great deal of psychic energy that just bled him dry, and by the time he left office he didn't have much psychic energy left.[3]

For his part, Brother Leo speaks of an even more subtle quality of Dom Edmund's: his ability to *empower* his men to accomplish the challenging tasks for which each was ideally suited but which, left to his own powers, he could not achieve. Most of them were not fully aware at the time of how he was helping. But looking back at all that was accomplished, Leo realized that Dom Edmund was for each of them a channel of God's own empowerment, a man who, in the words of St. Benedict, "is believed to hold the place of Christ in the monastery."[4]

Edmund's determination to set things right also showed in his impatience with the all too real insanity of many of the usages inherited from—or at least inspired by—Lestrange. He took great liberties in tailoring them to the needs and capacities of the community. The heroic circumstances of the post-fire period at the CCC camp and the later all-out construction program at Spencer provided excellent justification for making such changes, which were, in any case, outrageously overdue—even under normal circumstances. Though Dom Gabriel Sortais himself was to set in motion a process of reform in these matters in 1953, he nonetheless looked askance at the liberties Edmund was taking on his own initiative.

The qualities that seemed to set Dom Edmund in a higher sphere were paradoxically linked to another feature of his personality that was masked by them, namely his timidity. Despite the great effectiveness of his preaching and his chapter conferences, he was plagued by a sense of inadequacy in these and in other areas. He rarely felt comfortable meeting new people without being accompanied by some trusted companion. This tended to draw him even nearer to those monks whom he admired and trusted.

Dom Edmund's spiritual gifts were grafted onto a vibrant human personality, one that was sensitive to beauty in music and the arts. His care to make of the abbey a place of beauty and to foster high standards in the liturgy and its music bear witness. But another aspect of this human reality was the fact that he was subject to strong emotions that caused him sometimes to react in a sudden and exaggerated way to a variety of situations. We catch something of this in the private visitation reports sent to the General during Edmund's first years at Spencer, which testify to a blend of high spiritual ideals and a capacity for inspiring love with a hypersensitivity that could alarm those around him:

> The impression now of their monastery is one of over-ornateness. This, together with the tremendous improvements in the farm, both in machinery and in buildings, gives an overall impression of wealth.
>
> I mentioned this to Brother Blaise. He told Dom Edmund and the latter was tremendously upset—so much so that his stomach reacted. He suffered pains so severe that he was forced to lie down. . . . He was unable to come to the chapter for the closing of the Visitation.
>
> Dom James Fox, 1951[5]

> His good will is evident. Yet, nervous, due in part to sickness and to his preoccupations; for this reason it is not good to go against his ideas; he is given to making sudden grimaces.
>
> Dom Louis de Gonzague Le Pennuen, 1953[6]

> The Reverend Father is a very supernatural man. . . . Being very sensitive and having a nervous temperament, the Reverend Father sometimes makes rather hasty decisions and changes his officers too often. The community suffers somewhat from this state of affairs. . . .
>
> Dom Emmanuel Coutant, 1954[7]

> The majority of the religious have great love for their Reverend Father and are at ease in their relations with him. Several suffer from his great impressionability or are disturbed by the excessive importance that, in their opinion, his artistic temperament causes him to attribute to certain areas such as the chant or the carrying out of [liturgical] ceremonies. They also criticize him—with some justification—for making decisions too hastily or of changing them too easily. Being very sensitive, the Reverend Father accepts contradiction only with difficulty. Nonetheless, the Reverend Father does much good and is very regular despite the multiple concerns he has with the government of a large community. . . .
>
> Dom Emmanuel Coutant, 1955[8]

Despite these drawbacks, Edmund used the gifts he had from God with one end in view: to be a father to his monks and to inspire self-confidence in them. He wanted to be a refuge for them in times of self-questioning and self-doubt and to help them along the path of their own personal vocation as monastic members of Christ's Mystical Body. In light of that, most of his monks were willing (within limits!) to put up with his sometimes idiosyncratic behavior.

Edmund was particularly well endowed with an ability to understand human weakness and self-searching. Alongside his timidity and the humble opinion he had of his own gifts, there was an acute awareness of a pattern of contradictions that seemed to run like a thread though his entire life. What was a deeply felt personal reality became a dynamic force that shaped his central teaching for his monks: Trust in the loving mercy of God. As Dom Augustine remarked in his homily at the memorial Mass celebrated shortly after Edmund's death: "[There was a] total confidence that God will bring good out of everything, or, as he would frequently say, that God would draw straight with crooked lines . . . ."[9] He found an excellent example of this in the life of Blessed Marie-Thérèse de Soubiran, foundress of the Sisters of Marie Auxiliatrice. Unjustly expelled from the Congregation she had founded, this nun spent the rest of her life in a convent of another Order.

Dom Edmund belonged to a last generation of charismatic abbots in whose hands extensive powers had been invested, powers that were strengthened by the reign of an almost total silence among the members of the community and by their complete allegiance to himself as representative of Christ. Under these conditions it was possible for a superior to accomplish many things—not always without danger to all involved. Edmund was not alone in this; Dom James Fox and Dom Gabriel Sortais represented and defended the same mentality. While, under these conditions, it was possible for a superior to accomplish many things, such power was not without danger both for the one who wielded it and for the ones he hoped to serve.

But the world—and the monastic world—was changing as the 1950s came to a close. A significant segment of the Spencer community, namely those who had entered during Edmund's first ten years as superior, were coming to full maturity and were beginning to look beyond Spencer's boundaries for further inspiration. Study under Father Mulgrew and Father Dominic Hughes had a role to play in grounding these monks in the principles of theology, on which, after all, religious life itself ultimately depended. Those who went to Rome for advanced study would be closely in touch with the new spirit that was stirring even during those early days of John XXIII. Living in the same house with monks from other monasteries, they would be able to learn what life was like under other monastic skies and to exchange ideas with these newly discovered brothers in Christ. All of this would help to open up new perspectives concerning the nature of leadership in the monastic life.

With his increasingly bad health Dom Edmund retired in the summer of 1961, but even after the pressures of office were relaxed, instead of improving he suffered a series of strokes that set him even further back. He might well have thought that the end was near, but he was destined to live twenty-three more years as a simple monk. After a long period of recuperation at Snowmass, in 1966 he chose to spend the rest of his days at Azul. Here he shared in the menial labors of monastic life, and was often seen seated atop the monastery's *tractorcito* mowing the lawn. Towards the very end of his life he expressed a strong and insistent desire to return to Spencer, but just as final arrangements were being made, he died on July 27, 1984, like some latter-day Moses on his own Nebo, contradicted for one last time, but now headed for better things altogether.

One of the greatest surviving testimonies to Dom Edmund's vision of monastic life and to the teaching he gave his community is a letter he wrote from Azul on September 9, 1978, to Father Owen Hoey on the occasion of Father Owen's Golden Jubilee of entrance into the Valley. These words show him as a pastoral master, his thoughts still focused on one of his sheep, yet at the same time a truly reflective man well aware of his own nature. Indeed, there are no better words than these to testify to Dom Edmund's own great soul:

> There are times when I still find myself reminiscing fondly and gratefully upon those earlier years at the Valley and even Chepatchet [the CCC camp] [when we] were thrown together in God's providence—yourself in a subordinate capacity as a rule, while all the time I could not fail to recognize the far superior gifts with which God had endowed you. For yours was the precious gift of a simple humble constant fidelity to the adorable Will of God—a singleness of purpose which never willfully deviated one way or the other, pursuing calmly yet determinedly the ideal for which you had come to the monastery. Indeed, my father, you taught me more by your selfless example than I have ever learned from mere books. Often I would fondly refer to you as "Old Faithful"—words which come straight from my heart.

While at Chepatchet I sent you to head our new foundation at Holy Cross in Virginia; and eventually I asked you to assume the responsibility of Los Angeles, our first South American foundation in Argentina. This necessitated learning Spanish which you mastered fairly well in a surprisingly short time. This foundation bristled with problems of all kinds, not the least being the difference between the Argentine and the North American culture; as well as the added difficulty of embarking upon a construction program in a milieu quite different from that of Spencer or Snowmass, with practically everything in the making. You went down, took over, gave of your very best and were deeply loved by the community. Well do I remember my last visit to you accompanied by our dear Bro. Simon [at Azul in July, 1961]. So far as I could see the situation was being handled quite well. Yet that was but a flying visit. I was recalled to Chile the following day and shortly after handed in my resignation. I suffered a bad stroke the same month.

I was greatly surprised to learn a short while after this, that you had been recalled to Spencer and appointed Prior under Dom Thomas. Like yourself I leave all this matter in God's hands "who knows always what He is about" as Newman reminds us. You probably failed to give satisfaction to some few at the time down here, but God availed Himself of this occasion to achieve within your soul something great and lasting which He had planned throughout eternity. What might have seemed to constitute your two greatest failures in life have been actually, I'm convinced, the two most sanctifying graces of your entire life.

Now that God has done a great work in you, my dear, He means to achieve a far greater work *through* you whether your remaining life be long or short. This is true of every monk who lives out day by day St. Benedict's ideal: "to prefer nothing to the love of Christ!" To many a superficial observer your life is very simple and very ordinary, yet in God's eyes it is something extremely precious, and whether you realize it or not your apostolate to souls for whom Christ died is far-reaching. After all, the true apostolate is not what one says or does but what one is. Or we might capture even better the basic thought of St. Benedict by saying that our monastic life is not "something to be lived, but Someone to be loved"—that "someone" being, of course, Christ Jesus.

Though I haven't seen you since the time Simon and I bade farewell to you down here, I know you have come far in a spiritual way, and if you could but see what our dear Lord sees as He casts a loving glance at your beautiful soul, consecrated completely to His love, your soul would doubtless be radiant with amazement and purest joy. That joy awaits you on this occasion of your Golden Jubilee of entrance upon the Cistercian way of life. I rejoice with your two sisters to whom I ask you to convey my love. I rejoice too with the brethren of Spencer and our nuns at Wrentham, as well as with all who have known and loved you! If I can't be with you in person I yet will offer Mass on that day, in thanksgiving for all that God's Spirit has done for you over the years, for all the good you have yourself accomplished in the spiritual world of souls, not by anything outstanding, spectacular or unusual, but simply by being a perfectly docile and faithful instrument of grace in the hands of our God.

Pray for me, dearest father. God bless you, and Ad Multos Annos!

Yours,
Father Edmund

Abbreviations

AAB	Archives of the Abbey of Bellefontaine
AABalt	Archives of the Archdiocese of Baltimore (now housed in the Associated Archives at St. Mary's Seminary and University, Baltimore, Maryland)
AABoston	Archives of the Archdiocese of Boston
AAG	Archives of the Abbey of Gethsemani
AAGuad	Archives of the Abbey of Guadalupe
AAH	Archives of the Archdiocese of Halifax
AAMM	Archives of the Abbey of Mount Melleray
AAM, *Registre*	Archives of the Abbey of Melleray: *Registre des Vêtures, Professions et sépultures à l'usage du Monastère de la Ste Trinité de Notre Dame de la Trappe au Comté de Dorset District de Bath en Angleterre 1810*
ADA	Archives of the Diocese of Antigonish
AAK	Archives of the Diocese of Kingston, Ontario
AAS	Archives of St. Joseph's Abbey, Spencer, Massachusetts (without further qualification indicates material not yet catalogued)
AAS AC	Dom Edmund Futterer Correspondence exclusive of correspondence with OCSO and OSB monasteries

AAS ACM	Abbatial Correspondence with OCSO monasteries
AAS ACG	Spencer: Abbot General Correspondence 1950 –
AAS CD1	Spencer: Definitory Correspondence 1891 – 1959
AAS CD2	Spencer: Definitory Correspondence 1960 -
AAS Chronicles	Petit Clairvaux, Valley, Spencer: Chronicles, Newsletters, Chapter announcements
AAS CFI	Spencer: Correspondence with Father Immediates 1950 – 1999
AASS	Archives of the Abbey of Sint Sixtus
ArchLyonDoc	Document from the Archdiocesan archives of Lyons concerning Father Vincent de Paul Merle, now in the archives of the Abbey of Timadeuc (no shelfmark)
AAO	Archives of the Abbey of N.-D. du Lac at Oka
AAQ	Archives of the Archdiocese of Quebec
AAT	Archives of the Abbey of la Trappe
AATim	Archives of the Abbey of Timadeuc
ADP	Archives of the Diocese of Providence, Rhode Island
AOCSO Spencer	Archives of the Generalate of the Order of Cistercians of the Strict Observance: Documents concerning Petit Clairvaux, Our Lady of the Valley, and Spencer. The correspondence pertaining to this period has been gathered into two boxes: Spencer Lettres 1869-1951 and Spencer Lettres 1951-1961. For the period 1951-1963 additional material is found is two boxes marked "Spencer: Lettres de Dom Gabriel Sortais." The material from 1869 to 1951 was classified, described, and numbered by Father Théophile Sharding of Orval. References to documents from this period are cited according to this numbering.
AOCSO Spencer 1	Spencer: Lettres (1869-1951) cited by Father Théophile's archive number
AOCSO Spencer 2	Spencer: Lettres (1951-1961)
AOCSO SS 1	Spencer: Lettres de Dom Gabriel Sortais (1950-1963)

AOCSO List of Indults	Indults demandés par N.-D. du Petit Clairvaux et la Vallée. Undated typewritten document covering the period October 30, 1891 – November 30, 1949
AOCSO Visitation Reports	Visitation reports of Our Lady of the Valley and of Spencer filed by year under the name "Spencer"
ASB	Archives of the United States Province of the Society of St. Sulpice (now housed at the Associated Archives at St. Mary's Seminary and University, Baltimore, Maryland)
ASFX	Archives of the University of St. Francis Xavier, Antigonish, Nova Scotia
APF SRC	Archives of the Sacred Congregation of Propaganda Fide: Scritti e Riferiti nei Congressi, in the section "America Settentrionale, Canada etc." [Documents and Reports of meetings for North America, Canada, etc.]
APF SRCG	Archives of the Sacred Congregation of Propaganda Fide: Scritture originali riferite nelle congregazioni generali, [Original documents reported in General Congregations] in the section "America Settentrionale, Canada, Nuova Bretagna, Labrador, Terra Nuova" [North America, Canada, New Britain, Labrador, Newfoundland]
NSARM	The Nova Scotia Archives & Records Management, formerly PANS (Public Archives of Nova Scotia), Halifax, Nova Scotia

Notes

Introduction

1. The description of the Order's history depends largely on the accounts of Lekai, *The Cistercians* and Bouton, *Histoire* as well as the more recent publication of the early texts of the Order in Waddell, *Narrative and Legislative Texts*.

2. Waddell, *Narrative and Legislative Texts*, p. 451.

3. Lekai, *The Cistercians*, p. 140.

4. The present outline is based largely on life in the monasteries as outlined in the Constitutions of 1925 and the Book of Customs of 1926. These were to remain in effect from that time until (and beyond) 1958 when the present book ends. Since many features described in these documents were based on older traditions, they also serve as an approximate guide to life in the monastery during earlier periods, particularly from the time of the creation of the independent Order of Cistercians of the Strict Observance in 1892.

5. *Rule of St. Benedict* 63:13 (*RB 1980*, pp. 278-79).

6. In order to distinguish between the two types of "prior," the expression *titular prior* was used to designate the first superior of a priory, while the term *claustral prior* was used in the case of a prior in a monastery that had an abbot.

7. The number of members of this council varied throughout history. In the 1925 Constitutions of the Order this was to be "composed of at least three Religious holding office." In our text we refer to this council as the private council or simply the abbot's council (*Constitutions OCSO 1925*, c. 51). The Constitutions currently in force (*Constitutions OCSO 1990*) use the expression, "abbot's council" (c. 38) or, occasionally, "private council" (c. 36:1). In current usage at Spencer it is referred to as the "monastic council."

8. According to current legislation the cowl is only given after final or solemn profession. (*OCSO Constitutions 1990*. Monks, c. 12). The monastic tonsure in the form of a crown is no longer used.

The habit of the laybrother novice was brown. Instead of the full cloak, he wore a shoulder-length cape. Upon simple profession he received a leather belt and a full-length brown cloak. This habit did not change at the time of solemn profession.

9. Such were the provisions of the Constitutions of 1925 (*Constitutions OCSO 1925*, c. 168). Current legislation dictates that in the case of simple as well as solemn profession the candidate is admitted to profession by the abbot "with the consent of the conventual chapter." The number of votes needed is not determined. *OCSO Constitutions 1990:* Monks, cc. 51 and 54. Current practice at Spencer calls for a two-thirds majority in both cases.

Chapter One: The World of Dom Augustin de Lestrange

1. Krailsheimer, *Armand-Jean de Rancé,* pp. 4-5.

2. Ibid., 8-10, 15-28.

3. Candidates for religious life are frequently referred to as "vocations."

4. Gaillardin, *Les Trappistes* 1:300-345. He reports that during the period 1714-1790 there were 300 new professions.

5. Laffay, *Dom Augustin*, p. 67.

6. After their departure Dom Gérard Boulanger, last superior of la Trappe, also led a group of monks to Switzerland, where he founded two small monasteries, whose observance was more tempered than that of Lestrange. He died in 1795, however, having turned the direction of both communities over to Lestrange. See Laffay, *Dom Augustin*, p. 186. It should be noted that, apart from the Revolutionary crisis, the community of la Trappe was divided concerning the ideas of Lestrange, many fearing that he would take over the leadership of the community. Ibid., 45.

7. See *Réglemens*.

8. AAT 1:3 cited in Laffay, *Dom Augustin*, p. 193.

9. See Laffay, *Dom Augustin*, p. 196.

10. Secondary sources describe Lestrange's relation with Nagot during his seminary days in various terms. Thus for example: "Nagot, while he was at St. Sulpice, Paris, had under his guidance Louis de Lestrange. . . ." (*Notes of Fr. Reilly*, p. 1); "The superior [Lestrange] . . . was a former penitent of Nagot. . . ." (Kauffman, *Tradition and Transformation*, p. 77). Lestrange's letters to Nagot

(ASB RG1 Box 8) offer some indication of a debt which he felt that he owed to the older man. Thus in his letter of May 6, 1806: "[J]'ai l'honneur d'être avec tout le respect et l'attachement d'un fils pour son père mille fois tout à vous en notre seigneur . . . "[I have the honor of being with all the respect and attachment of a son for his father, a thousand times all yours in Our Lord . . .] or more strikingly in an undated letter probably written in 1811 when Nagot was gravely ill: "Quel bonheur pour moi si j'eusse pu vous voir encore une fois, comme je me le proposois, et profiter des derniers conseils de celui qui a tant de fois soustenu ma jeunesse." [How happy I would be had I been able to see you once more, as I had hoped, and to profit from the last counsels of one who on so many occasions was a support in my youth.]

In 1768 Nagot had been appointed superior of "la petite communauté" of St. Sulpice, where he had himself done his studies as a young man. He continued in this position until in 1789 he was made superior of the "petit séminaire" (Bertrand, *Bibliothèque Sulpicienne* 2:38). According to Kauffman, *Tradition and Transformation*, pp. 27-28 this community of seminarians known as the "robertins" was taken over by the Sulpicians in addition to their "grand" and "petit" seminaries during the regime of Leschassier as Superior General. It "housed non-aristocratic students who qualified for scholarships." During Nagot's tenure as superior of this house Lestrange pursued studies at St. Sulpice from 1772 until 1778, after which he spent little over two years as part of the community of priests serving at St. Sulpice in Paris. Thus it is possible that Lestrange lived in this small community, and this would indeed explain the close contacts suggested by the aforementioned letters.

11. ASB Rg1 Box 8, Letter 1, Lestrange to Nagot, June 1, 1792.

12. In 1793 Lestrange had already sent a group of monks to make a foundation in Spain. Santa Susanna, a former monastery near Saragossa, was chosen as a site. The foundation was, however, eventually removed from his jursidiction.

13. On the figure of de la Marche, see Kerbiriou, *Jean-François de la Marche*.

14. By way of excuse for having failed to write to the bishop on that earlier occasion, Lestrange explained that his first move had been to contact Cardinal de Bernis and Cardinal Antonelli concerning the project in the hope that they would pass on the suggestion to Bishop Hubert himself. Cf. AAT 52:6, de Bernis to Lestrange, July 4, 1794. This response to Lestrange's request reports that Cardinal Antonelli had insisted on the need for having the permission of the British crown for such a venture but promised to present the matter to the bishop of Quebec at such time as this permission would be obtained.

15. AAQ E. I:1d, Lestrange to Hubert, March 24, 1795.

16. AAQ R.L. 2:206-207, Hubert to Lestrange, July 11, 1795.

17. The city is today in Belarus near its border with Russia, not far from the Russian city of Smolensk.

18. AAQ R.L. 3:115, Denaut to de Calonne, July 7, 1800.

19. AAQ N.E. V:3, de Calonne to Plessis, August 14, 1800.

20. A coadjutor bishop serves as assistant to a diocesan bishop and has the right of succession when the See becomes vacant.

21. AAQ R.L. 3:114-115, Plessis to de Calonne, October 4, 1800.

22. It is not inconceivable that Lestrange in his predicament after the Russian expedition had first contacted de Calonne either personally or through Bishop de la Marche.

23. AAQ R.L. 3:153-154, Plessis to de Calonne, June 24, 1801.

24. See Kerbiriou, *Jean-François de La Marche*, pp. 455-456. Apparently after the refusal of permission to go to Canada, the bishop tried to obtain permission for Ireland but was once again unsuccessful.

25. The first monks returned on March 5, 1802, but it was not until May 1803 that the main body of the community, eighty-seven strong, was able to join them. See Courtray, *Histoire de la Valsainte*, pp. 400-401.

26. See ASB RG1 Box 18, Livre de Compte. Under the accounts of the "Fr. Superior of the Trappists" we find a record of expenses and credits dating from September 26, 1803 through January 12, 1808.

27. AABalt 8B M5, Lestrange to Carroll, March 3, 1803.

28. Laffay, *Dom Augustin*, p. 275.

29. Diary of Father Jean Tessier, S.S. cited in *TRAPPISTS—Notes of Fr. Wendell S. Reilly, S.S.* in ASB RG1 Box 8: Father Reilly's Notes on Trappists.

30. Many of the letters of Father Urbain are reproduced in Lindsay, *Un précurseur*. The first letter included is that of July 26, 1806, and the last, March 14, 1812. Unfortunately none of Bishop Plessis's letters to Father Urbain have survived, although it is often possible from Dom Urbain's responses to learn something of what Plessis had written.

31. See *Anonymous Life*.

32. The date of his entry into the monastery has not been recorded. His early dedication to a life of piety is evidenced from the fact that he had received the tonsure in Lyons on December 20, 1788. Cf. AATim, Undated document from the Archdiocese of Lyons attesting to Jacques Merles's reception of the tonsure and ordinations to various Minor Orders.

33. The account in the biography notes that his return to France occurred shortly after the fall of Robespierre, who was executed on this date. The records of the Lyons Archdiocese testify that a certain Merle received Minor Orders

and was ordained subdeacon in May 1795. No first name is indicated, however, and while this might have been Vincent, it is also possible that this was his brother Nicholas, who was also a priest.

34. This prelate had been removed from his diocese in the course of the Revolution. At this time he was living in hiding in Lyons. Later on, after the Concordat, the Diocese of Vienne itself was suppressed, and d'Aviau was made bishop of Bordeaux.

35. AATim, Undated document from the Archdiocese of Lyons attesting to the reception of the tonsure and of various ordinations of Jacques Merle.

36. Undated note, which the Petit Séminaire of Meximieux sent to the Abbey of Timadeuc (no shelfmark). Some time after, on August 3, 1804, the Council of the Archdiocese of Lyons decided to lay claim to his services as professor for the seminary of Meximieux and wrote accordingly to Lestrange. Nothing came of this, however. (AATim, ArchLyonsDoc).

37. Laffay, *Dom Augustin*, pp. 311 ff.

38. Ibid., p. 360.

39. "The judicious magistrate thought that he saw in him a 'very important person and, if I am not mistaken, a high-ranking cleric.'" (Ibid., 361, note 2)

40. Merle, *Mémoire*, p. 6. As of June 13, the case of the passports for the group of nuns was still pending (Laffay, *Dom Augustin*, p. 363). It is not known how this one nun's departure was finally arranged.

41. AABalt 8B M6, Lestrange to Carroll, June 15, 1811.

42. ASB RG1 Box 8, Lestrange to Nagot. Though undated, this second letter was clearly written on the occasion of Father Vincent de Paul's voyage. It was possibly written at the same time as the letter to Carroll, namely on the very day that Vincent sailed, and it is possible that Vincent himself was the bearer of the letters.

Unlike his earlier letter of March 3, 1803, written to Carroll on the occasion of Father Urbain Guillet's departure for America (AABalt 8B M5, Lestrange to Carroll, March 3, 1803), this letter makes no mention of the "apostolate" of the education of children.

43. Merle, *Mémoire*, p. 5 incorrectly specifies the year as 1812. On March 28, 1811 Vincent had received authorization from the French government to travel to America. Cf. Laffay, *Dom Augustin*, p. 360.

There seems to be some discrepancy in the sources concerning the date of the departure for Baltimore. According to Merle, *Mémoire*, p. 6 this took place on the 15th of the month, while a letter cited by Laffay, *Dom Augustin*, p. 363, note 3 says that it took place on the 12th.

Ruskowski, *French Émigré Priests*, pp. 18-19 says that one of the monks waiting in Boston was a Father Eugene, although he gives no source for this information.

44. Hamon, *Life of the Cardinal de Cheverus*, p. 162. Though the monks are not identified by name, it seems likely, as the author of the *Anonymous Life* of Vincent suggests, that the reference is to Vincent and his party. This same story appeared in an article in the *Halifax Herald* of October 22, 1892 (from the *Boston Republic*, n.d.). The original article could well have been inspired by Hamon's book.

45. AABalt 2-0-5, Cheverus to Carroll, October 16, 1811. It is clear from this letter that the sister was a member of Lestrange's Third Order.

46. Ibid.

47. Merle, *Mémoire*, p. 6.

48. On the first exploratory trip Vincent was accompanied by the son of the owner of the property. It is clear from his account that the later visit took place during the summer months, when the blueberries were on the bushes.

49. Sorin, *Compilation*, pp. 283-284 provides these names. He also suggests that they were destined for the mission of Father Urbain Guillet but for some reason joined Father Vincent instead. Merle, *Mémoire*, p. 14 describes the newly arrived brethren as three laybrothers who came "at the beginning of the winter of 1813."

50. Father Urbain (AAB D 102, L 63, Guillet to "Mon cher frère", ? 23, 1813) describes it simply as being "rather near to Baltimore." Unfortunately the month is not legible in the date on this letter. Since, however, Vincent's group had already been settled in their new home, it must have been written sometime in or after the summer of 1813, as the monks in Maryland had contracted their illnesses only after fine weather had set in and crops were promising to be good. The heading of the letter reads: "Chez M. J. F. Moranvillé, curé de la pointe à Baltimore."

51. Devitt, *History*, p. 219. The present church, which replaces the original one of 1795, dates from 1917 and is located on the Patuxent Naval Air Base which it serves as the station chapel for the Base. Next to it is located a cemetery with some 320 graves, none of which, however, seem to be graves of monks.

52. Anon., *Sesquicentennial Saint Patrick's Parish*, p. 61. Our information on Father Moranvillé's life before and after his contacts with the Trappists is based largely on this work.

53. AAB D 102, L 63, Guillet to "Mon cher frère," ? 23, 1813.

54. cited by Flick, *French Refugee Trappists*, pp. 111, 113, 114.

55. Father Urbain's letter also mentions the fact that he had found time to offer spiritual direction to a group of six women who had clustered around someone described as a "novice of the Order." This person had come from Europe, expecting to be joined by others nuns. It is not unlikely that this was none other than the sister who had accompanied Vincent from France and later followed him to Baltimore. Subsequently some of them seem to have joined the Sisters of Charity at Emmitsburg. Cf. Ruskowski, *French Émigré Priests*, p. 67. This group was also helped by Moranvillé who provided a house for them at Fell's Point. Cf. Ibid., p. 67.

Chapter Two: Adventures in Martinique and the United States

1. At Napoleon's bidding on Oct 11, 1811, the French Ambassador to Switzerland put pressure on la Valsainte itself. Although objections from the Swiss authorities delayed action, the final Mass was celebrated on April 12, 1812. A priest and two laybrothers were permitted to remain, presumably as caretakers, but they were forbidden to wear the habit. For the entire episode of Lestrange's stay near Bordeaux, see Laffay, *Dom Augustin*, pp. 359 ff.

2. Upper Canada was a distinct Canadian province from 1791 to 1840, located in what is now the southern part of the province of Ontario.

3. AAH Burke papers: Box II, File 176, Burke to "Monseigneur"(Plessis), February 9, 1813. Burke's letters to Plessis contained in these archives were all written in French.

4. AAQ R.L. 8:35, Plessis to Burke, March 16, 1813.

5. AAH Burke papers: Box II, File 176, Burke to "Monseigneur" (Plessis), July 6, 1813.

6. AAQ R.L. 8:96, Plessis to Burke, August 31, 1813.

7. Cf. Gaillardin, *Les Trappistes* II:243-244. According to Gaillardin, Chéneguy drowned in a shipwreck, but Halgouët, *Pierres d'attente* III:247 shows that this does not seem to have been the case.

8. Halgouët, *Pierres d'attente* III:252. Our information on the entire Martinique episode is based principally on section III (and note 17 of Section IV) of Halgouët's work. Despite the infinite patience with which he managed to piece together information from a variety of sources, the details of the story are by no means complete, nor always concordant.

9. Halgouët, *Pierres d'attente* IV:81, note 17.

10. Letter of Dom Antoine to Bishop Collingridge, December 7, 1813, cited by Halgouët, *Pierres d'attente* III:246.

11. Many years later in 1846 there were plans for Melleray to make a bona fide foundation in Martinique, but with the fall of the government of Louis Philippe in France, the project failed, and Melleray turned its attention to a new project: the foundation of Gethsemani in Kentucky. See Aprile, *Abbey of Gethsemani*, p. 48.

12. AAQ R.L. 9:190-91, Plessis to Bouvens, May 15, 1814.

13. Report of Dom Antoine to Propaganda Fide concerning Flynn, May 15, 1817, cited by Halgouët, *Pierres d'attente* III:261-62.

14. Cf. AABalt 8A S3, Lestrange to Carroll, October 10, 1813(?). The last digit of the year is not clear, but between the two possibilities of a "3" and a "5" the latter seems more likely and best fits the historical situation, since Lestrange did not arrive back on European shores until November 22, 1814. This letter written from "Stape-hill" makes it clear that Carroll and Lestrange had met, but there is no indication of when this was. In it Lestrange also mentions with regret that, due to lack of funds, he had not been able to purchase a property he had personally visited in Virginia. It is possible that the property referred to was the one Guillet had himself considered buying. (See AAB D 102, L 63, Guillet to "Mon cher frère," ? 23, 1813.) The main purpose of the letter was to warn Carroll about Flynn's activities on Ste. Croix island. On May 2, 1814 Lestrange had received from Carroll the faculties needed to hear Confessions (AAT 218:7-2).

15. AAB M 314, P. Romuald Tallon (1802-1839), *Notes réunies pour servir de mémoires à qui écrira l'histoire de L'abbaye de Bellefontaine* - 1839. Father Romuald entered Bellefontaine in 1822 and later became its cellarer. He drew up these notes on the monastery's beginnings on the basis of interviews with monks who had shared Father Urbain's life in America. Despite considerable inaccuracies, it gives a lively account of Urbain's group as it headed east.

16. Burrows, *Gotham*, p. 426.

17. Instead of "dollar" Lestrange uses the word "gourde," which at the time was commonly used for silver dollars in certain Caribbean countries. Cf. "gourde" in *Webster's Revised Unabridged Dictionary* (1913).

18. AABalt 8A S4, Lestrange to Carroll, July 25, 1814.

19. Vincent affirms that Lestrange brought with him to New York several monks who had accompanied him to Martinique (Merle, *Mémoire*, p. 17-18). Halgouët, *Pierres d'attente* III:259-62 manages to piece together available information concerning those who were known to have been on the expedition. Father Moranvillé, the ever faithful friend in Baltimore, accompanied Vincent's group to New York, "in order to arrange for their reception." (Anon., *Sesquicentennial Saint Patrick's Parish*, p. 61.)

20. ASB RG1, Box 8.

21. Merle, *Mémoire*, pp. 20-21.

22. AABalt 8A S4, Lestrange to Carroll, July 25, 1814. This letter explained that the person who had promised to provide the down payment on the New York property had suffered bankruptcy. It is clear from the tone of the letter (in which Lestrange tries to interest the bishop in certain religious items he is selling) that Lestrange had already decided to leave for France.

23. The departure would have been sometime after October 15 when the French consul in New York issued a single passport for Lestrange, his "secretary" Francis Hawkins, and a servant "Laurence." It should be noted that Urbain and his group left on a different boat. Cf. Bretonnière, *Vie de Dom Urbain*, pp. 288-289. It is not clear how these boats were able to leave from the port of New York, which was closed due to the British blockade.

24. AABalt 8-Q-5, Merle to Carroll, April 21, 1815. The ship had brought American prisoners to New York and was now returning to England.

25. AAB D 104 Petit Clairvaux 2. Only an extract of this letter has survived. There is no date, yet the apologetic tone of the account suggests that it would have been written for Lestrange not long after the event.

This delightful episode would undergo many transformations in the retelling. Many years later in 1892 the *Halifax Herald*, in connection with its reporting of the fire of that year, retold the story with a curious variant: "[Father Vincent] through hearing the confession of Monsignor Plessis, bishop of Quebec, who happened to be in Halifax at the time, lost his passage." Plessis, of course, had not even arrived in Halifax by this time. Cf. "Tracadie Trappists," *Halifax Herald*, October 22, 1892.

Chapter Three: The New World of Nova Scotia

1. Anselme Chiasson, O.F.M. Cap., ed., "Le Journal des visites pastorales en Acadie de Mgr Joseph-Octave Plessis, 1811, 1812, 1815," in *Cahiers de La Société Historique Acadienne* 11 (1980):131-265. The Journals for 1815 and 1816 were first published in 1903: Monseigneur Joseph-Octave Plessis, Evêque de Québec, *Journal des Visites Pastorales de 1815 et 1816 publié par Mgr Henri Têtu.* Québec, 1903.

2. Plessis, *Journal*, p. 184.

3. AAH Burke papers: Box II, File 176, Burke to "Monseigneur"(Plessis), July 6, 1813.

4. Johnston, *History* 1:70.

5. The *Journal* does not indicate that Plessis mentioned the plan or that Sherbrooke approved of it on this occasion, but Plessis states this in his letter of August 1, 1815 to Lestrange (AAQ R.L. 8:348).

6. NSARM RG1, Vol 430, No. 153, Plessis to Sherbrooke, July 27, 1815. Although he composed it in Halifax, Plessis did not send the letter until he had consulted Father Sigogne at St. Mary's Bay on his way home. It was sent to Sherbrooke from there with a covering letter affirming Sigogne's agreement to the plan.

7. Plessis does not bring this up in his letter to Sherbrooke but mentions it in his letter to Lestrange explaining the plan (AAQ R.L. 8:348-51, Plessis to Lestrange, August 6, 1815).

8. Vincent himself tells the story in Merle, *Memoir*, p. 65.

9. AAQ R.L. 8:348-51, Plessis to Lestrange, August 6, 1815.

10. AAQ R.L. 8:348, Plessis to Rev. Père Abbé Sup. de l'Ordre de la Trappe, August 1, 1815; AAQ R.L. 8:351, Plessis to Sherbrooke, August 4, 1815.

11. AAQ N.E. V-89, 1815, Vincent to Monseigneur [Plessis], August 16, 1815. The permission came in Augustin's own letter to Vincent of July 7, which has not survived but which is referred to in the present letter. No doubt it was written in response to the letter that Vincent had written to him explaining to him how he came to miss the ship back to Europe. Though Vincent did not ask for permission to remain, Lestrange, sensing the poignant tone of Vincent's letter, probably took the initiative to let him remain.

12. AAQ R.L. 8:351-52, Plessis to Merle, August 6, 1815.

13. AAQ R.L. 8:426, Plessis to Mignault, December 18, 1815.

14. Cf. Raddall, *Halifax, Warden of the North*, pp. 150-51 and Maclean, *Walk Historic Halifax*, pp. 41-42.

15. Merle, *Memoir*, pp. 31-32.

16. Several handwritten notes by Placide Gaudet in the diocesan archives of Quebec (AAQ N.E. V:131) offer brief descriptions of these visits. A first note indicates that Vincent had been in these missions before 1817, but there is no indication about how frequent this might have been. (Gaudet's notes are dated May 18, 1904.) Vincent visited St. Ann's church again in 1827. A letter to Jean Bourque of Eel Brook dated November 5, 1827, makes it clear that Vincent had just returned from a trip to St. Ann's church. (The letter is transcribed in Gaudet's notes, 31.)

17. AAQ N.E. I:105, Mignault to Plessis, October 3, 1815.

18. AAQ N.E. I:143, Mignault to Plessis, May 12, 1817.

Chapter Four: Chezzetcook and Beyond

1. Plessis during the 1815 visit mentions that an old Capuchin, Father Jacques, resident at Prospect had been making visits of several weeks there each year for twenty years but had had to discontinue them after 1811 because of ill health. Ronald Labelle, *Acadian Life*, p. 20 mentions the visits of the Irishman, Father Thomas Grace, during the period 1799-1801. Plessis, *Journal*, p. 193 seems to confuse the two, noting that Father Jacques was known popularly as Mr. Grace.

2. AAQ N.E. I:115, Mignault to Plessis, January 15, 1816.

3. AAQ N.E. I:117, Mignault to Plessis, January 28, 1817.

4. AAQ R.L. 8:449, Plessis to Mignault, January 29, 1816.

5. AAQ N.E. I:141, Mignault to Plessis, March 15, 1817. This sentence, and indeed the whole of the second half of the letter, is written in excellent English, showing what an asset Mignault was to Burke in his work with the Irish at Halifax.

6. AAQ N.E. V:93, Merle to Plessis, April 26, 1816. The parish records of West Chezzetcook show that Vincent's first recorded act of ministry there took place on September 6, 1815. Mignault's letter to Plessis of December 10 (AAQ N.E. I:113) explicitly says that Vincent spent Advent of 1815 at Chezzetcook. He was there again for two weeks in early April to permit the faithful to fulfill their Easter duties. (See AAQ N.E. I:123, Mignault to Plessis, April 2, 1816).

7. AAQ R.L. 8:529, Plessis to Mignault, August 18, 1816.

8. AAQ N.E. V:94, Merle to Plessis, September 19, 1816. He mentions the same plan in his letter of October 9 to Lestrange (AAT 218:11-19).

9. AAT 218:11-19, Merle to Lestrange, October 9, 1816. Lestrange's letter of September 11, 1816, has not survived. We know of its existence only from Vincent's reply. This passage gives us insight into Vincent's own inclinations towards living the solitude of the monastic life as well as his readiness to obey his superior and share in the work of the missions during this period of waiting.

Some time before 1817 Vincent apparently also made his way to the Argyle missions. See AAQ N.E. V:131. This is a handwritten document containing letters and various other pieces of information sent to Henri Têtu.

10. See AAQ R.L. 9:133, Plessis to Mignault, March 26, 1817; AAQ R.L. 9:144-45, Plessis to Burke, April 23, 1817.

11. AAQ N.E. V:97, Merle to Plessis, March 11, 1817.

12. AAQ N.E. I:139, Mignault to Plessis, March 11, 1817.

13. AAQ R.L. 9:143, Plessis to Merle, April 23, 1817.

14. AAQ R.L. 9:144-45, Plessis to Merle, April 23, 1817.

15. AAQ R.L. 9:155, Plessis to Mignault, May 7, 1817. The remark "keep for himself at least" referred to the fact that the Quebec missionaries had opted to return home rather than become incardinated in Nova Scotia.

16. AAQ R.L. 9:375, Plessis to Lejamtel, June 18, 1818. Bishops who served as assistants to local bishops or who depended directly on the Congregation of Propaganda Fide as in the case of the Vicar Apostolic of Nova Scotia were given the "title" of an ancient see that formerly had a Catholic bishop, clergy, and faithful but that now no longer had such. Thus, Bishop Burke was given the title of "Sion."

17. AAQ N.E. I:143, Mignault to Plessis, May 12, 1817. Lestrange wrote two letters to Vincent, one on September 30 and the other on December 16 of 1816. Neither of them has survived, so details of their contents are wanting, apart from the fact that Vincent was asked to stay on in Nova Scotia. We know of their existence from Vincent's remarks in his own letter to Lestrange of September 20, 1817 (AAT 218:11-11).

18. AAT 218:11-11, Merle to Lestrange, September 20, 1817.

19. AAQ N.E. I:143, Mignault to Plessis, May 12, 1817. Mignault's use of the first person plural ("We are going to begin . . .") is no doubt an expression of his enthusiasm for the project rather than an indication that he planned to be part of it. Indeed, he would be returning to Quebec in the course of the summer.

20. AAT 218:11-11, Merle to Lestrange, September 20, 1817.

21. Vincent's letter is cited in AAQ N.E. V:131.

22. AAQ N.E. V:100, Merle to Plessis, March 29, 1818.

23. Merle, *Memoir*, pp. 53 ff.

24. AAQ N.E. VI:75, Lejamtel to Plessis, May 12, 1818; AAQ VI:77, Lejamtel to Plessis, November 7, 1818.

25. AAQ N.E. VI:78, Lejamtel to Plessis, Dec 21, 1818. See also AAT 281:11-9, Merle to Lestrange, June 1, 1819.

26. AAQ N.E. V:103, Merle to Plessis, October 18, 1818.

27. AAT 281:11-9, Merle to Lestrange, June 1, 1819. The figures are given in arpents: 300 for the original purchase and 80 for the land cleared.

28. AAB D 104 Petit Clairvaux 10. Nothing is ever mentioned about the property at Antigonish that Burke had earmarked for the Trappists as far back as 1813 (AAQ N.E. IV:75, Burke to Plessis, July 6, 1813). One would expect that when Vincent was assigned to Tracadie, this property might have been finally offered to him. Perhaps by that time the bishop had used it for other purposes.

29. Letters of Merle to Lestrange of June 1, 1819 (AAT 281:11-9), June 9, 1821 (AAT 218:11-3), October 24, 1822 (AAT 218:11-14); Letter of Merle to Plessis, October 4, 1822 (AAQ N.E. V:113); Merle, *Memoir*, p. 66-67. Mention of the school appears in the documents of 1822.

30. AAQ N.E. IV:131, Burke to Plessis, November, 1818 (no day indicated).

31. AAQ N.E. V:106, Merle to Plessis, May 27, 1819. The archives of La Trappe contain a curious letter from Lestrange written on August 6, 1818, from Bellefontaine to some unnamed *curé* requesting him to care for a group of nuns on their way to Canada via England (AAT 218:2-7). There is no way of knowing whether these nuns were destined for Nova Scotia. In any case, it is not probable that the project was ever carried out.

32. AAT 218:11-6, Merle to Lestrange, 1820 (no other indication of date, but certainly not before June of this year). Rameau de Saint-Père writing in 1860 describes in these terms the church that he saw in Tracadie: "The present church was built forty-five years ago, but the sacristy area is the oldest part; it was the former church" ("Notes de Voyage de Rameau en Acadie 1860" in *Cahiers de la Société historique acadienne* IV:1, p. 34). This would put the construction of the church around 1815 and would justify Vincent's description of the building as the "new church." It further seems to corroborate his assertion that he himself created the sacristy area from the "former chapel." The church Vincent and Rameau de Saint-Père refer to was situated approximately a half-mile to the north of the present church, on a piece of land which extends out into the bay.

33. Johnston, *History* I:373 notes that Vincent had paid half by October, 1822.

34. AAT 218:11-9, Merle to Lestrange, June 1, 1819.

35. AAT 218:11-7, Merle to Lestrange, November 17, 1819; AAT 218:11-6 Merle to Lestrange, 1820 but otherwise undated (certainly after April 30); AAT 218:11-5 (1820, otherwise undated, but before June 2). Though Lestrange was to write Vincent on April 30, 1820 it was clear that Vincent's letters with the request to travel had not been received.

36. Laffay, *Dom Augustin*, p. 465.

37. A diocesan bishop is expected to visit the pope at regular intervals. According to current practice (*Code of Canon Law*, Canon 400) this takes place during the year when he submits a five-year report on the condition of his diocese. Amazingly Plessis's two visits to Lestrange seem to have left no trace in the journal Plessis kept during this trip. Nor are they mentioned in other sources save in a passing mention by Vincent in his letter to Lestrange of June 2, 1821 (AAT 218:11-4). Plessis took advantage of his trip to Europe to visit Sir John Sherbrooke at his home in England, ever mindful of the kindness of the former lieutenant-governor of Nova Scotia.

38. AAT 218:11-3, Merle to Lestrange (from Quebec), June 9, 1821.

39. Ibid.

40. AAQ N.E. V:11, Merle to Plessis, July 10, 1822.

41. There is no mention in the materials we have consulted of when the first attack occurred.

42. AAQ N.E. V:113, Merle to Plessis, October 4, 1822.

43. Ibid.

44. AAQ N.E. V:117, Merle to Plessis, April 8, 1823.

45. This letter from Lestrange has not survived but is mentioned by Vincent in his letter to Plessis of April 8, 1823 (AAQ N.E. V:117). Vincent's old friend from his days in Baltimore, Father Moranvillé, remained in contact with him in Nova Scotia and in 1817 promised to send him several candidates and even expressed a desire to come to join himself (AAQ N.E. I:143, Mignault to Plessis, May 12, 1817; AAT 218:11-11, Merle to Plessis, September 20, 1817). Later on, he became pessimistic about the prospects of success in Nova Scotia and proposed that Vincent move to Monsignor Flaget's diocese in Kentucky, where he promised to join him (AAT 218:11-13, Merle to Lestrange, October 2, 1821). This negative opinion concerning the foundation in Nova Scotia was shared by Dom Urbain Guillet, and it is possible that this influenced Lestrange to order Vincent to go to Kentucky.

46. AAQ R.L. 11:209, Plessis to Merle, May 30, 1823.

47. NSARM MG 100 Vol 239, #22, Merle to Sœur de la Croix, April 5, 1823. The *Notice sur le R. P. Vincent de Paul*, p. 27 makes the suggestion that the sisters returned to Nova Scotia in 1822 for another year's formation by Vincent himself before they were admitted to simple profession. This hypothesis is to be ruled out in the light of this letter of Vincent written in 1823.

48. Cf. Merle, *Memoir* 80. Vincent writing in Europe in 1824 describes them as still being in Pomquet at the time. The date of their arrival there is based on Johnson, *History* I:375.

49. AAQ N.E. V:116, Merle to Plessis, August 6, 1823.

50. In 1821 Father Angus Bernard MacEachern was consecrated bishop and appointed vicar-general of Bishop Plessis for the "fourth district" of the Diocese of Quebec, which included Cape Breton.

51. AAQ N.E. VI:83, Hudon to Plessis, March 30, 1824.

52. AAQ N.E. VI:84, Hudon to Plessis, September 24, 1824.

53. Ibid.

54. Letter of MacEachern to Father Paul Macpherson of August 31, 1835, reproduced in Johnston papers (ADA Rev AA Johnston MG 7.5/1 SLF2) apparently retranslated by Johnston into English from the Italian translation of the original found in *Acta Propaganda Fidei 1829*, ff. 254-255v.

55. AAQ N.E. VII:26, McKeagney to Plessis, July 23, 1823.

56. AAQ N.E. V:116, Merle to Plessis, August 6, 1823.

57. Vincent's letter to Plessis on July 10, 1822 (AAQ N.E. V:111) seems to suggest not only that McKeagney was possibly interested in joining Vincent, but that there had been some earlier contact between them. "This fine Irishman who is sincerely attached to you nonetheless aspires to another, more perfect vocation, but he does not wish to follow it without your consent." Later on in cryptic tones: "It must be admitted however that he is a subject who was somewhat 'stolen' (however cleverly) and I could ask for him back. I would not do this save with profound respect and granted that there would be no detriment to the glory of the Sovereign Master." McKeagney had been educated in Ireland before coming to America. He entered the Quebec seminary in September, 1820. It is not known how Vincent met him or why he felt he had a claim on him.

Chapter Five: Laying the Foundations for Petit Clairvaux

1. Even la Valsainte itself was reopened. On August 31, 1814, the decree of suppression was revoked, and on September 8 the monks were able to return. The old limitation of the number of monks to only twenty-four was once again in effect, however, and new demands were being made upon the community by the Swiss government. All of this, added to the promising hope of making new foundations in France itself after Napoleon's demise, led to the final closure of la Valsainte, and on December 13, 1815, the monks took their definitive leave.

2. Halgouët, *Pierres d'attente* III:257. The Lulworth community's problems could in part be traced to Thomas Power, who had accompanied Lestrange to Martinique. Upon returning to England, Power had converted to the Church of England and proceeded to launch a series of attacks against Lulworth, which caught the attention of the government. An inquest was made at the monastery around April 10, 1816. Those in charge of the inquiry were not unaware of the character as well as the precarious mental state of the accuser. Nonetheless, the British authorities took a stand of principle and indicated that the monks would have to leave.

3. The figures are based on Laffay, *Dom Augustin*, p. 403.

4. This was transferred in 1818 to its present location at the famous Marian sanctuary of Notre-Dame des Gardes.

5. Laffay, *Dom Augustin*, pp. 406-407.

6. Le Gard itself would be transferred to Sept-Fons, which after a fifty-year period was thus revived on November 1, 1845.

7. Ibid., pp. 46-61. In 1820 the office of *praeses generalis* was to pass to Dom Sisto Benigni on the occasion of the formation of the Italian Congregation of St. Bernard. Eventually the new figure would be responsible for confirming the election of all superiors of both Observances.

8. AAT 26:5 cited by Laffay, *Dom Augustin*, p. 459. Some compromise was made with regard to properties of religious communities in 1825.

9. Though he had asked Lestrange's permission to stop off in England to visit the sisters at Stapehill, there is no indication that he actually did so. He seems rather to have gone directly to France.

10. Father Marie-Joseph Dunand had also remained behind in America after the departure of the main body of Trappists for France in 1814. His efforts, however, were primarily in the missionary field.

11. *Relation de ce qui est arrivé à deux Religieux de la Trappe, pendant leur séjour auprès des sauvages.* Paris, 1824. Vincent's account is entitled: *Mémoire de ce qui est arrivé au P. Vincent de Paul, religieux de la Trappe: et ses observations lorsqu'il étoit en Amérique où il a passé environ dix ans avec l'agrément de son Supérieur.* 2000 copies were printed and were widely distributed in England, Ireland, Canada, and even Martinique (AAT 218:5).

12. *Annales de l'Association de la propagation de la foi.* Lyons, 1823-34. The author of the *Anonymous Life* cites the text *in extenso*, noting that it appeared during the "second year's issue" of the journal in 1826.

13. "Monastère de Sainte Anne [sic] en Amérique Australe en Nouvelle Écosse, *prope barbaras gentes nomine Micmacks. . . .*" AAT 19:1 cited by de Halgouët, *Pierres d'attente* series 2, II:202-203. Note the name used for the monastery. It had not yet received its definitive one: Petit Clairvaux.

14. Archives of Stapehill, Saulnier to de Chabannes, August 23, 1824, cited by de Halgouët, *Pierres d'attente* VI:37-38. The foundation in question (which was to become the monastery of Bricquebec) was proposed in response to a request from a diocesan priest, Father Onfroy, of Coutances who wanted to start a monastery. He applied to Lestrange for help but insisted that the future monastery follow the Observance of de Rancé. Amazingly, Lestrange accepted the condition. The project was eventually turned over to a monk of Port-du-Salut whose monastery followed the de Rancé Observance.

   In this text Dom Saulnier takes the opportunity to criticize Lestrange for his fickleness in dealing with Father Vincent but also for undertaking a de Rancé-style foundation after having denied his own subjects the mitigations which some of them desperately needed. As de Halgouët points out, this letter was written during a period when tension between Dom Saulnier and Lestrange was at its peak.

15. Most of our information on the life of Father Francis Xavier comes from AAB D 104 Petit Clairvaux 32, *Notice sur le P. François Xavier un des fondateur(s) du Monastère de N. D. du petit Clairvaux à Tracadie dans la Nouvelle Écosse*.

16. Later in life, writing to Dom Fulgence Guillaume of Bellefontaine on November 9, 1835, (AAB D 104 Petit Clairvaux 15) Father Francis Xavier attributed this changeover to Dom de Laprade: "I know well that it was Father Eugene, the abbot of Burlo, who caused the first stone to fall." See Laffay, *Dom Augustin*, pp. 254-55.

17. Letter of January 21, 1821 cited *in extenso* in AAB D 104 Petit Clairvaux 32, pp. 5-6.

18. This author suggests that because of his experience as a school teacher, Francis Xavier would be sufficiently versed in design as to be able to draw up plans for simple buildings such as might be required by the community. Ibid., p. 7.

19. Letter of January 4, 1822 cited *in extenso* in AAB D 104 Petit Clairvaux 32, pp. 7-8.

20. The *Notice concerning Rev. Fr. Vincent de Paul*, p. 28 indicates that Benoît was a cobbler, but the records of Aiguebelle show that he was indeed a farmer before entering. The register of personnel at la Trappe shows that Bruno entered as a choir novice, then passed to the laybrothers after six months in the monastery. He left for Bellefontaine on October 23, 1821.

21. Information on these brothers is found in the *History of Petit Clairvaux*, a document in the archives of Bellefontaine (AAB D.104-34, 3-4). This summary of the monastery's history was written by Father Ambroise Baugé, a French monk who had entered Bellefontaine but was later sent to Oka where he made profession in 1883. In 1885 he was sent to Petit Clairvaux where he remained until his return to Bellefontaine in 1887. Information on the founders of Petit Clairvaux is also to be found in *Notice concerning Fr. Vincent de Paul* and AAB D 104 Petit Clairvaux 32. The author of the *Anonymous Life* refers to Benoît as "père" [father]. Upon arrival in Cape Breton, however, Vincent informed Bishop Plessis that Father Francis Xavier and himself were the only priests in the group: "A priest of our Order and three simple religious are with me." The *History of Petit Clairvaux* refers to Benoît as a choir religious (Merle to Plessis, June 30, 1825 AAQ N.E. V:118).

22. AAB D 104 Petit Clairvaux 44, *Mémoire présenté au Chapitre Général de 1894* (*Memoir presented to the General Chapter of 1894*). This document indicates the date of departure from Bellefontaine. Vincent's own letter to Plessis written in Louisbourg (June 30, 1825) indicates the date of departure from

Rochefort. There is no indication of why they tarried so long. It is possible that the growing storm surrounding the figure of Lestrange caused them to wait. As a matter of fact, on May 7 Lestrange received a summons to come to Rome for questioning. This might explain why the founders left for Nova Scotia only on May 10. Of course, it is very possible that they could not find a suitable ship until that date.

23. AAB D 104 Petit Clairvaux 11. The document was made out to Brother Étienne Normand. Perhaps each member of the group received one, but only this one has survived.

24. The text actually mentions a "new Abbot General" although it simply refers to Lestrange's role as having been that of one concerned with the "general government" of his monasteries. Cf. de Halgouët, *Pierres d'attente* Series 2, 4:61.

25. AAQ N.E. V:118, Merle to Plessis, June 30, 1825 (written from Louisbourg).

26. Cf. Schrepfer, *Pioneer Monks* 37, taken up in Coté, *L'ordre de Cîteaux* 26. Immediately before mentioning the accident, Vincent indicates that his own group was composed of himself, another priest, and three simple brothers. Had the person who drowned been a monk, surely his name would have been mentioned, if not here, at least in the archives of Bellefontaine. In any case, the story is absent from the *Life*. Chiasson likewise makes no mention of it. (Cf. Chiasson, *Merle*, p. 627, Chiasson, *Fr. Vincent de Paul*. p. 32). It is probable that the idea originated with Schrepfer's account.

27. Letter of Father Simon Lawlor, August 16, 1827, cited by Johnston, *History* 1:454 without indication of the recipient of the letter or of the archival source.

28. AAQ N.E. V:119, Merle to Plessis, July 12, 1825.

29. AAQ N.E. V:118, Merle to Plessis, June 30, 1825.

30. AAQ N.E. V:119, Merle to Plessis, July 12, 1825.

31. Letter of Bishop MacEachern to Father Paul Macpherson, August 31, 1825, cited in *Johnston papers* under this date. MacEachern also expressed his enthusiasm for the project in a letter of October 17 of this year to Plessis (AAQ I.P.E: 95).

32. Father Hudon, while remaining pastor of Arichat, had taken l'Ardoise under his care after the departure of Father McKeagney on January 9, 1825. Since Hudon's name disappears from the record book after July 17, 1825, Johnston (*History* 1:441) states that Vincent took over the parish, and he assigns Vincent's tenure as pastor to the period from August 14, 1825, to June 3, 1826, at which time the parish reverted to the care of the pastor of Arichat. Johnston does not specify which source these dates are based on. A letter from Father A. Boudreau, pastor of l'Ardoise in 1944 to Father Schrepfer (Schrepfer papers) noted that the records of the parish suggest a continuous presence of

Father Vincent there from July 17, 1825, to November 24, 1826. Father Maranda writing from Arichat to Bishop Panet on January 2, 1828, (AAQ N.E. VI:92) recalls that the people of l'Ardoise guaranteed to provide Vincent with wood, potatoes, grain and fish.

33. Father Hubert Girroir, who was born in Tracadie on July 18 of this year, affirmed that he had been baptized by Father Francis Xavier, to whom he remained closely attached throughout his life. This would mean that probably already in the second half of July 1825 Francis Xavier was ministering in Tracadie. Unfortunately the pages pertinent to this period in time are missing from the records book of the parish of St. Peter's in Tracadie. As Johnston, *History* 1:493 points out, the first record in a parish book of the region around Tracadie signed by Francis Xavier appears in the Pomquet book on September 18, 1825. Thus it is possible that Francis Xavier made the transfer to Tracadie in a definitive way only in the fall.

34. AAQ N.E. XII:326-327, Plessis to Merle, September 9, 1825. Plessis raised the specter of a possible expulsion from the country, as had been the case at Lulworth.

35. A copy of the petition in French is found in the Bellefontaine archives (AAB D 104 Petit Clairvaux 14). In the margin there is the beginning of an English translation. The author of the *Life* maintains that the petition was drawn up under the direction of Lestrange at Bellefontaine before the founders left. He does not, however, cite the source of this information. The copy at Bellefontaine today clearly originated on this side of the Atlantic, or at least was copied there, since it is dated November 1825 (without indication of the day), and, as we have seen, it also served to record the arrival of Vincent's first postulant.

36. Many years later, on April 18, 1872, the monastery was officially incorporated. See *Statutes of Nova Scotia 1872*, pp. 193-94.

37. AAB D 104 Petit Clairvaux 14, Note on the reverse side of a copy of a letter of Merle to Kempt, November 1825 (date of month not indicated).

38. The spot is still visible on what is called today Salmon River Road, which leaves the village near the present-day Post Office.

39. The only documentary support for this is found in the Malloy *Annals* entry for September 1, 1825: "This is given as the date of the official opening or foundation of the Monastery of Petit Clairvaux, on which all the regular places were in existence and regular monastic life began." This work of Father Maurice Malloy is an attempt at reconstruction of an original manuscript (since destroyed by fire) drawn up by Dom John O'Connor, the superior of Our Lady of the Valley. Though Malloy's reconstruction is not free from error (and contains additional material from later sources), there is some possibility that the traditional date of founding was indeed passed down to the community by Dom John.

40. We have already encountered the name "Monastery of St. Ann" (cf. Note 13). Later still we find it referred to as "Our Lady of Loretto" (SRAS 4:760r) and in 1844 as the "Monastery of St. Bernard" (AAQ 71 CD PP Trappistes 1:7). It is only on September 22, 1846, (GT Côte 180-7) in a quasi official document sent to Rome by Father Vincent that we read: "Fait à Tracadie au Monastère de St. Bernard, dit le petit Clairvaux le 22 septembre 1846. . . ." [Drawn up at Tracadie at the Monastery of St. Bernard called petit Clairvaux on September 22, 1846.] For simplicity's sake we use the name "Petit Clairvaux" to refer to the monastery even during these early years.

41. Schrepfer, *Pioneer Monks*, p. 140 suggests that the constructions described in this passage took place only after Vincent's return from Europe. This would mean that the sisters took vows only then and not before Vincent's departure. Schrepfer describes the temporary convent as being "on the hill about half way between the Monastery and the present site of the convent." According to him, this building disappeared between 1835 and 1840.

42. APF SRC 4:224r., Merle to Propaganda, March 24, 1838.

43. Quinan functioned at first as a missionary priest in the area of Guysborough, Tracadie and Havre Boucher. In the summer of 1837 he undertook the assignment of resident pastor of Tracadie. Cf. Johnston, *History* 1:133.

44. We learn of the trip to Halifax and to Eel Brook from a letter he wrote to Jean Bourque on November 5, 1827, from Halifax. From this it is clear that he had visited the place sometime shortly before the letter itself was written. The letter is transcribed in a handwritten document by Placide Gaudet (AAQ N.E. V:131).

45. *Casket*, October 20, 1892. The epidemic was at its height in the fall. See Raddall, *Halifax, Warden of the North*, pp. 176-77.

46. The record book of l'Ardoise shows that he officiated at a marriage there on November 26, 1832. Maranda writing to Cazeau (AAQ N.E. VI:130 probably in 1832) noted his presence at Arichat. Another trip to Arichat is mentioned earlier in a letter of August 14, 1827, from Father Potvin to Bishop Panet of Quebec (AAQ N.E. VI:90).

Chapter Six: **A Dearth of Vocations**

1. Letter cited by Johnston, *History* 1:465 without further reference.

2. *Acadian Recorder* (Halifax) July 7, 1827.

3. The three petitions are found in NSARM RG 5 Vol 51:83,104; Vol 52:36 and RG 7 Vol 5:16. The majority of the local inhabitants who "signed" the second petition were illiterate; an "x" mark appears near their names, which had

been written out by someone else. It is interesting to note that among the signatories of the last three petitions we find the name of William Edge, thus attesting to his contact with the monastery during these years (1830–1832, at least). We had last encountered Edge in 1824, when he left Arichat to return to Tracadie in the course of the summer.

4. The *Petit Clairvaux Records Book* used by Vincent to record entries into the monastery indicates that Brother James entered the monastery in December of 1832, Brother Bernard in 1835 and Brother Charles in 1827. They all received the habit together on November 13, 1840.

5. *History of Petit Clairvaux*, p. 5.

6. AAT 190:10, Merle to Hercelin, March 28, 1848.

7. It is not clear just where the initiative for the foundation came from. It seems to have been Mount Melleray that supplied the Irish members, yet it was Bishop Walsh, vicar apostolic of the Midland district in England, who when approached by the benefactor of the new project, Ambrose de Lisle, consulted Dom Antoine of Melleray. The venerable abbot noted that he had no jurisdiction in England and apparently urged the bishop himself to take the matter in hand. When things were in readiness, Bishop Walsh appointed an Englishman, Father Odilo Woolfrey, superior of the new monastery. Odilo's brother, Norbert, also joined in the new venture (Lacey, *Second Spring*, p. 15).

8. The text of this decree is reproduced in an Appendix of Hermans, *Commentarium*, pp. 442–443.

9. AAB D 104 Petit Clairvaux 15, Kaiser to Guillaume, November 9, 1835. The letter mentions news they received from Father "Paul Augustin" at Lyons. This is possibly a reference to Father Augustin Pignard, chaplain of Vaise near Lyons, who assisted Lestrange during his dying moments.

It is curious that such an important and seemingly official letter was written by Francis Xavier rather than by Vincent himself, and that Francis Xavier could even go so far as to say, "...it was from Bellefontaine that I began this establishment with great difficulty." The reason for this might have been that, due to Vincent's frequent absences, the day-to-day running of the community rested on Francis's shoulders. Furthermore, Francis Xavier had lived a number of years at Bellefontaine and must have known Dom Fulgence Guillaume well, whereas Vincent's stay there was relatively brief. It is not impossible that the beginning of the letter, at least, was taken down by Francis Xavier from Vincent by dictation.

10. AAB D 104 Petit Clairvaux 15, Kaiser to Guillaume (abbot of Bellefontaine), November 9, 1835.

11. AAQ P.P.T. 1:4. "Vous, Monseigneur, et les Messieurs du Séminaire de Québec nous offriez l'emplacement de St. Joachim, maison et terres, pour y faire

un établissement de notre Ordre." [You, my Lord, and the priests of the seminary of Quebec offered us the site of St. Joachim, house and lands, to establish a house of our Order there.] There are today three place names in the province of Quebec that contain the name of St. Joachim (one, a town approximately 70 kilometers northwest of Quebec), but it is uncertain where the site referred to in this letter was.

12. AAQ PP.T. 1:4, Merle to Turgeon, January 28, 1836; AAQ PP.T. 1:5, Turgeon to Merle, March 15, 1836.

13. *Anonymous Life* 145. The main sources for Vincent's period in Europe are three letters: APF SRC f. 447r-v., Merle to Propaganda Fide, December 12, 1836; AAT 180:1, Merle to Hercelin, April 14, 1837, and a letter written to an unnamed bishop, April 13, 1837 (unidentified photocopy in Spencer archives). The last is a report to a bishop who took an interest in Vincent when he arrived in Paris (presumably after his stay at la Trappe). This could possibly be the Papal Nuncio or the bishop of Toul mentioned in his letter to Propaganda Fide. *Notice concerning Rev. Father Vincent de Paul*, p. 34, note 1, states that Vincent left for this trip in 1835, but this is contradicted by the fact that Vincent wrote to Bishop Turgeon from Tracadie on January 28, 1836 (AAQ PP.T. 1:4).

14. By December 12 he is already in Paris. APF SRC 3:f. 447r-v., Merle to Propaganda Fide, December 12, 1836.

15. Ibid.

16. The curious text "le Grand et le Tiers Ordre de la Trappe" [the Great and Third Order of la Trappe] reflects Lestangian terminology, according to which the traditional Order of Cîteaux became the "Great" Order, to which Lestrange had added a "Third" Order. One would have expected him to say "the Great and Third Orders of la Trappe."

The title "Reverend Father General of the Order of Cîteaux" used by Vincent refers to the new jurisdiction over the Congregation of the Cistercian Monks of Blessed Mary of la Trappe exercised by the President General of the Italian Congregation of St. Bernard. These powers were invested in one and the same person.

The somewhat gauche procedure of appealing to the Congregation of Propaganda Fide to present his letter to a lesser authority (the Abbot President) with a request that this person in turn address a petition back to the Holy See is perhaps explained as an attempt to put pressure on the President General.

17. The first contingent of monks had arrived at Mount St. Bernard in 1835.

18. Vincent was the only other priest at Mount St. Bernard at this time and during a rather serious illness of Dom Woolfrey priestly ministry in the monastery devolved on him alone.

19. AAT 180:1, Merle to Hercelin, April 14, 1837 (from Mount St. Bernard).

20. As a matter of fact Vincent's appeals to Melleray, Mount Melleray, and le Gard itself had not borne fruit. This period of uncertainty about the future of Petit Clairvaux is reflected in the reticence of a prospective postulant who was a priest of the Diocese of Quebec. Cf. AAQ PP.T. 6, Frère Marie Bernard to Turgeon, November 28, 1840.

21. AAB D 104 Petit Clairvaux 18:1, (Odilo) Woolfrey to Merle (at Vaise), October 24, 1837. Dom Woolfrey writing him there sends word that the church of Mount St. Bernard had been completed and was now in use.

22. Vincent informed Woolfrey of the plan in a letter of January 24, 1838 (AAB D 104 Petit Clairvaux 18:3). Woolfrey responded addressing his letter to Rome on February 9 of the same year. Thus he seems to have arrived there sometime in late January or early February.

23. APF SRC 4:91–94, MacKinnon to Propaganda, December 4, 1837.

24. APF SRC 4:222, Merle to Propaganda, March 15, 1838.

25. APF SRC 4:224r, Merle to Propaganda, March 24, 1838.

26. AAB D 104 Petit Clairvaux 19. Copy of decree of the Congregation of Propaganda Fide signed on April 9, 1838, and approved by the pope on April 30. The request concerning the Third Order was turned down somewhat later (APF SRC 4:313r, June 16, 1838).

27. *Anonymous Life* 161. The bishop's letter itself is not cited.

28. He wrote to Dom Woolfrey from Versailles and then on July 12 from Lyons, as we learn from a remark in Woolfrey's letter of July 24, 1838, written to him at Vaise (AAB D 104 Petit Clairvaux 18:4). On May 2, 1838, Maranda wrote to Cazeau saying that Father Vincent was expected back in Nova Scotia in the spring. By this time the decree had been issued, and Vincent would be free to come home. Yet it is possible that Vincent originally had plans for coming back sooner than he actually did.

29. AAB D 104 Petit Clairvaux 18:6, Woolfrey to Merle at Vaise, May 13, 1839. The area is today situated within the city limits of Lyons.

30. AAB D 104 Petit Clairvaux 20. The document is undated, and there is no indication of where it was composed. A note by the archivist, Father Ambroise Baugé, indicates that it was written in 1839.

31. *Anonymous Life* 159. It was perhaps also on this occasion that he visited the Seminary of Meximieux. The old seminary at Marboz where he had taught was transferred here in 1802. Such a visit is reported in a note concerning Vincent sent from this seminary to the Abbey of Timadeuc, although it mistakenly situates the visit in 1831.

32. AAT 140:1. The document has as its heading "Carte de visite, 1839" without further indication of date.

33. His presence in Havre is witnessed by Woolfrey's letter to him there August 27, 1839 (AAB D 104 Petit Clairvaux 18:8).

34. Vincent had written to him a year earlier in August of 1838, likewise receiving no answer.

Chapter Seven: Father Francis Xavier, Acting Superior

1. Francis Xavier's letter to Hercelin, which is our only source of information concerning Hercelin's letter, simply refers to the pastor of Arichat. Maranda, however, occupied this office from 1835 until his death in 1860, save for an interval of several months in 1840 (August 30-November 6). See Johnston, *Priests and Bishops*, p. 94. The date of Vincent's arrival is mentioned in Maranda's letter to Cazeau of June 26, 1840 (AAQ N.E. VI:103).

2. AAQ VI-136a, Maranda to Cazeau, May 24, 1836. "In the instructions you gave me when I left Quebec, you told me to keep you informed concerning everything that might pertain to religion in the mission that you assigned me." It is possible that Cazeau had a hand in Maranda's assignment to Arichat.

3. Ibid.

4. AAQ N.E. VI:138, Maranda to Cazeau, June, 1836. As in this case, Maranda's allusions are not always clear. Vincent had first encountered William Edge around 1821 when he presented himself as a candidate for the new monastery. Though he did not persevere, Edge remained in touch with Vincent during the years before Vincent's departure for Europe in 1823. In 1824 after a period spent in Arichat assisting with catechetical instruction he returned to Tracadie to teach school. The reference to him in this letter supposes that he was in Quebec, where Cazeau resided. It is not known whether he had gone to live in Lower Canada or was simply there on a visit.

5. AAQ N.E. VI:142, Maranda to Cazeau, September 27, 1836. "Il est, je crois, un peu dérangé." His reference to a trip to the United States might have simply been based on a confusion with Vincent's trip to Europe, but it is possible that either before leaving for Europe, or on the way there, Vincent had indeed gone to the United States to look for a spot to which the community might be transferred.

6. AAQ N.E. VI:136, Maranda to Cazeau, May 2, 1836. Though the original has the date 1836, Johnston suggests the year 1838. Perhaps he felt this was an error on the part of Maranda, since 1836 would have been too early for Vincent to be heading back, while 1838 would correspond to the fact that the Decree of Rome would have already been issued and Vincent would be free to return.

7. AAT 180:3, (Francis Xavier) Kaiser to Hercelin, September 1840 (without further indication of date).

8. APF SRC 4:760. The document is undated, but Vincent Hermans in a privately distributed commentary judged that it was probably sent in 1840. Yet it could not have been before 1842, the year in which Fr. Martin, who was one of the signatories of the document, arrived at Petit Clairvaux. Apparently, by this time, there had been some decision about what the name of the monastery should be. The name "Our Lady of Loretto" appears for the first time here. As noted in Chapter 5, the monastery's name was finalized only around 1846.

9. *History of Petit Clairvaux*, p. 4.

10. AAQ N.E. VI:171, Maranda to Cazeau, May 22, 1842. This period of "retirement" of Vincent is alluded to in Maranda's remark in 1842 to the effect that Vincent was "relegated to his convent for the past two years."

11. APF SRC 4:224r., Merle to Propaganda, March 24, 1838.

12. AAQ PP.T. 1:7, Merle to Turgeon, 1844 (without further specification of date).

13. The "Living Rosary" devotion was promoted by Pauline-Marie Jaricot, foundress of the Society of the Propagation of the Faith in Lyons. Vincent was in contact with her while in Lyons. The author of *Anonymous Life*, p. 160 suggested that the inspiration for starting a Living Rosary group at Petit Clairvaux might have come from this contact.

14. APF SRC 3:f. 447r-v., Merle to Propaganda, December 12, 1836; AAB D 104 Petit Clairvaux 20, Merle to Œeuvre de la Propagation de la Foi à Lyon, 1839 (no further date). The last person on the list is no doubt the promising young Mi'kmaq, much boasted about in the documents Vincent had presented in Rome and in Lyons. He was about 22 years of age, knew English and French and had begun to make progress in Latin with Father Francis Xavier's help. It was hoped that someday he would be ordained. However, he did not persevere, and it is not known what became of him.

15. The terms "frère donné" (donate brother), "oblat" (oblate) and "familier" (familiar) lacked canonical precision during this early period and were often used somewhat interchangeably. Cf. Hermans, *Commentarium*, p. 325-26. Delpal, *Être trappiste*, p.103-107 dealing with the period of interest to us points out that oblates unlike familiars and donate brothers received a religious habit and were buried in this habit according to the Cistercian Ritual, while the others were not.

16. Honorable mention goes to several of these familiars who persevered until death in the monastery: Patrick Brown, a blacksmith, entered during or before 1846, died early in 1848; Charles Syncox, a tailor, who entered in 1846 or ear-

lier and died on December 8, 1848; Laurence Brennan, who entered during or before 1848, left the monastery and was in the service of the bishop of Antigonish, then returned to Petit Clairvaux at some date not known, and died there on March 20, 1882.

17. AAB D 104 Petit Clairvaux 21, Letter of Introduction for Merle, June 26, 1841.

18. AAQ N.E. VI:142, Maranda to Cazeau, September 27, 1836. As we have seen above, Maranda might have been confused about Vincent's absence in Europe.

19. AAQ P.P.T. 1:7, Merle to Turgeon, 1844 (without further determination of date).

20. These figures are based on all those who entered the monasteries, regardless of whether or not they persevered.

21. AAQ N.E. VI:167, Maranda to Cazeau, April 22, 1842.

22. AAH Walsh papers: Box 3, File #207, F. Vincent (Merle) to Walsh, February 16, 1843.

23. Archives of the Abbey of Westmalle, Kaiser to Dom, March 16, 1857. The shelfmark is not visible on the photocopy we studied.

24. AAH Walsh papers: Box 3, File #207, F. Vincent (Merle) to Walsh, March 6, 1843.

25. The only mention we find in the sources concerning the rebuilding of the monastery is Fr. Ambroise Baugé's remark that a fundraising tour by Brother Cyprian provided money for the rebuilding after the fire. See *History of Petit Clairvaux*, p. 3.

26. APF SRC 4:515r-516, Merle to Cardinal Fransoni, October 19, 1840. As can be seen from this excerpt, Vincent does not enter directly into the Irish-Scots problem but rather stresses what had been a longstanding matter of concern to him, the poor state of religious life among the clergy.

27. Around 1886 the seat of the diocese was changed to Antigonish.

28. AAH Walsh papers: Box 3, File #207, F. Vincent (Merle) to Walsh, May 4, 1843.

29. It is interesting to note that it was Bishop Fraser who urged Vincent to write to Walsh both in connection with possible fundraising in Halifax as well as to ask for Walsh's advice concerning a possible future move.

30. AAQ N.E. VI:175, Maranda to Cazeau, April 27, 1844. There is no other record of a group having come from France for such a purpose, unless this is a confused reference to Cyprian, Michael or some other brother.

31. Johnston, *Priests and Bishops*, *p.*47. Martinus was already in the Tracadie area during the fall and winter of 1842-1843, and apparently residing at Petit Clairvaux, since he was one of the signatories of the petition to raise the monastery to the status of an abbey. Judging from Maranda's letter he had left for a year and by April of 1844 had returned to take up monastic life once again. *History of Petit Clairvaux*, p. 5 adds that Martinus came to Petit Clairvaux via Gethsemani and that he eventually left to go to the United States and then to England where he undertook the directorship of a hospital. According to this account he left around 1855.

32. APF SRCG Vol. 965, ff. 759-782. The text is cited from Johnston's Papers, where it appears with a note by Johnston: "From original written in Italian in Rome for Bishop Walsh." This seven-page document is a brief description of the principal districts of the Diocese of Halifax.

    Mention is made of the attempted sale of the property also in a letter of Vincent to Hercelin of March 28, 1848 (AAT 180:10).

33. In Johnston's summary there is no indication of the date of this document. He does, however, note the reference in the Vatican archives: APF SRC 5:516-517v. Volume 5 of this archive covers documents from 1842 to 1848. Johnston, *Priests and Bishops*, p. 47 says that Bishop Walsh brought Martinus to Nova Scotia in 1842. This serves as a point of departure for the undated document requesting the elevation of Petit Clairvaux to the status of an abbey (APF SRC 4:760r). Since Martinus was one of the signatories of this document, it could not have been written before 1842.

34. AAH Walsh papers: Box 3, File #207, F. Vincent (Merle) to Walsh, August 6, 1845. This letter written less than a month after Walsh had taken over Halifax asks the bishop's advice concerning an offer of land by a Mr. Mooney.

35. AAT 180:4, Merle to Hercelin, October 8, 1845. Vincent still refers to Walsh as Apostolic Administrator of Nova Scotia, even though Walsh formally took over as bishop on July 20 of this year.

36. APF SRC 6:215-224, Walsh to Fransoni, August 2, 1850.

37. *The Register* (Halifax), November 4, 1845.

38. AAT 180:7, Merle to Hercelin, September 23, 1846.

39. AAT 180:9, Francis Xavier to Hercelin, late February early March, 1846. There is no indication of where the letter was written.

40. AAT 180:7, Petition of Petit Clairvaux community to Rome, forwarded to Hercelin, September 22-23, 1846.

41. AAT 180:10, Merle to Hercelin, March 28, 1848.

42. The tag "New Reform" given to the followers of Lestrange did not sit well with them. As they saw it, they constituted the older branch of the Trappist movement, from which Darfeld had separated itself. Rome, however, based itself on the priority of de Rancé's reform (to which the Darfeld line had returned) with respect to Lestrange's later Observance.

43. According to the *History of Petit Clairvaux*, p. 7, around 1849 or 1850 the superior of Gethsemani, Dom Eutropius, paid a visit to Petit Clairvaux and urged the monks to join forces with his monks at Gethsemani, which he described as a true earthly paradise. According to the same account, on May 3, 1850, Francis Xavier, accompanied by Mother Anne Coté's brother, Amable, paid a visit to Gethsemani. They returned a month later, however, having decided to remain at Petit Clairvaux. Eutropius was to come later in 1854 on a fundraising tour. One wonders if Ambroise's sources are accurate, or if there is some confusion here with the 1854 visit.

44. Though the members of the Chapter were still reticent during the 1847 Chapter, the affiliation of Mount Melleray and Mount St. Bernard was officially approved by the Congregation of Propaganda Fide and duly announced during the 1848 Chapter of the Congregation. (*Acts GC 1835–1891*: p. [241]) During the 1849 Chapter the foundations of Gethsemani and New Melleray were approved.

Chapter Eight: Bishop MacKinnon and Petit Clairvaux

1. APF SRC 6:539=540v., MacKinnon-Fransoni, April 26, 1853. This document alludes to a letter from Fransoni to MacKinnon of December 4, 1852, which confirms the arrangement.

2. *History of Petit Clairvaux*, p. 5.

3. The report is dated June 21, 1853. The present passage is cited from a partial copy of this report found in the Schrepfer papers.

4. AAB D 104 Petit Clairvaux 23, Kaiser to "Cher Rd. Père," August 17, 1853. Ambroise's note suggests that it would have been written to Dom Fulgence, now functioning as Procurator General of the Congregation. Father Francis Xavier mentions a letter he received from Hercelin "with the usual expressions." Francis Xavier adds: "I thank him kindly for his good intentions, for I do as the bee, trying to suck out the honey, leaving the vermin for the spiders." Apparently the secretary of Hercelin had sent a warning concerning a certain Father Dominic, who will appear shortly in this account.

5. AAT 180:12, Theodore (Hercelin's secretary) to Cameron, July 20, 1854. This information is based on a partial deciphering of this poorly preserved letter. Hercelin's point of view was that Vincent had refused to obey the command

to return to France and join the monks at la Trappe, chosing instead to appeal directly to Rome. This resulted in a canonical arrangement which put his monastery under the jurisdiction of the local bishop instead of becoming subject to the Vicar General of the Congregation of Our Lady of la Trappe, namely Hercelin himself.

6. Johnston, *History* 2:275.

7. ADA MacKinnon papers, MacKinnon to (Hugh) MacDonald, January 23, 1855.

8. His name is also absent from an "Act of Civil Association" which the monastery drew up for civil purposes. Yet the name of Father Cyprian of Petit Clairvaux who was on loan to Gethsemani *was* inserted.

9. AAG Eutropius File, (Eutropius) Proust to "Révérendissime," December 26, 1853.

10. AAG (no shelfmark), *Arichat, Nova Scotia August 22, 1854*. Handwritten document consisting of a list of contributors from Arichat, Nova Scotia, to the building program of Gethsemani's first church on the occasion of the fundraising tour of Dom Eutropius and Father Dominic.

11. ADA MacKinnon papers, MacKinnon to Father Dominic, April 10, 1855.

12. Cited in AAK Phelan papers, Kaiser to Phelan, November 28, 1855.

13. Our information on what follows depends largely on the correspondence of Father Dominic (mostly with Bishop Phelan, Apostolic Administrator of the Diocese of Kingston, Ontario) during the period September 14, 1855, to March 10, 1856. We are grateful to the Rev. J. Appelman, MHM, assistant archivist of the Kingston diocese, who kindly provided us with a complete set of photocopies of these letters.

14. Johnston, *History* 2:279. Leaving at the beginning of September, he returned to Arichat in June 1856.

15. AAK Phelan papers, Kaiser to Phelan, September 14, 1855.

16. Ibid.

17. Father Vincent's Records Book indicates that he arrived at Petit Clairvaux from Newfoundland on October 9, 1850, but eventually left (no indication of date).

18. AAK Phelan papers, Kaiser to Phelan, November 28, 1855.

19. Ibid., Dominic to Phelan, December 13, 1855.

20. Ibid., Dominic to Phelan, December 14, 1855.

21. Ibid., Kaiser to Phelan, January 1, 1856.

22. AAK Dominic to Phelan, February 27, 1856.

23. Beyond the interest that this episode represents in itself, the correspondence of Father Dominic gives us some statistical information about the community as it was in 1855. Apart from Father Francis Xavier and the three professed laybrothers, there was a laybrother novice who had been there three years but had not taken vows. Of the professed, only Bernard is mentioned as being a possible candidate for Dominic's new community.

Dominic says that three choir monks accompanied him to Petit Clairvaux from Gethsemani. Two that are mentioned by name are Gregory and Malachy. Both of these names are well attested in various documents. Two other names appear in Dominic's letters: Anthony and Patrick. These two probably represent the laybrother novice and the other choir monk referred to in Dominic's generic descriptions, although there is no indication as to which was which. It goes without saying that the precise identification of these persons without indication of their family names is not possible.

24. *History of Petit Clairvaux*, p. 5. In the original the last sentence appears as a note in the margin.

25. We were unable to find any trace of this Gregory in Gethsemani's archives. Records of the monastery of le Gard now in the archives of Sept-Fons show that his name was Egide-Edouard Huybrechts and that he had made profession on October 29, 1834. In 1860 when this information was entered into another register of the abbey ("le grand livre"), he was said to be "à la Trappe d'Amérique [in the Trappist monastery of America]."

26. This letter has not been preserved, but it is mentioned in the Acts of the 1855 General Chapter of Congregation of the New Reform of la Trappe (*Acts GC 1835-1891*, p. 270).

27. AAB D 104 Petit Clairvaux 23, Kaiser to (Dom Fulgence) Guillaume, August 17, 1855.

28. AAT 180:13 (Francis Regis) de Martrin Donos to Gruyer, January 7, 1856; and AAT 180:14, MacKinnon to Gruyer, February 9, 1856.

29. AAT 180:15. This is an unsigned rough copy of the letter in the Archives of la Trappe.

30. Archives of Westmalle (no shelfmark), Kaiser to (Dom Martinus) Dom, March 16, 1857. The letter is written in another hand and only signed by Francis Xavier himself. It was perhaps written out by Brother Gregory, who eventually became secretary of the monastery. See Chapter 5 for Francis's description of the monastery. *History of Petit Clairvaux*, p. 5 affirms: "He proposed to the bishop of Arichat and to the community to appeal to Dom Martin, then Vicar General [of the Belgian Congregation] to obtain able personnel." Dom Martinus, in a document that he sent along with Father James,

affirms that he had been receiving requests for help from Father Francis Xavier about five years before the current one. An undated copy of this document is found in the Archives of Westmalle. (The photocopy which we were able to consult does not indicate a shelfmark.)

31. In the context of a conflict between le Gard and its foundation of Mont des Cats, le Gard founded Sint Sixtus with the prior and some others who refused obedience to the "Constitutional" bishop of Cambrai. In 1835 there was a reconciliation, and these monks were recalled to Mont des Cats, but by that time Rome was already in the process of erecting the Belgian Congregation, of which Sint Sixtus would become a member and was thus separated from the Congregation in France.

32. According to the Rule of St. Benedict, when a monk makes profession, he vows to dedicate himself for life to the specific community he has entered. In cases where circumstances make it imperative to change to another house, he is eventually required to make a new promise of "stability" in his new home.

33. Two contemporary letters attest to the fact of his severity in ruling the community. The strongest criticism that has come down to us appears in a letter of February 24, 1868, from the prior of Forges (Chimay), Dom Hyacinthe Bouteca to Cardinal Deschamps (Archives of the Archdiocese of Malines, fonds Dechamps: V). It clearly exaggerates the situation. James is called "a strange person, restless and ill at ease, who cannot live in peace with anyone, and who is a perpetual torment for himself and for those with whom he lives, who, in a word, can do nothing but cause trouble in a community."

34. The negative remarks concerning James are by no means conclusive. First of all, the tone of the letter of the prior of Chimay betrays a lack of objectivity. Secondly, it is not clear that Abbot Martinus removed James as prior of Sint Sixtus because of criticism. It might simply have been an opportunity to prepare the way for an election, now that it had become clear that its true prior, Francis, would not be returning. Finally, the accusation of James's exaggerated severity seems contradicted by the manner in which, in the future, James himself would criticize Father Andreas Leyten, the superior of Petit Clairvaux's own foundation in the province of Quebec. James would find Father Andreas's regime excessively severe given the rigors of Quebec's climate.

It is to the kindness of Father Alfons Vanden Broucke of Sint Sixtus that we owe the information concerning Dom James's early career as well the possible reasons for his being sent to Petit Clairvaux. Cf. AAS Sint Sixtus files, Vanden Broucke to Bourget, April 23, 1975. For the early history of Sint Sixtus see Vanden Broucke, *Abbaye de Saint-Sixte.*

35. AAT 180:9, Francis Xavier to Hercelin, late February early March, 1846.

Chapter Nine: **A New Beginning**

1. The monastery of Sint Sixtus in southern Belgium is frequently mentioned in the literature by the French version of its name: Saint-Sixte.

2. The excerpts of these letters of James provided in this work were translated by the author from a French text kindly provided by Father Alphonse Vanden Broucke, who himself translated into French the Flemish originals found in the archives of Sint Sixtus.

3. AASS Tracadie A1, (James) Deportemont to (Dositheus) Kempeneers, January 28, 1858.

4. AASS Tracadie A2, Deportemont to Kempeneers, February 24, 1858.

5. *History of Petit Clairvaux*, p. 6.

6. AASS Tracadie A3, Deportemont to Kempeneers, March 10, 1858. The letter speaks of "one of our good choir brothers who speaks English and French well." *History of Petit Clairvaux*, p. 7 identifies him as Cyprian. This latter document mistakenly situated Cyprian's arrival a year after James had come to Nova Scotia.

7. AASS Tracadie A4, Deportemont to Kempeneers, February 17, 1858.

8. Brothers Bernard and Clement would go to Petit Clairvaux's foundation of St.-Esprit at Sainte-Justine in the province of Quebec. When it closed, Bernard returned to Petit Clairvaux, but Clement returned to Europe where he became a Carthusian.

9. *Casket*, March 24, 1892 notes that Arsenius was ordained two years after his arrival in Nova Scotia in 1858. It seems likely that the two would have been ordained together. In any case in MacKinnon's report to Rome on January 12, 1860 they both appear as priests.

10. Ibid.

11. This is based on the fact that his name appears after that of the superior in the census of 1871, 1881, and 1891. In the first case he is specifically identified as subprior. Vanden Broucke, *Personnel envoyé*, p. 1 notes that he held this office at the time of his death.

12. These were Father Andreas Leyten, solemnly professed monk of Sint Sixtus, Brother Francis, choir religious, an unnamed laybrother postulant, and Brother Idesbald Baeken, solemnly professed of Westmalle. In a letter of May 27, 1925, Father Gildas of Oka calls attention to the fact that Brother Francis's testimonial letter from the bishop of Harlem notes that he had entered religion only on March 1, 1859. It is possible that the date refers instead to his profession. Otherwise, we must assume that he came to Nova Scotia as a choir novice.

13. The priest was, of course, Father Francis Xavier himself. Of the brothers, Charles, James, Bernard were laybrothers, while Malachy, Daniel, and Gregory were choir monks. Daniel was ordained priest sometime before the 1871 census was taken.

14. The expressions "solemnly professed" and "simply professed" refer respectively to those who had made solemn or temporary profession. See Introduction.

15. The three brothers were: Brother Edmund Ruys who had come as a lay-brother novice of Sint Sixtus. (He subsequently went to the foundation of St.-Esprit but returned to Petit Clairvaux on July 13, 1872 after the closure of St.-Esprit); Brother Matthew De Wilde and Brother Pachomius Leloup, both of whom came as solemnly professed brothers from Sint Sixtus.

16. Information on this venture, both the sequence of events leading to the foundation as well as details of its later history, is found in an undated, type-written document now in the archives of the Abbey of Timadeuc, entitled "*Notre-Dame du Saint-Esprit, Diocèse de Québec (1862-1872) à Sainte-Justine, Province de Québec, Comté Langevin, Canada.*" The most complete modern study of the foundation is found in the publication *125e Sainte-Justine 1862-1872*, which appeared in 1987 on the occasion of the 125th anniversary of the parish. The pages dedicated to the history of the monastery (23-60) are the work of Dom Armand Veilleux, O.C.S.O., himself a native of the town of Sainte-Justine.

17. AASS Tracadie A41, Deportemont to Kempeneers, February 17, 1862. At this time Bishop Baillargeon was serving as administrator of the archdiocese of Quebec. He would become its archbishop only in 1867.

18. Father Bernard and Father Andrew accompanied them only part of the way, then returned to Sainte-Claire. Andrew joined the other brothers later.

19. See *Sainte-Justine 1862-1987*, p. 31.

20. AAQ, Registre d'Insinuations P:238v-239, cited in *Sainte-Justine 1862-1987*, p. 31.

21. The ordination is reported in *Casket*, November 6, 1862. According to the account of *Sainte-Justine 1862-1987*, p. 31 he remained at Sainte-Justine for six or seven months. If this is accurate, it would mean that he returned to Sainte-Justine after assisting at Father John Baptist's ordination in Nova Scotia on November 1, 1862.

22. AASS Tracadie A5, Deportemont to Kempeneers, August 19, 1863.

23. Brother Hilarion is mentioned in AAB *Chouteau Ordo Notes*, 1894.

24. AASS Tracadie A9, (Paul) Meulemeester to Kempeneers, March 23, 1865.

25. It is not known when Bernard went to St.-Esprit, but he was not among the first two groups sent there.

26. AASS Tracadie A6, (Brother Bernard) Van Nieuwenhuise to Très Révérend Père, January 23, 1866.

27. Dominic Schietecatte after his resignation as abbot returned to Sint Sixtus along with Brother Anthony Counen and Brother Bernard Ghys who had come with him. Brothers Ambroise and Joachim persevered at Petit Clairvaux. Brother Bruno eventually left monastic life. The surnames of these last three are not in preserved records.

28. AASS Tracadie A15, (Jean-Baptiste) Doughe to Father Prior, June 16, 1868.

29. AASS Tracadie A18, Deportemont to Kempeneers, March 10, 1868.

30. AAG, Berger file, Gruyer to Berger, *Instructions du Chapitre Général, au Révérend Père Dom Benoît, pour la mission qui lui est confiée en Amérique,* 1862 (no further determination of date).

31. Even less challenging was the monastery of Staouéli in North Africa in the shadow of the French colonial presence there.

32. Ibid.

33. AAO 12-8, Handwritten notes based on the reminiscences of Sr. Génevière Monbourquette. These are found in the same folder as a letter of Oger to the General, Dom Sebastian Wyart on July 5, 1898.

34. AAB D 104 Petit Clairvaux 25-c, Berger to Gruyer, November 2, 1876; 25-a, Berger to Salasc, May 30, 1882; 25-b, Berger to Salasc, August 16, 1882. These letters written by Benedict to the Vicar Generals many years later witness to Berger's early impressions of Petit Clairvaux. In AAB D 104 Petit Clairvaux 25-a he relates that his first visit to the monastery took place "seventeen years ago," which puts us in 1865.

35. The visit of Dom Benedict is described in *History of Petit Clairvaux*, p. 8, but it is difficult to date it. The text simply says that it took place.

36. APF SRC 8:250r., Deportemont to Cardinal Barnabo, December 7, 1866.

37. AAS, Photocopy of an unidentified document from the Vatican Archives with description, "Vol 25, 1867b," Letter to the Bishop Administrator of the Diocese of Quebec.

38. These included Westmalle, Sint Sixtus, Achel, and Scourmont.

39. AASS Tracadie A18, Deportemont to Kempeneers, March 10, 1868.

40. AASS Tracadie A21, Deportemont to Kempeneers, November 3, 1868.

41. Ibid.

42. AASS Tracadie A22, Deportemont to Kempeneers, October 18, 1869.

43. AASS Tracadie A25, Deportement to Kempeneers, August 8, 1870.

Chapter Ten: Petit Clairvaux, an Abbey

1. *History of Petit Clairvaux*, p. 9 is our only source of information on this visitation.

2. Ibid., pp. 12–14.

3. Charles Brean also made a drawing of the building based on his recollections. (This is now found in the Schrepfer papers donated to the Spencer archives by the Augustinians after the closure of St. Augustine's monastery.) The attempt to render this in a three dimensional way, however, makes the drawing hard to interpret, save that it was a four-sided structure with an open area at the center, such as was described by Ambroise. Brean noted faithfully, however, an architectural detail: the keystones with crosses over the windows. Schrepfer used both the drawing as well as Brean's verbal description in making his own reconstruction drawing.

4. This seems to have been the opinion of the Augustinians who took over the property after it was vacated by the Trappists.

5. The name of the sisters' chaplain, Father Edward Vaughan (a diocesan priest of Ottawa), appears by mistake among those of the laybrothers. In any case, it seems likely that he resided near the convent itself.

6. The exact date of Patrick Delaney's ordination is not known. Johnston cites a document (APF SRC 15 with no indication of folia) of March 15, 1877, which affirms that there were seven priests there at the time. This number is confirmed by a report made by MacKinnon to Propaganda on March 15, 1877. This report is mentioned in ADA Johnston Papers under this date.

7. As secretary he signs a document of obedience given to Father Francis Xavier de Brie upon his departure for Lower Canada (APF SRC 8:740r).

8. The bishop's letter is found in APF SRC 12:248r–249; for the General's Chapter's position see *Acts GC 1835–1891*, p. 400.

9. APF SRC 12:493–494, November 14, 1873.

10. *Statutes of Nova Scotia 1872*, p. 193.

11. The monks in question were Father Gerard, the choir brother, Placid (later to be ordained priest in 1889), and the laybrother Isdebald. This small house known as Our Lady of the Immaculate Conception was situated in Old Monroe in the Diocese of St. Louis. After the closure of St.-Esprit, the monks of Old Monroe appealed to the Congregation of Sept-Fons to be admitted

into it, but nothing came of this. See Hermans, *Actes* (1873):115. By 1875, the only remaining monks were Father Gerard and Brother Placid, and it was finally decided to abandon the project. Father Placid returned to Petit Clairvaux, and Father Gerard remained to become the first pastor of the parish, which was also dedicated to the Immaculate Conception.

12. AAQ R.L. 30:59–60, Taschereau (successor of Bishop Baillargeon) to de Martein (Procurator of the Trappists), October 10, 1871.

13. AAQ P.P.T. I:30A, Deportemont to Taschereau, June 13, 1872.

14. APF SRC 12:259r–260v, de Martein to Congregation of Propaganda, January 10, 1873.

15. *History of Petit Clairvaux*, p. 11. It is not known what circumstances led to the differing calculations of the monastery's acreage reported in various texts cited in this work.

16. The General Chapter of 1876 took exception to the fact that Dom Benedict as Father Immediate was not called on to preside over the election in accordance with the provisions of the Constitutions.

17. The allusion here seems to be to the fact that the word *prior* should rather be in the accusative: *priorem* if it is to modify the word *Jacobum*. The phrase, as it stands, could mean that *Jacobum* was the person voted for, and the *prior* was the voter.

18. ADA Cameron Papers, Rough draft of letter of Cameron in Italian, to "Padre Reverendissimo" (undated but relating to the election of May 3, 1876). The letter no doubt was addressed to the President General of the Cistercians in Rome, who had the right of confirming abbatial elections. Though the young monk in question is not named, it seems rather certain that this was Father Augustine Lubbe who was indeed ordained by Bishop Cameron shortly before the event of the election. In 1886 he was to request a dispensation from his vows, but this never materialized, and he eventually transferred to the monastery of Tilburg in 1894, then in 1907 to Westmalle, where he died in 1927. An interesting note found at the end of this letter of Cameron is that the younger monks by their votes showed themselves in favor of Dom James rather than Dominic.

19. See ADA Cameron Papers, Berger to Cameron, May 13, 1876, and ADA Cameron papers, Deportemont to Cameron, May 25, 1876.

20. *Acts GC 1835–1891*, p. 429.

21. *History of Petit Clairvaux*, p. 12.

22. AAB D 104 Petit Clairvaux 25-c, Berger to Gruyer, November 2, 1876. This is a copy of the original letter in the archives of Bellefontaine.

23. APF SRC 11:271r–272r, MacKinnon to Propaganda, April 13, 1869. This is found in translation in Johnston papers as ff. 287–288 and is reproduced here.

24. The only source we have for this move is the account of Ambroise, *History of Petit Clairvaux*, p. 3. This information was later taken up in the *Casket* of June 26, 1919 and in Schrepfer, *Pioneer Monks*, p. 140.

25. AAB D 104 Petit Clairvaux 26-3, Coté to Chouteau, February 1, 1876.

26. AAB D 104 Petit Clairvaux 26-4, Coté to Chouteau, April 12, 1876.

27. ADA Cameron Papers, Girroir to Cameron, January 4, 1878; Sisters of Tracadie to Cameron, December 18, 1878; Amable Coté and Geneviève Matthé to Cameron, January 3, 1879. Though the two documents drawn up by the Sisters and by Coté seem to correspond in content to those described in Girroir's letter to the bishop, they both date from a year later. It is not inconceivable that these two dates are mistaken in light of the fact that this whole episode straddled the end of one year and the beginning of the next. It is also possible that they represent a new updated form possibly requested by the bishop and/or the General Chapter after the resolution taken during its 1878 session.

28. *Acts GC 1835–1891*, p. 438.

29. See Johnston, *History* 2:537.

30. AAB D 104 Petit Clairvaux 25-c, Berger to "Mon Très Révérend Père" (Salasc), August 16, 1882.

31. AAB *Chouteau Ordo Notes*, 1882 under the heading "Filiation du Petit-Clairvaux."

32. AAB *Chouteau Ordo Notes*, 1881 under the date May 5, 1883.

33. *Acts GC 1835–1891*, p. 489.

34. "That in order to avert the sacrifice of our property, we have come to the conclusion to petition Your Lordship to allow us to transfer ourselves under the protection of the Abbey of Petit Clairvaux, Tracadie, and that a transfer of our property be also made to said Abbey of Petit Clairvaux to help towards our support." ADA Cameron Papers, *Memorial of the Superioress and Sisters of the Trappistine Convent at Tracadie to His Lordship the Bishop of Arichat*, November 20, 1885. *History of Petit Clairvaux*, p. 10 notes that the final signing of this contract took place only in early March of 1886.

Chapter Eleven: Bellefontaine, Motherhouse of Petit Clairvaux

1. This same property had been already offered in 1862 to Father Andrew Leyton of Petit Clairvaux, when he was searching for a property to make a

foundation. As we saw, however, he turned it down and eventually began at Sainte-Justine, the foundation that became St.-Esprit.

2. AAB D 104 Petit Clairvaux 25, Transcribed excerpt of a letter of Dom Benedict to the "Abbot of la Grande Trappe", May 30, 1881. At this time, la Trappe was without an abbot. The role of Vicar General had been confided to Dom Eugene of Aiguebelle on a provisional basis. On August 6, 1881, Dom Étienne Salasc was elected abbot of la Trappe and Vicar General.

3. We henceforth refer to the monastery simply as Oka, the name by which it is commonly known today.

4. He notes as another advantage—as he as he saw it: "The advantages that Petit Clairvaux would perhaps derive from having a Father Immediate from France." (Ibid.)

5. AAB D 104 Petit Clairvaux 25-a, Berger to Salasc, May 30, 1882.

6. *Acts GC 1835–1891*, p. 476.

7. AAB D 104 Petit Clairvaux 25-b, Berger to "Mon très Révérend Père," August 16, 1882.

8. AAB D 104 Petit Clairvaux 25-a, Berger to (Dom Étienne) Salasc (abbot of la Trappe), August 16, 1882. The reference to 1849 is perhaps due to the decision of the General Chapter of that year which suppressed all reference to the usages of Dom Augustine de Lestrange in favor of the primitive usages of Cîteaux.

9. AAO 1-20, (Dom Dominic) Schietecatte to Lehaye, August 31, 1882. Dominic's letters preserved in this folder are simply addressed to "Mon Révérend Père" or some such expression. Father Guillaume was superior until September 6, 1886, when Father Antoine Oger arrived.

10. AAB *Chouteau Ordo Notes*, 1883, April 28.

11. The monastery's faithful friend, Father Girroir, died on December 21, 1883.

12. AAO 1-20, Schietecatte to Lehaye, June 5, 1885.

13. Cf. the decision of the General Chapter of 1886 in *Acts GC 1835–1891*, p. 239.

14. AAO 1-20, Schietecatte to Lehaye, October 17, 1885.

15. AAB D 104 Petit Clairvaux 34:3–4. His description of the monastery is found in *History of Petit Clairvaux*, pp. 12–15.

16. In days before central heating became common in monasteries, the calefactory was a room that was kept heated, so that in the course of the day the monks could go there to warm up.

17. To our knowledge, there are no earlier documents which would help to determine which of these names was in use first.

18. Archives of St. Augustine's Monastery, Schrepfer papers, (Father Maurice) Malloy to Schrepfer, September 1, 1942. Malloy affirms that this information is based on the recollections of Dom John O'Connor.

19. *Acts GC 1835–1891*, p. 239. The decision seems never to have been carried out. The title "Révérendissime" (Most Reverend) was reserved for the Vicar General of the Congregation and later for the Abbot General of the Cistercians of the Strict Observance.

20 For the most part this tallies with Father Ambroise's count in 1885–1886 save that there was one less choir professed and the laybrother oblate seems to have left.

21. This money was paid to the monastery of Staouéli to settle part of Petit Clairvaux's debt to that monastery. In a note found among the Schrepfer papers, there is mention of an ordination that took place on June 29 at Petit Clairvaux of two diocesan priests (Father Colin MacKinnon II and Father Alex Beaton) and of an unnamed monk. One wonders if there is a mistake of dates here and that the monk in question was none other than Father Ambroise.

22. See letters of Schietecatte to Oger on October 31, 1887, February 5 and July 18, 1888, and February 9, 1890. The dossier on Brother Alphonse is a large one. Apart from other letters, documents 6 to 20 in the archives of the Generalate of the Order concerning Petit Clairvaux-Valley-Spencer have to do with him. By a curious turn of events Chouteau was forced by the Abbot General to pay his return fare to Canada (AAO 160, Chouteau to Oger, December 4, 1890). AAO 160 consists of transcripts of various letters, none of which has an individual shelf mark. All are filed by date.)

23. Ibid., Schietecatte to Oger, January 10, 1890.

24. AAO 160, Chouteau to Oger, October 25 and November 23, 1887.

25. AAO 1-20, Schietecatte to Oger, March 15, 1888.

26. AAO 160, Chouteau to Oger, November 2, 1888.

27. *Acts GC 1835–1891*, p. 526.

28. "This gives the community a self-contained block of holdings" seems to be the sense of the French: "ce qui rend la communauté complètement chez elle." *History of Nova Scotia*, p. 14 notes that by 1884–1885 the monastery's holdings added up to seven hundred acres, including the lands of the sisters that they had received.

29. AAB *Chouteau Ordo Notes*, 1889.

30. AAO 160, Chouteau to Oger, November 23, 1889.

31. Ibid., Chouteau to Oger, September 28, 1889.

32. It is not known if he also died from the grippe. Concerning these deaths see *Casket,* March 17, 1892, and March 24, 1892.

Chapter Twelve: Crisis

1. In 1946 the number of definitors was raised to six. In *Constitutions OCSO 1990* (St. 84:1.A) the definitory was replaced by the "permanent council of the Abbot General," and the members were once again reduced to four. The function of the new entity remained essentially the same. Currently the members of the council are once again five, but the criterion of choice is defined thus: "These members are chosen because of their competence and, among other things, their capacity to be open to different cultures." More significantly, membership now includes both monks and nuns. In early Cistercian times the definitory had been a group of abbots whose function was to determine the final formulation of resolutions that had been discussed at each General Chapter. Cf. Hermanns, *Commentarium,* p. 127 ff.

2. NSARM MG 100 Vol. 239 22T, (Dom John) O'Connor to (Ms. A. M.) Kinnear (of the Public Archives of Nova Scotia), February 2, 1929. Father John's memory obviously did not serve him well on all points. The abbot was not present at the fire but was at the General Chapter. October 4 seems to be the correct date of the fire, as the *Casket* reported on October 6. The *Presbyterian Witness* of October 8 mistakenly affirmed that it had taken place on October 3.

3. In 1893 Dom Chouteau forwarded to Dominic a gift of 7,000 francs from a Father René Herbault in France. See AAB *Chouteau Ordo Notes,* 1893.

4. AAO 9-61, (Edward) Chaux-Bourbon to Oger, April 27, 1893.

5. AAO 1-21, Schietecatte to Oger, March 17, 1893.

6. Dominic's letters to Oger during this period are dated March 14 and 17, 1893, and May 6, 1893.

7. The correspondence referred to in this paragraph is based on a brief summary made by Chouteau in the *Ordo Notes* for 1894 of letters that he himself had written.

8. AAB *Chouteau Ordo Notes,* 1894, entry without further indication of date.

9. Ibid., April 6, 1894.

10. AAO 160, Chouteau to Oger, April 12, 1894.

11. AAB *Chouteau Ordo Notes,* April 1, 1894.

12. AAB *Chouteau Ordo Notes,* April 14, 1894.

13. Concerning Brother John, Chouteau before the opening of the visitation recorded in his notes: "Father John [O'Connor] does not understand human nature. He is a bit crazy." ("Le P. Jean ne connaît pas les hommes; il a l'esprit un peu braqué.") The reading *braqué* is not certain but seems the likeliest. In informal language the word *braqué* means "a bit crazy" or "birdbrained." Perhaps this was intended. (AAB *Chouteau Ordo Notes,* 1894, April 5.)

14. ADA Cameron Papers, Chouteau to Cameron, April 7, 1894.

15. NSARM MG100 Vol. 239:22 P, O'Connor to Kinnear, February 2, 1929.

16. AAO 1-22, "Community of Oka" to Schietecatte, June 8, 1895, and AAO 1-21, Schietecatte to Oger, June 12, 15, and 20, 1895.

17. *Acts of General Chapter of 1895,* p. 5.

18. See AAB *Chouteau Ordo Notes,* 1895 under this date; also AAO 1-21, Schietecatte to Oger, June 20, 1895. There is no mention of the visitation in Oka's *Chronique* for this year.

19. AOCSO List of Indults, July 3, 1896. Permission was given verbally so as not to cause a stir among the local bishops.

20. NSARM MG100 Vol. 239:22 P, O'Connor to Kinnear, February 2, 1929. Once again Dom John's memory played him false. The fire took place in 1896, not 1897 as he says. This explains why he speaks of having spent five years in the provisional quarters created after the first fire. The community was in them for only four years since the 1896 fire destroyed these quarters also. The *Casket* of October indicated the day of the month as being the second; John describes it as having happened at "the beginning of the month of October." Chouteau notes that he heard the news on October 4.

21. Mention of these letters appears in the AAB *Chouteau Ordo Notes,* 1896.

22. Chouteau was mistaken concerning the dates. As we have seen, the first fire occurred on October 4, 1892, and the second on October 2, 1896.

23. AAO 160, Chouteau to Oger, November 19, 1896.

24. AAO 160, Chouteau to Wyart, November 19, 1896.

25. The *Chronique* of Oka for 1897 indicates that the visitation at Oka opened on May 6 and was followed by others at Mistassini, Prairies, New Melleray, and Gethsemani, no mention being made of Petit Clairvaux. In the light of this itinerary it seems likely that Petit Clairvaux was visited first. The *Chronique* does not mention the day of the visitors' departure for France and Ireland, but they were back by July, for Dom Eugène visited Dom Chouteau at Bellefontaine on July 22.

26. The letters that passed between Chouteau and Vachette are simply mentioned by Chouteau in his *Ordo Notes* for 1897 under the appropriate dates.

27. ADA Cameron Papers, Wyart to Cameron, September 23, 1897.

28. AAO 1-21, Schietecatte to Oger, December 14, 1897. The offer is reported in this letter.

29. AAO 1-21, Schietecatte to Oger, March 4, 1898.

30. AOCSO Spencer 21, O'Connor to Wyart, January 13, 1898.

31. AAO 2-12, List of expenses of Petit Clairvaux covered by Oka.

32. AOCSO Spencer 38, Oger to Marre, January 13, 1912. Dom Augustin Marre was elected General in 1904.

33. See AAO 1-21, Schietecatte to Oger, May 10 and May 14, 1898.

Chapter Thirteen: Enter Father John Mary Murphy

1. AOCSO Spencer 22, Oger to Wyart, July 1, 1898 (first letter).

2. AAO 12-08, Oger to "Most Reverend Father" (Wyart), July 5, 1898.

3. AAO 12-08, Oger to "Reverend Father" (Dom Ferdinandus Broechoven, abbot of Westmalle), July 3, 1898; AAO 12-08, Oger to Broechoven (undated letter written shortly after July 5, 1898).

4. Brother Raphael transferred to Oka on July 18, 1898. He died there on March 11, 1902.

5. AOCSO Spencer 24, Oger to Wyart, July 1, 1898 (second letter).

6. AOCSO Spencer 25, Conaghan to Wyart , July 4, 1898.

7. Ibid., Murphy to Oger, July 20, 1898.

8. Ibid., Murphy to Oger, July 29, 1898.

9. AAO 160, Symphorien to Oger, July 20, 1898.

10. AAO 2-3, Murphy to (Pacôme) Gaboury. There is nothing in this letter to suggest a possible date.

11. AAO 12-8, Oger to Wyart, July 5, 1898 (first draft); AOCSO Spencer 26 is the final version sent to the General.

12. According to AAO 160, Symphorien to Oger, July 20, 1898, there was at the time also a well-disposed lay postulant.

13. AAO 160, Oger to Chouteau, August 1, 1898.

14. On July 5 Oger had written to Dom Ferdinand, the abbot of Westmalle, asking for permission for Dominic and the brothers to come to Westmalle. By July 9 there would not have been enough time for an answer to reach Oger. Perhaps the abbot had offered to receive them even before Oger's letter arrived.

15. AAO 2-3, Murphy to Gaboury, June 10, 1899.

16. AAO 2-7, Murphy to Oger, July 20, 1898.

17. AAO 2-3, Murphy to Gaboury, June 10, 1899.

18. AAO 2-7, Murphy to Oger, July 20, 1898.

19. Ibid., Murphy to Oger, July 28, 1898.

20. Ibid., Murphy to Oger, August 26, 1898.

21. AAO *Chronique*, September 12, 1898. He later went to Mistassini (at some date not recorded) and eventually returned to Oka on November 9, 1899. This brother is not to be confused with the Brother John Baptist Jochems who returned to Belgium in 1898 and was received at Sint Sixtus on December 19, 1898.

22. AAO 10-13, Schietecatte to Oger, September 14, 1898. Dominic registers having received the news of Columban's departure but does not mention where exactly he had gone. He was skeptical about the future, however: "I can only congratulate Rev. James Cunningham (ex prior) [Columban's legal name, to which he presumably reverted upon leaving the monastery] for having obtained a good place in the United States; he is indeed worthy. Please God that he might keep it for many years, but I fear very much that he will arrive at your monastery after a short time with his same faults. I hope that you laid down good conditions with him before his departure and that P.C. will not have anything to do with him in the future." The name of the diocese is not mentioned elsewhere in the available sources.

23. AAO 2-2, Murphy to Oger, January 9, 1899.

24. AAO 160, Symphorien to Oger, October 13, 1898.

25. Ibid., Chouteau to Oger, September 4, 1898.

26. Ibid., Chouteau to Oger, September 28, 1898.

27. AAO *Chronique*, September 3, 1898.

28. AAO 2-7, Murphy to Oger, October 22, 1898,

29. AAO 2-4, Murphy to "Father Prior," December 14, 1898.

30. In 1892 Bellefontaine founded the monastery of Prairies near Winnipeg, Canada.

31. BIO 1 and 2 relate that they were accompanied on the return trip to Oka by Murphy. The *Chronique* of Mistassini, however, makes no mention of his presence, and the two Oka biographies of Murphy fail to indicate when and how Murphy arrived there in the first place.

32. He would be back, however, in six months, only to leave again for Oka on September 1 of the same year. After further goings and comings elsewhere, he left Oka definitively on July 16, 1901.

33. AAO 2-4, Murphy to Beauregard (Prior of Oka), December 14, 1898.

34. AAO 2-3, Murphy to Gaboury, January 30, 1899.

35. AAO 2-7, Murphy to Oger, January 9, 1899. The letter bears the date 1898, but this is clearly wrong since its contents clearly indicate that John Mary is functioning as superior at Petit Clairvaux. He arrived there only during the summer of 1898. The benefactor in question was a certain Mr. Reid. It is clear from a later letter to Oger (AAO 2-2, July 5, 1899) that Tetreau had a specific property in mind; this is referred to as "Tetreau's farm." It was presumably a country property outside the city.

36. AAO 2-1, Murphy to Oger, August 13, 1895.

37. Ibid.

38. AAO 12-18, Oger to "Mon Révérendissime Père," July 5, 1898.

39. AAO 10-13 Schietecatte to Oger, November 5, 1898; AAO 3-24, Murphy to Oger, April 5, 1900.

40. Not long after his arrival Caillault wrote to Dom Oger in an attempt to regularize his situation (AAO 2-4, Caillault to Oger, February 2, 1899). In April the Procurator General of the Order applied to the Roman Congregation of Propaganda Fide but was told that the matter should be taken care of by the Ordinary (AOCSO List of Indults, May 28, 1899). It is not known what the outcome of this was, but Caillault eventually transferred to Rhode Island with the community and continued his garden work there.

41. AAO 2-3, Murphy to Gaboury, June 4 and July 4, 1899.

42. AAO, Régistre des Choristes. Towards the beginning of 1901 he spent two months at New Melleray but returned once again to Oka.

43. AAO 2-2, Murphy to Oger, July 4, 1899.

44. AAO 2-3, Murphy to Gaboury, June 4 and July 4, 1899.

45. AOCSO, List of Indults, January 20, 1899.

46. AAO 2-2, Murphy to Oger, July 5 and July 13, 1899.

47. Ibid., Murphy to Oger, July 5, 1899.

48. Ibid., Murphy to Oger, August 11, 1899.

49. *Acts of the General Chapter of 1899*, p. 12.

50. Ibid., p. 4. For the first time the *Acts of the General Chapter of 1903* bear the title, *Acts of the General Chapter of the Order of Reformed Cistercians or the Order of Cistercians of the Strict Observance. 1903.* With the appearance of the new Constitutions in 1990, the Order's name was changed once again: *Cistercian Order of the Strict Observance.*

51. AAO 2-2, Murphy to Oger, October 4, 1899.

52. An undated letter in Murphy's dossier for 1899 (AAO 2-2) gives as his point of contact in Boston, Mr. J. McGinnis, 30 Court St., Boston. This is probably the person in question.

53. AAO 160, Chouteau to Oger, October 14, 1899.

54. AAO 2-2, Murphy (at Cîteaux) to Oger, September 15, 1899.

55. Ibid., Murphy to Oger, December 4, 1899.

56. AOCSO Valley 60, Chouteau to Marre, July 9, 1912. In this polemical mood, Chouteau failed to give due credit for the many fine men Oger *did* send to Petit Clairvaux.

57. *Murphy BIO 1 and 2* speak of him as returning to Petit Clairvaux from Kingston, Ontario on October 22. It is possible that he had gone there from Oka and returned to Petit Clairvaux after his European trip only at this time.

58. AAO (Remi) Baron to Oger, October 28, 1899.

59. AAO 2-2, Murphy to Oger, December 3, 1899.

60. Ibid., Murphy to Oger, December 12, 1899.

61. Ibid., Murphy to Oger, December 21, 1899.

62. Even earlier John Mary's collaborator in Oka's fundraising program, Father Alban, had visited Providence on November 16, 1892, as Bishop Harkins noted in his diary: "Father Alban—Trappist from Oka Monastery—came about 5 and spent night." (ADP *Diary of Bishop Harkins*) This would be the bishop's first recorded contact with the Trappists.

63. AAO 1-24 but I do not have the date of the letter in question.

64. There is no indication in Murphy's correspondence to indicate how he came into contact with Bishop Harkins.

65. AAO 2-2, Murphy to Oger, December 25, 1899.

66. Ibid., Murphy to Oger, December 27, 1899. Oger's letter to him was written on December 21, not 22 as Murphy states here.

67. Ibid.

68. *Providence Visitor*, December 3, 1899. Note the overblown title given to Murphy by the author of the article.

69. Hayman, *Catholicism in Rhode Island*, p. 26. ADP Bishop Harkins' Diary, January 8, 1900.

70. AAO 2-2, Murphy to Oger, January 12, 1900.

71. BIO 2 records that from January 24 to 26 Oger and Murphy were "away from the monastery [Oka]" and that Murphy left Oka for PC on January 27. This presumably means that Murphy went to Canada, although this is not explicitly said.

72. AAO 2-2, Murphy to Oger, January 12, 1900.

73. *Providence Visitor*, February 24, 1900.

74. *ProJo*, March 4, 1900.

75. AAO 3-24, Murphy to Oger, March 21, 1900.

76. Ibid., April 1, 1900.

77. Ibid., March 21, 1900; April 1, 1900.

78. Angus McRyan came down on April 9, but it is not certain whether any others came also.

Chapter Fourteen: **Our Lady of the Valley**

1. The original property at the time of the sale is described in the town records as the "Abigail Whipple Homestead Farm, otherwise known as Bishop Harkins Brook Farm." The actual transfer of property did not occur until September 26, 1902, when it was sold to the "Cistercian Agricultural Society" for $3,000.

2. A contemporary article on the monastery in the *Providence Journal* of October 20, 1901, describes it as being "one mile north of the 'new' village of Lonsdale." On the new village of Lonsdale see Balfour and Koutsogiane, *Cumberland by the Blackstone*, pp. 63-66.

3. A 1906 map of the area labels the railway station in this new part of Lonsdale as "Lonsdale Station."

4. For the first time in 1919 the monastery's letterhead begins to bear the address, "The Cistercian Monastery, Diamond Hill Road, Valley Falls, RI." Technically, the monastery was not situated within the boundaries of any of the then existing villages of the town of Cumberland.

5. *Providence Sunday Tribune*, July 13, 1913:32.

6. AAO 3-24, Murphy to Oger, April 31, 1900. This gives as return address "Father Thos. Grace, Broadway, Providence." In this he also speaks of helping out in the parish. A letter of September 26, 1955, from Joseph Shea to Dom Edmund Futterer (AAS AC "S" files, Shea to Futterer) says that Murphy spent his first night in Providence at the home of his father, the architect Dennis J. Shea, along with "Angus." Yet Angus did not arrive from Nova Scotia until April 12, more than two weeks after Murphy himself. Thus this probably refers to another occasion, perhaps when Murphy went to meet Angus upon his arrival in Providence.

7. AAO 3-24, Murphy to Oger, April 11, 1900.

8. *The Cistercian Order*, p. 73.

9. The sketch map sent by Murphy to Oger shows nine rooms of which the two corner ones on the front (south) side of the building are somewhat larger. The one at the western end is the kitchen, while the one adjacent to the door-way on the east is called "Hall." None of the other rooms have descriptive titles.

10. AAO 3-24, Murphy to Oger, April 26, 1900. The movements of Murphy during the latter part of this month are difficult to determine. The letter of April 26 finds him at St. James Church in Providence—on his way to Tracadie. Yet a letter of April 31 says that he had just arrived in Providence on April 26. An article in an unidentified newspaper in the Spencer archives notes that when he arrived in Providence in the summer of 1900 he lived for a time with the Pastor of Holy Trinity Church in Central Falls.

11. It seems that the project of buying an existing barn and moving it to the site of the monastery farm had been ruled out.

12. There had been a number of diocesan priests residing at Petit Clairvaux, who had been sent there for disciplinary reasons. Bishop Harkins was reticent about receiving them and finally permitted only these two to come to Rhode Island, on condition that they say Mass only in the monastery.

13. AAO 3-24, Murphy to Oger, March 22, 1900.

14. *ProJo*, July 31, 1940. This obituary of Brother Richard supplies the details about his trip with the livestock.

15. AAO 3-24, Murphy to Oger, July 18, 1900. A letter of Murphy to Oger of August 14 of this year makes it clear that Oger had made a request for monetary assistance from Lonsdale, based no doubt on its good fortune of having received such a handsome sum. Murphy promised to send help out the following year but at the time of writing current needs were such that he could not spare anything.

16. The earliest ledger preserved from the Valley shows for December 1902 that the monastery was in possession of bonds for $10,000. It seems likely that this corresponds to what remained of the gift of the Canadian widow after the expenses incurred on the building of the first, temporary monastery. This figure remained on the ledger until sometime between July 1 and October 1, 1922.

17. AAO 3-24, Murphy to Oger, August 1, 1900. The brothers in question are not specified in this letter. These would have included Brothers Aloysius Van Enschot, Paul Le Chartier, Anthony Chisholm, and Francis MacKinnon, and a Brother Patrick who did not remain until profession. Brother Richard Torpey, however, was not included in this group; his absence is noted in this same letter.

18. All along Father John Mary placed great trust in Brother Richard, having left him in charge of temporalities while he was away at the General Chapter in 1899. When news of the foundation of Masses arrived, he shared it only with Richard, waiting until things were settled to inform the community.

19. Malloy, *Annals*, 1930. "Father John O'Connor, fresh from his ordination by Archbishop Bruchési on July 6, 1900, in Montreal, rejoined the busy little community for the last month of its existence in Nova Scotia, to lend the help of his strong young arms in final preparations for departure." There is no other record of this event, and if it is correct, one must assume that John returned to Oka once again, only to leave for Lonsdale on January 30 of the following year.

Father Maurice Malloy, who entered Our Lady of the Valley in 1933, kept in a journal an almost daily account of his life in the monastery (Malloy, *Journal*). He was also asked to help redact a final version of the Annals of the monastery written by his superior, Dom John O'Connor (Malloy, *Annals*). This brief, year by year account of events in the life of the community from the time of its opening in 1900 up through 1939 was reconstructed by Dom John on the basis of notes and of his own memories.

20. AAO 3-24, Report of the Abbey of Petit Clairvaux, August 29, 1900. The ledger for December 1901 shows that the interest on the $10,000 bonds was being used to pay off a loan granted by the Sisters of the Presentation. These interest payments ended sometime between December 1910 and Feb. 1, 1912.

21. AAO 2-31, O'Connor to Oger, February 2, 1901.

22. Ibid., O'Connor to Father Bernard, March 21, 1901.

23. It is not known exactly when Brother Richard arrived. According to AAO 3-24 (Murphy to Oger, August 14, 1900) Father John Mary was expecting him towards the end of August, 1900. It is unlikely that he would have tarried much longer after shipping the household goods from Tracadie. These seemed to have been on their way to Lonsdale by the middle of August of the same year.

24. AAO 3-25, Murphy to Oger, March 4, 1901; AOCSO List of Indults, May 30, 1901.

25. He had arrived there by March 19, as we learn from AAO 3-25, Murphy to Oger, March 19, 1901.

26. AAO 10-13, Schietecatte to Oger, December 21, 1900.

27. ADA Cameron Papers, (Dom Bernard) Chevalier to Cameron, March 2, 1901; AAO 10-16, Chevalier to Oger, December 21, 1900; ADA Cameron Papers, Chevalier to Cameron, January 3, 1901.

28. AAO 3-26, Murphy to Oger, June 2, 1903.

29. "I would really like to have your Father Master here and from this point of view I would not be angry if the Cistercians were expelled from France. This is personal interest only!" AAB Petit Clairvaux (no shelfmark), Murphy to Chouteau, December 23, 1903.

30. AAB *Chouteau Ordo Notes*, March 28, 1901. The visit was limited to a single full day. On the twenty-ninth he continued on to Boston en route to Oka.

31. AAO 10-13, (Oger?) to "Mon Révérendissime Père," undated. The document is clearly a rough draft with corrections and additions and is unsigned. It is not certain that it was ever sent. Unfortunately, it is also undated. It was probably written sometime during the first half of 1901, given the fact that the whole question of the canonical erection of the Lonsdale monastery was very much to the fore by summertime, as well as at the General Chapter in September. There seems to be no trace of such a letter in the archives of the Generalate in Rome.

32. AAO 3-25, Murphy to Oger, November 30, 1901. The same judgment concerning Oger's conduct towards Petit Clairvaux (as well as towards Mistassini) appears some years later in a letter of Dom Chouteau of Bellefontaine to the Abbot General, Dom Augustine Marre (AOCSO Spencer 60, Chouteau to Marre, July 9, 1912). Murphy's letter to Dom Oger is in French, but the text of the letter of Dom Louis is cited in what was presumably the original English version. The expressions "Abbot Anthony" and "Dom Antoine" obviously refer to the same person: Dom Oger. (Dom Louis was a priest, despite his use of "Brother" in the signature.)

33. See Chapter 8, note 32.

34. AAO 3-27, Murphy to Gaboury, May 20, 1901. On January 12 of the new year, Father Remi Baron finally decided to make his stability at the Valley, while Father Alberic Crotty would follow suit only on August 28 of the following year. Father Theophane returned to Oka on February 27, 1901 for reasons of health.

35. The bishop's covering letter (AAO 12-11) is dated July 12, 1901. Oger's covering letter (AOCSO Spencer 29) is dated July 15, 1901.

36. *Acts of General Chapter of 1901*, p. 6.

37. AAB *Chouteau Ordo Notes,* September 15, 1901. The letter itself was lost in the fire of 1950. The text cited is Chouteau's own summary of the letter in his *Ordo Notes.* Chouteau, of course, is wrong in speaking of the proposed "erection as an abbey," since the abbey had never really lost its abbatial status.

38. Thus AAO 3-26, April 23, 1902, April 14, 1903, May 6, 1903, and June 2, 1903, December 9, 1903. On November 12, 1903, he discussed with Oger the question of the novice master. On December 23, 1903, he also shared with Chouteau the question of the novices, even looking forward to the possibility that Bellefontaine's own novice master might be coming to the Valley if the monks of the French monastery were forced to flee.

39. AAO 3-25, Murphy to Oger, October 2, 1901.

Chapter Fifteen: Early Years

1. AAO 3-25, Murphy to Oger, July 18, 1901. Malloy, *Annals,* 1901, incorrectly affirms that he arrived on July 1. He was still at Oka as late as July 4, when he left to accompany the Abbot of Timadeuc to Petit Clairvaux (AAO *Murphy Bio 2*).

2. AAB *Chouteau Ordo Notes,* 1901.

3. AAO 3-25, Murphy to Oger, October 2, 1901.

4. Malloy, *Annals,* 1901 notes that in the course of this year the cattle suffered from what seems to have been hoof and mouth disease.

5. Brother Zephyrin Quinn, a simply professed laybrother of Oka, also came and eventually made his solemn profession on July 27, 1901 but returned to Oka in January 1902. Various biographical notes in Oka's archives testify to the community's admiration for his piety and his devoted service to the monastery's guests. Other monks of Oka were sent to try out life at the Valley, but none of them stayed. Brother Theophane, already a sick man, arrived on March 4, 1901. By May 1902 Murphy had to report that he was "pretty far gone in consumption" (AAO 3-26, Murphy to Pacôme, May 8, 1902). Murphy asked repeatedly for the English-speaking Brother Sebastian, but it is not known if he ever came. The presence of a Brother Sebastian is attested in *ProJo,* July 7, 1913:3, but it is not certain if this is the one in question. Oka's records show that by 1904 twelve of Oka's choir monks and one laybrother (Brother Zéphyrin) had gone either to Petit Clairvaux or the Valley, at least for some period of time.

6. AAO 3-25, Murphy to Oger, September 23, 1901.

7. AAO 3-26, Murphy to Oger, September 24, 1901.

8. AAS Personnel list for 1921 notes these dates.

9. His profession is alluded to in a personnel list of 1921. It is not clear if he was forced to make a second novitiate or not.

10. An earlier article on March 4, 1900, told of plans for the transfer from Nova Scotia.

11. AAO 3-26, Murphy to Oger, January 7, 1902.

12. The short north and south sides of the building also had revetment. A photograph of the north side taken after the fire of 1950 shows traces of fieldstone revetment near the roof line, whereas the lower area corresponding to a space occupied by a wooden building attached to it was of brick. An eyewitness reports that the south wall also had brick revetment. The west side of the building was of wood.

13. AAO 3-26, Murphy to Pacôme, February 14, 1902, notes that the builder's plan was to begin work on April 15. A later article in the *Pawtucket Evening Times* of December 20, 1902, confirms this date. Malloy, *Annals,* 1902 claims that the work began on March 1 of that year.

14. AAO 3-23, Murphy to Gaboury, May 8, 1902.

15. AAO 3-26, Murphy to Oger, May 13, 1902. "As you know we have debentures for 10,000 dollars which bring in 4½%. We have at hand $3,000 and $5,000 at [?] Timadeuc making a total of $18,000. I explained all to Bishop Harkins and he advised me to borrow $18–20,000 at 4% and to leave the debentures of $10,000 in the Bank and the interests of this sum will serve to help pay the interests on the sum borrowed. I submit this proposal for your approbation. Please answer as soon as you can. The bishop permits me to take out the first mortgage with whoever consents to lend us the sum needed, and he would be himself content with the second. He says that its being in his name would be only for form."

16. This is mentioned in two letters. In the first (AAO 3-26, Murphy to Oger, March 17, 1903) there is question of $8,000. In the second (AAO 3-26, Murphy to "Brother Bruno" [of Oka]), March 25, 1903, a figure of "$10,000" is indicated. This was the final figure decided upon. It appears in the Valley ledger in April, 1903.

17. Malloy, *Annals,* 1902.

18. AAO 3-26, Murphy to Oger, March 17, 1903. The letter was written in French, but the last words "poor old Father . . . so foolish" are in English. Choir monks who were professed were sometimes called "Father," even though they were not priests.

19. AAB Petit Clairvaux (no shelfmark), Murphy to Chouteau, December 23, 1903.

20. AAS, Photocopies of handwritten notes of Father Guénolé of Timadeuc.

21. He sent a list suggesting possible names. Oger, however, suggested other names, whom Murphy did not know. AAO 3-26, Murphy to Oger, November 13, 1902; AAO 3-26, Murphy to Oger, December 30, 1902.

22. AAO 3-26, Murphy to Oger, December 30, 1902; Malloy, *Annals,* 1902 provides the day of entry.

23. ADP Bishop Harkins' Journal, March 28, 1903. *Providence Visitor,* March 28, 1903.

24. Malloy, *Annals,* 1903.

25. The exact location of this guesthouse for ladies has never been determined. Malloy, *Annals,* 1902, claims that it was "on the southeastern extremity of the property." However, sometime in 1933 or later Father Benedict Barré brought his novices to visit an abandoned site near the northwestern extremity of the property which he said was the site of the ladies' guesthouse. The building itself seems to have disappeared early in the history of the Valley. A photograph of the building has survived. A cellar hole and nearby wellhead near the northeastern extremity of the former Valley property might conceivably be the site of this guesthouse.

26. Dom Chouteau's enthusiastic account of his 1904 visit (AAB *Chouteau Ordo Notes,* 1904) gives the impression that there were several bathtubs, but this is inaccurate, as the plans of Murphy and Hindle show.

27. AAO 3-26, Murphy to Oger, April 14, 1903.

28. Ibid., Murphy to Oger, June 2, 1903. Obrecht's signature in the account books is dated May 30, and Murphy's letter to Oger on June 2 indicates that the visitation had ended.

29. AAO 2-8, List of those sent to Petit Clairvaux from Oka. Brother Ignace Müller and Brother Francis D'Assisi Courschene came in 1904.

30. AAO 3-26, Murphy to Oger, November 12, 1903.

31. AAO 3-27, Murphy to Gaboury, May 20, 1901.

32. AAB *Chouteau Ordo Notes,* 1904.

33. AOCSO Spencer 32, Oger to "Mon Révérendissime Père," May 8, 1907.

34. AAO 3-26, Murphy to Oger, January 11, 1904.

35. AAO 2-8 reports that he left Oka for the Valley on May 7. In 1913 he transferred to Gethsemani and died there on March 28, 1927.

36. The expression "dames à journée" is not clear. It perhaps refers to ladies who worked as volunteers or who were employed "by the day" to assist in caring for visitors to the monastery.

37. The farm referred to seems to be the one that Murphy had rented to the west of the original property and that he would indeed purchase in 1909, although Chouteau's incorrectly cites its size as 105 arpents rather than 105 *acres.* The Cumberland town records show that the precise size was 105.97 acres. The overall property holding is reported as being 500 arpents or about 442 acres, a decidedly exaggerated figure. The initial holding purchased from Bishop Harkins was 222.5 acres and the property acquired in 1909 was 105.97 acres, which taken together would be equivalent to only 328.48 arpents.

38. AAS AC Denis Shea file, Shea to Murphy, June 5, 1905. For this stone the monastery received from Shea $105.63 in addition to $20 in alms. From the time of the arrival the monks were faced with the prospect of clearing their land of rocks. An article in *ProJo,* July 7, 1913:3 notes in connection with this: "Stones were disposed of to the town for use at the crusher." The impression one gets is that this was more a means of disposal than profit. Various oral sources speak of the monastery's stone as having been used for paving in the neighboring villages.

39. Malloy, *Annals,* 1903. Malloy also notes that numbers are down to fourteen in the community this year. It should be remembered, however, that these yearly figures cited by Malloy should be seen in the light of the many comings and goings of postulants and novices in the course of the monastery's history.

40. AOCSO Spencer 30, Murphy to Marre, June 12, 1904.

41. By September 1904 the debt no longer appeared on the ledger.

42. The community moved to the site of the Quarr Abbey in 1908 and began construction of a new monastery that same year.

43. *Acts of General Chapter of 1905*, p. 10. Several months after the chapter, on January 6, 1906, Murphy paid a visit to the bishop which is described in these terms in the bishop's Diary: "Spoke of evil reports about house—he [Murphy] has deposed Father Remi from office of prior." As usual, the bishop's stenographic style makes it difficult to gather much information from these remarks. Were they in any way related to the chapter's observations about the monastery? The word, "prior" used of Father Remi is obviously to be taken in the sense of second superior. Father John Mary paid another visit to the bishop on January 17 of the same year. In the bishop's words: "Father Murphy—Trappist—states that according to instruction received from the General Chapter no priest who has given scandal on account of immorality or drunkenness can be received in Cumberland." The Acts of the General Chapter make no reference to this matter. Not all the deliberations of the chapter appear

in these Acts, however, and it is possible, of course, that this was communicated to John Mary verbally or by some document apart from the Acts themselves. The priests in question are hardly the old priests who had been living at Petit Clairvaux. As we have seen, two of them were permitted to come to the Valley, while the others were not. More likely, it has to do with local priests being sent there for purposes of penance.

The chapter's insistence on the priests' refraining from outside pastoral work is mirrored in remarks made to Bishop Harkins in the course of another visit which Murphy paid him on June 6, 1906: "Father Murphy—Trappist— the General is unwilling to have priests go out to help in parish work." The same was reiterated in a later visit on June 6 of the same year.

44. *Murphy Bio 1 and 2.* Malloy asserts that Oger put an end to these practices on the occasion of his visitation, even before they were brought up at the chapter during the next month.

45. AAO 2-10, Villeneuve to Oger, February 23, 1904.

46. *Acts of General Chapter of 1904,* p. 15.

47. Materials in the archives of Timadeuc make it clear that the composition of the "Life" referred to was entrusted to the secretary of the monastery, Father Etienne Ozenne (d. 1911). These include large sections in manuscript form of the *Anonymous Life* of Vincent. More telling, various documents certifying data reported in the Life are found here: copies of Vincent's baptismal certificate, attestation of ordination, and a letter from the rector of seminary of Meximieux where he had taught.

48. *Acts of General Chapter of 1904,* pp. 12, 21.

49. *Casket,* March 16, 1905. It is clear from the tone of the document as a whole that the monks of Petit Clairvaux, though arriving on the scene many years after the death of Father Vincent, were themselves happy to promote the cause of Vincent's beatification. An oral tradition at Timadeuc, however, asserts that the main impetus for the beatification process came from the local Church.

Chapter Sixteen: The Valley 1905–1910

1. AOCSO Spencer 27, Murphy to Chambon (Procurator General of the Order), October 3, 1905. This 1905 document constitutes the first detailed surviving community list that has come down to us. From this we see that Father Francis Quézel who had come from Oka in May 1904 changed his stability to the Valley on July 14, 1905, not long before this document was sent to Rome.

2. "Sanation" is a legal term indicating the retroactive validation of an act performed without proper authorization.

3. Typical truncated formula used in such documents.

4. AOCSO *Rescripts* I:231 (no. 70517 Congregation of Propaganda Fide). The remark, "the General Chapter of 1899 decided that for that small community a more fitting location be sought, care being taken to follow all that is laid down concerning the transfer and the erection of monasteries," does not correspond to what is said in the Acts of the Chapter of 1899. Indeed, had the chapter or at least the curia of the Order insisted on (or even mentioned) the Valley's duty to follow "all that is laid down concerning the transfer and the erection of monasteries" much confusion would have been avoided.

5. Malloy, *Annals*, 1907, notes that during the course of the year, "There was some technical error in the transfer of the community from Nova Scotia, and we lost our abbatial standing—so a Visitor from abroad told us this year." Nowhere in the official documents do we find mention of the loss of abbatial standing as related to the question of the irregularity that was cleared up by the sanation. As we have shown, whatever culpability there might have been in the matter seems rather to lie with the Order's curia in Rome and/or with Dom Oger, who might be seen as having failed to regulate the practice of the Valley in the matter of receptions of habit and professions. Judging from his letters, Murphy seems to have been faithful in reporting these to his Father Immediate.

6. Malloy's *Annals* describe the ice pond as being at the point where the stream bends to the south. Cf. Malloy, *Annals*, 1906. There seems to be no trace left of this today. The pond now visible to the west of the monastery buildings is usually referred to in Malloy as the reservoir. The icehouses were constructed near the main barn.

7. *Acts of General Chapter of 1906*, p. 16. Among other things, the chapter also clarified, in response to a request made by Father John Mary, that accommodations could be provided in a guesthouse for female relatives of the religious.

8. Dom Joseph-Marie Hercelin, Abbot of la Trappe, with whom Vincent had to deal.

9. AATim (no shelfmark), Lehodey to "Mon Révérend et bien cher Père," September, 1906 (day of month illegible). The reference to "the letter to Dom Joseph-Marie" is to AAT 180-3, Kaiser to Hercelin, September, 1840 (day of month not indicated).

10. *Acts of the General Chapter of 1909*, p. 6.

11. AAS Visitation Cards, 1907. The visitation card is a report of the visitation drawn up by the superior who carries out the visit. This is the first visitation card of Spencer's history that has survived.

12. Malloy situates the election on April 2 in contradiction to the date on the *Instrument of election* itself and in the AAO, *Murphy Bio 1 and 2*. Oger's visit to the bishop is mentioned in Bishop Harkins' Diary, May 2, 1907.

13. The ones chosen were the pastors of St. Mary's Church in Providence and of Precious Blood Church in Woonsocket.

14. AAS *Instrumentum Electionis,* Our Lady of the Valley, May 4, 1907. This document does not record the name of the person who got the other vote.

15. AOCSO Spencer 32, Oger to Marre, May 4, 1907.

16. Spencer archives, *Instrumentum confirmationis et installationis*; *ProJo,* August 21, 1907. Malloy, *Annals,* 1907 notes that shortly after the election the bishop made a "ceremonial visit" to the monastery.

17. The visitation is mentioned in *Murphy Bio 1 and 2.*

18. Malloy, *Annals,* 1909.

19. *Cumberland Book* 113:350. Sale of property to "the "Cistercian Agricultural Society." May 18, 1909.

Chapter Seventeen: Last Years of Dom John Mary Murphy

1. The first members of the Commission were Dom John Mary, Father John O'Connor, and Father Francis Quézel. John Mary's signature, however, appears for the last time on September 30, 1911. All the signatures disappear from December 31, 1912, to January 2, 1914, no doubt in the wake of the confusion generated by the last illness and death of Dom John Mary on July 6, 1913. On January 2, 1914, the signatures begin again and the signatees become Father John O'Connor, Father Remi Baron, and Father Augustine Herran. On April 1, 1916, Father Benedict Barré replaces Father Augustine as signatee, a move that was confirmed during a visit of Obrecht in May 1917, when at a meeting of the Commission of Accounts, the private council, and Obrecht himself, Father Benedict was officially made a member of the Commission. From January 1, 1929, Father Michael Holland replaces Father Remi as signatee, while on January 1, 1931, Father Aelred Walsh replaces Father Remi.

2. AOCSO Spencer 33, Oger to Marre, March 10, 1911. The preceding year Bishop Harkins noted in connection with a visit Oger and Murphy paid to him on June 13, 1907: "[Father Murphy] . . . suffering from varicose veins—[I] advised him to go to Hospital. He is unwilling."

3. Malloy, *Annals,* 1911.

4. It is not clear when exactly Murphy was taken to St. Joseph's Hospital. In his account Malloy simply describes this as "early this year."

5. AOCSO Spencer 35, Oger to Marre, January 13, 1912.

6. Ibid. A second letter written the same day is also in this archive.

7. AOCSO Spencer 40, Gaboury to Oger, February 2, 1912.

8. AOCSO Spencer 41, Oger to Marre, February 4, 1912 (covering letter sent with Father Pacôme's letter to Oger).

9. AOCSO Spencer 38, Oger to Marre, January 30, 1912. A letter of Father John O' Connor to the General of January 18, 1912 seems to suggest that Murphy is home, where he is being attended to by two monks as well a lay nurse. Thus is it not clear exactly when Murphy went for his three-month stay at the Providence hospital.

10. AOCSO Valley 39, Chouteau to Marre, January 30, 1912.

11. AOCSO Spencer 43, Oger to Marre, February 15, 1912. The letter of February 1 is mentioned in this letter.

12. Cited in AOCSO Spencer 44, Oger to Murphy, February 15, 1912.

13. AOCSO Spencer 47, Murphy to Marre, February 23. The letter was written for him by Father Alberic.

14. AOCSO Spencer 53, Oger to Marre, March 19, 1912. See also AOCSO Spencer 51, Oger to Marre, March 3, 1912.

15. AOCSO Spencer 54, Oger to Marre, March 24, 1912.

16. AOCSO Spencer 55, Oger to Marre, March 26, 1912. In light of Murphy's exceptional accomplishments in the transfer from Nova Scotia and the initial organization of the Valley, Oger's assessment of Murphy's superiorship as not successful seems decidedly off the mark.

17. AOCSO Spencer 56, Oger to Marre, April 19, 1912.

18. Ibid.

19. Malloy, *Annals*, 1912. It is not clear when he received Extreme Unction. Easter of 1912 fell on April 7, and it is possible that he received the sacrament in the hospital itself.

20. AOCSO Spencer 65, Baron to Marre, August 29, 1912. Father Remi was apparently serving as secretary at this time.

21. *Acts of General Chapter of 1912*, pp. 15–16.

22. At this same Chapter Obrecht received the charge of visiting the monasteries of the Order in China and Japan. Cf. *GethAnnals* 1912:133.

23. AAS Murphy papers, Murphy to Shea, November 15, 1912.

24. Malloy, *Annals*, 1912 and 1913 notes that Father Benedict Barré was ordained deacon in 1912.

25. *ProJo,* July 7, 1913:3; *Providence Visitor,* July 11:1. The "retrospective" appears in the *Providence Sunday Tribune,* "Making the Wilderness to Bloom."

26. *Acts of General Chapter of 1913,* p. 5. These included a slight prolongation of sleep on Sundays and feastdays, removal of the cowl during periods of free time during the summer months, and to limit the use of chanting on weekdays to the Offices of Prime, Vespers, and the Salve Regina following Compline.

27. In 1913 Father John O'Connor was present at Gethsemani for the Immaculate Conception. The Pontifical Mass that day was celebrated by Dom Chouteau, who was visiting Gethsemani on the occasion of his coming to North America to visit Bellefontaine's foundation of Our Lady of the Prairies in Canada. On this occasion Father John made a good impression as a speaker. Indeed, over the years Obrecht would come to appreciate John's talents more and more. The Gethsemani Annals relate: "The Father, who has considerable talents as a speaker, addressed us on the history and needs of his house, transferred from Petit Clairvaux in Nova Scotia. He asked for help. One of our Fathers was exchanged for the one he brought to us." (*GethAnnals* 1913:141) The monk in question was Fr. Francis Xavier Quézel. The one sent from Gethsemani to replace him was Father Aloysius Connolly, who died at the Valley on March 26, 1932.

Chapter Eighteen: Increasing Stability under Dom John O'Connor

1. AAG *Annals,* 1914:150; Valley Account Books, signature of Obrecht on June 24, 1914.

2. AAG *Annals,* 1915:159; 1916:168; 1917:176.

3. Ibid., 1916:168.

4. AAB Petit Clairvaux (no shelfmark), Baron to "Mon très Révérend Père" (Chouteau), November 1, 1917.

5. AAO 2-13, Act of sale of Petit Clairvaux, June 16, 1919.

6. Schrepfer, *Pioneer Monks,* p. 95. As far as we know there is no record of exactly when the transfer took place.

7. ValleyAccount Books, October 5, 1918.

8. ADP, Bishop Hickey's Diary, August 30, 1922.

9. AAG *Annals,* 1918:182.

10. Dom Obrecht left early and found himself already in Europe when the postponement of the chapter was announced. He decided instead to spend some time in his native Alsace. (AAG *Annals,* 1919) It is possible that the same thing happened to Father John O'Connor, since Malloy relates that John spent

a week at Mt. Melleray while in Europe attending the General Chapter that year. This, however, does not seem likely, since as late as October 20, 1919, John's travel plans were still up in the air, as we learn from his letter of that date to Dom Pacôme of Oka. Malloy's information on the period from 1916 to 1922 was extremely sketchy, and it is possible that he was projecting backward later visits that O'Connor frequently made to houses in Europe on the occasion of his attendance at General Chapters.

11. The word used here is *tourteaux*. These solid remains of various grains or seeds from which oil has been pressed are used as fodder for animals.

12. AAB 3 J ch 371. P. A. Moussion. 1920, P. Antoine Moussion, *Journal de voyage aux États-Unis et au Canada décembre 1919 – mai 1920.*

13. It is also the only account of personnel that has survived for this year.

14. Malloy, *Annals*, 1920.

15. The only information we have concerning this visitation appears in AAG *Annals*, 1920:195.

16. On the occasion of his trip to the Valley for the election, Dom Obrecht visited his friend Cardinal Dougherty of Philadelphia who had just been made cardinal on March 7, 1921. Obrecht would be a frequent visitor to the Cardinal on his way east for visitations at the Valley and as he headed to Europe for the General Chapter.

17. Malloy, *Annals*, 1919.

18. AAG *Annals*, 1921:200. Dom John arrived on December 6 and stayed until December 13.

19. This plan is outlined in "Trappist Monks Reclaim Unproductive Land," *ProJo*, May 8, 1921.

20. See ADP Bishop Hickey's Journal, February 18, April 4.

21. Malloy, *Annals*, 1922. By the time O'Connor received this permission to spend $75,000 on the church, he already had at least $50,000 in bonds and in cash, and this figure would continue to increase until 1925 when it reached approximately $75,000. The books show that between January 25, 1925, and January 26, 1926, this money was no longer present.

22. There are no records in the archives of the Royal Canadian Mounted Police of his having served there.

23. *ProJo*, May 8, 1921. The monastery soon also caught the attention of the *Boston Globe*, which featured an article on it in its Sunday edition on October 30, 1921. Little by little Michael would be entrusted with other important responsibilities. In June 1923 he was chosen to accompany Dom Chouteau of

Bellefontaine to Our Lady of Prairies stopping on the way for a visit at Gethsemani (AAG *Annals*, 1923:192). It is not clear if Michael met Dom Chouteau at the boat in New York or if the French abbot had paid a visit to the Valley and that it was from there that they set out.

24. In addition to these arduous farms labors, in 1923 Michael resumed his priestly studies, which had been interrupted by his illness.

25. Malloy, *Annals*, 1923.

26. Town of Cumberland, *Book of Deeds* under various dates. A convenient summary description of the entire holdings of the abbey by the time of its sale to the Franciscan Friars of the Atonement in 1951 is found in Book 113:350-57. The transactions took place on September 21, 25 and October 11, 1923.

27. According to AAG *Annals*, 1923 (un-numbered page) Obrecht left Gethsemani with Father Robert acting as secretary on April 23 and returned home on May 8.

28. ADP Bishop Hickey's Journal, September 17, 1923.

29. AAG Valley files, Dougherty to O'Connor, December 31, 1923.

30. Malloy, *Annals*, 1924.

31. *ProJo*, July 6, 1925.

32. Malloy, *Annals*, 1924.

33. AAG *Annals*, 1924:249 ff.

34. Ibid., 1924:10,19.

35. *Acts of General Chapter of 1924*, pp. 19-20.

36. Malloy, *Annals*, 1925. A *ProJo* article of June 21, 1925 notes that the contractor was a J. A. Savoie of Woonsocket. This was presumably the one newly chosen.

   The springtime also brought the year's regular visitation which lasted from April 13 to May 12. See AAG *Annals*, 1925:13, 35.

37. AAO 3-28, O'Connor to Gaboury, April 26. Unfortunately Dom John forgot to indicate the year on his letter. The letter appears last in the Oka archive folder, immediately after one written on March 22, 1929. It is possible that the present letter also dates from this year. However, this seems very late for such an action to occur.

38. *ProJo*, June 12, 27; July 6, 7, 1925.

39. *ProJo*, July 11, 1925.

40. Ibid., July 6, 1925, cites this figure but indicates that the construction contract was for $130,000 due to the contribution of materials and labor by the monks. *ProJo*, August 1, 1926, written as the building was nearing completion also mentions the figure of $200,000. Obviously, these figures based on a newspaper account must be taken with caution.

41. AAO 3-28, O'Connor to Gaboury, October 7, 1925. Malloy, *Annals*, 1925 only mentions that four men were injured, indicating incorrectly that no one was killed.

42. Malloy, *Annals*, 1926.

43. AAO 3-28, February 9 (O'Connor to Gaboury) and 15 (Gaboury to O'Connor).

44. *ProJo*, April 25, 1926, claimed that four had died of the influenza, but Brother Mary Ryan died of a heart condition on February 15, *before* the epidemic began.

45. Ibid., April 25, 1926.

46. AAO 3-28, O'Connor to Gaboury, July 17, year not given. The letter in question is found in the Oka archives between one of February 12, 1925, and another of October 27 of the same year. The letter refers to the arrival of the model choir stall which had not been sent as late as February 15, 1926. For this reason it is preferable to situate the letter in 1926 rather than 1925. The news of O'Connor's illness accords well with what we learn of the "serious illness" that prompts Dom Obrecht in May to bring John to Gethsemani for a rest. The present letter would have been written after his return to the Valley.

47. *Woonsocket Call*, December 10, 1926:2.

48 *ProJo*, March 20, 1927. This article is the only source of information we have concerning this act of the bishop. The bishop's journal has an entry on August 26, 1927: "Father J. M. O'Connor, Prior at Monastery, O. L. of the Valley. Gave $5000 from C. C. F." The whole entry is a long one that records various contacts of the bishop on that day, and it is not even clear if the second incomplete sentence cited here refers to the monastery at all, although this seems probable. Somewhat earlier we learn from the monastery's account books that between the end of May 1926 and October 26 two notes were taken out adding up to $30,000. It is possible that the present transaction is linked to the sum mentioned in the *ProJo* article cited.

It is impossible today to arrive at an accurate accounting of all the expenses that went into the building of the abbey church.

49. By this time Father Michael had become the official public relations figure in dealing with the press, and we get a somewhat overblown picture of his role in the planning and realization of the building: "Envisaged by Father Michael years before the first stone of its impressive solidity was taken from the hillside

of the monastery quarry, the completed edifice is a tribute to his grasp of the artistic, combined with the practical. . . ."

50. *Pawtucket Times,* February 26, 1927. The dedication took place only on November 21, 1928.

51. AAG *Annals,* 1927:50.

52. Ibid., 1928:53. Along the way Obrecht had also brought the General to the celebration in honor of Cardinal Dougherty's jubilee.

53. *ProJo,* June 12, 1928. There is no mention in the sources of Obrecht accompanying the General to New York. Concerning Benedict's visit to Gethsemani, we read in AAG *Annals,* June 21, 1928:56: "It has been the principle of Dom Edmond to bring to Geth from time to time one or other of the brethren of the Valley in order to knot closely together the motherhouse and its filiation."

Chapter Nineteen: A New Church

1. The full rite of "Dedication of a Church" was never carried out at the Valley. The present ceremony was simply a solemn blessing.

2. *ProJo,* November 22, 1928:8.

3. The activities on this level seemed to vary considerably throughout history, and it is impossible to say exactly what went on here immediately after the opening of the building. At later periods, the cider press was located here along with the wine cellar, and the laundry.

4. The clerestory windows on the north side also showed some irregularities since the old 1902 building had been tied into the new one. This meant that the last two windows were walled up, although once again the jambs of these blind windows reflected those of the windows in the south clerestory. Likewise, on the north side the last three bays were also provided with blind arches.

5. The name "jube" was based on the first word of the request for a blessing which the reader made to the abbot before beginning to read: "Jube, Domne, benedicere." [Pray, Lord, a blessing!] This type of structure was not unique to Cistercian churches but was common in other churches, particularly where there were choirs of monks or canons.

6. A cross originally donated to Dom John by his relatives for the main altar of the church was eventually moved to a position in the south transept. From there it was transferred to the jube at a later time. (Such crosses placed on the jube would give rise to the expression, "rood screen" as applied to the screening structure as a whole.) Later on, it was moved once again when a copy of the Limpias crucifix replaced it on the jube. The old cross was then placed against the window on the east wall of the church in the tribune of the retreatants.

7. These stalls were venerable relics that had been brought from Petit Clairvaux. The space in the brothers' choir was further reduced by the presence of two confessionals that had been built around the screen separating this choir from the guests' chapel.

8. The following year a door was opened in the north transept, leading into the new wing of the monastery then under construction. It seems likely that provisions were already made for this when the church itself was being built.

Provision must also have been made at the time of the church's construction for a doorway at ground level in the north transept that would eventually lead to a sacristy on the ground floor of the proposed wing.

9. The crucifix had been offered to Dom John by his relatives.

10. *ProJo,* April 14, 1929:8.

11. AAG *Annals,* 1929:57, 62.

12. Ibid., 1929:57.

13. AOCSO *Visitation Reports* 1929:3. The points noted here are found under the heading of "Observations."

Chapter Twenty: **The 1930s: Enter Malloy**

1. Malloy, *Journal,* October 16, 1930.

2. Ibid., October 20, 1930.

3. Ibid., October 7, 1930. The prostration and the prayers mentioned refer to the prayers offered in church for a monk returning from a journey.

4. Malloy, *Journal,* July 15, 1933.

5. AOCSO List of Indults, April 28, 1930. The General Chapter of 1930 also confirmed this Indult. See *Acts of General Chapter of 1930,* p. 6. It is not clear why this was necessary since the Indult had already been issued. Perhaps the chapter had to confirm its use. In any case the building program was well under way before the chapter began.

The old cemetery was situated on the site chosen for the new building, and it was necessary to move the bodies of those buried there to a new site to the southwest of the new church.

6. Hindle's name no longer appears on the plans for this building.

7. Malloy notes that on January 12, 1931: "I also almost finished revising the architect's sketch of a future porter's lodge...." Work on this building, however, was not begun until late 1936. Concerning the master plan, we read in Malloy, *Journal,* December 9, 1932: "Rev. Father gave me the plans of remaining monastery buildings to alter in half a dozen places. May the good God through

the help of St. Joseph hasten the day when we shall see them completed and in use!" The reproduction of an elevation of the main facade of the new building in *ProJo*, July 1, 1932, shows that the actual plans were already in existence at that time, at least in part.

8. An article in *ProJo*, January 6, 1933 announced that the booklet had been published that week. It also indicated that there were no immediate plans for beginning with the construction of the buildings shown. Rather, "The preparation of the pamphlet was prompted by the interest of many friends of the monastery in the plans for the proposed retreat house."

9. *ProJo*, July 1, 1932. The "Cenacle" in Newport, Rhode Island was already having great success in offering retreats for women.

10. Malloy, *Journal*, April 27, 1934.

11. Ibid., October 24, 1935.

12. The present shape of the novitiate building has been modified by later revisions. The link between the west wing and the building has most recently been destroyed in connection with the construction of a new building for the Cumberland Public Library. This was completed and opened to the public in March 2000. Yet older photos show traces of the fact that certain elements of the main cloister area of the proposed north wing were being provided for in the link that was constructed between it and the west wing. See Figure 32.

13. On the 1931 list he does appear as cellarer. The following years, however, he is described as sub-cellarer, no doubt due to the fact that the then current practice of the Order was to restrict the office of cellarer to choir monks. Nonetheless, no "cellarer" is listed for the monastery throughout this period until 1943, when, after the appointment of Fr Edmund as superior *ad nutum*, Father Paulinus Fitzgerald is named to the office.

14. The only other monk sent to Gethsemani for studies after this would be Father John Mary Cefai, who left for Gethsemani on January 17, 1933, and after a rather lengthy stay was ordained there on December 21, 1935, returning to the Valley only on April 20, 1936.

15. See Malloy, *Journal*, August 11, 1931: "Short interview with C. about course of studies. Until now there has apparently been no course; he marvels that the monastery kept going, says that the work is God's will and will advance."

16. "On Sunday, January 18, we had for the first time a 'Missa Festiva' with deacon, subdeacon and incense. Henceforth we are to follow the ceremonial for all the different grades of High Mass." Malloy, *Annals*, 1931.

17. In the course of 1933 it was decided that these responsories would be sung on four occasions each year: Christmas, Easter and "two summer feasts." (No doubt one of these would be the Assumption on August 15.)

18. All of these changes were made at the behest of the Father Immediate. See specific years in Malloy, *Annals.*

19. Malloy, *Journal,* January 26, 1933.

20. The session took place on April 13–16, 1936.

21. Malloy, *Journal,* April 29, 1933.

22. On October 22 not long after his entrance Malloy relates his "editing" of a "history of this place" consigned to him by Dom John. He had finished the work in a week and soon began typing it. (Cf. October 22, 31, and December 13 in the *Journal.*) On December 8, 1930, Dom John's "Annals of Our Lady of the Valley" were being read in the refectory. These were described by Malloy as "very brief accounts of the chief events of each year, full of varied interest and showing literary beauty in the occasional descriptions." (Malloy, *Journal,* December 8, 1930). On December 15 we read: "Rev. Father gave me the diary of two European trips to 'edit' as a supplement of the 'Annals' referred to on December 8." As late as July 16, 1934, he was still at work on the latter project. By October 13 it had been completed, and it was decided to read it in the refectory.

23. Malloy, *Journal,* October13, 1934. This document written in the hand of Malloy himself is presently in the archives of Our Lady of Guadalupe Abbey.

24. It would seem that Aelred was working as secretary even earlier, for his name appears as one of the signatees of the financial committee in the account books on June 30, 1931.

25. AAG *Annals,* May 18, 1933:94. Presumably he met Dom Corentin at the boat in New York. Dom Corentin would visit the Valley on his way back east in June.

26. Malloy, *Journal,* July 31, 1933.

27. Ibid., September 28, 1934. The visitation lasted from September 30 to October 6.

28. Malloy, *Journal,* May 6, 1936.

29. AAS Transcription of fragment of letter from AOCSO (shelfmark not identified), O'Connor to (Anthony) Daly, April 24, 1937. There is no record of an answer from Daly.

30. Malloy, *Journal,* July 7, 1938.

31. Ibid., April 18, 1939.

32. Malloy, *Annals,* 1937.

33. Malloy, *Journal,* April 6, 1937.

34. Ibid., April 5, 1937.

35. Ibid., June 2, 1937.

36. AAMM (no shelfmark), O'Connor to O'Connell, January 15, 1938.

37. Malloy, *Annals,* 1938.

Chapter Twenty-One: **The Decline of Father John**

1. Malloy, *Journal,* June 29, 1939.

2. In the course of 1939 Father John Mary Cefai, who had never really settled down after his return from studies at Gethsemani, had begun to behave strangely. This turned out to be a ploy to facilitate his departure from the monastery. And in February 1940 he obtained an indult of secularization and went to work as a diocesan priest.

3. AAG Valley files, Dunne to Smets, July 4, 1940.

4. AAG Valley files, Dunne to Smets, August 10, 1940.

5. Malloy, *Journal,* October 28, November 20, 1940.

6. Ibid., December 30, 1940.

7. Ibid., August 22, 1941. The Trappists were known for their strict (although not absolute) silence. Sign language was extensively used to obviate the need for speech. This often caused more confusion and distraction than if they had spoken.

8. The WPA was in operation between 1936 and 1940. This building was certainly in existence by 1939 when it appears on an aerial photograph made that year.

The conversion of the building is mentioned in AAG Valley files, Futterer to Dunne, April 11, 1944. On this occasion Dom Edmund noted that the structure was put up "three years ago at a cost of $7,000" and that the cost of conversion would come to $2,000.

9. AOCSO Spencer Correspondence 1941, Dunne to Smets, December 2, 1941.

10. Malloy, *Journal,* July 5, 1942.

11. Reported by Father Aelred in AAG Dunne files, Walsh to Dunne, September 12, 1942.

12. AOCSO Spencer Correspondence 1943, Dunne to Nogues, undated. Though undated this document best fits the period following the 1943 visitation than that of 1942, since it was written as soon as Frederic returned home and consequently was unaware that John's first request had been turned down.

13. AAG Valley files, Dunne to (Dom Anthony) Daly (definitor), July 12, 1943.

14. AOCSO Spencer 68, Dunne to Barbaroux, September 25, 1943.

15. Malloy, *Journal*, September 1-2, 1943. The mention of "2 Rev. Fr." probably refers to Dom Frederic and Dom John.

16. AAG Valley files, Dunne to Barbaroux, September 25, 1943. This letter narrates for the definitory the sequence of events leading up to Dom Frederic's September 1 visit to the Valley.

17. AAG Valley files, Futterer to Dunne, October 8, 1943.

18. Archives of the Congregation of Religious 4997/43; AOCSO List of Indults, November 9, 1943; Archive of Apostolic Delegate to the United States (no protocol number visible on photocopy). By this appointment Father Edmund became in effect a superior ad nutum. However, since the appointment came directly from the Holy See and not the Order, the Holy See itself would need to consent to any change in his status. In such cases an appointee is named a superior *ad nutum Sanctae Sedis*.

19. See AAG Valley files, Futterer to Dunne, December 20, 1943, where Dom Edmund described his office as "undercellerar."

20. AAG Valley files, Futterer to Dunne, December 20, 1943.

21. Earlier on, the monastery had made a first step towards mechanization with the purchase of a caterpillar tractor (which was of little use in agricultural operations save to drag heavy loads) and a Pierce Arrow truck. The first mention of the plan to purchase a tractor is found in AAG Valley files, Futterer to Dunne, January 20, 1944.

22. The information of the workings of the farm during this period is based on various interviews with Brother Dominic Mihm and Brother Leo Gregory.

23. AAG Valley files, Futterer to Dunne, February 15, 1944. Edmund himself seemed genuinely impressed with the way both of these men received the changes, as we read in AAG Valley files, Futterer to Dunne, December 20, 1943: "I think Father Michael and Father Aelred have a reserve of a spiritual strength wholly unsuspected; they have given general edification." Later on Edmund could report that Michael was doing well and was "affable, good natured and respectful" (AAG Valley files, Futterer to Dunne, February 15, 1944).

24. Malloy, *Journal*, June 24, 1944.

25. We also owe the details concerning dairy activities to interviews with Brother Leo Gregory as well as Brother Dominic.

26. Ibid., September 9, 1944. He notes that the old barn having been cleaned, sprayed and whitewashed was being used for grading and storing apples.

27. During this postwar period Brother Leo was to make good use of war surplus material, thanks to the high priority held by war veterans who had entered the monastery after their stint in the service. There was also the added advantage of discounts offered to religious organizations.

28. Malloy, *Journal*, October 2, 1944.

29. Cumberland Town Hall Records of Deeds, Book 113:354–357: Hamel property (May 1), Angell woods and orchards (June 12), Waterman farm (August 8), Fogarty property (July 12). We learn from Malloy (*Journal*, May 25, 1944) that the plan had won the approval of both Dom Frederic and the Apostolic Delegate, although only the Angell property is mentioned there. The purchase of the Angell property was already being considered as far back as April 14 (AAS Typed statement of the Secretary, Father Ambrose Davidson). On May 30 permission was granted by the Apostolic Delegate to borrow $2,040 to buy land (Archives of the Apostolic Delegate of the USA, Document G-16627/44).

30. A note of caution was sounded by Father Ambrose in his letter to Dunne explaining the reasons for his resignation as secretary. He complained that the question of the purchase of the Angell land was laid before the chapter one morning without any possibility of discussion and that votes were taken in the afternoon. "We are partners in a first-class, Yankee hard-deal. . . . Angell is selling us the tail-end of what he does not want, and we are paying more for the tail end than the assessed value of the whole" (AAG Valley files, Davidson to Dunne, May 27, 1944).

31. The document found in AAG in the Valley files is without heading or date. The state of affairs described there shows that the letter must have been written sometime between August 8 and October 2. While the Waterman property had already been purchased (on August 8), the new laundry building had not yet been begun. This latter was voted on by the Valley chapter only in October 2. Work began several days later, but it dragged on over a number of months.

32. AAG Valley files, Financial Statements of March 31, 1944 and May 28, 1944.

33. AAG Valley files, O'Leary to Dunne, undated, but written certainly after January 6 when Dom Celsus arrived at the Valley.

34. See Malloy, *Journal*, February 27, March 5, April 12, 1945.

35. AAG Valley files, Futterer to Dunne, March 2, 1945.

36. AAG Valley files, Futterer to Dunne, April 20, 1945. On May 4 the Apostolic Delegate confirmed permission for the monastery to spend $35,000 on these projects.

37. AOCSO, File folder unknown, Dunne to "Padre Procuratore," April 26, 1945 (from a copy in the archives of AAS). The approval of the Holy See was communicated by the definitory to Dom Frederic on May, 24, 1945.

38. On July 4 Father Michael Holland wrote a letter to the General, asking for an "extraordinary Visitation of our monastery by a major Superior" before permitting the elevation of the monastery to the status of abbey (AOCSO Spencer 75).

39. Father Malloy, who was assigned the task of communicating with the press concerning the election, made the faux pas of revealing the results of the voting, which according to law should have remained secret. For this he was chided by Father Owen. In the future the new abbot would remain wary about too much press coverage of the monastery's news.

40. No doubt a letter was also sent to Dom Edmund, but this would have been lost in the fire of 1950.

Chapter Twenty-Two: Dom Edmund Futterer, Abbot

1. AOCSO Spencer 78, Futterer to Nogues, November 13, 1945. The new oak floor was installed by October 27, 1945. While the installation was going on, a temporary altar had been placed in the transept. The tabernacle was installed on December 13. See also the entries in Malloy's *Journal* for April 4–5, 1946, and January 23, September 24, and October 23, 1947.

2. AOCSO Spencer 78, Futterer to Nogues, November 13, 1945.

3. Malloy, *Journal*, November, 25, 1945.

4. The ambitious building was also to have a chapel with eleven altars for the use of visiting priests. Nothing was to come of the whole project, however.

5. Malloy, *Journal*, April 21, 1946.

6. *Acts of the General Chapter of 1946*, p. 28. It is difficult to imagine what this property might have been, since there were no sizable portions of land available in the immediate vicinity of the monastery. There is no record of such a transaction having taken place after the Chapter. On the other hand, one would have expected some mention of his plans for the new guesthouse, but the Acts of the meeting make no mention of this.

7. AAG Valley files, Futterer to Dunne, July 9, 1947. An outline of these initial steps taken in connection with the proposed convent is found in AAG Valley files, Hoey to Dunne, September 9, 1947.

8. Act of definitory on July 29, 1946, reported in *Acts of the General Chapter of 1947*, p. 6.

9. Malloy, *Journal*, May 27, 1946.

10. Ibid., July 6, 1947.

11. Ibid., June 30, 1946. The statistics on the numbers are found in AAG Valley files, Futterer to Dunne, July 9, 1946.

12. Malloy, *Journal*, April 21, 1946.

13. *Act of the definitory* reported in *Acts of the General Chapter of 1947*, p. 6.

14. Malloy *Journal*, June 30, 1946.

15. Ibid., August 8, 1946.

16. AABoston, Futterer to Cushing, August 21, 1946; (Secretary of the Archbishop) to Futterer, August 26, 1946.

17. AABoston, O'Connell to Cushing, September 5, 1946. It is not known if anything came of this proposed meeting.

18. Plans for this racetrack in Lonsdale for "midget cars" were afoot in the spring of 1947. Angry letters of protest were sent to the town authorities concerning the project, several of which affirmed that the monks too would object if they could speak out. An article in *ProJo* (May 6, 1947), which reports on these events, cites Brother Leo as having made the declaration, "We have no objection to Mr. McNulty's project. I don't feel that the noise of the midget autos would disturb the monks." Unfortunately the opposite turned out to be true. Perhaps the reason for this benign attitude was the fact that the impresario of the project was the monastery's friend, Edward A. McNulty. The racetrack was eventually called the "Lonsdale Speedway." It was still functioning well into the 1950s.

19. Malloy, *Journal*, November 10, 1946. This entry has an addition made on November 11 in which these words are cited.

20. Hawes to (Dom Michael) Hanbury, November 5, 1946, cited in Taylor, *Between Devotion and Design*, p. 340. Additional information concerning Hawes plans is based on sources cited in the same work on pp. 340–342.

21. Anson, *The Hermit*, p. 146.

22. AAS Hawes file.

23. Malloy, *Journal*, November 14, 1946.

24. Ibid., January, *passim*.

25. Interviews of Father Laurence Bourget, *passim*.

26. Malloy, *Journal*, March 21, 1947.

27. AOCSO Spencer 94.5 *Mémoire confidentiel pour le Révérendissime Père Abbé Général*, May 23, 1949.

28. Malloy, *Journal*, May 23, 1947. In a later entry Malloy mentions several other notables, who advised the community to move, among them Dom Celsus of Mount Melleray and Dom Columban of Achel (Malloy, *Journal*, August 29, 1948).

29. The text as it appears in the *Collectanea* is in French: "Non content de ses trois cents Trappistes de Gethsémani et des deux filiales, Notre-Dame de la Vallée et Notre Dame du Saint-Esprit, notre cher révérend Père Abbé désire susciter des Trappistines aux États-Unis, et il a accepté la paternité d'un monastère de Cisterciennes dans l'archidiocèse de Boston; bien des difficultés sont en vue, mais elles ne diminuent pas son courage, car la Croix augmente sa confiance; déjà des postulantes se proposent pour la fondation des Trappistines." *Collectanea* April, 1947.

30. AAG Dunne to Hoey, September 5, 1947.

31. Ibid., Hoey to Dunne, September 9, 1947.

32. Ibid., Dunne to Futterer, September 19, 1947.

33. Father Raymond, O.C.S.O., *Burnt Out Incense.* (New York, 1949), pp. 418–19.

34. Malloy, *Journal*, October 28, 1947.

35. *ProJo*, September 30, October 19, October 21, 1947. Father Owen was given the honor of blessing the new acquisition: "O Lord, who by thy angels did lessen the fires of Babylon for the sake of the three children . . ."

36. *ProJo*, April 5, 1948. By the end of the year we learn that Father Stephen had been made fire chief (Malloy, *Journal*, December 8, 1948).

37. AAO 2-3, Futterer to Gaboury, October 21, 1947.

38. Private interview with Brother Leo Gregory.

39. AAG Valley files, Dunne to Abbot General, December 1, 1947.

40. Malloy, *Journal*, November 26, 1947.

41. "Cumberland Monks Run Foul of Traffic Law in Indiana," undated clipping from an unidentified newspaper in Spencer's archives.

42. This seems to correspond to an architectural drawing of Malloy now in the archives of Guadalupe, which shows that, despite some later revision, this plan corresponds in a general way to what was actually carried out.

43. AOCSO List of Indults, February 22, 1948.

44. AAG Spencer files, Hoey to Fox, April 20, 1948. We also learn from this letter that Dom Edmund already had in mind a *second* foundation to be made when financial resources would become available.

45. Unidentified newspaper article in Spencer archives.

46. It eventually had to be removed because of decay, but its wood was used as material for a number of carvings.

47. Malloy, *Journal*, February 22, 1948.

48. Ibid., April 28, 1948.

49. *ProJo*, October 3, 1948. Malloy reports seeing the stone being used on October 13 (*Journal*, 1948).

50. Malloy, *Journal*, March 19, June 14, 1948. Other improvements at the Valley this year included the removal of the unsightly old water tower on March 29, and the renovation of the infirmary including the installation of an operating room on September 10.

Chapter Twenty-Three: Spencer on the Horizon

1. The copy of the *Previews* listing that has survived is undated, but the fact that the original price shown has been cancelled in favor of a lower one suggests that the booklet went through more than one printing.

2. Malloy, *Journal*, August 28, 1948.

3. An outline of these contacts is presented in AOCSO Spencer 94.5, Minutes of Private Council Meeting at Spencer, July 21, 1948. See also Dom Edmund's first letter to the Bishop in connection with the matter: AAS Transfer to Spencer dossier, Futterer to O'Leary, May 29, 1948.

4. Text of Dom Edmund's presentation to the chapter cited in AOCSO Spencer 94.5, Minutes of the Private Council Meeting, February 15, 1949.

5. AAS Transfer to Spencer dossier, *Concerning the transfer of the Abbey of Our Lady of the Valley from Rhode Island to Massachusetts.* Undated.

6. *Acts of General Chapter of 1948*, p. 21.

7. AAS Transfer to Spencer dossier, Report of the Meeting of the Conventual Chapter, August 29, 1948.

8. AAG Spencer files, Futterer to Fox, January 3, 1949.

9. Ibid., Futterer to Fox, March 26, 1949. The second visit to Texas was at least partially in response to an invitation by a local bishop concerning the possibility of a foundation there.

10. AOCSO Spencer 94.5, Minutes of the Private Council Meeting, February 15, 1949.

11. Ibid., Minutes of the Private Council Meeting, February 17, 1949. John Duggan, president of Chapman Valve Manufacturing Company in Springfield, Massachusetts, was a friend of Brother Leo. Contrary to Leo's hopes Duggan was not forthcoming with funds.

12. Ibid., Minutes of the Private Council Meeting, February 18, 1949.

13. Ibid.

14. AAG Spencer files, Futterer to Fox, March 26, 1949.

15. AAS Transfer to Spencer dossier, Haffert to (Harry) John, April 29, 1949. Brother Leo maintains that Peter Grace also visited with Sagendorph in order to help bring the price down. There is no written record of this, however.

16. At the time the matter was proposed to a vote of the Valley Chapter the price was indicated as $175,000. By the time of the *Previews* listing it had dropped to $145,000 and, in a later listing of the same firm, to $120,000.

17. AAS Transfer to Spencer dossier, Handwritten notes of Dom Edmund, obviously drawn up in view of a phone call to Harry John. Though not dated, these make reference to Haffert's visit in late April.

18. AOCSO Visitation Reports, Spencer 1949 under the heading "VI. Observations et Suggestions." Normally such documents would be sent by the visitor to the Abbot General, along with a more formal report on the visitation. In this case it is the Abbot General himself who is setting down his impressions. Two versions of the report for this 1949 visitation have survived: an apparently earlier one totally handwritten, the other with many of the entries typed. In both cases the material under "VI. Observations et Suggestions" is handwritten and consists of simple notes, some of them incomplete sentences.

19. Ibid. The earlier version adds further comment to the suggestive mention of the phrase "houses of pleasure": "music hall [in English in the original] – houses of ill repute [maisons de nuit] – girls, dancing." This seems like an overblown description of the barroom and the nearby polka parlor!

A second memorandum from certain officers of the community was presented to the General on May 24. It stressed the fact that the encroachment of the town on the monastery was less important than the attitude of some in the community towards "the world."

20. AAS Transfer to Spencer dossier, *Statement on the "Spencer Proposal" and Transfer*, undated but clearly written within a month of the purchase of Alta Crest.

21. These latter details are mentioned in a later letter of Edmund to the General, in which he recalled discussions that had taken place at the May visitation (AOCSO Spencer 94.8, Futterer to Nogues, August 12, 1949).

22. After all of the excitement of the previous months, on July 31 Dom Edmund's health began to fail, and the doctors insisted upon complete rest. He was transferred to the infirmary, although by October 26 he had made considerable improvement (AAG Spencer files, Fox to Futterer, October 26, 1949).

Chapter Twenty-Four: **The New Home: A First Move**

1. Much of the information on the early history of the farm is based on Fiske, *History of Spencer* 34–37, as well as on certain research materials which the author has kindly made available to readers at the Richard Sugden Library in Spencer.

2. Among these were also the Hayes and the John P. Day farms.

3. The name of this road has varied throughout its history. We generally refer to it according to its more recent name: Alta Crest Road.

4. Fiske, *History of Spencer*, p. 35.

5. *Spencer New Leader*, January 4, 1907.

6. The early version of this building appears in old photographs. Its exterior was finished in what seems to be a kind of stucco with half-timbering, with a series small windows set high up in its walls. There seems to be little doubt that the new building was set up at least partially on the foundations of the earlier one, even though there is no direct evidence apart from the photographs that this was the case. No architectural plans survive for this structure, and no other information is available concerning its architects.

7. The Manning farmhouse had disappeared by the time the property was purchased by the monks.

8. See Malloy, *Journal*, August 28, 1948, which noted: "The owner wants to sell, as income tax and the cost of labor make dairying unprofitable now."

9. *Catalog for the Alta Crest Farms Milking Herd Dispersal*, undated.

10. Unfortunately the *Previews* booklet on the property is undated.

11. Father Laurence has the impression that the building was to be constructed on Manning Hill, unlike the Eggers and Higgins monastery. (Taped interview of Father Laurence Bourget, March 7, 2001).

12. The building proposed to the vote of Spencer's conventual chapter on August 29, 1948, was described as having "one, two, or three wings with complete cloister" (AAS Transfer to Spencer dossier, Report of Chapter Meeting, August 29, 1948).

13. Ibid., *Supplementary Report on Financial Condition of Our Lady of the Valley,* October 31, 1949.

14. It is not clear when the deeds were indeed passed. *ProJo* reported on July 2, 1949, that "negotiations were said to be completed today"; in its July 16 issue it speaks of the purchase having taken place "yesterday."

15. AAS Transfer to Spencer dossier, *Purchase Agreement*: 2.

16. AAG Spencer files, Futterer to Fox, January 3, 1949.

17. AAS Transfer to Spencer dossier, Futterer to Nogues, August 13, 1949. There is no way of knowing which of the architects Edmund is referring to, Eggers and Higgins or Meacham. Edmund was in touch with Meacham by mid-September, yet the Eggers and Higgins plan had already been in existence about a month.

18. AAS Transfer to Spencer dossier, Futterer to Nogues, August 13, 1949; Nogues to Futterer, August 24, 1949.

19. AOCSO Spencer 94.12, Futterer to Nogues, September 2, 1949. The report itself (94.12a) is dated September 3.

20. AOCSO Spencer 94.20, Notes of the commission of the General Chapter of 1949 assigned to study Spencer's request for a loan of $400,000, undated.

21. AOCSO Spencer 94.11, *Supplementary Report on financial condition of O. L. of the Valley,* October 31, 1949.

22. On December 12, 1949, another set of drawings had been produced by Maginnis and Walsh, but variations from their original plan of November 3, 1949, seem slight. The name of the abbey now begins to appear on the drawings as "Holy Cross Abbey."

23. AAS Transfer to Spencer dossier, *Petition au Définitoire au sujet du transfer* [*sic*] *à Spencer.* February 15, 1950.

24. Father Paul Schiebler's diary, which is preserved in the monastery's archives, covers in detail the period extending from February 1 to April 5. This is followed by eight additional entries relative to scattered days between June 27, 1950, and January 6, 1951. It is crucial for our knowledge of the happenings at Spencer during the months of February and March 1950.

25. AAS Father Paul Shiebler papers, *Diary,* February 12, 1950.

26. Ibid., February 16, 28, 1950.

27. Ibid., March 13, 1950.

28. The new barn was in the planning phase in mid-February, 1950, as we learn from AAS Transfer to Spencer dossier, *Petition to the definitory,* February 15, 1950:1–2.

29. Bishop Wright had been ordained as Auxiliary Bishop of Boston in 1947.

30. Ibid., *Diary*, March 9, 1950.

31. There was even an intermediate step! After the Bishop's objection the next choice was "Mount St. Joseph," as we learn in AAS Transfer to Spencer Box, Futterer to Nogues, March 20, 1950.

32. "Bishop Approves Trappists' Plans for Abbey in Spencer," *Worcester Daily Telegram*, March 16, 1950.

33. John McMahon was a wealthy mill owner from Providence who had purchased an elegant house with surrounding land in Franklin, Massachusetts, as a second home. Some of his land was sold to the Valley as part of the lands for the convent. He was to prove a good friend to the nuns from the time of their arrival. Upon his death they inherited all of his land in Franklin as well as the house, which would become the guesthouse.

34. Malloy, *Journal*, March 19, 1949. The cornerstone was carved by the Howard Benson Co. of Newport, R.I.

35. AAG Spencer files, Futterer to Fox, March 26, 1949.

36. Malloy, *Journal, March 26*, 1949.

37. Ibid., *May 7 ,* 1949.

38. From this time forth, Malloy's comments on happenings at the Valley are far fewer in number and are, in any case, secondhand.

39. Sister Michael Howe had originally entered St. Romuald and made her perpetual vows there. Later she transferred to Glencairn in view of becoming part of the Wrentham foundation. Several of the sisters later changed their names: Stephen to Stephanie, Celsus to Andrée, Andrew to Grace, and Emmanuel to Carol. At this period those professed were in perpetual rather than solemn vows.

40. The details of this trip were kindly provided by Sister Carol Holohan of Wrentham.

41. In accordance with Canon law the nuns were more restricted to the "enclosure" of their monastery than were the monks.

42. Recollections of those still living differ in their versions of the details of this visit. One person seems to remember that the sisters spent the entire day there, assisting also at Mass; others did not remember assisting at Vespers and Benediction. All agree however on the fact of the meal!

43. AAS Wrentham files, *Declaration of the definitory on Wrentham,* January 14, 1950.

Chapter Twenty-Five: The Fire

1. AAS Newspapers, Unidentified clipping. The present account of the fire is based on interviews of the monks who experienced it as well as articles that appeared in the following newspapers: *Providence Journal* (March 22, 23, 24, 26, 27, 28, 1950), *Providence Visitor* (March 23, 1950), *Pawtucket Times* (March 22, 23, 1950), *Woonsocket Call* (March 22, 1950).

2. AAS ACM Mt. Melleray file, Futterer to O'Connell, April 24, 1950.

3. One of the guests in the monastery that night noted: "…even during the day we noticed that we were smelling gas around the dining area, near the lift that brought the food up from the kitchen. This is where the odor was prominent during the day." (Taped interview of Mr. Laurent Doire, August 30, 1999) This might suggest the possibility of the fire originating in the basement, but as we have seen, Brother Michael found that there were no flames in the basement when he went down there to inspect the situation after the fire was already well under way.

4. The monastery was raised to the status of abbey in 1969.

5. This count is based on a personnel list for the Valley in AAS Personnel Lists.

6. AAS ACG Nogues file, Futterer to Nogues, March 27, 1950. In actual fact fewer than 40 remained at the Valley.

7. Ibid.

8. AAS CFI Fox file, Futterer to Fox, March 31, 1950; an unidentified and undated newspaper clipping relates that debris was being used "on a Douglas Pike project at Twin Rivers, Smithfield [Rhode Island]."

Chapter Twenty-Six: Our Lady of Refuge: The CCC Camp

1. AAS Taped Interview of Brother Bernard Matthews, April 25, 2001.

2. Taped Interview of Fr. Richard Gans, August 3, 2000.

3. Malloy, *Journal,* November 25, 1945: "Father Prior told me of progress of vestment industry under F. Alberic." Later on March 6, 1949, Malloy relates that Brother Blaise "returns to the vestment department." A community list indicating work assignments at the camp shows eight persons as working in the "Holy Rood Guild." The names of Father Alberic and Brother Blaise do not appear on the list, the latter being much occupied with the restoration project at the Valley.

4 . AAS AC Maginnis file, Maginnis to "Father John," June 2, 1950.

5. AAS Transfer to Spencer dossier, Futterer to Gondal, March 19, 1950.

6. Brother Leo, *Seven Foundations*, p. 26. It is not clear whether Hidden Valley had already been found before the fire and was indeed the one referred to by Dom Edmund in his letter of March 19 to the definitory.

7. The property had been purchased in 1748 by his relative, Ralph Wormeley IV. It is rumored that the young George Washington, then a surveyor, tipped Wormeley off that the property was up for sale. It was his son John who first called the plantation "Cool Spring." We owe this information to the kindness of Dom Robert Barnes, abbot of Berryville, and its historian, Brother James Sommers.

8. The owner later made a proposal of selling his livestock and farm equipment along with the property itself, but this proved to be impossible from his point of view. At some time during this month Harry John pledged to give $50,000 towards this purchase, a pledge which he redeemed on January 6, 1952.

9. AAS Visitation Cards, 1950.

10. AOCSO Visitation Reports, Spencer 1950.

11. AAS ACM Mount Melleray file, April 24, 1950.

12. AAS ACM Oka file, Gaboury to Futterer, April 5, 1950.

13. AAS CFI Fox file, Futterer to Fox, July 31, 1950.

14. AAS ACM Glencairn file, Shaw to Futterer, August 12, 1950.

15. AOCSO Spencer 110, *Rapport sommaire sur les moyens proposés pour le rétablissement de la Communauté de Notre Dame de la Vallée – à l'état du 6-IX-50.* This otherwise untitled document was probably brought to the chapter by Edmund himself.

16. AAS AC Cushing file, Cushing to Hoey, September 23, 1950.

17. Had not Mother St. John passed away by this time, she would have been a very likely candidate for the election. This relatively young sister died at the age of 38 on May 15, 1950, to the distress of the entire community.

18. Dom Edmund himself dropped in frequently and even came for a longer stay when he contracted pneumonia at the camp. Interested visitors often came up the Alta Crest Road to see how things were going, and it was Father Thomas who greeted them and chatted about the plans. He also remembers receiving certain less formal visits from some of the Ayrshire cattle, which would on occasion peer into the windows of the building.

19. The abbey's records show that some new cows were purchased in the course of 1950. It is not clear whether this took place at the Valley before the fire or at Spencer. The latter possibility seems less likely in view of the upcoming purchase of the Broad Rock herd in 1951.

20. Overestimating the abbey's future capacity for milk production, additional building tiles were purchased with a view to creating a new wing for the barn further south and along the same axis, but these were eventually sold to a farmer nearby, who used them for constructing a barn of his own. Additional silos were also purchased for this extension but were eventually sold on auction.

21. AAS AC H. John file, Futterer to H. John, August 7, 1950.

22. AAS ACM Oka file, Futterer to Gaboury, October 6, 1950.

23. AAS Plans and Elevations, *Revised Kitchen drawing for Trappist Monastery. Spencer, Mass. September 12, 1950.* The original drawing (*Proposed Kitchen drawing for Trappist Monastery, Spencer, Mass.*) was drawn up on May 8, 1950. Both drawings indicate Father Paul, O.C.S.O. as the contact person, even though by September 12 Brother Blaise Drayton had long taken over the direction of the project.

24. AAS CFI Fox file, Futterer to Fox, October 30, 1950.

25. AAS ACG Nogues file, Futterer to Nogues, October 31, 1950.

26. AAB Coutant files, Futterer to Coutant, January 30, 1953.

27. AAS AC Peter Grace file, Grace to Futterer, October 30, 1950.

Chapter Twenty-Seven: A New Beginning

1. AAS Taped Interview of Fr. Thomas Keating, July 15, 1999.

2. AAS Taped Interview of Br. Jerome Collins, May 18, 2001.

3. In a last effort to reverse the decision Spencer appealed once again to the Cardinal in November, and a meeting was held in New York between Graymoor, Spencer, and the Cardinal, but nothing came of it.

4. AAS Taped Interview of Fr. Thomas Keating, July 15, 1999.

5. AAS CD1 Futterer to Gondal, May 28, 1951. There was only one negative vote.

6. Reported in the *Acts of General Chapter of 1951*, p. 6.

7. AAS CD1 Memorandum of Futterer to definitory, August 27, 1951.

8. AAS AC (Leo) Gregory to (Charles) Grace, August 22, 1951.

9. See AAS CFI Fox file, Futterer to Fox, November 19, 1952; Br. Leo, *Seven Foundations*, p. 30.

10. AOCSO Visitation Reports, Spencer 1951.

11. AOCSO Visitation Reports, Spencer 1951, attached letter, Fox to Nogues, August 31, 1951.

12. *Acts of the General Chapter of 1951,* p. 19.

13. AAS ACG Sortais file, Sortais to Futterer, September 15, 1951. The Abbot Vicar was chosen by the General Chapter to substitute for the Abbot General in case of death or resignation. He was to convoke an extraordinary General Chapter for the election of a new General within three months. (*Constitutions OCSO 1924,* Chapter 2:28, p. 12.

14. AAS CD1 Sortais (Abbot Vicar) to Futterer, September 15, 1951. This letter of Sortais to Futterer of September 15 is the only document we have that makes mention of earlier plans having been sent to the definitory.

15. AAS AC Meacham file, Meacham to Futterer, October 13, 1951.

16. Ibid., Futterer to Meacham, October 23, 1951.

17. AAS ACG, Sortais file, Futterer to Sortais, November 8, 1951

18. Though they bear the name of Meacham, these drawings are unfortunately undated. Yet the covering letter sent along with them clearly make reference to four of the pieces of this set (AAS ACG, Sortais file, Futterer to Sortais, November 1, 1951). It is possible that Meacham had managed to finish only these four by October 28 but had continued his work after this date.

19. One would like to know more about the even earlier phase of discussions during which the monastic planners thrashed out questions that had eventually been decided by November 1, and that no longer appear even on Meacham's earliest plans.

Chapter Twenty-Eight: Building a Monastery

1. AAS AC Oechsler file, Bourget to Oechsler, June 5, 1952.

2. AAS AC H. John file, Futterer to H. John, April 23, 1952.

3. AAS, Chapter talk of Dom Gabriel Sortais at Spencer, May 1, 1952.

4. The visitation card is a report made to the community, in the form of an exhortation concerning areas where the visitor feels improvement is needed. Congratulation is offered concerning the positive aspects of the community's life.

5. AOCSO Visitation Reports, Spencer, 1952.

6. AAS CFI Fox file, Fox to Futterer, May 21, 1952.

7. AAS ACG Sortais file, Sortais to Futterer, May 23, 1952.

8. Ibid., Sortais to Futterer, June 5, 1952.

9. Ibid., Futterer to Sortais, June 9, 1952.

10. Ibid., Sortais to Futterer, June 5, 1952.

11. Ibid., Futterer to Sortais, June 14, 1952.

12. Ibid., June 2, 1952.

13. AAS AC Oechsler file, Futterer to Oechsler, July 21, 1952. Oechsler had been a friend and benefactor of the monastery since the 1930s. He also served as notary at Dom Edmund's election as abbot in 1945.

14. AAS ACG Sortais file, Futterer to Sortais, August 7, 1952.

15. Ibid., Sortais to Futterer, September 10, 1952.

16. Work on the foundations for the entire complex would continue independently of the aboveground building throughout the first half of August.

17. AAS ACM Conyers file, Futterer to McGann, August 13, 1952.

18. AAS Taped interview of Alan Hudon, March 4, 2002.

19. AAS ACM Conyers file, Futterer to McGann, August 13, 1952.

20. *Acts of the General Chapter of 1952*, p. 17.

21. At Spencer the rooms used for the conferences given to the laybrothers and the novices were called "chapter rooms" on the model of the true chapter room of the monastery. This new laybrothers' chapter room served also as common room for the brothers.

22. AAS AC H. John file, Futterer to H. John, March 11, 1953; De Rancé Inc. to Futterer, March 19, 1953.

23. This window came to be known as the Salve window, because it is the object of special veneration each evening at the end of Compline when the antiphon "Salve Regina" is sung in honor of Mary.

24. AAS Furnishings-Stained Glass 2, J. Nicolas to Drayton, undated.

25. In the light of this it seems unlikely that the round apse window shown in Hovsepian's 1951 rendering of the proposed interior of Spencer's church was the result of an early Nicolas proposal, although this cannot be ruled out. In any case, there is no record of such in the file of correspondence with Joep in the Spencer archives. It seems more likely that the idea of a round window in Spencer's apse would have been inspired by what Dom Edmund saw of Joep's work at Orval.

26. AAS ACG Sortais file, Sortais to Futterer, December 4, 1952. A copy of Dom Edmund's letter to the General has not survived in Spencer's archives, but its contents may be deduced from this answer of the General.

27. The votes were taken on December 27, 1952, and January 20, 1953, for two separate properties. See *Guadalupe Chronicle* 1:56–57.

28. *Acts of the General Chapter of 1953,* pp. 5–6.

29. AAS AC Peter Grace file, Sortais to (Peter) Grace, August 26, 1952 (translated copy of original).

30. AAS ACG Sortais file, Futterer to Sortais, February 7, 1953.

31. Ibid., Sortais to Futterer, February 5, 1953. Before he learned that Dom Louis de Gonzague had been delegated for the visitation, Edmund had written to Dom Emmanuel suggesting that the delegation be given to Dom Pacôme of Oka (AAB Coutant files, Futterer to Coutant, February 11, 1953). Judging by the dates, the letters must have crossed.

32. AAS CFI Fox file, Futterer to Fox, April 1, 1953. The expression "Regular Places" was often used in the usages of the Order to refer to the main communal areas of the monastery.

33. The author identifies himself as a simply professed laybrother who was "close to Reverend Father." Furthermore, the final sentence notes that the conversations reported had been "retold in the language of Brother Blaise."

34. The Memorandum relates events that took place on April 18–19 and is filed under these dates in AAS ACG Sortais file for 1953.

35. Brother Leo, *Dom Edmund Futterer,* p. 15. The monastery of Miraflores was not yet in existence in 1953. The comparison was one that Brother Leo made in 1993 at the time of writing. Ibid., p. 26. The monastery at la Dehesa in Chile was transferred to Miraflores in 1966.

36. Ibid., p. 26.

37. AAS CD1 Le Pennuen to Futterer, September 24, 1951.

38. AOCSO Visitation Reports, Spencer 1953.

39. AAB Coutant files, Hoey to Coutant, May 16, 1953.

40. AAS ACG Sortais file, Sortais to Futterer, May 21, 1953. The prior, Father Owen Hoey, also wrote to Dom Emmanuel (AAB Coutant files, Hoey to Coutant, May 16, 1953).

41. AAS ACG Sortais file, Sortais to Futterer, May 21, 1953.

42. AAS ACM Oka file, Futterer to (Camille) Doucet of Oka, June 5, 1953.

43. AAS AC Oechsler file, Futterer to Oechsler, June 29, 1953. See also ACM Oka File, Futterer to Doucet, June 5, 1953.

44. AAS *Notes of Brother Blaise* undated.

45. AAS AC Oechsler file, Futterer to Oechsler, June 29, 1953.

Chapter Twenty-Nine: Settling In to the New Home

1. Cf. Kinder, *Cistercian* Europe, p. 309. Since all members of the community now share the common rooms of the monastery, the laybrothers' room currently serves as meeting place for various councils and for novitiate classes.

2. Immediately behind the monks' choir there is a small space reserved for the infirm, a traditional feature in Cistercian churches. The low dividing wall is situated behind this space.

3. The rood beam was normally placed on top of the screen between the two choirs when there was no jube platform.

4. These Valley windows were composed of three adjacent panels, which had to be redistributed to make double paneled ones in order to fit the width of the Spencer windows.

5. This window was created by Robert Barrie of St. Andrew's Stained Glass Studios in Providence, Rhode Island, who was also responsible for fitting the stained glass from the Valley into the new windows of Spencer's church as well as the creation of other windows for the new monastery.

6. The pattern for this window was designed by Brother Blaise and executed by Robert Barrie.

7. AAS CFI Fox file, "Prior" to Fox, September 4, 1953; AAB Coutant files, Futterer to Coutant, September 2, 1953 and Hoey to Coutant, August 28, 1953. The latter document mentions that Edmund had hoped to spend a week in Lourdes before the chapter.

8. AAB Coutant file, Hoey to Coutant, September 7 and November 26, 1953.

9. Ibid., Hoey to Coutant, November 26, 1953.

10. The "discipline" was a small whip used on Fridays for self-flagellation.

11. *Acts of the General Chapter of 1953*, pp. 13, 27. The November 9, 1953 Decree of Rome is referred to in *Acts of the General Chapter of 1956*, p. 20.

12. Practically speaking this contained all of the Offices save Vigils.

13. The ceiling beams of the church were not stained until March 1954 (AAS AC Oechsler file, Futterer to Oechsler, March 5, 1954).

14. AAS ACG Sortais file, Futterer to Sortais, September 3, 1953.

15. Ibid., Futterer to Sortais, September 3, 1953; Sortais to Futterer, September 10, 1953.

16. AAB Coutant file, Futterer to Coutant, January 16, 1954.

17. AAS CFI Fox file, Futterer to Fox, August 16, 1954.

18. AAS AC Oechsler file, Futterer to Oechsler, August 19, 1955.

19. AAS CD1 Futterer to Daly, November 17, 1953.

20. AAS Furnishings-Stained Glass 2, Suzanne Nicolas to Drayton, June 24, 1954.

21. The first mention of these is found in AAS Furnishings-Stained Glass 2, Suzanne Nicolas to Drayton, August 1, 1955; there is no exact documentation as to when they were delivered.

22. One was hospitalized on May 4, the other on August 21.

23. AOCSO Visitation Reports, Spencer 1954.

Chapter Thirty: **A New Foundation**

1. AAS AC Vehr file, Futterer to Vehr, March 20, 1954.

2. AAB Coutant file, Futterer to Coutant, April 6, 1954 and August 9, 1954.

3. AAS AC Archdiocese of San Francisco file, Futterer to Mitty, March 21, 1955.

4. Ibid., Futterer to Mitty, April 5, 1955.

5. AAS ACG Sortais file, Sortais to Futterer, August 5, 1955. Edmund's letter to the General has not survived in Spencer's archives.

6. AAS AC Archdiocese of San Francisco file, Hoey to Mitty, September 19, 1955. See also Brother Leo in *Seven Foundations*, p. 33.

7. AAS Wrentham files, *Return of Irish Foundresses from Wrentham to Glencairn in 1955.* Undated document prepared by Sister Gertrude Kelly (around November 1, 1999).

8. Here it was stated explicitly that, in addition to its recitation once a month and on the "Great Anniversaries," the Office of the Dead would also be celebrated on November 2, and on the occasion of the death of a member of the community, while the body was being waked in the church.

9. See *Acts of the General Chapter of 1955*, pp. 14–15.

10. Brother Leo, *Seven Foundations*, p. 34. Brother Leo uses the authorial "we" in this passage. He was accompanied on this trip only by Don Joslyn.

11. AAB Coutant file, Futterer to Coutant, November 14, 1955.

12. AAS AC H. J. file, Futterer to John, November 14, 1955.

13. Brother Leo, *Seven Foundations*, p. 34.

14. AOCSO Visitation Reports, Spencer 1955. The following two citations are from this same text.

15. AAS ACG Sortais file, Sortais to Futterer, February 16, 1956.

16. Ibid., Futterer to Sortais, December 26, 1955.

17. The reference is to Dom Edmund's acceptance of the fact that the permission for a California foundation was awarded during that chapter to Gethsemani instead of to Spencer.

18. Ibid., Sortais to Futterer, January 3, 1956.

19. Ibid., Futterer to Sortais, January 9, 1956.

20. Ibid., Futterer to Coutant, February 3, 1956.

21. Note in Spencer archives. Brother Leo maintains that as early as December Father James was sent to stay at Snowmass in the Le Moy ranch house with a small group of men (Brother Leo, *Seven Foundations*, p. 34–35).

22. AAS ACG Sortais file, Sortais to Futterer, February 16, 1956.

23. AAB Coutant file, Futterer to Coutant, February 28, 1956; the decision of the definitory appears in *Acts of the General Chapter of 1956*, p. 5.

24. AAS CD1 Futterer to Moore, April 14, 1956.

25. AAS ACG Sortais file, Sortais to Futterer, May 17, 1956.

26. *Guadalupe Chronicle* 1:96; AAS ACG Sortais file, Futterer to Sortais, June 22, 1956.

Chapter Thirty-One: **The Order Updates**

1. AAB Coutant file, Futterer to Coutant, August 3, 1956. Father Edward McCorkell and Father William O'Connor were two priests of the Spencer community sent to Berryville as part of a program aimed at preparing the community for independent status.

2. Ibid., Futterer to Coutant, October 8, 1956.

3. AOCSO SS 1, Drayton to Sortais, November 23, 1956.

4. AAB Coutant file, Futterer to Coutant, November 28, 1956.

5. AAS Abbatial Correspondence, Larrain file. Futterer to Larrain, December 27, 1956.

6. AAS Abbatial Correspondence, Larrain file, Larrain to (Leo) Gregory, December 8, 1956. The letter was composed in English.

7. AAS CD1 Futterer to Sortais, March 22, 1957.

8. This and the following citations are from AAS CD1 Moore to Futterer, May 22, 1957.

9. The "Decree on Unification" also provided for a subdivision in the case of those who opted for full monastic status, namely a) those who would in some measure participate in the Divine Office and b) those who would not. The Latin terms used to describe these categories have a curious ring to the ears of English speakers: *choro addicti* and *choro non addicti,* which one might be tempted to translate as, "addicted to choir" and "not addicted to choir"! The distinction no longer appears in *Constitutions OCSO 1990.*

10. Merton, *Dancing in the Water of Life,* pp. 70–71. The sentence, "This is what more of them, or more of the real brothers, actually want—quite the contrary," is hard to interpret. In any case, it seems from the context of the whole passage that those whom Merton describes as having "genuine brothers' vocations" are in favor of the "old way." We are grateful to Paul Pearson, Director and Archivist of the Thomas Merton Center at Bellarmine University, for verifying the manuscript version of the text and to Jonathan Montaldo for communicating this information to us.

11. For the text of the report see *Acts of the General Chapter of 1957,* pp. 11-13.

12. AAS AC H. John file, H. John to Futterer, April 7, 1958. The donation was open-ended ("to be used for your general purposes"), but Edmund's letter of thanks shows that it was interpreted as part of Harry's ongoing help for Snowmass (AAS AC H. John file, Futterer to H. John, April 11, 1958).

13. AAS Definitory files, Futterer to Holohan, April 30, 1958.

14. Dom Eugene was invited back to preach the 1960 retreat.

15. AAS CD1 Futterer to Gondal, February 28, 1958.

16. They arrived there on March 19, 1958.

17. AAB Coutant file, Futterer to Coutant, November 25, 1957.

18. By March 20 he had returned to Rome.

19. Ibid., Moore to Coutant, March 8, 1958.

20. AOCSO Visitation Reports, Spencer 1958. Dom Augustine composed this text in French. The person referred to as "Father Master of the choir novices" was Father Thomas Aquinas Keating.

21. AAB Coutant file, Moore to Coutant, March 8, 1958.

22. Ibid.

23. AAS ACG Sortais file, Futterer to Sortais, May 24, 1958.

24. AAS ACG Sortais file, Sortais to Futterer, March 17, 1958.

25. Ibid., Futterer to Sortais, March 17, 1958.

26. By January 1959 the cow barn was being totally restructured to house 400 pigs.

27. AAS CD1 Futterer to Holohan, May 17, 1958. The grade cows were installed in the old Allen barn. Brother Alberic O'Connor who was in charge of the operation notes that these cows were insufficient to supply the needs of the monastery, and that he and Brother Dominic were able to quietly sell them and acquire a small herd of pedigreed cows.

28. AAS Taped interview of Father Richard Gans, August 4, 2000. Brothers Joachim and Eugene Cody (who were blood brothers) worked on the farm with Richard.

Chapter Thirty-Two: South America Looms

1. Brother Leo, *Seven Foundations*, pp. 36–39.

2. Ibid., pp. 40–41.

3. Ibid., pp. 43–44.

4. Ibid., p. 44.

5. AAS ACG Sortais file, Futterer to Sortais, May 24, 1958.

6. AAS CD1 Futterer to Holohan, April 30, 1958.

7. AAS ACG Sortais file, Sortais to Futterer, June 2, 1958.

8. AAS Undated document read at the presentation to the chapter of Spencer. Cf. also AAS AC Acosta file, Futterer to Acosta, June 9, 1958. This latter document confirms that Don Pablo also communicated this news by letter. Brother Leo, *Seven Foundations*, pp. 45–46 maintains incorrectly that Don Pablo decided to offer the land only *after* his visit to the United States, which took place in August and September.

9. These were documents sent to Dom Emmanuel to enable him to obtain a visa for the projected trip to the United States as a visitor.

10. AAB Coutant file, Futterer to Coutant, June 8, 1958.

11. For some reason, these documents are filed together with Dom Augustine Moore's Report to the General on the 1958 Visitation of Spencer (AOCSO Visitation Reports, Spencer 1958).

12. The text of the photocopy is not clear between the words "à parler" and "m'emmener voir Snowmass."

13. AOCSO, Visitation Reports, Spencer 1958, Attached documents: Coutant to Sortais, June 20, 1958. The following citations are from this first letter unless otherwise noted.

14. Ibid., Coutant to Sortais, June 23, 1958.

15. Ibid.

16. AOCSO, Visitation Reports, Spencer 1958, Attached documents: Coutant to Sortais, June 20, 1958.

17. Ibid., Coutant to Sortais, June 23, 1958.

18. AAS ACG Sortais file, Futterer to Sortais, June 15, 1958.

19. Ibid., Sortais to Futterer, June 27, 1958.

20. Decision of the definitory reported in *Acts of the General Chapter of 1958*, p. 6. The Acts of the General Chapter nowhere record an official approval for the foundation of Azul as such. The only item relative to Azul's early days is the one cited here relating the chapter's confirmation on September 12, 1958, of the definitory's earlier approval (on June 4 of the same year) of Spencer's accepting the land in Azul.

21. AAS ACG Sortais file, Futterer to Sortais, July 21, 1958. See also AAS CD1 Futterer to Holohan, July 8, 1958 and August 21, 1958.

22. Brother Leo, *Seven Foundations*, p. 45.

23. See AAS AC Acosta file, correspondence of June 16 and 23, 1958.

24. Despite this fact, those who worked on the job have no recollection of a person by this name playing a role on site during the actual construction. Mr. Louis Shine (the former Father James Shine) recalls that Mr. Ernesto Holmberg, a contractor in Buenos Aires, was consulted on the work.

25. AAS CD1 Futterer to Holohan, August 21, 1958 and October 6, 1958.

26. Brother Leo, *Dom Edmund Futterer*, p. 12.

27. AAS Taped interview of Brother Conrad Irrgang, January 15, 2002. Señor Ernesto Homberg recalls that in 1958 Father Benedict spent three days working in his studio drawing up plans for a monastery, which he described as being in "California style." We owe the latter information to the kindness of Father Ceferino Leardi, a monk of Azul, who reported a conversation he had with the engineer in February 2002.

28. AAS AC Cletus Keating file, T. Keating to Brother Alan, August 30, 1958 (letter accompanying the check for these funds); Futterer to C. Keating, September 3, 1958.

Chapter Thirty-Three: **Retrospect**

1. AAS Taped conference of Father Laurence Bourget on the occasion of the death of Dom Edmund Futterer on July 27, 1984, undated.

2. Ibid.

3. AAS Taped interview of Alan Hudon, March 5, 2002.

4. *Rule of St. Benedict* 2:2 in *RB 1980*, p. 173.

5. AOCSO Visitation Reports, Spencer 1951, attached letter: Fox to Nogues, August 31, 1951.

6. AOCSO Visitation Reports, Spencer 1953.

7. Ibid., Spencer 1954.

8. Ibid., Spencer 1955. The following two citations are from this same text.

9. AAS Tape recording of Homily by Dom Augustine Roberts after the death of Dom Edmund, undated.

Bibliography

Acts GC 1835–1891 = Vincent Hermans, *Actes des chapitres généraux des Congrégations Trappistes au XIXe siècle* (Extracts from *Analecta Cisterciensia* 1971-1974). Rome, 1975.

Acts of the General Chapters of 1892, etc. The Acts of individual General Chapters from 1892 to 1960 were published after each Chapter in a standardized format at Cîteaux, France from 1892 to 1899, at la Trappe, France in 1900, and subsequently at Westmalle, Belgium.

Anson, *The Hermit* = Peter Anson, *The Hermit of Cat Island.* New York, 1957.

Aprile, *The Abbey of Gethsemani* = Dianne Aprile, *The Abbey of Gethsemani: Place of Peace and Paradox.* Louisville, 1998.

Balfour and Koutsogiane, *Cumberland by the Blackstone* = David W. Balfour and Joyce Hindle Koutsogiane, *Cumberland by the Blackstone: 250 Years of Heritage.* Virginia Beach, Virginia, 1997.

Beitzell, *The Jesuit Missions* = Edwin Warfield Beitzell, *The Jesuit Missions of St. Mary's County, Maryland,* 2nd ed. Abell, Maryland, 1976.

Bertrand, *Bibliothèque sulpicienne* = L. Bertrand, *Bibliothèque sulpicienne ou histoire littéraire de la Compagnie de Saint-Sulpice,* 3 vols. Paris, 1900.

Boudreaux, Ephrem, *Le Petit Clairvaux: Cent ans de vie cistercienne à Tracadie en Nouvelle-Écosse, 1818-1919,* N. p., 1980.

Bouton, Jean de la Croix, O.C.S.O., *Histoire de l'ordre de Cîteaux,* 3 vols., reprint from *Fiches « cisterciennes »,* Westmalle, 1959-1968.

Bretonnière, *Vie de Dom Urbain* = Bretonnière, Hermeland, *Vie de Dom Urbain Guillet fondateur de la Trappe de Bellefontaine,* La Chapelle-Montligeon, 1899.

Brother Leo, *Seven Foundations* = [Brother Leo Gregory], *Seven Foundations, 1947-1960,* 2nd ed. Spencer, 1990.

Brother Leo, *Dom Edmund Futterer* = [Brother Leo Gregory], *Dom Edmund Futterer, 1938-1984.* Tanti Lomas, Argentina, 1993.

Burrows, *Gotham* = Edwin G. Burrows, *Gotham: A History of New York City to 1898.* New York, 1999.

Chiasson, *Fr. Vincent de Paul* = Paulette M. Chiasson, "Father Vincent de Paul Merle: Unusual Trappist, Unlikely Missionary," *Nova Scotia Historical Review* 8 (1988): 21-41.

Chiasson, *Merle* = Paulette Chiasson, "Merle, Vincent de Paul" in *Dictionary of Canadian Biography* 8:625-628. Toronto, 1985.

Cistercian Order = Anon., *The Cistercian Order: Its Object, Its Rule.* Cambridge, Massachusetts, 1905.

Code of Canon Law = *The Code of Canon Law: A Text and Commentary,* eds. James A. Coriden, Thomas J. Green, and Donald E. Heintschel. New York, 1985.

Constitutions OCSO 1925 = *Constitutions of the Order of Cistercians of the Strict Observance.* Dublin, 1925.

Constitutions OCSO 1990 = *Constitutions and Statutes of the Monks and Nuns of the Cistercian Order of the Strict Observance and Other Legislative Documents.* Rome, 1990. Ongoing updates appear on the Order's website, http://www.ocso.org/net/cstst-en.htm.

Cook, *St. Patrick's Cathedral* = Leland Cook, *St. Patrick's Cathedral: A Centennial History.* New York, 1979.

Coté, *L'Ordre de Cîteaux* = André Coté, « L'Ordre de Cîteaux et son établissement dans la Province de Québec, depuis la Révolution française jusqu'à 1935 », Thèse, Maîtrise ès arts, University of Laval, Quebec, 1971.

Courtray, *Histoire de la Valsainte* = D. A. Courtray, *Histoire de la Valsainte,* Fribourg, 1914.

Cuyler, *Pigeon Hill* = Cornelius M. Cuyler, S.S., "Pigeon Hill," *The Borromean,* November, 1947: 5-6, 23.

Devitt, *History* = Edward I. Devitt, S. J., "History of the Maryland Province," *The Woodstock Letters* 60 (1931): 218-19.

Dilhet, *État* = Jean Dilhet, *État de l'église catholique ou Diocèse des États-Unis de l'Amérique septentrionale,* translated and annotated by Patrick W. Browne. Washington, D.C., 1922.

Dunand, *Lettre* = « Lettre ou Journal du R. P. Marie Joseph [Dunand] Écrit pour son Supérieur le R. P. Abbé de la Trappe, Dom Augustin de Lestrange, en 1823, etc.; concernant ses voyages, et la mission qu'il a faite dans la Louisiane et dans le pays des Illinois, depuis l'année 1805 », in *Relation de ce qui est arrivé,* pp. 85-168.

Fiske, *History of Spencer* = Jeffrey H. Fiske, *History of Spencer, Massachusetts, 1875-1975.* Spencer, 1990.

Flick, *French Refugee Trappists* = Lawrence Francis Flick, "The French Refugee Trappists in the United States," *The Records of the American Catholic Historical Society of Philadelphia* 1 (1884-86): 86-116.

Gaillardin, *Les Trappistes* = Casimir Gaillardin, *Les Trappistes, ou, L'Ordre de Cîteaux au XIXe siècle. Histoire de la Trappe depuis sa fondation jusqu'à nos jours, 1140-1844,* 2 vols. Paris, 1844.

Halgouët, *Pierres d'attente* = Jérôme du Halgouët, *Pierres d'attente pour une histoire de l'Ordre dans la première moitié du XIXème siècle,* « I. Le Fondateur disparu : J.-B. Desnoyers », *Cîteaux* 17 (1966): 89-118; « II. Un havre de paix dans la tourmente : Lulworth », *Cîteaux* 18 (1967): 51-74; « III. Le Hourvari de la Martinique », *Cîteaux* 18 (1967): 240-262; « IV. Histoire d'une mitre », *Cîteaux* 19 (1968): 74-93; « V. La Tête froide de la réforme », *Cîteaux* 20 (1969): 38-68; « VI. Dom Antoine supérieur général », *Cîteaux* 21 (1970): 23-61; « VII. Anne Nicolas Charles Saulnier de Beauregard », *Cîteaux* 21 (1970): 279-299; « VIII. La Raison d'État », *Cîteaux* 22 (1971): 61-92; « IX. Fin d'un règne », *Cîteaux* 23 (1972): 91-113; « Deuxième série. Le procès. I. « Le Différend Saussol », *Cîteaux* 26 (1975): 57-81; « Deuxième série. Le procès. II. La Dominante... », *Cîteaux* 26 (1975): 185-215; « Deuxième série. Le procès. III. Questo geloso affare », *Cîteaux* 26 (1975): 284-315; « Deuxième série. Le procès. IV. Sanctissimus annuit ... », *Cîteaux* 27 (1976): 56-84.

_____, « François Thomas Alexandre Bodé, jeune homme de quelque talent », *Cîteaux* 28 (1977): 48-93; 306-346.

_____, « Les Débuts de la renaissance cistercienne du XIXe siècle », *Collectanea cisterciensia* 45 (1983): 139-148.

Hamon, *Life of the Cardinal de Cheverus* = M. Hamon (J. Huen-Dubourg), *Life of the Cardinal de Cheverus, Archbishop of Bordeaux,* trans. Robert M. Walsh. Philadelphia, 1839.

Hanington, *Every Popish Person* = J. Brian Hanington, *Every Popish Person: The Story of Roman Catholicism in Nova Scotia and the Church of Halifax, 1604-1984.* Halifax, 1984.

Hayman, *Catholicism in Rhode Island* = Robert W. Hayman, *Catholicism in Rhode Island and the Diocese of Providence, 1886-1921.* Providence, 1995.

Hermans, *Actes* = Vincent Hermans, *Actes des chapitres généraux des Congrégations des Trappistes au XIXᵉ siècle (1835-1891),* Rome, 1975.

Hermans, *Commentarium* = Vincent Hermans, *Commentarium historico-practicum in codicis canones de religiosis,* Rome, 1961.

Hoffman, *Arms and the Monk* = M. M. Hoffman, *Arms and the Monk.* Dubuque, 1952.

Horn, *The Barns* = Walter Horn and Ernest Born, *The Barns of the Abbey of Beaulieu at Its Granges of Great Coxwell and Beaulieu-St. Leonards.* Berkeley and Los Angeles, 1965.

Jennings, *Tending the Flock* = John Jennings, *Tending the Flock: Bishop Joseph-Octave Plessis and Roman Catholics in early 19ᵗʰ century New Brunswick.* Fredericton, New Brunswick, 1998.

Johnston, *History* = Angus Anthony Johnston, *A History of the Catholic Church in Eastern Nova Scotia,* 2 vols. Antigonish, 1960 (Volume 1) and 1972 (Volume 2).

Johnston, *Priests and Bishops* = A. A. Johnston, *Antigonish Diocese: Priests and Bishops, 1786-1925,* ed. Kathleen M. MacKenzie. Antigonish, 1994.

Kauffman, *Tradition and Transformation* = Christopher J. Kauffman, *Tradition and Transformation in Catholic Culture: The Priests of Saint Sulpice in the United States from 1791 to the Present.* New York, 1988.

Kerbiriou, *Jean-François de la Marche* = Louis Kerbiriou, *Jean-François de la Marche, évêque-comte de Léon (1729-1806): Étude sur un diocèse breton et sur l'émigration,* Quimper-Paris, 1924.

Kervignant, M. T., *Des moniales face à la Révolution française (1790-1816). Aux origines des Cisterciennes-Trappistines,* Paris, 1989.

Kinder, *Cistercian Europe* = Terryl N. Kinder, *Cistercian Europe: Architecture of Contemplation.* English edition. Grand Rapids, 2002.

Krailsheimer, *Armand-Jean de Rancé* = A. J. Krailsheimer, *Armand-Jean de Rancé, Abbot of la Trappe.* Oxford, 1974.

Labelle, *Acadian Life* = Ronald Labelle, *Acadian Life in Chezzetcook.* Lawrencetown, Nova Scotia, 1995.

Lacey, *Second Spring* = Andrew C. Lacey, *Second Spring of Charnwood Forest.* Loughborough, 1985.

Laffay, *Dom Augustin* = Augustin-Hervé Laffay, *Dom Augustin de Lestrange et l'avenir du monachisme (1754-1827)*, Paris, 1998.

Laurent, Laval, *Québec et l'église aux États-Unis sous mgr. Briand et mgr. Plessis*, Catholic University of America Studies in Sacred Theology 88A. Washington, D.C., 1945.

Lekai, *The Cistercians* = Louis J. Lekai, *The Cistercians: Ideals and Reality*. Kent, Ohio, 1977.

Lindsay, *Un précurseur* = L. Lindsay, « Un précurseur de la Trappe du Canada, Dom Urbain Guillet: Sa vie aventureuse et merveilleuse, Sa correspondance avec Mgr Plessis », *La Nouvelle France* 10 (1911): 417-428; 453-463; 541-552; 13 (1914): 456-464; 14 (1915): 121-130; 370-376; 15 (1916): 134-137; 207-215; 16 (1917): 227-233; 274-276; 17 (1918): 185-189; 219-228.

Maclean, *Walk Historic Halifax* = Grant Maclean, *Walk Historic Halifax: An Historic Walking Guide to Halifax*. Halifax, 1996.

Maes, Camillus P., *The Life of Rev. Charles Nerinckx*. Cincinnati, 1880.

Mattingly, Sister Mary Ramona, "The Catholic Church on the Kentucky Frontier, 1785-1812." Ph.D diss., Catholic University of America, Washington, D.C., 1936.

Merle, *Mémoire* = « Mémoire de ce qui est arrivé au P. Vincent de Paul, religieux de la Trappe: et ses observations lorsqu'il étoit en Amérique où il a passé environ dix ans avec l'agrément de son Supérieur » in *Relation de ce qui est arrivé*, pp. 4-84.

Merton, Thomas, *Dancing in the Water of Life*. The Journals of Thomas Merton, Volume 5 (1963-1965), ed. Robert E. Daggy. San Francisco, 1997.

O'Brien, Cornelius, S.J., *Memoirs of Bishop Burke*. Ottawa, 1894.

Odyssée monastique. Dom A. de Lestrange et les Trappistes pendant la révolution, Soligni, 1898.

Oury, Dom Guy, O.S.B., *Dom Gabriel Sortais (1902-1963)*, Solesmes, 1975.

Plessis, *Journal* = Anselme Chiasson, O.F.M. Cap., ed., « Le Journal des visites pastorales en Acadie de Mgr. Joseph-Octave Plessis, 1811, 1812, 1815 », in *Cahiers de la Société historique acadienne* 11 (1980): 10-311.

Plessis, Joseph-Octave, *Journal des visites pastorales de 1815 et 1816 publié par Henri Têtu*, Quebec, 1903.

Pope, A. M., *Memoir of Father Vincent de Paul, Religious of La Trappe*. (Translation of Merle, *Mémoire*.) Charlottetown, Prince Edward Island, 1886.

Raddall, *Halifax Warden of the North* = Thomas H. Raddall, *Halifax, Warden of the North*. Halifax, 1993.

RB 1980 = *RB 1980: The Rule of St. Benedict in Latin and English with Notes*, ed. Timothy Fry, O.S.B. Collegeville, 1981.

Réglemens = *Réglemens de la Maison-Dieu de Notre-Dame de la Trappe, par M. L'abbé de Rancé, son digne Réformateur, mis en nouvel ordre et augmentés des Usages particuliers de la Maison-Dieu de la Val-sainte de Notre-Dame de la Trappe au canton de Fribourg en Suisse...*, 2 vols. Fribourg, 1794.

Regulations OCSO 1926 = *Regulations of the Order of Cistercians of the Strict Observance*. Dublin, 1926.

Relation de ce qui est arrivé à deux religieux de la Trappe, pendant leur séjour auprès des sauvages, Paris, 1824.

Reid, Jennifer, *Myth, Symbol and Colonial Encounter: British and Mi'kmaq in Acadia, 1700-1867*. Ottawa, 1995.

Ruskowski, *French Émigré Priests* = Leo F. Ruskowski, *French Émigré Priests in the United States, 1791-1815. Studies in American Church History* 32. Washington, D.C., 1940.

Sainte-Henriette, Sœur, C.N.D. (D.-A. Lemire-Marsolais), *Histoire de la Congrégation de Notre-Dame de Montréal*, 2 vols. Montreal, 1910.

Schauinger, *Badin* = J. Herman Schauinger, *Stephen T. Badin: Priest in the Wilderness*. Milwaukee, 1956.

Schrepfer, *Pioneer Monks* = Luke Schrepfer, O.S.A., *Pioneer Monks in Nova Scotia*. N. p., 1947.

Simpson, Robert V., *North Cumberland: A History*. N.p., 1975.

Statutes of Nova Scotia: 1872. Halifax, 1872.

Ste.-Justine 1862-1987 = *125ème Sainte-Justine, 1862-1987*, Sainte-Justine, 1987.

Taylor, *Between Devotion and Design* = John J. Taylor, *Between Devotion and Design: The Architecture of John Cyril Hawes, 1876-1956*. Crawley, Australia, 2000.

Upton, Leslie Francis Stokes, *Micmacs and Colonists*. Vancouver, 1979.

Vanden Broucke, *Abbaye de Saint-Sixte* = Alfons Vanden Broucke, *Abbaye de Saint-Sixte. Histoire de la fondation, 1826-1831-1836*, Sixtina 8. Westvleteren, Belgium, 2000.

Vanden Broucke, *Personnel envoyé* = Alfons Vanden Broucke, *Personnel envoyé à Tracadie*. Typewritten list of monks of Sint Sixtus sent to Tracadie, including selected information concerning them. AAO, no shelfmark.

Waddell, *Narrative and Legislative Texts* = Chrysogonus Waddell, *Narrative and Legislative Texts from Early Cîteaux*. Cîteaux: Commentarii cistercienses. Studia et Documenta IX (1999).

Short titles for archival documents

AAG, *List of Contributors* = AAG, Document listing contributors to the building program of Our Lady of Gethsemani during the years 1851-52.

Anonymous Life = AAO A 1221, *Le R. P. Vincent de Paul, trappiste et missionnaire, 1768-1853*. Page numbers are inconsistent in the original. Citations are indicated by page numbers in the transcription of the manuscript in the archives of Spencer (AAS, *Life of Fr. Vincent de Paul*).

Chouteau Ordo Notes = AAB M 318 Dom Chouteau, Ordos annotés (1870-1929). Notes written by Dom Jean-Marie Chouteau of Bellefontaine in his copies of the yearly Liturgical Ordo of the Cistercian Order.

Floor Plans Valley = AAS, Plans and Drawings, *Floor Plans of Completed Buildings and Proposed Additions to the Cistercian Monastery of Our Lady of the Valley. Valley Falls, R.I.*

Guadalupe Chronicle = AAGuad, *Annals of the Abbey of Our Lady of Guadalupe.*

Hermans, *Description of Documents* = AAS Vincent Hermans, Typewritten list of documents relative to the monastery of Petit Clairvaux in the Vatican archives.

History of Petit Clairvaux = AASS, *Histoire de N. D. du Petit Clairvaux depuis sa fondation jusqu'en 1885-1886. Extrait des notes du P. Ambroise,* Typewritten document in the Archives of Sint Sixtus consisting of excerpts of *N.-D. du Petit Clairvaux* (AAB D.104-34, 3-4).

Le R. P. Vincent de Paul, trappiste et missionnaire (1768-1853) = AAO A 1021 (Copy of various uncataloged materials from AATim).

Malloy, *Annals* = AAGuad, Malloy, *Annals of the Abbey of Our Lady of the Valley.* Typewritten document, which attempts "…to reconstruct the Annals of Our Lady of the Valley, of which two copies—one in manuscript by Father John O'Connor (Superior and Titular Prior 1913 to 1943), the other a typed copy of Father John's manuscript—perished in the fire of March 21, 1950." (Ibid., p. 1) After an initial section entitled, "Preliminaries," covering significant events in the life of the community from before its transfer to

Rhode Island, the Annals proper cover from 1900 to 1939. For some reason the work of reconstruction was not completed. The years 1930-1939 draw on Malloy's own experience of life at the Valley.

Malloy, *Journal* = AAGuad, Maurice Malloy, *Journal*. Manuscript in 20 vols. covering the period from his early years until March 6, 1960, only four months before his death on July 11 of the same year. The earlier volumes of the diary contain mostly notations of dates on which various events took place. After September 3, 1930, however, the entries become increasingly descriptive of life at the Abbey of Our Lady of the Valley. The folia in all these volumes are unnumbered; references made to this document in our text are simply indicated by the date of specific entries.

Murphy BIO 1 and 2 = AAO 1252. Two anonymous accounts of Dom John-Mary Murphy's life.

Notes of Fr. Reilly = ASB RG1, Box 8, *Notes of Fr. Wendell S. Reilly, S.S.*

Notice concerning Rev. Fr. Vincent de Paul = AAB 104 Petit Clairvaux 31, *Notice sur le R. P. Vincent de Paul fondateur du couvent des sœurs trappistines de N.-D. des Sept Douleurs, paroisse [de] Pomquète et sur le R. P. François-Xavier coopérateur du P. Vincent dans la fondation du Monastère de N.-D. du Petit Clairvaux à Tracadie dans la Nouvelle Écosse, Amérique Septentrionale*, which is a transcription of Sorin, *Compilation* 2: 242-281.

Petit Clairvaux Records Book = AAS, Manuscript notebook with entries by Fr. Vincent de Paul, Fr. Francis-Xavier, and others, with records of community personnel for both Petit Clairvaux and the convent of Sisters.

Romuald, *Notes réunies* = AAB M. 314-1, P. Romulad Tallon, *Notes réunies pour servir de mémoires à qui écrira l'histoire de l'Abbaye de Bellefontaine.*

Sorin, *Compilation* = AAB 308, Bernard Sorin, *Compilation sur Bellefontaine et sa communauté*. Manuscript in two parts. Bellefontaine, 1887. Partial transcription of second part in AAB 104 Petit Clairvaux: 23 and 24.

Index

W

X

Z

Photo Credits

1. Archives of the Abbey of la Trappe
5. Archives of the Parish of St. Patrick's Church, Baltimore, Maryland
6. Archdiocese of Halifax Archives, Photograph Collection, Bishop Edmund Burke, Every *Popish Person*, p.63
8. Eugène Hamel *after* John James, Monseigneur Joseph-Octave Plessis. Oil on board. 30.7 x 25.6 cm. Musée nationale des beaux-arts du Québec no. 99.443
13. Archives of the Abbey of la Trappe
14. Archdiocese of Halifax Archives, Photograph Collection, Archbishop William Walsh daguerreotype File 1 #10
16. Archives of the Abbey of Westmalle
17. Archives of the Abbey of Westmalle
18. Archives of Sint Sixtus
54. Archives of the Abbey of Notre-Dame du Lac at Oka
60. Archives of the Abbey of Notre-Dame du Lac at Oka

All other illustrations are in the archives of St. Joseph's Abbey, Spencer, Massachusetts.

Text Credits

Diary entry for February 4, 1964, pp. 70-71 from *Dancing in the Water of Life: The Journals of Thomas Merton*. Volume five 1963-1965 by Thomas Merton and Edited by Robert E. Daggy. Copyright © 1997 by The Merton Legacy Trust. Reprinted by permission of HarperCollins Publishers Inc. *1825-1958.

Jeffrey H. Fiske, *History of Spencer, Massachusetts: 1875-1975*. Spencer, 1990. Paragraph "Sagendorph's agricultural interests...," p. 35 quoted on p. 319 of this work with permission of the author.